THE **GUINNESS** BOOK OF
TENNIS
FACTS & FEATS

THE **GUINNESS** BOOK OF
TENNIS
FACTS & FEATS

Lance Tingay

GUINNESS SUPERLATIVES LIMITED
2 CECIL COURT, LONDON ROAD, ENFIELD, MIDDLESEX

Also by Lance Tingay

The Bedside Barsetshire
Tennis: a Pictorial History
Royalty and Lawn Tennis
100 Years of Wimbledon

Editor Alex E Reid
Design and layout Roger Daniels

Published in Great Britain by
Guinness Superlatives Ltd.,
2 Cecil Court, London Road, Enfield, Middlesex EN2
6DJ.

Filmset, printed and bound in Great Britain by
Redwood Burn Limited, Trowbridge, Wiltshire

British Library Cataloguing in Publication Data

Tingay, Lance
    The Guinness book of tennis facts and feats.
    1. Tennis – Dictionaries
    I. Title
    796.342′0321   GV995

    ISBN 0–85112–268–X
    ISBN 0–85112–289–2 Pbk

'Guinness' is a registered trade mark of
Guinness Superlatives Ltd

LIST OF COUNTRY ABBREVIATIONS USED

Arg	Argentina	Fra	France	NZ	New Zealand
Aus	Australia/Australasia	FRG	West Germany	Pak	Pakistan
Aut	Austria	GB	Great Britain	Par	Paraguay
Bel	Belgium	Ger	Germany	Per	Peru
Ber	Bermuda	Gre	Greece	Phi	Philippines
Bra	Brazil	HK	Hong Kong	Pol	Poland
Brit WI	British West Indies	Hol	Holland/Netherlands	Por	Portugal
Bul	Bulgaria	Hun	Hungary	Rho	Rhodesia
Bur	Burma	Ind	India	Rom	Romania
Can	Canada	Ina	Indonesia	SA	South Africa
Chi	Chile	Ire	Ireland	Spa	Spain
Chn	China	Isr	Israel	Swe	Sweden
Col	Colombia	Ita	Italy	Swi	Switzerland
Cze	Czechoslovakia	Jap	Japan	Tai	Taiwan
Den	Denmark	Kor	Korea	Uru	Uruguay
Ecu	Ecuador	Lux	Luxembourg	USA	United States
Egy	Egypt	Mal	Malaysia	USSR	Soviet Union
Fin	Finland	Mex	Mexico	Ven	Venezuela
		Mon	Monaco	Vnm	Vietnam
		Nor	Norway	Yug	Yugoslavia

ACKNOWLEDGEMENTS

The author wishes to make grateful acknowledgement to the following individuals and sources of reference:

Ayres' Lawn Tennis Almanack 1908–1938; Dunlop Lawn Tennis Almanack 1939–1958; International Lawn Tennis Almanack 1960, 1961; Cooper's Annual of Lawn Tennis 1959–1961; World of Tennis 1969 to date; Spalding's Lawn Tennis Annual 1919–1931; USTA Yearbook 1951 to date. *Lawn Tennis & Badminton; Tenis World; Tennis Today; American Lawn Tennis; World Tennis; Tennis; Tennis de France; Tennis Club. The Encyclopaedia of Tennis* (Max Robertson); *Official Encyclopaedia of Tennis* (USTA); *Modern Encyclopaedia of Tennis* (Bud Collins); *The Encyclopaedia of Lawn Tennis* (Maurice Brady); *Tennis, Lawn Tennis, Rackets, Fives* (Badminton Library); *Uber Europas Tennisfelder* (Edgar Joubert); *The Tennis Players* (Tom Todd). Steve Flink; Stan Greenberg; Alan Little, Tom Todd and Valerie Warren of The Wimbledon Lawn Tennis Museum; The All England Lawn Tennis Club; Queen's Club; Lawn Tennis Association; US Tennis Association; International Tennis Federation.

Colour captions:

Page 1. **Bjorn Borg of Sweden, a champion of champions. Uniquely he won the Wimbledon singles five years 1976 to 1980.**

Page 2. **The old and the new. Queen's Club in 1897 with the real tennis courts in the background. The modern scene is much the same.**

CONTENTS

INTRODUCTION

This work presumes on the part of the reader an interest in the facts of lawn tennis and, that being the case, I hope it will be found, like that Victorian jigsaw map of the Holy Land, instructive and amusing.

I have spent a lifetime recording facts and opinion about the great game, unequalled in my view because of its uniquely rich combination of the athletic and artistic and with an appeal shared by men and women. Whether a match be good or not so good (and, indeed, whether a player behaves well or ill) is a matter of opinion.

This is a compilation of the facts and feats in lawn tennis since its beginnings in the 1870's and covers rather more than one hundred years. The facts are not new. Some of the feats and superlatives are, if not new in themselves, presented for the first time.

Statistics in lawn tennis were not much dealt with before the commercial promotion and sponsorship that came with the open era after 1968. Since then the Americans, brought up on the statistical mania of baseball and American football beside which the cricketer is but a child, have codified current results hugely. But much ground prior to 1968 is virgin territory.

Because much of my research has been new I must beg indulgence for such errors that may have crept in. Correction will be gratefully received.

The early facts, let alone the feats, of lawn tennis are not always easily found. Some have disappeared without a trace and I will mention one. My friend, Alan Little, whose avocation is librarian of the Wimbledon Museum, set out to amass *all* the results in the Wimbledon Championships 1877 to date. It was a worthy cause.

None the less he did not succeed. There was, it seems, in the early days a mixed doubles the score sheet for which was never passed to the referee. The gap will remain and when in the future some computer is programmed to cope with Wimbledon's statistics it will be less accurate than it should.

The contents list should clarify the basic arrangement of the work, which starts with the origins of lawn tennis and then deals with the game in general. Of the specialised sections the most comprehensive are those dealing with Wimbledon and the Davis Cup.

The nationality given after the name of a player is that of the country for which the player is competing at that particular time. As is customary, nationalities are not given of those playing in matches or championships held in their own country.

Origin and Structure

LAWN TENNIS – AND TENNIS

Lawn tennis, with which this book is concerned, derives its name from the sport from which it originated, tennis. This ancient game, played by Henry V and of which Henry VIII was reputedly champion of England, was and still is played in a stone court-yard.

Tennis was taken out of doors and played on a lawn. Because of that its name became lawn tennis to distinguish it the better from the venerable pastime which has since become known variously as real tennis, court tennis or royal tennis. But lawn tennis does not have to be played on a lawn to be properly so named. Whether on clay or cement or wood or carpet or what you will lawn tennis is still lawn tennis.

In recent years official ruling bodies have bowed to the semantic fashion of the age by dropping 'lawn' and keeping only 'tennis' in their titles. In 1977 the International Lawn Tennis Federation became the International Tennis Federation. At the same time 53 of the 101 Federation members have retained 'lawn tennis' as the name of the sport they administer. They include The Lawn Tennis Association of Great Britain.

The game of tennis is still played in England, Scotland, France, the United States and Australia. It is out of respect for this ancient and delightful sport that many insist on using the more accurate description 'lawn tennis' for the more popular game. The antiquity of tennis may be emphasised by recording the 24 variant spellings it has had over the centuries:

Teneis	Tennes	Tenyce
Tenes	Tennice	Tenys
Tenetz	Tennies	Tenyse
Teneys	Tennis	Tenyys
Tenez	Tennise	Tinneis
Tenice	Tennys	Tinnies
Tenise	Tennyse	Tinnis
Tenisse	Tennysse	Tynes

THE FIRST CHAMPIONS

1877

The world's first lawn tennis champion was **Spencer William Gore**, winner of the men's singles in The Lawn Tennis Championships at Wimbledon when on Thursday, 19 July 1877, he beat William Marshall.

Gore, a rackets player and keen cricketer, was not enthusiastic about the game at which he was the pioneer champion and the only other appearance he made was to defend, unsuccessfully, his title the following year. He wrote:

> That anyone who has really played well at cricket, tennis, or even rackets, will ever seriously give his attention to lawn tennis, beyond showing himself to be a promising player, is extremely doubtful; for in all probability the monotony of the game as compared with others would choke him off before he had time to excel in it.

Gore, born in Wimbledon 10 March 1850, was a surveyor. He died 19 April 1906 at Ramsgate, Kent. He was the son of the Hon C A Gore and Lady Augusta L P Ponsonby, Dowager Countess of Kerry. He was at Harrow 1863–69 and captain of cricket in 1869. His brother became Bishop of Birmingham in 1905.

1878

The first **men's doubles** championships were those of Scotland and won by **A Graham Murray and C C Maconochie** on an indoor court at Raeburn Place in Edinburgh.

Murray, born in 1849, was later Viscount Dunedin and a lawyer of the highest distinction. He was successively Advocate-Depute, Sheriff of Perthshire, Solicitor-General, Secretary for Scotland, Lord Advocate, MP, Lord Justice-General and Lord President. His full title was the Rt Hon Viscount Dunedin, PC, GCVO, KC, LL D of Edinburgh, Glasgow and Aberdeen, DCL of Oxford, Keeper of the Great Seal, and

The unique champion—Spencer Gore, Wimbledon's first winner in 1877.

Wimbledon in 1877. With four courts occupied the scene can only have bee[n] 16 or 17 July.

Lord of Appeal.

Maconochie, born in 1852, was also a lawyer and became Sheriff of the Lothians.

They won the title for the first three years, 1878, 1879 and 1880 but detailed records have not survived. The following year they played through as far as the final (in an entry of eight pairs) and were beaten, 6–1 6–3 6–1, by J G and W Horn.

1879

The **first woman champion** was **May Langrishe**. The inaugural Irish Championships of 1879 pioneered a women's singles championship. There was an entry of seven and Miss Langrishe won the final 6–2 0–6 8–6 against Miss D Meldon. She was born, in Ireland, 31 December 1864, and was, when the tournament ended on 10 June 1879 just **14 years 161 days old**. She won the title again in 1883 and 1886. She died in 1939.

The **first mixed doubles champions** were found in the same year when the Irish also pioneered this event. **E Elliott and Miss Costello** take precedence as the first in the world of their kind. They won the title from a field of nine pairs. They were probably Irish but no knowledge seems to have survived the years.

1882

The **first women's doubles champions** were **May Langrishe** and her older sister **Miss B Langrishe**. They won the women's doubles event staged at the Northern Lawn Tennis Championships in Manchester. The West of England Championships at Bath also pioneered a women's doubles in the same year and was won by Miss G B Gibbs and Miss Constable.

THE WORLD'S FIRST TOURNAMENT

The first lawn tennis tournament in the world, as far as can be judged on surviving records, wa[s] held in **August 1876** on a court laid down by Wil liam Appleton in Nahant, Massachusetts. It wa[s] played on handicap on a round robin basis There were two players on scratch, James Dwight and F D Sears Jr, each of whom played against 11 other players until a final between them. Rackets scoring was used.

Dwight (scratch) beat H Curtis (receive 4 15–8, beat D Curtis (receive 4) 15–8, beat [I] Curtis (receive 5) 15–8, beat B Grant (receive 7 15–7, beat W Otis (receive 7) 15–8, beat H [C] Otis (receive 9) 15–10, beat Guild (receive 11 15–13, beat Merriam (receive 11) 15–11, bea[t] Ellis (receive 12) 15–12, beat Greenoug[h] (receive 13) 15–13, beat Post (receive 13) 15–13.

It can be seen that Dwight lost four points a[t] most in any match and no points at all in five o[f] them. The progress of Sears has not survived.

In the final Dwight was the victor. Here the best of three sets was played and Dwight bea[t] Sears 12–15 15–7 15–13.

The world's first tournament open to all comer[s] was 'The Lawn Tennis Championship Meetin[g] for 1877', promoted by the All England Croque[t] and Lawn Tennis Club, universally known a[s] Wimbledon.

MILESTONES

1859 Summer. Major Harry Gem, solicitor, an[d] Mr J B Perera, merchant, began playing their adaptation of tennis on the lawn o[f] the latter's house, Fairlight, Ampton Road Edgbaston, Birmingham, England.

Dr. James Dwight, the founding father of American tennis. He played at Wimbledon in 1884.

1868 23 July. The founding of the All England Croquet Club at a meeting in the offices of *The Field*, 346 Strand, London. The founding members were Capt R F Dalton, J Hinde Hale, Rev A Law, S H Clarke Maddock and Walter Jones Whitmore with John Walsh in the chair.

1870 June. Opening of the All England Croquet Club between Worple Road and the London and South Western Railway, Wimbledon. A committee meeting was held on the club premises for the first time on 24 June.

1872 Summer. Major Gem and Mr Perera, together with Dr Frederick Haynes and Dr Arthur Tomkins, founded in Leamington, Warwickshire, the Leamington Lawn Tennis Club, **the world's first lawn tennis club**.

1874 23 February. Major Walter Clopton Wingfield entered a patent registration for a 'New and Improved Court for Playing the

Ancient Game of Tennis'. It was publicised as 'Sphairistike, or, Lawn Tennis' in March.

August. **Lawn tennis first played in the USA** by Dr James Dwight and F R Sears Jr on a court at Nahant, Mass.

1875 25 February. The All England Club agreed a motion 'That one ground be set apart for Lawn Tennis and Badminton during the ensuing season'. Capt R F Dalton, J M Heathcote and Henry Jones were appointed to the sub-committee. An outlay of £25 for lawn tennis was approved on 8 April.

3 March. A meeting convened by the MCC inviting all interested parties to standardise the rules of lawn tennis. The agreed code was issued on 29 May.

Summer. The Staten Island Cricket and Baseball Club laid down a lawn tennis court, making it **the first lawn tennis club in the USA.**

An American tournament of the 1880's at New Brighton, Staten Island, New York. Sketched by H. A. Ogden.

1877 14 April. The All England Croquet Club changed its name to the All England Croquet and Lawn Tennis Club.

2 June. The All England Club committee agreed 'That a public meeting be held on July 10th and following days to compete for the Championships in Lawn Tennis'.

30 June. The All England Club committee resolved that 'In future no courts for lawn tennis be marked out but 26 yards by 9 yards or, for four handed games, as at Princes, 26 yards by 12 yards'.

9 July. **Start of The Lawn Tennis Championships.** The winner on Thursday, 19 July was Spencer William Gore, a surveyor, aged 27, from Wimbledon. 21 players competed. Founding of the New Orleans Lawn Tennis Club, the oldest surviving club in the USA.

1878 **The world's first men's doubles championship** instituted with the Scottish Championships at Raeburn Place in Edinburgh. The winners were A Graham Murray (later Viscount Dunedin) and C C Maconochie, both lawyers.

1879 **The world's first women's singles and mixed doubles championships** instituted with the Irish Championships in Dublin. May Langrishe won the women's singles, E Elliot and Miss Costello the mixed.

The first tournament staged in Australia, the Victorian Championships in Melbourne. Winner was A F Robinson.

1880 An **American Championship** staged at the Staten Island Cricket and Baseball Club. In the final O E Woodhouse, a British player from the Ealing Club, beat J F Hellmuth of Canada 15–11 14–15 15–9 10–15 (rackets scoring), an aggregate of 54 points to 50.

1881 21 May. **The US Lawn Tennis Association founded** at a meeting in the Fifth Avenue Hotel, New York City. There were 33 clubs represented and the convening clubs were the Staten Island Cricket and Baseball Club, the Beacon Park Athletic Association of Boston and the All Philadelphia Lawn Tennis Committee.

31 August. **The US National Championships, men's singles and doubles, inaugurated** at the Newport Casino, Newport, Rhode Island. Richard D Sears, aged 19 years 10 months, won the singles from an entry of 25.

Dodgson created 'Alice in Wonderland'.

1883 **The first international contest** staged at the All England Club, Wimbledon. For the British Isles William and Ernest Renshaw beat J S and C M Clark, representing the USA, first by 6–4 8–6 3–6 6–1 and, a week later, by 6–3 6–2 6–3.

1884 The first overseas challenge at Wimbledon. There were three Americans, James Dwight, Richard Sears and A L Rives. E L Williams, born in South Africa, also competed.

Wimbledon staged a women's singles and men's doubles championship for the first time, both being held at the conclusion of the men's singles. The women's singles in the Victorian Championships initiated tournament play for women in Australia. Winner was Miss Mackenzie.

1887 **The US National Women's Singles Championship was inaugurated** at the Philadelphia Cricket Club. The first champion was the 17-year-old Ellen Hansell.

1888 26 January. **The Lawn Tennis Association founded.** The inaugural meeting, called on the initiative of H S Scrivener and G W Hillyard, was at the Freemasons' Tavern, Great Queen Street, London, with Capt J C Hobbs, of the Northern Lawn Tennis Association, in the chair. At least 80 were present. The LTA presented its first balance sheet on 6 December. It showed an income of £45 7s, expenditure of £20 3s 11d. The first honorary secretary was Herbert Chipp.

1889 The first overseas challenge in the US Championships at Newport. It was by E G Meers of the Chiswick Park Club, London. He won three rounds and lost in the semi-final to Oliver Campbell.

1891 A national championship had its first overseas winner when Mabel Cahill, from Ireland, won the US women's singles in Philadelphia.

The French Championships began, entry being open to members of French clubs. The South African Championships started.

1892 The first full scale international contest was staged between England and Ireland at Ballsbridge, Dublin. The format comprised men's doubles only and Ireland won 5–4.

1896 **The Olympic Games in Athens with lawn tennis for men.** J P Boland (Ire) and F Traun (Ger) were the gold medalists.

1899 The All England Club changed its name to its present title the All England Lawn Tennis and Croquet Club. 'Croquet' had been dropped from the title in 1882.

1900 **The first Davis Cup tie** was staged at the Longwood Cricket Club, Boston, Mass. The USA beat the British Isles easily. The American side had Dwight F Davis, the

above **The 'new' Wimbledon. The singles final of 1924, Jean Borotra v Rene Lacoste. The electric scoreboard had yet to be installed. That was in 1927.**

left **Norman Brookes, a great Australian. He was the first man from overseas to win Wimbledon in 1907.**

founder of the trophy, as a playing captain.

The Olympic Games in Paris included lawn tennis events for women. The first woman gold medalist was Charlotte Cooper (GB).

1902 **The US National men's championships had their first overseas winner.** The British Hugh Lawrence & Reginald Frank Doherty won the doubles at Newport. In the challenge round they beat Holcombe Ward and Dwight Davis 11–9 12–10 6–4. Reggie Doherty won the All-Comers' singles and lost in the challenge round to William Larned.

1903 The US National singles title went overseas. It was won by Laurie Doherty. He beat Larned 6–3 6–0 10–8 in the challenge round and lost no set at any stage.

1905 **A Wimbledon title had its first overseas winner** when May Sutton (USA) won the women's singles at her first attempt.

The Australian Championships were staged for the first time.

1907 **The men's singles at Wimbledon went overseas for the first time,** won by Norman E Brookes of Australia.

1913 1 March. **The International Lawn Tennis Federation founded** in Paris. Founding members were Australasia, Austria, Belgium, British Isles, Denmark, France, Germany, Holland, Russia, South Africa, Sweden and Switzerland.

1915 The US National men's singles championship staged for the first time at the West

Side Club, Forest Hills, New York.

1921 16 August. Molla Mallory (USA) beat Suzanne Lenglen (Fra) 6–2 30–love, retired, in the second round of the US women's singles championship, staged for the first time at the West Side Club, Forest Hills, New York. The only time, 1919 to 1926, that Mlle Lenglen was ever beaten in a singles.

1922 The All England Club moved from Worple Road to Church Road, Wimbledon, at a cost of £140 000. The capacity of the new Centre Court was about 14 000.

The US National Championships introduced seeding for the first time.

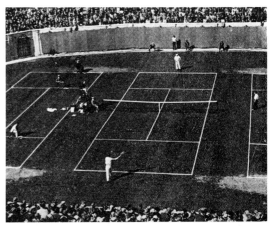

The Stadium Court at the West Side Club, Forest Hills, N.Y., in 1927. The singles final between William Tilden and Rene Lacoste.

1923 The Stadium Court was opened at the West Side Club, Forest Hills, New York, with a capacity of about 17 000. The inaugural event was the Wightman Cup contest between British and American women. Hazel Wightman was the playing captain of the home side, an easy winner.

1924 Lawn tennis was played for the last time in the Olympic Games, held in Paris. All gold medalists were American, Helen Wills, Hazel Wightman, Vincent Richards, Frank Hunter and Norris Williams.
The USA joined the International Lawn Tennis Federation.
Partial seeding by nationality introduced at Wimbledon.

1925 The French Championships became open to all amateurs.
The women's singles at Wimbledon was won by Suzanne Lenglen (Fra) for the total loss of five games. She played five matches. In winning all three titles she lost only one set, taking 209 games out of 261, 80 per cent.

1927 France won the Davis Cup, becoming the first nation to break the dominance of the USA, Great Britain and Australia.
Full merit seeding introduced at Wimbledon.

1928 The Stade Roland Garros opened at Auteuil, Paris, with its centre court seating about 14 000.

1938 **First achievement of the 'Grand Slam',** by Don Budge (USA). By winning the French singles in June he became the current holder of the championships of Australia, France, Wimbledon and the USA. All five Wimbledon events were won by Americans for the first time and Budge was triple champion for the second year in succession.

1953 Maureen Connolly (USA) became, on winning the French title in June, the first woman to take the 'Grand Slam'.

1963 **The Federation Cup inaugurated.** The USA were the first winners at Queen's Club, London.
The first commercially sponsored tournament, the Kent Championships at Beckenham, with Messrs Rothmans as sponsors.

1968 **Open lawn tennis** brought about at a special general meeting of the ILTF in Paris on 30 March. The first open tournament was the British Hard Court Championships at Bournemouth, England, 22 to 27 April. see p 214.

1970 The Grand Prix Series inaugurated, spon-

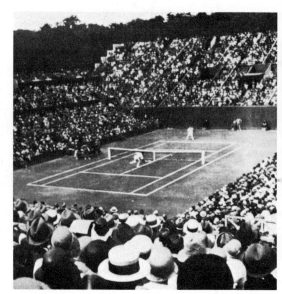

The Stade Roland Garros in 1929. Jean Borotra v William Tilden in the Davis Cup.

J. Donald Budge, arguably the greatest player of all time. He won the first 'Grand Slam' in 1938.

sored by Pepsi-Cola. First winner was Cliff Richey (USA). He won two of the 20 qualifying tournaments, was finalist in three and semi-finalist in three also. Richey's prize was $25 000. The Grand Prix Masters' tournament was held in Tokyo and held entirely as a round robin. Winner was Stan Smith (USA) with a prize of $10 000.

The tie-break was authorised as an experiment by the ILTF. The nine-point 'sudden death' method was first used, unofficially, in the US Pro Indoor Championships in Philadelphia in January and later used officially in the US Open Championships at Forest Hills.

1971 **The tie-break** used for the first time at Wimbledon. The system (12 points up with a two points lead) was later incorporated into the rules of the game by the ILTF.

The Virginia Slims circuit of tournaments inaugurated in the USA. It marked the start of the growth of the earnings of women players to amounts comparable with those earned by men.

1972 The Challenge Round of the Davis Cup abolished, all nations having to play through.

The Association of Tennis Professionals was founded in September. First President was Cliff Drysdale (SA).

1973 **The Wimbledon boycott.** Following the suspension by the ILTF of the Yugoslav Nikki Pilic and the refusal of his entry for the Wimbledon Championships the Association of Tennis Professionals called on its members to withdraw their Wimbledon entries and 79 members did so. Just three members defied the ATP's call, Roger Taylor of Great Britain, Ilie Nastase of Romania and Ray Keldie of Australia, and they were subsequently fined. Despite the absence of nearly all the leading men the Wimbledon Championships had its second highest attendance, 300 172.

1974 South Africa won the Davis Cup with a walk-over in the final round from India.

1975 The surface for the US Open Championships at the West Side Club, Forest Hills, New York, was changed from grass to hard courts.

1978 The venue for the US Open Championships moved from the West Side Club to the National Tennis Centre, Flushing Meadow, New York, with cement courts.

1981 The Davis Cup became commercially sponsored. The 16 leading nations competed on a non-zonal basis for the trophy. The remaining nations continued to compete in zones with the winners of the four zonal regions earning promotion to replace the four relegated nations coming down from the top section.

1982 The Wimbledon Championships rescheduled from 12 to 13 playing days by being extended to Sunday.

ORIGINS OF SCORING

In its cradle days both rackets and tennis scoring were used for lawn tennis. With rackets scoring a game comprised 15 aces which could be won only by the server who remained 'hand in' until the loss of a rally.

Tennis scoring was adopted for the first Wimbledon Championships in 1877 and became the standard. The origins of the 15, 30 and 40 and so on belong to the venerable game and are not known with certainty.

One thing is sure. The origins are medieval and French. Remembering that until the beginning of the nineteenth century tennis was scored with the steps, 15, 30 and *45*, two explanations merit consideration.

One is that the currency of the period was divided into 60 smaller units, 15 of which were staked by the gallants of the court on the outcome of each rally, or, rather, rest, to use the proper term.

The other, more generally favoured, is based on the presence of a clock face at the end of the tennis court. A quarter move of the appropriate hand was made after each rest, with the score being called as 15, 30 or 45 as the case might be. As the hand was moved to 60, making the complete circuit, this was the game.

The size and shape of the court became standardised with the Wimbledon Championships. The standardisation of the ball took longer. It was the manufacture of the rubber ball, which became possible in the mid-nineteenth century, that made practicable the transition of court tennis to the lawn. It was covering the rubber ball with cloth that enabled lawn tennis to progress from a pastime into a sport.

The best of five sets has been the orthodox distance for championship play from the first, though there have been many departures from the norm. Women not infrequently played the best of five sets until after the turn of the century. Advantage sets were the norm in all rounds by that time.

THE TIE-BREAK

The first important change in scoring was initiated in the US Professional Indoor Championships in Philadelphia in early 1970 when the 'Sudden Death' nine-point system was used without official sanction. At six games all each player alternated with two service points in a best of nine points series. If level at four points all then the last serving player had a third service point with the receiver having choice of sides. Then the outcome of the one rally decided the set, or match, to either player.

The theoretical weakness of the system was the possibility of a player going from start to finish without losing a single point on service and yet being beaten.

In the summer of 1970 the International Federation sanctioned the experimental use of the tie-break, the system being left to each national association. The US Association favoured the nine-point system. Great Britain and other nations adopted a 12-point method. In this the service changes after the initial point and then after every two. The game is won by the player first reaching a total of seven points unless the score be level at six points all in which case a lead of two points must be established.

This 12-point system was used first at Wimbledon in 1971. From 1975 it became part of the rules of the game as an optional scoring method, to be used at six or eight games all.

The **longest tie break** was in the first round of the singles in 1973 when Bjorn Borg (Swe) beat Premjit Lal (Ind) 6–3 6–4 9–8. The third set tie break was **20–18**, that is **38 points**.

Mark Cox (GB) beat Roy Emerson (Aus) 4–6 7–6 7–6 in the third round of the Rawlings Tournament in Dallas, Texas, in 1971 when the second set tie break was **19–17**, a total of **36 points**.

The **longest tie break involving women** was in 1978 when in the second round of the mixed doubles in the US Open at Flushing Meadow when Andy Lucchesi and Mareen Louie (both USA) beat Horace Reid and Diane Desfor (both USA) 6–2 6–7 7–6. The third set tie break was **18–16**, that is **34 points**.

In the Wimbledon men's singles final of 1980 Bjorn Borg (Swe) beat John McEnroe (USA) 1–6 7–5 6–3 6–7 8–6. The fourth set tie break was **18–16, 34 points**.

The **longest tie break** recorded in a **women's singles** was in the first round at Wimbledon in 1982 when Virginia Wade (GB) beat Jo Durie (GB) 3–6 7–6 6–2, the tie break in the second set extending to **15–13, 28 points**.

ORIGINS OF SEEDING

Seeding is the placing of selected players in a tournament in certain places in the draw in order to prevent their meeting until the later stages. It was first done in the US National Championships of 1922 after the passing of a regulation at the annual meeting of the USLTA on **4 February 1922**. It provided for home and overseas players to be seeded separately.

Two notable happenings of the 1921 season added weight to the arguments in favour of seeding. In the women's singles championship of the previous summer the two leading contenders for the title, Molla Mallory, the top US player, and Suzanne Lenglen, at that time three times Wimbledon champion, met in the second round, Mlle Lenglen not having played a match.

In the men's singles 'Big Bill' Tilden and 'Little Bill' Johnston, the clear cut rivals for the leadership of the American game (and finalists for the two preceding years) met in the round of the last 16, bringing the event to its logical climax with three rounds to go. Tilden beat Johnston in four sets and did not subsequently lose a set.

Seeding was first adopted in the **Wimbledon Championships in 1924**. Each nation was allowed to nominate up to four players in the singles (and two pairs in the doubles) who were then drawn to fall in different quarters of the draw. **In 1927 seeding on merit** was adopted, selected players being placed in fixed positions.

THE CHALLENGE ROUND SYSTEM

Traditionally the challenge round system of conducting tournaments was taken for granted. The champion, having been found, stood out the following year until his challengers had played out among themselves an All Comers' event to decide the best to assail the supremacy of the defending champion.

As with the introduction of seeding the USLTA moved first with the change. In **1912** the Challenge Round in the men's singles was abolished and in 1919 in the women's singles also.

At Wimbledon the Challenge Round was abolished in **1922** when the All England Club moved from Worple Road to Church Road. It never had applied in the women's and mixed doubles, events given full championship status only in 1913.

The Challenge Round system was maintained in the Davis Cup 1900 to 1971 and 60 Challenge Round ties were played. The decisive tie became the Final Round from **1972**, the USA giving up its right to stand out.

DEVELOPMENT OF COURT AND EQUIPMENT

	THE COURT				THE BALL			THE RACKET
Date and Authority	**Dimensions**	**Height of Net Sides**	**Centre**	**Service line from net**	**Weight**	**Diameter**		
c 1872 Leamington Club	90′ by 36′ *27·43 m by 10·97 m*	Level 4′ *1·22m*		—	$1\frac{1}{4}$–$1\frac{3}{4}$ oz *35·4–49·6 g*	—		Not defined
Feb 1874 Wingfield	60′ by 30′ *18·29 m by 9·14 m* (hour glass 21′ *6·40 m* at centre)	4′8″ *1·42 m* at centre		—	$1\frac{1}{3}$ oz *37·7 g*	$2\frac{1}{2}$″ *6·35 cm*		Not defined
1874 Germains	60′ by 30′ *18·29 m by 9·14 m* Lawn Tennis	6′ *1·83 m*	4′ 8″ *1·42 m*	15′ *4·57 m*	$1\frac{1}{8}$–$1\frac{1}{4}$ oz *31·9–35·4 g*	$2\frac{1}{4}$″ *5·72 cm*		Not defined
Aug 1874 Wingfield	84′ by 36′ *25·60 by 10·97 m* (hour glass 21′ *6·40 m* at centre)	4′8″ *1·42 m* at centre		18′ *5·49 m*	$1\frac{1}{3}$ oz *37·7 g*	$2\frac{1}{2}$″ *6·35 cm*		Not defined
Nov 1874 Wingfield	84′ by 39′ *25·60 m by 11·89 m* (hour glass 21′ *6·40 m* at centre)	4′4″ *1·32 m* at centre		18′ *5·49 m*	$1\frac{1}{3}$ oz *37·7 g*	$2\frac{1}{2}$″ *6·35 cm*		Not defined
1875 MCC	78′ by 30′ *23·77 m by 9·14 m* (hour glass 24′ *7·32 m* at centre)	5′ *1·52 m*	4′ *1·22 m*	26′ *7·92 m*	$1\frac{1}{2}$ oz *42·5 g*	$2\frac{1}{4}$–$2\frac{5}{8}$″ *5·72–6·67 cm*	Flannel covered	Not defined
1877 All England Club	78′ by 27′ *23·77 m by 8·23 m*	5′ *1·52 m*	3′3″ *0·99 m*	26′ *7·92 m*	$1\frac{1}{4}$–$1\frac{1}{2}$ oz *35·4–42·5 g*	$2\frac{1}{4}$–$2\frac{5}{8}$″ *5·72–6·67 cm*	Flannel covered	Not defined
1878 All England Club & MCC	*78′ by 27′* *23·77 m by 8·23 m*	4′9″ *1·45 m*	3′ *0·91 m*	22′ *6·71 m*	$1\frac{3}{4}$–2 oz, *49·6–56·7 g*	$2\frac{1}{4}$–$2\frac{5}{8}$″ *5·72–6·67 cm*	Flannel covered	Not defined
1880 All England Club & MCC	78′ by 27′ *23·77 m by 8·23 m* singles 78′ by 36′ *23·77 m by 10·97 m* doubles	4′ *1·22 m*	3′ *0·91 m*	21′ *6·40 m*	$1\frac{7}{8}$–2 oz *53·2–56·7 g*	$2\frac{1}{2}$–$2\frac{9}{16}$″ *6·35–6·51 cm*	Flannel covered	Not defined
1882 All England Club & MCC	as above	3′6″ *1·07 m*	3′ *0·91 m*	as above	as above	as above	Flannel covered	Not defined
1921 ILTF	as above	as above		as above	$1\frac{15}{16}$–$2\frac{1}{16}$ oz. *54·9–58·5 g*	$2\frac{1}{2}$–$2\frac{5}{8}$″ *6·35–6·67 cm*	Flannel covered	Not defined
1923 ILTF	as above	as above		as above	2–$2\frac{1}{16}$ oz *56·7–58·5 g*	as above	Flannel covered	Not defined
1973 ILTF	as above	as above		as above	as above	as above	White *or* yellow sanctioned	Not defined
1978 ILTF	as above	as above		as above	as above	as above	White *or* yellow sanctioned	Defined to consist of a frame of any material, weight, size or shape and of stringing which must connect with the frame, be interlaced and without attachments that alter the flight of the ball.

DEFINITION OF THE RACKET

It was more than 100 years after the origin of lawn tennis that any rule was made governing the racket. On 1 October 1977 the management committee of the International Tennis Federation, using emergency powers, forbade the use of the double stringing which had become popular with some tournament players in the preceding months.

At the annual general meeting of the Federation on 13 July 1978 in Stockholm a new rule was decreed:

> The racket shall consist of a frame and a stringing. The frame may be of any material, weight, size or shape. The strings must be alternately interlaced or bonded where they cross and each string must be connected to the frame.
>
> If there are attachments, they must be used only to prevent wear and tear and must not alter the flight of the ball. The density at the centre must be at least equal to the average density of the stringing.
>
> Note to the Rule. The spirit of this rule is to prevent undue spin on the ball that would result in a change in the character of the game. The stringing must be made so that the moves between the strings will not exceed what is possible for instance with 18 mains and 18 crosses uniformly spaced and interlaced in a stringing area of 75 square inches.

A qualification was made on 8 July 1981. It limited the frame of the racket to a length of 32 inches *81·28 cm*, including the handle, and its width to 12·5 inches *31·75 cm*. It further limited the strung surface to 15·5 inches *39·37 cm* by 11·5 inches *29·21 cm*.

SERVING SPEED

The records are not satisfactory because of the difficulty of making adequate measurement during play under normal conditions. Ideally the measurement would be of speed during actual competitive play.

For instance one would like to know the speed of the ball when the American Ellsworth Vines aced the British Bunny Austin to win the match point of the Wimbledon singles final of 1932. Those who saw the point aver that the only clear evidence of the ball falling into court was the puff of chalk from the service line and that there was no real sight of the ball from the time it was hit by Vines' racket until it dropped out of the stop netting. Austin declared he did not

Roscoe Tanner from Lookout Mountain, Tennessee, a fast server and a left hander. Tanner had his best success in reaching the Wimbledon singles final in 1979.

know if the ball passed him on the backhand or forehand side.

Objective evidence of service speed is harder to come by. The figures arrived at before the modern electronic aids must be held suspect.

In September 1976 the American **Scott Carnahan** was credited with 137 mph *220 km/h* at a trial in Los Angeles.

In March 1981 *Horst Goepper,* a lawn tennis coach (and mathematician) of Weinheim, West Germany, claimed a serving speed of **199·53 mph** *321·11 km/h.* The increase over previous speeds seemed enormous.

'Big Bill' Tilden, in 1931, was credited with 163·3 mph *262·8 km/h.* **Lester Stoefen,** American also, was credited with 131 mph *211 km/h* in the 1930's. In the post-war game **Jack Kramer** was accorded 110 mph *177 km/h* and **Richard Gonzales** 112 mph *180 km/h.*

LAWN TENNIS CLUBS

The **oldest lawn tennis club in the world** was the Leamington Lawn Tennis Club in the grounds of the Manor House Hotel, Leamington, Warwickshire, England. It was founded by Major T H Gem, Mr J B Perera, Dr A Wellesley Tomkins and Dr F Haynes in 1872. It is now defunct.

The **oldest surviving club** is the All England Lawn Tennis and Croquet Club, Wimbledon. It was founded as the All England Croquet Club in 1868 and became the All England Croquet and Lawn Tennis Club when lawn tennis was introduced in 1877.

The **first club in which lawn tennis was played in the USA** was the Staten Island Cricket and Baseball Club, arguably in 1874.

The **oldest surviving club in the USA** is the New Orleans Lawn Tennis Club, founded in 1876.

The **first club in France** was the Decimal Club, Neuilly-sur-Seine, founded in 1877 and now defunct. The **oldest surviving club in France** is the Tennis-Club de Dinard, founded in 1878.

The **oldest club in Ireland** is the Fitzwilliam Club, Dublin, founded in 1877.

The **oldest club in Scotland** is the Perth Lawn Tennis Club, founded in 1881.

The **oldest tournament site** is the Newport Casino, Newport, RI, USA, where the US National Championships were first played in 1881.

The **first floodlit court** was at Cheltenham in 1881.

The **biggest club** is the Santa Ana Tennis Club, Santa Ana, California. It has **55 courts.**

The **biggest club in Great Britain** is the Hurlingham Club, Fulham, London. It has 20 grass and 20 hard courts, a total of **40.**

The **most northerly** club in the world is at **Hammerfest, Norway.** Its latitude is 70 degrees 35 minutes North. It has one outdoor court and a membership (in 1980) of 29.

The **most southerly** club is at **Punta Arenas, Chile.** The latitude is 53 degrees 10 minutes South. Membership in 1980 was approximately 120.

In **Australasia the most southerly club is at Bluff, New Zealand,** near the tip of South Island, with a membership in 1980 of 46. Its latitude is 46 degrees 37 minutes South.

LAWN TENNIS ASSOCIATIONS

The **oldest national association** is the United States Tennis Association. It was founded, as the US National Lawn Tennis Association, at a meeting in the Fifth Avenue Hotel, New York City, on 21 May 1881.

The **Lawn Tennis Association** (of Great Britain) was founded at a meeting at the Freemasons' Tavern, Great Queen Street, London, on 26 January 1888.

The **International Tennis Federation** was founded, as the International Lawn Tennis Federation, in Paris on 26 October 1912. The first formal meeting was in Paris on 1 March 1913. The founding nations were Australasia, Austria, Belgium, British Isles, Denmark, France, Germany, Holland, Russia, South Africa, Sweden and Switzerland.

ATTENDANCE RECORDS

The **highest daily attendance** for a lawn tennis event was on Wednesday 27 June 1979 for the Wimbledon Championships. The number of spectators was—38 291

The **highest number** of spectators attending **one specific match** was on 20 September 1973 at the Astrodome, Houston, Texas, to watch a singles in which Billie Jean King beat Bobbie Riggs—30 472

The **highest number** of spectators **attending a Davis Cup tie** was on 27 December 1954, the first day of the Challenge Round tie between Australia and the USA, at the White City, Sydney—25 578

The **highest number** of spectators attending **one session of an indoor tournament** was on the evening of 15 January 1981 when Bjorn Borg met John McEnroe in the Grand Prix Masters' Tournament at Madison Square Garden, New

York. The attendance was—19 103

The **highest overall attendance at a tournament** was for the Wimbledon Championships 1981. Over 12 sessions it was—358 250

PRIZE MONEY

The following tables estimate the amount of prize money, in US dollars, earned by the ten leading men and ten leading women year by year. Precise accuracy is not claimed. The figures are informed calculations made variously by the US Tennis Association, the Association of Tennis Professionals and the Women's Tennis Association. Money earned from exhibition matches has been excluded. Prize money began to be paid with the onset of open lawn tennis on 22 April 1968 but no calculations were made for that year.

1969
Men

R G Laver (Aus)	$124 000
A D Roche (Aus)	70 045
T S Okker (Hol)	65 451
R S Emerson (Aus)	62 129
J D Newcombe (Aus)	52 610
K R Rosewall (Aus)	46 796
R A Gonzales (USA)	46 288
M C Riessen (USA)	43 441
F S Stolle (Aus)	43 160
A R Ashe (USA)	42 030

1970
Men

Laver	$201 453
Ashe	141 018
Rosewall	140 455
C Richey (USA)	97 000
Emerson	96 485
S R Smith (USA)	95 251
Newcombe	78 251
Gonzales	77 365
C Graebner (USA)	68 000
Roche	61 797

Women

No reliable estimates were made of the earnings of the women players until 1971. It was calculated that Margaret Court was the top prize money earner in 1970 and had earned 'more than $60 000'.

1971
Men

Laver	$292 717
Rosewall	138 371

Okker	120 465
I Nastase (Rom)	114 000
Ashe	104 642
Smith	103 806
Newcombe	101 514
Riessen	81 310
Graebner	75 400
Richey	75 000

Women

Mrs L W King (USA)	$117 000
F Durr (Fra)	65 000
R Casals (USA)	62 000
Mrs D E Dalton (Aus)	33 867
K Melville (Aus)	29 767
Mrs P F Jones (GB)	26 148
Mrs B M Court (Aus)	26 000
E Goolagong (Aus)	25 000
S V Wade (GB)	24 000
Mrs K Gunter (USA)	15 300

1972
Men

Nastase	$176 000
Smith	142 300
Rosewall	132 950
Newcombe	120 600
Ashe	119 775
Laver	100 200
Okker	90 004
J S Connors (USA)	90 000
Riessen	74 436
E C Drysdale (SA)	68 433

Women

King	$119 000
Casals	70 000
Melville	55 000
Gunter	50 800
Court	47 000
Durr	46 000
Goolagong	42 000
Wade	32 800
W Overton (USA)	30 000
K M Krantzcke (Aus)	19 312

1973
Men

Nastase	$228 750
Smith	218 647
Okker	178 215
Connors	156 400
Newcombe	151 675
Ashe	141 206
Laver	140 325
Rosewall	120 420
M Orantes (Spa)	97 175
B E Gottfried (USA)	87 710

Women

Court	$204 400
King	194 700
C M Evert (USA)	152 002
Goolagong	108 127
Casals	104 375
Melville	61 200
Wade	60 100
Gunter	48 292
Durr	40 727
B F Stove (Hol)	40 019

1974
Men

Connors	$281 309
G Vilas (Arg)	274 327
Newcombe	273 299
B Borg (Swe)	215 229
Nastase	190 752
Ashe	165 194
Smith	163 326
Orantes	139 857
Laver	134 600
R Ramirez (Mex)	127 425

Women

Evert	$261 460
King	173 225
Goolagong	102 506
Wade	85 389
Casals	72 389
J M Heldman (USA)	60 511
Melville	56 022
Durr	41 227
O Morozova (USSR)	40 877
Stove	40 249

1975
Men

Connors	$600 273
Ashe	338 327
Orantes	271 066
Vilas	247 372
Borg	229 875
Ramirez	210 850
Nastase	210 793
Gottfried	171 130
Laver	165 321
J Alexander (Aus)	158 650

Women

Evert	$412 977
M Navratilova (Cze)	185 518
Wade	153 576
Mrs R A Cawley (Miss E Goolagong)	145 254

King	124 900
Court	105 646
Durr	80 602
Stove	65 195
Morozova	64 527
Casals	62 302

1976
Men

Connors	$686 335
Nastase	576 705
Ramirez	465 942
Borg	424 420
Ashe	373 886
Orantes	361 884
H Solomon (USA)	253 432
Vilas	250 726
E Dibbs (USA)	239 821
W Fibak (Pol)	234 039

Women

Evert	$343 165
Cawley	209 952
Wade	159 213
Casals	128 685
Navratilova	128 535
Stove	98 358
S Barker (GB)	92 483
Durr	70 830
King	70 470
Mrs M Guerrant (USA)	45 910

1977
Men

Vilas	$800 642
Connors	622 657
Gottfried	478 988
Borg	345 661
R L Stockton (USA)	311 856
Nastase	396 956
Dibbs	283 691
V Gerulaitis (USA)	274 324
Ramirez	245 007
R Tanner (USA)	129 465

Women

Evert	$453 134
Navratilova	275 317
King	274 149
Stove	229 162
Wade	193 476
Barker	180 458
Mrs G Reid (Miss K Melville)	139 567
Casals	126 139
W M Turnbull (Aus)	98 568
Durr	92 703

1978
Men

Dibbs	$582 872
Ramirez	450 110
J P McEnroe (USA)	445 024
Fibak	383 843
Nastase	367 422
Gerulaitis	359 095
Solomon	354 732
Connors	353 307
Borg	348 386
Gottfried	312 205

Women

Navratilova	$450 757
Evert	354 486
Wade	270 027
Reid	208 766
Turnbull	189 583
Stove	177 243
Cawley	160 844
V Ruzici (Rom)	151 379
King	149 492
R Marsikova (Cze)	88 894

1979
Men

Borg	$1 019 345
McEnroe	1 005 238
Connors	701 340
Gerulaitis	414 515
Vilas	374 195
P Fleming (USA)	353 315
Tanner	263 433
Dibbs	249 293
Fibak	234 452
Solomon	222 078

Women

Navratilova	$747 548
Mrs J M Lloyd (Miss C M Evert)	564 398
T A Austin (USA)	541 676
Turnbull	317 463
D Fromholtz (Aus)	265 990
King	185 804
Stove	182 006
Barker	175 452
Cawley	171 573
Wade	146 283

1980
Men

McEnroe	$972 369
Borg	731 762
I Lendl (Cze)	593 906
Connors	570 060
G Mayer (USA)	397 156
Vilas	378 217

Fibak	368 073
Gerulaitis	340 820
Gottfried	296 800
Smith	277 675

Women

Navratilova	766 487
Austin	717 378
Lloyd	457 533
H Mandlikova (Cze)	379 642
Turnbull	345 413
King	298 413
A Jaeger (USA)	260 496
Cawley	218 606
Ruzici	197 936
P H Shriver (USA)	182 104

1981
Men

McEnroe	$991 000
Lendl	846 037
Connors	405 872
Vilas	402 261
J L Clerc (Arg)	327 375
Gerulaitis	283 475
H Gunthardt (Swi)	278 642
P McNamara (Aus)	273 066
E Teltscher (USA)	267 630
Tanner	245 380

Women

Navratilova	$865 437
Lloyd	572 162
Austin	453 409
Jaeger	392 115
Shriver	366 530
Mandlikova	339 602
Turnbull	225 161
A E Smith (USA)	192 311
S Hanika (FRG)	190 898
Ruzici	179 115

RICHEST TOURNAMENT

The **world's richest tournament** was staged in Dubai, United Arab Emirates, 19–23 November 1980. The total prize money for the Dubai Golden Tournament was **$680 000** for a field of 16 men players. The first prize for the singles (won by the Pole, Wojtek Fibak) was $125 000, this reward being for winning five matches in all. Second prize was $100 000, third $75 000 and fourth $50 000 with twelve other players getting $25 000 each for taking part in three round robin matches. Doubles winners shared $15 000.

For Fibak his earnings averaged $968·9 per game.

The Game on Court

THE LONGEST MATCHES

The longest matches as measured by the number of games are shown in the tables below.

The longest match in Great Britain was the men's singles at Wimbledon in 1969 (see table) of 112 games.

The longest men's doubles in Great Britain was in 1966 in the first round at Wimbledon in which Nikki Pilic (Yug) and Gene Scott (USA) beat Cliff Richey (USA) and Torben Ulrich (Den) 19–21 12–10 6–4 4–6 9–7, a total of 98 games.

The longest women's singles in Great Britain was in 1968 (see table) and comprised 60 games.

The longest women's doubles in Great Britain was in 1970 at Hoylake when in the second round Evonne Goolagong and Pat Edwards (both Aus) beat Patti Hogan (USA) and Fay Toyne-Moore (Aus) 9–11 7–5 12–10, a total of 54 games.

The longest mixed doubles in Great Britain was in 1967 at Wimbledon when in the quarter-final Ken Fletcher (Aus) and Maria Bueno (Bra) beat Alex Metreveli and Anna Dmitrieva (both USSR) 6–8 7–5 16–14, a total of 56 games.

MEN'S MATCHES OF 100 GAMES OR MORE

Event		Occasion	Players	Score	Total
1967	Men's Doubles	Newport Casino, RI, Tournament. Second Round.	R Dell & R Leach beat T Mozur & L Schloss (all USA)	3–6 49–47 22–20	147
1968	Men's Doubles	US Indoor Champs, Salisbury. Quarter-final.	M Cox & R K Wilson (GB) beat R Holmberg & C Pasarell (USA)	2–6 2–6 17–19 30–28	144
1949	Men's Doubles	S California Champs, LA. Final	R Falkenburg & F R Schroeder beat F Gonzales & H Stewart (all USA)	36–34 2–6 4–6 6–4 19–17	135
1966	Men's Singles	King's Cup, Warsaw.	R Taylor (GB) beat W Gasoriek (Poland)	27–29 31–29 6–4	126
1973	Men's Doubles	Davis Cup, American Zone Final, Little Rock, Arkansas.	S R Smith & E Van Dillen (USA) beat P Cornejo & J Fillol (Chi)	7–9 37–39 8–6 6–1 6–3	122
1969	Men's Singles	Wimbledon Champs, First Round.	R Gonzales beat C Pasarell (both USA)	22–24 1–6 16–14 6–3 11–9	112
1967	Men's Singles	Meadow Club Tournament, Qualifying Round.	R Knight beat M Sprengelmeyer (both USA)	32–30 3–6 19–17	107
1967	Men's Doubles	Meadow Club Tournament, Second Round.	T Mozur & L Schloss (USA) beat C Bovett (GB) & B Seewagen (USA)	7–5 48–46	106
1966	Men's Doubles	US Doubles Champs, Boston. Third Round.	M Lara & J Loyo-Mayo (Mex) beat L Garcia (Mex) & M Santana (Spa)	10–12 24–22 11–9 3–6 6–2	105
1967	Men's Doubles	US Doubles Champs, Boston. Quarter-final.	E C Drysdale & R J Moore (SA) beat R Emerson (Aus) & R Barnes (Bra)	29–31 8–6 3–6 8–6 6–2	105
1969	Men's Doubles	Merion Club Tournament. Semi-final.	W Bowrey (Aus) & J Osborne (USA) beat T Addison & R Keldie (Aus)	3–6 43–41 7–5	105
1941	Men's Doubles	US Doubles Champs, Boston. Second Round.	R Bobbitt & B M Grant beat E Amarck & R Hippenstiel (all USA)	14–12 15–17 6–4 4–6 13–11	102
1964	Men's Doubles	US Doubles Champs, Boston. First Round.	R Galloway & D White beat L Roemer & H Sweeney (all USA)	6–4 17–15 4–6 18–20 7–5	102
1934	Men's Doubles	Buffalo Indoor, Semi-final.	G McAuliff & C Sutter beat G M Lott & F X Shields (all USA)	12–14 14–12 25–23	100
1955	Men's Singles	Lyons Indoor, Final.	J Drobny (Egy) v J E Patty (USA)	21–19 8–10 21–21 divided	100

Event	Occasion	Players	Score	Total
1969 Men's Singles	US Open, New York. First Round.	F D Robbins beat R Dell (both USA)	22–20 9–7 6–8 8–10 6–4	100
1969 Men's Doubles	Phoenix Tournament. Quarter-final.	J Loyo-Mayo (Mex) & R C Lutz (USA) beat W Bond & R Leach (USA)	19–17 33–31	100
1982 Men's Singles	Davis Cup, American Zone. Caracas.	H Fritz (Can) beat J Andrew (Ven)	16–14 11–9 9–11 4–6 11–9	100

WOMEN'S MATCHES OF 60 GAMES OR MORE

Event	Occasion	Players	Score	Total
1964 Women's Doubles	S. Orange Tournament, Semi-final.	Miss C Caldwell & Miss N Richey beat Miss J Bricka & Miss C Hanks (all USA)	31–33 6–1 6–4	81
1948 Mixed Doubles	US National Champs, NY, Semi-final.	(WF Talbert) & Miss M E Osborne beat (R Falkenburg) & Miss G Moran (all USA)	27–25 5–7 6–1	71
1970 Mixed Doubles	Pacific NW Champs, Tacona, Quarter-final.	(E Jackson) & Miss D Irish beat (R Hill) & Miss S Ride (all USA)	7–5 2–6 25–23	68
1966 Women's Singles	Piping Rock Tournament, First round.	K Blake (USA) beat E Subirats (Mex)	12–10 6–8 14–12	62
1972 Mixed Doubles	Armed Forces Champs, Moscow, Final.	(P Lamp) & Miss D Yushka beat (V Korotkov) & Miss S Shriniskaya (all USSR)	9–11 8–6 15–13	62
1968 Women's Singles	Dewar Cup, Crystal Palace, London. Quarter-final.	Miss M A Eisel (USA) beat Miss P M Walkden (SA)	7–9 7–5 17–15	60
1969 Women's Singles	Kingston, Jamaica, Tournament. First round.	Miss K Pigeon (USA) beat Miss K M Krantzcke (Aus)	17–15 2–6 11–9	60

LONGEST FINALS IN MAJOR CHAMPIONSHIPS

Men's Singles	Women's Singles	Men's Doubles	Women's Doubles	Mixed Doubles
Australia				
1927	1956	1966	1926	1933
G L Patterson beat J B Hawkes 3–6 6–4 3–6 18–16 6–3	Miss M Carter beat Mrs T D Long 3–6 6–2 9–7	R S Emerson & F S Stolle beat J D Newcombe & A D Roche 7–9 6–3 6–8 14–12 12–10	Mrs P O'Hara Wood & Miss E F Boyd beat Miss D Akhurst & Miss M Cox 6–3 6–8 8–6	J H & Mrs Crawford beat H E Vines (USA) & Mrs J Van Ryn (USA) 3–6 7–5 13–11
71 games	33 games	**87 games**	37 games	45 games
France				
1927	1955	1934	1955	1958
R Lacoste beat W T Tilden (USA) 6–4 4–6 5–7 6–3 11–9	Miss A Mortimer (GB) beat Mrs D P Knode (USA) 2–6 7–5 10–8	J Borotra & J Brugnon beat J H Crawford (Aus) & V B McGrath (Aus) 11–9 6–3 2–6 4–6 9–7	Mrs J C Fleitz (USA) & Miss D R Hard (USA) beat Miss S J Bloomer (GB) & Miss P E Ward (GB) 7–5 6–8 13–11	N Pietrangeli (Ita) & Miss S J Bloomer (GB) beat R N Howe (Aus) & Miss L Coghlan (Aus) 9–7 6–8 6–2
61 games	38 games	1971 A R Ashe (USA) & M C Riessen (USA) beat T Gorman (USA) & S R Smith (USA) 6–8 4–6 6–3 6–4 11–9	**50 games**	38 games
		63 games		

Men's Singles	Women's Singles	Men's Doubles	Women's Doubles	Mixed Doubles
Wimbledon 1954 J Drobny (Egy) beat K R Rosewall (Aus) 13–11 4–6 6–2 9–7 58 games	1970 Mrs B M Court (Aus) beat Mrs L W King (USA) 14–12 11–9 46 games	1968 J D Newcombe (Aus) & A D Roche (Aus) beat K R Rosewall (Aus) & F S Stolle (Aus) 3–6 8–6 5–7 14–12 6–3 70 games	1933 Mme R Mathieu (Fra) & Miss E Ryan (USA) beat Miss F James & Miss A M Yorke 6–2 11–9 6–4 1967 Miss R Casals (USA) & Mrs L W King (USA) beat Miss M E Bueno (Bra) & Miss N Richey (USA) 9–11 6–4 6–2 38 games	1949 E W Sturgess (SA) & Mrs S P Summers (SA) beat J E Bromwich (Aus) & Miss A L Brough (USA) 9–7 9–11 7–5 **48 games**
USA 1949 R A Gonzales beat F R Schroeder 16–18 2–6 6–1 6–2 6–4 67 games	1898 Miss J P Atkinson beat Miss M Jones 6–3 5–7 6–4 2–6 7–5 **51 games** but 1948 Mrs W du Pont beat Miss A L Brough 6–4 4–6 15–13 **48 games**	1946 G Mulloy & W F Talbert beat W D McNeill & F Guernsey 3–6 6–4 2–6 6–3 20–18 74 games	1926 Miss E Ryan & Miss E Goss beat Miss M K Browne & Mrs A H Chapin 3–6 6–4 12–10 1953 Miss S J Fry & Miss D J Hart beat Mrs W D du Pont & Miss A L Brough 6–3 7–9 9–7 41 games	1959 N A Fraser (Aus) & Mrs W du Pont beat R Mark (Aus) & Miss J Hopps 7–5 13–15 6–2 **48 games**

LONGEST FINAL DAYS

BOURNEMOUTH

Eric Sturgess (SA) took part in five matches on the last day of the British Hard Court Championships at the West Hants Club, Bournemouth, 1 May 1948. He beat I Tloczynski (Pol) 6–2 6–3 6–1 to win the men's singles final. In the men's doubles semi-final he and R van Meegeren (Hol) beat C Spychala (Pol) and Tloczynski 6–1 6–0 1–6 3–6 7–5 and, in the final, F Kukuljevic (Yug) and J S Olliff (GB) 7–5 6–0 6–1. In mixed doubles Sturgess partnered Jean Quertier (GB) to beat Paddy Roberts and Betty Hilton (both GB) 6–2 6–2 in the semi-final and J R Mansell and Miss E A Middleton (both GB) 6–2 7–5 in the final. Total: **15 sets, 126 games.**

WIMBLEDON

Louise Brough (USA) took part in three finals on the last day of the Wimbledon Championships 2 July 1949. In the singles she beat Margaret du Pont (USA) 10–8 1–6 10–8. In women's doubles Miss Brough and Margaret du Pont beat Gussy Moran and Pat Todd (both USA) 8–6 7–5. In mixed doubles Miss Brough partnered John Bromwich (Aus) and they lost to Eric Sturgess and Sheila Summers (both SA) 7–9 11–9 5–7. Total: **8 sets, 117 games.** She occupied the Centre Court for 5 hours 20 minutes.

LONG SETS

The **longest set** was played in a men's doubles in 1967 when in the second round of the Newport, RI, tournament R Dell and R Leach beat T Mozur and L Schloss (all USA) 3–6 **49–47** 22–20, a total of **96 games.**

The **longest set in a men's singles** was in the third round of the Heart of America tournament, Kansas City, 1968, when John Brown (Aus) beat Bill Brown (USA) **36–34** 6–1, a total of **70 games.**

The **longest set in a women's doubles** was in the semi-final of the Eastern Grass Championships at South Orange, N J, in August 1964 when Nancy Richey and Carol Caldwell beat Justina Bricka and Carol Hanks (all USA) **31–33** 6–1 6–4, a total of **64 games.**

The **longest set in a mixed doubles** was in the semi-final of the US National Championships at Forest Hills, 1948, when William Talbert and

Margaret du Pont beat Bob Falkenburg and Gussy Moran (all USA) **27–25** 5–7 6–1, a total of **52 games**.

The **longest set in a women's singles** was in the Wightman Cup contest at the Cleveland Skating Club, Cleveland, Ohio, 1963, when Billie Jean Moffitt (USA) beat Christine Truman (GB) 6–4 **19–17**, a total of **36 games**.

The **longest set between juniors** was in the British Junior Covered Court Championships at Queen's Club, London, 1959, when R B B Avory and J Baker won a boys' doubles against W J King and R Taylor (all GB) 6–4 **28–26**, a total of **54 games**.

LONG GAMES AND LONG RALLIES

The **longest game** on record was played between A Fawcett of Rhodesia and K Glass of Great Britain in the men's singles in the Surrey Grass Court Championships in Surbiton, England, in May 1975. It extended for **37 deuces (80 points)**.

The **longest game between women** was probably between Billie Jean King of the USA and Virginia Wade in the semi-final of the Italian Championships on the centre court at the Foro Italico in Rome on 26 April 1970. Mrs King, saving two match points at 4–5 in the second set, beat Miss Wade 3–6 7–5 6–3 and went on to take the championship. With Mrs King 6–5 in the second set the next game lasted 22 minutes and extended for **21 deuces (48 points)**.

The **longest recorded rally** was played 13 November 1977 between two 11-year-old girls, Cari Hagey and Colette Kavanagh in the Anaheim Junior Championships, California when, after slightly more than five hours, Miss Hagey won 2–6 6–4 6–2. The opening point of the second set lasted **51½ minutes** and it was estimated that the ball crossed the net **1,029 times**. The second set started at 10.30 am and finished at 2.05 pm, having lasted 3 hours 35 minutes. Both players were from La Jolla, California.

Two juniors, Inderjit Singh and A R Mitter, played a rally of **924 strokes** lasting **38 minutes**, in the boys' singles semi-final in the Calcutta Hard Court Championships in 1958.

In the State Centre Junior Championships in Northern California, in April 1981 Gus Anderson and Eric Gottlieb, playing an under 18 singles match that Anderson won 6–2 6–2, had a rally lasting **48 minutes**. The match lasted 2 hours 30 minutes in all. The number of times the ball crossed the net was not estimated.

In the Philadelphia Clay Court Championships at the Cynwyd Club on 23 June 1981 Ken

Phelan and Dr Richard Cohen, playing the match point by which Phelan won 6–1 6–3 with a drop shot, had a rally of **2,095 strokes** that lasted **29 minutes 25 seconds**.

In the final of the women's singles at Bordighera, Italy, in 1930, the British Phyllis Satterthwaite, the winner, had a rally against the Italian Lucia Valerio of **450 strokes** that lasted **19 minutes**.

The **longest recorded rally between top class men** was in the London Championships at Queen's Club, 1920 when Gordon Lowe of Great Britain and Bitsy Norton of South Africa exchanged more than **200 shots**.

Note. All records about the number of shots and the time of a rally must be viewed with some scepticism. Such figures are rarely made a matter of precise measurement.

SHORT MATCHES

Possibly the **shortest five set match** was the men's singles final of the Carlton Club tournament at Cannes on 24 January 1927 when H Cochet (Fra) beat J Brugnon (Fra) 1–6 6–1 6–0 1–6 6–0. A contemporary account reads: 'Brugnon won the first and fourth sets by brilliant volleying; but after each fell back and Cochet took the initiative.' The total was **33 games**.

Possibly the **shortest finish to a five set match** was a quarter-final of the men's singles in the British Hard Court Championships at Bournemouth on 26 April 1938 when Kho Sin Kie (Chn) beat W C Choy (Chn). Kho Sin Kie trailed 4–6 4–6 0–1 and won **18 successive games** to triumph 4–6 4–6 6–1 6–0 6–0. The same players provided the final in 1939 (with Kho Sin Kie winning 7–5 6–1 6–4), the **only all Chinese final** of a major tournament.

Forty-eight straight points in a tournament singles were won by Hazel Hotchkiss, later Mrs G W Wightman (USA) in Seattle in 1910 when she beat Miss Huiskamp 6–0 6–0. A like pointless victory was had by Pauline Betz (USA) against Miss C Wolf in the Tri-State tournament, Pennsylvania, in 1943.

The **greatest number of points in sequence** was probably by the Indian Mohammed Sleem at Eastbourne in 1924. In a handicap singles he owed 40 and gave 30, needing seven points to win each game. He won **52 consecutive points**.

Possibly **the most one sided team match** was an Under-14 contest at Devonshire Park, Eastbourne, on 7, 8 and 9 July 1975. Teams were 10-a-side, six boys and four girls. Italy beat Great Britain **65–nil**. The British team comprised M J Bates, P S J Farrell, N Gerbard, K E G Gilbert,

P E Hughesman, S J Taylor, Miss M A Barton, Miss K J Brasher, Miss S G Davies and Miss T Heath.

SLOW AND QUICK MATCHES

The **longest overall duration of a match** was the final of the men's doubles of the Italian Championships 1976. In Rome on 30 May Brian Gottfried (USA) and Raul Ramirez (Mex) were two sets all with Geoff Masters and John Newcombe (Aus) when bad light stopped play. Gottfried and Ramirez won the match 7–6 5–7 6–3 3–6 6–3 when they won the final set in Houston, Texas, on 15 September. Duration of the match was **108 days.**

R Salvet (Fra) beat R Contet (Fra) 7–5 5–7 9–7 in a club competition at the Stade Roland Garros, Paris, in 1950 and, extended over three evenings, the match duration was **8 hours 15 minutes.**

In the fifth and decisive rubber of the quarter-final Davis Cup tie in St Louis in July 1982 John McEnroe (USA) beat Mats Wilander (Swe) 8–7 6–2 15–17 3–6 8–6 after **6 hours 32 minutes.**

In February 1968 in the men's doubles quarter-final of the US Indoor Championships at Salisbury, Maryland, Mark Cox and Bobby Wilson (GB) beat Charlie Pasarell and Ron Holmberg (USA) 26–24 17–19 30–28 (a total of 144 games) when the duration was **6 hours 23 minutes.**

F G Lowe (GB) beat A Zerlendi (Gre) 14–12 8–10 5–7 6–4 6–4 in the second round of the men's singles in the Olympic Games in Antwerp in 1920 after a playing time of **5 hours 45 minutes.** There were many interruptions. Darkness postponed the match after 2 hours on the first day. The ball boys arbitrarily delayed by leaving to have lunch at the end of the third set the next day. There was a hold up of 7 minutes in the final set when, without objection from anyone, Lowe was allowed to have cramp relieved by massage. The exact time of the match from start to finish was not recorded but it was about **24 hours.**

The Wimbledon men's singles final in 1982, in which Jimmy Connors (USA) beat John McEnroe (USA) 3–6 6–3 6–7 7–6 6–2, lasted **4 hours 14 minutes.**

Mrs H Doleschell (Can) beat Mlle C Mercelis (Bel) 9–11 5–7 6–3 in the Canadian Championships in Toronto in 1953 after **4 hours.**

In the third round of the women's singles in the French Championships 1972 Kerry Melville (Aus) beat Pam Teeguarden (USA) 9–4 4–6 16–14 after **3 hours 55 minutes.**

The **shortest authenticated** time on record was on 13 June 1914 in the Kent Championships at Beckenham when in the men's doubles final Norman Brookes (Aus) and Tony Wilding (NZ) beat Arthur Gore and Herbert Roper Barrett (GB) 6–2 6–1 in **16 minutes.**

J E Harper (Aus) beat a dental student J Sandiford (GB) 6–0 6–0 for the loss of only one point in the Sutton tournament in 1946 on his 32nd birthday on 9 April in **18 minutes.**

The **quickest best of five sets** match on record was played in an international on Davis Cup lines between the USA and Great Britain at the Northern LT Club, Manchester, when Bill Tilden (USA) beat D M Greig (GB) on 16 June 1927 by 6–0 6–0 6–2 in **22 minutes.** (The same match played in the 1980's could legally occupy 15 minutes in the change of ends.)

In the Wimbledon women's singles final of 1922 Suzanne Lenglen beat Molla Mallory 6–2 6–0 in **25 minutes.**

A record of the time of the 1911 final, when Dorothea Lambert Chambers beat Dora Boothby 6–0 6–0, has not survived.

The **quickest men's singles final at Wimbledon** was that of 1881 when William Renshaw beat Rev. John Hartley 6–0 6–1 6–1 in **37 minutes.** At that time it was customary to change ends only at the end of each set.

Note: The timing of matches has to be treated with caution. It has never been a matter of official measurement and only in recent years has it been done with precision. Since 1980 and the sanction of an interval of 90 seconds for the change over period, together with the allowance of a 30 seconds interval between points, the match duration has increased considerably.

FIRST OVERSEAS WINNERS

The first player to win a tournament overseas was **O E Woodhouse** of England, and a member of the Ealing Club, Middlesex, when he won the 'Championship of America' at the Staten Island Cricket and Baseball Club in **September 1880.**

The first to win a British tournament from overseas was **James Dwight** (USA) when he won the men's singles in the Northern Championships in Manchester in **June 1885.**

The first woman to win a tournament overseas was **Mabel Cahill** of Ireland who won the US women's singles championships in Philadelphia in **1891.** The first woman from overseas to win a British tournament was **May Sutton** (of California though born in Plymouth, Devon) when she won the Northern Championship in Manchester in **June 1905.**

SHORTEST FINALS IN MAJOR CHAMPIONSHIPS

Men's Singles	Women's Singles	Men's Doubles	Women's Doubles	Mixed Doubles
Australia				
1926	1962	1947	1971	1922
J B Hawkes beat J Willard 6–1 6–3 6–1	Miss M Smith beat Miss J Lehane 6–0 6–2	A K Quist & J E Bromwich beat F A Sedgman & G Worthington 6–1 6–3 6–1	Mrs B M Court & Miss E Goolagong beat Miss L Hunt and Mrs J Emerson 6–0 6–0	J B Hawkes & Miss E F Boyd beat H S Utz & Mrs Utz 6–1 6–1
23 games	14 games	23 games	**12 games**	
				1936
				H C Hopman & Mrs Hopman beat A A Kay & Miss M Blick 6–2 6–0
				14 games
France				
1977	1926	1953	1980	1947
G Vilas (Arg) beat B E Gottfried (USA) 6–0 6–3 6–0	Mlle S Lenglen beat Miss M K Browne (USA) 6–1 6–0	L A Hoad (Aus) & K R Rosewall (Aus) beat M Rose (Aus) & C Wilderspin (Aus) 6–2 6–1 6–1	Miss K Jordan (USA) & Miss A E Smith (USA) beat Miss I Madruga (Arg) & Miss A Villagran (Arg) 6–1 6–0	E W Sturgess (SA) & Mrs P Summers (SA) beat C Carallulis (Rom) & Miss J Jedrezejowska (Pol) 6–0 6–0
21 games	13 games	**22 games**	13 games	**12 games**
Wimbledon				
1881	1911	1910	1953	1919
W Renshaw beat J T Hartley 6–0 6–1 6–1	Mrs R Lambert Chambers beat Miss D Boothby 6–0 6–0	M J G Ritchie & A F Wilding (NZ) beat A W Gore & H Roper Barrett 6–1 6–1 6–2	Miss S J Fry (USA) & Miss D J Hart (USA) beat Miss M Connolly (USA) & Miss J Sampson (USA) 6–0 6–0	R Lycett & Miss E Ryan (USA) beat A Prebble & Mrs R Lambert Chambers 6–0 6–0
	12 games	**22 games**	**12 games**	**12 games**
1936				
F J Perry beat G Von Cramm (Ger) 6–1 6–1 6–0				
20 games				
USA				
1974	1887	1885	1946	1915
J S Connors beat K R Rosewall (Aus) 6–1 6–0 6–1	Miss E Hansell beat Miss L Knight 6–1 6–0	J S Clark & R D Sears beat W P Knapp & H W Slocum 6–3 6–0 6–2	Miss A L Brough & Miss M E Osborn beat Mrs D Prentiss & Mrs P C Todd 6–2 6–0	H C Johnson & Mrs G W Wightman beat I C Wright & Miss M Bjurstedt 6–0 6–1
20 games				13 games
	1916	1909	1960	
	Miss M Bjurstedt beat Mrs E Raymond 6–0 6–1	F B Alexander & H H Hackett beat G J James & M E McLoughlin 6–4 6–1 6–0	Miss M E Bueno (Bra) & Miss D R Hard beat Miss D M Catt (GB) & Miss A S Haydon (GB) 6–1 6–1	
	13 games		14 games	
		1949		
		J E Bromwich (Aus) & O W Sidwell (Aus) beat F A Sedgman (Aus) & G Worthington (Aus) 6–4 6–0 6–1		
		23 games		

FIRST OPEN WINNERS

The **world's first open champions** were the British Hard Court Champions of 1968 after the world's first open tournament at Bournemouth, 22 to 27 April played without distinction between professionals and amateurs. They were:

Men's singles: Ken Rosewall (Aus), winning £1,000.
Women's singles: Virginia Wade (GB), winning £300.
Men's doubles: Roy Emerson (Aus) and Rod Laver (Aus), winning £250 each.
Women's doubles: Christine Janes and Nell Truman (GB), winning £50 each.
Mixed doubles: Bob Howe (Aus) and Virginia Wade, winning £40 each.

The **first 'open' match** in a tournament was in the men's singles first round in the British Hard Court Championships on 22 April 1968 when Owen Davidson (Aus) beat his pupil John Clifton (GB) 6–2 6–3 4–6 8–6.

The **first 'amateur' to beat a 'professional'** was on 24 April 1968 at Bournemouth when Mark Cox (GB) beat Richard Gonzales (USA) 0–6 6–2 4–6 6–3 6–3.

KINDRED ACHIEVEMENT

High lawn tennis skill has often belonged to members of the same family. It can be argued that genetic factors are involved. A more obvious cause is environmental. Be that as it may, brothers were notable in the early days of the game with the twins William and Ernest Renshaw ranking as the inventors of modern technique in the 1880's. Another pair of twins, C G and E R Allen were famous. More so were the brothers Herbert and Wilfred Baddeley and, resoundingly, Reggie and Laurie Doherty. In the first women's singles final at Wimbledon in 1884 Maud Watson beat her sister Lilian.

In the USA the Clark brothers, J S and C M, were front runners among the pioneers. So, among the women, were Ellen and Grace Roosevelt. Later R D and G L Wrenn were among the top rank and so were Howard and Robert Kinsey.

The geneticists can find ammunition for their case with the fathers and sons who have been at the top. There have been at least eight instances where a son has followed his father into his national Davis Cup team.

DAVIS CUP: FATHER AND SON

Name	Father	Years	Son	Years	Nation
BERTRAM	Max	1935	Byron	1974–78	South Africa
DE BORMAN	Paul	1904–19	Leopold	1930–39	Belgium
HAILLET	Robert	1952–60	Jean-Louis	1977–80	France
KRISHNAN	Ramanathan	1953–69	Ramesh	1981	India
MOTTRAM	Anthony	1947–55	Christopher*	1975–81	Great Britain
PAISH	Geoff	1947–55	John	1972	Great Britain
ULRICH†	Einer	1924–38	Torben	1948–77	Denmark
			& Jorgen	1958–71	Denmark
WASHER	Jean	1921–27	Phillippe	1946–61	Belgium

* The mother of 'Buster' Mottram is Joy Mottram, née Gannon, British Wightman Cup player 1947–52.
† The Ulrichs must be the outstanding Davis Cup family. Einer and his two sons together played 225 rubbers, winning 109, with Torben and Jorgen sharing six doubles out of 75. Out of the 94 ties in which Denmark took part 1921 to 1977 the Ulrichs took part in 79.

WIGHTMAN CUP: MOTHER AND DAUGHTER

Name	Mother	Years	Daughter	Years	Nation
BUNDY	May (Sutton)	1925	Dorothy*	1937–39	USA

* The father of Dorothy Bundy (later Mrs Cheney) was T C Bundy, US Davis Cup player 1911–14.

KINDRED CHAMPIONS

	Titles Won	Years
BROTHERS—Men's Doubles		
E & W Renshaw (GB)	Wimbledon	1884–86, 1888, 1889
H & W Baddeley (GB)	Wimbledon	1891, 1894–96
C B & S R Neel (USA)	US Champ	1896
H L & R F Doherty (GB)	Wimbledon	1897–1901, 1903–05
	US Champ	1902, 1903
	Brit. Cov. Court	1898–1903, 1906
	Olympic Gold	1900
A & M Vacherot (Fra)	French	1901
H & R Kinsley (USA)	US Champ	1924
SISTERS—Women's Doubles		
Misses B & M Steedman (GB)	All England	1889, 1900
Misses E C & G W Roosevelt (USA)	US Champ	1900
Misses L & M Marriott (GB)	All England	1891
Mlles J & C Matthey (Fra)	French	1909
Mlles B & S Amblard (Fra)	French	1913, 1914
BROTHER & SISTER—Mixed Doubles		
A & Miss C Dod (GB)	All England	1892
M & Mlle Meny (Fra)	French	1910
J & Miss T A Austin (USA)	Wimbledon	1980
HUSBAND & WIFE—Mixed Doubles		
Mr & Mrs G Greville (GB)	Brit. Cov. Court	1904
Mr & Mrs C Hobart (USA)	US Champ	1905
Herr & Frau H Schomburgk (Ger)	German	1921
Mr & Mrs L A Godfree (GB)	Wimbledon	1926
Mr & Mrs J H Crawford (Aus)	Australian	1931–33
Mr & Mrs H C Hopman (Aus)	Australian	1936, 1937, 1939
Mr & Mrs A R Mills (GB)	Brit. Hard Court	1963

(Note. Mrs Charles Tuckey played in the mixed doubles with her son Raymond Tuckey in the Wimbledon Championship 1931, winning one round, and in 1932.

Tony Mottram, in the final of the mixed doubles in the German Championships 1953, partnered Pat Ward to beat Jean Borotra and Mrs Tony Mottram 2–6 6–4 6–3.)

JUNIOR KINDRED CHAMPIONS

	Titles Won	Years
SISTERS—Girls' Doubles		
Sarah & Mianne Palfrey	US Champ	1926, 1928, 1929
	US Indoor Champ	1927–1929
Sarah & Joanna Palfrey	US Indoor Champ	1930
BROTHER & SISTER—Mixed Doubles		
H W & Miss J W Austin	British	1921
J W & Miss B Nuthall	British	1926
R C & Miss J Nicoll	British	1938

The most successful lawn tennis playing family was arguably the four Sutton sisters, **May, Ethel, Florence and Violet** Sutton of San Francisco, daughters of a British naval captain who emigrated from Plymouth, Devon.

In the 1913 US ranking list Ethel rated two and Florence three. Violet, the first to have success, won the Pacific Coast Championship in 1899 and 1900. That championship was dominated by the sisters 1899 to 1912, May taking the singles eight times, Florence three times and Violet twice. They won 26 Pacific Coast titles in all.

May was the most notable, being US Champion in 1904, Wimbledon Champion 1905 and 1907. As Mrs T C Bundy she played in the Wightman Cup in 1925. She ranked fifth in the US in 1928 when aged 41.

Her daughter, **Dorothy Bundy** (whose father was an American Davis Cup player in 1911 and 1914) played in the Wightman Cup 1937, 1938 and 1939. As Mrs Cheyney she won no less than 116 US National titles, mainly age group 1940–82.

VICTORY FROM THE BRINK: MATCH POINTS

The **highest number of match points saved** in world class play was **18.** This mammoth sequence of salvation was achieved by Wilmer Allison (USA) in the opening rubber of the Inter-Zone Final of the Davis Cup in Paris on 18 July 1930. He beat Giorgio de Stefani (Ita) 4–6 7–9 6–4 8–6 10–8 after trailing 2–5 in the fourth set and by 1–5 in the fifth.

Adriano Panatta (Ita) uniquely **won two major championships in succession,** the Italian and the French in 1976, **after being match point down in the opening rounds** of both. In the Italian Championships in Rome he won the first round against Kim Warwick (Aus) 3–6 6–4 7–6 having been within a point of losing 11 times. He went on to win the title. The next week in the first round of the French Championships in Paris he beat Pavel Hutka (Cze) 2–6 6–2 6–2 0–6 12–10 after being match point behind at 9–10 in the final set. He went on to become French champion.

Robert Haillet (Fra) beat Budge Patty (USA) in the fourth round of the French Championships in Paris in 1958 by 7–5 in the fifth set after **Patty had led 5–love, 40–love,** and had had a further match point at 5–4, 40–30. He won 5–7 7–5 10–8 4–6 7–5.

Humphrey Truman (GB) saved match points in the third, fourth and fifth sets in beating B Katz (Rho) in the qualifying round of the Wimbledon Qualifying singles in 1962. Truman won 4–6 1–6 11–9 8–6 10–8. The sequence was ironic. In the first round of the championships proper G Hernandez (Phi) beat Truman 5–7 4–6 6–4 14–12 6–2 after Truman was at match point in the fourth set.

Peter McNamara and Paul McNamme, both of Australia, **saved match points in the third, fourth and fifth sets** in beating Sherwood Stewart and Ferdie Taygan, both of the USA 2–6 4–6 7–6 7–5 7–6 in their round robin contest in the World Championship Tennis Doubles tournament at the National Exhibition Centre, Birmingham, England, on 7 January 1982. They salvaged two match points in the third set, three in the fourth and two in the fifth, making seven in all before winning from a deficit of 1–4 in the final set tie break.

Helga Schultze (FRG) beat Janine Lieffrig (Fra) by 4–6 11–9 12–10 in the first round of the women's singles at Wimbledon in 1966 after saving **11 match points** in all.

ALL FIVE CONTINENTS

There were three occasions when **all five continents were represented** at the quarter-final stages of a major championship. All were in the men's singles. In the first instance it was less a matter of representation in the 'last eight' as in the 'last nine' since the challenge round system still pertained.

Wimbledon Championships 1920

Africa	C R Blackbeard (SA)
America	C S Garland (USA), W T Tilden (USA), R N Williams (USA)
Asia	Z Shimidzu (Jap)
Australia	G L Patterson (Aus) —standing out champion
Europe	R Lycett (GB), T M Mavrogordato (GB), N Willford (GB)

French Championships 1952

Africa	E W Sturgess (SA)
America	G Mulloy (USA), J E Patty (USA), R Savitt (USA)
Asia	F Ampon (Phi)
Australia	K McGregor (Aus), F A Sedgman (Aus)
Europe	J Drobny (Cze)

Wimbledon Championships 1981

Africa	J C Kriek (SA)
America	J S Connors (USA), J P McEnroe (USA), T S Mayotte (USA)
Asia	V Amritraj (Ind)
Australia	R J Frawley (Aus), P McNamara (Aus)
Europe	B Borg (Swe)

JUNIOR ACHIEVEMENT

The most striking junior achievement was by the American **Earl Buchholz** in 1958. He brought off a **Grand Slam** of titles by winning the boys' singles championship of Australia, France, Wimbledon and the United States. The first three were international events held in conjunction with the senior tournament. The American title was his own domestic one.

Wimbledon and France initiated the practice

of staging a junior tournament in association with the main events in 1947. It was, though, many years before such junior singles were recognised as 'official'. The United States followed in 1953.

The **most titles,** if they can be called such, have been won by the American **Billy Martin.** He won the boys' singles at both Wimbledon and New York in 1973 and repeated the performance in 1974.

The first player to win the French junior event in Paris and follow it by winning at Wimbledon was **Joan Cross** of South Africa in 1959.

Brother and sister were successful when Ilse Buding won the French girls' singles in 1957 and her brother Inge Buding the boys' singles in France also in 1959 and 1960. They were French residents but had German qualifications.

The overwhelming majority of junior champions have not gone on to win the senior championship where they did so well as youngsters. The following are the exceptions:

	Junior Champion	Full Champion
French Championships		
Ken Rosewall	1952	1953, 1968
Roy Emerson	1954	1963, 1967
Andres Gimeno	1955	1972
Francoise Durr	1960	1967
Mima Jausovec	1973	1977
Hana Mandlikova	1978	1981
Mats Wilander	1981	1982
Wimbledon		
Ann Haydon	1956	1969
Karen Hantze	1960	1962
Bjorn Borg	1972	1976–80

INTERNATIONAL JUNIOR CHAMPIONS Winners in the Three Major Championships

BOYS

Year	French Championships	Wimbledon Championships	USA Championships
1947	J Brichant (Bel)	K Nielsen (Den)	
1948	K Nielsen (Den)	S Stockenberg (Swe)	
1949	J C Molinari (Fra)	S Stockenberg (Swe)	
1950	R Dubuisson (Fra)	J A T Horn (GB)	
1951	H Richardson (USA)	J Kupferburger (SA)	
1952	K R Rosewall (Aus)	R K Wilson (GB)	
1953	J N Grinda (Fra)	W A Knight (GB)	
1954	R S Emerson (Aus)	Ramanathan Krishnan (Ind)	
1955	A Gimeno (Spa)	M P Hann (GB)	
1956	M Belkhodja (Fra)	R Holmberg (USA)	
1957	A Arilla (Spa)	J I Tattersall (GB)	
1958	E Buchholz (USA)	E Buchholz (USA)	
1959	I Buding (FRG)	T Lejus (USSR)	
1960	I Buding (FRG)	A R Mandelstam (SA)	
1961	J D Newcombe (Aus)	C E Graebner (USA)	
1962	J D Newcombe (Aus)	S J Matthews (GB)	
1963	N Kalogeropolous (Gre)	N Kalogeropolous (Gre)	
1964	C Richey (USA)	I El Shafei (Egy)	
1965	G D Battrick (GB)	V Korotkov (USSR)	
1966	V Korotkov (USSR)	V Korotkov (USSR)	
1967	P Proisy (Fra)	M Orantes (Spa)	
1968	P Dent (Aus)	J G Alexander (Aus)	
1969	A Munoz (Spa)	B Bertram (SA)	
1970	J Gerrero (Spa)	B Bertram (SA)	
1971	C Barazzutti (Ita)	R Kreiss (USA)	
1972	C J Mottram (GB)	B Borg (Swe)	
1973	V Pecci (Par)	W Martin (USA)	W Martin (USA)
1974	C Casa (Fra)	W Martin (USA)	W Martin (USA)
1975	C Roger-Vasselin (Fra)	C J Lewis (NZ)	H Schoenfield (USA)
1976	H Gunthardt (Swi)	H Gunthardt (Swi)	R Ycaza (Ecu)
1977	J P McEnroe (USA)	V Winitsky (USA)	V Winitsky (USA)
1978	I Lendl (Cze)	I Lendl (Cze)	P Hjertquist (Swe)
1979	Ramesh Krishnan (Ind)	Ramesh Krishnan (Ind)	S Davis (USA)
1980	H Leconte (Fra)	T Tulasne (Fra)	M Falberg (USA)
1981	M Wilander (Swe)	M Anger (USA)	T Hoegstedt (Swe)
1982	T Benhabiles (Fra)	P Cash (Aus)	P Cash (Aus)

GIRLS Year	French Championships	Wimbledon Championships	USA Championships
1948		O Miskova (Cze)	
1949		C Mercellis (Bel)	
1950		L Cornell (GB)	
1951		L Cornell (GB)	
1952		F ten Bosch (Hol)	
1953	C Brunon (Fra)	D Kilian (SA)	
1954	B de Chambre (Fra)	V A Pitt (GB)	
1955	J Redl (Aut)	S M Armstrong (GB)	
1956	E Launay (Fra)	A S Haydon (GB)	
1957	I Buding (FRG)	M Arnold (USA)	
1958	F Gordignani (Ita)	S M Moore (USA)	
1959	J Cross (SA)	J Cross (SA)	
1960	F Durr (Fra)	K Hantze (USA)	
1961	R A Ebbern (Aus)	G Baksheeva (USSR)	
1962	K Denings (Aus)	G Baksheeva (USSR)	
1963	D M Salfati (Fra)	D M Salfati (Fra)	
1964	N Seghers (Fra)	J Bartkowicz (USA)	
1965	E Emanuel (SA)	O Morozova (USSR)	
1966	O de Roubin (Fra)	B Lindstrom (Fin)	
1967	C Molesworth (GB)	J Salome (Hol)	
1968	L Hunt (Aus)	K Pigeon (USA)	
1969	K Sawamatsu (Jap)	K Sawamatsu (Jap)	
1970	V A Burton (GB)	S A Walsh (USA)	
1971	E Granatourova (USSR)	M V Kroschina (USSR)	
1972	R Tomanova (Cze)	I Kloss (SA)	
1973	M Jausovec (Yug)	A Kiyomura (USA)	
1974	M Simionescu (Rom)	M Jausovec (Yug)	I Kloss (SA)
1975	R Marsikova (Cze)	N Y Chmyriova (USSR)	N Y Chmyriova (USSR)
1976	M Tyler (GB)	N Y Chmyriova (USSR)	M Kruger (SA)
1977	A E Smith (USA)	L Antonoplis (USA)	C Casabianca (Arg)
1978	H Mandlikova (Cze)	T A Austin (USA)	L Siegel (USA)
1979	L Sandin (Swe)	M L Piatek (USA)	A Moulton (USA)
1980	K Horvath (USA)	D Freeman (Aus)	S Mascarin (USA)
1981	B Gadusek (USA)	Z Garrison (USA)	Z Garrison (USA)
1982	M Maleeva (Bul)	C Tanvier (Fra)	B Herr (USA)

MISCELLANEOUS ACHIEVEMENTS

The Australian born Gail Sherriff won the French women's doubles championship under **three different identities.** In 1967 she won as **Miss Gail Sherriff** with Francoise Durr. In 1970 and 1971 she won with the same partner as **Mme J B Chanfreau.** In 1976 she won with Florella Bonicelli as **Mme J Lovera.**

British tournament records prior to 1914 featured a prominent player whose successive identities were Miss Batty Bellew, Mrs Nutcombe-Quick and Mrs Crundell-Punnett.

Minda Ochoa, 15 years old, **beat her mother, Elisa Ochoa,** 6–3 3–6 6–4, to win the Philippines women's singles championship in 1935. Elisa had been the champion four times.

Harry Hopman, Australia's Davis Cup captain 1938–1968, reached the Australian Championships men's doubles final (with James Willard)

Gail Sherriff, whose forehand was formidable. She played for both Australia and France in the Federation Cup.

in 1930 and again (with Frank Sedgman) in 1948. His wife, **Nell Hopman**, won the Australian mixed title with him in 1930 and the French women's doubles title (with Maureen Connolly) in 1954, a gap of 24 years between Grand Slam titles.

Hans Redl first played in the Davis Cup for Austria in 1937. Subsequently, after surviving the siege of Stalingrad, he played in 1948, 1949 and 1955 as **a one armed player**. He reached the last 16 of the singles at Wimbledon in 1947. The service rule, permitting the throw up of the ball from the racket strings in the case of players so handicapped, was brought in because of him.

Eric Peters was the **only British player to beat Bill Tilden**. He did so in the Carlton tournament, Cannes, in February 1930, winning in the second round by 9–7 8–6. Tilden was 37, Peters 26.

Seventeen successive double faults, probably a record in a major championship, were served by Miss M H de Amorin (Bra) at the start of her first match at Wimbledon in 1957. She was beaten 6–3 4–6 6–1 by Mrs L B E Thung (Hol) in the second round.

The **highest altitude** at which a Davis Cup tie has been played is 11 916 feet (352 metres). It is at the La Paz Tennis Club, Bolivia.

L E Burgess played in the Edgbaston, Birmingham, tournament for **50 years** from 1888.

The **tightest stringing** is believed to be in the rackets used by **Bjorn Borg**, who has them strung to a tension of **80 pounds**.

The **lightest known stringing** among first class players was by **Beppe Merlo,**who played Davis Cup for Italy 1951 to 1965. He did his own stringing to a tension of only **47 pounds**.

The **heaviest racket** was probably used by **Don Budge**, the Grand Slam winner of 1938. It was **16 ounces**.

John Bromwich, the Wimbledon singles finalist of 1948 and doubles champion in both that year and 1950, used a racket weighing only 12½ **ounces,** the **lightest** known among leading men players.

Old time coaches took pride in holding a **large number of balls in one hand** to enable them to serve without interruption. The record was claimed by **William Frederick White**, the lawn tennis and squash rackets coach at the Merion Cricket Club, Philadelphia, when on 5 May 1930 he held **13 balls**.

MEN *v* WOMEN

In 1883 the Leicester Club championships men's singles had **two women** in the entry. **Mrs F Watts** survived one round.

The first Hungarian Championship, staged in Budapest in 1894, was unrestricted. With both men and women competing the singles was won by **Miss Paulina Palffy.**

Mixed singles were staged for Red Cross funds at the Cannes Beau Site Club in 1916. Suzanne Lenglen beat the amateur B Marion Crawford 6–1 6–0. The professional T Burke beat Mlle Lenglen 5–7 3–0 retired.

At the Cannes Club the same year a mixed handicap singles was staged. In the final Mlle Lenglen (owe 30) beat C P Hatch (owe 3/6) 6–2 6–1.

In 1917 at the Beau Site Club in Cannes Mlle Lenglen and Marion Crawford won a doubles final against T Burke and C P Hatch 6–2 7–5.

In San Diego 13 May 1973 Bobby Riggs beat Margaret Court 6–2 6–1. In Houston 20 September 1973 Billie Jean King beat Riggs 6–4 6–3 6–3 before a crowd of 30 492, winning $100 000.

In Palm Springs, California, 9 May 1981 Riggs (aged 63) and Pancho Segura (aged 59) beat Miss K Latham (aged 28) and Miss S Margolin (aged 22) 7–6 6–4 7–6. At the time Miss Latham's ranking on the Women's Tennis Association's computer ranking list was 41 and that of Miss Margolin 35.

THE 21 GREATEST MATCHES 1877–1977

In 1980 the American magazine *Tennis* conducted a survey by a panel of eight judges of the 20 greatest matches of all time. The panel comprised Edwin S Baker, Florence Blanchard, Allison Danzig, Will Grimely, Mary Hare, Roy McKelvie, Lance Tingay and Ted Tinling, the first four being American, the last four British.

The unanimity over the best match was striking, six judges placing the Budge *v* Von Cramm match of 1937 at the top. The other two placed it second.

The composite list was:
1 Don Budge (USA) beat Gottfried Von Cramm (Ger) 6–8 5–7 6–4 6–2 8–6, Inter-Zone Davis Cup final, Wimbledon, 1937. Budge was 22, von Cramm 28. It was the fifth and deciding rubber of the tie and Budge was behind 1–4 in the final set.
2 Suzanne Lenglen (Fra) beat Helen Wills (USA) 6–3 8–6, final of the Carlton Tournament, Cannes, February 1926. Mlle Lenglen was 26, Miss Wills 20. It was the only singles meeting between them.
3 Henri Cochet (Fra) beat Bill Tilden (USA) 2–6 4–6 7–5 6–4 6–3, semi-final Wimbledon

Ernest and William Renshaw playing in the final set at Wimbledon in 1882.

Some English players in 1884. Standing from left: E de S H Browne, Rev John Hartley, C W Grinstead, Miss Maud Watson, Herbert Lawford, William Renshaw. Seated: Ernest Renshaw and Miss Watson.

The Foro Italico in Rome, one of the game's most famous (and exhausting) arenas.

The West Hants Club, Bournemouth, with its three types of court, grass, indoor and hard. Home of the British Hard Court Championships.

The match that became history. Suzanne Lenglen (left) and Helen Wills before their singles at Cannes in 1926.

1927. Cochet was 25, Tilden 34. Cochet recovered from 1–5, 15–15 in the third set, taking 17 consecutive points.

4 Jack Crawford (Aus) beat Ellsworth Vines (USA) 4–6 11–9 6–2 2–6 6–4, Wimbledon final 1933. Crawford was 25, Vines 21.

5 Ken Rosewall (Aus) beat Rod Laver (Aus) 4–6 6–0 6–3 6–7 7–6, final WCT Finals, Dallas, Texas, 1972. Rosewall was 37, Laver 33.

6 Suzanne Lenglen (Fra) beat Dorothea Lambert Chambers (GB) 10–8 4–6 9–7, Wimbledon Challenge Round 1919. Mlle Lenglen was 20, Mrs Lambert Chambers 40. Mlle Lenglen saved two match points at 5–6 in the third set.

7 Fred Perry (GB) beat Don Budge (USA) 2–6 6–2 8–6 1–6 10–8, final US Championship, Forest Hills, NY, 1936. Perry was 27, Budge 21.

8 Margaret Court (Aus) beat Billie Jean King (USA) 14–12 11–9, Wimbledon final, 1970. Mrs Court was 27, Mrs King 26.

9 Arthur Ashe (USA) beat Jimmy Connors (USA) 6–1 6–1 5–7 6–4, Wimbledon final, 1975. Ashe was 29, Connors 22.

10 Pancho Gonzales (USA) beat Charlie Pasarell (USA) 22–24 1–6 16–14 6–3 11–9, first round Wimbledon, 1969, saving seven match points in the final set. Gonzales was 41, Pasarell 25.

11 Pancho Gonzales (USA) beat Ted Schroeder (USA) 16–18 2–6 6–1 6–2 6–4, final US Championships, Forest Hills, 1949. Gonzales was 21, Schroeder 28.

12 Bjorn Borg (Swe) beat Vitas Gerulaitis (USA) 6–4 3–6 6–3 3–6 8–6, Wimbledon semi-final, 1977. Borg was 21, Gerulaitis 22.

13 René Lacoste (Fra) beat Bill Tilden (USA) 11–9 6–3 11–9, final US Championships, Forest Hills, 1927. Lacoste was 23, Tilden 34.

14 Maureen Connolly (USA) beat Doris Hart (USA) 8–6 7–5, final Wimbledon, 1953. Miss Connolly was 18, Miss Hart 28.

15 René Lacoste (Fra) beat Bill Tilden (USA) 6–3 4–6 6–3 6–2, Davis Cup Challenge Round, Philadelphia, 1927. The fourth rubber, bringing France level to two all before their eventual triumph. Lacoste was 23, Tilden 34.

16 Lew Hoad (Aus) beat Tony Trabert (USA) 13–11 6–3 2–6 3–6 7–5, Davis Cup Challenge Round, Melbourne, 1953. The fourth rubber, bringing Australia level at two all before their eventual victory. Hoad was 19, Trabert 23.

17 Bill Tilden (USA) beat René Lacoste (Fra) 1–6 6–4 6–4 2–6 6–3, Davis Cup Challenge Round, Paris, 1928. Tilden was 35, Lacoste 24.

18 Jaroslav Drobny (Egy) beat Budge Patty (USA) 8–6 16–18 3–6 8–6 12–10, third round Wimbledon, 1953. Drobny saved three match points in the fourth and three in the fifth. Drobny was 31, Patty 29.

19 Billie Jean King (USA) beat Bobby Riggs (USA) 6–4 6–3 6–3, Houston, Texas, 1973. The most famous confrontation between man and woman player. Mrs King was 29, Riggs 55.

20 Helen Wills Moody (USA) beat Helen Jacobs (USA) 6–3 3–6 7–5, Wimbledon final 1935, saving match point in the third set. Mrs Moody was 29, Miss Jacobs 26.

To which I would add, as a post-centenary classic of outstanding quality:

21 Bjorn Borg (Swe) beat John McEnroe (USA) 1–6 7–5 6–3 6–7 8–6, Wimbledon final, 1980. The fourth set tie break was 18–16. Borg was 24, McEnroe 21.

ANCIENT AND MODERN

Were the champions of the past as good as those of today? Were they better?

A clear line of ascendancy indicating the superiority of the former champions may be constructed:

MEN

Spencer Gore, the first Wimbledon Champion, beat (6–1 6–2 6–4 Wimbledon final 1877)

William Marshall, who beat (6–5 5–6 6–4 6–1 Wimbledon semi-final 1877)

L R Erskine, who beat (6–3 6–1 6–3 Wimbledon semi-final 1878)

Herbert Lawford, who beat (8–6 6–1 8–6 Wimbledon quarter-final 1886)

Willoughby Hamilton, who beat (6–3 6–0 6–1, Wimbledon quarter-final 1890)

Wilfred Baddeley, who beat (6–4 6–2 6–2 Wimbledon quarter-final 1897)

Laurie Doherty, who beat (6–0 6–3 10–8 US Championships challenge round 1903)

William Larned, who beat (6–4 6–4 6–2 US Championships challenge round 1911)

Maurice McLoughlin, who beat (6–2 6–4 6–0 US Championships quarter-final 1915)

Frank Hunter, who beat (7–5 3–6 6–3 6–4 US Championships quarter-final 1928)

Jack Crawford, who beat (6–1 1–6 6–2 3–6 6–3 Australian Championships semi-final 1935)

Adrian Quist, who beat (6–3 6–2 6–3 Australian Hard Court Championships final 1947)

Frank Sedgman, who beat (4–6 6–2 6–2 Wembley 1960)

Alex Olmedo, who beat (6–4 6–3 6–4 Wimbledon final 1959)

Rod Laver, who beat (7–6 6–2 Houston final 1974)

Bjorn Borg, designated World Champion by the ITF 1978–1980.

WOMEN

May Langrishe, the first woman champion in 1879, beat (Irish Championships final 1886)

Miss L Martin, who beat (7–5 6–0 Irish Championships final 1889)

Blanche Hillyard, who beat (3–6 8–6 6–3 Wimbledon quarter-final 1912)

Elizabeth Ryan, who beat (6–3 6–3 Seabright tournament final 1925)

Helen Wills Moody, who beat (6–2 6–1 Wimbledon quarter-final 1938)

Kay Stammers, who beat (7–5 2–6 6–3 Wimbledon semi-final 1939)

Sarah Fabyan, who beat (6–3 6–4 US Championships semi-final 1945)

Louise Brough, who beat (6–3 8–6 Wimbledon semi-final 1955)

Darlene Hard, who beat (at the Essex tournament, Manchester, Mass., 1960)

Billie Jean King, who beat (6–3 6–2 US Championships semi-final 1971)

Chris Evert, who, as Mrs J M Lloyd, was named World Champion by the ITF for 1978, 1980.

QED

On the other hand it may be that the modern champions are better. The following may help:

MEN

Bjorn Borg beat (7–6 3–6 5–7 7–6 6–2 Dallas 1976)

Rod Laver, who beat (4–6 9–7 6–3 Wembley 1965)

Frank Sedgman, who beat (7–5 6–3 1–6 6–4 Italian Championships final 1952)

Jaroslav Drobny, who beat (7–5 6–3 6–2 British Covered Court Championships semi-final 1950)

Henri Cochet, who beat (3–6 8–6 6–3 6–1 French Championships final 1930)

Bill Tilden, who beat (10–8 6–4 1–6 6–4 Davis Cup challenge round, Auckland, 1920)

Norman Brookes, who beat (6–3 9–7 6–2 Wimbledon semi-final 1905)

Arthur Gore, who beat (6–3 4–6 3–6 7–5 6–1 Wimbledon semi-final 1899)

Harold Mahony, who beat (6–2 6–8 5–7 8–6 6–3 Wimbledon challenge round 1896)

Wilfred Baddeley, who beat (6–0 6–1 6–1 Wimbledon semi-final 1891)

Ernest Renshaw, who beat (in the Prince's Club tournament 1881)

William Renshaw, who beat (6–0 6–1 6–1 Wimbledon challenge round 1881)

John Hartley, who beat (by walkover Wimbledon challenge round 1879)

Frank Hadow, who beat (7–5 6–1 9–7 Wimbledon challenge round 1878)

Spencer Gore, the first champion.

WOMEN

Chris Lloyd beat (6–3 7–5 US Championships semi-final 1977)

Billie Jean King, who beat (6–4 19–17 Wightman Cup, Cleveland, 1963)

Christine Truman, who beat (2–6 6–3 6–4 Wightman Cup, Wimbledon, 1958)

Althea Gibson, who beat (6–3 6–2 US Championships final 1957)

Louise Brough, who beat (6–4 6–2 Wightman Cup, Forest Hills, 1947)

Kay Stammers who beat (6–0 6–4 Beckenham semi-final 1935)

Helen Wills Moody, who beat (6–1 6–1 Wimbledon semi-final 1928)

Elizabeth Ryan, who beat (7–5 6–2 Chiswick Park final 1920)

Dorothea Lambert Chambers, who beat (6–3 4–6 6–2 Felixstowe 1912)

Blanche Hillyard, who beat (6–4 6–1 Wimbledon semi-final 1891)

May Langrishe, the first champion.

QED

The Traditional Championships

WIMBLEDON
THE LAWN TENNIS CHAMPIONSHIPS

Wimbledon in 1906. Tea on the lawns!

Wimbledon, the proper title for which is The Lawn Tennis Championships, had its beginning on 2 June 1877 when the committee of the All England Croquet and Lawn Tennis Club, then situated just off Worple Road, Wimbledon, approved a motion, proposed by J H Walsh and seconded by B C Evelegh, 'that a public meeting be held on July 10th and following days to compete for The Championships in lawn tennis, and that a sub-committee composed of Messrs J Marshall, H Jones and C G Heathcote be appointed to draw up rules for its management.'

The committee did just that, laying down the rules of lawn tennis which have remained unchanged, except in minor detail, since. In the event the tournament started on Monday 9 July. It was the first tournament in the world open to all comers, the complication of professionalism,

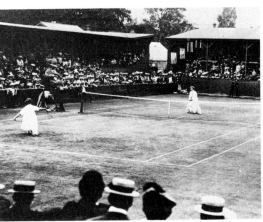

Wimbledon in 1907. May Sutton (USA) v Connie Wilson (GB) in the All-Comers' Final.

which bothered the game until 1968, not then having come into existence.

From 1913 to 1923 the tournament, by edict of the International Lawn Tennis Federation, carried the title of 'The World Championships on Grass'. The embellishment was happily dropped when the USA made it a condition of their belatedly joining the Federation in 1924.

WIMBLEDON SUPERLATIVES

MOST SETS AND GAMES

The **greatest number of games** played by a competitor in one year was by Bobby Riggs (USA) in 1939. In becoming triple champion he won 19 matches, 51 sets to 9, a total of 60, and 361 games to 220, a total of **581 games**.

The **greatest number of games by a woman** was by Billie Jean King (USA) in becoming triple champion for the second time in 1975. She won 17 matches, 34 sets to 4, 231 games to 126, a total of **357 games**.

Jean Borotra on the volley. The picture shows him at Wimbledon in 1932.

The **greatest number of sets played** in the men's singles was by Jean Borotra (Fra) as losing finalist in 1927. Only one of his seven matches ended in three sets, three went to four and three went the full distance. In all he played **30 sets**. His games totalled 283 which was 23 more than the total of the champion Henry Cochet. (If the three qualifying rounds played by John McEnroe (USA) in 1977 be included the record number of sets was played that year. He played **31 sets** in all, of which 8 were in the qualifying rounds, and a total of 308 games.)

Wimbledon from the air. An early view taken about 1929.

The **greatest number of games** played in the men's singles was by Ashley Cooper (Aus) as champion in 1958. His total over 28 sets was **31?** games.

The **greatest number of games** played in the women's singles was by Martina Navratilova (Cze) as title winner in 1979. She won 14 sets to 3, 96 games to 59, a total of **155 games**.

The **greatest number of games** played in the men's doubles was by the champions, Ross Case and Geoff Masters (both Aus), in 1977 when over 26 sets the total was **297 games**.

The **greatest number of games** in the women's doubles was played by Mima Jausovec (Yug) and Virginia Ruzici (Rom) as losing finalists in 1978 when over 15 sets they engaged in **168 games**.

The **greatest number of games** played in the mixed doubles was in 1981 with the win of Frew McMillan (SA) and Betty Stove (Hol). In 17 sets they totalled **172 games**.

MATCHES PLAYED

The **greatest number of matches** played in the Wimbledon Championships was **411** in 1938. The field comprised:

Men's singles	128
Women's singles	96
Men's doubles	64
Women's doubles	48
Mixed doubles	81

making a requirement of 412 matches but there was one walk-over.

The **biggest field** at Wimbledon was in 1963, made up by:

en's singles	128
'omen's singles	96
en's doubles	68
'omen's doubles	48
lixed doubles	80
otal	420

The requirement was 415 matches but in the vent there were 17 walks-over in all and 398 atches were played.

he biggest fields in the individual events ere:

Ien's singles	133 in 1923
Jomen's singles	97 in 1937
Ien's doubles	68 in 1963
Jomen's doubles	50 in 1973
lixed doubles	81 in 1938
	and 1947

.nce 1977 the field has comprised:

Ien's singles	128
Jomen's singles	96
en's doubles	64
Jomen's doubles	48
lixed doubles	48

iving a requirement of 379 matches.

OUNGEST COMPETITORS

he youngest competitor in the Wimbledon hampionships is believed to have been the ustrian Mita Klima. She was 13 when she layed in 1907, losing in the first round of the 'omen's singles, 6–1 6–2, to Mrs O'Neil. Her 14 ear old sister Willy Klima lost in the same und, 6–0 6–2, to Miss A M Morton. In the 'omen's doubles the sisters were beaten, 6–2 –3, in their opening match by Miss M Coles nd Miss M Slocock. Nor did either sister win a atch in the mixed doubles. Mita partnered er compatriot C von Wesseley to lose 6–1 7–5 the British pair X E Casdagli and Mrs Sterry. Jilly also paired with a fellow Austrian and she nd R Kinzl were beaten 6–1 6–4 by the British A Thomas and Miss A N G Greene.

The youngest player to win a match in the Jimbledon Championships was Kathy Rinaldi, f Jensen Beach, Florida. She was 14 years 92 ays old when, in 1981, she won her first round 'omen's singles 6–3 2–6 9–7 against Sue Rollin-on of South Africa, surviving a match point in e third set.

The youngest seed in the Wimbledon Cham-ionships was Andrea Jaeger of Chicago in 980. She was 15 years 19 days old at the start f the meeting where she was seeded number

14 in the women's singles. She surpassed her seeding expectation by reaching the quarter-finals.

Lottie Dod as a 13 year old. Two years later she was the champion of Wimbledon.

YOUNG CHAMPIONS

	Champion-ship	Date	Age Years/Days
WOMEN			
Lottie Dod	Singles	1887	15· 285
Tracy Austin (USA)	Mixed	1980	17· 206
Billie Jean Moffit (USA)	Doubles	1961	17· 227
Maureen Connolly (USA)	Singles	1952	17· 291
Karen Hantze (USA)	Doubles	1961	18· 208
Maria Bueno (Bra)	Doubles	1958	18· 266
Rosemary Casals (USA)	Doubles	1967	18· 294
Lesley Turner (Aus)	Mixed	1961	18· 326
Pam Shriver (USA)	Mixed	1981	19· 000
Chris Evert (USA)	Singles	1974	19· 196
Karen Susman (2) (USA)	Singles	1962	19· 208
Martina Navratilova (Cze)	Doubles	1976	19· 258
Maria Bueno (2) (Bra)	Singles	1959	19· 266
Maud Watson	Singles	1884	19· 283
Ann Kiyomura (USA)	Doubles	1975	19· 317
Evonne Goolagong (Aus)	Singles	1971	19· 336
MEN			
Dennis Ralston (USA)	Doubles	1960	17· 341
Lew Hoad (Aus)	Doubles	1953	18· 223
Ken Rosewall (Aus)	Doubles	1953	18· 244
Wilfred Baddeley	Singles	1891	19· 175
Wilfred Baddeley (2)	Doubles	1891	19· 180
Herbert Baddeley	Doubles	1891	19· 180
Sidney Wood (USA)	Singles	1931	19· 256

The **youngest pair** to be **men's doubles champions** was Lew Hoad and Ken Rosewall in 1953 with combined ages of **18 years 223 days** and **18 years 244 days**, i.e. **37 years 102 days**.

The **youngest pair** was Billie Jean Moffitt and Karen Hantze in 1961 with combined ages of **36 years 70 days**.

The **youngest man** to be **mixed doubles champion** was Rod Laver, the winner in 1959 at the age of **20 years 298 days**.

Second youngest man was John Austin in 1980 at 22 years 340 days. The **youngest pair** as mixed champions was John Austin and Tracy Austin in 1980 with combined ages of **40 years 171 days**.

OLDEST CHAMPIONS

	Champion-ship	Date	Age Years/Days
WOMEN			
Margaret du Pont (USA)	Mixed	1962	44· 125
Elizabeth Ryan (USA)	Doubles	1934	42· 151
Agatha Morton	Doubles	1914	40· 123
Hazel Wightman (USA)	Doubles	1924	37· 198
Charlotte Sterry	Singles	1908	37· 282
Blanche Hillyard	Singles	1900	36· 242
Margaret du Pont (2) (USA)	Doubles	1954	36· 150
Betty Stove (Hol)	Mixed	1981	36· 110
Agnes Tuckey	Mixed	1913	35· 361
Dorothea L. Chambers	Singles	1914	35· 334
Winifred McNair	Doubles	1913	35· 329
Billie Jean King (USA)	Doubles	1979	35· 227
Mary Browne (USA)	Doubles	1926	35· 29
Ethel Larcombe	Mixed	1914	35· 28
MEN			
Gardnar Mulloy (USA)	Doubles	1957	43· 236
Arthur Gore	Singles	1909	41· 184
Arthur Gore (2)	Doubles	1909	41· 181
Leslie Godfree	Mixed	1926	41· 67
Charles Dixon	Doubles	1913	40· 147
Major Ritchie	Doubles	1910	39· 257
Roper Barrett	Doubles	1913	39· 222
Bob Hewitt (SA)	Mixed	1979	39· 180
Frew McMillan (SA)	Mixed	1981	39· 45
Bob Hewitt (2) (SA)	Doubles	1978	38· 181
Jacques Brugnon (Fra)	Doubles	1933	38· 58
Adrian Quist (Aus)	Doubles	1950	37· 166
William Tilden (USA)	Singles	1930	37· 145
Brian Gilbert	Mixed	1924	37· 353
Randolph Lycett	Doubles Mixed	1923	36· 314
Norman Brookes (Aus)	Doubles	1914	36· 234
Norman Brookes (2) (Aus)	Singles	1914	36· 232
Herbert Lawford	Singles	1887	36· 53
Frew McMillan (2) (SA)	Doubles	1978	36· 49
Frank Hunter (USA)	Mixed	1929	35· 8

The **oldest pair as men's doubles champions** was H. Roper Barrett, 39 years 222 days, and Charles Dixon, 40 years 147 days, with a combined age in 1913 of 80 years 4 days.

Lew Hoad of Australia, one of the all time greats. He won his first Wimbledon title at 18.

The **oldest pair** to be **women's doubles champions** was Mary Browne and Elizabeth Ryan in 1926 when their combined ages, **35 years 29 days** and **34 years 147 days**, came to **69 years 176 days**.

The **oldest pair** as **mixed champions** was Neale Fraser and Margaret du Pont in 1962 with ages, **27 years 270 days** and **44 years 155 days**, totalling **72 years 60 days**.

FAMILY COMPETITORS

What was probably the greatest number and most diverse array of family relationships occurred in the Wimbledon Championships of 1979. There were seven sets of brothers, two sets of sisters, four married couples, two sets of brother and sister and a father and son.

They were:

BROTHERS
Anand and Vijay **Amritraj** both played in the singles. Together they were in the men's doubles. A third brother, Ashok, played in the mixed. They were from Madras, India.

David and Dick **Bohrnstedt** of the USA played together in the men's doubles.

Charles and Michael **Fancutt** of Australia were in the mixed doubles.

and France respectively, played together in the mixed.

Brian and Kathy **Teacher,** both American, were both singles competitors but neither played in the mixed.

BROTHER AND SISTER

John and Tracy **Austin** both played in singles and were partners in the mixed doubles.

Vitas and Ruta **Gerulaitis** were a second American set of siblings. Both played in the singles but neither played in the mixed.

he most recent in a long line of twins, **Tim (on the right)** nd Tom Gullikson, born in La Crosse, Wisconsin, USA, 8 eptember 1951.

Alvara and Jaime **Fillol,** from Chile, played in he singles and together in the men's doubles.

Tim and Tom **Gullikson,** identical twins from Wisconsin, played together in the men's doubles. In singles Tim beat John McEnroe in the ourth round to avenge the loss of Tom in the hird.

David and John **Lloyd,** each a British Davis Cup player, both played in the singles. John partnered their youngest brother, Tony, in the men's doubles.

Alexander and Gene **Mayer,** from New York, played in the singles and together in the men's doubles.

There were two sets of three brothers, and six sets of brothers in the doubles.)

SISTERS

Barbara and Kathy **Jordan,** from King of Prussia, Pennsylvania, competed in the singles and separately in the doubles.

Marcie and Mareen **Louie,** of San Francisco, were each in the singles and together in the doubles.

HUSBAND AND WIFE

John and Chris **Lloyd,** the former British, the latter American. They did not play in the mixed doubles.

Peter and Cynthia **Doerner,** from Australia, played together in the mixed.

Patricio and Michelle **Rodriguez,** from Chile

Champions as brother and sister. John and Tracy Austin who won the mixed at Wimbledon in 1980.

FATHER AND SON

Geoff **Paish,** British Davis Cup player 1947–1955, competed in the senior invitation men's doubles. His son John, British Davis Cup player in 1972, played in the championship doubles.

MOTHER AND SON PARTNERSHIP

Mrs Charles Tuckey and her son Raymond Tuckey competed together in the mixed doubles in 1931, winning one match, and in 1932, when Mrs Tuckey was a few days short of being 55 years old. Mrs Tuckey was the mixed champion in 1913. Raymond Tuckey, a regular Army officer, won the men's doubles in 1936. He was a British Davis Cup player. His younger sister, Kay Tuckey, was a British Wightman Cup player.

TRIPLE CHAMPIONS

Not until 1913 could a Wimbledon competitor take part in three full championship events singles, doubles and mixed. However, a women's doubles was staged from 1899 to 1907 and mixed doubles from 1900 to 1912 with lack of championship status a technicality. Accordingly was possible from 1900 to 1907 for a player to be unbeaten in three events. The inclusion of Mr Sterry below is made with this qualification.

		Matches Won	Sets Won	Sets Lost	Games Won	Games Lost	Partner
1901 Mrs A Sterry	Singles	6	12	0	72	25	
(GB)	Doubles	3	6	2	43	29	Mrs G W Hillyard
	Mixed	5	10	2	66	40	H L Doherty
		14	28	4	181	94	
							Average loss of games per set 2·93
1920 Mlle S Lenglen	Singles	1	2	0	12	3	
(Fra)	Doubles	5	10	0	60	13	Miss E Ryan
	Mixed	6	12	0	74	29	G L Patterson
		12	24	0	146	45	
							Average loss of games per set 1·87
1922 Mlle S Lenglen	Singles	6	12	0	75	20	
(Fra)	Doubles	5	10	0	61	14	Miss E Ryan
	Mixed	6	12	0	72	25	P O'Hara Wood
		17	34	0	208	59	
							Average loss of games per set 1·73
1925 Mlle S Lenglen	Singles	5	10	0	60	5	
(Fra)	Doubles	6	12	0	72	16	Miss E Ryan
	Mixed	6	12	1	77	31	J Borotra
		17	34	1	209	52	
							Average loss of games per set 1·48
1937 J D Budge	Singles	7	21	1	140	68	
(USA)	Doubles	6	18	4	135	81	G Mako
	Mixed	6	12	2	78	35	Miss A Marble
		19	51	7	353	184	
							Average loss of games per set 3·17
1938 J D Budge	Singles	7	21	0	129	48	
(USA)	Doubles	6	18	1	120	64	G Mako
	Mixed	6	12	0	74	30	Miss A Marble
		19	51	1	323	142	
							Average loss of games per set 2·73
1939 Miss A Marble	Singles	6	12	0	72	21	
(USA)	Doubles	5	10	1	66	23	Mrs M Fabyan
	Mixed	6	12	2	83	42	R L Riggs
		17	34	3	221	86	
							Average loss of games per set 2·32
1939 R L Riggs	Singles	7	21	3	147	92	
(USA)	Doubles	5	18	4	131	86	E T Cooke
	Mixed	6	12	2	83	42	Miss A Marble
		19	51	9	361	220	
							Average loss of games per set 3·66

Charlotte Sterry, in 1901 the first of the triple Wimbledon champions.

Alice Marble, triple Wimbledon champion in 1939. She was triple US Champion 1938, 1939 and 1940.

Frank Sedgman of Australia. The last man to be triple Wimbledon champion in 1952.

		Matches Won	Sets Won	Lost	Games Won	Lost	Partner
1948 Miss A L Brough (USA)	Singles	5	*11	1	70	29	
	Doubles	5	10	1	64	26	Mrs W du Pont
	Mixed	6	12	2	82	42	J E Bromwich
		17	33	4	216	97	
							Average loss of games per set **2·622**
1950 Miss A L Brough (USA)	Singles	6	12	2	80	34	
	Doubles	5	10	1	67	30	Mrs W du Pont
	Mixed	6	12	1	87	54	E W Sturgess
		17	34	4	234	118	
							Average loss of games per set **3·105**
1951 Miss D J Hart (USA)	Singles	7	14	0	86	34	
	Doubles	5	10	0	67	23	Miss S J Fry
	Mixed	6	12	1	81	35	F A Sedgman
		18	36	1	234	92	
							Average loss of games per set **2·486**
1952 F A Sedgman (Aus)	Singles	7	21	2	136	57	
	Doubles	6	18	3	138	75	K McGregor
	Mixed	6	12	1	77	35	Miss D J Hart
		19	51	6	251	167	
							Average loss of games per set **2·929**
1967 Mrs L W King (USA)	Singles	5	10	0	63	28	
	Doubles	6	12	1	81	39	Miss R Casals
	Mixed	5	10	1	64	28	O K Davidson
		16	32	2	208	95	
							Average loss of games per set **2·794**
1973 Mrs L W King (USA)	Singles	6	12	2	83	50	
	Doubles	5	10	1	67	38	Miss R Casals
	Mixed	6	12	1	81	38	O K Davidson
		17	34	4	231	126	
							Average loss of games per set **3·315**

* In one match, the quarter-final, her opponent retired injured before the end of the first set.

THE CENTURIONS

The elite of the Wimbledon Championships can be measured by the number of matches won. The following have won 100 or more matches in the course of their careers:

	Titles Won	Pl'd	Matches Lost	Won
Mrs L W King (USA) (1961–82)				
Singles	6	104	14	90
Doubles	10	84	11	73
Mixed	4	64	13	51
	20	252	38	**214**
Miss E Ryan (USA) (1912–34)				
Singles	–	61	15	46
Doubles	12	77	4	73
Mixed	7	80	10	70
	19	218	29	**189**
J Borotra (Fra) (1922–64)				
Singles	2	65	10	55
Doubles	3	88	31	57
Mixed	1	68	28	40
	6	221	69	**152**
Miss A L Brough (USA) (1946–57)				
Singles	4	63	7	56
Doubles	5	43	4	39
Mixed	4	49	5	44
	13	155	16	**139**
Mrs B M Court (Aus) (1961–75)				
Singles	3	60	9	51
Doubles	2	45	8	37
Mixed	5	51	4	47
	10	156	21	**135**
R A J Hewitt (Aus & SA) (1959–79)				
Singles	–	53	19	34
Doubles	5	83	15	68
Mixed	2	35	8	27
	7	171	42	**129**
R S Emerson (Aus) (1954–71)				
Singles	2	74	14	60
Doubles	3	72	12	60
Mixed	–	8	2	6
	5	154	28	**126**
Miss D J Hart (USA) (1946–55)				
Singles	1	51	8	43
Doubles	4	42	6	36
Mixed	5	49	4	45
	10	142	18	**124**
Mrs R Lambert Chambers (GB) (1900–27)				
Singles	7	40	8	32
Doubles*	2	54	14	40
Mixed*	3	67	15	52
	12	161	37	**124**
Miss S V Wade (GB) (1962–82)				
Singles	1	76	20	56
Doubles	–	67	20	47
Mixed	–	40	19	21
	1	183	59	**124**

	Titles Won	Pl'd	Matches Lost	Won
N A Fraser (Aus) (1954–76)				
Singles	1	51	13	38
Doubles	2	57	11	46
Mixed	1	48	12	36
	4	156	36	**120**
Mrs P F Jones (GB) (1956–69)				
Singles	1	70	13	57
Doubles	–	45	13	32
Mixed	1	39	10	29
	2	154	36	**118**
Miss M E Bueno (Bra) (1958–80)				
Singles	3	57	8	49
Doubles	5	42	5	37
Mixed	–	37	8	29
	8	136	21	**115**
Mrs L A Godfree (GB) (1919–34)				
Singles	2	49	11	38
Doubles	–	46	12	34
Mixed	2	52	12	40
	4	147	35	**112**
A W Gore (GB) (1888–1927)				
Singles	3	90	26	64
Doubles	1	58	26	32
Mixed*	1	22	8	14
	5	170	60	**110**
J D Newcombe (Aus) (1961–82)				
Singles	3	56	11	45
Doubles	6	65	12	53
Mixed	–	12	4	8
	9	133	27	**106**
Mme R Mathieu (Fra) (1926–47)				
Singles	–	60	14	46
Doubles	3	47	12	35
Mixed	–	34	13	21
	3	141	39	**102**
H Roper Barrett (GB) (1898–1926)				
Singles	–	48	12	36
Doubles	3	60	17	43
Mixed*	1	33	11	22
	4	141	40	**101**

*(including the event prior to 1913 before it was technically a "championship").

Bob Hewitt, a stalwart who changed his allegiance from Australia to South Africa.

In terms of stalwart prowess, i.e. numbers of matches played as distinct from the numbers won, the aristocrat list becomes:

	Matches Played	Won
Billie Jean King (USA)	252	214
Jean Borotra (Fra)	221	152
Elizabeth Ryan (USA)	218	189
Virginia Wade	183	124
Bob Hewitt (Aus/SA)	171	129
Arthur Gore	170	110
Dorothea Lambert Chambers	161	124
Margaret Court (Aus)	156	135
Neale Fraser (Aus)	156	120
Louise Brough (USA)	155	139
Roy Emerson (USA)	154	126
Ann Jones	154	118
Kitty Godfree	147	112
Doris Hart (USA)	142	124
Simone Mathieu (Fra)	141	102
Roper Barratt	141	101
Maria Bueno (Bra)	136	115
John Newcombe (Aus)	133	106

The following *played* more than a century of matches:

Randolf Lycett	122	97
Kay Menzies	122	89
Budge Patty (USA)	116	88
Rod Laver (Aus)	115	97
Chris Lloyd (USA)	113	93
Evonne Cawley (Aus)	112	89
Ken Rosewall (Aus)	108	88
Dorothy Round	106	80
Angela Mortimer	105	72
Vic Seixas (USA)	103	82

MOST DECISIVE CHAMPIONS

MEN'S SINGLES

Jack Kramer in 1947 won the title 21 sets to 1, 130 games to 37, his loss in games being **22·15%**.

Don Budge in 1938 won 21 sets to nil, 129 games to 48, a loss of **27·12%**.

Tony Trabert in 1955 won 21 sets to nil, 131 games to 60, losing **31·41%**.

Bjorn Borg in 1976 won 21 sets to nil, 133 games to 70, losing **34·48%**.

Chuck McKinley in 1963 won 21 sets to nil, 140 games to 82, losing **36·94%**.

Tony Trabert, who lost no sets in winning Wimbledon in 1955.

Jack Kramer, the Wimbledon champion with the lowest percentage loss of games.

WOMEN'S SINGLES*

Suzanne Lenglen in 1925 won 10 sets to nil, 60 games to 5, a loss of **7·69%**.

Suzanne Lenglen in 1923 won 12 sets to nil, 72 games to 11, losing **13·25%**.

Helen Wills Moody in 1932 won 12 sets to nil, 72 games to 13, losing **15·29%**.

* This data excludes the challenge round days prior to 1922. Strictly the most decisive victory in the women's singles was gained by Dorothea Lambert Chambers in 1911 when, playing only the challenge round as the defending champion, she beat Dora Boothby 6–0 6–0, thus gaining the title 2 sets to nil, 12 games to nil, a loss of **0%**.

MEN'S DOUBLES*

Tom Brown and Jack Kramer won in 1946 by 18 sets to 1, 111 games to 47, the percentage of lost games being **29·74%**.

Bob Hewitt and Frew McMillan in 1967 won 18 sets to nil, 120 games to 61, a loss of **33·7%**.

Bob Falkenburg and Jack Kramer in 1947 won 18 sets to nil, 115 games to 59, losing **33·9%**.

* The old challenge rounds excluded. The most decisive men's doubles championship was achieved in 1899 by **Laurie and Reggie Doherty** when they successfully defended in the challenge round 19 games to 7, losing just **26·92%**.

WOMEN'S DOUBLES

Shirley Fry and Doris Hart in 1953 won 8 sets to nil, 48 games to 4, losing **7·69%**.

Suzanne Lenglen and Elizabeth Ryan in 1923 won 10 sets to nil, 60 games to 11, losing **15·49%**.

MIXED DOUBLES

Pat O'Hara Wood and Suzanne Lenglen won in 1922 12 sets to nil, 72 games to 25, a loss of **25·77%**.

Lesley and Kitty Godfree won in 1926 12 sets to nil, 73 games to 30, a loss of **29·12%**.

MOST EXTENDED CHAMPIONS

MEN'S SINGLES

Ted Schroeder lost most sets in 1949 with his tally **21 sets to 8**. He won 172 games to 119, a losing percentage of **40·89%**.

Ashley Cooper in 1958 took 21 sets to 7 but had a higher percentage of loss in games, winning 172 games to 140, a losing percentage of **44·87%**.

Henri Cochet won in 1927 by 21 sets to 7, 146 games to 114, a percentage loss of **43·84%**. Uniquely he trailed two sets to nil in the quarter-final, semi-final and final rounds.

WOMEN'S SINGLES

Martina Navratilova won in 1979 by 14 sets to 3, 96 games to 59, her game loss percentage being **38·06%**.

Dorothy Round in 1931 won 14 sets to 3, 96 games to 49, a losing game percentage of **33·79%**.

MEN'S DOUBLES

Rafael Osuna and Antonio Palafox in 1963 won 18 sets to 8, 154 games to 124, a loss rate of **44·6%**.

Ross Case and Geoff Masters in 1977 took 18 sets to 8, 165 games to 132, a losing percentage of **44·44%**.

WOMEN'S DOUBLES

Kathy Jordan and Anne Smith in 1980 won 10 sets to 4, the highest number of sets conceded by the champions. They won 74 games to 48, a loss rate of **39·34%**.

Ann Kiyomura and Kazuko Sawamatsu suffered the highest percentage loss of games in 1975, winning 10 sets to 3 but 79 games to 66, a loss rate of **45·51%**.

MIXED DOUBLES

Frew McMillan and Betty Stove won in 1981 12 sets to 5, unique in losing so many. They won 99 games to 73, a loss rate of **42·44%**.

George Lott and Anna Harper won in 1931 by 10 sets to 4, 77 games to 56, a game loss rate of **42·10%**.

Champions the hard way. Frew McMillan and Betty Stove when they won the Wimbledon mixed in 1981, losing 5 sets.

PLATE WINNERS AS CHAMPIONS

The consolation plate for players beaten in the early rounds of the singles was begun for men in 1896 and for women in 1933. Three men, Arthur Gore, Herbert Baddeley and Henri Cochet, and one woman, Freda James, were plate winners when they already had the status as Wimbledon Champions, Gore and Cochet in the singles.

Men	Women	Year Winner of Plate	Year of Championship(s)
Arthur Gore		1896, 1903	Singles 1901, 08, 09
			Doubles 1909
Herbert Baddeley		1897	Doubles 1891, 94, 95, 96
Tony Wilding (NZ)		1907	Singles 1910, 11, 12, 13
			Doubles 1907, 08, 10, 14
Henri Cochet (Fra)		1932	Singles 1927, 29
			Doubles 1926, 28
	Freda James	1937	Doubles 1935, 36
Eric Sturgess (SA)		1947	Mixed 1949, 50
Neale Fraser (Aus)		1955	Singles 1960
			Doubles 1959, 61
			Mixed 1962
	Francoise Durr (Fra)	1963	Mixed 1976
	Evonne Goolagong (Aus)	1970	Singles 1971, 80
			Doubles 1974
	Helen Gourley (Aus)	1973	Doubles 1978

JUNIOR WINNERS AS SUBSEQUENT CHAMPIONS

The following Wimbledon Champions had their first successes at Wimbledon in the junior tournament.

Boys	Girls	Year Winner of Junior Event	Year of Championship
	Ann Haydon	1956	Singles 1969
			Mixed 1969
	Karen Hantze (USA)	1960	Singles 1962
			Doubles 1961, 62
	Kazuki Sawamatsu (Jap)	1969	Doubles 1975
Bjorn Borg (Swe)		1972	Singles 1976, 77, 78, 79, 80
	Ann Kiyomura (USA)	1973	Doubles 1975
	Tracy Austin (USA)	1978	Mixed 1980

MULTIPLE CHAMPIONS
Players Winning Seven or more Titles

	Singles	Championships Won Doubles	Mixed	Total
Mrs L W King (USA) (1961–79)	6	10	4	20
Miss E Ryan (USA) (1914–34)	–	12	7	19
Mlle S Lenglen (Fra) (1919–25)	6	6	3	15
H L Doherty (GB) (1897–1905)	5	8	–	13
Miss A L Brough (USA) (1946–55)	4	5	4	13
Mrs F S Moody (USA) (1927–38)	8	3	1	12
W Renshaw (GB) (1881–89)	7	5	–	12
R F Doherty (GB) (1897–1905)	4	8	–	12
Mrs B M Court (Aus) (1953–75)	3	2	5	10
Miss D J Hart (USA) (1947–55)	1	4	5	10
J D Newcombe (Aus) (1965–74)	3	6	–	9
A F Wilding (NZ) (1907–14)	4	4	–	8
Miss M E Bueno (Bra) (1958–66)	3	5	–	8
Mrs R Lambert Chambers (GB) (1903–14)	7	–	–	7
R G Laver (Aus) (1959–69)	4	1	2	7
Mrs W du Pont (USA) (1947–62)	1	5	1	7
Miss R Casals (USA) (1967–73)	–	5	2	7
Miss D R Hard (USA) (1957–63)	–	4	3	7
R A J Hewitt (Aus & SA) (1962–79)	–	5	2	7

Jimmy Connors, the only champion to be a left hander and double fisted.

Jaroslav Drobny, one of the six left handers to be men's singles champion at Wimbledon. Now British he was born a Czech but he had an Egyptian passport as champion.

UNORTHODOX CHAMPIONS
Left Handers and Double Handers

Thirty Wimbledon Championships were completed before the first left hander won a title, Norman Brookes in 1907. There was only one other, Brian Gilbert, the mixed champion of 1924, after the first fifty years. A double fisted player did not take a championship until 1947 when John Bromwich won the mixed. He was unusual among the unorthodox in being double fisted on the forehand rather than the backhand, though less so than Frew McMillan with a double grip on both wings.

Left Handers	Double Handers	Year of First Title
Men		
N E Brookes (Aus)		1907
J B Gilbert (GB)*		1924
	J E Bromwich (Aus)*	1947
J Drobny (Cze)		1954
	R N Howe (Aus)*	1958
N A Fraser (Aus)		1959
R G Laver (Aus)		1959
A D Roche (Aus)*		1965
	F D McMillan (SA)*	1967
O K Davidson (Aus)*		1967
J S Connors (USA)	J S Connors	1973
	B Borg (Swe)	1976
J P McEnroe (USA)		1979
	P McNamee (Aus)*	1980
Women		
Miss K E Stammers (GB)*		1935
Mrs P F Jones (GB)		1969
	Mrs J M Lloyd (USA)	1974
Miss M Navratilova (Cze)		1976
	Miss T A Austin (USA)*	1980

* Doubles champion only.

The invincible Maureen Connolly; champion at her first attempt in 1952, she was never subsequently beaten in singles.

Frank Hadow, the champion at his first attempt in 1878 and who never returned.

SINGLES WINNERS AT FIRST ATTEMPT

1877 S W Gore (inaugural year)	
1878 P F Hadow	
1979 J T Hartley	
1884	Miss M E E Watson (inaugural year)
1887	Miss C Dod
1905	Miss M G Sutton
1919 G L Patterson	Mlle S Lenglen
1920 W T Tilden	
1932 H E Vines	
1939 R L Riggs (triple champion)	
1946	Miss P M Betz
1949 F R Schroeder	
1951 R Savitt	
1952	Miss M C Connolly

Of the above the following were unbeaten in singles at any time:

		Winning years
Hadow		1878 (without losing a set)
	Miss Dod	1887, 1888, 1891, 1892, 1893
	Mlle Lenglen*	1919, 1920, 1921, 1922, 1923, 1925
Riggs		1939
	Miss Betz	1946 (without losing a set)
Schroeder		1949
	Miss Connolly	1952, 1953, 1954

* Mlle Lenglen retired ill in 1924 and 1926.

RESULTS

MEN'S SINGLES

	CHALLENGE ROUND			ALL COMERS' FINAL		
Year	Champion	Loser	Score	Winner	Loser	Score
1877	S W Gore			S W Gore	W C Marshall	6–1 6–2 6–4
1878	P F Hadow	S W Gore	7–5 6–1 9–7	Hadow	L Erskine	6–4 6–4 6–4
1879	J T Hartley		w.o.	Hartley	V St Leger Goold	6–3 6–4 6–2
1880	J T Hartley	H F Lawford	6–3 6–2 2–6 6–3	Lawford	O E Woodhouse	7–5 6–4 6–0
1881	W Renshaw	J T Hartley	6–0 6–1 6–1	W Renshaw	R T Richardson	6–4 6–2 6–3
1882	W Renshaw	E Renshaw	6–1 2–6 4–6 6–2 6–2	E Renshaw	R T Richardson	7–5 6–3 2–6 6–3
1883	W Renshaw	E Renshaw	2–6 6–3 6–3 4–6 6–3	E Renshaw	D Stewart	0–6 6–3 6–0 6–2
1884	W Renshaw	H F Lawford	6–0 6–4 9–7	Lawford	C W Grinstead	7–5 2–6 6–2 9–7
1885	W Renshaw	H F Lawford	7–5 6–2 4–6 7–5	Lawford	E Renshaw	5–7 6–1 0–6 6–2 6–4
1886	W Renshaw	H F Lawford	6–0 5–7 6–3 6–4	Lawford	E W Lewis	6–2 6–3 2–6 4–6 6–4
1887	H F Lawford		w.o.	Lawford	E Renshaw	1–6 6–3 3–6 6–4 ȯ–4
1888	E Renshaw	H F Lawford	6–3 7–5 6–0	E Renshaw	E W Lewis	7–9 6–1 8–6 6–4
1889	W Renshaw	E Renshaw	6–4 6–1 3–6 6–0	W Renshaw	H S Barlow	3–6 5–7 8–6 10–8 8–6
1890	W J Hamilton	W Renshaw	6–8 6–2 3–6 6–1 6–1	Hamilton	H S Barlow	2–6 6–4 6–4 4–6 7–5
1891	W Baddeley		w.o.	Baddeley	J Pim	6–4 1–6 7–5 6–0
1892	W Baddeley	J Pim	4–6 6–3 6–3 6–2	J Pim	E W Lewis	2–6 5–7 9–7 6–3 6–2
1893	J Pim	W Baddeley	3–6 6–1 6–3 6–2	Pim	H S Mahony	9–7 6–3 6–0
1894	J Pim	W Baddeley	10–8 6–2 8–6	W Baddeley	E W Lewis	6–0 6–1 6–0
1895	W Baddeley		w.o.	Baddeley	W V Eaves	4–6 2–6 8–6 6–2 6–3
1896	H S Mahony	W Baddeley	6–2 6–8 5–7 8–6 6–3	Mahony	W V Eaves	6–2 6–2 11–9
1897	R F Doherty	H S Mahony	6–4 6–4 6–3	R F Doherty	W V Eaves	6–3 7–5 2–0 ret'd
1898	R F Doherty	H L Doherty	6–3 6–3 2–6 7–5 6–1	H L Doherty	H S Mahony	6–1 6–2 4–6 2–6 14–12
1899	R F Doherty	A W Gore	1–6 4–6 6–2 6–3 6–3	Gore	S H Smith	3–6 6–2 6–1 6–4
1900	R F Doherty	S H Smith	6–8 6–3 6–1 6–2	Smith	A W Gore	6–4 4–6 6–2 6–1
1901	A W Gore	R F Doherty	4–6 7–5 6–4 6–4	Gore	C P Dixon	6–4 6–0 6–3
1902	H L Doherty	A W Gore	6–4 6–3 3–6 6–0	H L Doherty	M J G Ritchie	8–6 6–3 7–5
1903	H L Doherty	F L Riseley	7–5 6–3 6–0	Riseley	M J G Ritchie	1–6 6–3 8–6 13–11
1904	H L Doherty	F L Riseley	6–1 7–5 8–6	Riseley	M J G Ritchie	6–0 6–1 6–2
1905	H L Doherty	N E Brookes (Aus)	8–6 6–2 6–4	Brookes	S H Smith	1–6 6–4 6–1 1–6 7–5
1906	H L Doherty	F L Riseley	6–4 4–6 6–2 6–3	Riseley	A W Gore	6–3 6–3 6–4
1907	N E Brookes (Aus)		w.o.	Brookes	A W Gore	6–4 6–2 6–2
1908	A W Gore		w.o.	Gore	H Roper Barrett	6–3 6–2 4–6 3–6 6–4
1909	A W Gore	M J G Ritchie	6–8 1–6 6–2 6–2 6–2	Ritchie	H Roper Barrett	6–2 6–3 4–6 6–4
1910	A F Wilding (NZ)	A W Gore	6–4 7–5 4–6 6–2	Wilding	B C Wright	4–6 4–6 6–3 6–2 6–3
1911	A F Wilding (NZ)	H Roper Barrett	6–4 4–6 2–6 6–2 ret'd	Barrett	C P Dixon	5–7 4–6 6–4 6–3 6–1
1912	A F Wilding (NZ)	A W Gore	6–4 6–4 4–6 6–4	Gore	A H Gobert (Fra)	9–7 2–6 7–5 6–1
1913	A F Wilding (NZ)	M E McLoughlin (USA)	8–6 6–3 10–8	McLoughlin	S N Doust	6–3 6–4 7–5
1914	N E Brookes (Aus)	A F Wilding (NZ)	6–4 6–4 7–5	Brookes	O Froitzheim (Ger)	6–2 6–1 5–7 4–6 8–6
1915–1918 not held						
1919	G L Patterson (Aus)	N E Brookes (Aus)	6–3 7–5 6–2	Patterson	A R F Kingscote	6–2 6–1 6–3
1920	W T Tilden (USA)	G L Patterson (Aus)	2–6 6–3 6–2 6–4	Tilden	Z Shimidzu (Jap)	6–4 6–4 13–11
1921	W T Tilden (USA)	B I C Norton (SA)	4–6 2–6 6–1 6–0 7–5	Norton	M Alonso (Spa)	5–7 4–6 7–5 6–3 6–3

Challenge Round abolished.

	FINAL			SEMI-FINALS		
1922	G L Patterson (Aus)	R Lycett	6–3 6–4 6–2	Patterson	J O Anderson (Aus)	6–1 3–6 7–9 6–1 6–3
				Lycett	J B Gilbert	8–6 9–7 6–3
1923	W M Johnston (USA)	F T Hunter (USA)	6–0 6–3 6–1	Johnston	B I C Norton (SA)	6–4 6–2 6–4
				Hunter	F G Lowe	6–3 7–5 6–4
1924	J Borotra (Fra)	R Lacoste (Fra)	6–1 3–6 6–1 3–6 6–4	Borotra	L Raymond (SA)	6–2 6–4 7–5
				Lacoste	R N Williams (USA)	6–1 3–6 6–2 6–3
1925	R Lacoste (Fra)	J Borotra (Fra)	6–3 6–3 4–6 8–6	Lacoste	J O Anderson (Aus)	6–4 7–5 6–1
				Borotra	H Cochet (Fra)	5–7 8–6 6–4 6–1

Year	FINAL Champion	Loser	Score	SEMI-FINALS Winner	Loser	Score
1926	J Borotra (Fra)	H Kinsey (USA)	8–6 6–1 6–3	Borotra	H Cochet (Fra)	2–6 7–5 2–6 6–3 7–5
				Kinsey	J Brugnon (Fra)	6–4 4–6 6–3 3–6 9–7
1927	H Cochet (Fra)	J Borotra (Fra)	4–6 4–6 6–3 6–4 7–5	Cochet	W T Tilden (USA)	2–6 4–6 7–5 6–4 6–3
				Borotra	R Lacoste (Fra)	6–4 6–3 1–6 1–6 6–2
1928	R Lacoste (Fra)	H Cochet (Fra)	6–1 4–6 6–4 6–2	Lacoste	W T Tilden (USA)	2–6 6–4 2–6 6–4 6–3
				Cochet	C Boussus (Fra)	11–9 3–6 6–2 6–3
1929	H Cochet (Fra)	J Borotra (Fra)	6–4 6–3 6–4	Cochet	W T Tilden (USA)	6–4 6–1 7–5
				Borotra	H W Austin	6–1 10–8 5–7 6–1
1930	W T Tilden (USA)	W L Allison (USA)	6–3 9–7 6–4	Tilden	J Borotra (Fra)	0–6 6–4 4–6 6–0 7–5
				Allison	J H Doeg (USA)	6–3 4–6 8–6 3–6 7–5
1931	S B Wood (USA)	F X Shields (USA)	w.o.	Wood	F J Perry	4–6 6–2 6–4 6–2
				Shields	J Borotra (Fra)	7–5 3–6 6–4 6–4
1932	H E Vines (USA)	H W Austin	6–4 6–2 6–0	Vines	J H Crawford (Aus)	6–2 6–1 6–3
				Austin	J Satoh (Jap)	7–5 6–2 6–1
1933	J H Crawford (Aus)	H E Vines (USA)	4–6 11–9 6–2 2–6 6–4	Crawford	J Satoh (Jap)	6–3 6–4 2–6 6–4
				Vines	H Cochet (Fra)	6–2 8–6 3–6 6–1
1934	F J Perry	J H Crawford (Aus)	6–3 6–0 7–5	Perry	S B Wood (USA)	6–3 3–6 7–5 5–7 6–3
				Crawford	F X Shields (USA)	2–6 4–6 6–4 6–3 6–4
1935	F J Perry	G von Cramm (Ger)	6–2 6–4 6–4	Perry	J H Crawford (Aus)	6–2 3–6 6–4 6–4
				von Cramm	J D Budge (USA)	4–6 6–4 6–3 6–2
1936	F J Perry	G von Cramm (Ger)	6–1 6–1 6–0	Perry	J D Budge (USA)	5–7 6–4 6–3 6–4
				von Cramm	H W Austin	8–6 6–3 2–6 6–3
1937	J D Budge (USA)	G von Cramm (Ger)	6–3 6–4 6–2	Budge	F A Parker (USA)	2–6 6–4 6–4 6–1
				von Cramm	H W Austin	8–6 6–3 12–14 6–1
1938	J D Budge (USA)	H W Austin	6–1 6–0 6–3	Budge	F Puncec (Yug)	6–2 6–1 6–4
				Austin	H Henkel (Ger)	6–2 6–4 6–0
1939	R L Riggs (USA)	E T Cooke (USA)	2–6 8–6 3–6 6–3 6–2	Riggs	F Puncec (Yug)	6–2 6–3 6–4
				Cooke	H Henkel (Ger)	6–3 4–6 6–4 6–4
1940–1945 not held						
1946	Y Petra (Fra)	G E Brown (Aus)	6–2 6–4 7–9 5–7 6–4	Petra	T P Brown (USA)	4–6 4–6 6–3 7–5 8–6
				G E Brown	J Drobny (Cze)	6–4 7–5 6–2
1947	J A Kramer (USA)	T P Brown (USA)	6–1 6–3 6–2	Kramer	D Pails (Aus)	6–1 3–6 6–1 6–0
				T P Brown	J E Patty (USA)	6–3 6–3 6–3
1948	R Falkenburg (USA)	J E Bromwich (Aus)	7–5 0–6 6–2 3–6 7–5	Falkenburg	G Mulloy (USA)	6–4 6–4 8–6
				Bromwich	J Asboth (Hun)	6–3 14–12 6–2
1949	F R Schroeder (USA)	J Drobny (Cze)	3–6 6–0 6–3 4–6 6–4	Schroeder	E W Sturgess (SA)	3–6 7–5 5–7 6–1 6–2
				Drobny	J E Bromwich (Aus)	6–1 6–3 6–2
1950	J E Patty (USA)	F A Sedgman (Aus)	6–1 8–10 6–2 6–3	Patty	E V Seixas (USA)	6–3 5–7 6–2 7–5
				Sedgman	J Drobny (Egy)	3–6 3–6 6–3 7–5 6–2
1951	R Savitt (USA)	K McGregor (Aus)	6–4 6–4 6–4	Savitt	H Flam (USA)	1–6 15–13 6–3 6–2
				McGregor	E W Sturgess (SA)	6–4 3–6 6–3 7–5
1952	F A Sedgman (Aus)	J Drobny (Egy)	4–6 6–2 6–3 6–2	Sedgman	M G Rose (Aus)	6–4 6–4 7–5
				Drobny	H Flam (USA)	6–2 6–4 0–6 8–10 6–4
1953	E V Seixas (USA)	K Nielsen (Den)	9–7 6–3 6–4	Seixas	M G Rose (Aus)	6–4 10–12 9–11 6–4 6–3
				Nielsen	J Drobny (Egy)	6–4 6–3 6–2
1954	J Drobny (Egy)	K R Rosewall (Aus)	13–11 4–6 6–2 9–7	Drobny	J E Patty (USA)	6–2 6–4 4–6 9–7
				Rosewall	M A Trabert (USA)	3–6 6–3 4–6 6–1 6–1
1955	M A Trabert (USA)	K Nielsen (Den)	6–3 7–5 6–1	Trabert	J E Patty (USA)	8–6 6–2 6–2
				Nielsen	K R Rosewall (Aus)	11–9 6–2 2–6 6–4
1956	L A Hoad (Aus)	K R Rosewall (Aus)	6–2 4–6 7–5 6–4	Hoad	H Richardson (USA)	3–6 6–4 6–2 6–4
				Rosewall	E V Seixas (USA)	6–2 4–6 7–5 6–4
1957	L A Hoad (Aus)	A J Cooper (Aus)	6–2 6–1 6–2	Hoad	S Davidson (Swe)	6–4 6–4 7–5
				Cooper	N A Fraser (Aus)	1–6 14–12 6–3 8–6
1958	A J Cooper (Aus)	N A Fraser (Aus)	3–6 6–3 6–4 13–11	Cooper	M G Rose (Aus)	7–9 6–2 6–2 6–3
				Fraser	K Nielsen (Den)	6–4 6–4 17–19 6–4
1959	A Olmedo (USA)	R G Laver (Aus)	6–4 6–3 6–4	Olmedo	R S Emerson (Aus)	6–4 6–0 6–4
				Laver	B MacKay (USA)	11–13 11–9 10–8 7–9 6–3
1960	N A Fraser (Aus)	R G Laver (Aus)	6–4 3–6 9–7 7–5	Fraser	R Krishnan (Ind)	6–3 6–2 6–2
				Laver	N Pietrangeli (Ita)	4–6 6–3 8–10 6–2 6–4
1961	R G Laver (Aus)	C R McKinley (USA)	6–3 6–1 6–4	Laver	R Krishnan (Ind)	6–2 8–6 6–2
				McKinley	M J Sangster	6–4 6–4 8–6
1962	R G Laver (Aus)	M F Mulligan (Aus)	6–2 6–2 6–1	Laver	N A Fraser (Aus)	10–8 6–1 7–5
				Mulligan	J G Fraser (Aus)	6–3 6–2 6–2
1963	C R McKinley (USA)	F S Stolle (Aus)	9–7 6–1 6–4	McKinley	W P Bungert (FRG)	6–2 6–4 8–6
				Stolle	M Santana (Spa)	8–6 6–1 7–5

	FINAL			SEMI-FINALS		
Year	Champion	Loser	Score	Winner	Loser	Score
1964	R S Emerson (Aus)	F S Stolle (Aus)	6–4 12–10 4–6 6–3	Emerson	W P Bungert (FRG)	6–3 15–13 6–0
				Stolle	C R McKinley (USA)	4–6 10–8 9–7 6–4
1965	R S Emerson (Aus)	F S Stolle (Aus)	6–2 6–4 6–4	Emerson	R D Ralston (USA)	6–1 6–2 7–9 6–1
				Stolle	E C Drysdale (SA)	6–3 6–4 7–5
1966	M Santana (Spa)	R D Ralston (USA)	6–4 11–9 6–4	Santana	O K Davidson (Aus)	6–2 4–6 9–7 3–6 7–5
				Ralston	E C Drysdale (SA)	6–8 8–6 3–6 7–5 6–3
1967	J D Newcombe (Aus)	W P Bungert (FRG)	6–3 6–1 6–1	Newcombe	N Pilic (Yug)	9–7 4–6 6–3 6–4
				Bungert	R Taylor	6–4 6–8 2–6 6–4 6–4
1968	R G Laver (Aus)	A D Roche (Aus)	6–3 6–4 6–2	Laver	A R Ashe (USA)	7–5 6–2 6–4
				Roche	C E Graebner (USA)	9–7 8–10 6–4 8–6
1969	R G Laver (Aus)	J D Newcombe (Aus)	6–4 5–7 6–4 6–4	Laver	A R Ashe (USA)	2–6 6–2 9–7 6–0
				Newcombe	A D Roche (Aus)	3–6 6–1 14–12 6–4
1970	J D Newcombe (Aus)	K R Rosewall (Aus)	5–7 6–3 6–2 3–6 6–1	Newcombe	A Gimeno (Spa)	6–3 8–6 6–0
				Rosewall	R Taylor	6–3 4–6 6–3 6–3
1971	J D Newcombe (Aus)	S R Smith (USA)	6–3 5–7 2–6 6–4 6–4	Newcombe	K R Rosewall (Aus)	6–1 6–1 6–3
				Smith	T W Gorman (USA)	6–3 8–6 6–2
1972	S R Smith (USA)	I Nastase (Rom)	4–6 6–3 6–3 4–6 7–5	Smith	J Kodes (Cze)	3–6 6–4 6–1 7–5
				Nastase	M Orantes (Spa)	6–3 6–4 6–4
1973	J Kodes (Cze)	A Metreveli (USSR)	6–1 9–8 6–3	Kodes	R Taylor	8–9 9–7 5–7 6–4 7–5
				Metreveli	A A Mayer (USA)	6–3 3–6 6–3 6–4
1974	J S Connors (USA)	K R Rosewall (Aus)	6–1 6–1 6–4	Connors	R L Stockton (USA)	4–6 6–2 6–3 6–4
				Rosewall	S R Smith (USA)	6–8 4–6 9–8 6–1 6–3
1975	A R Ashe (USA)	J S Connors (USA)	6–1 6–1 5–7 6–4	Ashe	A D Roche (Aus)	5–7 6–4 7–5 8–9 6–4
				Connors	L R Tanner (USA)	6–4 6–1 6–4
1976	B Borg (Swe)	I Nastase (Rom)	6–4 6–2 9–7	Borg	L R Tanner (USA)	6–4 9–8 6–4
				Nastase	R Ramirez (Mex)	6–2 9–7 6–3
1977	B Borg (Swe)	J S Connors (USA)	3–6 6–2 6–1 5–7 6–4	Borg	V Gerulaitis (USA)	6–4 3–6 6–3 3–6 8–6
				Connors	J P McEnroe (USA)	6–3 6–3 4–6 6–4
1978	B Borg (Swe)	J S Connors (USA)	6–2 6–2 6–3	Borg	T S Okker (Hol)	6–4 6–4 6–4
				Connors	V Gerulaitis (USA)	9–7 6–2 6–1
1979	B Borg (Swe)	L R Tanner (USA)	6–7 6–1 3–6 6–3 6–4	Borg	J S Connors (USA)	6–2 6–3 6–2
				Tanner	P Dupre (USA)	6–3 7–6 6–3
1980	B Borg (Swe)	J P McEnroe (USA)	1–6 7–5 6–3 6–7 8–6	Borg	B E Gottfried (USA)	6–2 4–6 6–2 6–0
				McEnroe	J S Connors (USA)	6–3 3–6 6–3 6–4
1981	J P McEnroe (USA)	B Borg (Swe)	4–6 7–6 7–6 6–4	McEnroe	R J Frawley (Aus)	7–6 6–4 7–5
				Borg	J S Connors (USA)	0–6 4–6 6–3 6–0 6–4
1982	J S Connors (USA)	J P McEnroe (USA)	3–6 6–3 6–7 7–6 6–4	Connors	M R Edmondson (Aus)	6–4 6–3 6–1
				McEnroe	T S Mayotte (USA)	6–3 6–1 6–2

Ricardo Gonzales, the hero of Wimbledon's longest match in 1969. He was 41 years old.

The **longest match** was in 1969 when, on 24 and 25 June in the first round Ricardo Gonzales (USA) beat Charlie Pasarell (USA) 22–24 1–6 16–14 6–3 11–9, a total of **112 games**. (Its duration was 5 hours 12 minutes and it was interrupted overnight after the first two sets.)

The **second longest** was in 1953 when in the third round Jaroslav Drobny (Cze) beat Budge Patty (USA) 8–6 16–18 3–6 8–6 12–10, a total of **93 games**. (Its duration was 4 hours 15 minutes and Drobny saved six match points.)

The **longest final** was in 1954 when Jaroslav Drobny (Cze) beat Ken Rosewall (Aus) 13–11 4–6 6–2 9–7, a total of **58 games**.

The **second longest final** was in 1896 when Harold Mahony (Ire) beat Wilfred Baddeley (GB) 6–2 6–8 5–7 8–6 6–3, a total of **57 games**.

The **longest All Comers' final** was in 1889 when William Renshaw beat Harry Barlow (both GB) 3–6 5–7 8–6 10–8 8–6, a total of **67 games**.

The **longest semi-final** was 1959 when Rod Laver (Aus) beat Barry MacKay (USA) 11–13 11–9 10–8 7–9 6–3, a total of **87 games**.

The **longest quarter-final** was in 1921 when Z Shimidzu (Jap) beat Randolph Lycett (GB) 6–3 9–11 3–6 6–2 10–8 and in 1971 when Ken Rosewall (Aus) beat Cliff Richey (USA) 6–8 5–7 6–4 9–7 7–5, a total of **64 games**.

The **longest set played in a singles** was 24–22, a total of **46 games**. (It was played twice, by Gonzales and Pasarell in the longest match (see above) and in 1962 when Nicola Pietrangeli (Ita) beat Nikki Pilic (Yug) 24–22 6–2 6–4.)

The **longest set played in a final** was 13–11, a total of **24 games**. (It was played twice, by Drobny and Rosewall as above and in 1958 when Ashley Cooper beat Neale Fraser (both Aus) 3–6 6–3 6–4 13–11.)

The **longest set in a semi-final** was in 1958 when Neale Fraser (Aus) beat Kurt Nielsen (Den) 6–4 6–4 17–19 6–4, a total of **36 games**.

The **longest set in a quarter-final** was in 1924 when Louis Raymond (SA) beat William Washburn (USA) 6–0 7–5 17–15, a total of **32 games**.

WOMEN'S SINGLES

	FINAL				SEMI-FINALS		
Year	Winner	Loser	Score		Winner	Loser	Score
1884	Miss M Watson	Miss L Watson	6–8 6–3 6–3		Miss M Watson	Miss B Bingley	3–6 6–4 6–2
					Miss L Watson	Miss M Leslie	6–4 6–1
1885	Miss M Watson	Miss B Bingley	6–1 7–5		Miss M Watson	Miss E F Hudson	6–0 6–1
					Miss Bingley	Miss E Gurney	6–1 6–2

Challenge Round Instituted.

	CHALLENGE ROUND				ALL COMERS' FINAL		
1886	Miss B Bingley	Miss M Watson	6–3 6–3		Miss Bingley	Miss A Tabor	6–2 6–0
1887	Miss C Dod	Miss B Bingley	6–2 6–0		Miss Dod	Mrs C J Cole	6–2 6–3
1888	Miss C Dod	Mrs G W Hillyard	6–3 6–3		Mrs Hillyard	Miss Howes	6–1 6–2
1889	Mrs G W Hillyard		w.o.		Mrs Hillyard	Miss H B G Rice	4–6 8–6 6–4
1890	Miss H B G Rice		w.o.		Miss Rice	Miss M Jacks	6–4 6–1
1891	Miss C Dod		w.o.		Miss Dod	Mrs G W Hillyard	6–2 6–1
1892	Miss C Dod	Mrs G W Hillyard	6–1 6–1		Mrs Hillyard	Miss M Shackle	6–1 6–4
1893	Miss C Dod	Mrs G W Hillyard	6–8 6–1 6–4		Mrs Hillyard	Miss M Shackle	6–3 6–2
1894	Mrs G W Hillyard		w.o.		Mrs Hillyard	Miss L Austin	6–1 6–1
1895	Miss C Cooper		w.o.		Miss Cooper	Miss H Jackson	7–5 8–6
1896	Miss C Cooper	Mrs W H Pickering	6–2 6–3		Mrs Pickering	Miss L Austin	4–6 6–3 6–3
1897	Mrs G W Hillyard	Miss C Cooper	5–7 7–5 6–2		Mrs Hillyard	Mrs W H Pickering	6–2 7–5
1898	Miss C Cooper		w.o.		Miss Cooper	Miss L Martin	6–4 6–4
1899	Mrs G W Hillyard	Miss C Cooper	6–2 6–3		Mrs Hillyard	Mrs N Durlacher	7–5 6–8 6–1
1900	Mrs G W Hillyard	Miss C Cooper	4–6 6–4 6–4		Miss Cooper	Miss L Martin	8–6 5–7 6–1
1901	Mrs A Sterry	Mrs G W Hillyard	6–2 6–2		Mrs Sterry	Miss L Martin	6–3 6–4
1902	Miss M E Robb	Mrs A Sterry	7–5 6–1		Miss Robb	Miss A M Morton	6–2 6–4
	(Replay after abandonment at 4–6 13–11)						
1903	Miss D K Douglass		w.o.		Miss Douglass	Miss E W Thomson	4–6 6–4 6–2
1904	Miss D K Douglass	Mrs A Sterry	6–0 6–3		Mrs Sterry	Miss A M Morton	6–3 6–3
1905	Miss M G Sutton (USA)	Miss D K Douglass	6–3 6–4		Miss Sutton	Miss C M Wilson	6–3 8–6
1906	Miss D K Douglass	Miss M G Sutton (USA)	6–3 9–7		Miss Douglass	Mrs A Sterry	6–2 6–2
1907	Miss M G Sutton (USA)	Mrs R Lambert Chambers	6–1 6–4		Miss Sutton	Miss C M Wilson	6–4 6–2
1908	Mrs A Sterry		w.o.		Mrs Sterry	Miss A M Morton	6–4 6–4
1909	Miss D P Boothby		w.o.		Miss Boothby	Miss A M Morton	6–4 4–6 6–8
1910	Mrs R Lambert Chambers	Miss D P Boothby	6–2 6–2		Mrs Lambert Chambers	Miss E G Johnson	6–4 6–2
1911	Mrs R Lambert Chambers	Miss D P Boothby	6–0 6–0		Miss Boothby	Mrs G Hannam	6–2 7–5
1912	Mrs D R Larcombe		w.o.		Mrs Larcombe	Mrs A Sterry	6–3 6–1
1913	Mrs R Lambert Chambers		w.o.		Mrs Lambert Chambers	Mrs R J McNair	6–0 6–4
1914	Mrs R Lambert Chambers	Mrs D R Larcombe	7–5 6–4		Mrs Larcombe	Miss E Ryan	6–3 6–2
1915–1918 not held							
1919	Mlle S Lenglen (Fra)	Mrs R Lambert Chambers	10–8 4–6 9–7		Mlle Lenglen	Mrs P Satterthwaite	6–1 6–1

	CHALLENGE ROUND			**ALL COMERS' FINAL**		
Year	Winner	Loser	Score	Winner	Loser	Score
1920	Mlle S Lenglen (Fra)	Mrs R Lambert Chambers	6–3 6–0	Mrs Lambert Chambers	Miss E Ryan (USA)	6–2 6–1
1921	Mlle S Lenglen (Fra)	Miss E Ryan (USA)	6–2 6–0	Miss Ryan	Mrs P Satterthwaite	6–1 6–0

Challenge Round abolished.

	FINAL			**SEMI-FINALS**		
Year	Winner	Loser	Score	Winner	Loser	Score
1922	Mlle S Lenglen (Fra)	Mrs F I Mallory (USA)	6–2 6–0	Mlle Lenglen	Mrs G Peacock (Ind)	6–4 6–1
				Mrs Mallory	Mrs A E Beamish	6–2 6–2
1923	Mlle S Lenglen (Fra)	Miss K McKane	6–2 6–2	Mlle Lenglen	Mrs A E Beamish	6–0 6–0
				Miss McKane	Miss E Ryan (USA)	1–6 6–2 6–4
1924	Miss K McKane	Miss H N Wills (USA)	4–6 6–4 6–4	Miss McKane	Mlle S Lenglen (Fra)	w.o.
				Miss Wills	Mrs P Satterthwaite	6–2 6–1
1925	Mlle S Lenglen (Fra)	Miss J Fry	6–2 6–0	Mlle Lenglen	Miss K McKane	6–0 6–0
				Miss Fry	Mme M Billout (Fra)	6–2 4–6 6–3
1926	Mrs L A Godfree	Sta E de Alvarez (Spa)	6–2 4–6 6–3	Mrs Godfree	Mlle D Vlasto (Fra)	6–4 6–0
				Sta de Alvarez	Mrs F I Mallory (USA)	6–2 6–2
1927	Miss H N Wills (USA)	Sta E de Alvarez (Spa)	6–2 6–4	Miss Wills	Miss J Fry	6–3 6–1
				Sta de Alvarez	Miss E Ryan (USA)	2–6 6–0 6–4
1928	Miss H N Wills (USA)	Sta E de Alvarez (Spa)	6–2 6–3	Miss Wills	Miss E Ryan (USA)	6–1 6–1
				Sta de Alvarez	Miss D Akhurst (Aus)	6–2 6–0
1929	Miss H N Wills (USA)	Miss H H Jacobs (USA)	6–1 6–2	Miss Wills	Miss E A Goldsack	6–2 6–0
				Miss Jacobs	Miss J Ridley	6–2 6–2
1930	Mrs F S Moody (USA)	Miss E Ryan (USA)	6–2 6–2	Mrs Moody	Mme R Mathieu (Fra)	6–3 6–2
				Miss Ryan	Frl C Aussem (Ger)	6–3 0–6 4–4 ret'd
1931	Frl C Aussem (Ger)	Frl H Krahwinkel (Ger)	7–2 7–5	Frl Aussem	Mme R Mathieu (Fra)	6–0 2–6 6–3
				Frl Krahwinkel	Miss H H Jacobs (USA)	10–8 0–6 6–4
1932	Mrs F S Moody (USA)	Miss H H Jacobs (USA)	6–3 6–1	Mrs Moody	Miss M Heeley	6–2 6–0
				Miss Jacobs	Mme R Mathieu (Fra)	7–5 6–1
1933	Mrs F S Moody (USA)	Miss D E Round	6–4 6–8 6–3	Mrs Moody	Frl H Krahwinkel (Ger)	6–4 6–3
				Miss Round	Miss H H Jacobs (USA)	4–6 6–4 6–2
1934	Miss D E Round	Miss H H Jacobs (USA)	6–2 5–7 6–3	Miss Round	Mme R Mathieu (Fra)	6–4 5–7 6–2
				Miss Jacobs	Miss J Hartigan (Aus)	6–2 6–2
1935	Mrs F S Moody (USA)	Miss H H Jacobs (USA)	6–3 3–6 7–5	Mrs Moody	Miss J Hartigan (Aus)	6–3 6–3
				Miss Jacobs	Fru S Sperling (Ger)	6–3 6–0
1936	Miss H H Jacobs (USA)	Fru S Sperling (Ger)	6–2 4–6 7–5	Miss Jacobs	Miss J Jedrzejowska (Pol)	6–4 6–2
				Fru Sperling	Mme R Mathieu (Fra)	6–3 6–2
1937	Miss D E Round	Miss J Jedrzejowska (Pol)	6–2 2–6 7–5	Miss Round	Mme R Mathieu (Fra)	6–4 6–0
				Miss Jedrzejowska	Miss A Marble (USA)	8–6 6–2
1938	Mrs F S Moody (USA)	Miss H H Jacobs (USA)	6–4 6–0	Mrs Moody	Fru S Sperling (Ger)	12–10 6–4
				Miss Jacobs	Miss A Marble (USA)	6–4 6–4
1939	Miss A Marble (USA)	Miss K E Stammers	6–2 6–0	Miss Marble	Fru S Sperling (Ger)	6–0 6–0
				Miss Stammers	Mrs M Fabyan (USA)	7–5 2–6 6–3
1940–1945 not held						
1946	Miss P M Betz (USA)	Miss A L Brough (USA)	6–2 6–4	Miss Betz	Miss D Bundy (USA)	6–2 6–3
				Miss Brough	Miss M E Osborne (USA)	8–6 7–5
1947	Miss M E Osborne (USA)	Miss D J Hart (USA)	6–2 6–4	Miss Osborne	Mrs S P Summers (SA)	6–1 6–2
				Miss Hart	Miss A L Brough (USA)	2–6 8–6 6–4
1948	Miss A L Brough (USA)	Miss D J Hart (USA)	6–3 8–6	Miss Brough	Mrs P C Todd (USA)	6–3 7–5
				Miss Hart	Mrs W D du Pont (USA)	6–4 2–6 6–3
1949	Miss A L Brough (USA)	Mrs W D du Pont (USA)	10–8 1–6 10–8	Miss Brough	Mrs P C Todd (USA)	6–3 6–0
				Mrs du Pont	Mrs H P Rihbany (USA)	6–2 6–2
1950	Miss A L Brough (USA)	Mrs W D du Pont (USA)	6–1 3–6 6–1	Miss Brough	Miss D J Hart (USA)	6–4 6–3
				Mrs du Pont	Mrs P C Todd (USA)	8–6 4–6 8–6
1951	Miss D J Hart (USA)	Miss S J Fry (USA)	6–1 6–0	Miss Hart	Miss B Baker (USA)	6–3 6–1
				Miss Fry	Miss A L Brough (USA)	6–4 6–2
1952	Miss M C Connolly (USA)	Miss A L Brough (USA)	7–5 6–3	Miss Connolly	Miss S J Fry (USA)	6–4 6–3
				Miss Brough	Mrs P C Todd (USA)	6–3 3–6 6–1
1953	Miss M C Connolly (USA)	Miss D J Hart (USA)	8–6 7–5	Miss Connolly	Miss S J Fry (USA)	6–1 6–1
				Miss Hart	Mrs D P Knode (USA)	6–2 6–2
1954	Miss M C Connolly (USA)	Miss A L Brough (USA)	6–2 7–5	Miss Connolly	Mrs E C S Pratt (USA)	6–1 6–1
				Miss Brough	Miss D J Hart (USA)	2–6 6–3 6–3
1955	Miss A L Brough (USA)	Mrs J G Fleitz (USA)	7–5 8–6	Miss Brough	Miss D R Hard (USA)	6–3 8–6
				Mrs Fleitz	Miss D J Hart (USA)	6–3 6–0

Year	FINAL Winner	Loser	Score	SEMI-FINALS Winner	Loser	Score
1956	Miss S J Fry (USA)	Miss A Buxton	6–3 6–1	Miss Fry	Miss A L Brough (USA)	6–4 4–6 6–3
				Miss Buxton	Miss P E Ward	6–1 6–4
1957	Miss A Gibson (USA)	Miss D R Hard (USA)	6–3 6–2	Miss Gibson	Miss C C Truman	6–1 6–1
				Miss Hard	Mrs D P Knode (USA)	6–2 6–3
1958	Miss A Gibson (USA)	Miss A Mortimer	8–6 6–2	Miss Gibson	Miss A S Haydon	6–2 6–0
				Miss Mortimer	Mrs S Kormoczi (Hun)	6–0 6–1
1959	Miss M E Bueno (Bra)	Miss D R Hard (USA)	6–4 6–3	Miss Bueno	Miss S M Moore (USA)	6–2 6–4
				Miss Hard	Miss S Reynolds (SA)	6–4 6–4
1960	Miss M E Bueno (Bra)	Miss S Reynolds (SA)	8–6 6–0	Miss Bueno	Miss C C Truman	6–0 5–7 6–1
				Miss Reynolds	Miss A S Haydon	6–3 2–6 6–4
1961	Miss A Mortimer	Miss C C Truman	4–6 6–4 7–5	Miss Mortimer	Miss S Reynolds (SA)	11–9 6–3
				Miss Truman	Miss R Schuurman (SA)	6–4 6–4
1962	Mrs J R Susman (USA)	Mrs V Sukova (Cze)	6–4 6–4	Mrs Susman	Miss A S Haydon	8–6 6–1
				Mrs Sukova	Miss M E Bueno (Bra)	6–4 6–3
1963	Miss M Smith (Aus)	Miss B J Moffitt (USA)	6–3 6–4	Miss Smith	Miss D R Hard (USA)	6–3 6–3
				Miss Moffitt	Mrs P F Jones	6–4 6–4
1964	Miss M E Bueno (Bra)	Miss M Smith (Aus)	6–4 7–9 6–3	Miss Bueno	Miss L R Turner (Aus)	3–6 6–4 6–4
				Miss Smith	Miss B J Moffitt (USA)	6–3 6–4
1965	Miss M Smith (Aus)	Miss M E Bueno (Bra)	6–4 7–5	Miss Smith	Miss C C Truman	6–4 6–0
				Miss Bueno	Miss B J Moffitt (USA)	6–4 5–7 6–3
1966	Mrs L W King (USA)	Miss M E Bueno (Bra)	6–3 3–6 6–1	Mrs King	Miss M Smith (Aus)	6–3 6–3
				Miss Bueno	Mrs P F Jones	6–3 9–11 7–5
1967	Mrs L W King (USA)	Mrs P F Jones	6–3 6–4	Mrs King	Miss K M Harter (USA)	6–0 6–3
				Mrs Jones	Miss R Casals (USA)	2–6 6–3 7–5
1968	Mrs L W King (USA)	Miss J A M Tegart (Aus)	9–7 7–5	Mrs King	Mrs P F Jones	4–6 7–5 6–2
				Miss Tegart	Miss N Richey (USA)	6–3 6–1
1969	Mrs P F Jones	Mrs L W King (USA)	3–6 6–3 6–2	Mrs Jones	Mrs B M Court (Aus)	10–12 6–3 6–2
				Mrs King	Miss R Casals (USA)	6–1 6–0
1970	Mrs B M Court (Aus)	Mrs L W King (USA)	14–12 11–9	Mrs Court	Miss R Casals (USA)	6–4 6–1
				Mrs King	Mlle F Durr (Fra)	6–3 7–5
1971	Miss E F Goolagong (Aus)	Mrs B M Court (Aus)	6–4 6–1	Miss Goolagong	Mrs L W King (USA)	6–4 6–4
				Mrs Court	Mrs D E Dalton (Aus)	4–6 6–1 6–0
1972	Mrs L W King (USA)	Miss E F Goolagong (Aus)	6–3 6–3	Mrs King	Miss R Casals (USA)	6–2 6–4
				Miss Goolagong	Miss C M Evert (USA)	4–6 6–3 6–4
1973	Mrs L W King (USA)	Miss C M Evert (USA)	6–0 7–5	Mrs King	Miss E F Goolagong	6–3 5–7 6–3
				Miss Evert	Mrs B M Court (Aus)	6–1 1–6 6–1
1974	Miss C M Evert (USA)	Mrs O Morozova (USSR)	6–0 6–4	Miss Evert	Miss K A Melville (Aus)	6–2 6–3
				Mrs Morozova	Miss S V Wade	1–6 7–5 6–4
1975	Mrs L W King (USA)	Mrs R A Cawley (Aus)	6–0 6–1	Mrs King	Miss C M Evert (USA)	2–6 6–2 6–3
				Mrs Cawley	Mrs B M Court (Aus)	6–4 6–4
1976	Miss C M Evert (USA)	Mrs R A Cawley (Aus)	6–3 4–6 8–6	Miss Evert	Miss M Navratilova (Cze)	6–3 4–6 6–4
				Mrs Cawley	Miss S V Wade	6–1 6–2
1977	Miss S V Wade	Miss B F Stove (Hol)	4–6 6–3 6–1	Miss Wade	Miss C M Evert (USA)	6–2 4–6 6–1
				Miss Stove	Miss S Barker	6–4 2–6 6–4
1978	Miss M Navratilova (Cze)	Miss C M Evert (USA)	2–6 6–4 7–5	Miss Navratilova	Mrs R A Cawley (Aus)	2–6 6–4 6–4
				Miss Evert	Miss S V Wade	8–6 6–2
1979	Miss M Navratilova (Cze)	Mrs J M Lloyd (USA)	6–4 6–4	Miss Navratilova	Miss T A Austin (USA)	7–5 6–1
				Mrs Lloyd	Mrs R A Cawley (Aus)	6–3 6–2
1980	Mrs R A Cawley (Aus)	Mrs J M Lloyd (USA)	6–1 7–6	Mrs Cawley	Miss T A Austin (USA)	6–3 0–6 6–4
				Mrs Lloyd	Miss M Navratilova (Cze)	4–6 6–4 6–2
1981	Mrs J M Lloyd (USA)	Miss H Mandlikova (Cze)	6–2 6–2	Mrs Lloyd	Miss P H Shriver (USA)	6–3 6–1
				Miss Mandlikova	Miss M Navratilova (Cze)	7–5 4–6 6–1
1982	Miss M Navratilova (USA)	Mrs J M Lloyd (USA)	6–1 3–6 6–2	Miss Navratilova	Miss B Bunge (FRG)	6–2 6–2
				Mrs Lloyd	Mrs L W King (USA)	7–6 2–6 6–3

The **longest match** was in 1948 in the second round when Mlle A Weiwers (Lux) beat Mrs Rita Anderson (GB) 8–10 14–12 6–4, a total of **54 games**.

The **second longest match**, and the **longest final**, was 1902 when Muriel Robb beat Charlotte Sterry (both GB) 7–5 6–1 after abandonment of an overnight score of 4–6 13–11, a total of **53 games**.

The **longest final, measured normally**, was in 1970 when Billie Jean King beat Margaret Court 14–12 11–9, a total of **46 games**.

The **second longest final** was 1919 when Suzanne Lenglen (Fra) beat Dorothea Lambert Chambers (GB) 10–8 4–6 9–7, a total of **44 games**.

The **longest All Comers' final** was 1889 when Blanche Hillyard (GB) beat Helena Rice (Ire) 4–6 8–6 6–4 and 1909 when Dora Boothby beat

Agatha Morton (both GB) 6–4 4–6 8–6, a total of **34 games**.

The **longest semi-final** was in 1966 when Maria Bueno (Bra) beat Ann Jones (GB) 6–3 9–11 7–5, a total of **41 games**.

The **longest quarter-final** was 1954 when Betty Pratt (USA) beat Shirley Fry (USA) 6–4 9–11 6–3, a total of **39 games**.

The **longest set**, played on three occasions, is 14–12, a total of **26 games**. (It was played in the record 1960 final above.)

The **longest set** played in the **semi-finals** or **quarter-finals** is 12–10, a total of **22 games**.

MEN'S DOUBLES

Year	FINAL Winners	Losers	Score	SEMI-FINALS Winners	Losers	Score
1879*	L R Erskine & H F Lawford	F Durant & G E Tabor	4–6 6–4 6–5 6–2 3–6 5–6 10–8**	Erskine & Lawford	L H Mulholland & A J Mullholland	5–6 6–5 6–2 6–4 6–5**
				Durant & Tabor	W F Wells Cole & E B Hill	6–4 6–2 6–1 6–3**
1880*	E Renshaw & W Renshaw	C J Cole & O E Woodhouse	6–1 6–4 6–0 6–8 6–3	Renshaw & Renshaw	J Comber & R-W Braddell	6–4 6–3 6–1 6–2
				Cole & Woodhouse		bye
1881*	E Renshaw & W Renshaw	W J Down & H L Vaughan	6–0 6–0 6–4	Renshaw & Renshaw	J Comber & R W Braddell	4–6 6–1 6–2 6–4
				Down & Vaughan	C J Cole & D Stewart	8–10 6–0 0–6 6–2 6–1
1882*	J T Hartley & R T Richardson	J G Horn & C B Russell	6–2 6–1 6–0	Hartley & Richardson	E Renshaw & W Renshaw	6–3 6–5 6–2
				Horn & Russell	M G Lascelles & A S Rashleigh	6–2 6–4 2–6 6–3
1883*	C W Grinstead & C E Weldon	R T Milford & C B Russell	3–6 6–1 6–3 6–4	Grinstead & Weldon	E Renshaw & W Renshaw	w.o.
				Mitford & Russell	T R Deykin & F R Pinhorn	6–5 3–6 6–4 6–3
1884	E Renshaw & W Renshaw	E W Lewis & E L Williams	6–3 6–1 1–6 6–4	Renshaw & Renshaw	J Dwight (USA) & R D Sears (USA)	6–0 6–1 6–2
				Lewis & Williams		bye
1885	E Renshaw & W Renshaw	C E Farrer & A J Stanley	6–3 6–3 10–8	Renshaw & Renshaw	J Dwight (USA) & E W Lewis	4–6 6–1 6–4 6–4
				Farrer & Stanley	C H A Ross & W C Taylor	6–3 8–6 6–2

Challenge Round Instituted.

Year	CHALLENGE ROUND Winners	Losers	Score	ALL COMERS' FINAL Winners	Losers	Score
1886	E Renshaw & W Renshaw	C E Farrer & A J Stanley	6–3 6–3 4–6 7–5	Farrer & Stanley	P Bowes-Lyon & H W W Wilberforce	7–5 6–3 6–1
1887	P Bowes-Lyon & H W W Wilberforce		w.o.	Bowes-Lyon & Wilberforce	E Barrett-Smith & J H Crispe	7–5 6–3 6–2
1888	E Renshaw & W Renshaw	P Bowes-Lyon & H W W Wilberforce	2–6 1–6 6–3 6–4 6–3	Renshaw & Renshaw	E G Meers & A G Ziffo	6–3 6–2 6–2
1889	E Renshaw & W Renshaw	G W Hillyard & E W Lewis	6–4 6–4 3–6 0–6 6–1	Hillyard & Lewis	A W Gore & G R Mewburn	6–2 6–1 6–3
1890	J Pim & F O Stoker		w.o.	Pim & Stoker	G W Hillyard & E W Lewis	6–0 7–5 6–4
1891	H Baddeley & W Baddeley	J Pim & F O Stoker	6–1 6–3 1–6 6–2	Baddeley & Baddeley	H S Barlow & E Renshaw	4–6 6–4 7–5 0–6 6–2
1892	H S Barlow & E W Lewis	H Baddeley & W Baddeley	4–6 6–2 8–6 6–4	Barlow & Lewis	H S Mahony & J Pim	8–10 6–3 5–7 11–9 6–1
1893	J Pim & F O Stoker	H S Barlow & E W Lewis	4–6 6–3 6–1 2–6 6–0	Pim & Stoker	H Baddeley & W Baddeley	6–2 4–6 6–3 5–7 6–2
1894	H Baddeley & W Baddeley		w.o.	Baddley & Baddeley	H S Barlow & C H Martin	5–7 7–5 4–6 6–3 8–6
1895	H Baddeley & W Baddeley	W V Eaves & E W Lewis	8–6 5–7 6–4 6–3	Eaves & Lewis	W G Bailey & C F Simond	6–4 6–4 6–3

* The 'Oxford University Doubles Championship', played at Noreham Gardens, Oxford. The trophies were given to Wimbledon.
** The best of seven sets was played throughout.

	CHALLENGE ROUND			ALL COMERS' FINAL		
Year	Winners	Losers	Score	Winners	Losers	Score
1896	H Baddeley & W Baddeley	R F Doherty & H A Nisbet	1–6 3–6 6–4 6–2 6–1	R F Doherty & Nisbet	C G Allen & E R Allen	3–6 7–5 6–4 6–1
1897	H L Doherty & R F Doherty	H Baddeley & W Baddeley	6–4 4–6 8–6 6–4	Doherty & Doherty	C H L Cazalet & S H Smith	6–2 7–5 2–6 6–2
1898	H L Doherty & R F Doherty	C Hobart (USA) & H A Nisbet	6–4 6–4 6–2	Hobart & Nisbet	G W Hillyard & S H Smith	2–6 6–2 6–2 6–3
1899	H L Doherty & R F Doherty	C Hobart (USA) & H A Nisbet	7–5 6–0 6–2	Hobart & Nisbet	A W Gore & H Roper Barrett	6–4 6–1 8–6
1900	H L Doherty & R F Doherty	H A Nisbet & H Roper Barrett	9–7 7–5 4–6 3–6	Nisbet & Roper Barrett	F L Riseley & S H Smith	6–2 2–6 6–8 8–6 6–2
1901	H L Doherty & R F Doherty	D F Davis (USA) & H Ward (USA)	4–6 6–2 6–3 9–7	Davis & Ward	H Roper Barrett & G M Simond	7–5 6–4 6–4
1902	F L Riseley & S H Smith	H L Doherty & R F Doherty	4–6 8–6 6–3 4–6 11–9	Riseley & Smith	C H L Cazalet & G W Hillyard	7–5 2–6 6–8 6–3 6–1
1903	H L Doherty & R F Doherty	F L Riseley & S H Smith	6–4 6–4 6–4	Doherty & Doherty	H S Mahony & M J G Ritchie	8–6 6–2 6–2
1904	H L Doherty & R F Doherty	F L Riseley & S H Smith	6–3 6–4 6–3	Riseley & Smith	G A Caridia & A W Gore	6–3 6–4 6–3
1905	H L Doherty & R F Doherty	F L Riseley & S H Smith	6–2 6–4 6–8 6–3	Riseley & Smith	N E Brookes (Aus) & A W Dunlop (Aus)	6–2 1–6 6–2 6–3
1906	F L Riseley & S H Smith	H L Doherty & R F Doherty	6–8 6–4 5–7 6–3 6–3	Riseley & Smith	C H L Cazalet & G M Simond	6–2 6–2 5–7 6–4
1907	N E Brookes (Aus) & A F Wilding (NZ)		w.o.	Brookes & Wilding	K Behr (USA) & B C Wright (USA)	6–4 6–4 6–2
1908	M J G Ritchie & A F Wilding (NZ)		w.o.	Ritchie & Wilding	A W Gore & H Roper Barrett	6–1 6–2 1–6 1–6 9–7
1909	A W Gore & H Roper Barrett		w.o.	Gore & Roper Barrett	S N Doust (Aus) & H A Parker (NZ)	6–2 6–1 6–4
1910	M J G Ritchie & A F Wilding (NZ)	A W Gore & H Roper Barrett	6–1 6–1 6–2	Ritchie & Wilding	K Powell & R B Powell (Can)	9–7 6–0 6–4
1911	M Decugis (Fra) & A H Gobert (Fra)	M J G Ritchie & A F Wilding (NZ)	9–7 5–7 6–3 2–6 6–2	Decugis & Gobert	S Hardy (USA) & J C Parke	6–2 6–1 6–2
1912	C P Dixon & H Roper Barrett	M Decugis (Fra) & A H Gobert (Fra)	3–6 6–3 6–4 7–5	Dixon & Roper Barrett	A E Beamish & J C Parke	6–8 6–4 3–6 6–3 6–4
1913	C P Dixon & H Roper Barrett	H Kleinschroth (Ger) & F W Rahe (Ger)	6–2 6–4 4–6 6–2	Kleinschroth & Rahe	A E Beamish & J C Parke	6–3 6–2 6–4
1914	N E Brookes (Aus) & A F Wilding (NZ)	C P Dixon & H Roper Barrett	6–1 6–1 5–7 8–6	Brookes & Wilding	A H Lowe & F G Lowe	6–2 8–6 6–1
1915–1918 not held						
1919	P O'Hara Wood (Aus) & R V Thomas (Aus)		w.o.	O'Hara Wood & Thomas	R W Heath (Aus) & R Lycett	6–4 6–2 4–6 6–2
1920	C S Garland (USA) & R N Williams (USA)		w.o.	Garland & Williams	A R F Kingscote & J C Parke	4–6 6–4 7–5 6–2
1921	R Lycett & M Woosnam		w.o.	Lycett & Woosnam	A H Lowe & F G Lowe	6–3 6–0 7–5

Challenge Round abolished.

	FINAL			SEMI-FINALS		
1922	J O Anderson (Aus) & R Lycett	P O'Hara Wood (Aus) & G L Patterson (Aus)	3–6 7–9 6–4 6–3 11–9	Anderson & Lycett	G C Caner (USA) & D Mathey (USA)	6–2 6–3 6–2
				O'Hara Wood & Patterson	B I C Norton (SA) & H Roper Barrett	6–1 3–6 5–7 6–3 15–13
1923	L A Godfree & R Lycett	E Flaquer (Spa) & Count de Gomar (Spa)	6–3 6–4 3–6 6–3	Godfree & Lycett	L S Deane (Ind) & A H Fyzee (Ind)	8–6 6–4 6–3
				Flaquer & de Gomar	J Borotra (Fra) & R Lacoste (Fra)	11–9 4–6 6–4 3–6 7–5
1924	F T Hunter (USA) & V Richards (USA)	W M Washburn (USA) & R N Williams (USA)	6–3 3–6 8–10 8–6 6–3	Hunter & Richards	L Raymond (SA) & P D B Spence (SA)	6–4 6–4 6–2
				Washburn & Williams	L A Godfree & R Lycett	4–6 12–10 6–3 7–7 ret'd.

Year	FINAL Winners	Losers	Score	SEMI-FINALS Winners	Losers	Score
1925	J Borotra (Fra) & R Lacoste (Fra)	R Casey (USA) & J Hennessey (USA)	6–4 11–9 4–6 1–6 6–3	Borotra & Lacoste	H L de Morpurgo (Ita) & B von Kehrling (Hun)	11–9 7–9 6–1 6–1
				Casey & Hennessey	J Brugnon (Fra) & H Cochet (Fra)	7–5 5–7 9–7 6–4
1926	J Bugnon (Fra) & H Cochet (Fra)	H Kinsey (USA) & V Richards (USA)	7–5 4–6 6–3 6–2	Brugnon & Cochet	B von Kehrling (Hun) & C E van Lennep (Hol)	9–7 6–4 6–2
				Kinsey & Richards	H W Austin & R Lycett	7–5 6–4 6–4
1927	F T Hunter (USA) & W T Tilden (USA)	J Brugnon (Fra) & H Cochet (Fra)	1–6 4–6 8–6 6–3 6–4	Hunter & Tilden	H W Austin & R Lycett	6–0 10–8 6–4
				Brugnon & Cochet	J Condon (SA) & L Raymond (SA)	6–1 6–2 7–5
1928	J Brugnon (Fra) & H Cochet (Fra)	J B Hawkes (Aus) & G L Patterson (Aus)	13–11 6–4 6–4	Brugnon & Cochet	J Hennessey (USA) & G M Lott (USA)	11–9 6–4 3–6 7–5
				Hawkes & Patterson	F T Hunter (USA) & W T Tilden (USA)	7–9 7–9 6–4 6–4 10–8
1929	W L Allison USA) & J Van Ryn (USA)	I G Collins & J C Gregory	6–4 5–7 6–3 10–12 6–4	Allison & Van Ryn	F T Hunter (USA) & W T Tilden (USA)	6–3 12–10 6–3
				Collins & Gregory	J Hennessey (USA) & G M Lott (USA)	4–6 7–5 6–1 4–6 7–5
1930	W L Allison (USA) & J Van Ryn (USA)	J H Doeg (USA) & G M Lott (USA)	6–3 6–3 6–2	Allison & Van Ryn	I G Collins & J C Gregory	4–6 7–5 6–3 6–3
				Doeg & Lott	J Brugnon (Fra) & H Cochet (Fra)	8–6 3–6 6–3 6–1
1931	G M Lott (USA) & J Van Ryn (USA)	J Brugnon (Fra) & H Cochet (Fra)	6–2 10–8 9–11 3–6 6–3	Lott & Van Ryn	G P Hughes & F J Perry	6–4 11–9 6–4
				Brugnon & Cochet	F X Shields (USA) & S B Wood (USA)	6–4 7–5 6–2
1932	J Borotra (Fra) & J Brugnon (Fra)	G P Hughes & F J Perry	6–0 4–6 3–6 7–5 7–5	Borotra & Brugnon	W L Allison (USA) & J Van Ryn (USA)	6–3 6–2 6–4
				Hughes & Perry	C Boussus (Fra) & A Merlin (Fra)	8–6 6–1 6–3
1933	J Borotra (Fra) & J Brugnon (Fra)	R Nunoi (Jap) & J Satoh (Jap)	4–6 6–3 6–3 7–5	Borotra & Brugnon	N G Farquharson (SA) & V G Kirby (SA)	5–7 3–6 6–4 6–3 6–4
				Nunoi & Satoh	E Nourney (Ger) & G von Cramm (Ger)	7–5 3–6 6–4 6–1
1934	G M Lott (USA) & L R Stoefen (USA)	J Borotra (Fra) & J Brugnon (Fra)	6–2 6–3 6–4	Lott & Stoefen	H C Hopman (Aus) & D Prenn (Ger)	6–4 4–6 6–3 8–6
				Borotra & Brugnon	I G Collins & F H D Wilde	7–5 3–6 6–2 6–4
1935	J H Crawford (Aus) & A K Quist (Aus)	W L Allison (USA) & J Van Ryn (USA)	6–3 5–7 6–2	Crawford & Quist	J D Budge (USA) & G Mako (USA)	6–2 13–11 6–3
				Allison & Van Ryn	G P Hughes & C R D Tuckey	4–6 6–4 6–2 6–2
1936	G P Hughes & C R D Tuckey	C E Hare & F H D Wilde	6–4 3–6 7–9 6–1 6–4	Hughes & Tuckey	W L Allison (USA) & J Van Ryn (USA)	7–5 6–4 3–6 11–9
				Hare & Wilde	J Borotra (Fra) & J Brugnon (Fra)	6–1 4–6 6–1 6–4
1937	J D Budge (USA) & G Mako (USA)	G P Hughes & C R D Tuckey	6–0 6–4 6–8 6–1	Budge & Mako	H Henekl (Ger) & G von Cramm (Ger)	4–6 4–6 6–2 6–4 6–3
				Hughes & Tuckey	L Hecht (Cze) & R Menzel (Cze)	6–2 6–2 6–4
1938	J D Budge (USA) & G Mako (USA)	H Henkel (Ger) & G von Metaxa (Ger)	6–4 3–6 6–3 8–6	Budge & Mako	G P Hughes & F H D Wilde	6–2 6–4 12–10
				Henkel & von Metaxa	F Kukuljevic & J Pallada	7–5 6–2 6–4
1939	E T Cooke (USA) & R L Riggs (USA)	C E Hare & F H D Wilde	6–3 3–6 6–3 9–7	Cooke & Riggs	J Borotra (Fra) & J Brugnon (Fra)	6–4 2–6 6–4 6–3
				Hare & Wilde	J S Olliff & R A Shayes	6–2 6–4 6–4
1940–1945 not held						
1946	T P Brown (USA) & J A Kramer (USA)	G E Brown (Aus) & D Pails (Aus)	6–4 6–4 6–2	T P Brown & Kramer	J E Patty (USA) & F Segura (USA)	6–3 6–3 6–3
				G E Brown & Pails	D Mitic (Yug) & J Pallada (Yug)	6–2 6–4 6–3

Year	FINAL Winners	Losers	Score	SEMI-FINALS Winners	Losers	Score
1947	R Falkenburg (USA) & J A Kramer (USA)	A J Mottram & O W Sidwell (Aus)	8–6 6–3 6–3	Falkenburg & Kramer	G E Brown (Aus) & C F Long (Aus)	10–8 6–4 6–4
				Mottram & Sidwell	J E Bromwich (Aus) & D Pails (Aus)	6–3 6–3 7–5
1948	J E Bromwich (Aus) & F A Sedgman (Aus)	T P Brown (USA) & G Mulloy (USA)	5–7 7–5 7–5 9–7	Bromwich & Sedgman	R Falkenburg (USA) & F A Parker (USA)	6–2 6–8 4–6 6–4 6–1
				T P Brown & Mulloy	L Bergelin (Swe) & J E Harper (Aus)	1–6 6–3 4–6 6–4 8–6
1949	R A Gonzales (USA) & F A Parker (USA)	G Mulloy (USA) & F R Schroeder (USA)	6–4 6–4 6–2	Gonzales & Parker	J E Patty (USA) & E W Sturgess (SA)	6–3 6–1 3–6 5–7 7–5
				Mulloy & Schroeder	G E Brown (Aus) & O W Sidwell (Aus)	6–4 3–6 6–8 6–3 9–7
1950	J E Bromwich (Aus) & A K Quist (Aus)	G E Brown (Aus) & O W Sidwell (Aus)	7–5 3–6 6–3 3–6 6–2	Bromwich & Quist	J Drobny (Egy) & E W Sturgess (SA)	6–4 3–6 6–3 6–4
				G E Brown & Sidwell	J E Patty (USA) & M A Trabert (USA)	6–4 6–4 6–3
1951	K McGregor (Aus) & F A Sedgman (Aus)	J Drobny (Egy) & E W Sturgess (SA)	3–6 6–2 6–3 3–6 6–3	McGregor & Sedgman	J E Patty (USA) & H Richardson (USA)	6–4 6–2 6–3
				Drobny & Sturgess	G Mulloy (USA) & R Savitt (USA)	4–6 6–4 6–3 6–4
1952	K McGregor (Aus) & F A Sedgman (Aus)	E V Seixas (USA) & E W Sturgess (SA)	6–3 7–5 6–4	McGregor & Sedgman	J Drobny (Egy) & J E Patty (USA)	6–3 6–4 7–9 6–4
				Seixas & Sturgess	L A Hoad (Aus) & K R Rosewall (Aus)	6–4 8–6 6–8 7–5
1953	L A Hoad (Aus) & K R Rosewall (Aus)	R N Hartwig (Aus) & M G Rose (Aus)	6–4 7–5 4–6 7–5	Hoad & Rosewall	J Brichant (Bel) & P Washer (Bel)	4–6 6–0 6–4 3–6 6–1
				Hartwig & Rose	G Mulloy (USA) & E V Seixas (USA)	14–16 6–3 6–3 6–4
1954	R N Hartwig (Aus) & M G Rose (Aus)	E V Seixas (USA) & M A Trabert (USA)	6–4 6–4 3–6 6–4	Hartwig & Rose	G Mulloy (USA) & J E Patty (USA)	4–6 6–4 6–2 6–1
				Seixas & Trabert	L A Hoad (Aus) & K R Rosewall (Aus)	6–3 7–5 3–6 4–6 8–6
1955	R N Hartwig (Aus) & L A Hoad (Aus)	N A Fraser (Aus) & K R Rosewall (Aus)	7–5 6–4 6–3	Hartwig & Hoad	M G Rose (Aus) & G A Worthington (Aus)	7–9 6–4 6–4 2–6 6–1
				Fraser & Rosewall	E V Seixas (USA) & M A Trabert (USA)	6–2 1–6 6–1 4–6 6–3
1956	L A Hoad (Aus) & K R Rosewall (Aus)	N Pietrangeli (Ita) & O Sirola (Ita)	7–5 6–2 6–1	Hoad & Rosewall	R N Howe (Aus) & A Larsen (USA)	4–6 6–2 7–5 6–3
				Pietrangeli & Sirola	A J Cooper (Aus) & N A Fraser (Aus)	6–4 6–4 8–6
1957	G Mulloy (USA) & J E Patty (USA)	N A Fraser (Aus) & L A Hoad (Aus)	8–10 6–4 6–4 6–4	Mulloy & Patty	R Becker & R N Howe (Aus)	9–7 7–5 6–3
				Fraser & Hoad	N Pietrangeli (Ita) & O Sirola (Ita)	14–12 1–6 8–6 6–3
1958	S Davidson (Swe) & U Schmidt (Swe)	A J Cooper (Aus) & N A Fraser (Aus)	6–4 6–4 8–6	Davidson & Schmidt	N Pietrangeli (Ita) & O Sirola (Ita)	8–6 3–6 6–3 7–5
				Cooper & Fraser	B MacKay (USA) & M G Rose (Aus)	3–6 8–6 7–5 7–5
1959	R S Emerson (Aus) & N A Fraser (Aus)	R G Laver (Aus) & R Mark (Aus)	8–6 6–3 14–16 9–7	Emerson & Fraser	L Legenstein (Yug) & T Ulrich (Den)	6–3 8–6 6–4
				Laver & Mark	N Pietrangeli (Ita) & O Sirola (Ita)	6–4 6–4 6–3
1960	R H Osuna (Mex) & R D Ralston (USA)	M G Davies & R K Wilson	7–5 6–3 10–8	Osuna & Ralston	R G Laver (Aus) & R Mark (Aus)	4–6 10–8 15–13 4–6 11–9
				Davies & Wilson	R A J Hewitt (Aus) & M F Mulligan (Aus)	3–6 6–3 6–2 6–4
1961	R S Emerson (Aus) & N A Fraser (Aus)	R A J Hewitt (Aus) & F S Stolle (Aus)	6–4 6–8 6–4 6–8 8–6	Emerson & Fraser	K N Fletcher (Aus) & J D Newcombe (Aus)	10–8 11–9 6–1
				Hewitt & Stolle	R G Laver (Aus) & R Mark (Aus)	4–6 10–8 6–3 6–4
1962	R A J Hewitt (Aus) & F S Stolle (Aus)	B Jovanovic (Yug) & N Pilic (Yug)	6–2 5–7 6–2 6–4	Hewitt & Stolle	J G Fraser (Aus) & R G Laver (Aus)	8–5 5–7 7–5 6–2
				Jovanovic & Pilic	R S Emerson (Aus) & N A Fraser (Aus)	4–6 6–3 6–4 6–4

Year	FINAL Winners	Losers	Score	SEMI-FINALS Winners	Losers	Score
1963	R H Osuna (Mex) & A Palafox (Mex)	J C Barclay (Fra) & P Darmon (Fra)	4–6 6–2 6–2 6–2	Osuna & Palafox	G L Forbes (SA) & A A Segal (SA)	6–3 5–7 6–4 6–4
				Barclay & Darmon	R S Emerson (Aus) & M Santana (Spa)	6–2 7–5 3–6 6–3
1964	R A J Hewitt (Aus) & F S Stolle (Aus)	R S Emerson (Aus) & K N Fletcher (Aus)	7–5 11–9 6–4	Hewitt & Stolle	R H Osuna (Mex) & A Palafox (Mex)	6–2 6–2 6–3
				Emerson & Fletcher	I S Crookenden (NZ) & L A Gerard (NZ)	14–12 6–2 6–1
1965	J D Newcombe (Aus) & A D Roche (Aus)	K N Fletcher (Aus) & R A J Hewitt (Aus)	7–5 6–3 6–4	Newcombe & Roche	R D Ralston (USA) & H Richardson (USA)	5–7 14–12 6–8 7–5 6–4
				Fletcher & Hewitt	C E Graebner (USA) & M C Riessen (USA)	7–5 6–4 6–4
1966	K N Fletcher (Aus) & J D Newcombe (Aus)	W W Bowrey (Aus) & O K Davidson (Aus)	6–3 6–4 3–6 6–3	Fletcher & Newcombe	C E Graebner (USA) & M C Riessen (USA)	6–3 7–5 6–1
				Bowrey & Davidson	M Cox & A R Mills	6–2 6–4 9–7
1967	R A J Hewitt (SA) & F D McMillan (SA)	R S Emerson (Aus) & K N Fletcher (Aus)	6–2 6–3 6–4	Hewitt & McMillan	W W Bowrey (Aus) & O K Davidson (Aus)	6–2 10–8 6–2
				Emerson & Fletcher	P W Curtis & G R Stilwell	6–4 8–6 4–6 5–7 9–7
1968	J D Newcombe (Aus) & A D Roche (Aus)	K R Rosewall (Aus) & F S Stolle (Aus)	3–6 8–6 5–7 14–12 6–3	Newcombe & Roche	R S Emerson (Aus) & R G Laver (Aus)	6–3 8–6 2–6 7–5
				Rosewall & Stolle	R A J Hewitt (SA) & F D McMillan (SA)	6–2 6–3 6–4
1969	J D Newcombe (Aus) & A D Roche (Aus)	T S Okker (Hol) & M C Riessen (USA)	7–5 11–9 6–3	Newcombe & Roche	R A J Hewitt (SA) & F D McMillan (SA)	3–6 6–3 14–12 6–2
				Okker & Riessen	R S Emerson (Aus) & R G Laver (Aus)	6–3 3–6 6–3 6–4
1970	J D Newcombe (Aus) & A D Roche (Aus)	K R Rosewall (Aus) & F S Stolle (Aus)	10–8 6–3 6–1	Newcombe & Roche	R A J Hewitt (SA) & F D McMillan (SA)	7–5 8–6 5–7 5–7 6–4
				Rosewall & Stolle	I Nastase (Rom) & I Tiriac (Rom)	6–4 3–6 10–8 0–6 6–3
1971	R S Emerson (Aus) & R G Laver (Aus)	A R Ashe (USA) & R D Ralston (USA)	4–6 9–7 6–8 6–4 6–4	Emerson & Laver	J G Alexander (Aus) & P C Dent (Aus)	6–4 3–6 6–3 6–4
				Ashe & Ralston	C E Graebner (USA) & T Koch (Bra)	8–9 6–3 8–6 6–4
1972	R A J Hewitt (SA) & F D McMillan (SA)	S R Smith (USA) & E van Dillen (USA)	6–2 6–2 9–7	Hewitt & McMillan	J R Cooper (Aus) & N A Fraser (Aus)	8–6 4–6 9–8 6–2
				Smith & van Dillen	P Cornejo (Chi) & J Fillol (Chi)	9–7 6–1 6–4
1973	J S Connors (USA) & I Nastase (Rom)	J R Cooper (Aus) & N A Fraser (Aus)	3–6 6–3 6–4 8–9 6–1	Connors & Nastase	J Fassbender (FRG) & K Meiler (FRG)	9–7 3–6 6–4 6–3
				Cooper & Fraser	D A Lloyd & J G Paish	3–6 6–3 6–2 6–4
1974	J D Newcombe (Aus) & A D Roche (Aus)	R C Lutz (USA) & S R Smith (USA)	8–6 6–4 6–4	Newcombe & Roche	J S Connors (USA) & I Nastase (Rom)	3–6 4–6 6–3 6–2 6–4
				Lutz & Smith	E C Drysdale (SA) & T S Okker (Hol)	3–6 6–1 7–5 9–7
1975	V Gerulaitis (USA) & A A Mayer (USA)	C Dowdeswell (Rho) & A J Stone (Aus)	7–5 8–6 6–4	Gerulaitis & Mayer	J Fassbender (FRG) & H J Pohmann (FRG)	8–9 3–6 6–3 6–3 6–3
				Dowdeswell & Stone	R D Crealy (Aus) & N Pilic (Yug)	9–8 3–6 4–6 9–8 6–3
1976	B E Gottfried (USA) & R Ramirez (Mex)	R L Case (Aus) & G Masters (Aus)	3–6 6–3 8–6 2–6 7–5	Gottfried & Ramirez	A Amritraj (Ind) & V Amritraj (Ind)	6–3 7–5 8–6
				Case & Masters	R C Lutz (USA) & S R Smith (USA)	6–4 6–3 6–4
1977	R L Case (Aus) & G Masters (Aus)	J G Alexander (Aus) & P C Dent (Aus)	6–3 6–4 3–6 8–9 6–4	Case & Masters	M Cox & E C Drysdale (SA)	6–1 6–4 6–1
				Alexander & Dent	R J Carmichael (Aus) & B Teacher (USA)	8–9 6–1 9–7 3–6 6–4
1978	R A J Hewitt (SA) & F D McMillan (SA)	P Fleming (USA) & J P McEnroe (USA)	6–1 6–4 6–2	Hewitt & McMillan	J G Alexander (Aus) & P C Dent (Aus)	9–7 7–5 6–4
				Fleming & McEnroe	W Fibak (Pol) & T S Okker (Hol)	1–6 6–3 9–7 6–4

	FINAL				SEMI-FINALS		
Year	Winners	Losers	Score		Winners	Losers	Score
1979	P Fleming (USA) & J P McEnroe (USA)	B E Gottfried (USA) & R Ramirez (Mex)	4–6 6–4 6–2 6–2		Fleming & McEnroe	R A J Hewitt (SA) & F D McMillan (SA)	6–3 7–6 6–1
					Gottfried & Ramirez	J Sadri (USA) & T Wilkison (USA)	6–4 2–6 7–5 3–6 6–3
1980	P McNamara (Aus) & P McNamee (Aus)	R C Lutz (USA) & S R Smith (USA)	7–6 6–3 6–7 6–4		McNamara & McNamee	P Fleming (USA) & J P McEnroe (USA)	6–3 6–2 6–3
					Lutz & Smith	A A Mayer (USA) & G Mayer (USA)	6–4 6–4 2–6 1–6 8–6
1981	P Fleming (USA) & J P McEnroe (USA)	R C Lutz (USA) & S R Smith (USA)	6–4 6–4 6–4		Fleming & McEnroe	T S Okker (Hol) & R L Stockton (USA)	6–3 6–2 6–4
					Lutz & Smith	P McNamara (Aus) & P McNamee (Aus)	6–4 2–6 4–6 7–6 6–4
1982	P McNamara (Aus) & P McNamee (Aus)	P Fleming (USA) & J P McEnroe (USA)	6–3 6–2 (best of 3 sets)		McNamara & McNamee	S E Stewart (USA) & F Taygan (USA)	4–6 6–4 6–7 7–6 6–4
					Fleming & McEnroe	K Curren (SA) & S Denton (USA)	6–2 6–4 2–6 6–3

The **longest match** was in 1966 when in the first round Nikki Pilic (Yug) and Gene Scott (USA) beat Cliff Richey (USA) and Torben Ulrich (Den) 19–21 12–10 6–4 4–6 9–7, a total of **98 games**.

The **second longest match** was in 1950 in the quarter-final; Budge Patty and Tony Trabert (both USA) beat Frank Sedgman and Ken McGregor (both Aus) 6–4 31–29 7–9 6–2, a total of **94 games**, and in 1968 (see longest set below).

The **longest final** was 1968 when John Newcombe and Tony Roche beat Ken Rosewall and Fred Stolle (all Aus) 3–6 8–6 5–7 14–12 6–3, a total of **70 games**.

The **second longest final** was 1959; Roy Emerson and Neale Fraser beat Rod Laver and Bob Mark (all Aus) 8–6 6–3 14–16 9–7, a total of **69 games**.

In the first final in the Oxford event, 1879 L R Erskine and H F Lawford played the best of seven sets against F Durrant and G E Tabor to win 4–6 6–4 6–5 6–2 3–6 5–6 10–8, a total of **77 games**.

The **longest All Comers' final** was in 1892 when H S Barlow and E W Lewis (both England) beat H S Mahony and J Pim (both Ire) 8–10 6–3 5–7 11–9 6–1, a total of **66 games**.

The **longest semi-final** was in 1960; Rafael Osuna (Mex) and Dennis Ralston (USA) beat Rod Laver and Bob Mark (both Aus) 4–6 10–8 15–13 4–6 11–9, a total of **86 games**.

The **longest set** was in 1968 in the second round when Pancho Segura (USA but born Ecuador) and Alex Olmedo (USA but born Peru) beat Gordon Forbes and Abe Segal (both SA) 32–30 5–7 6–4 6–4, a total of **62 games**, with match total equalling second longest above, a total of **94 games**.

The **longest set in a final** was the 16–14 in the 1959 final recorded as the second longest above, a total of **30 games**.

WOMEN'S DOUBLES

	FINAL				SEMI-FINALS		
Year	Winners	Losers	Score		Winners	Losers	Score
1899*	Mrs G W Hillyard & Miss B Steedman	Mrs N Durlacher & Mrs W H Pickering	6–4 2–6 6–4		Hillyard & Steedman	Miss E J Bromfield & Mrs Kirby	6–1 6–0
					Durlacher & Pickering	Miss L Austin & Miss C Cooper	2–6 6–3 6–3
1900*	Mrs W H Pickering & Miss M E Robb	Mrs G W Hillyard & Miss L Martin	2–6 6–4 6–4		Pickering & Robb	Mrs G Greville & Miss B Tulloch	6–2 6–3
					Hillyard & Martin	Miss E J Bromfield & Miss D K Douglass	4–6 6–4 7–5
1901*	Mrs G W Hillyard & Mrs A Sterry	Miss D C Adams & Mrs W H Pickering	6–3 6–0		Hillyard & Sterry	Miss T Lowther & Miss M E Robb	5–7 6–3 6–3
					Adams & Pickering	Mrs G E Evered & Miss E M Stawell-Brown	6–3 6–2

* Not holding status as a full championship event.

Year	FINAL Winners	Losers	Score	SEMI-FINALS Winners	Losers	Score
1902*	Miss A M Morton & Mrs A Sterry	Miss H Lane & Miss C M Wilson	w.o.	Morton & Sterry	Mrs G W Hillyard & Miss B Steedman	7–5 6–3
				Lane & Wilson	Mrs G Greville & Miss E W Thomson	4–6 7–5 10–8
1903*	Miss D K Douglass & Mrs W H Pickering	Miss H Lane & Miss C M Wilson	6–2 6–1	Douglass & Pickering	Miss A N G Greene & Miss E R Morgan	6–1 1–6 6–3
				Lane & Wilson	Miss E J Bromfield & Miss A M Morton	6–1 6–8 6–3
1904*	Miss W A Longhurst & Miss E W Thomson	Miss D K Douglass & Mrs A Sterry	6–4 3–6 7–5	Longhurst & Thomson	Miss A Farrington & Miss M B Squire	6–0 6–2
				Douglass & Sterry	Mrs G Greville & Mrs R J Winch	6–2 6–4
1905*	Miss W A Longhurst & Miss E W Thomson	Miss A M Morton & Miss M G Sutton	6–3 6–3	Longhurst & Thomson	Miss H Lane & Miss C M Wilson	6–3 9–7
				Morton & Sutton	Miss D P Boothby & Miss E M Stawell-Brown	6–4 6–1
1906*	Mrs G W Hillyard & Miss M G Sutton (USA)	Miss A M Morton & Mrs A Sterry	10–8 6–4	Hillyard & Sutton	Miss W A Longhurst & Miss E W Thomson	3–6 6–2 6–4
				Morton & Sterry	Miss M E Brown & Miss V M Pinckney	6–4 6–3
1907*	Mrs R Lambert Chambers & Miss C L Wilson	Miss A M Morton & Mrs A Sterry	7–9 6–3 6–2	Lambert Chambers & Wilson	Miss M Coles & Miss W M Slocock	w.o.
				Morton & Sterry	Miss D P Boothby & Miss C H E Meyer	6–4 3–6 6–4
1908–1912 not held						
1913	Mrs R J McNair & Miss D P Boothby	Mrs R Lambert Chambers & Mrs A Sterry	4–6 2–4 ret'd	McNair & Boothby	Mrs D R Larcombe & Mrs E G Parton	6–3 6–4
				Lambert Chambers & Sterry	Mrs Armstrong & Miss O B Manser	6–3 2–6 6–3
1914	Miss A M Morton & Miss E Ryan (USA)	Mrs G Hannam & Mrs D R Larcombe	6–1 6–3	Morton & Ryan	Mrs R Lambert Chambers & Mrs A Sterry	6–4 6–1
				Hannam & Larcombe	Miss V M Pinckney & Mlle M Broquedis (Fra)	6–2 6–0
1915–1918 not held						
1919	Mlle S Lenglen (Fra) & Miss E Ryan (USA)	Mrs R Lambert Chambers & Mrs D R Larcombe	4–6 7–5 6–3	Lenglen & Ryan	Mrs R J McNair & Mrs E G Parton	6–2 6–1
				Lambert Chambers & Larcombe	Mrs A Hall & Miss E D Holman	6–1 6–2
1920	Mlle S Lenglen (Fra) & Miss E Ryan (USA)	Mrs R Lambert Chambers & Mrs D R Larcombe	6–4 6–0	Lenglen & Ryan	Mrs Armstrong & Miss O B Manser	6–1 6–0
				Lambert Chambers & Larcombe	Mrs A E Beamish & Miss H Hogarth	6–1 6–1
1921	Mlle S Lenglen (Fra) & Miss E Ryan (USA)	Mrs A E Beamish & Mrs G Peacock (Ind)	6–1 6–2	Lenglen & Ryan	Miss P L Howkins & Miss D C Shepherd	6–2 6–0
				Beamish & Peacock	Mrs Craddock & Miss M McKane	6–2 6–1
1922	Mlle S Lenglen (Fra) & Miss E Ryan (USA)	Miss K McKane & Mrs A D Stocks	6–0 6–4	Lenglen & Ryan	Mrs A C Geen & Mrs R J McNair	6–0 6–1
				McKane & Stocks	Miss E D Holman & Mrs J L Leisk	w.o.
1923	Mlle S Lenglen (Fra) & Miss E Ryan (USA)	Miss J Austin & Miss E L Colyer	6–3 6–1	Lenglen & Ryan	Mrs R Lambert Chambers & Miss K McKane	6–1 6–2
				Austin & Colyer	Miss E F Rose & Mrs J S Youle	8–6 6–4
1924	Mrs G Wightman (USA) & Miss H N Wills (USA)	Mrs B C Covell & Miss K McKane	6–4 6–4	Wightman & Wills	Miss E Goss (USA) & Mrs M Z Jessup (USA)	8–6 6–4
				Covell & McKane	Mrs R Lambert Chambers & Mrs D C Shepherd-Barron	6–4 3–6 6–4
1925	Mlle S Lenglen (Fra) & Miss E Ryan (USA)	Mrs A V Bridge & Mrs C G McIlquham	6–2 6–2	Lenglen & Ryan	Mrs A E Beamish & Miss E R Clarke	6–0 6–2
				Bridge & McIlquham	Mrs R Lambert Chambers & Miss E H Harvey	6–1 2–6 6–4

* Not holding status as a full championship event.

Year	FINAL Winners	Losers	Score	SEMI-FINALS Winners	Losers	Score
1926	Miss M K Browne (USA) & Miss E Ryan (USA)	Mrs L A Godfree & Miss E L Colyer	6–1 6–1	Browne & Ryan	Mrs A E Beamish & Miss E R Clarke	6–2 6–3
				Godfree & Colyer	Mrs Jackson Fielden & Miss N Welch	6–2 6–3
1927	Miss H N Wills (USA) & Miss E Ryan (USA)	Miss E L Heine (SA) & Mrs G Peacock (Ind)	6–3 6–2	Wills & Ryan	Mrs L A Godfree & Miss B Nuthall	6–2 6–2
				Heine & Peacock	Miss E H Harvey & Mrs C G McIlquham	5–7 6–2 6–1
1928	Miss P Saunders & Mrs M Watson	Miss E Bennett & Miss E H Harvey	6–2 6–3	Saunders & Watson	Mrs R Lycett & Miss E Ryan (USA)	6–3 6–1
				Bennett & Harvey	Miss D Akhurst (Aus) & Miss E Boyd (Aus)	6–8 6–3 6–2
1929	Mrs L R C Mitchell & Mrs M Watson	Mrs B C Covell & Mrs D C Shepherd-Barron	6–4 8–6	Michell & Watson	Miss E H Harvey & Mrs C G McIlquham	6–4 5–7 6–2
				Covell & Shepherd-Barron	Miss B Nuthall & Miss E Ryan (USA)	6–4 3–6 9–7
1930	Mrs F S Moody (USA) & Miss E Ryan (USA)	Miss E Cross (USA) & Miss S Palfrey (USA)	6–2 9–7	Moody & Ryan	Mme S Henrotin (Fra) & Mlle J Sigart (Bel)	6–2 6–0
				Cross & Palfrey	Miss B Feltham & Miss M Heeley	8–6 6–2
1931	Mrs D C Shepherd-Barron & Miss P E Mudford	Mlle D Metaxa (Fra) & Mlle J Sigart (Bel)	3–6 6–3 6–4	Shepherd-Barron & Mudford	Mrs L A Godfree & Miss D E Round	7–5 3–6 6–3
				Metaxa & Sigart	Mrs F Whittingstall & Miss B Nuthall	4–6 8–6 6–4
1932	Mlle D Metaxa (Fra) & Mlle J Sigart (Bel)	Miss H H Jacobs (USA) & Miss E Ryan (USA)	6–4 6–3	Metaxa & Sigart	Mrs P Holcroft-Watson & Miss E H Harvey	7–5 6–2
				Jacobs & Ryan	Mlle L Payot (Swi) & Miss M A Thomas (USA)	6–1 6–2
1933	Mme R Mathieu (Fra) & Miss E Ryan (USA)	Miss F James & Miss A M Yorke	6–2 9–11 6–4	Mathieu & Ryan	Mrs J P Pittman & Miss J C Ridley	6–1 4–6 6–4
				James & Yorke	Mrs L A Godfree & Mrs L R C Michell	5–7 6–0 6–4
1934	Mme R Mathieu (Fra) & Miss E Ryan (USA)	Mrs D B Andrus (USA) & Mme S Henrotin (Fra)	6–3 6–3	Mathieu & Ryan	Mlle L Payot (Swi) & Miss M A Thomas (USA)	7–5 6–0
				Andrus & Henrotin	Mrs L A Godfree & Miss M C Scriven	6–3 12–10
1935	Miss F James & Miss K E Stammers	Mme R Mathieu (Fra) & Fru S Sperling (Ger)	6–1 6–4	James & Stammers	Mrs R E Haylock & Mrs J S Kirk	6–3 6–0
				Mathieu & Sperling	Mme J de Meulemeester (Bel) & Mrs P D Howard (Fra)	6–4 8–6
1936	Miss F James & Miss K E Stammers	Mrs M Fabyan (USA) & Miss H H Jacobs (USA)	6–2 6–1	James & Stammers	Mrs D B Andrus (USA) & Mme S Henrotin (Fra)	6–0 6–4
				Fabyan & Jacobs	Miss J Ingram & Mrs M R King	6–4 6–3
1937	Mme R Mathieu (Fra) & Miss A M Yorke	Mrs M R King & Mrs J B Pittman	6–3 6–3	Mathieu & Yorke	Miss E M Dearman & Miss J Ingram	7–5 6–3
				King & Pittman	Mrs D B Andrus (USA) & Mme S Henrotin (Fra)	6–3 6–4
1938	Mrs M Fabyan (USA) & Miss A Marble (USA)	Mme R Mathieu (Fra) & Miss A M Yorke	6–2 6–3	Fabyan & Marble	Mrs E L Heine-Miller (SA) & Miss M Morphew (SA)	7–5 6–4
				Mathieu & Yorke	Mrs D B Andrus (USA) & Mme S Henrotin (Fra)	3–6 6–3 6–4
1939	Mrs M Fabyan (USA) & Miss A Marble (USA)	Miss H H Jacobs (USA) & Miss A M Yorke	6–1 6–0	Fabyan & Marble	Mrs S H Hammersley & Miss K E Stammers	8–6 6–3
				Jacobs & Yorke	Miss J Nicoll & Miss B Nuthall	5–7 6–4 11–9
	1940–1945 not held					
1946	Miss A L Brough (USA) & Miss M E Osborne (USA)	Miss P M Betz (USA) & Miss D J Hart (USA)	6–3 2–6 6–3	Brough & Osborne	Mrs P C Todd (USA) & Miss D Bundy (USA)	6–4 6–2
				Betz & Hart	Mrs E W A Bostock & Mrs M Menzies	3–6 6–3 6–4
1947	Miss D J Hart (USA) & Mrs P C Todd (USA)	Miss A L Brough (USA) & Miss M E Osborne (USA)	3–6 6–4 7–5	Hart & Todd	Mrs E W A Bostock & Mrs B E Hilton	6–0 6–1
				Brough & Osborne	Mrs N W Blair & Mrs M Menzies	6–2 6–1

Year	FINAL Winners	Losers	Score	SEMI-FINALS Winners	Losers	Score
1948	Miss A L Brough (USA) & Mrs W du Pont (USA)	Miss D J Hart (USA) & Mrs P C Todd (USA)	6–3 3–6 6–3	Brough & du Pont	Mrs H P Rihbany (USA) & Miss B Scofield (USA)	7–5 6–0
				Hart & Todd	Mrs N W Blair & Mrs E W A Bostock	6–4 8–6
1949	Miss A L Brough (USA) & Mrs W du Pont (USA)	Miss G Moran (USA) & Mrs P C Todd (USA)	8–6 7–5	Brough & du Pont	Miss J Gannon & Mrs B E Hilton	6–2 6–2
				Moran & Todd	Miss S J Fry (USA) & Mrs H P Rihbany (USA)	6–0 7–5
1950	Miss A L Brough (USA) & Mrs W du Pont (USA)	Miss S J Fry (USA) & Miss D J Hart (USA)	6–4 5–7 6–1	Brough & du Pont	Mrs M Buck (USA) & Miss N Chaffee (USA)	6–1 6–3
				Fry & Hart	Mrs T D Long (Aus) & Mrs A J Mottram	6–0 6–2
1951	Miss S J Fry (USA) & Miss D J Hart (USA)	Miss A L Brough (USA) & Mrs W du Pont (USA)	6–3 13–11	Fry & Hart	Miss B Baker (USA) & Miss N Chaffee (USA)	6–0 6–2
				Brough & du Pont	Mrs G Davidson (USA) & Miss B Rosenquest (USA)	6–1 6–3
1952	Miss S J Fry (USA) & Miss D J Hart (USA)	Miss A L Brough (USA) & Miss M C Connolly (USA)	8–6 6–3	Fry & Hart	Miss J S V Partridge & Mrs I Rinkel-Quertier	7–5 6–3
				Brough & Connolly	Mrs T D Long (Aus) & Mrs P C Todd (USA)	5–7 6–1 6–4
1953	Miss S J Fry (USA) & Miss D J Hart (USA)	Miss M C Connolly (USA) & Miss J Sampson (USA)	6–0 6–0	Fry & Hart	Miss H Fletcher & Mrs I Rinkel-Quertier	6–0 6–0
				Connolly & Sampson	Miss A Mortimer & Miss J A Shilcock	6–2 6–3
1954	Miss A L Brough (USA) & Mrs W du Pont (USA)	Miss S J Fry (USA) & Miss D J Hart (USA)	4–6 9–7 6–3	Brough & du Pont	Mrs W Brewer (Ber) & Miss K Hubble (USA)	6–1 6–1
				Fry & Hart	Miss A Mortimer & Miss J A Shilcock	6–2 6–1
1955	Miss A Mortimer & Miss J A Shilcock	Miss S J Bloomer & Miss P E Ward	7–5 6–1	Mortimer & Shilcock	Miss F Muller (Aus) & Mrs L A Hoad (Aus)	6–2 6–1
				Bloomer & Ward	Mrs J Fleitz (USA) & Miss D R Hard (USA)	6–3 9–7
1956	Miss A Buxton & Miss A Gibson (USA)	Miss F Muller (Aus) & Miss D G Seeney (Aus)	6–1 8–6	Buxton & Gibson	Miss A L Brough (USA) & Miss S J Fry (USA)	7–5 6–4
				Fuller & Seeney	Miss A Mortimer & Miss J A Shilcock	6–4 6–2
1957	Miss A Gibson (USA) & Miss D R Hard (USA)	Mrs K Hawton (Aus) & Mrs T D Long (Aus)	6–1 6–2	Gibson & Hard	Miss S Reynolds (SA) & Miss R Schuurman (SA)	6–2 6–2
				Hawton & Long	Miss Y Ramirez (Mex) & Miss R M Reyes (Mex)	7–5 6–2
1958	Miss M E Bueno (Bra) & Miss A Gibson (USA)	Mrs W du Pont (USA) & Miss M Varner (USA)	6–3 7–5	Bueno & Gibson	Mrs K Hawton (Aus) & Mrs T D Long (Aus)	6–3 6–2
				du Pont & Varner	Miss Y Ramirez (Mex) & Miss R M Reyes (Mex)	6–2 6–3
1959	Miss J Arth (USA) & Miss D R Hard (USA)	Mrs J Fleitz (USA) & Miss C C Truman	2–6 6–2	Arth & Hard	Miss S Reynolds (SA) & Miss R Schuurman (SA)	6–0 6–2
				Fleitz & Truman	Miss Y Ramirez (Mex) & Miss R M Reyes (Mex)	8–6 6–1
1960	Miss M E Bueno (Bra) & Miss D R Hard (USA)	Miss S Reynolds (SA) & Miss R Schuurman (SA)	6–4 6–0	Bueno & Hard	Miss K Hantze (USA) & Miss J S Hopps (USA)	3–6 6–1 6–4
				Reynolds & Schuurman	Mrs K Hawton (Aus) & Miss J Lehane (Aus)	7–5 6–1
1961	Miss K Hantze (USA) & Miss B J Moffitt (USA)	Miss J Lehane (Aus) & Miss M Smith (Aus)	6–3 6–4	Hantze & Moffitt	Miss S M Moore (USA) & Miss L R Turner (Aus)	6–3 6–0
				Lehane & Smith	Miss M L Hunt (SA) & Miss L M Hutchings (SA)	6–1 6–1
1962	Miss B J Moffitt (USA) & Mrs J R Susman (USA)	Mrs L E G Price (SA) & Miss R Schuurman (SA)	5–7 6–3 7–5	Moffitt & Susman	Miss J Bricka (USA) & Miss M Smith (Aus)	6–3 6–4
				Price & Schuurman	Miss M E Bueno (Bra) & Miss D R Hard (USA)	6–3 6–3
1963	Miss M E Bueno (Bra) & Miss D R Hard (USA)	Miss R A Ebbern (Aus) & Miss M Smith (Aus)	8–6 9–7	Bueno & Hard	Miss A Dmitrieva (USSR) & Miss J A M Tegart (Aus)	6–4 9–7
				Ebbern & Smith	Mrs P F Jones & Miss R Schuurman (SA)	7–5 3–6 6–3

Year	FINAL Winners	Losers	Score	SEMI-FINALS Winners	Losers	Score
1964	Miss M Smith (Aus) & Miss L R Turner (Aus)	Miss B J Moffitt (USA) & Mrs Susman (USA)	7–5 6–2	Smith & Turner	Mrs P Haygarth (SA) & Mrs P F Jones	6–3 6–2
				Moffitt & Susman	Miss M E Bueno (Bra) & Miss R A Ebbern (Aus)	4–6 6–2 6–3
1965	Miss M E Bueno (Bra) & Miss B J Moffitt (USA)	Mlle F Durr (Fra) & Mlle J Lieffrig (Fra)	6–2 7–5	Bueno & Moffitt	Mrs C E Graebner (USA) & Miss N Richey (USA)	6–4 6–2
				Durr & Lieffrig	Frl E Buding (FDR) & Frl H Schultze (FDR)	6–4 7–5
1966	Miss M E Bueno (Bra) & Miss N Richey (USA)	Miss M Smith (Aus) & Miss J A M Tegart (Aus)	6–3 4–6 6–4	Bueno & Richey	Miss K M Krantzcke (Aus) & Miss K A Melville (Aus)	6–2 6–3
				Smith & Tegart	Mrs P F Jones & Miss S V Wade	10–8 6–4
1967	Miss R Casals (USA) & Mrs L W King (USA)	Miss M E Bueno (Bra) & Miss N Richey (USA)	9–11 6–4 6–2	Casals & King	Mrs P F Jones & Miss S V Wade	6–1 6–4
				Bueno & Richey	Miss J A M Tegart (Aus) & Miss L R Turner (Aus)	4–6 6–4 6–4
1968	Miss R Casals (USA) & Mrs L W King (USA)	Mlle F Durr (Fra) & Mrs P F Jones	3–6 6–4 7–5	Casals & King	Mrs W W Bowrey (Aus) & Miss J A M Tegart (Aus)	1–6 6–1 10–8
				Durr & Jones	Mrs J A G Lloyd & Miss F V MacLennan	6–1 6–0
1969	Mrs B M Court (Aus) & Miss J A M Tegart (Aus)	Miss P S A Hogan (USA) & Miss M Michel (USA)	9–7 6–2	Court & Tegart	Mrs P W Curtis & Miss V J Ziegenfuss (USA)	6–4 6–4
				Hogan & Michel	Miss K M Krantzcke (Aus) & Miss K A Melville (Aus)	4–6 6–2 7–5
1970	Mrs R Casals (USA) & Mrs L W King (USA)	Mlle F Durr (Fra) & Miss S V Wade	6–2 6–3	Casals & King	Miss K M Krantzcke (Aus) & Miss K A Melville (Aus)	6–2 8–6
				Durr & Wade	Miss H F Gourlay (Aus) & Miss P M Walkden (SA)	6–4 0–6 6–3
1971	Miss R Casals (USA) & Mrs L W King (USA)	Mrs B M Court (Aus) & Miss E F Goolagong (Aus)	6–3 6–2	Casals & King	Mme J B Chanfreau (Fra) & Mlle F Durr (Fra)	4–6 6–4 6–4
				Court & Goolagong	Mrs P W Curtis & Miss V J Ziegenfuss (USA)	6–2 6–4
1972	Mrs L W King (USA) & Miss B F Stove (Hol)	Mrs D E Dalton (Aus) & Mlle F Durr (Fra)	6–2 4–6 6–3	King & Stove	Miss W M Shaw & Mrs G M Williams	7–5 3–6 6–3
				Dalton & Durr	Miss R Casals (USA) & Miss S V Wade	6–4 6–1
1973	Miss R Casals (USA) & Mrs L W King (USA)	Mlle F Durr (Fra) & Miss B F Stove (Hol)	6–1 4–6 7–5	Casals & King	Miss E F Goolagong (Aus) & Miss J A Young (Aus)	7–5 7–5
				Durr & Stove	Miss F Bonicelli (Uru) & Miss L Fernandez (Col)	7–5 8–6
1974	Miss E F Goolagong (Aus) & Miss M Michel (USA)	Miss H F Gourlay (Aus) & Miss K M Krantzcke (Aus)	2–6 6–4 6–3	Goolagong & Michel	Miss C M Evert (USA) & Mrs O Morozova (USSR)	7–5 6–2
				Gourlay & Krantzcke	Miss J Anthony (USA) & Miss M Schallau (USA)	9–8 6–2
1975	Miss A K Kiyomura (USA) & Miss K Sawamatsu (Jap)	Mlle F Durr (Fra) & Miss B F Stove (Hol)	7–5 1–6 7–5	Kiyomura & Sawamatsu	Mme J B Chanfreau (Fra) & Miss H F Gourlay (Aus)	8–6 6–8 6–2
				Durr & Stove	Miss R Casals (USA) & Mrs L W King (USA)	2–6 8–6 6–2
1976	Miss C M Evert (USA) & Miss M Navratilova (Cze)	Mrs L W King (USA) & Miss B F Stove (Hol)	6–1 3–6 7–5	Evert & Navratilova	Miss D A Boshoff (SA) & Miss I S Kloss (SA)	8–6 8–6
				King & Stove	Miss L J Charles & Miss S Mappin	6–4 6–3
1977	Mrs R L Cawley (Aus) & Miss J C Russell (USA)	Miss M Navratilova (Cze) & Miss B F Stove (Hol)	6–3 6–3	Cawley & Russell	Miss L J Charles & Miss S Mappin	6–3 6–4
				Navratilova & Stove	Mlle F Durr (Fra) & Miss S V Wade	6–8 6–2 6–2
1978	Mrs G E Reid (Aus) & Miss W M Turnbull (Aus)	Miss M Jausovec (Yug) & Miss V Ruzici (Rom)	4–6 9–8 6–3	Reid & Turnbull	Miss S Barker & Mrs T E Guerrant (USA)	6–3 6–2
				Jausovec & Ruzici	Mlle F Durr (Fra) & Miss S V Wade	6–4 6–4
1979	Mrs L W King (USA) & Miss M Navratilova (Cze)	Miss B F Stove (Hol) & Miss W M Turnbull (Aus)	5–7 6–3 6–2	King & Navratilova	Mlle F Durr (Fra) & Miss S V Wade	6–2 6–4
				Stove & Turnbull	Miss M Jausovec (Yug) & Miss V Ruzici (Rom)	6–1 7–5

	FINAL			SEMI-FINALS		
Year	Winners	Losers	Score	Winners	Losers	Score
1980	Miss K Jordan (USA) & Miss A E Smith (USA)	Miss R Casals (USA) & Miss W M Turnbull (Aus)	4–6 7–5 6–1	Jordan & Smith	Mrs L W King (USA) & Miss M Navratilova (Cze)	6–2 4–6 6–4
				Casals & Turnbull	Miss C S Reynolds (USA) & Miss P G Smith (USA)	6–7 7–6 6–0
1981	Miss M Navratilova (Cze) & Miss P H Shriver (USA)	Miss K Jordan (USA) & Miss A E Smith (USA)	6–3 7–6	Navratilova & Shriver	Miss S Barker & Miss A K Kiyomura (USA)	6–3 6–7 6–2
				Jordan & Smith	Miss R D Fairbank (SA) & Miss T J Harford (SA)	6–1 6–2
1982	Miss M Navratilova (USA) & Miss P H Shriver (USA)	Miss K Jordan (USA) & Miss A E Smith (USA)	6–4 6–1	Navratilova & Shriver	Miss B Bunge (FRG) & Miss C Kohde (FRG)	6–3 6–4
				Jordan & Smith	Miss R Casals (USA) & Miss W M Turnbull (Aus)	6–2 2–6 6–4

The **longest match** was in 1933 when in the first round Pat Brazier and Christabel Wheatcroft beat Mildred Nonwiler and Betty Soames (all GB) 11–9 5–7 9–7, a total of **48 games**.

The **second longest** match was in the first round in 1921 when Miss Houghton and Mrs Jackson beat Mrs Middleton and Miss Dransfield (all GB) 6–3 2–6 16–14, a total of **47 games**.

The **longest final** was played in 1933 when Simone Mathieu (Fra) and Elizabeth Ryan (USA) beat Freda James and Billie Yorke (both GB) 6–2 9–11 6–4 and in 1967 when Rosemary Casals and Billie Jean King (both USA) beat Maria Bueno (Bra) and Nancy Richey (USA) 9–11 6–4 6–2, a total of **38 games**.

The **second longest final** was 1978; Kerry Reid and Wendy Turnbull (both Aus) beat Mima Jausovec (Yug) and Virginia Ruzici (Rom) 4–6 9–8 6–3, a total of **36 games**.

The **longest semi-final** was in 1939 when Helen Jacobs (USA) and Billie Yorke (GB) beat Jean Nicoll and Betty Nuthall (both GB) 5–7 6–4 11–9, a total of **42 games**.

The **longest set** was the 16–14 in the second longest match above, a total of **30 games**.

The **longest set in a final** was in 1951 when Shirley Fry and Doris Hart beat Louise Brough and Margaret du Pont (all USA) 6–3 13–11, a total of **24 games**.

MIXED DOUBLES

	FINAL			SEMI-FINALS		
Year	Winners	Losers	Score	Winners	Losers	Score
1900*	H A Nisbet & Mrs W H Pickering	H Roper Barrett & Miss E J Bromfield	8–6 6–3	Nisbet & Mrs Pickering	C H L Cazalet & Miss M E Robbs	7–5 6–8 6–3
				Roper Barrett & Miss Bromfield	E D Black & Miss C Cooper	6–3 6–2
1901*	H L Doherty & Mrs A Sterry	W C Eaves & Mrs N Durlacher	6–2 6–3	H L Doherty & Mrs Sterry	G W Hillyard & Mrs Hillyard	3–6 7–5 6–1
				Eaves & Mrs Durlacher	G Greville & Mrs Greville	w.o.
1902*	H L Doherty & Mrs A Sterry	C H L Cazalet & Miss M E Robbs	6–4 6–3	H L Doherty & Mrs Sterry	R F Doherty & Miss B Steedman	0–1 (sets) ret'd
				Cazalet & Miss Robb	C H Martin & Miss D K Douglass	6–2 6–1
1903*	S H Smith & Miss E W Thomson	C Hobart (USA) & Miss E J Bromfield	6–2 6–3	Smith & Miss Thomson	E D Robinson & Miss M Stonham	6–2 6–3
				Hobart & Miss Bromfield	F L Riseley & Miss D K Douglass	w.o.
1904*	S H Smith & Miss E W Thomson	W V Eaves & Mrs R J Winch	7–5 12–10	Smith & Miss Thomson	H N Marrett & Miss H Lane	6–2 6–2
				Eaves & Mrs Winch	G Greville & Mrs Greville	6–4 2–6 6–4
1905*	A W Gore & Miss C M Wilson	A F Wilding (NZ) & Miss E W Thomson	8–6 6–4	Gore & Miss Wilson	R F Doherty & Miss G S Eastlake Smith	6–3 4–6 6–3
				Wilding & Miss Thomson	S H Adams & Miss D P Boothby	6–0 6–0

* Not holding status as a full championship event.

Jimmy Connors first won the Wimbledon singles in 1974. His second success in 1982 came as a joyful bonus.

Martina Navratilova (right) with her coach and mentor Renee Richards.

Martina Navratilova, outstanding advocate of the serve and volley tactics.

Chris Lloyd, never less than a semi-finalist and often a champion.

Year	FINAL Winners	Losers	Score	SEMI-FINALS Winners	Losers	Score
1906*	A F Wilding (NZ) & Miss D K Douglass	A W Gore & Miss E W Thomson	4–6 6–2 6–3	Wilding & Miss Douglass Gore & Miss Thomson	R F Doherty & Miss G S Eastlake Smith G W Hillyard & Miss M G Sutton	4–6 6–2 7–5 6–3 3–6 8–6
1907*	B C Wright (USA) & Miss M G Sutton (USA)	A D Prebble & Miss D P Boothby	6–1 6–3	Wright & Miss Sutton Prebble & Miss Boothby	N Durlacher & Miss A M Morton W V Eaves & Miss T Lowther	w.o. 6–3 7–5
1908*	A F Wilding (NZ) & Mrs R Lambert Chambers	H Roper Barrett & Mrs A Sterry	6–4 6–3	Wilding & Mrs Lambert Chambers Roper Barrett & Mrs Sterry	A D Prebble & Miss D P Boothby A W Gore & Mrs J F Luard	6–1 6–0 5–7 6–4 6–3
1909*	H Roper Barrett & Miss A M Morton	A D Prebble & Miss D P Boothby	6–2 7–5	Roper Barrett & Miss Morton Prebble & Miss Boothby	C P Dixon & Miss A N G Greene J B Ward & Miss M Coles	11–9 6–3 6–1 7–5
1910*	S N Doust (Aus) & Mrs R Lambert Chambers	R B Powell (Can) & Mrs A Sterry	6–2 7–5	Doust & Mrs Lambert Chambers Powell & Mrs Sterry	E Gwynne Evans & Miss A G Ransome H Roper Barrett & Mrs E S Lamplough	6–1 6–2 6–1 6–4
1911*	T M Mavrogordato & Mrs E G Parton	S N Doust (Aus) & Mrs R Lambert Chambers	6–2 6–4	Mavrogordato & Mrs Parton Doust & Mrs Lambert Chambers	R B Powell (Can) & Mrs A Sterry J B Ward & Miss M Coles	7–5 6–1 6–1 6–2
1912*	J C Parke & Mrs D R Larcombe	A D Prebble & Miss D P Boothby	6–4 6–2	Parke & Mrs Larcombe Prebble & Miss Boothby	T M Mavrogordato & Mrs E G Parton S N Doust (Aus) & Mrs G W Hillyard	8–6 6–2 7–5 6–2
1913	Hope Crisp & Mrs C O Tuckey	J C Parke & Mrs D R Larcombe	3–6 5–3 ret'd	Crisp & Mrs Tuckey Parke & Mrs Larcombe	N S B Kidson & Mrs O'Neill T M Mavrogordato & Mrs E G Parton	6–2 6–3 6–3 6–4
1914	J C Parke & Mrs D R Larcombe	A F Wilding (NZ) & Mlle M Broquedis (Fra)	4–6 6–4 6–2	Parke & Mrs Larcombe Wilding & Mlle Broquedis	Hope Crisp & Mrs C O Tuckey H Aitken & Mrs G Hannam	4–6 6–2 6–2 6–3 4–6 6–3
1915–1918 not held						
1919	R Lycett & Miss E Ryan (USA)	A D Prebble & Mrs R Lambert Chambers	6–0 6–0	Lycett & Miss Ryan Prebble & Mrs Lambert Chambers	R V Thomas (Aus) & Mrs D R Larcombe M Decugis & Miss L Addison	6–2 6–3 6–1 6–0
1920	G L Patterson (Aus) & Mlle S Lenglen (Fra)	R Lycett & Miss E Ryan (USA)	7–5 6–3	Patterson & Mlle Lenglen Lycett & Miss Ryan	A E Beamish & Mrs Beamish B I C Norton (SA) & Mrs D R Larcombe	6–1 6–4 6–3 6–4
1921	R Lycett & Miss E Ryan (USA)	M Woosnam & Miss P L Howkins	6–3 6–1	Lycett & Miss Ryan Woosnam & Miss Howkins	A E Beamish & Mrs D R Larcombe M Alonso (Spa) & Mrs R J McNair	6–4 6–1 6–1 6–4
1922	P O'Hara Wood (Aus) & Mlle S Lenglen (Fra)	R Lycett & Miss E Ryan (USA)	6–4 6–3	O'Hara Wood & Mlle Lenglen Lycett & Miss Ryan	C J Tindell Green & Mrs J S Youle J B Gilbert & Mrs R J McNair	6–2 6–2 6–2 6–1
1923	R Lycett & Miss E Ryan (USA)	L S Deane (Ind) & Mrs D C Shepherd-Barron	6–4 7–5	Lycett & Miss Ryan Deane & Mrs Shepherd-Barron	J Washer (Bel) & Mlle S Lenglen (Fra) V Richards (USA) & Mrs F I Mallory (USA)	7–5 6–3 5–7 6–3 6–4

* not holding status as a full championship event.

Year	FINAL Winners	Losers	Score	SEMI-FINALS Winners	Losers	Score
1924	J B Gilbert & Miss K McKane	L A Godfree & Mrs D C Shepherd-Barron	6–3 3–6 6–3	Gilbert & Miss McKane	E T Lamb & Miss E H Harvey	6–2 6–4
				Godfree & Mrs Shepherd-Barron	M Woosnam & Mrs B C Covell	6–4 4–6 6–4
1925	J Borotra (Fra) & Mlle S Lenglen (Fra)	H L de Morpurgo (Ita) & Miss E Ryan (USA)	6–3 6–3	Borotra & Mlle Lenglen	R Lycett & Mrs Lycett	6–4 5–7 6–3
				Morpurgo & Miss Ryan	J D P Wheatley & Mrs R Lambert Chambers	9–7 6–4
1926	L A Godfree & Mrs Godfree	H Kinsey (USA) & Miss M K Browne (USA)	6–3 6–4	Godfree & Mrs Godfree	V Richards (USA) & Mrs E Ryan (USA)	7–5 6–4
				Kinsey & Miss Browne	A Berger & Mrs F M Strawson	5–7 6–4 6–0
1927	F T Hunter (USA) & Miss E Ryan (USA)	L A Godfree & Mrs Godfree	8–6 6–0	Hunter & Miss Ryan	L Raymond (SA) & Miss E L Heine (SA)	6–3 6–4
				Godfree & Mrs Godfree	D M Greig & Mrs M Watson	6–3 6–4
1928	P D B Spence (SA) & Miss E Ryan (USA)	J H Crawford (Aus) & Miss D Akhurst (Aus)	7–5 6–4	Spence & Miss Ryan	F T Hunter (USA) & Miss H N Wills (USA)	4–6 6–4 6–3
				Crawford & Miss Akhurst	E F Moon (Aus) & Mrs P O'Hara Wood (Aus)	6–3 7–5
1929	F T Hunter (USA) & Miss H N Wills (USA)	I G Collins & Miss J Fry	6–1 6–4	Hunter & Miss Wills	N G Farquharson (SA) & Miss E L Heine (SA)	6–8 6–2 6–3
				Collins & Miss Fry	J C Gregory & Miss E Ryan (USA)	6–2 6–3
1930	J H Crawford (Aus) & Miss E Ryan (USA)	D Prenn (Ger) & Frl H Krahwinkel (Ger)	6–1 6–3	Crawford & Miss Ryan	H Cochet (Fra) & Mrs F Whittingstall	6–3 7–9 6–4
				Prenn & Frl Krahwinkel	G R O Crole-Rees & Miss P E Mudford	4–6 6–3 6–3
1931	G M Lott (USA) & Mrs L A Harper (USA)	I G Collins & Miss J C Ridley	6–3 1–6 6–1	Lott & Mrs Harper	F J Perry & Miss M Heeley	1–6 3–4 ret'd
				Collins & Miss Ridley	P D B Spence (SA) & Miss B Nuthall	4–6 6–4 6–4
1932	E Maier (Spa) & Miss E Ryan (USA)	H C Hopman (Aus) & Mlle J Sigart (Bel)	7–5 6–2	Maier & Miss Ryan	H Cochet (Fra) & Mrs F Whittingstall	7–5 3–6 6–1
				Hopman & Mlle Sigart	J Brugnon (Fra) & Mme R Mathieu (Fra)	6–4 6–4
1933	G von Cramm (Ger) & Frl H Krahwinkel (Ger)	N G Farquharson (SA) & Miss M Heeley	7–5 8–6	Von Cramm & Frl Krahwinkel	C H Kingsley & Mrs L A Godfree	6–3 8–6
				Farquharson & Miss Heeley	J Borotra (Fra) & Miss B Nuthall	8–6 11–9
1934	R Miki (Jap) & Miss D E Round	H W Austin & Mrs D C Shepherd-Barron	3–6 6–4 6–0	Miki & Miss Round	H G N Lee & Miss F James	6–3 6–2
				Austin & Mrs Shepherd-Barron	J S Olliff & Miss J Ingram	6–4 6–1
1935	F J Perry & Miss D E Round	H C Hopman (Aus) & Mrs Hopman (Aus)	7–5 4–6 6–2	Perry & Miss Round	A K Quist (Aus) & Miss J Jedrzejowska (Pol)	6–1 6–3
				Hopman & Mrs Hopman	G von Cramm (Ger) & Fru S Sperling (Ger)	6–4 6–4
1936	F J Perry & Miss D E Round	J D Budge (USA) & Mrs M Fabyan (USA)	7–9 7–5 6–4	Perry & Miss Round	F H D Wilde & Miss M Whitmarsh	6–4 1–6 6–3
				Budge & Mrs Fabyan	C E Malfroy (NZ) & Fru S Sperling (Ger)	6–4 6–3
1937	J D Budge (USA) & Miss A Marble (USA)	Y Petra (Fra) & Mme R Mathieu (Fra)	6–4 6–1	Budge & Miss Marble	G Mako (USA) & Miss J Jedrzejowska (Pol)	6–3 6–2
				Petra & Mme Mathieu	D Prenn (Ger) & Miss E M Dearman	6–2 6–4
1938	J D Budge (USA) & Miss A Marble (USA)	H Henkel (Ger) & Mrs M Fabyan (USA)	6–1 6–4	Budge & Miss Marble	R A Shayes & Miss J Saunders	6–4 6–2
				Henkel & Mrs Fabyan	A D Russell (Arg) & Miss F James	6–3 1–6 6–3
1939	R L Riggs (USA) & Miss A Marble (USA)	F H D Wilde & Miss N B Brown	9–7 6–1	Riggs & Miss Marble	C E Malfroy (NZ) & Miss B Nuthall	3–6 6–2 6–4
				Wilde & Miss Brown	E T Cooke (USA) & Mrs M Fabyan (USA)	6–3 7–5

	FINAL Winners	Losers	Score	SEMI-FINALS Winners	Losers	Score
1940–1945 not held						
1946	T P Brown (USA) & Miss A L Brough (USA)	G E Brown (Aus) & Miss D Bundy (USA)	6–4 6–4	T P Brown & Miss Brough	H C Hopman (Aus) & Miss M E Osborne (USA)	6–3 6–3
				G E Brown & Miss Bundy	J E Patty (USA) & Miss P M Betz (USA)	12–10 6–2
1947	J E Bromwich (Aus) & Miss A L Brough (USA)	C F Long (Aus) & Mrs N W Bolton (Aus)	1–6 6–4 6–2	Bromwich & Miss Brough	L Bergelin (Swe) & Miss D J Hart (USA)	6–4 6–2
				Long & Mrs Bolton	T P Brown (USA) & Miss M E Osborne (USA)	7–5 6–2
1948	J E Bromwich (Aus) & Miss A L Brough (USA)	F A Sedgman (Aus) & Miss D J Hart (USA)	6–2 3–6 6–3	Bromwich & Miss Brough	J Drobny (Cze) & Mrs P C Todd (USA)	5–7 6–1 8–6
				Sedgman & Miss Hart	T P Brown (USA) & Mrs W du Pont (USA)	6–4 3–6 6–3
1949	E W Sturgess (SA) & Mrs S P Summers (SA)	J E Bromwich (Aus) & Miss A L Brough (USA)	9–7 9–11 7–5	Sturgess & Mrs Summers	O W Sidwell (Aus) & Mrs W du Pont (USA)	6–4 7–9 6–3
				Bromwich & Miss Brough	G A Worthington (Aus) & Mrs T D Long (Aus)	6–1 6–2
1950	E W Sturgess (SA) & Miss A L Brough (USA)	G E Brown (Aus) & Mrs P C Todd (USA)	11–9 1–6 6–4	Sturgess & Miss Brough	F A Sedgman (Aus) & Miss D J Hart (USA)	6–2 9–7
				G E Brown & Mrs Todd	G A Worthington (Aus) & Mrs T D Long (Aus)	9–7 6–4
1951	F A Sedgman (Aus) & Miss D J Hart (USA)	M G Rose (Aus) & Mrs N W Bolton (Aus)	7–5 6–2	Sedgman & Miss Hart	K McGregor (Aus) & Mrs W du Pont (USA)	6–2 4–6 6–3
				Rose & Mrs Bolton	E W Sturgess (SA) & Miss A L Brough (USA)	7–5 6–2
1952	F A Sedgman (Aus) & Miss D J Hart (USA)	E Morea (Arg) & Mrs T D Long (Aus)	4–6 6–3 6–4	Sedgman & Miss Hart	D W Candy (Aus) & Mrs P C Todd (USA)	6–2 6–3
				Morea & Mrs Long	K McGregor (Aus) & Miss A L Brough (USA)	6–3 7–5
1953	E V Seixas (USA) & Miss D J Hart (USA)	E Morea (Arg) & Miss S J Fry (USA)	9–7 7–5	Seixas & Miss Hart	L A Hoad (Aus) & Miss J Sampson (USA)	6–3 7–5
				Morea & Miss Fry	G A Worthington (Aus) & Miss P E Ward	6–2 6–2
1954	E V Seixas (USA) & Miss D J Hart (USA)	K R Rosewall (Aus) & Mrs W du Pont (USA)	5–7 6–4 6–3	Seixas & Miss Hart	M A Otway (NZ) & Miss J F Burke (NZ)	6–4 6–1
				Rosewall & Mrs du Pont	L A Hoad (Aus) & Miss M C Connolly (USA)	6–8 6–4 6–4
1955	E V Seixas (USA) & Miss D J Hart (USA)	E Morea (Arg) & Miss A L Brough (USA)	8–6 2–6 6–3	Seixas & Miss Hart	L A Hoad (Aus) & Mrs Hoad (Aus)	6–3 9–7
				Morea & Miss Brough	N A Fraser (Aus) & Miss B Penrose (Aus)	7–9 6–4 6–4
1956	E V Seixas (USA) & Miss S J Fry (USA)	G Mulloy (USA) & Miss A Gibson (USA)	2–6 6–2 7–5	Seixas & Miss Fry	R N Howe (Aus) & Miss D R Hard (USA)	6–3 7–5
				Mulloy & Miss Gibson	T T Fancutt (SA) & Miss D G Seeney (Aus)	6–4 6–4
1957	M G Rose (Aus) & Miss D R Hard (USA)	N A Fraser (Aus) & Miss A Gibson (USA)	6–4 7–5	Rose & Miss Hard	L Ayala (Chi) & Mrs T D Long (Aus)	3–6 6–3 6–2
				Fraser & Miss Gibson	R S Emerson (Aus) & Miss M Hellyer (Aus)	6–4 6–4
1958	R N Howe (Aus) & Miss L Coghlan (Aus)	K Nielsen (Den) & Miss A Gibson (USA)	6–3 13–11	Howe & Miss Coghlan	F Contreras (Mex) & Miss R M Reyes (Mex)	6–4 6–4
				Nielsen & Miss Gibson	W A Knight & Miss S J Bloomer	7–5 6–3
1959	R G Laver (Aus) & Miss D R Hard (USA)	N A Fraser (Aus) & Miss M E Bueno (Bra)	6–4 6–3	Laver & Miss Hard	W A Knight & Miss Y Ramirez (Mex)	6–2 5–7 6–2
				Fraser & Miss Bueno	R Mark (Aus) & Miss J Arth (USA)	6–3 6–2
1960	R G Laver (Aus) & Miss D R Hard (USA)	R N Howe (Aus) & Miss M E Bueno (Bra)	13–11 3–6 8–6	Laver & Miss Hard	R Mark (Aus) & Miss J S Hopps (USA)	4–6 6–1 6–2
				Howe & Miss Bueno	J Javorsky (Cze) & Miss V Puzejova (Cze)	6–1 2–6 6–4
1961	F S Stolle (Aus) & Miss L R Turner (Aus)	R N Howe (Aus) & Frl E Buding (FDR)	11–9 6–2	Stolle & Miss Turner	J Javorsky (Cze) & Mrs V Sukova (Cze)	7–5 6–3
				Howe & Frl Buding	E Morea (Arg) & Miss M Smith (Aus)	6–3 6–2

Year	FINAL Winners	Losers	Score	SEMI-FINALS Winners	Losers	Score
1962	N A Fraser (Aus) & Mrs W du Pont (USA)	R D Ralston (USA) & Miss A S Haydon	2–6 6–3 13–11	Fraser & Mrs du Pont	F S Stolle (Aus) & Miss L R Turner (Aus)	4–6 6–3 6–4
				Ralston & Miss Haydon	R N Howe (Aus) & Miss M E Bueno (Bra)	6–3 8–10 6–
1963	K N Fletcher (Aus) & Miss M Smith (Aus)	R A J Hewitt (Aus) & Miss D R Hard (USA)	11–9 6–4	Fletcher & Miss Smith	R D Ralston (USA) & Mrs P F Jones	6–1 7–5
				Hewitt & Miss Hard	F S Stolle (Aus) & Miss L R Turner (Aus)	5–7 6–2 6–2
1964	F S Stolle (Aus) & Miss L R Turner (Aus)	K N Fletcher (Aus) & Miss M Smith (Aus)	6–4 6–4	Stolle & Miss Turner	T S Okker (Hol) & Miss T Groenman (Hol)	2–6 6–2 6–3
				Fletcher & Miss Smith	F A Froehling (USA) & Miss J Bricka (USA)	7–5 6–3
1965	K N Fletcher (Aus) & Miss M Smith (Aus)	A D Roche (Aus) & Miss J A M Tegart (Aus)	12–10 6–3	Fletcher & Miss Smith	R D Ralston (USA) & Miss M E Bueno (Bra)	7–5 6–4
				Roche & Miss Tegart	F S Stolle (Aus) & Miss L R Turner (Aus)	6–3 11–9
1966	K N Fletcher (Aus) & Miss M Smith (Aus)	R D Ralston (USA) & Mrs L W King (USA)	4–6 6–3 6–3	Fletcher & Miss Smith	F S Stolle (Aus) & Mlle F Durr (Fra)	6–1 7–5
				Ralston & Mrs King	F D McMillan (SA) & Miss A M Van Zyl (SA)	6–4 6–4
1967	O K Davidson (Aus) & Mrs L W King (USA)	K N Fletcher (Aus) & Miss M E Bueno (Bra)	7–5 6–2	Davidson & Mrs King	F D McMillan (SA) & Miss A M Van Zyl (SA)	6–3 3–6 6–1
				Fletcher & Miss Bueno	R O Ruffels (Aus) & Miss K M Krantzcke (Aus)	6–3 6–1
1968	K N Fletcher (Aus) & Mrs B M Court (Aus)	A Metreveli (USSR) & Miss O Morozova (USSR)	6–1 14–12	Fletcher & Mrs Court	O K Davidson (Aus) & Mrs L W King (USA)	6–4 9–7
				Metreveli & Miss Morozova	F S Stolle (Aus) & Mrs P F Jones	6–3 12–10
1969	F S Stolle (Aus) & Mrs P F Jones	A D Roche (Aus) & Miss J A M Tegart (Aus)	6–3 6–2	Stolle & Mrs Jones	K N Fletcher (Aus) & Mrs B M Court (Aus)	11–9 11–9
				Roche & Miss Tegart	R O Ruffels (Aus) & Miss K M Krantzcke (Aus)	6–4 7–5
1970	I Nastase (Rom) & Miss R Casals (USA)	A Metreveli (USSR) & Miss O Morozova (USSR)	6–3 4–6 9–7	Nastase & Miss Casals	F D McMillan (SA) & Mrs D E Dalton (Aus)	5–7 6–2 6–4
				Metreveli & Miss Morozova	D Irvine (Rho) & Miss H F Gourlay (Aus)	9–11 6–3 6–
1971	O K Davidson (Aus) & Mrs L W King (USA)	M C Riessen (USA) & Mrs B M Court (Aus)	3–6 6–2 15–13	Davidson & Mrs King	I Nastase (Rom) & Miss R Casals (USA)	6–4 6–1
				Riessen & Mrs Court	F D McMillan (SA) & Mrs D E Dalton (Aus)	7–5 6–3
1972	I Nastase (Rom) & Miss R Casals (USA)	K G Warwick (Aus) & Miss E F Goolagong (Aus)	6–4 6–4	Nastase & Miss Casals	C E Graebner (USA) & Mrs L W King (USA)	9–8 7–6
				Warwick & Miss Goolagong	P J Cramer (SA) & Mrs Q C Pretorious (SA)	6–4 6–3
1973	O K Davidson (Aus) & Mrs L W King (USA)	R Ramirez (Mex) & Miss J S Newberry (USA)	6–3 6–2	Davidson & Mrs King	A Metreveli (USSR) & Mrs O Morozova (USSR)	5–7 7–5 6–1
				Ramirez & Miss Newberry	J R Cooper (Aus) & Miss K M Krantzcke (Aus)	6–1 6–4
1974	O K Davidson (Aus) & Mrs L W King (USA)	M J Farrell & Miss L J Charles	6–3 9–7	Davidson & Mrs King	A D Roche (Aus) & Mlle F Durr (Fra)	3–6 6–3 6–4
				Farrell & Miss Charles	N A Fraser (Aus) & Miss H F Gourlay (Aus)	7–9 8–6 6–2
1975	M C Riessen (USA) & Mrs B M Court (Aus)	A J Stone (Aus) & Miss B F Stove (Hol)	6–4 7–5	Riessen & Mrs Court	J Kodes (Cze) & Miss M Navratilova (Cze)	5–7 6–3 6–2
				Stone & Miss Stove	A Metreveli (USSR) & Mrs O Morozova (USSR)	2–6 6–4 6–4
1976	A D Roche (Aus) & Mlle F Durr (Fra)	R L Stockton (USA) & Miss R Casals (USA)	6–3 2–6 7–5	Roche & Mlle Durr	F D McMillan (SA) & Miss B F Stove (Hol)	6–3 6–3
				Stockton & Miss Casals	R A J Hewitt (SA) & Miss G R Stevens (SA)	6–3 9–8
1977	R A J Hewitt (SA) & Miss G R Stevens (SA)	F D McMillan (SA) & Miss B F Stove (Hol)	3–6 7–5 6–4	Hewitt & Miss Stevens	P C Dent (Aus) & Mrs L W King (USA)	5–7 6–4 7–5
				McMillan & Miss Stove	R D Ralston (USA) & Miss M Navratilova (Cze)	5–7 6–4 12–10

Year	FINAL Winners	Losers	Score	SEMI-FINALS Winners	Losers	Score
1978	F D McMillan (SA) & Miss B F Stove (Hol)	R O Ruffels (Aus) & Mrs L W King (USA)	6–2 6–2	McMillan & Miss Stove	A D Roche (Aus) & Mlle F Durr (Fra)	7–5 6–3
				Ruffels & Mrs King	A J Stone (Aus) & Miss D Fromholtz (Aus)	6–3 6–4
1979	R A J Hewitt (SA) & Miss G R Stevens (SA)	F D McMillan (SA) & Miss B F Stove (Hol)	7–5 7–6	Hewitt & Miss Stevens	J D Newcombe (Aus) & Mrs R A Cawley (Aus)	6–7 6–4 6–4
				McMillan & Miss Stove	K G Warwick (Aus) & Miss B Nagelsen (USA)	6–2 2–6 6–2
1980	J R Austin (USA) & Miss T A Austin (USA)	M R Edmondson (Aus) & Miss D Fromholtz (Aus)	4–6 7–6 6–3	Austin & Miss Austin	F D McMillan (SA) & Miss B F Stove (Hol)	6–4 6–2
				Edmondson & Miss Fromholtz	R L Case (Aus) & Miss W M Turnbull (Aus)	7–6 6–4
1981	F D McMillan (SA) & Miss B F Stove (Hol)	J R Austin (USA) & Miss T A Austin (USA)	4–6 7–6 6–3	McMillan & Miss Stove	L C Leeds (USA) & Miss S L Acker (USA)	4–6 6–1 6–2
				Austin & Miss Austin	A D Roche (Aus) & Miss B Bunge (FRG)	6–2 7–6
1982	K Curren (SA) & Miss A E Smith (USA)	J M Lloyd & Miss W M Turnbull (Aus)	2–6 6–3 7–5	Curren & Miss Smith	C Strode (USA) & Miss A Temesvari (Hun)	6–4 7–5
				Lloyd & Miss Turnbull	C M Johnstone (Aus) & Miss P J Whytcross (Aus)	6–4 6–0

The **longest match** was in 1967 in the quarter-final when Ken Fletcher (Aus) and Maria Bueno (Bra) beat Alex Metreveli and Anna Dmitrieva (both USSR) 6–8 7–5 16–14, a total of **56 games**.

The **second longest match** was in 1963; in the second round Bob Dixon and Cathy Lyon (both GB) beat O K French (Aus) and Miss A L K Barclay (Can) 2–6 9–7 15–13, a total of **52 games**.

The **longest final** was 1949; Eric Sturgess and Sheila Summers (both SA) beat John Bromwich (Aus) and Louise Brough (USA) 9–7 9–11 7–5, a total of **48 games**.

The **second longest final** was 1960 when Rod Laver (Aus) and Darlene Hard (USA) beat Bob Howe (Aus) and Maria Bueno (Bra) 13–11 3–6 8–6, a total of **47 games**.

The **longest semi-final** was in 1977 when Frew McMillan (SA) and Betty Stove (Hol) beat Dennis Ralston (USA) and Martina Navratilova (Cze) 5–7 6–4 12–10, a total of **44 games**.

The **longest set** was in 1931 when Harry Lee and Phylis King (both GB) beat Norman Farquharson (SA) and Helen Jacobs (USA) **17–15** 6–1, a total of **32 games**.

The **longest set in a final** was 1971 when Owen Davidson (Aus) and Billie Jean King (USA) beat Marty Riessen (USA) and Margaret Court (Aus) 3–6 6–2 **15–13**, a total of **28 games**.

CHAMPIONSHIPS WON FROM MATCH POINT

1889 Men's singles
William Renshaw in All Comers' Final beat Harry Barlow 3–6 5–7 8–6 10–8 8–6 after six match points in the fourth set at 2–5 and 6–7.

The immortal William Renshaw. He changed tennis from a pastime into a sport.

1889 Women's singles*
Blanche Hillyard in All Comers' Final beat Lena Rice 4–6 8–6 6–4 after three match points in the second set.

1895 Men's singles*
William Baddeley in All Comers' Final beat Willoughby Eaves 4–6 2–6 8–6 6–2 6–3 from 5–6, 30–40 in the third set.

1901 Men's singles
Arthur Gore beat George Hillyard in the quarter-final by 6–1 2–6 4–6 8–6 6–2 after a match point in the fourth set.

Blanche Bingley, later Mrs George Hillyard. She competed at Wimbledon in the inaugural women's year of 1884 and won six times in all.

1908 Men's doubles*

Major Ritchie and Tony Wilding in All Comers' Final beat Arthur Gore and Roper Barrett 6–1 6–2 1–6 1–6 9–7 after match point in the fifth set.

1919 Women's singles*

Suzanne Lenglen in the Challenge Round beat Dorothea Lambert Chambers 10–8 4–6 9–7 after two match points in the third set at 5–6, 15–40.

1921 Men's singles*

William Tilden in the Challenge Round beat Brian Norton 4–6 2–6 6–1 6–0 7–5 after two match points in the fifth set at 4–5.

1926 Women's doubles

Mary Browne and Elizabeth Ryan in the second round beat Suzanne Lenglen and Didi Vlasto 3–6 9–7 6–2 after two match points in the second set.

1927 Men's singles*

Henri Cochet in the final beat Jean Borotra 4–6 4–6 6–3 6–4 7–5 after six match points in the fifth set, one at 2–5 and five at 3–5.

1927 Men's doubles*

Frank Hunter and William Tilden in the final beat Jacques Brugnon and Henri Cochet 1–6 4–6 8–6 6–3 6–4 after two match points in the third set at 4–5.

1932 Women's doubles

Doris Metaxa and Josane Sigart in the first round beat Mary Heeley and Freda James 2–6 6–4 7–5 after three match points in the third set.

1935 Women's singles*

Helen Moody in the final beat Helen Jacobs 6–3 3–6 7–5 after a match point in the third set at 3–5.

1935 Men's doubles*

Jack Crawford and Adrian Quist in the final beat Wilmer Allison and John Van Ryn 6–3 5–7 6–2 5–7 7–5 after a match point in the fifth set.

1947 Women's doubles*

Doris Hart and Pat Todd in the final beat Louise Brough and Miss Margaret Osborne 3–6 6–4 7–5 after three match points in the third set at 3–5, 0–40.

1948 Men's singles*

Bob Falkenburg in the final beat John Bromwich 7–5 0–6 6–2 3–6 7–5 after three match points in the fifth set at 3–5, 15–40 and advantage Bromwich.

1949 Men's singles

Ted Schroeder in the quarter-final beat Frank Sedgman 3–6 6–8 6–3 6–2 9–7 after two match points in the fifth set, one at 4–5 and one at 5–6.

1954 Women's doubles*

Louise Brough and Margaret du Pont in the final beat Shirley Fry and Doris Hart 4–6 9–7 6–3 after two match points in the second set at 3–5.

1960 Men's singles

Neale Fraser in the quarter-final beat Earl Buchholz 4–6 6–3 4–6 15–15 retired after six match points in the fourth set.

1960 Mixed doubles*

Rod Laver and Darlene Hard in the final beat Bob Howe and Maria Bueno 13–11 3–6 8–6 after three match points in the third set at 4–5.

1976 Mixed doubles*

Tony Roche and Francoise Durr in the final beat Dick Stockton and Rosemary Casals 6–3 2–6 7–5 after a match point at 4–5 in the third set.

1978 Women's doubles*

Kerry Reid and Wendy Turnbull in the final beat Mima Jausovec and Virginia Ruzici 4–6 9–8 6–3 after two match points in the tie break of the second set.

1980 Mixed doubles*

John and Tracy Austin in the final beat Mark Edmondson and Dianne Fromholtz 4–6 7–6 6–3 after a match point at 4–5 in the second set, after two match points at 4–6 in the second set tie break.

* Matches in which the losers, had they won, would have taken the title.

MEN'S SINGLES CONSOLATION PLATE

FINALS

Year	Winner	Finalist	Score
1896	A W Gore	H L Doherty	1–6 6–2 7–5
1897	H Baddeley	A E Crawley	6–1 6–3 5–7 6–2
1898	G W Hillyard	A C Pearson	6–3 8–6
1899	W V Eaves	G W Hillyard	w.o.
1900	G Greville	E D Black	6–2 4–6 6–3
1901	P G Pearson	H W Davies	6–1 4–6 6–2 7–5
1902	B Hillyard	C R D Pritchett	8–6 6–1
1903	A W Gore	C Hobart (USA)	7–5 6–3
1904	G Greville	B Hillyard	6–3 6–0
1905	W V Eaves	B Murphy	6–3 6–2
1906	G W Hillyard	T M Mavrogordato	6–2 6–4
1907	A F Wilding (NZ)	C von Wesseley (Aut)	6–3 6–4
1908	O Kreuzer (Ger)	V R Gauntlett (SA)	6–3 6–4
1909	R B Powell (Can)	H A Parker (NZ)	3–6 6–3 6–1
1910	A H Gobert (Fra)	P M Davson	6–4 6–4
1911	A H Lowe	J C Parke	6–0 8–6
1912	F M Pearson	F E Barritt (Aus)	6–0 10–8
1913	F G Lowe	F F Roe	8–10 6–3 6–3
1914	C P Dixon	R W F Harding	6–1 6–2
1915–1918 not held			
1919	F R L Crawford	M Woosnam	6–4 5–7 7–5
1920	F G Lowe	C P Dixon	1–6 8–6 6–3
1921	J B Gilbert	F M B Fisher (NZ)	7–5 4–6 6–0
1922	B I C Norton (SA)	R C Wertheim (Aus)	6–2 6–2
1923	J Washer (Bel)	M J G Ritchie	6–3 6–4
1924	J Condon (SA)	J M Hillyard	7–5 6–2
1925	B von Kehrling (Hun)	R George (Fra)	6–3 6–4
1926	J B Gilbert	F R L Crawford	10–8 6–2
1927	A Gentien (Fra)	O G N Turnbull	1–6 6–2 6–0
1928	M Sleem (Ind)	J B Gilbert	6–3 6–3
1929	E G Chandler (USA)	W H Powell	6–4 6–1
1930	E du Plaix (Fra)	C E Malfroy (NZ)	6–1 8–6
1931	V G Kirby (SA)	G L Rogers (Ire)	2–6 6–3 6–3
1932	H Cochet (Fra)	T Kuwabara (Jap)	6–2 6–4
1933	F H D Wilde	J D P Wheatley	6–4 6–4
1934	H W Artens (Aus)	C R D Tuckey	5–7 7–5 6–1
1935	J Yamagishi (Jap)	J Lesueur (Fra)	6–2 6–2
1936	D N Jones (USA)	I G Collins	6–0 6–2
1937	W Sabin (USA)	N G Farquharson (SA)	2–6 6–0 6–3
1938	D W Butler	O Szigeti (Hun)	6–1 8–10 6–3
1939	D McNeill (USA)	J van den Eynde (Bel)	8–6 6–2
1940–1945 not held			
1946	R Abdesselam (Fra)	C Spychala (Pol)	7–5 6–3
1947	E W Sturgess (SA)	A J Mottram	6–3 6–3
1948	F Ampon (Phi)	H Weiss (Arg)	11–9 6–4
1949	E H Cochell (USA)	G P Jackson (Ire)	4–6 6–3 6–1
1950	G L Paish	J Brichant (Bel)	6–4 6–4
1951	N M Cockburn (SA)	K H Ip (HK)	7–5 5–7 10–8
1952	L Ayala (Chi)	N Kumar (Ind)	8–6 6–2
1953	G L Paish	J W Ager (USA)	4–6 6–0 7–5
1954	H W Stewart (USA)	A Vieira (Bra)	8–6 6–4
1955	N A Fraser (Aus)	R N Howe (Aus)	6–2 7–5
1956	H W Stewart (USA)	G Mulloy (USA)	4–6 6–4 6–4
1957	G L Forbes (SA)	A Segal (SA)	10–8 11–13 6–3
1958	P Remy (Fra)	J N Grinda (Fra)	6–3 11–9
1959	J Javorsky (Cze)	M Fox (USA)	6–3 6–2
1960	T Ulrich (Den)	O Sirola (Ita)	6–4 7–5

FINALS

Year	Winner	Finalist	Score
1961	J Ulrich (Den)	N Kumar (Ind)	6–4 10–12 6–3
1962	J A Douglas (USA)	A Segal (SA)	3–6 6–2 6–3
1963	E L Scott (USA)	I S Crookenden (NZ)	w.o.
1964	R K Wilson	W W Bowrey (Aus)	6–4 6–3
1965	O K Davidson (Aus)	T S Okker (Hol)	6–3 8–6
1966	R Taylor	R N Howe (Aus)	6–4 2–6 7–5
1967	J H McManus (USA)	E L Scott (USA)	6–3 6–2
1968	G Battrick	H S Fitzgibbon (USA)	6–4 3–6 7–5
1969	T Koch (Bra)	R O Ruffels (Aus)	6–1 6–3
1970	R R Maud (SA)	R R Barth (USA)	6–4 6–3
1971	R D Crealy (Aus)	P Cornejo (Chi)	6–3 6–4
1972	K G Warwick (Aus)	no finalist	w.o.
1973	J G Clifton	S G Messmer (USA)	6–4 4–6 6–1
1974	T I Kakulia (USSR)	P C Kronk (Aus)	6–3 7–5
1975	T Koch (Bra)	V Gerulaitis (USA)	6–3 6–2
1976	B E Fairlie (NZ)	R Taylor	4–6 6–3 6–4
1977	M C Riessen (USA)	G E Reid (Aus)	6–4 5–7 9–7
1978	D H Collings (Aus)	T Wilkison (USA)	3–6 9–8 6–4
1979	P C Kronk (Aus)	M R Edmondson (Aus)	6–7 6–2 6–4
1980	S Glickstein (Isr)	P Dominguez (Fra)	6–3 7–6
1981	D Carter (Aus)	C M Johnstone (Aus)	6–3 6–4
1982	not held		

WOMEN'S CONSOLATION PLATE

FINALS

Year	Winner	Finalist	Score
1933	Mlle C Rosambert (Fra)	Mlle J Goldschmidt (Fra)	6–4 6–1
1934	Miss L Valerio (Ita)	Miss J Saunders	7–5 6–3
1935	Miss L Valerio (Ita)	Miss A E L McOstrich	6–2 1–6 6–0
1936	Miss F S Ford	Miss M Riddell	6–4 6–4
1937	Miss F James	Miss M E Lumb	6–0 7–5
1938	Miss D Stevenson (Aus)	Miss J Hartigan (Aus)	6–4 6–4
1939	Mrs R D McKelvie	Mlle A Weiwers (Lux)	6–4 4–6 6–2
1940–1945	not held		
1946	Miss J Jedrzejowska (Pol)	Miss P A O'Connell	6–4 7–5
1947	Miss J Jedrzejowska (Pol)	Mrs N W Blair	6–2 7–5
1948	Mrs H Weiss (Arg)	Miss E M Wilford	6–1 5–7 7–5
1949	Mrs A Bossi (Ita)	Miss B Gullbrandson (Swe)	6–0 7–5
1950	Miss K L A Tuckey	Miss B Rosenquest (USA)	6–4 6–1
1951	Mrs F Bartlett (SA)	Miss G E Woodgate	3–6 6–1 6–2
1952	Mrs B Abbas (Egy)	Miss G C Hoahing	0–6 6–4 6–3
1953	Miss M P Harrison	Miss E G Lombard (Ire)	1–6 6–3 6–3
1954	Miss R Walsh	Miss P A Hird	6–2 7–5
1955	Miss F Muller (Aus)	Miss L L Delix (USA)	6–4 6–4
1956	Mrs T D Long (Aus)	Frl I Buding (Ger)	6–3 6–4
1957	Miss M B Hellyer (Aus)	Miss R Schuurman (SA)	6–4 6–4
1958	Miss S Reynolds (SA)	Miss M B Hellyer (Aus)	6–2 6–2
1959	Mrs C W Brasher	Mrs M Sladek (Can)	3–6 6–3 7–5
1960	Miss D M Catt	Mrs J W Cawthorne	6–3 6–2
1961	Miss R H Bentley	Miss A Dmitrieva (USSR)	6–4 3–6 6–3
1962	Miss M L Gerson (SA)	Miss M B Hellyer (Aus)	6–2 6–1
1963	Mlle F Durr (Fra)	Miss A Dmitrieva (USSR)	6–1 6–3
1964	Mrs V Sukova (Cze)	Miss J Bricka (USA)	0–6 6–3 6–3
1965	Miss A Dmitrieva (USSR)	Miss F E Truman	6–1 6–2
1966	Miss P M Walkden (SA)	Mrs J G A Lloyd	6–4 6–0

FINALS

Year	Winner	Finalist	Score
1967	Miss P S A Hogan (USA)	Miss G V Sherriff (Aus)	6–2 9–7
1968	Miss S V Wade	Miss K M Harter (USA)	6–2 12–10
1969	Miss B A Grubb (USA)	Miss L A Rossouw (SA)	6–3 4–6 6–4
1970	Miss E F Goolagong (Aus)	Miss L Liem (Ina)	6–2 6–1
1971	Mrs M R Wainwright	Miss B F Stove (Hol)	6–4 0–6 6–2
1972	Miss K M Krantzcke (Aus)	Miss S A Walsh (USA)	6–4 6–1
1973	Miss H F Gourlay (Aus)	Miss V A Burton	6–1 4–6 6–1
1974	Miss M V Kroschina (USSR)	Miss L J Beaven	6–3 8–6
1975	Miss D L Fromholtz (Aus)	Miss V A Burton	6–4 6–2
1976	Miss M Wikstedt (Swe)	Miss B Bruning (USA)	4–6 6–3 6–3
1977	Miss Y Vermaak (SA)	Miss S Mappin	6–2 7–5
1978	Mrs T E Guerrant (USA)	Miss H Strachanova (Cze)	6–2 8–6
1979	Miss S Barker	Miss S Simmonds (Ita)	7–6 6–0
1980	Miss R D Fairbank (SA)	Miss S A Walsh (USA)	6–4 6–2
1981	Miss S E Saliba (Aus)	Miss P Casale (USA)	6–3 6–3
1982	Miss C C Monteiro (Bra)	Miss R L Blount (USA)	6–3 2–6 6–2

JUNIOR EVENTS BOYS' SINGLES

Year	Winner	Runner-up	Final Score
1947	K Nielsen (Den)	S Davidson (Swe)	(round robin)
1948	S Stockenberg (Swe)	D Vad (Hun)	6–4 6–4
1949	S Stockenberg (Swe)	J A T Horn	6–2 6–1
1950	J A T Horn	K Moubarek (Egy)	6–3 6–4
1951	J Kupferburger (SA)	K Moubarek (Egy)	8–6 6–4
1952	R K Wilson	T Fancutt (SA)	6–3 6–3
1953	W A Knight	R Krishnan (Ind)	6–4 6–2
1954	R Krishnan (Ind)	A J Cooper (Aus)	6–2 7–5
1955	M P Hann	J E Lundquist (Swe)	6–0 11–9
1956	R Holmberg (USA)	R G Laver (Aus)	6–1 6–1
1957	J I Tattersall	I Ribiero (Bra)	6–3 6–4
1958	E Buchholz (USA)	P J Lall (Ind)	6–1 6–3
1959	T Lejus (USSR)	R W Barnes (Bra)	6–2 6–4
1960	A R Mandelstam (SA)	J Mukerjea (Ind)	1–6 8–6 6–4
1961	C E Graebner (USA)	E Blanke (Aut)	6–3 9–7
1962	S J Matthews	A Metreveli (USSR)	10–8 3–6 6–4
1963	N Kalogeropoulos (Gre)	I El Shafel (Egy)	6–4 6–3
1964	I El Shafei (Egy)	V Korotkov (USSR)	6–2 6–3
1965	V Korotkov (USSR)	C Goven (Fra)	6–2 3–6 6–3
1966	V Korotkov (USSR)	B E Fairlie (NZ)	6–3 11–9
1967	M Orantes (Spa)	M Estep (USA)	6–2 6–0
1968	J D Alexander (Aus)	J Thamin (Fra)	6–1 6–2
1969	B Bertram (SA)	J D Alexander (Aus)	7–5 5–7 6–4
1970	B Bertram (SA)	F Gebert (Ger)	6–0 6–3
1971	R Kreiss (USA)	S A Warboys	2–6 6–4 6–3
1972	B Borg (Swe)	C J Mottram	6–3 4–6 7–5
1973	W Martin (USA)	C Dowdeswell (Rho)	6–2 6–4
1974	W Martin (USA)	Ashok Amritraj (Ind)	6–2 6–1
1975	C J Lewis (NZ)	R Ycaza (Ecu)	6–1 6–4
1976	H Guenthardt (Swi)	P Elter (Ger)	6–4 7–5
1977	V Winitsky (USA)	E Teltscher (USA)	6–1 1–6 8–6
1978	I Lendl (Cze)	J Turpin (USA)	6–3 6–4
1979	R Krishan (Ind)	D Siegler (USA)	6–0 6–2
1980	T Tulasne (Fra)	H D Beutel (FRG)	6–4 3–6 6–4
1981	M Anger (USA)	P Cash (Aus)	7–6 7–5
1982	P Cash (Aus)	H Sundstrom (Swe)	6–4 6–7 6–3

GIRLS' SINGLES

Year	Winner	Runner-up	Final Score
1948	O Miskova (Cze)	V Rigollet (Swi)	6–4 6–4
1949	C Mercellis (Bel)	J S V Partridge	6–3 6–4
1950	L Cornell	A Winther (Nor)	6–2 6–4
1951	L Cornell	S Lazzarino (Ita)	6–3 6–4
1952	F ten Bosch (Hol)	R Davar (Ind)	5–7 6–1 7–5
1953	D Kilian (SA)	V A Pitt	7–5 6–3
1954	V A Pitt	C Monnot (Fra)	5–7 6–3 6–2
1955	S M Armstrong	B de Chambure (Fra)	6–2 6–4
1956	A S Haydon	I Buding (FRG)	6–3 6–4
1957	M Arnold (USA)	R M Reyes (Mex)	6–4 6–4
1958	S M Moore (USA)	A Dmitrieva (USSR)	6–2 6–4
1959	J Cross (SA)	D Schuster (Aut)	6–0 6–1
1960	K Hantze (USA)	L M Hutchings (SA)	6–4 6–4
1961	G Baksheeva (USSR)	K D Chabot (USA)	6–4 8–6
1962	G Baksheeva (USSR)	E P Terry (NZ)	6–2 6–3
1963	D M Salfati (Fra)	K Dening (Aus)	6–4 6–1
1964	J Bartkowicz (USA)	E Subirats (Mex)	6–3 6–1
1965	O Morozova (USSR)	R Giscafre (Arg)	6–3 6–3
1966	B Lindstrom (Fin)	J Congdon	7–5 6–3
1967	J Salome (Hol)	M Strandberg (Swe)	6–4 6–2
1968	K Pigeon (USA)	L Hunt (Aus)	6–4 6–3
1969	K Sawamatsu (Jap)	B Kirk (SA)	6–3 1–6 7–5
1970	S A Walsh (USA)	M Kroschina (USSR)	8–6 6–4
1971	M Kroschina (USSR)	S Minford (Ire)	6–4 6–4
1972	I Kloss (SA)	G L Coles	6–4 4–6 6–4
1973	A K Kiyomura (USA)	M Navratilova (Cze)	6–4 7–5
1974	M Jausovec (Yug)	M Simionescu (Rom)	7–5 6–4
1975	N Y Chmyriova (USSR)	R Marsikova (Cze)	6–4 6–3
1976	N Y Chmyriova (USSR)	M Kruger (SA)	6–3 2–6 6–1
1977	L Antonoplis (USA)	Mareen Louie (USA)	7–5 6–1
1978	T A Austin (USA)	H M Mandlikova (Cze)	6–0 3–6 6–4
1979	M L Piatek (USA)	A A Moulton (USA)	6–1 6–3
1980	D Freeman (Aus)	S Leo (Aus)	7–6 7–5
1981	Z Garrison (USA)	R Uys (SA)	6–4 3–6 6–0
1982	C Tanvier (Fra)	H Sukova (Cze)	6–2 7–5

SEEDING

There was no seeding until 1924 when a modified form was introduced. Overseas associations nominated up to four men and four women who were then drawn into different quarters of the singles draw.

Merit seeding was introduced in 1927, taking priority over the national seeding but combined with it. It made for an involved draw. National seeding ceased with the open lawn tennis from 1968.

YOUNGEST AND OLDEST SEEDS

The **youngest seed** in the Wimbledon Championships was Andrea Jaeger (USA), number 14 in the women's singles in 1980. She was **15 years 19 days**.

The second youngest seed was Tracy Austin (USA), number nine in the women's singles in 1978. Her age was **15 years 196 days**.

The **youngest man** to be seeded was Bjorn Borg (Swe), number six in the singles in 1973. His age was **17 years 19 days**.

The second youngest man was Lew Hoad (Aus), the number six of 1953. His age was **18 years 211 days**.

The **oldest player** to be seeded in the singles was Ricardo Gonzales (USA), the number 12 seed in 1969. He was **41 years 45 days**.

The second oldest was William Tilden (USA), the number two seed (and champion) in 1930. His age was **37 years 133 days**.

The **oldest woman** to be seeded in singles was Billie Jean King (USA), the number 12 in 1982. Her age was **38 years 211 days**.

The second oldest woman was Margaret du

Pont (USA), the fifth seed in 1954. She was **36 years 109 days.**

(In 1962 Mrs du Pont was seeded number 3 in the mixed doubles with Neale Fraser (Aus), with whom she won the event. She was **44 years 113 days.**)

MOST SEEDED SINGLES PLAYERS

	Times Seeded	Years	Range of Rating	Times Number One
MEN				
Roy Emerson (Aus)	12	1959–70	1–10	4
Wilfred Austin (GB)	10	1930–39	1–7	1
Jaroslav Drobny (Cze, Egy)	10	1947–56	2–11	–
Ken Rosewall (Aus)	10	1953–56, 68–75	1–9	1
John Newcombe (Aus)	10	1965–71, 74, 76, 78	1–16	1
Jimmy Connors (USA)	10	1973–82	1–5	2
Stan Smith (USA)	9	1969–72, 74–77, 80	1–16	1
Ilie Nastase (Rom)	9	1970–78	1–9	1
Bjorn Borg (Swe)	9	1973–81	1–6	4
WOMEN				
Billie Jean King (USA)	17	1964–75, 77–80, 82	1–12	3
Virginia Wade (GB)	14	1967–80	3–7	–
Margaret Court (Aus)	12	1961–72, 75	1–5	8
Helen Jacobs (USA)	11	1928–37, 39	1–8	2
Simone Mathieu (Fra)	11	1929–39	2–7	–
Louise Brough (USA)	11	1946–52, 54–57	1–4	4
Chris Lloyd (USA)	11	1972–82	1–4	5
Maria Bueno (Bra)	10	1958–60, 62–68	1–7	2
Ann Jones (GB)	10	1959–64, 66–69	3–8	–
Kerry Reid (Aus)	10	1969, 70, 72–79	4–10	–
Evonne Cawley (Aus)	10	1971–76, 78–80, 82	1–16	1
Hilde Sperling (Ger)	9	1931–39	2–6	–
Doris Hart (USA)	9	1946–48, 50–55	1–7	2
Angela Mortimer (GB)	9	1953–57, 59–62	2–7	–

TOP SEEDING IN THREE EVENTS

Just three players, Don Budge in 1938, Louise Brough in 1950 and Frank Sedgman in 1952 have been seeded number one in all three events, singles, doubles and mixed, and gone on to justify that high expectation. The following lists those players who have been made triple favourites:

Year		Singles	Doubles	Mixed
1929	Henri Cochet	Won	Lost quarter-final	Lost quarter-final
1938	Don Budge	Won	Won	Won
1949	Louise Brough	Won	Won	Lost final
1950	Louise Brough	Won	Won	Won
1951	Louise Brough	Lost semi-final	Lost final	Lost semi-final
1952	Frank Sedgman	Won	Won	Won
1952	Doris Hart	Lost quarter-final	Won	Won
1955	Doris Hart	Lost semi-final	Lost 1st match	Won
1964	Margaret Smith	Won	Won	Lost final
1966	Margaret Smith	Lost semi-final	Lost final	Won
1968	Billie Jean King	Won	Won	Lost semi-final
1969	Margaret Court	Lost semi-final	Won	Lost semi-final
1970	Margaret Court	Won	Scratched quarter-final	Scratched 1st round
1974	Billie Jean King	Lost quarter-final	Lost quarter-final	Won

Henri Cochet.

PERFORMANCE OF TOP SEEDS

MEN'S SINGLES Year Top Seed		WOMEN'S SINGLES Top Seed	
1927	R Lacoste	Lost semi-final	Miss H Wills	Won
1928	H Cochet	Lost final	Miss H Wills	Won
1929	H Cochet	Won	Miss H Wills	Won
1930	H Cochet	Lost quarter-final	Mrs F S Moody	Won
1931	J Borotra	Lost semi-final	Frl C Aussem	Won
1932	H Cochet	Lost 2nd round	Mrs F S Moody	Won
1933	H E Vines	Lost final	Mrs F S Moody	Won
1934	J H Crawford	Lost final	Miss H H Jacobs	Lost final
1935	F J Perry	Won	Miss D E Round	Lost quarter-final
1936	F J Perry	Won	Miss D E Round	Lost quarter-final
1937	J D Budge	Won	Miss H H Jacobs	Lost quarter-final
1938	J D Budge	Won	Mrs F S Moody	Won
1939	H W Austin	Lost quarter-final	Miss A Marble	Won
1946	D Pails	Lost quarter-final	Miss P M Betz	Won
1947	J A Kramer	Won	Miss M E Osborne	Won
1948	F A Parker	Lost 4th round	Mrs W du Pont	Lost semi-final
1949	F R Schroeder	Won	Miss A L Brough	Won
1950	F A Sedgman	Lost final	Miss A L Brough	Won
1951	F A Sedgman	Lost quarter-final	Miss A L Brough	Lost semi-final
1952	F A Sedgman	Won	Miss D J Hart	Lost quarter-final
1953	K R Rosewall	Lost quarter-final	Miss M C Connolly	Won
1954	M A Trabert	Lost semi-final	Miss M C Connolly	Won
1955	M A Trabert	Won	Miss D J Hart	Lost semi-final
1956	L A Hoad	Won	Miss A L Brough	Lost semi-final
1957	L A Hoad	Won	Miss A Gibson	Won
1958	A J Cooper	Won	Miss A Gibson	Won
1959	A Olmedo	Won	Miss C C Truman	Lost 4th round
1960	N A Fraser	Won	Miss M E Bueno	Won
1961	N A Fraser	Lost 4th round	Miss S Reynolds	Lost semi-final
1962	R G Laver	Won	Miss M Smith	Lost first match
1963	R S Emerson	Lost quarter-final	Miss M Smith	Won
1964	R S Emerson	Won	Miss M Smith	Lost final
1965	R S Emerson	Won	Miss M E Bueno	Lost final
1966	R S Emerson	Lost quarter-final	Miss M Smith	Lost semi-final
1967	M Santana	Lost 1st round	Mrs L W King	Won
1968	R G Laver	Won	Mrs L W King	Won
1969	R G Laver	Won	Mrs L W King	Lost final
1970	R G Laver	Lost 4th round	Mrs B M Court	Won
1971	R G Laver	Lost quarter-final	Mrs B M Court	Lost final
1972	S R Smith	Won	Miss E F Goolagong	Lost final
1973	I Nastase	Lost 4th round	Mrs B M Court	Lost semi-final
1974	J D Newcombe	Lost quarter-final	Mrs L W King	Lost quarter-final
1975	J S Connors	Lost final	Miss C M Evert	Lost semi-final
1976	A R Ashe	Lost 4th round	Miss C M Evert	Won
1977	J S Connors	Lost final	Miss C M Evert	Lost semi-final
1978	B Borg	Won	Miss C M Evert	Lost final
1979	B Borg	Won	Miss M Navratilova	Won
1980	B Borg	Won	Miss M Navratilova	Lost semi-final
1981	B Borg	Lost final	Mrs J M Lloyd	Won
1982	J P McEnroe	Lost final	Miss M Navratilova	Won

MEN'S DOUBLES Year Top Seeds		WOMEN'S DOUBLES Year Top Seeds	
1927	J Brugnon & H Cochet	Lost final	1927 Miss E Ryan & Miss H N Wills	Won
1928	F T Hunter & W T Tilden	Lost quarter-final	1928 Mrs R Lycett & Miss E Ryan	Lost semi-final
1929	J Brugnon & H Cochet	Lost quarter-final	1929 Miss B Nuthall & Miss E Ryan	Lost semi-final
1930	J H Doeg & G M Lott	Lost final	1930 Mrs F S Moody & Miss E Ryan	Won
1931	G M Lott & J Van Ryn	Won	1931 Miss B Nuthall & Mrs E F Whittingstall	Lost semi-final
1932	W L Allison & J Van Ryn	Lost semi-final	1932 Miss B Nuthall & Mrs E F Whittingstall	Lost 3rd round
1933	J Borotra & J Brugnon	Won	1933 Mme R Mathieu & Miss E Ryan	Won

Year Top Seeds		Year Top Seeds	
1934 J Borotra & J Brugnon	Lost final	1934 Mme R Mathieu & Miss E Ryan	Won
1935 W L Allison & J Van Ryn	Lost final	1935 Mrs D B Andrus & Mme S Henrotin	Lost 3rd round
1936 J D Budge & G Mako	Lost 3rd round	1936 Miss F James	
		& Miss K E Stammers	Won
1937 G P Hughes & C R D Tuckey	Lost final	1937 Miss F James	
		& Miss K E Stammers	Lost quarter-final
1938 J D Budge & G Mako	Won	1938 Mme R Mathieu & Miss A M Yorke	Lost final
1939 H Henkel & G Von Metaxa	Lost 2nd round	1939 Mrs M Fabyan & Miss A Marble	Won
1946 G E Brown & D Pails	Lost final	1946 Miss A L Brough	
		& Miss M E Osborne	Won
1947 J A Kramer & R Falkenburg	Won	1947 Miss A L Brough	
		& Miss M E Osborne	Lost final
1948 R Falkenburg & F A Parker	Lost semi-final	1948 Miss A L Brough & Mrs W du Pont	Won
1949 G Mulloy & F R Schroeder	Lost final	1949 Miss A L Brough & Mrs W du Pont	Won
1950 G Mulloy & W F Talbert	Lost 3rd round	1950 Miss A L Brough & Mrs W du Pont	Won
1951 K McGregor & F A Sedgman	Won	1951 Miss A L Brough & Mrs W du Pont	Lost final
1952 K McGregor & F A Sedgman	Won	1952 Miss S J Fry & Miss D J Hart	Won
1953 L A Hoad & K R Rosewall	Won	1953 Miss S J Fry & Miss D J Hart	Won
1954 R N Hartwig & M G Rose	Won	1954 Miss S J Fry & Miss D J Hart	Lost final
1955 E V Seixas & M A Trabert	Lost semi-final	1955 Mrs G Davidson & Miss D J Hart	Lost 1st match
1956 L A Hoad & K R Rosewall	Won	1956 Miss A L Brough & Miss S J Fry	Lost semi-final
1957 N A Fraser & L A Hoad	Lost final	1957 Miss A Gibson & Miss D R Hard	Won
1958 A J Cooper & N A Fraser	Lost final	1958 Miss A Gibson & Miss M E Bueno	Won
1959 R S Emerson & N A Fraser	Won	1959 Miss J Arth & Miss D R Hard	Won
1960 R S Emerson & N A Fraser	Lost quarter-final	1960 Miss M E Bueno & Miss D R Hard	Won
1961 R S Emerson & N A Fraser	Won	1961 Miss S Reynolds	
		& Miss R Schuurman	Lost quarter-final
1962 R S Emerson & N A Fraser	Lost semi-final	1962 Miss M E Bueno & Miss D R Hard	Lost semi-final
1963 R A J Hewitt & F S Stolle	Lost 3rd round	1963 Miss R Ebben & Miss M Smith	Lost final
1964 C R McKinley & R D Ralston	Lost quarter-final	1964 Miss M Smith & Miss L R Turner	Won
1965 R S Emerson & F S Stolle	Lost 3rd round	1965 Miss M Smith & Miss L R Turner	Lost 3rd round
1966 R S Emerson & F S Stolle	Scratched 3rd round	1966 Miss M Smith & Miss J A M Tegart	Lost final
1967 J D Newcombe & A D Roche	Lost quarter-final	1967 Miss M E Bueno & Miss N Richey	Lost final
1968 R S Emerson & R G Laver	Lost semi-final	1968 Miss R Casals & Mrs L W King	Lost semi-final
1969 J D Newcombe & A D Roche	Won	1969 Mrs B M Court & Miss J A M Tegart	Won
1970 J D Newcombe & A D Roche	Won	1970 Mrs B M Court & Mrs D E Dalton	Scratched quarter-final
1971 J D Newcombe & A D Roche	Lost 1st round	1971 Miss R Casals & Mrs L W King	Won
1972 R A J Hewitt & F D McMillan	Won	1972 Mrs L W King & Miss B F Stove	Won
1973 J S Connors & I Nastase	Won	1973 Miss R Casals & Mrs L W King	Won
1974 J S Connors & I Nastase	Lost semi-final	1974 Miss R Casals & Mrs L W King	Lost quarter-final
1975 B E Gottfried & R Ramirez	Lost 2nd round	1975 Mrs R A Cawley & Miss M Michel	Lost 2nd round
1976 B E Gottfried & R Ramirez	Won	1976 Mrs L W King & Miss B F Stove	Lost final
1977 B E Gottfried & R Ramirez	Lost 1st round	1977 Miss M Navratilova	
		& Miss B F Stove	Lost final
1978 R A J Hewitt & F D McMillan	Won	1978 Mrs L W King & Miss M Navratilova	Lost quarter-final
1979 P Fleming & J P McEnroe	Won	1979 Mrs L W King & Miss M Navratilova	Won
1980 P Fleming & J P McEnroe	Lost semi-final	1980 Mrs L W King & Miss M Navratilova	Lost semi-final
1981 P Fleming & J P McEnroe	Won	1981 Miss K Jordan & Miss A E Smith	Lost final
1982 P Fleming & J P McEnroe	Lost final	1982 Miss M Navratilova	
		& Miss P H Shriver	Won

MIXED DOUBLES

Year Top Seeds		Year Top Seeds	
1927 L A Godfree & Mrs Godfree	Lost final	1939 E T Cooke & Mrs M Fabyan	Lost semi-final
1928 H Cochet & Miss E Bennett	Lost quarter-final	1946 H C Hopman & Miss M E Osborne	Lost semi-final
1929 H Cochet & Miss E Bennett	Lost quarter-final	1947 J E Bromwich & Miss A L Brough	Won
1930 W T Tilden & Frl C Aussem	Scratched quarter-final	1948 J E Bromwich & Miss A L Brough	Won
1931 H Cochet & Mrs E F Whittingstall	Lost 4th round	1949 J E Bromwich & Miss A L Brough	Lost final
1932 H E Vines & Mrs F S Moody	Lost 3rd round	1950 E W Sturgess & Miss A L Brough	Won
1933 E Maier & Miss E Ryan	Lost quarter-final	1951 E W Sturgess & Miss A L Brough	Lost final
1934 G von Cramm & Fru S Sperling	Lost 3rd round	1952 F A Sedgman & Miss D J Hart	Won
1935 G von Cramm & Fru S Sperling	Lost semi-final	1953 E V Seixas & Miss D J Hart	Won
1936 F J Perry & Miss D E Round	Won	1954 E V Seixas & Miss D J Hart	Won
1937 J D Budge & Miss A Marble	Won	1955 E V Seixas & Miss D J Hart	Won
1938 J D Budge & Miss A Marble	Won	1956 E V Seixas & Miss S J Fry	Won

Year Top Seeds

1957	E V Seixas & Miss A L Brough	Lost 4th round
1958	N A Fraser & Mrs W du Pont	Retired 1st match
1959	W A Knight & Miss Y Ramirez	Lost semi-final
1960	R G Laver & Miss D R Hard	Won
1961	F S Stolle & Miss L R Turner	Won
1962	F S Stolle & Miss L R Turner	Lost semi-final
1963	F S Stolle & Miss L R Turner	Lost semi-final
1964	K N Fletcher & Miss M Smith	Lost final
1965	F S Stolle & Miss L R Turner	Lost semi-final
1966	K N Fletcher & Miss M Smith	Won
1967	O K Davidson & Mrs L W King	Won
1968	O K Davidson & Mrs L W King	Lost semi-final
1969	K N Fletcher & Mrs B M Court	Lost semi-final

Year Top Seeds

1970	M C Riessen & Mrs B M Court	Scratched
1971	M C Riessen & Mrs B M Court	Lost final
1972	K Warwick & Miss E F Goolagong	Lost final
1973	I Nastase & Miss R Casals	Scratched quarter-final
1974	O K Davidson & Mrs L W King	Won
1975	M C Riessen & Mrs B M Court	Won
1976	A A Mayer & Mrs L W King	Lost 2nd round
1977	F D McMillan & Miss B F Stove	Lost final
1978	F D McMillan & Miss B F Stove	Won
1979	F D McMillan & Miss B F Stove	Lost final
1980	F D McMillan & Miss B F Stove	Lost semi-final
1981	J R Austin & Miss T A Austin	Lost final
1982	F D McMillan & Miss B F Stove	Lost 3rd round

SEEDING POSITION OF WINNERS AND RUNNERS-UP

Year	Men's Singles		Women's Singles		Men's Doubles		Women's Doubles		Mixed Doubles	
	Champ.	R-up.	Champ.	R-up.	Champ.	R-up.	Champ.	R-up.	Champ.	R-up.
1927	4	3	1	4	3	1	1	2	4	1
1928	2	1	1	2	2	4	3	3	2	—
1929	1	2	1	5	—	4	2	3	2	—
1930	2	—	1	8	2	1	1	4	2	—
1931	7	3	1	4	1	2	—	4	—	—
1932	2	6	1	5	4	3	4	2	4	6
1933	2	1	1	2	1	—	1	—	—	4
1934	2	1	2	1	2	1	1	—	—	—
1935	1	2	4	3	2	1	3	2	3	—
1936	1	2	2	5	3	—	1	2	1	2
1937	1	2	7	4	2	1	2	—	1	2
1938	1	2	1	—	1	4	2	1	1	2
1939	2	6	1	6	2	4	1	2	2	—
1946	5	3	1	3	2	1	1	2	3	2
1947	1	3	1	3	1	—	2	1	1	3
1948	7	2	2	4	3	2	1	2	1	4
1949	1	6	1	2	3	1	1	2	4	1
1950	5	1	1	2	2	4	1	2	1	4
1951	6	7	3	4	1	4	2	1	2	—
1952	1	2	2	4	1	4	1	2	1	—
1953	2	—	1	2	1	3	1	2	1	4
1954	11	3	1	4	1	2	2	1	1	3
1955	1	—	2	3	2	3	4	3	1	2
1956	1	2	5	6	1	—	3	—	1	3
1957	1	2	1	5	—	1	1	2	4	2
1958	1	4	1	—	—	1	1	—	4	2
1959	1	—	6	4	1	4	1	3	3	2
1960	1	3	1	8	—	—	1	4	1	2
1961	2	8	7	6	1	—	—	3	1	4
1962	1	—	8	—	2	—	2	4	3	—
1963	4	—	1	—	—	—	2	1	2	—
1964	1	6	2	1	3	4	1	2	2	1
1965	1	2	2	1	2	4	2	—	2	—
1966	4	6	4	2	—	4	2	1	1	3
1967	3	—	1	3	2	4	3	1	1	2
1968	1	15	1	7	4	2	1	3	4	—
1969	1	6	4	1	1	6	1	—	4	3
1970	2	5	1	2	1	6	2	4	—	—
1971	2	4	3	1	—	—	1	2	3	1
1972	1	2	2	1	1	2	1	3	2	1

Year	Men's Singles		Women's Singles		Men's Doubles		Women's Doubles		Mixed Doubles	
	Champ.	R-up	Champ.	R-up	Champ.	R-up	Champ.	R-up	Champ.	R-up
1973	2	4	2	4	1	2	1	3	2	1
1974	3	9	2	8	4	3	–	–	1	–
1975	6	1	3	4	–	–	–	–	1	–
1976	4	3	1	2	1	–	2	1	–	–
1977	2	1	3	7	7	–	–	1	–	1
1978	1	2	2	1	1	–	4	7	1	2
1979	1	5	1	2	1	7	1	2	2	1
1980	1	2	4	3	7	4	4	2	–	6
1981	2	1	1	2	1	3	2	1	2	1
1982	2	1	1	2	3	1	1	2	4	3

GROWTH OF THE OVERSEAS CHALLENGE

Note: In this context Irish players, prior to 1922, are not regarded as from overseas since the British Isles functioned as a single entity until that time. If this were not so Helena Rice would be listed as the first overseas finalist in the women's singles in 1889 and the first overseas holder of that title in 1890, the same year in which Joshua Pim and Frank Stoker could be held as overseas winners of the men's doubles.

The following all refer to first time happenings.

1884 The **first overseas challenge** (comprising the Americans J Dwight, R D Sears, and A L Rives, with the South African E L Williams.

The **first overseas finalist** with Williams partnering the British E W Lewis in the men's doubles.

1900 The **first overseas challenge by a woman,** Marion Jones of the USA.

1905 The **first overseas champion,** with May Sutton (USA) winning the *women's singles.* (Miss Sutton was, however, British born. The first overseas born player to win the event was the French Suzanne Lenglen in 1919.)

The first overseas **finalist in the men's singles,** Norman Brookes (Aus).

1907 The **men's singles** (Norman Brookes) and the **men's doubles** (Brookes and Tony Wilding of New Zealand) went overseas. Since Miss Sutton won the women's singles for the second time as well **all championship titles** (only three title events were then played) went overseas.

1913 **Both men's singles finalists** were from overseas, Tony Wilding of New Zealand and Maurice McLoughlin of the USA.

One of the early overseas challengers at Wimbledon, Tony Wilding of New Zealand won the men's doubles in 1907 with Norman Brookes of Australia and was a singles finalist in 1913.

1914 The first overseas **women's doubles champion**, Elizabeth Ryan (USA) with the British Agatha Morton.

1919 The first **overseas pair** as **women's doubles champions**, Miss Ryan and Suzanne Lenglen of France.
Miss Ryan became the first overseas holder of the **mixed doubles**, partnering the British Randolph Lycett.

1920 All **five championship titles** taken overseas.
Gerald Patterson and Mlle Lenglen were the first overseas pair to win the **mixed doubles.**

1921 The **women's singles** title match entirely overseas, Mlle Lenglen against Miss Ryan.
The **last four** in the **men's singles** was entirely overseas, together with the standing out champion.

1925 The **mixed doubles final** was **entirely overseas**, Jean Borotra and Mlle Lenglen of France playing Baron Morpurgo of Italy and Miss Ryan.

1927 The **last eight** of the **men's singles** was entirely from overseas.
Final of the **women's doubles** was all overseas, Miss Ryan and Helen Wills Moody against the South Africans Bobbie Heine and Gwen Peacock.

1928 The **last four** in the **women's singles** was exclusively from overseas.

1930 All **five finals** were contested by overseas players.

1947 The **last 16** in the **men's singles** was entirely overseas.

1951 **Semi-finals** in **all five events** filled from overseas.

1965 **All seeding positions** in **all five events** filled by overseas players.

1978 **Last 32** places in **men's singles** filled from overseas.

1980 **Last eight** in **women's singles** filled by overseas players.

THE NATIONS AT WIMBLEDON 1877–1982

A record of the nationality of the Champions and of the number of championships won, nation by nation.

Nationality & Year of First Win		Number of Champions			Singles Only			Number of Championships Won					
								Singles		Doubles*			
		Men	Women	Total	Men	Women	Total	Men's	Women's	Men's	Women's	Mixed	Total
British[1]	1877	33	26	59	14	14	28	35	36	30½	8½	9	119
American	1905	40	31	71	19	14	33	23	35	18½	36½	23	136
Australian	1907	29	8	37	10	2	12	19	5	25½	4	16	69½
New Zealand	1907	1	–	1	1	–	1	4	–	2	–	–	6
French	1911	7	4	11	4	1	5	7	6	6	5	2½	26½
S African	1928	4	2	6	–	–	–	–	–	3	–	5½	8½
German	1931	1	2	3	–	1	1	–	1	–	–	1	2
Spanish	1932	2	–	2	1	–	1	1	–	–	–	½	1½
Belgian	1932	–	1	1	–	–	–	–	–	–	½	–	½
Japanese	1935	1	1	2	–	–	–	–	–	–	½	½	1
Czech[2]	1954	2	1	3	2	1	3	2	3	–	2	–	7
Swedish	1958	3	–	3	1	–	1	5	–	1	–	–	6
Brazilian	1958	–	1	1	–	1	1	–	3	–	2½	–	5½
Mexican	1960	3	–	3	–	–	–	–	–	2	–	–	2
Romanian	1972	1	–	1	–	–	–	–	–	½	–	1	1½
Dutch	1972	–	1	1	–	–	–	–	–	–	½	1	1½
Totals		127	78	205	52	34	86	96	89	89	60	60	394

* Each doubles title shared by two players, hence the ½ championship.
[1] includes Ireland 1877–1921.
[2] includes J Drobny, designated as Egyptian when champion in 1954, and Miss M Navratilova, American 1982.

WIMBLEDON'S PRIZES

1877

Only a men's singles championship was involved, though the restriction to men was not specifically mentioned. The prospectus read:
'The following prizes will be open to competition by all Amateur Lawn Tennis Players, viz:
1. The Champion Gold Prize: with a silver challenge cup value 25 guineas (given by the proprietors of the *Field*) to be competed for annually on conditions to be laid down by the Committee.
2. The Silver Prize.
3. Smaller prizes, if a sufficient number enter.'

1967

By the time of the last amateur Wimbledon the

prize list had grown considerably.

Men's Singles. 'The Winner will become the holder, for the year only, of the Challenge Cup presented by King George V and also of the Challenge Cup presented by the All England Club. The First Prize is a piece of silver, known as "The Renshaw Cup" annually presented by the surviving members of the family of the late Ernest and William Renshaw. A Second Prize will be given, value £30, and two Third Prizes, value £16 each. The winner will receive silver replicas of the two Challenge Cups. A Silver Medal will be presented to the Runner-up and a Bronze Medal to each defeated Semi-finalist.'

Women's Singles. 'The Winner will become the holder, for the year only, of the Challenge Trophy presented by the All England Club. First Prize, value £30. Second Prize, value £20. Two Third Prizes, value £10 each. The winner will receive a silver replica of the trophy. A Silver Medal will be presented to the Runner-up and a Bronze medal to each defeated Semi-finalist.'

Third Prizes value £10 each. The Winners will receive silver replicas of the Challenge Cup. A Silver Medal will be presented to each of the Runners-up and a Bronze Medal to each defeated Semi-finalist.'

Mixed Doubles. 'The Winners will become the holders, for the year, of the Challenge Cup presented by the family of the late Mr S H Smith. Two First Prizes value £20 each. Two Second Prizes, value £16 each. Four Third Prizes, value £10 each. The Winners will receive silver replicas of the Challenge Cup. A Silver Medal will be presented to each of the Runners-up and a Bronze Medal to each of the defeated Semi-finalists.'

1968

The first open championships listed the same prizes. There was, however, prize money for those 'who elected to play for it'. This was:

Men's Singles
Winner: £2000. Runner-up: £1300
Minimum—1st round loser: £50

The original men's singles trophy. **Evonne Cawley with the women's singles trophy.** **The Renshaw Cup for the All-Comers' singles, now one of the champion's trophies.**

Men's Doubles. 'The winning pair will become the holders, for the year only, of the Challenge Cups, presented by the Oxford University Lawn Tennis Club and the late Sir Herbert Wilberforce. Two First Prizes, value £20 each. Two Second Prizes, value £16 each. Four Third Prizes, value £10 each. The Winners will receive silver replicas of the Challenge Cups. A Silver Medal will be presented to each of the Runners-up and a Bronze Medal to each defeated semi-finalist.'

Women's Doubles. 'The Winners will become the holders, for the year, of the Challenge Cup presented by HRH Princess Marina, Duchess of Kent. Two First Prizes, value £20 each. Two Second Prizes, value £16 each. Four

Women's Singles
Winner: £750. Runner-up: £450
Minimum—1st round loser: £25
Men's Doubles
Winners: £800. Runners-up: £500
Minimum—Quarter-final losers: £180
Women's Doubles
Winners: £500. Runners-up: £300
Minimum—Quarter-final losers: £100
Mixed Doubles
Winners: £450. Runners-up: £300
Minimum—Quarter-final losers: £100

(All doubles prizes shared between both players).
The total prize money awarded was £26 150.

1982

The same cups and medals were at stake but prizes of varying value, which had been awarded in the form of vouchers, were no longer on offer. The prize money was:

Men's Singles
  Winner: £41 667. Runner-up: £20 833
  Minimum—1st round losers: £556
Women's Singles
  Winner: £37 500. Runner-up: £18 750
  Minimum—1st round losers: £428
Men's Doubles
  Winners: £16 666. Runners-up: £8334
  Minimum—1st round losers: £140
Women's Doubles
  Winners: £14 450. Runners-up: £7226
  Minimum—1st round losers: £100
Mixed Doubles
  Winners: £6750. Runners-up: £3400
  Minimum—3rd round losers: £400

The total prize money, including plate event, veterans' event and percentage to the bonus pool of the men's Grand Prix and the women's International Series, was £593 366.

WIMBLEDON'S CROWD CAPACITY

The crowd, on a rather wet day, for the climax of the first Championship in 1877 was assessed as 200. Two movable grandstands were erected round the Centre Court first in 1880. There was a crowd of 8000 for the finals of 1919. The move of the All England Club from its original ground in Worple Road to its present site in Church Road was made in 1922.

Total attendance exceeded 200 000 for the first time in 1932. In 1967 300 000 was broken for the first time.

In 1981, with the rebuilding of the stands on Court One, the crowd capacity was brought to a peak. The stand accommodation was:

	Seating	Standing room
Centre Court	11 579	2750
Court One	6350	1500
Court No. 2	2020	1000
Court No. 3	800	
Court No. 6	250	
Court No. 7	250	
Court No. 13	1450	
Court No. 14	740	
Benching on other outside courts	1000	
Total	24 439	5250

The highest daily totals have been:

	First Week	Year	Second Week	Year
Monday	32 075	1981	34 875	1981
Tuesday	33 693	1978	31 345	1981
Wednesday	38 291	1979	29 672	1982
Thursday	37 161	1981	24 265	1980
Friday	37 290	1975	19 254	1980
Saturday	33 295	1981	19 162	1981

The record total attendance was in 1981 with 207 282 attending the first week and **358 152** in all.

THE WIMBLEDON SURPLUS

The Wimbledon Championships were originally promoted exclusively by the All England Croquet and Lawn Tennis Club and the inaugural meeting in 1877 is reputed to have produced a profit of £10. Except for one occasion (1895 when there was a loss of £33) there has always been a surplus.

The tournament is now promoted by the Wimbledon Management Committee, a joint body with members from the All England Club and the British Lawn Tennis Association. By an agreement of 1934 the surplus from The Lawn Tennis Championships, less a small sum amounting to little more than £1000, belongs to the LTA.

In 1934 the surplus was £9054. Prior to 1939 the peak figure was £12 693 in 1938.

It exceeded £20 000 for the first time in 1949. £50 000 was reached, though not sustained, for the first time in 1953. Prior to the first Open Wimbledon in 1968 the biggest surplus was £57 509 in 1956.

Since 1968 the surplus has been:

1968	£35 960
1969	£93 684
1970	£57 345
1971	£65 836
1972	£63 331
1973	£56 401
1974	£84 054
1975	£121 001
1976	£183 969
1977	£401 224
1978	£435 063
1979	£306 501
1980	£411 455
1981	£1 067 860
1982	£1 530 585

UNITED STATES OF AMERICA

THE US CHAMPIONSHIPS

Four national championships, those of Wimbledon, Scotland, Ireland and Victoria (then a colony on its own) have a longer continuous history than those of the United States. Only Wimbledon would claim prestige to match venerability.

There was an American Championship, open to all comers, in September 1880 at the Staten Island Cricket and Baseball Club. It was won by the English O E Woodhouse from the West Middlesex Club, Ealing. He beat Canadian, J F Helmuth, in the final. Rackets scoring was used.

Laurie and Reggie Doherty winning the US men's doubles title at Newport.

The first 'official' US Championships were in 1881, following the formation of the US National Lawn Tennis Association. Beginning on 31 August 1881 the inaugural US National Championships were held on the grass courts at the Newport Casino, Newport, Rhode Island. The events were men's singles and doubles and Wimbledon rules were adopted. Richard Sears won the singles from an entry of 25.

Entry was restricted to American residents. Immediately following the tournament another, open to all, was arranged, mainly to accommodate J J Cairnes, a British player. Cairnes and Sears reached the final from an entry of 23 and Cairnes beat Sears 4–6 6–2 6–1 6–3.

The 'American residents only' rule was maintained in 1882. The next year the restriction was to members of American clubs. In 1884 it became an international tournament. The first overseas player of note to compete was the British E G Meers in 1889. He reached the All Comers' semi-finals.

American women staged a championship at the Philadelphia Cricket Club in 1887. By the fol-

lowing year they had received the approval of the US National Association. Their rules of entry have not survived. The winner in 1891 was Mabel Cahill from Ireland. The women inaugurated their doubles in 1890, the mixed in 1892.

The separation of events for men and women became established in American tradition. The first time the men's and women's singles were played together at the same venue at the same time was 1935. The first time all five championships were staged together was in 1942 as a war time measure and only temporarily. Only in the last two years of the US National Championships, the 88th title event being the final one in 1969, at the Longwood Cricket Club, Boston, did the tournament function as most others then.

The 1968 and 1969 championships were a

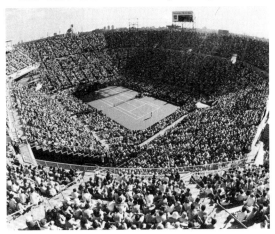

The Stadium Court at the National Tennis Centre, Flushing Meadow, New York.

curious duplication. The long standing amateur only rule was maintained. At the same time in 1968 there began at the West Side Club, New York, the US Open Championships.

VENUES

There was never a question with the Open meeting of all events not being held together. No mixed doubles were staged in the first year.

In 1975 a radical change of surface was made. Grass was abandoned for a loose-surface hard court, grey-green in colour, not unlike the shale hard court of Europe in playing characteristics.

There was a change of venue in 1978 from the West Side Club, Queen's, New York, to the National Tennis Centre, Flushing Meadow, in the same New York borough. The surface was changed as well, to a non-porous cement.

Mabel Cahill, the Irish winner of the US women's singles in 1891, 1892.

William Larned, US champion five times in a row 1907–11.

Betty Nuthall, first British winner of the US women's singles in 1930.

US NATIONAL CHAMPIONSHIPS

Venue	Event	Years
Newport Casino, Newport, RI	Men's singles	1881–1914
	Men's doubles	1881–1914
Philadelphia Cricket Club	Women's singles	1887–1920
	Women's doubles	1890–1920
	Mixed doubles	1892–1920
West Side Club, New York	Men's singles	1915–1920, 1924–1967
	Men's doubles	1915, 1916, 1942–1945
	Women's singles	1921–1967
	Women's doubles	1921–1934, 1942–1945
	Mixed doubles	1942–1967
Germantown Cricket Club, Philadelphia	Men's singles	1921–1923
	Men's doubles	1934
	Mixed doubles	1934
Longwood Cricket Club, Boston	Men's singles	1968, 1969
	Men's doubles	1918–1933, 1935–1941, 1946–1969
	Women's singles	1968, 1969
	Women's doubles	1935–1941, 1946–1969
	Mixed doubles	1921–1933, 1935–1941, 1968, 1969

US OPEN CHAMPIONSHIPS

West Side Club, New York	All events	1967–1977
National Tennis Centre, Flushing Meadow, New York	All events	1978 et seq.

AMERICAN SUPERLATIVES

YOUNGEST AND OLDEST

The **youngest champion** was Vincent Richards. He won the **men's doubles** with Big Bill Tilden in 1918 when his age was **15 years 139 days**.

Vincent Richards was also the **youngest mixed doubles** champion when in 1919 he won with Marion Zinderstein at **16 years 93 days**.

The **youngest woman to be champion** was, presumptively because of uncertain records, Tracy Austin, singles winner in 1979 at **16 years 271 days**.

The **youngest women's doubles champion** was May Sutton in 1904 at **17 years 350 days**.

The **youngest woman** to win the **mixed** was Betty Nuthall in 1929 at **18 years 102 days**.

The **youngest men's singles champion** was Oliver Campbell. He won in 1890 at the age of **19 years 190 days**.

The **oldest champion** was Margaret du Pont in 1960. She won the **mixed** doubles with Neale Fraser when she was **42 years 166 days**.

The **oldest women's doubles** champion was Hazel Wightman in 1928 at **41 years 257 days**.

The **oldest male champion** was Bob Hewitt when he won the **mixed** doubles in 1979 at the age of **39 years 240 days**.

The **oldest men's singles champion** was William Larned. His last win was in 1911 when he was **38 years 242 days**.

The oldest winner of the **women's singles** was Maud Barger-Wallach. She won in 1908 at the age of **37 years 244 days**.

The oldest **men's doubles** winner was Hewitt in 1977 at **37 years 243 days**.

(Note: For the above records, and those on pages 93–109 the US Nationals, 1881–1969, and the US Open Championships, 1967 et seq., are treated as one championship.)

THE LONGEST

The **longest matches** in the US Championships were both in the men's doubles at the Longwood Club, Boston. In 1966 in the third round Morcelo Lara and Joaquin Loyo-Mayo (both Mex) beat Manuel Santana (Spa) and L Garcia (Mex) 10–12 24–22 11–9 3–6 6–2. In 1967 in the quarter-final Cliff Drysdale and Ray Moore (both SA) beat Roy Emerson (Aus) and Ron Barnes (Bra) 29–31 8–6 3–6 8–6 6–2. Each had a total of **105 games**.

The **longest singles** was a men's singles at Forest Hills in 1969 in the first round when F D Robbins (USA) beat Dick Dell (USA) 22–20 9–7 6–8 8–10 6–4, a total of **100 games**.

The **longest women's match** was the **singles challenge round** of 1898 when, with the best of five sets being played, Juliette Atkinson beat Marion Jones (both USA) 6–3 5–7 6–4 2–6 7–5, the total being **51 games**.

The **longest men's singles final** was in 1949. Ricardo Gonzales (USA) beat Ted Schroeder (USA) 16–18 2–6 6–1 6–2 6–4, a total of **67 games**.

The **longest men's doubles final** was in 1946 when Gardner Mulloy and William Talbert (both USA) beat F Guernsey and W D McNeill (both USA) 3–6 6–4 2–6 6–3 20–18, the total being **74 games**.

The longest **women's doubles final** was 1920 when Eleanor Goss and Marion Zinderstein beat Helen Baker and Eleanor Tennant (all USA) 13–11 4–6 6–3, the total being **43 games**.

The **longest mixed doubles final** was in 1959. Neale Fraser (Aus) and Margaret du Pont (USA) beat Bob Mark (Aus) and Janet Hopps (USA) 7–5 13–15 6–2, a total of **48 games**.

THE SHORTEST

The **shortest men's singles final** was in 1974

when Jimmy Connors (USA) beat Ken Rosewall (Aus) 6–1 6–0 6–1, a total of **20 games**.

The **shortest women's singles finals** were played in 1887 (Ellen Hansell beat Laura Knight 6–1 6–0), in 1909 (Hazel Hotchkiss beat Maud Barger-Wallach 6–0 6–1), in 1916 (Mona Bjurstedt beat Louise Raymond 6–0 6–1) and in 1964 (Maria Bueno beat Carole Graebner 6–1 6–0), each only **13 games**.

The **shortest women's doubles finals** were 1946 (Louise Brough and Margaret Osborne beat Mrs D Arnold-Prentiss and Pat Todd 6–2 6–0) and 1960 (Maria Bueno and Darlene Hard beat Deidre Catt and Ann Haydon 6–1 6–1), each only **14 games**.

The **shortest mixed doubles final** was 1915 when Harry Johnson and Hazel Wightman beat Irving Wright and Molla Bjurstedt 6–0 6–1, the total being **13 games**.

In the men's doubles final the loser took the issue to 23 games only on four different occasions.

The **most eccentric score in a final** was in the men's doubles of 1971. John Newcombe (Aus) and Roger Taylor (GB) recorded their win against Stan Smith and Erik van Dillen (both USA) by 6–7 6–3 7–6 4–6 **5–3** (tie break). Because of darkness the fifth set was not played; instead was substituted a best of nine point tie break. No known rule covered the compromise.

(All the records relating to the doubles above are based on facts as far as they are known. More complete early records might necessitate amendment.)

CHAMPIONSHIPS WON FROM MATCH POINT

1901 Women's singles
Elizabeth Moore in All Comers' Final beat Marion Jones 4–6 1–6 9–7 9–7 6–3 after a match point in the third set.

1906 Men's singles
William Clothier in the quarter-final beat Fred Alexander 8–6 6–2 4–6 1–6 7–5 after three match points at 2–5, 0–40, in the fifth set.

1923 Mixed doubles*
William Tilden and Molla Mallory in the final beat John Hawkes and Kitty McKane 6–3 2–6 10–8 after two match points in the third set.

1926 Women's singles*
Molla Mallory in the final beat Elizabeth Ryan 4–6 6–4 9–7 after a match point at 6–7 in the third set.

1932 Men's singles
Ellsworth Vines in the semi-final beat Cliff Sutter 4–6 8–10 12–10 10–8 6–1 after four match points in the fourth set.

1936 Men's singles*
Fred Perry in the final beat Don Budge 2–6 6–2 8–6 1–6 10–8 after two match points at 4–5 in the fifth set.

1938 Women's singles
Alice Marble in the semi-final beat Sarah Fabyan 5–7 7–5 7–5 after two match points at 2–5 in the second set.

1942 Women's singles
Pauline Betz in the semi-final beat Margaret Osborne after a match point at 3–5 in the third set.

1946 Men's doubles*
Gardner Mulloy and William Talbert in the semi-final beat Robert Falkenburg and Frank Parker after two match points at 4–5 in the fifth set; in the final they beat Frank Guernsey and Donald McNeill* 3–6 6–4 2–6 6–3 20–18 after seven match points in the fifth set.

1947 Women's singles
Louise Brough in the semi-final beat Nancye Bolton 4–6 6–4 7–5 after two match points in the third set.

1948 Women's singles*
Margaret du Pont in the final beat Louise Brough 4–6 6–4 15–13 after a match point at 5–6 in the third set.

1948 Mixed doubles*
Tom Brown and Louise Brough in the semi-final beat Frank Sedgman and Doris Hart 6–2 5–7 8–6 after match point in the third set.

1953 Women's doubles*
Shirley Fry and Doris Hart in the final beat Louise Brough and Margaret du Pont 6–3 7–9 9–7 after two match points at 2–5 in the third set.

1954 Women's singles*
Doris Hart in the final beat Louise Brough 6–8 6–1 8–6 after three match points in the third set.

1963 Men's doubles*
Chuck McKinley and Dennis Ralston in the final beat Rafael Osuna and Antonio Palafox 9–7 4–6 5–7 6–3 11–9 after two match points at 5–6 in the fifth set.

1970 Men's doubles
Pierre Barthes and Nikki Pilic in the semi-final beat Patricio Cornejo and Jaime Fillol 6–7 6–7 7–6 7–6 7–5 after a match point in the fourth set.

1975 Men's singles
Manuel Orantes in the semi-final beat Guillermo Vilas 4–6 1–6 7–5 7–5 6–4 after three match points at 1–5 and two at 2–5 in the fourth set.

1976 Mixed doubles*
Phil Dent and Billie Jean King in the final beat Frew McMillan and Betty Stove 3–6 6–2 7–5 after a match point at 4–5 in the third set.

1979 Men's doubles
Peter Fleming and John McEnroe in the third round beat Bruce Manson and Andrew Pattison 4–6 7–5 6–3 after a match point at 3–5 in the second set.

* Matches in which the losers, had they won, would have taken the title.

William Tilden, the first man to be triple US Champion.

Vic Seixas, triple US Champion 1954 and Wimbledon singles winner in 1953.

Richard Dudley Sears, the first US National Champion.

TRIPLE CHAMPIONS

US NATIONAL CHAMPIONSHIPS*

Men	Women	Year
	Miss M Cahill (Ire)	1892
	Miss J P Atkinson (USA)	1895
	Miss H V Hotchkiss (USA)	1909
	Miss H V Hotchkiss (USA)	1910
	Miss H V Hotchkiss (USA)	1911
	Miss M K Browne (USA)	1912
	Miss M K Browne (USA)	1913
	Miss M K Browne (USA)	1914
	Miss M Bjurstedt (Nor)	**1917
W T Tilden (USA)		1922
W T Tilden (USA)		1923
	Miss H N Wills (USA)	1924
	Miss H N Wills (USA)	1928
	Miss H H Jacobs (USA)	1934
D Budge (USA)	Miss A Marble (USA)	1938
	Miss A Marble (USA)	1939
	Miss A Marble (USA)	1940
	Mrs E T Cooke (USA)	1941
	Miss A L Brough (USA)	1947
	Mrs W du Pont (USA)	1950
F A Sedgman (Aus)		1951
E V Seixas (USA)	Miss D J Hart (USA)	1954
K R Rosewall (Aus)		1956
N A Fraser (Aus)		1959
N A Fraser (Aus)		1960
	Mrs L W King (USA)	1967

US OPEN CHAMPIONSHIPS

	Mrs B M Court (Aus)	1970

* The triple champions emerging from the US Nationals won their titles at different times and different venues.
** In this case the events were all played at the same time.

MULTIPLE CHAMPIONS

Players Winning 10 or more titles in their Careers.

	Championships Won			
	Singles	Doubles	Mixed	Total
Mrs W D du Pont (USA) (1941–60)	3	13	8	24
Mrs B M Court (Aus) (1961–75) (including 1968 and 1969 when she won titles in both championships)	7	7	8	22
Miss A L Brough (USA) (1942–57)	1	12	4	17
W T Tilden (USA) (1913–29)	7	5	4	16
Mrs G W Wightman (USA) (1909–28)	4	6	6	16
Mrs M Fabyan (USA) (1930–45)	2	9	4	15
R D Sears (USA) (1881–87)	7	6	–	13
Mrs F S Moody (USA) (1922–31)	7	4	2	13
Mrs L W King (USA) (1964–80)	4	5	4	13
Miss J P Atkinson (USA) (1894–1902)	3	7	3	13
Miss A Marble (USA) (1936–40)	4	4	4	12
Miss M K Browne (USA) (1912–35)	3	5	4	12
Miss D J Hart (USA) (1951–55)	2	4	5	11
Mrs F Mallory (USA) (1915–26)	7	1	2	10

RESULTS: NATIONAL CHAMPIONSHIPS

MEN'S SINGLES

	FINAL			SEMI-FINALS		
Year	Winner	Loser	Score	Winner	Loser	Score

Played at The Casino, Newport, RI.

Year	Winner	Loser	Score	Winner	Loser	Score
1881	R D Sears	W E Glyn	6–0 6–3 6–2	Sears	Gray	6–3 6–0
				Glyn	Shaw	6–2 6–2
1882	R D Sears	C M Clark	6–1 6–4 6–0	Sears		bye
				Clark	Gray	6–3 6–2
1883	R D Sears	J Dwight	6–2 6–0 9–7	Sears	F Keene	6–0 6–0
				Dwight	R F Conover	6–4 6–3

Challenge Round instituted.

	CHALLENGE ROUND			ALL COMERS' FINAL		
1884	R D Sears	H A Taylor	6–0 1–6 6–0 6–2	Taylor	W V S Thorne	6–4 4–6 6–1 6–4
1885	R D Sears	G M Brinley	6–3 4–6 6–0 6–4	Brinley	W P Knapp	6–3 6–3 3–6 6–4
1886	R D Sears	R L Beeckman	4–6 6–1 6–3 6–4	Beeckman	H A Taylor	2–6 6–3 6–4 6–2
1887	R D Sears	H W Slocum	6–1 6–3 6–2	Slocum	H A Taylor	12–10 7–5 6–4
1888	H W Slocum		w.o.	Slocum	H A Taylor	6–4 6–1 6–0
1889	H W Slocum	Q A Shaw	6–3 6–1 4–6 6–2	Shaw	O S Campbell	1–6 6–4 6–3 6–4
1890	O S Campbell	H W Slocum	6–2 4–6 6–3 6–1	Campbell	W P Knapp	8–6 0–6 6–2 6–3
1891	O S Campbell	C Hobart	2–6 7–5 7–9 6–1 6–2	Hobart	F H Hovey	6–4 3–6 6–4 6–8 6–0

	CHALLENGE ROUND			**ALL COMERS' FINAL**		
Year	**Winner**	**Loser**	**Score**	**Winner**	**Loser**	**Score**
1892	O S Campbell	F H Hovey	7–5 3–6 6–3 7–5	Hovey	W A Larned	6–0 6–2 7–5
1893	R D Wrenn		w.o.	Wrenn	F H Hovey	6–4 3–6 6–4 6–4
1894	R D Wrenn	M F Goodbody (GB)	6–8 6–1 6–4 6–4	Goodbody	W A Larned	4–6 6–1 3–6 7–5 6–2
1895	F H Hovey	R D Wrenn	6–3 6–2 6–4	Hovey	W A Larned	6–1 9–7 6–4
1896	R D Wrenn	F H Hovey	7–5 3–6 6–0 1–6 6–1	Wrenn	W A Larned	4–6 3–6 6–4 6–4 6–3
1897	R D Wrenn	W V Eaves (GB)	4–6 8–6 6–3 2–6 6–2	Eaves	H A Nisbet (GB)	7–5 6–3 6–2
1898	M D Whitman		w.o.	Whitman	D F Davis	3–6 6–2 6–2 6–1
1899	M D Whitman	J P Paret	6–1 6–2 3–6 7–5	Paret	D F Davis	7–5 8–10 6–3 2–6 6–4
1900	M D Whitman	W A Larned	6–4 1–6 6–2 6–2	Larned	G L Wrenn	6–3 6–2 6–2
1901	W A Larned		w.o.	Larned	B C Wright	6–2 6–8 6–4 6–4
1902	W A Larned	R F Doherty (GB)	4–6 6–2 6–4 8–6	R F Doherty	M D Whitman	6–1 3–6 6–3 6–0
1903	H L Doherty (GB)	W A Larned	6–0 6–3 10–8	H L Doherty	W J Clothier	6–3 6–2 6–3
1904	H Ward		w.o.	Ward	W J Clothier	10–8 6–4 9–7
1905	B C Wright	H Ward	6–1 6–2 11–9	Wright	C Hobart	6–4 6–1 6–3
1906	W J Clothier	B C Wright	6–3 6–0 6–4	Clothier	K H Behr	6–2 6–4 6–2
1907	W A Larned		w.o.	Larned	R LeRoy	6–2 6–2 6–4
1908	W A Larned	B C Wright	6–1 6–2 8–6	Wright	F B Alexander	6–3 6–3 6–3
1909	W A Larned	W J Clothier	6–1 6–2 5–7 1–6 6–1	Clothier	M E McLoughlin	7–5 6–4 9–11 6–3
1910	W A Larned	T C Bundy	6–1 5–7 6–0 6–8 6–4	Bundy	B C Wright	6–8 6–3 6–3 10–8
1911	W A Larned	M E McLoughlin	6–4 6–4 6–2	McLoughlin	B C Wright	6–4 4–6 7–5 6–3

Challenge Round abolished.

	FINAL			**SEMI-FINALS**		
1912	M E McLoughlin	W F Johnson	3–6 2–6 6–2 6–4 6–2	McLoughlin	W J Clothier	8–6 6–2 3–6 6–4
				Johnson	K H Behr	4–6 6–0 6–3 6–2
1913	M E McLoughlin	R N Williams	6–4 5–7 6–3 6–1	McLoughlin	W F Johnson	6–0 7–5 6–1
				Williams	N W Niles	6–4 7–5 3–6 6–1
1914	R N Williams	M E McLoughlin	6–3 8–6 10–8	Williams	E F Fottrell	6–4 6–3 6–2
				McLoughlin	W J Clothier	6–4 6–4 6–3

Played at the West Side Club, Forest Hills, NY.

1915	W M Johnston	M E McLoughlin	1–6 6–0 7–5 10–8	Johnston	R N Williams	5–7 6–4 5–7 6–2 6–2
				McLoughlin	T R Pell	6–2 6–0 7–5
1916	R N Williams	W M Johnston	4–6 6–4 0–6 6–2 6–4	Williams	C J Griffin	6–3 6–3 6–3
				Johnston	R L Murray	6–2 6–3 6–1
1917	National Patriotic Tournament without championship status.					
	(R L Murray	N W Niles	5–7 8–6 6–3 6–3	Murray	J R Strachan	4–6 6–3 6–3 6–1
				Niles	R N Williams	6–2 4–6 6–4 6–3)
1918	R L Murray	W T Tilden	6–3 6–1 7–5	Murray	S H Voshell	6–4 6–3 8–6
				Tilden	I Kumagae	6–2 6–2 6–0
1919	W M Johnston	W T Tilden	6–4 6–4 6–3	Johnston	W F Johnson	2–6 6–1 6–3 6–3
				Tilden	R N Williams	6–1 7–5 6–3
1920	W T Tilden	W M Johnston	6–1 1–6 7–5 5–7 6–3	Tilden	W F Johnson	14–12 6–4 6–4
				Johnston	G C Kaner	6–3 4–6 8–6 6–4

Played at the Germantown Cricket Club, Philadelphia.

1921	W T Tilden	W F Johnson	6–1 6–3 6–1	Tilden	W E Davis	10–8 6–2 6–1
				Johnson	J O Anderson (Aus)	6–4 3–6 8–6 6–3
1922	W T Tilden	W M Johnston	4–6 3–6 6–2 6–3 6–4	Tilden	G L Patterson (Aus)	4–6 6–4 6–3 6–1
				Johnston	V Richards	8–6 6–2 6–1
1923	W T Tilden	W M Johnston	6–4 6–1 6–4	Tilden	B I C Norton (SA)	6–3 7–5 6–2
				Johnston	F T Hunter	6–4 6–2 7–5

Played at the West Side Club, Forest Hills, NY.

1924	W T Tilden	W M Johnston	6–1 9–7 6–2	Tilden	V Richards	4–6 6–2 8–6 4–6 6–4
				Johnston	G L Patterson (Aus)	6–2 6–0 6–0
1925	W T Tilden	W M Johnston	4–6 11–9 6–3 4–6 6–3	Tilden	V Richards	6–8 6–4 6–4 6–1
				Johnston	R N Williams	7–5 6–3 6–2
1926	R Lacoste (Fra)	J Borotra (Fra)	6–4 6–0 6–4	Lacoste	H Cochet (Fra)	2–6 4–6 6–4 6–4 6–3
				Borotra	V Richards	3–6 6–4 4–6 8–6 6–2
1927	R Lacoste (Fra)	W T Tilden	11–9 6–3 11–9	Lacoste	W M Johnston	6–2 2–6 6–4 6–1
				Tilden	F T Hunter	14–12 6–1 4–6 9–7
1928	H Cochet (Fra)	F T Hunter	4–6 6–4 3–6 7–5 6–3	Cochet	F X Shields	6–2 8–6 6–4
				Hunter	G M Lott	6–8 6–4 6–3 6–4
1929	W T Tilden	F T Hunter	3–6 6–3 4–6 6–2 6–4	Tilden	J H Doeg	4–6 6–2 2–6 6–4 6–3
				Hunter	F Mercur	6–4 6–8 6–4 6–3
1930	J H Doeg	F X Shields	10–8 1–6 6–4 16–14	Doeg	W T Tilden	10–8 6–3 3–6 12–10
				Shields	S B Wood	6–2 6–3 4–6 6–3

	FINAL			SEMI-FINALS		
Year	Winner	Loser	Score	Winner	Loser	Score
1931	H E Vines	G M Lott	7–9 6–3 9–7 7–5	Vines	F J Perry (GB)	4–6 3–6 6–4 6–4 6–3
				Lott	J H Doeg	7–5 6–3 6–0
1932	H E Vines	H Cochet (Fra)	6–4 6–4 6–4	Vines	C Sutter	4–6 8–10 12–10 10–8 6–1
				Cochet	W L Allison	6–1 10–12 4–6 6–3 7–5
1933	F J Perry (GB)	J H Crawford (Aus)	6–3 11–13 4–6 6–0 6–1	Perry	L R Stoefen	6–3 6–2 6–2
				Crawford	F X Shields	7–5 6–4 6–3
1934	F J Perry (GB)	W L Allison	6–4 6–3 3–6 1–6 8–6	Perry	V G Kirby	6–2 2–6 6–4 6–2
				Allison	S B Wood	8–6 6–2 6–3
1935	W L Allison	S B Wood	6–2 6–2 6–3	Allison	F J Perry (GB)	7–5 6–3 6–3
				Wood	B M Grant	6–2 4–6 12–10 6–2
1936	F J Perry (GB)	J D Budge	2–6 6–2 8–6 1–6 10–8	Perry	B M Grant	6–4 3–6 7–5 6–2
				Budge	F A Parker	6–4 6–3 6–3
1937	J D Budge	G von Cramm (Ger)	6–1 7–9 6–1 3–6 6–1	Budge	F A Parker	6–2 6–1 6–3
				Von Cramm	R L Riggs	0–6 8–6 6–8 6–3 6–2
1938	J D Budge	G Mako	6–3 6–8 6–2 6–1	Budge	S B Wood	6–3 6–3 6–3
				Mako	J E Bromwich (Aus)	6–3 7–5 6–4
1939	R L Riggs	W Van Horn	6–4 6–2 6–4	Riggs	J R Hunt	6–1 6–2 4–6 6–1
				Van Horn	J E Bromwich (Aus)	2–6 4–6 6–2 6–4 8–6
1940	W D McNeill	R L Riggs	8–6 6–8 6–3 7–5	McNeill	J A Kramer	6–1 5–7 6–4 6–3
				Riggs	J R Hunt	4–6 6–3 5–7 6–3 6–4
1941	R L Riggs	F Kovacs	5–7 6–1 6–3 6–3	Riggs	F R Schroeder	6–4 6–4 1–6 9–11 7–5
				Kovacs	W D McNeill	6–4 6–2 10–8
1942	F R Schroeder	F A Parker	8–6 7–5 3–6 4–6 6–2	Schroeder	G Mulloy	9–7 6–3 6–4
				Parker	F Segura	6–1 6–1 2–6 6–2
1943	J R Hunt	J A Kramer	6–3 6–8 10–8 6–0	Hunt	W F Talbert	3–6 6–4 6–2 6–4
				Kramer	F Segura	2–6 6–4 7–5 6–3
1944	F A Parker	W F Talbert	6–4 3–6 6–3 6–3	Parker	W D McNeill	6–4 3–6 6–2 6–2
				Talbert	F Segura	3–6 6–3 6–0 6–8 6–3
1945	F A Parker	W F Talbert	14–12 6–1 6–2	Parker	E T Cooke	6–1 8–6 7–5
				Talbert	F Segura	7–5 6–3 6–4
1946	J A Kramer	T P Brown	9–7 6–3 6–0	Kramer	R Falkenburg	6–0 6–4 6–4
				Brown	G Mulloy	6–4 6–2 6–4
1947	J A Kramer	F A Parker	4–6 2–6 6–1 6–0 6–3	Kramer	J Drobny (Cze)	3–6 6–3 6–0 6–1
				Parker	J E Bromwich (Aus)	6–3 4–6 6–3 6–8 8–6
1948	R A Gonzales	E W Sturgess (SA)	6–2 6–3 14–12	Gonzales	J Drobny (Cze)	8–10 11–9 6–0 6–3
				Sturgess	H Flam	9–7 6–3 6–2
1949	R A Gonzales	F R Schroeder	16–18 2–6 6–1 6–2 6–4	Gonzales	F A Parker	3–6 9–7 6–3 6–2
				Schroeder	W F Talbert	2–6 6–4 4–6 6–4 6–4
1950	A Larsen	H Flam	6–3 4–6 5–7 6–4 6–3	Larsen	R Savitt	6–2 10–8 7–9 6–2
				Flam	G Mulloy	2–6 6–2 9–11 6–1 6–3
1951	F A Sedgman (Aus)	E V Seixas	6–4 6–1 6–1	Sedgman	A Larsen	6–1 6–2 6–0
				Seixas	R Savitt	6–0 3–6 6–3 6–2
1952	F A Sedgman (Aus)	G Mulloy	6–1 6–2 6–3	Sedgman	M G Rose (Aus)	6–3 6–3 6–4
				Mulloy	H Richardson	10–8 6–0 8–6
1953	M A Trabert	E V Seixas	6–3 6–2 6–3	Trabert	K R Rosewall (Aus)	7–5 6–3 6–3
				Seixas	L A Hoad (Aus)	7–5 6–4 6–4
1954	E V Seixas	R N Hartwig (Aus)	3–6 6–2 6–4 6–4	Seixas	H Richardson	6–3 12–14 8–6 6–2
				Hartwig	K E Rosewall (Aus)	6–4 6–3 6–4
1955	M A Trabert	K R Rosewall (Aus)	9–7 6–3 6–3	Trabert	L A Hoad (Aus)	6–4 6–2 6–1
				Rosewall	E V Seixas	6–4 6–4 7–5
1956	K R Rosewall (Aus)	L A Hoad (Aus)	4–6 6–2 6–3	Rosewall	E V Seixas	10–8 6–0 6–3
				Hoad	N A Fraser (Aus)	15–13 6–2 6–4
1957	M J Anderson (Aus)	J R Cooper (Aus)	10–8 7–5 6–4	Anderson	S Davidson (Swe)	5–7 6–2 4–6 6–3 6–4
				Cooper	H Flam	6–1 7–5 6–4
1958	A J Cooper (Aus)	M J Anderson (Aus)	6–2 3–6 4–6 10–8 8–6	Cooper	N A Fraser (Aus)	8–6 8–6 6–1
				Anderson	U Schmidt (Swe)	6–4 7–5 6–2
1959	N A Fraser (Aus)	A Olmedo	6–3 5–7 6–2 6–4	Fraser	B Bartzen	6–3 6–2 6–2
				Olmedo	R Holmberg	15–13 6–4 3–6 6–1
1960	N A Fraser (Aus)	R G Laver (Aus)	6–4 6–4 10–8	Fraser	R D Ralston	11–9 6–3 6–2
				Laver	E Buchholz	4–6 5–7 6–4 6–2 7–5
1961	R S Emerson (Aus)	R G Laver (Aus)	7–5 6–3 6–2	Emerson	R H Osuna (Mex)	6–3 6–2 3–6 5–7 9–7
				Laver	M J Sangster (GB)	13–11 7–5 6–4
1962	R G Laver (Aus)	R S Emerson (Aus)	6–2 6–4 5–7 6–4	Laver	R H Osuna (Mex)	6–1 6–3 6–4
				Emerson	C R McKinley	4–6 6–4 6–3 6–2

	FINAL				SEMI-FINALS		
Year	Winner	Loser	Score		Winner	Loser	Score
1963	R H Osuna (Mex)	F A Froehling	7–5 6–4 6–2		Osuna	C R McKinley	6–4 6–4 10–8
					Froehling	R Barnes (Bra)	6–3 6–1 6–4
1964	R S Emerson (Aus)	F S Stolle (Aus)	6–4 6–1 6–4		Emerson	C R McKinley	7–5 11–9 6–4
					Stolle	R H Osuna (Mex)	6–3 8–6 6–3
1965	M Santana (Spa)	E C Drysdale (SA)	6–2 7–9 7–5 6–1		Santana	A R Ashe	2–6 6–4 6–2 6–4
					Drysdale	R H Osuna (Mex)	6–3 4–6 6–4 6–1
1966	F S Stolle (Aus)	J D Newcombe (Aus)	4–6 12–10 6–3 6–4		Stolle	R S Emerson (Aus)	6–4 6–1 6–1
					Newcombe	M Santana (Spa)	6–3 6–4 6–8 8–6
1967	J D Newcombe (Aus)	C E Graebner	6–4 6–4 8–6		Newcombe	E L Scott	6–4 6–3 6–3
					Graebner	J Leschly (Den)	3–6 3–6 7–5 6–4 7–5

Played at the Longwood Cricket Club, Boston.

	FINAL				SEMI-FINALS		
1968	A R Ashe	R C Lutz	4–6 6–3 8–10 6–0 6–4		Ashe	J McManus	6–4 6–3 14–16 6–3
					Lutz	C E Graebner	6–4 7–5 6–4
1969	S R Smith	R C Lutz	9–7 6–3 6–1		Smith	C Pasarell	2–6 6–2 8–6 13–15 6–4
					Lutz	A R Ashe	6–4 4–6 10–8 6–8 6–4

WOMEN'S SINGLES

Year	Winner	Loser	Score

(The championship was decided on a challenge round basis 1887 to 1918. * indicates the All-Comers' Finals which became the title match in the absence of a defending holder.)

Played at the Philadelphia Cricket Club, Philadelphia.

Year	Winner	Loser	Score
1887	Miss E Hansell	Miss L Knight	6–1 6–0
1888	Miss B L Townsend	Miss M Wright	*6–2 6–2
1889	Miss B L Townsend	Miss L D Vorhees	7–5 6–2
1890	Miss E C Roosevelt	Miss B L Townsend	6–2 6–2
1891	Miss M E Cahill (Ire)	Miss E C Roosevelt	6–4 1–6 6–4
1892	Miss M E Cahill (Ire)	Miss E H Moore	5–7 6–3 6–4 4–6 6–2
1893	Miss A M Terry	Miss A M Schultz	*6–1 6–3
1894	Miss H R Helwig	Miss A M Terry	7–5 3–6 6–0 3–6 6–3
1895	Miss J P Atkinson	Miss H R Helwig	6–4 6–2 6–1
1896	Miss E H Moore	Miss J P Atkinson	6–4 4–6 6–3 6–2
1897	Miss J P Atkinson	Miss E H Moore	6–3 6–3 4–6 3–6 6–3
1898	Miss J P Atkinson	Miss M Jones	6–3 5–7 6–4 2–6 7–5
1899	Miss M Jones	Miss M Banks	*6–1 6–1 7–5
1900	Miss M McAteer	Miss E Parker	*6–2 6–2 6–0
1901	Miss E H Moore	Miss M McAteer	6–4 3–6 7–5 2–6 6–2
1902	Miss M Jones	Miss E H Moore	6–1 1–0 ret'd.
1903	Miss E H Moore	Miss M Jones	7–5 8–6
1904	Miss M G Sutton	Miss E H Moore	6–1 6–2
1905	Miss E H Moore	Miss H Homans	*6–4 5–7 6–1
1906	Miss H Homans	Mrs M Barger-Wallach	*6–4 6–3
1907	Miss E Sears	Miss C B Neely	*6–3 6–2
1908	Mrs M Barger-Wallach	Miss E Sears	6–2 1–6 6–3
1909	Miss H V Hotchkiss	Mrs M Barger-Wallach	6–0 6–1
1910	Miss H V Hotchkiss	Miss L Hammond	6–4 6–2
1911	Miss H V Hotchkiss	Miss F Sutton	8–10 6–1 6–3
1912	Miss M K Browne	Miss E Sears	*6–4 6–2
1913	Miss M K Browne	Miss D Green	6–2 7–5
1914	Miss M K Browne	Miss M Wagner	6–2 1–6 6–1
1915	Miss M Bjurstedt	Mrs G W Wightman	*4–6 6–2 6–0
1916	Miss M Bjurstedt	Mrs E Raymond	6–0 6–1
1917	National Patriotic Tournament without championship status		
	(Miss M Bjurstedt	Miss M Vanderhoef	4–6 6–0 6–2)
1918	Miss M Bjurstedt	Miss E E Goss	6–4 6–3

Challenge Round abolished.

1919	Mrs G W Wightman	Miss M Zinderstein	6–1 6–2
1920	Mrs F I Mallory	Miss M Zinderstein	6–3 6–1

Played at the West Side Club, Forest Hills, NY.

1921	Mrs F I Mallory	Miss M K Browne	4–6 6–4 6–2

Year	Winner	Loser	Score
1922	Mrs F I Mallory	Miss H N Wills	6–3 6–1
1923	Miss H N Wills	Mrs F I Mallory	6–2 6–1
1924	Miss H N Wills	Mrs F I Mallory	6–1 6–3
1925	Miss H N Wills	Miss K McKane (GB)	3–6 6–0 6–2
1926	Mrs F I Mallory	Miss E Ryan	4–6 6–4 9–7
1927	Miss H N Wills	Miss B Nuthall (GB)	6–1 6–4
1928	Miss H N Wills	Miss H H Jacobs	6–2 6–1
1929	Miss H N Wills	Mrs P H Watson (GB)	6–4 6–2
1930	Miss B Nuthall (GB)	Mrs L A Harper	6–4 6–1
1931	Mrs F S Moody	Mrs E F Whittingstall (GB)	6–4 6–1
1932	Miss H H Jacobs	Miss C A Babcock	6–2 6–2
1933	Miss H H Jacobs	Mrs F S Moody	8–6 3–6 3–0 ret'd.
1934	Miss H H Jacobs	Miss S Palfrey	6–1 6–4
1935	Miss H H Jacobs	Mrs M Fabyan	6–2 6–4
1936	Miss A Marble	Miss H H Jacobs	4–6 6–3 6–2
1937	Sta A Lizana (Chi)	Miss J Jedrzejowska (Pol)	6–4 6–2
1938	Miss A Marble	Miss N Wynne (Aus)	6–0 6–3
1939	Miss A Marble	Miss H H Jacobs	6–0 8–10 6–4
1940	Miss A Marble	Miss H H Jacobs	6–2 6–3
1941	Mrs E T Cooke	Miss P M Betz	7–5 6–2
1942	Miss P M Betz	Miss A L Brough	4–6 6–1 6–4
1943	Miss P M Betz	Miss A L Brough	6–3 5–7 6–3
1944	Miss P M Betz	Miss M E Osborne	6–3 8–6
1945	Mrs E T Cooke	Mss P M Betz	3–6 8–6 6–4
1946	Miss P M Betz	Miss D J Hart	11–9 6–3
1947	Miss A L Brough	Miss M E Osborne	8–6 4–6 6–1
1948	Mrs W du Pont	Miss A L Brough	4–6 6–4 15–13
1949	Mrs W du Pont	Miss D J Hart	6–4 6–1
1950	Mrs W du Pont	Miss D J Hart	6–3 6–3
1951	Miss M C Connolly	Miss S J Fry	6–3 1–6 6–4
1952	Miss M C Connolly	Miss D J Hart	6–3 7–5
1953	Miss M C Connolly	Miss D J Hart	6–2 6–4
1954	Miss D J Hart	Miss A L Brough	6–8 6–1 8–6
1955	Miss D J Hart	Miss P E Ward (GB)	6–4 6–2
1956	Miss S J Fry	Miss A Gibson	6–3 6–4
1957	Miss A Gibson	Miss A L Brough	6–3 6–2
1958	Miss A Gibson	Miss D R Hard	3–6 6–1 6–2
1959	Miss M E Bueno (Bra)	Miss C C Truman (GB)	6–1 6–4
1960	Miss D R Hard	Miss M E Bueno (Bra)	6–4 10–12 6–4
1961	Miss D R Hard	Miss A S Haydon (GB)	6–3 6–4
1962	Miss M Smith (Aus)	Miss D R Hard	9–7 6–4
1963	Miss M E Bueno (Bra)	Miss M Smith (Aus)	7–5 6–4
1964	Miss M E Bueno (Bra)	Mrs C E Graebner	6–1 6–0
1965	Miss M Smith (Aus)	Miss B J Moffitt	8–6 7–5
1966	Miss M E Bueno (Bra)	Miss N Richey	6–3 6–1
1967	Mrs L W King	Mrs P F Jones (GB)	11–9 6–4

Played at the Longwood Cricket Club, Boston.

Year	Winner	Loser	Score
1968	Mrs B M Court (Aus)	Miss M E Bueno (Bra)	6–2 6–2
1969	Mrs B M Court (Aus)	Miss S V Wade (GB)	4–6 6–3 6–0

MEN'S DOUBLES

Year	Winners	Finalists	Score

(* indicates All Comer's final, holders not defending.)

Played at the Newport Casino, Rhode Island.

Year	Winners	Finalists	Score
1881	C M Clark & F W Taylor	A Van Rennselaer & A E Newbold	6–5 6–4 6–5
1882	J Dwight & R D Sears	W Nightingale & G M Shields	6–2 6–4 6–4
1883	J Dwight & R D Sears	A Van Rennselaer & A E Newbold	6–0 6–2 6–2
1884	J Dwight & R D Sears	A Van Rennselaer & W V R Berry	6–4 6–1 8–10 6–4
1885	J S Clark & R D Sears	W P Knapp & H W Slocum	6–3 6–0 6–2
1886	J Dwight & R D Sears	G M Brinley & H A Taylor	7–5 5–7 7–5 6–4

Year Winners	Finalists	Score
Played at the Orange LTC, New Jersey.		
1887 J Dwight & R D Sears	H W Slocum & H A Taylor	6–4 3–6 2–6 6–3 6–3
Played at the Staten Island Cricket Club, NY.		
1888 O S Campbell & V G Hall	C Hobart & E P MacMullen	6–4 6–2 6–4
1889 H W Slocum & H A Taylor	O S Campbell & V G Hall	6–1 6–3 6–2
Played at the Newport Casino, Rhode Island.		
1890 V G Hall & C Hobart	C W Carver & J A Ryerson	6–3 4–6 6–2 2–6 6–3
Challenge Round instituted		
1891 O S Campbell & R P Huntington	V G Hall & C Hobart	6–3 6–4 8–6
1892 O S Campbell & R P Huntington	V G Hall & E L Hall	6–4 6–2 4–6 6–3
Played at the St George Club, Chicago.		
1893 C Hobart & F H Hovey	O S Campbell & R P Huntington	6–3 6–4 4–6 6–2
Played at the Newport Casino, Rhode Island.		
1894 C Hobart & F H Hovey	C B Neel & S R Neel	6–3 8–6 6–1
1895 M G Chase & R D Wrenn	C Hobart & F H Hovey	7–5 6–1 8–6
1896 C B Neel & S R Neel	M G Chase & R D Wrenn	6–3 1–6 6–1 3–6 6–1
1897 L E Ware & P Sheldon	H S Mahony (GB) & H A Nisbet (GB)	*11–13 6–2 9–7 1–6 6–1
1898 L E Ware & P Sheldon	D F Davis & H Ward	1–6 7–5 6–4 4–6 7–5
1899 D F Davis & H Ward	L E Ware & P Sheldon	6–4 6–4 6–3
1900 D F Davis & H Ward	F B Alexander & R D Little	6–4 9–7 12–10
1901 D F Davis & H Ward	L E Ware & B C Wright	6–3 9–7 6–1
1902 H L Doherty (GB) & R F Doherty (GB)	D F Davis & H Ward	11–9 12–10 6–4
1903 H L Doherty (GB) & R F Doherty (GB)	L Collins & L H Waldner	7–5 6–3 6–3
1904 H Ward & B C Wright	K Collins & R D Little	*1–6 6–2 3–6 6–4 6–1
1905 H Ward & B C Wright	F B Alexander & H H Hackett	6–3 6–1 6–2
1906 H Ward & B C Wright	F B Alexander & H H Hackett	6–3 3–6 6–3 6–3
1907 F B Alexander & B C Wright	W J Clothier & W A Larned	*6–3 6–1 6–4
1908 F B Alexander & H H Hackett	R D Little & B C Wright	6–1 7–5 6–2
1909 F B Alexander & H H Hackett	G J James & M E McLoughlin	6–4 6–1 6–0
1910 F B Alexander & H H Hackett	T C Bundy & T W Hendrick	6–1 8–6 6–3
1911 R D Little & G F Touchard	F B Alexander & H H Hackett	7–5 13–15 6–2 6–4
1912 T C Bundy & M E McLoughlin	R D Little & G F Touchard	3–6 6–2 6–1 7–5
1913 T C Bundy & M E McLoughlin	C J Griffin & J R Strachan	6–4 7–5 6–1
1914 T C Bundy & M E McLoughlin	G M Church & D Mathey	6–4 6–2 6–4
Played at the West Side Club, Forest Hills, NY.		
1915 C J Griffin & W M Johnston	T C Bundy & M E McLoughlin	6–2 3–6 4–6 6–3 6–3
1916 C J Griffin & W M Johnston	W Dawson & M E McLoughlin	6–4 6–3 5–7 6–3
1917 National Patriotic tournament without championship status.		
(F B Alexander & H A Throckmorton	H C Johnson & I C Wright	11–9 6–4 6–4)
Challenge Round abolished.		
1918 V Richards & W T Tilden	F B Alexander & B C Wright	6–3 6–4 3–6 2–6 6–2
Played at the Longwood Cricket Club, Boston.		
Challenge Round restored.		
1919 N E Brookes (Aus) & G L Patterson (Aus)	V Richards & W T Tilden	8–6 6–3 4–6 6–2
Challenge Round abolished.		
1920 C J Griffin & W M Johnston	W E Davis & R Roberts	6–2 6–2 6–3
1921 V Richards & W T Tilden	W M Washburn & R N Williams	13–11 12–10 6–1
1922 V Richards & W T Tilden	P O'Hara Wood (Aus) & G L Patterson (Aus)	4–6 6–3 6–4
1923 B I C Norton (SA) & W T Tilden	W M Washburn & R N Williams	3–6 6–2 6–3 5–7 6–2
1924 H Kinsey & R Kinsey	P O'Hara Wood (Aus) & G L Patterson (Aus)	7–5 5–7 7–9 6–3 6–4
1925 V Richards & R N Williams	J B Hawkes (Aus) & G L Patterson (Aus)	6–2 8–10 6–4 11–9
1926 V Richards & R N Williams	A H Chapin & W T Tilden	6–4 6–8 11–9 6–3
1927 F T Hunter & W T Tilden	W M Johnston & R N Williams	10–8 6–3 6–3
1928 J F Hennessey & G M Lott	J B Hawkes (Aus) & G L Patterson (Aus)	6–2 6–1 6–2
1929 J H Doeg & G M Lott	B Bell & L N White	10–8 16–14 6–1
1930 J H Doeg & G M Lott	W L Allison & J Van Ryn	8–6 6–3 4–6 13–15 6–4
1931 W L Allison & J Van Ryn	B Bell & G S Mangin	6–4 8–6 6–3
1932 K Gledhill & H E Vines	W L Allison & J Van Ryn	6–4 6–3 6–2
1933 G M Lott & L R Stoefen	F A Parker & F X Shields	11–13 9–7 9–7 6–3

Year	Winners	Finalists	Score

Played at the Germantown Cricket Club, Philadelphia.
| 1934 | G M Lott & L R Stoefen | W L Allison & J Van Ryn | 6–4 9–7 3–6 6–4 |

Played at the Longwood Cricket Club, Boston.
1935	W L Allison & J Van Ryn	J D Budge & G Mako	6–4 6–2 3–6 2–6 6–1
1936	J D Budge & G Mako	W L Allison & J Van Ryn	6–4 6–2 6–4
1937	G Von Cramm (Ger) & H Henkel (Ger)	J D Budge & G Mako	6–4 7–5 6–4
1938	J D Budge & G Mako	J E Bromwich (Aus) & A K Quist (Aus)	6–3 6–2 6–1
1939	J E Bromwich (Aus) & A K Quist (Aus)	J H Crawford (Aus) & H C Hopman (Aus)	8–6 6–1 6–4
1940	J A Kramer & F R Schroeder	G Mulloy & H J Prussoff	6–4 8–6 9–7
1941	J A Kramer & F R Schroeder	G Mulloy & W Sabin	9–7 6–4 6–2

Played at the West Side Club, Forest Hills, NY.
1942	G Mulloy & W F Talbert	F R Schroeder & S B Wood	9–7 7–5 6–1
1943	J A Kramer & F A Parker	D Freeman & W F Talbert	6–2 6–4 6–4
1944	R Falkenburg & W D McNeill	F Segura & W F Talbert	7–5 6–4 3–6 6–1
1945	G Mulloy & W F Talbert	R Falkenburg & J Tuero	12–10 8–10 12–10 6–2

Played at the Longwood Cricket Club, Boston.
1946	G Mulloy & W F Talbert	F Guernsey & W D McNeill	3–6 6–4 2–6 6–3 20–18
1947	J A Kramer & F R Schroeder	O W Sidwell (Aus) & W F Talbert	6–4 7–5 6–3
1948	G Mulloy & W F Talbert	F A Parker & F R Schroeder	1–6 9–7 6–3 3–6 9–7
1949	J E Bromwich (Aus) & O W Sidwell (Aus)	F A Sedgman (Aus) & G A Worthington (Aus)	6–4 6–0 6–1
1950	J E Bromwich (Aus) & F A Sedgman (Aus)	G Mulloy & W F Talbert	7–5 8–6 3–6 6–1
1951	K McGregor (Aus) & F A Sedgman (Aus)	D W Candy (Aus) & M G Rose (Aus)	10–8 6–4 4–6 7–5
1952	M G Rose (Aus) & E V Seixas	K McGregor (Aus) & F A Sedgman (Aus)	3–6 10–8 10–8 6–8 8–6
1953	R N Hartwig (Aus) & M G Rose (Aus)	G Mulloy & W F Talbert	6–4 4–6 6–2 6–4
1954	E V Seixas & M A Trabert	L A Hoad (Aus) & K R Rosewall (Aus)	3–6 6–4 8–6 6–3
1955	K Kano (Jap) & A Miyagi (Jap)	G Moss & W Quillian	6–2 6–3 3–6 1–6 6–4
1956	L A Hoad (Aus) & K R Rosewall (Aus)	H Richardson & E V Seixas	6–2 6–2 3–6 6–4
1957	A J Cooper (Aus) & N A Fraser (Aus)	G Mulloy & J E Patty	4–6 6–3 9–7 6–3
1958	A Olmedo & H Richardson	S Giammalva & B MacKay	6–4 3–6 6–3 6–4
1959	R S Emerson (Aus) & N A Fraser (Aus)	E Buchholz & A Olmedo	3–6 6–3 5–7 6–4 7–5
1960	R S Emerson (Aus) & N A Fraser (Aus)	R G Laver (Aus) & R Mark (Aus)	9–7 6–2 6–4
1961	C R McKinley & R D Ralston	R H Osuna (Mex) & A Palafox (Mex)	6–3 6–4 2–6 13–11
1962	R H Osuna (Mex) & A Palafox (Mex)	C R McKinley & R D Ralston	6–4 10–12 1–6 9–7 6–3
1963	C R McKinley & R D Ralston	R H Osuna (Mex) & A Palafox (Mex)	9–7 4–6 5–7 6–3 11–9
1964	C R McKinley & R D Ralston	M J Sangster (GB) & G R Stilwell (GB)	6–3 6–2 6–4
1965	R S Emerson (Aus) & F S Stolle (Aus)	F A Froehling & C M Pasarell	6–4 10–12 7–5 6–3
1966	R S Emerson (Aus) & F S Stolle (Aus)	C E Graebner & R D Ralston	6–4 6–4 6–4
1967	J D Newcombe (Aus) & A D Roche (Aus)	W W Bowrey (Aus) & O K Davidson (Aus)	6–8 9–7 6–3 6–3
1968	R C Lutz & S R Smith	R A J Hewitt (SA) & R J Moore (SA)	6–4 6–4 9–7
1969	R D Crealy (Aus) & A J Stone (Aus)	W W Bowrey (Aus) & C M Pasarell	9–11 6–3 7–5

WOMEN'S DOUBLES

Year	Winners	Losers	Score

Played at the Philadelphia Cricket Club, Philadelphia.
1890	Miss E C Roosevelt & Miss G W Roosevelt	Miss B L Townsend & Miss M Ballard	6–1 6–2
1891	Miss M E Cahill (Ire) & Mrs W F Morgan	Miss E C Roosevelt & Miss G W Roosevelt	2–6 8–6 6–4
1892	Miss M E Cahill (Ire) & Miss A M McKinley	Miss A H Harris & Miss A R Williams	6–1 6–3
1893	Miss H Butler & Miss A M Terry	Miss A L Schultz & Miss Stone	6–4 6–3
1894	Miss J P Atkinson & Miss H R Helwig	Miss A R Williams & Miss A C Wistar	6–4 7–5
1895	Miss J P Atkinson & Miss H R Helwig	Miss E H Moore & Miss A R Williams	6–2 6–2 12–10
1896	Miss J P Atkinson & Miss E H Moore	Miss A R Williams & Miss A C Wistar	6–4 7–5
1897	Miss J P Atkinson & Miss K Atkinson	Mrs F Edwards & Miss E J Rastall	6–2 6–1 6–1
1898	Miss J P Atkinson & Miss K Atkinson	Miss C B Neely & Miss M Weimer	6–1 2–6 4–6 6–1 6–2
1899	Miss J W Craven & Miss M McAteer	Miss M Banks & Miss E J Rastall	6–1 6–1 7–5
1900	Miss H Champlin & Miss E Parker	Miss M McAteer & Miss M Weimer	9–7 6–2 6–2
1901	Miss J P Atkinson & Miss M McAteer	Miss M Jones & Miss E H Moore	w.o.
1902	Miss J P Atkinson & Miss M Jones	Miss M Banks & Miss N Closterman	6–2 7–5
1903	Miss E H Moore & Miss C B Neely	Miss M Jones & Miss M Hall	6–4 6–1 6–1
1904	Miss M Hall & Miss M G Sutton	Miss E H Moore & Miss C B Neely	3–6 6–3 6–3
1905	Miss H Homans & Miss C B Neely	Miss V Maule & Miss M F Oberteuffer	6–0 6–1
1906	Mrs L S Coe & Mrs D S Platt	Miss C Boldt & Miss H Homans	6–4 6–4

Year	Winners	Losers	Score
1907	Miss C B Neely & Miss M Weimer	Miss E Wildey & Miss N Wildey	6–1 2–6 6–4
1908	Miss M Curtis & Miss E Sears	Miss C B Neely & Miss M Steever	6–3 5–7 9–7
1909	Miss H V Hotchkiss & Miss E E Rotch	Miss D Green & Miss L Moyes	6–1 6–1
1910	Miss H V Hotchkiss & Miss E E Rotch	Miss A Browning & Miss E Wildey	6–4 6–4
1911	Miss H V Hotchkiss & Miss E Sears	Miss D Green & Miss F Sutton	6–4 4–6 6–2
1912	Miss M K Browne & Miss D Green	Mrs M Barger-Wallach & Mrs F. Schmitz	6–2 5–7 6–0
1913	Miss M K Browne & Mrs R H Williams	Miss D Green & Miss E Wildey	12–10 2–6 6–3
1914	Miss M K Browne & Mrs R H Williams	Mrs E Raymond & Miss E Wildey	8–6 6–2
1915	Miss E Sears & Mrs G W Wightman	Mrs G L Chapman & Mrs M McLean	10–8 6–2
1916	Miss M Bjurstedt & Miss E Sears	Mrs E Raymond & Miss E Wildey	4–6 6–2 10–8
1917	National Patriotic Tournament without championship status		
	(Miss M Bjurstedt & Miss E Sears	Mrs R LeRoy & Miss P Walsh	6–2 6–4)
1918	Miss E E Goss & Miss M Zinderstein	Miss M Bjurstedt & Mrs J Rogge	7–5 8–6
1919	Miss E E Goss & Miss M Zinderstein	Miss E Sears & Mrs G W Wightman	9–7 9–7
1920	Miss E E Goss & Miss M Zinderstein	Miss H Baker & Miss E Tennant	13–11 4–6 6–3

Played at the West Side Club, Forest Hills, NY.

Year	Winners	Losers	Score
1921	Miss M K Browne & Mrs L Williams	Miss H Gilleaudeau & Mrs L G Morris	6–3 6–2
1922	Mrs J B Jessup & Miss H N Wills	Mrs F I Mallory & Miss E Sigourney	6–4 7–9 6–3
1923	Mrs B C Covell (GB) & Miss K McKane (GB)	Miss E E Goss & Mrs G W Wightman	2–6 6–2 6–1
1924	Mrs G W Wightman & Miss H N Wills	Miss E E Goss & Mrs J B Jessup	6–4 6–3
1925	Miss M K Browne & Miss H N Wills	Mrs T C Bundy & Miss E Ryan	6–4 6–3
1926	Miss E E Goss & Miss E Ryan	Miss M K Browne & Mrs A H Chapin	3–6 6–4 12–10
1927	Mrs L A Godfree (GB) & Miss E H Harvey (GB)	Miss J Fry (GB) & Miss B Nuthall (GB)	6–1 4–6 6–4
1928	Mrs G W Wightman & Miss H N Wills	Miss E Cross & Mrs L A Harper	6–2 6–2
1929	Mrs L R C Michell (GB) & Mrs P H Watson (GB)	Mrs B C Covell (GB) & Mrs D C Shepherd-Barron (GB)	2–6 6–3 6–4
1930	Miss B Nuthall (GB) & Miss S Palfrey	Miss E Cross & Mrs L A Harper	3–6 6–3 7–5
1931	Miss B Nuthall (GB) & Mrs E F Whittingstall (GB)	Miss H H Jacobs & Miss D E Round (GB)	6–2 6–4
1932	Miss H H Jacobs & Miss S Palfrey	Miss A Marble & Mrs M Painter	8–6 6–1
1933	Miss F James (GB) & Miss B Nuthall (GB)	Mrs F S Moody & Miss E Ryan	w.o.
1934	Miss H H Jacobs & Miss S Palfrey	Mrs D B Andrus & Miss C A Babcock	4–6 6–3 6–4

Played at the Longwood Cricket Club, Boston.

Year	Winners	Losers	Score
1935	Miss H H Jacobs & Mrs M Fabyan	Mrs D B Andrus & Miss C A Babcock	6–4 6–2
1936	Miss C A Babcock & Mrs J Van Ryn	Miss H H Jacobs & Mrs M Fabyan	9–7 2–6 6–4
1937	Mrs M Fabyan & Miss A Marble	Miss C A Babcock & Mrs J Van Ryn	7–5 6–4
1938	Mrs M Fabyan & Miss A Marble	Miss J Jedrzejowska (Pol) & Mme R Mathieu (Fra)	6–8 6–4 6–3
1939	Mrs M Fabyan & Miss A Marble	Mrs S H Hammersley (GB) & Miss K E Stammers (GB)	7–5 8–6
1940	Mrs M Fabyan & Miss A Marble	Miss D M Bundy & Mrs J Van Ryn	6–4 6–3
1941	Mrs E T Cooke & Miss M E Osborne	Miss D M Bundy & Miss D J Hart	3–6 6–1 6–4

Played at the West Side Club, Forest Hills, NY.

Year	Winners	Losers	Score
1942	Miss A L Brough & Miss M E Osborne	Miss P M Betz & Miss D J Hart	9–7 6–2 6–1
1943	Miss A L Brough & Miss M E Osborne	Miss P M Betz & Miss D J Hart	6–4 6–3
1944	Miss A L Brough & Miss M E Osborne	Miss P M Betz & Miss D J Hart	4–6 6–4 6–3
1945	Miss A L Brough & Miss M E Osborne	Miss P M Betz & Miss D J Hart	6–4 6–4

Played at the Longwood Cricket Club, Boston.

Year	Winners	Losers	Score
1946	Miss A L Brough & Miss M E Osborne	Mrs D Arnold-Prentiss & Mrs P C Todd	6–2 6–0
1947	Miss A L Brough & Miss M E Osborne	Miss D J Hart & Mrs P C Todd	5–7 6–3 7–5
1948	Miss A L Brough & Mrs W du Pont	Miss D J Hart & Mrs P C Todd	6–4 8–10 6–1
1949	Miss A L Brough & Mrs W du Pont	Miss D J Hart & Miss S J Fry	6–4 8–6
1950	Miss A L Brough & Mrs W du Pont	Miss D J Hart & Miss S J Fry	6–2 6–2
1951	Miss D J Hart & Miss S J Fry	Miss N Chaffee & Mrs P C Todd	6–4 6–2
1952	Miss D J Hart & Miss S J Fry	Miss A L Brough & Miss M C Connolly	10–8 6–4
1953	Miss D J Hart & Miss S J Fry	Miss A L Brough & Mrs W du Pont	6–3 7–9 9–7
1954	Miss D J Hart & Miss S J Fry	Miss A L Brough & Mrs W du Pont	6–4 6–4
1955	Miss A L Brough & Mrs W du Pont	Miss D J Hart & Miss S J Fry	6–3 1–6 6–3
1956	Miss A L Brough & Mrs W du Pont	Miss S J Fry & Mrs B Pratt	6–3 6–0
1957	Miss A L Brough & Mrs W du Pont	Miss A Gibson & Miss D R Hard	6–2 7–5
1958	Miss J Arth & Miss D R Hard	Miss M E Bueno (Bra) & Miss A Gibson	2–6 6–3 6–4
1959	Miss J Arth & Miss D R Hard	Miss M E Bueno (Bra) & Miss S H Moore	6–2 6–3
1960	Miss M E Bueno (Bra) & Miss D R Hard	Miss D M Catt (GB) & Miss A S Haydon (GB)	6–1 6–1
1961	Miss D R Hard & Miss L R Turner (Aus)	Frl E Buding (FRG) & Miss Y Ramirez (Mex)	6–4 5–7 6–0
1962	Miss M E Bueno (Bra) & Miss D R Hard	Miss B J Moffitt & Mrs J R Susman	4–6 6–3 6–2
1963	Miss R A Ebbern (Aus) & Miss M Smith (Aus)	Miss M E Bueno (Bra) & Miss D R Hard	4–6 10–8 6–3
1964	Miss B J Moffitt & Mrs J R Susman	Miss M Smith (Aus) & Miss L R Turner (Aus)	3–6 6–2 6–4
1965	Mrs C E Graebner & Miss N Richey	Miss B J Moffitt & Mrs J R Susman	6–4 6–4

Year	Winners	Losers	Score
1966	Mis M E Bueno (Bra) & Miss N Richey	Miss R Casals & Mrs L W King	6–3 6–4
1967	Miss R Casals & Mrs L W King	Miss M A Eisel & Mrs D Fales	4–6 6–3 6–4
1968	Miss M E Bueno (Bra) & Mrs B M Court (Aus)	Miss S V Wade (GB) & Mrs G M Williams (GB)	6–3 7–5
1969	Mrs B M Court (Aus) & Miss S V Wade (GB)	Mrs P W Curtis & Miss V Ziegenfuss	6–1 6–3

MIXED DOUBLES

Year	Winners	Finalists	Score
Played at the Philadelphia Cricket Club, Philadelphia.			
1887*	J S Clark & Miss V Stokes	not known	not known
1888*	J S Clark & Miss M Wright	P Johnson & Miss A Robinson	1–6 6–5 6–4 6–3
1889*	J S Clark & Miss M Wright	not known	not known
1890*	R Beach & Miss M E Cahill (Ire)	not known	not known
1891*	M R Wright & Miss M E Cahill (Ire)	C T Lee & Miss G W Roosevelt	6–4 6–0 7–5
* not recognised as an official championship.			
1892	C Hobart & Miss M E Cahill (Ire)	R Beach & Miss E H Moore	6–1 6–3
1893	C Hobart & Miss E C Roosevelt	R N Wilson & Miss Bankson	6–1 4–6 10–8 6–1
1894	E P Fischer & Miss J P Atkinson	A Remak & Mrs McFaddon	6–2 6–2 6–1
1895	E P Fischer & Miss J P Atkinson	M Fielding & Miss A R Williams	4–6 6–1 6–2
1896	E P Fischer & Miss J P Atkinson	M Fielding & Miss A R Williams	6–2 6–3 6–3
1897	D L Magruder & Miss L Henson	R A Griffin & Miss M Banks	6–4 6–3 7–5
1898	E P Fischer & Miss C B Neely	J A Hill & Miss H Chapman	not known
1899	A L Hoskins & Miss E J Rastall	J P Gardner & Miss J W Craven	6–4 6–0 ret'd
1900	A Codman & Miss M J Hunnewell	G Atkinson & Miss T Shaw	11–9 6–3 6–1
1901	R D Little & Miss M Jones	C Stevens & Miss M McAteer	6–4 6–4 7–5
1902	W C Grant & Miss E H Moore	A L Hoskins & Miss E J Rastall	6–2 6–1
1903	H F Allen & Miss H Chapman	W H Rowland & Miss C B Neely	6–4 7–5
1904	W C Grant & Miss E H Moore	F B Dallas & Miss M Sutton	6–2 6–1
1905	C Hobart & Mrs Hobart	E B Dewhurst & Miss E H Moore	6–2 6–4
1906	E B Dewhurst & Miss S Coffin	J B Johnson & Miss M Johnson	6–3 7–5
1907	W F Johnson & Miss M Sayres	H M Tilden & Miss N Wildey	6–1 7–5
1908	N W Niles & Miss E E Rotch	R D Little & Miss L Hammond	6–4 4–6 6–4
1909	W F Johnson & Miss H V Hotchkiss	R D Little & Miss L Hammond	6–2 6–0
1910	J R Carpenter & Miss H V Hotchkiss	H M Tilden & Miss E Wildey	6–2 6–2
1911	W F Johnson & Miss H V Hotchkiss	H M Tilden & Miss E Wildey	6–4 6–4
1912	R N Williams & Miss M K Browne	W J Clothier & Miss E Sears	6–4 2–6 11–9
1913	W T Tilden & Miss M K Browne	C S Rogers & Miss D Green	7–5 7–5
1914	W T Tilden & Miss M K Browne	J R Rowland & Miss M Myers	6–1 6–4
1915	H C Johnson & Mrs G W Wightman	I C Wright & Miss M Bjurstedt	6–0 6–1
1916	W E Davis & Miss E Sears	W T Tilden & Miss F A Ballin	6–4 7–5
1917	National Patriotic Tournament without championship status		
	(I C Wright & Miss M Bjurstedt)	W T Tilden & Miss F A Ballin	10–12 6–1 6–3)
1918	I C Wright & Mrs G W Wightman	F B Alexander & Miss M Bjurstedt	6–2 6–4
1919	V Richards & Miss M Zinderstein	W T Tilden & Miss F A Ballin	2–6 11–9 6–1
1920	W F Johnson & Mrs G W Wightman	C Biddle & Mrs F I Mallory	6–4 6–3
Played at the Longwood Cricket Club, Boston.			
1921	W M Johnston & Miss M K Browne	W T Tilden & Miss F I Mallory	3–6 6–4 6–3
1922	W T Tilden & Mrs F I Mallory	H Kinsey & Miss H N Wills	6–4 6–3
1923	W T Tilden & Mrs F I Mallory	J B Hawkes (Aus) & Miss K McKane (GB)	6–3 2–6 10–8
1924	V Richards & Miss H N Wills	W T Tilden & Mrs F I Mallory	6–8 7–5 6–0
1925	J B Hawkes (Aus) & Miss K McKane (GB)	V Richards & Miss E H Harvey (GB)	6–2 6–4
1926	J Borotra (Fra) & Miss E Ryan	R Lacoste (Fra) & Mrs G W Wightman	6–4 7–5
1927	H Cochet (Fra) & Miss E Bennett (GB)	R Lacoste (Fra) & Mrs G W Wightman	2–6 6–0 6–2
1928	J B Hawkes (Aus) & Miss H N Wills	E F Moon (Aus) & Miss E Cross	6–1 6–3
1929	G M Lott & Miss B Nuthall (GB)	H W Austin (GB) & Mrs B C Covell (GB)	6–3 6–3
1930	W L Allison & Miss E Cross	F X Shields & Miss M Morrill	6–4 6–4
1931	G M Lott & Miss B Nuthall (GB)	W L Allison & Mrs L A Harper	6–3 6–3
1932	F J Perry (GB) & Miss S Palfrey	H E Vines & Miss H H Jacobs	6–3 7–5
1933	H E Vines & Miss E Ryan	G M Lott & Miss S Palfrey	11–9 6–1
Played at the Germantown Cricket Club, Philadelphia.			
1934	G M Lott & Miss H H Jacobs	L R Stoefen & Miss E Ryan	4–6 13–11 6–2

Year	Winners	Finalists	Score
Played at the Longwood Cricket Club, Boston.			
1935	E Maier (Spa) & Mrs M Fabyan	R Menzel (Cze) & Miss K E Stammers (GB)	6–3 3–6 6–4
1936	G Mako & Miss A Marble	J D Budge & Mrs M Fabyan	6–3 6–2
1937	J D Budge & Mrs M Fabyan	Y Petra (Fra) & Mme S Henrotin (Fra)	6–2 8–10 6–0
1938	J D Budge & Miss A Marble	J E Bromwich (Aus) & Miss T Coyne (Aus)	6–1 6–2
1939	H C Hopman (Aus) & Miss A Marble	E T Cooke & Mrs M Fabyan	9–7 6–1
1940	R L Riggs & Miss A Marble	J A Kramer & Miss D M Bundy	9–7 6–1
1941	J A Kramer & Mrs E T Cooke	R L Riggs & Miss P M Betz	4–6 6–4 6–4
Played at the West Side Club, Forest Hills, NY.			
1942	F R Schroeder & Miss A L Brough	A D Russell (Arg) & Mrs P C Todd	3–6 6–1 6–4
1943	W F Talbert & Miss M E Osborne	F Segura & Miss P M Betz	10–8 6–4
1944	W F Talbert & Miss M E Osborne	W D McNeill & Miss D M Bundy	6–2 6–3
1945	W F Talbert & Miss M E Osborne	R Falkenburg & Miss D J Hart	6–4 6–4
1946	W F Talbert & Miss M E Osborne	R Kimbell & Miss A L Brough	6–3 6–4
1947	J E Bromwich (Aus) & Miss A L Brough	F Segura & Miss G Moran	6–3 6–1
1948	T P Brown & Miss A L Brough	W F Talbert & Mrs W du Pont	6–4 6–4
1949	E W Sturgess (SA) & Miss A L Brough	W F Talbert & Mrs W du Pont	4–6 6–3 7–5
1950	K McGregor (Aus) & Mrs W du Pont	F A Sedgman (Aus) & Miss D J Hart	6–4 3–6 6–3
1951	F A Sedgman (Aus) & Miss D J Hart	M G Rose (Aus) & Miss S J Fry	6–3 6–2
1952	F A Sedgman (Aus) & Miss D J Hart	L A Hoad (Aus) & Mrs T D Long (Aus)	6–3 7–5
1953	E V Seixas & Miss D J Hart	R N Hartwig (Aus) & Miss J Sampson	6–2 4–6 6–4
1954	E V Seixas & Miss D J Hart	K R Rosewall (Aus) & Mrs W du Pont	4–6 6–1 6–1
1955	E V Seixas & Miss D J Hart	G Mulloy & Miss D J Fry	7–5 5–7 6–2
1956	K R Rosewall (Aus) & Mrs W du Pont	L A Hoad (Aus) & Miss D R Hard	9–7 6–1
1957	K Nielsen (Den) & Miss A Gibson	R N Howe (Aus) & Miss D R Hard	6–3 9–7
1958	N A Fraser (Aus) & Mrs W du Pont	A Olmedo & Miss M E Bueno (Bra)	6–4 3–6 9–7
1959	N A Fraser (Aus) & Mrs W du Pont	R Mark (Aus) & Miss J S Hopps	7–5 13–15 6–2
1960	N A Fraser (Aus) & Mrs W du Pont	A Palafox (Mex) & Miss M E Bueno (Bra)	6–3 6–2
1961	R Mark (Aus) & Miss M Smith (Aus)	R D Ralston & Miss D R Hard	w.o.
1962	F S Stolle (Aus) & Miss M Smith (Aus)	F A Froehling & Miss L R Turner (Aus)	6–5 6–2
1963	K N Fletcher (Aus) & Miss M Smith (Aus)	E Rubinoff & Miss J A M Tegart (Aus)	3–6 8–6 6–2
1964	J D Newcombe (Aus) & Miss M Smith (Aus)	E Rubinoff & Miss J A M Tegart (Aus)	10–8 4–6 6–3
1965	F S Stolle (Aus) & Miss M Smith (Aus)	F A Froehling & Miss J A M Tegart (Aus)	6–2 6–2
1966	O K Davidson (Aus) & Mrs D Fales	E Rubinoff & Miss C Aucampt	6–3 6–1
1967	O K Davidson (Aus) & Mrs L W King	S R Smith & Miss R Casals	6–3 6–2
Played at the Longwood Cricket Club, Boston.			
1968	P W Curtis (GB) & Miss M A Eisel	R N Perry & Miss T A Fretz	6–4 7–5
1969	P Sullivan & Miss P S A Hogan	T Addison (Aus) & Miss K Pigeon	6–4 2–6 12–10

The British Virginia Wade, winner of the first US Open in 1968. In 1977 she took the Wimbledon singles.

Arthur Ashe, the first black man to be US Champion. He won the inaugural open title in 1968.

top Hana Mandlikova, one of the great Czechs. Champion of France 1981.

above Tracy Austin, a precocious American champion.

top Billie Jean King, 20 times a Wimbledon champion.

above Pam Shriver, one of the game's keen volleyers.

Bjorn Borg and his wife, Marianne, formerly Miss Simionescu of the Romanian Federation Cup team.

Margaret Court, Australia's greatest woman player and Grand Slam winner in 1970.

Virginia Wade, top player of Great Britain for more than a decade. Wimbledon champion in 1977.

RESULTS: OPEN CHAMPIONSHIPS

MEN'S SINGLES

FINAL				SEMI-FINALS		
Year	Winner	Loser	Score	Winners	Losers	Score

Played at the West Side Club, Forest Hills, NY on grass courts.

1968	A R Ashe	T S Okker (Hol)	14–12 5–7 6–3 3–6 6–3	Ashe	C E Graebner	4–6 8–6 7–5 6–2
				Okker	K R Rosewall	8–6 6–4 6–8 6–1
1969	R G Laver (Aus)	A D Roche (Aus)	7–9 6–2 6–2 6–1	Laver	A R Ashe	8–6 6–3 14–12
				Roche	J D Newcombe	3–6 6–4 4–6 6–3 8–6
1970	K R Rosewall (Aus)	A D Roche (Aus)	2–6 6–4 7–6 6–3	Rosewall	J D Newcombe	6–3 6–4 6–3
				Roche	C Richey	6–2 7–6 6–1
1971	S R Smith	J Kodes (Cze)	3–6 6–3 6–2 7–6	Smith	T S Okker	7–6 6–3 3–6 2–6 6–3
				Kodes	A R Ashe	7–6 3–6 4–6 6–3 6–4
1972	I Nastase (Rom)	A R Ashe	3–6 6–3 6–7 6–4 6–3	Nastase	T W Gorman	4–6 7–6 6–2 6–1
				Ashe	C Richey	6–1 6–4 7–6
1973	J D Newcombe (Aus)	J Kodes (Cze)	6–4 1–6 4–6 6–2 6–3	Newcombe	K R Rosewall	6–4 7–6 6–3
				Kodes	S R Smith	7–5 6–7 1–6 6–1 7–5
1974	J S Connors	K R Rosewall (Aus)	6–1 6–0 6–1	Connors	L R Tanner	7–6 7–6 6–4
				Rosewall	J D Newcombe	6–7 6–4 7–6 6–3

Played at the West Side Club, Forest Hills, NY on Har-Tru courts.

1975	M Orantes (Spa)	J S Connors	6–4 6–3 6–3	Orantes	G Vilas	4–6 1–6 6–2 7–5 6–4
				Connors	B Borg	7–5 7–5 7–5
1976	J S Connors	B Borg (Swe)	6–4 3–6 7–6 6–4	Connors	G Vilas	6–4 6–2 6–1
				Borg	I Nastase	6–3 6–3 6–4
1977	G Vilas (Arg)	J S Connors	2–6 6–3 7–6 6–0	Vilas	H Solomon	6–2 7–6 6–2
				Connors	C Barazzutti	7–5 6–3 7–5

Played at the National Tennis Centre, Flushing Meadow, NY on cement courts.

1978	J S Connors	B Borg (Swe)	6–4 6–2 6–2	Connors	J P McEnroe	6–2 6–2 7–5
				Borg	V Gerulaitis	6–3 6–2 7–6
1979	J P McEnroe	V Gerulaitis	7–5 6–3 6–3	McEnroe	J S Connors	6–3 6–3 7–5
				Gerulaitis	L R Tanner	3–6 2–6 7–6 6–3 6–3
1980	J P McEnroe	B Borg (Swe)	7–6 6–1 6–7 5–7 6–4	McEnroe	J S Connors	6–4 5–7 0–6 6–3 7–6
				Borg	J Kriek	4–6 4–6 6–1 6–1 6–1
1981	J P McEnroe	B Borg (Swe)	4–6 6–2 6–4 6–3	McEnroe	V Gerulaitis	5–7 6–3 6–2 4–6 6–3
				Borg	J S Connors	6–2 7–5 6–4
1982	J S Connors	I Lendl (Cze)	6–3 6–2 4–6 6–4	Connors	G Vilas	6–1 3–6 6–2 6–3
				Lendl	J P McEnroe	6–4 6–4 7–6

WOMEN'S SINGLES

FINAL				SEMI-FINALS		
Year	Winner	Loser	Score	Winners	Losers	Score

Played at the West Side Club, Forest Hills, NY on grass courts.

1968	Miss S V Wade (GB)	Mrs L W King	6–4 6–2	Miss Wade	Mrs P F Jones (GB)	7–5 6–1
				Mrs King	Miss M E Bueno (Bra)	3–6 6–4 6–2
1969	Mrs B M Court (Aus)	Miss N Richey	6–2 6–2	Mrs Court	Miss S V Wade (GB)	7–5 6–0
				Miss Richey	Miss R Casals	7–5 6–3
1970	Mrs B M Court (Aus)	Miss R Casals	6–2 2–6 6–1	Mrs Court	Miss N Richey	6–1 6–3
				Miss Casals	Miss S V Wade (GB)	6–2 6–7 6–2
1971	Mrs L W King	Miss R Casals	6–4 7–6	Mrs King	Miss C M Evert	6–3 6–2
				Miss Casals	Miss K Melville (Aus)	6–4 6–3
1972	Mrs L W King	Miss K Melville (Aus)	6–3 7–5	Mrs King	Mrs B M Court (Aus)	6–4 6–4
				Miss Melville	Miss C M Evert	6–4 6–2
1973	Mrs B M Court (Aus)	Miss E F Goolagong (Aus)	7–6 5–7 6–2	Mrs Court	Miss C M Evert	7–6 2–6 6–2
				Miss Goolagong	Frau H Masthoff (FDR)	6–1 4–6 6–4
1974	Mrs L W King	Miss E F Goolagong (Aus)	3–6 6–3 7–5	Mrs King	Miss J M Heldman	2–6 6–3 6–1
				Miss Goolagong	Miss C M Evert	6–0 6–7 6–3

	FINAL			SEMI-FINALS		
Year	Winner	Loser	Score	Winners	Losers	Score

Played at the West Side Club, Forest Hills, NY on Har-Tru courts.

1975	Miss C M Evert	Mrs R A Cawley (Aus)	5–7 6–4 6–2	Miss Evert	Miss M Navratilova (Cze)	6–4 6–4
				Mrs Cawley	Miss S V Wade (GB)	7–5 6–1
1976	Miss C M Evert	Mrs R A Cawley (Aus)	6–3 6–0	Miss Evert	Miss M Jausovec (Yug)	6–3 6–1
				Mrs Cawley	Miss D Fromholtz (Aus)	7–6 6–0
1977	Miss C M Evert	Miss W M Turnbull (Aus)	7–6 6–2	Miss Evert	Miss B F Stove (Hol)	6–3 7–5
				Miss Turnbull	Miss M Navratilova (Cze)	2–6 7–5 6–

Played at the National Tennis Centre, Flushing Meadow, NY on cement.

1978	Miss C M Evert	Miss P H Shriver	7–5 6–4	Miss Evert	Miss W M Turnbull (Aus)	6–3 6–0
				Miss Shriver	Miss M Navratilova (Cze)	7–6 7–6
1979	Miss T A Austin	Mrs J M Lloyd	6–4 6–3	Miss Austin	Miss M Navratilova (Cze)	7–5 7–5
				Mrs Lloyd	Mrs L W King	6–1 6–0
1980	Mrs J M Lloyd	Miss H Mandlikova (Cze)	5–7 6–1 6–1	Mrs Lloyd	Miss T A Austin	4–6 6–1 6–
				Miss Mandlikova	Miss A Jaeger	6–1 3–6 7–
1981	Miss T A Austin	Miss M Navratilova (Cze)	1–6 7–6 7–6	Miss Austin	Miss B Potter	6–1 6–3
				Miss Navratilova	Mrs J M Lloyd	7–5 4–6 6–
1982	Mrs J M Lloyd	Miss H Mandlikova (Cze)	6–3 6–1	Mrs Lloyd	Miss A Jaeger	6–1 6–2
				Miss Mandlikova	Miss P H Shriver	6–4 2–6 6–

MEN'S DOUBLES

	FINAL			SEMI-FINALS		
Year	Winners	Losers	Score	Winners	Losers	Score

Played at the West Side Club, Forest Hills, NY, on grass courts.

1968	R C Lutz & S R Smith	A R Ashe & A Gimeno (Spa)	11–9 6–1 7–5	Lutz & Smith	J H Osborne & J H McManus	6–4 6–3 6–2
				Ashe & Gimeno	C E Graebner & C M Pasarell	6–4 3–6 4–6 20–18 14–12
1969	K R Rosewall (Aus) & F S Stolle (Aus)	C M Pasarell & R D Ralston	2–6 7–5 13–11 6–3	Rosewall & Stolle	T S Okker (Hol) & M C Riessen	6–1 10–8 6–4
				Pasarell & Ralston	R S Emerson (Aus) & R G Laver (Aus)	w.o.
1970	P Barthes (Fra) & N Pilic (Yug)	R S Emerson (Aus) & R G Laver (Aus)	6–3 7–6 4–6 7–6	Barthes & Pilic	P Cornejo (Chi) & J Fillol (Chi)	6–7 6–7 7–6 7–6 7–5
				Emerson & Laver	K R Rosewall (Aus) & F S Stolle (Aus)	6–1 6–1 7–6
1971	J D Newcombe (Aus) & R Taylor (GB)	S R Smith & E Van Dillen	6–7 6–3 7–6 4–6 5–3 (tie break)	Newcombe & Taylor	R A J Hewitt (SA) & F D McMillan (SA)	7–6 6–1 ret'd
				Smith & Van Dillen	T S Okker (Hol) & M C Riessen	6–4 6–2 6–2
1972	E C Drysdale (SA) & R Taylor	O K Davidson (Aus) & J D Newcombe (Aus)	6–4 7–6 6–4	Drysdale & Taylor	I Nastase (Rom) & M Orantes (Spa)	6–4 6–4 6–2
				Davidson & Newcombe	S R Smith & E Van Dillen	6–7 7–6 6–1 7–5
1973	O K Davidson (Aus) & J D Newcombe (Aus)	R G Laver (Aus) & K R Rosewall (Aus)	7–5 2–6 7–5 7–5	Davidson & Newcombe	T S Okker (Hol) & M C Riessen	7–6 6–7 6–2 7–6
				Laver & Rosewall	T W Gorman & R Ramirez (Mex)	6–3 7–6 7–6
1974*	R C Lutz & S R Smith	P Cornejo (Chi) & J Fillol (Chi)	6–3 6–3	Lutz & Smith	S Ball (Aus) & R Keldie (Aus)	6–4 6–4
				Cornejo & Fillol	J D Newcombe (Aus) & A D Roche (Aus)	6–7 6–3 7–6

Played at the West Side Club, Forest Hills, NY, on Har-Tru courts.   Played over the best of three sets throughout.

1975	J S Connors & I Nastase (Rom)	T S Okker (Hol) & M C Riessen	6–4 7–6	Connors & Nastase	R L Stockton & E Van Dillen	6–4 6–4
				Okker & Riessen	F McNair & S Stewart	7–5 7–5
1976	T S Okker (Hol) & M C Riessen	P Kronk (Aus) & C Letcher (Aus)	6–4 6–4	Okker & Riessen	C Dowdeswell (Rho) & C Kachel (Aus)	6–3 7–6
				Kronk & Letcher	R O Ruffels & A J Stone	6–4 6–3

* All except quarter-final round played as the best of three sets.

Year	FINAL Winners	Losers	Score	SEMI-FINALS Winners	Losers	Score
1977	R A J Hewitt (SA) & F D McMillan (SA)	B E Gottfried & R Ramirez (Mex)	6–4 6–0	Hewitt & McMillan	R Carmichael (Aus) & B Teacher	6–2 4–6 6–3
				Gottfried & Ramirez	K Warwick (Aus) & S Ball (Aus)	6–4 6–1

Played at the National Tennis Center, Flushing Meadow, NY, on cement courts.

Year	FINAL Winners	Losers	Score	SEMI-FINALS Winners	Losers	Score
1978	R C Lutz & S R Smith	M C Riessen & S Stewart	1–6 7–5 6–3	Lutz & Smith	W Fibak (Pol) & T S Okker (Hol)	7–6 5–7 7–6
				Riessen & Stewart	M R Edmondson (Aus) & J Marks (Aus)	6–3 6–4
1979	P Fleming & J P McEnroe	R C Lutz & S R Smith	6–2 6–4	Fleming & McEnroe	M C Riessen & S Stewart	6–4 6–4
				Lutz & Smith	R S Emerson (Aus) & F S Stolle (Aus)	7–5 3–6 7–5
1980*	R C Lutz & S R Smith	P Fleming & J P McEnroe	7–6 3–6 6–1 3–6 6–3	Lutz & Smith	M C Riessen & S Stewart	6–2 6–1 6–1
				Fleming & McEnroe	P McNamara (Aus) & P McNamee (Aus)	4–6 6–3 7–6 6–1
1981	P Fleming & J P McEnroe	H Gunthardt (Swi) & P McNamara (Aus)	w.o.	Fleming & McEnroe	J D Newcombe (Aus) & F S Stolle (Aus)	6–2 6–2 5–7 6–7 7–6
				Gunthardt & McNamara	F Buehning & F Taygan	7–6 7–6 6–4
1982**	K Curren (SA) & S Denton	V Amaya & H Pfister	6–2 6–7 5–7 6–2 6–4	Curren & Denton	Tim/Tom Gullikson	6–3 6–2 6–4
				Amaya & Pfister	B E Gottfried & R Ramirez (Mex).	6–3 6–4 6–3

WOMEN'S DOUBLES

Played at the West Side Club, Forest Hills, NY, on grass courts.

Year	FINAL Winners	Losers	Score	SEMI-FINALS Winners	Losers	Score
1968	Miss M E Bueno (Bra) & Mrs B M Court (Aus)	Miss R Casals & Mrs L W King	4–6 9–7 8–6	Miss Bueno & Mrs Court	Mlle F Durr (Fra) & Mrs P F Jones (GB)	6–1 8–6
				Miss Casals & Mrs King	Miss S V Wade (GB) & Mrs G M Williams (GB)	12–10 6–4
1969	Mlle F Durr (Fra) & Miss D R Hard	Mrs B M Court (Aus) & Miss S V Wade (GB)	0–6 6–3 6–4	Mlle Durr & Miss Hard	Mrs P W Curtis & Miss V Ziegenfuss	6–3 3–6 6–1
				Mrs Court & Miss Wade	Miss R Casals & Mrs L W King	9–7 9–7
1970	Mrs B M Court (Aus) & Mrs D E Dalton (Aus)	Miss R Casals & Miss S V Wade (GB)	6–3 6–4	Mrs Court & Mrs Dalton	Mme J B Chanfreau (Fra) & Mlle F Durr (Fra)	7–6 6–7 7–5
				Miss Casals & Miss Wade	Mrs C E Graebner & Miss K Melville (Aus)	6–2 6–2
1971	Miss R Casals & Mrs D E Dalton (Aus)	Mme J B Chanfreau (Fra) & Mlle F Durr (Fra)	6–3 6–3	Miss Casals & Mrs Dalton	Mrs K Gunter & Miss K Melville (Aus)	6–3 6–0
				Mme Chanfreau & Mlle Durr	Mrs M A Eisel & Miss V Ziegenfuss	6–4 6–0
1972	Mlle F Durr (Fra) & Miss B F Stove (Hol)	Mrs B M Court (Aus) & Miss S V Wade (GB)	6–3 1–6 6–3	Mlle Durr & Miss Stove	Miss R Casals & Mrs L W King	7–6 3–6 6–4
				Mrs Court & Miss Wade	Miss E F Goolagong (Aus) & Miss L Hunt (Aus)	7–6 7–5
1973	Mrs B M Court (Aus) & Miss S V Wade (GB)	Miss R Casals & Mrs L W King	3–6 6–3 7–5	Mrs Court & Miss Wade	Miss E F Goolagong (Aus) & Miss J Young (Aus)	6–0 6–4
				Miss Casals & Mrs King	Miss C M Evert & Mrs O Morozova (USSR)	6–2 6–1
1974	Miss R Casals & Mrs L W King	Mlle F Durr (Fra) & Miss B F Stove (Hol)	7–6 6–7 6–4	Miss Casals & Mrs King	Miss L Hunt (Aus) & Miss S V Wade (GB)	6–1 5–7 6–1
				Mlle Durr & Miss Stove	Miss E F Goolagong (Aus) & Miss M Michel	6–3 5–7 6–4

* Best of five sets in semi-finals and final only.

** Best of five sets from quarter-finals on.

Year	FINAL Winners	Losers	Score	SEMI-FINALS Winners	Losers	Score

Played at the West Side Club, Forest Hills, NY, on Har-Tru courts.

Year	FINAL Winners	Losers	Score	SEMI-FINALS Winners	Losers	Score
1975	Mrs B M Court (Aus) & Miss S V Wade (GB)	Miss R Casals & Mrs L W King	7–5 2–6 7–6	Mrs Court & Miss Wade	Mlle F Durr (Fra) & Miss B F Stove (Hol)	6–1 6–2
				Miss Casals & Mrs King	Miss C M Evert & Miss M Navratilova (Cze)	3–6 6–4 6–
1976	Miss D A Boshoff (SA) & Miss I Kloss (SA)	Mrs O Morozova (USSR) & Miss S V Wade (GB)	6–1 6–4	Miss Boshoff & Miss Kloss	Miss M Jausovec (Yug) & Miss V Ruzici (Rom)	6–1 7–6
				Mrs Morozova & Miss Wade	Mrs T E Guerrant & Miss A Kiyomura	6–2 6–4
1977	Miss M Navratilova (Cze) & Miss B F Stove (Hol)	Miss R Richards & Miss B Stuart	6–1 7–6	Miss Navratilova & Miss Stove	Mrs G E Reid (Aus) & Miss G Stevens (SA)	6–4 6–4
				Miss Richards & Miss Stuart	Miss L Forood & Miss R Giscafre (Arg)	7–5 5–7 6–

Played at the National Tennis Center, Flushing Meadow, NY, on cement courts.

Year	FINAL Winners	Losers	Score	SEMI-FINALS Winners	Losers	Score
1978	Mrs L W King & Miss M Navratilova (Cze)	Mrs G E Reid (Aus) & Miss W M Turnbull (Aus)	7–6 6–4	Mrs King & Miss Navratilova	Mlle F Durr (Fra) & Miss S V Wade (GB)	6–2 6–3
				Mrs Reid & Miss Turnbull	Miss B Nagelsen & Miss P H Shriver	6–4 1–6 7–
1979	Miss B F Stove (Hol) & Miss W M Turnbull (Aus)	Mrs L W King & Miss M Navratilova (Cze)	7–5 6–3	Miss Stove & Miss Turnbull	Miss R Casals & Mrs J M Lloyd	6–2 7–5
				Mrs King & Miss Navratilova	Miss J Anthony & Miss S Acker	6–2 7–5
1980	Mrs L W King & Miss M Navratilova (Cze)	Miss P H Shriver & Miss B F Stove (Hol)	7–6 7–5	Mrs King & Miss Navratilova	Miss A Jaeger & Miss R Marsikova (Cze)	6–2 6–3
				Miss Shriver & Miss Stove	Miss K Jordan & Miss A Smith	7–6 6–3
1981	Miss K Jordan & Miss A E Smith	Miss R Casals & Miss W M Turnbull (Aus)	6–3 6–3	Miss Jordan & Miss Smith	Miss H Mandlikova (Cze) & Miss P Teeguarden	3–6 6–2 6–1
				Miss Casals & Miss Turnbull	Miss M Navratilova & Miss P H Shriver	7–6 4–6 6–4
1982	Miss R Casals & Miss W M Turnbull (Aus)	Miss B Potter & Miss S A Walsh	6–4 6–4	Miss Casals & Miss Turnbull	Miss B Bunge (FRG) & Miss C Kohde (FRG)	6–4 6–1
				Miss Potter & Miss Walsh	Miss M Navratilova & Miss P H Shriver	7–5 2–6 6–4

MIXED DOUBLES

Year	FINAL Winners	Losers	Score	SEMI-FINALS Winners	Losers	Score
1968	Event not held					

Played at the West Side Club, Forest Hills, NY, on grass courts.

Year	FINAL Winners	Losers	Score	SEMI-FINALS Winners	Losers	Score
1969	M C Riessen & Mrs B M Court (Aus)	R D Ralston & Mlle F Durr (Fra)	7–5 6–3	Riessen & Mrs Court	T Ulrich (Den) & Miss J M Heldman	6–3 6–2
				Ralston & Mlle Durr	P W Curtis (GB) & Mrs Curtis	6–1 6–1
1970	M C Riessen & Mrs B M Court (Aus)	F D McMillan (SA) & Mrs D E Dalton (Aus)	6–4 6–4	Riessen & Mrs Court	R D Ralston & Mlle F Durr (Fra)	6–3 6–7 6–3
				McMillan & Mrs Dalton	R Taylor (GB) & Miss F E Truman (GB)	7–5 6–3
1971	O K Davidson (Aus) & Mrs L W King	R R Maud (SA) & Miss B F Stove (Hol)	6–3 7–5	Davidson & Mrs King	F D McMillan (SA) & Mrs D E Dalton (Aus)	6–3 2–6 6–2
				Maud & Miss Stove	I Nastase (Rom) & Miss R Casals	w.o.
1972	M C Riessen & Mrs B M Court (Aus)	I Nastase (Rom) & Miss R Casals	6–3 7–5	Riessen & Mrs Court	R J Carmichael (Aus) & Miss L Hunt (Aus)	6–7 6–3 6–3
				Nastase & Miss Casals	O K Davidson (Aus) & Mrs L W King	4–6 6–4 7–6
1973	O K Davidson (Aus) & Mrs L W King	M C Riessen & Mrs B M Court (Aus)	6–3 3–6 7–6	Davidson & Mrs King	F D McMillan (SA) & Miss R Casals	7–5 6–3
				Riessen & Mrs Court	J S Connors & Miss C M Evert	6–4 7–6

	FINAL			SEMI-FINALS		
Year	Winners	Losers	Score	Winners	Losers	Score
1974	G Masters (Aus) & Miss P Teeguarden	J S Connors & Miss C M Evert	6–1 7–6	Masters & Miss Teeguarden	O K Davidson (Aus) & Mrs L W King	7–6 6–4
				Connors & Miss Evert	R Keldie (Aus) & Miss R Giscafre (Arg)	7–6 7–5

Played at the West Side Club, Forest Hills, NY, on Har-Tru courts.

	FINAL			SEMI-FINALS		
1975	R L Stockton & Miss R Casals	F S Stolle (Aus) & Mrs L W King	6–3 6–7 6–3	Stockton & Miss Casals	M C Riessen & Mrs B M Court (Aus)	7–6 3–6 6–3
				Stolle & Mrs King	A Metreveli (USSR) & Mrs O Morozova (USSR)	3–6 6–3 6–4
1976	P C Dent (Aus) & Mrs L W King	F D McMillan (SA) & Miss B F Stove (Hol)	3–6 6–2 7–5	Dent & Mrs King	R L Stockton & Miss R Casals	6–2 7–6
				McMillan & Miss Stove	G Masters (Aus) & Miss L Hunt (Aus)	6–3 6–4
1977	F D McMillan (SA) & Miss B F Stove (Hol)	V Gerulaitis & Mrs L W King	6–2 3–6 6–3	McMillan & Miss Stove	B Walts & Mrs K K Shaw	7–5 3–6 6–3
				Gerulaitis & Mrs King	R A J Hewitt (SA) & Miss G Stevens (SA)	4–6 6–3 7–6

Played at the National Tennis Center, Flushing Meadow, NY, on cement courts.

	FINAL			SEMI-FINALS		
1978	F D McMillan (SA) & Miss B F Stove (Hol)	R O Ruffels (Aus) & Mrs L W King	6–3 7–6	McMillan & Miss Stove	R A J Hewitt (SA) & Miss W M Turnbull (Aus)	4–6 7–6 6–2
				Ruffels & Mrs King	S R Smith & Miss A E Smith	7–6 6–4
1979	R A J Hewitt (SA) & Miss G Stevens (SA)	F D McMillan (SA) & Miss B F Stove (Hol)	6–3 7–5	Hewitt & Miss Stevens	I Nastase (Rom) & Miss R Richards	6–0 6–4
				McMillan & Miss Stove	W Scanlon & Miss M Navratilova (Cze)	7–6 6–3
1980	M C Riessen & Miss W M Turnbull (Aus)	F McMillan (SA) & Miss B F Stove (Hol)	7–6 6–2	Riessen & Miss Turnbull	S Denton & Miss C Reynolds	2–6 7–5 6–3
				McMillan & Miss Stove	K Curren (SA) & Miss A E Smith	6–4 7–5
1981	K Curren (SA) & Miss A E Smith	S Denton & Miss J Russell	6–4 7–6	Curren & Miss Smith	R L Stockton & Miss B Bunge (FDR)	6–4 3–6 6–4
				Denton & Miss Russell	M Purcell & Miss P G Smith	7–6 6–4
1982	K Curren (SA) & Miss A E Smith	F Taygan & Miss B Potter	6–7 7–6 7–6	Curren & Miss Smith	C Dunk & Miss B Jordan	6–1 7–6
				Taygan & Miss Potter	S E Stewart & Miss C Reynolds	6–2 6–4

PERFORMANCE OF TOP SEEDS

	MEN'S SINGLES		WOMEN'S SINGLES	
Year	Top Seed		Top Seed	
1968	R G Laver	Lost 4th round	Mrs L W King	Lost final
1969	R G Laver	Won	Mrs P F Jones	Scratched
1970	R G Laver	Lost 4th round	Mrs B M Court	Won
1971	J D Newcombe	Lost 1st round	Mrs L W King	Won
1972	S R Smith	Lost quarter-final	Mrs L W King	Won
1973	S R Smith	Lost semi-final	Mrs L W King	Lost 3rd round
1974	J S Connors	Won	Miss C M Evert	Lost semi-final
1975	J S Connors	Lost final	Miss C M Evert	Won
1976	J S Connors	Won	Miss C M Evert	Won
1977	B Borg	Lost 4th round	Miss C M Evert	Won
1978	B Borg	Lost final	Miss M Navratilova	Lost semi-final
1979	B Borg	Lost quarter-final	Mrs J M Lloyd	Lost final
1980	B Borg	Lost final	Miss T A Austin	Lost semi-final
1981	J P McEnroe	Won	Mrs J M Lloyd	Lost semi-final
1982	J P McEnroe	Lost semi-final	Miss M Navratilova	Lost quarter-final

MEN'S DOUBLES
Year Top Seeds

1968	J D Newcombe & A D Roche	Lost quarter-final
1969	J D Newcombe & A D Roche	Retired in quarter-final
1970	J D Newcombe & A D Roche	Lost first match
1971	A R Ashe & A D Ralston	Scratched 3rd round
1972	T S Okker & M C Riessen	Lost 3rd round
1973	T S Okker & M C Riessen	Lost semi-final
1974	J D Newcombe & A D Roche	Lost semi-final
1975	B E Gottfried & R Ramirez	Lost 3rd round
1976	B E Gottfried & R Ramirez	Lost 2nd round
1977	R A J Hewitt & F D McMillan	Won
1978	R A J Hewitt & F D McMillan	Lost quarter-final
1979	P Fleming & J P McEnroe	Won
1980	P Fleming & J P McEnroe	Lost final
1981	P Fleming & J P McEnroe	Won
1982	P Fleming & J P McEnroe	Lost quarter-final

WOMEN'S DOUBLES
Year Top Seeds

1968	Miss R Casals & Mrs L W King	Lost final
1969	Miss R Casals & Mrs L W King	Lost semi-final
1970	Mrs B M Court & Mrs D E Dalton	Won
1971	Miss R Casals & Mrs D E Dalton	Won
1972	Miss R Casals & Mrs L W King	Lost semi-final
1973	Miss R Casals & Mrs L W King	Lost final
1974	Miss E F Goolagong & Miss M Michel	Lost semi-final
1975	Miss C M Evert & Miss M Navratilova	Lost semi-final
1976	Mrs L W King & Miss B F Stove	Lost quarter-final
1977	Miss M Navratilova & Miss B F Stove	Won
1978	Mrs L W King & Miss M Navratilova	Won
1979	Miss B F Stove & Miss W M Turnbull	Won
1980	Mrs L W King & Miss M Navratilova	Won
1981	Miss M Navratilova & Miss P H Shriver	Lost semi-final
1982	Miss M Navratilova & Miss P H Shriver	Lost semi-final

MIXED DOUBLES
Year Top Seeds

1968	no event	
1969	R S Emerson & Mrs L W King	Scratched 3rd round
1970	M C Riessen & Mrs B M Court	Won
1971	O K Davidson & Mrs L W King	Won
1972	I Nastase & Miss R Casals	Lost final
1973	O K Davidson & Mrs L W King	Won
1974	O K Davidson & Mrs L W King	Lost semi-final
1975	M C Riessen & Mrs B M Court	Lost semi-final
1976	R L Stockton & Miss R Casals	Lost semi-final
1977	R A J Hewitt & Miss G Stevens	Lost semi-final
1978	F D McMillan & Miss B F Stove	Won
1979	R A J Hewitt & Miss G Stevens	Won
1980	M C Riessen & Miss W M Turnbull	Won
1981	F D McMillan & Miss B F Stove	Lost 2nd round
1982	K Curren & Miss A E Smith	Won

EEDING POSITION OF WINNERS AND RUNNERS-UP

Year	Men's Singles		Women's Singles		Men's Doubles		Women's Doubles		Mixed Doubles	
	Champ.	R-up	Champ.	R-up	Champ.	R-up	Champ.	R-up	Champ.	R-up
1968	5	8	6	1	6	7	3	1	not held	
1969	1	3	2	6	5	–	2	3	2	5
1970	3	4	1	2	8	6	1	2	1	3
1971	2	–	1	2	7	6	1	2	1	–
1972	4	6	1	9	6	–	4	2	2	1
1973	10	6	2	4	3	1	2	1	1	2
1974	1	5	2	5	2	8	2	3	–	3
1975	3	1	1	4	7	–	3	4	4	2
1976	1	2	1	2	4	–	5	3	3	2
1977	4	2	1	12	1	2	1	–	2	3
1978	2	1	2	16	3	8	1	2	1	2
1979	3	4	3	1	1	4	1	2	1	2
1980	2	1	3	9	2	1	1	4	1	2
1981	1	2	3	4	1	2	2	3	3	4
1982	2	3	2	5	3	5	3	5	1	2

MOST DISRUPTED CHAMPIONSHIP

The most disrupted major championship was probably the US National Men's Doubles title meeting at the Longwood Cricket Club, Boston, 1955. Scheduled from Monday 15 August to Sunday 21 August, the tournament, after 2 days, was disrupted by 3 days of heavy rain brought by a hurricane code named 'Diane'. The grass courts were flooded. At one time, on the lowest level of courts, the water was over the height of the net posts.

By the first Saturday the first round of the men's doubles in an entry of 50 pairs had not been completed. To add to the discomfiture of the organisers the imminence of the Davis Cup Challenge Round between the US and Australia in New York on the following Friday caused the respective captains to withdraw the members of their teams. There was further rain in the second week.

The upshot was the withdrawal of three pairs in the first round, of four in the second, of no less than five in the third (which meant only three matches at that stage instead of eight) and of two in the quarter-final—14 in all. In addition there was a withdrawal by another pair at match point.

The damp courts also brought a large number of long sets. The longest was 16–14. There were five at 14–12, one at 13–11, four at 12–10, five at 11–9, three at 10–8, six at 9–7, seven at 8–6 and nine at 7–5.

The eventual winners from the emasculated field when the event finished one week late were the unseeded Kosei Kamo and Atsushi Miyagi of Japan.

JUNIOR CHAMPIONS

The **most prolific winner** of national junior championships was **Tracy Austin**. Born 12 December 1962, she won her first national title, the US Public Parks Under 12 singles in 1972 when 9 years old. On 20 August 1978 she won the US National Championship, girls' singles and doubles, to achieve **27 titles**. She was 15 years 251 days old. She won 17 singles, 10 girls' doubles. Her most prolific year was 1977 when she became US Junior Clay Court Champion, Under 16 singles and doubles, US National Junior Champion, Under 18 singles and Under 16 doubles, US Junior Indoor Champion, Under 16 singles and doubles.

Miss Austin's success brought her ranking status first in 1974 when she was number 1 among the Under 12's. In 1975 she ranked number 1 in the Under 14's, a status she maintained in 1976. In 1977 she was ranked number 4 in the senior list, the youngest player to achieve the top ten. She was 14. At the same time she was rated number 1 in the Under 18 list but number 2 in the Under 16 list. In 1978 she was rated number 1 in both the Under 16 and Under 18 lists and number 3 in the senior list as she was again in 1979. She was number 1 in 1980.

The **most prolific winner** of national junior titles **among boys** was **Scott Davis**. His first success was in 1975 when he won the boys' doubles in the Under 14 US Indoor Championships. In 1980 he won singles and doubles in the US Junior Grass Court Championships at Tuscaloosa, Alabama, to have his **22nd success**. He took 6 titles in 1980, his best total in one year. He was born 27 August 1962.

FRANCE

THE FRENCH CHAMPIONSHIPS

The French Championships vie with the American Championships as the most important and prestigious international meeting after Wimbledon. The surface is 'Terre Battue', known in Great Britain as hard courts and in the USA as clay. On that surface it is unquestionably the premier individual event.

The sequence of the champions may be recorded as far back as 1891. The tournament was then held on the grounds of the sports society of the Île de Puteaux on the Seine. Entry was restricted to representatives of French clubs. The first men's singles champion, J Briggs, seems to have been British. So were the men's doubles victors of 1896, F N Warden and Wynes.

The championships were, though, virtually closed national meeting. In 1925, following th cessation of the 'World Hard Court Champior ships', which had been staged mainly in Pari from 1912 to 1923 and after the Olympic Game events at the Stade Colombes in 1924, th French Championships took on full inter national status.

The championships found their home at th Stade Roland Garros, Auteuil, Paris, in 1928, th stadium having been constructed primaril with a view to staging the defence of the Davi Cup. The ground was magnificently restored i 1980 following a failure to finance a complet rebuilding.

In 1968 the French meeting was the first o the major tournaments to be staged as an 'oper meeting', with prize money and unrestricted entry to all classes of players.

The Île de Puteaux in 1909. The first French Championships were held there in 1891.

The Centre Court at the Stade Roland Garros in Paris, the most important tennis venue in France.

FRENCH SUPERLATIVES

The **longest singles** was in the semi-final in 1951 when Eric Sturgess beat Ken McGregor 10–8 7–9 8–6 5–7 9–7, with Sturgess saving a set point in both the first and third sets and with the match, because of rain, being spread over three days. The total was **76 games**.

The **longest women's singles** was in the third round in 1972 when Kerry Melville beat Pam Teeguarden 9–7 4–6 16–14 after 3 hours 55 minutes and saving two match points in the third set. The total was **56 games**.

The **longest finals** were in the men's doubles, in 1934 when Jean Borotra and Jacques Brugnon beat Jack Crawford & Vivian McGrath 11–9 6–3 2–6 4–6 9–7 and in 1971 when Arthur Ashe & Marty Riessen beat Tom Gorman & Stan Smith

6–8 4–6 6–3 6–4 11–9, a total of **63 games**.

The **longest men's singles final** was 1927 when René Lacoste beat Bill Tilden 6–4 4–6 5–7 6–3 11–9, a total of **61 games**.

The **longest women's doubles final** was 1955 when Beverley Fleitz & Darlene Hard beat Shirley Bloomer & Pat Ward 7–5 6–8 13–11, a total of **50 games**.

The **longest women's singles final** was 1955 when Angela Mortimer beat Dorothy Knode 2–6 7–5 10–8, a total of **38 games**.

The **longest mixed final** was 1958. Nicola Pietrangeli & Shirley Bloomer beat Bob Howe & Lorraine Coghlan 9–7 6–8 6–2, a total of **38 games**.

The **shortest final** was the mixed doubles of 1947 when Eric Sturgess & Sheila Summers beat Carol Carallulis & Jadwiga Jedrzejowska

6–0 6–0, a total of **12 games.**

The shortest women's singles final was 1926 when Suzanne Lenglen beat Mary Browne 6–1 6–0, a total of **13 games.**

The shortest women's doubles final was 1980. Kathy Jordan & Anne Smith beat Ivanna Madruga & Adriana Villagran 6–1 6–0, a total of **13 games.**

The shortest men's singles final was in 1977 when Guillermo Vilas beat Brian Gottfried 6–0 6–3 6–0, a total of **21 games.**

The shortest men's doubles final was 1953. Lew Hoad & Ken Rosewall beat Melvin Rose & Clive Wilderspin 6–2 6–1 6–1, a total of **22 games.**

The **youngest champion** was Andrea Jaeger. In 1981 she won the mixed doubles with Jimmy Arias when her age was **15 years 339 days.**

The **youngest male champion** was Jimmy Arias who won the mixed doubles in 1981, as above, with Miss Jaeger, when he was **16 years 296 days.**

The **youngest singles winner** was M Wilander, men's singles champion in 1982 when his age was **17 years 288 days.**

The **youngest winner of the women's singles** was Christine Truman. She was champion in 1959 at the age of **18 years 139 days.**

The **oldest winner** was Elizabeth Ryan. In 1934 she won the women's doubles with Simone Mathieu at the age of **42 years 88 days.**

The **oldest singles winner** was Andres Gimeno in 1972 when he was men's singles champion at **34 years 301 days.**

The **oldest winner of the women's singles** was Suzi Kormoczi in 1958 when she was **33 years 284 days.**

CHAMPIONSHIPS WON FROM MATCH POINT

1927 Men's singles*
René Lacoste in the final beat Bill Tilden 6–4

Angela Mortimer of Torquay, champion of France. She was also champion of Australia—and Wimbledon.

4–6 5–7 6–3 11–9 after two match points at 8–9 in the fifth set.

1934 Men's singles*
Gottfried von Cramm in the final beat Jack Crawford 6–4 7–9 3–6 7–5 6–3 after a match point at 4–5 in the fourth set.

1934 Men's doubles*
Jean Borotra and Jacques Brugnon in the final beat Jack Crawford and Vivian McGrath 11–9 6–3 2–6 4–6 9–7 after a match point at 5–6 in the fifth set.

1939 Men's doubles*
C Harris and W D McNeill in the final beat Jean Borotra and Jacques Brugnon 4–6 6–4 6–0 2–6 10–8 after three match points in the fifth set.

1946 Women's singles*
Margaret Osborne in the final beat Pauline Betz 1–6 8–6 7–5 after two match points at 5–6 in the second set.

1950 Women's doubles*
Shirley Fry and Doris Hart in the final beat Louise Brough and Margaret du Pont 1–6 7–5 6–2 after a match point in the second set.

1957 Women's doubles*
Shirley Bloomer and Darlene Hard in the final beat Yola Ramirez and Rosa Maria Reyes 7–5 4–6 7–5 after three match points in the third set.

1962 Men's singles
Rod Laver in the quarter-final beat Martin Mulligan 6–4 3–6 2–6 10–8 6–2 after a match point in the fourth set.

1962 Women's singles*
Margaret Smith in the final beat Lesley Turner 3–6 6–3 7–5 after a match point at 3–5 in the third set.

1976 Men's singles
Adriano Panatta in the first round beat Pavel Hutka 2–6 6–2 6–2 0–6 12–10 after a match point at 9–10 in the fifth set.

* Matches in which the losers, had they won, would have taken the title.

TRIPLE CHAMPIONS

No man has yet won all three events. The period 1891 to 1925, when the French meeting was restricted, is not included.

1925 Suzanne Lenglen
1926 Suzanne Lenglen
1938 Simone Mathieu
1952 Doris Hart (USA)
1954 Maureen Connolly (USA)
1964 Margaret Smith (Aus)

Christine Truman of Woodford, champion of France. She lost to Angela Mortimer in the Wimbledon final of 1961.

Françoise Durr, an outstanding player of France. She won nine French championships in the period 1967–73.

MULTIPLE CHAMPIONS

Players Winning Six or more Titles	Championships Won			
	Singles	Doubles	Mixed	Total
Mrs B M Court (Aus) (1962–73)	5	4	4	13
Mme R Mathieu (1933–39)	2	6	2	10
Miss D J Hart (USA) (1948–53)	2	5	3	10
H Cochet (1926–30)	4	3	2	9
Mlle F Durr (1967–73)	1	5	3	9
R S Emerson (Aus) (1960–67)	2	6	–	8
J Borotra (1927–36)	1	5	2	8
J Brugnon (1927–34)	–	5	2	7
B Borg (Swe) (1974–81)	6	–	–	6
Mrs F S Moody (USA) (1928–32)	4	2	–	6
Mrs J M Lloyd (USA) (1974–80)	4	2	–	6
Mlle S Lenglen (1925, 26)	2	2	2	6

RESULTS

MEN'S SINGLES

	FINAL			SEMI-FINALS		
Year	Winner	Loser	Score	Winner	Loser	Score
Played at the Stade Francais, St Cloud.						
1925	R Lacoste	J Borotra	7–5 6–1 6–4	Lacoste	S M Jacob (Ind)	6–2 6–1 3–6 6–4
				Borotra	J Washer (Bel)	6–2 6–1 6–3
Played at the Racing Club of France, Auteuil.						
1926	H Cochet	R Lacoste	6–2 6–4 6–3	Cochet	V Richards (USA)	6–1 6–4 6–4
				Lacoste	J Borotra	8–6 3–6 6–2 6–4
Played at the Stade Francais, St Cloud.						
1927	R Lacoste	W T Tilden (USA)	6–4 4–6 5–7 6–3 11–9	Lacoste	P D B Spence (SA)	6–1 6–3 6–2
				Tilden	H Cochet	9–7 6–3 6–2
Played at the Stade Roland Garros, Auteuil.						
1928	H Cochet	R Lacoste	5–7 6–3 6–1 6–3	Cochet	J Borotra	6–3 2–6 7–5 6–4
				Lacoste	J B Hawkes (Aus)	6–2 6–4 6–4
1929	R Lacoste	J Borotra	6–3 2–6 6–0 2–6 8–6	Lacoste	W T Tilden (USA)	6–1 6–0 5–7 6–3
				Borotra	H Cochet	6–3 5–7 7–5 5–7 6–4
1930	H Cochet	W T Tilden (USA)	3–6 8–6 6–3 6–1	Cochet	H L de Morpurgo (Ita)	7–5 6–1 6–2
				Tilden	J Borotra	2–6 6–2 6–4 4–6 6–3
1931	J Borotra	C Boussus	2–6 6–4 7–5 6–4	Borotra	J Satoh (Jap)	10–8 2–6 5–7 6–1 6–2
				Boussus	G P Hughes (GB)	6–1 4–6 6–2 6–3
1932	H Cochet	G de Stefani (Ita)	6–0 6–4 4–6 6–3	Cochet	M Bernard	6–1 6–0 6–4
				Stefani	R Menzel (Cze)	6–3 2–6 7–5 6–4
1933	J H Crawford (Aus)	H Cochet	8–6 6–1 6–3	Crawford	J Satoh (Jap)	6–0 6–2 6–2
				Cochet	H G N Lee (GB)	9–11 6–3 6–3 6–3
1934	G von Cramm (Ger)	J H Crawford (Aus)	6–4 7–9 3–6 7–5 6–3	Von Cram	G de Stefani (Ita)	3–6 6–4 6–1 3–6 6–2
				Crawford	C Boussus	6–3 2–6 7–5 6–4
1935	F J Perry (GB)	G von Cramm (Ger)	6–3 3–6 6–1 6–3	Perry	J H Crawford (Aus)	6–3 8–6 6–3
				Von Cramm	H W Austin (GB)	6–2 5–7 6–1 5–6 6–0
1936	G von Cramm (Ger)	F J Perry (GB)	6–0 2–6 6–2 2–6 6–0	Von Cramm	M Bernard	7–5 6–1 6–1
				Perry	C Boussus	6–4 7–5 5–7 6–2
1937	H Henkel (Ger)	H W Austin (GB)	6–1 6–4 6–3	Henkel	B Destremau	6–1 6–4 6–3
				Austin	C Boussus	7–5 6–2 1–6 6–3

	FINAL			SEMI-FINALS		
Year	Winner	Loser	Score	Winner	Loser	Score
1938	J D Budge (USA)	R Menzel (Cze)	6–3 6–2 6–4	Budge	J Pallada (Yug)	6–2 6–3 6–3
				Menzel	F Puncec (Yug)	6–4 6–4 6–4
1939	W D McNeill (USA)	R L Riggs (USA)	7–5 6–0 6–3	McNeill	E T Cooke (USA)	6–2 7–5 7–9 6–2
				Riggs	O Szigeti (Hun)	6–3 6–0 6–4
1940–1945 not held						
1946	M Bernard	J Drobny (Cze)	3–6 2–6 6–1 6–4 6–3	Bernard	Y Petra	5–7 6–2 6–3 5–7 6–2
				Drobny	T P Brown (USA)	7–5 3–6 6–4 5–7 6–2
1947	J Asboth (Hun)	E W Sturgess (SA)	8–6 7–5 6–4	Asboth	T P Brown (USA)	6–2 6–2 6–1
				Sturgess	M Bernard	3–6 2–6 6–3 8–6 6–3
1948	F A Parker (USA)	J Drobny (Cze)	6–4 7–5 5–7 8–6	Parker	E W Sturgess (SA)	6–2 6–2 6–1
				Drobny	J E Patty (USA)	2–6 6–3 4–6 6–4 6–3
1949	F A Parker (USA)	J E Patty (USA)	6–3 1–6 6–1 6–4	Parker	E W Sturgess (SA)	6–2 6–1 6–4
				Patty	R A Gonzales (USA)	6–4 6–3 3–6 6–3
1950	J E Patty (USA)	J Drobny (Egy)	6–1 6–2 3–6 5–7 7–5	Patty	W F Talbert (USA)	2–6 6–4 4–6 6–4 13–11
				Drobny	E W Sturgess (SA)	6–4 7–5 3–6 12–10
1951	J Drobny (Egy)	E W Sturgess (SA)	6–3 6–3 6–3	Drobny	F A Sedgman (Aus)	6–0 6–3 6–1
				Sturgess	K McGregor (Aus)	10–8 7–9 8–6 5–7 9–7
1952	J Drobny (Egy)	F A Sedgman (Aus)	6–2 6–0 3–6 6–4	Drobny	K McGregor (Aus)	6–3 6–0 4–6 6–3
				Sedgman	E W Sturgess (SA)	7–5 6–2 8–6
1953	K R Rosewall (Aus)	E V Seixas (USA)	6–3 6–4 1–6 6–2	Rosewall	E Morea (Arg)	2–6 6–2 6–4 0–6 6–2
				Seixas	J Drobny (Egy)	6–3 6–2 3–6 6–3
1954	M A Trabert (USA)	A Larsen (USA)	6–4 7–5 6–1	Trabert	J E Patty (USA)	6–1 7–5 6–4
				Larsen	E Morea (Arg)	6–4 6–3 6–4
1955	M A Trabert (USA)	S Davidson (Swe)	2–6 6–1 6–4 6–2	Trabert	H Richardson (USA)	6–1 2–2 ret'd
				Davidson	G Merlo (Ita)	6–3 6–3 6–2
1956	L A Hoad (Aus)	S Davidson (Swe)	6–4 8–6 6–3	Hoad	G Merlo (Ita)	6–4 7–5 6–4
				Davidson	A J Cooper (Aus)	6–2 9–7 5–7 6–3
1957	S Davidson (Swe)	H Flam (USA)	6–3 6–4 6–4	Davidson	A J Cooper (Aus)	6–4 2–6 2–6 6–2 6–3
				Flam	M G Rose (Aus)	4–6 6–4 4–6 6–2 7–5
1958	M G Rose (Aus)	L Ayala (Chi)	6–3 6–4 6–4	Rose	J Brichant (Bel)	10–8 6–1 6–3
				Ayala	A J Cooper (Aus)	9–11 4–6 6–4 6–2 7–5
1959	N Pietrangeli (Ita)	E C Vermaak (SA)	3–6 6–3 6–4 6–1	Pietrangeli	N A Fraser (Aus)	7–5 6–3 7–5
				Vermaak	L Ayala (Chi)	6–2 6–1 6–4
1960	N Pietrangeli (Ita)	L Ayala (Chi)	3–6 6–3 6–4 4–6 6–3	Pietrangeli	R Haillet	6–4 7–5 7–5
				Ayala	O Sirola (Ita)	6–4 6–0 6–2
1961	M Santana (Spa)	N Pietrangeli (Ita)	4–6 6–1 3–6 6–0 6–2	Santana	R G Laver (Aus)	3–6 6–2 4–6 6–4 6–0
				Pietrangeli	J E Lundquist (Swe)	6–4 6–4 6–4
1962	R G Laver (Aus)	R S Emerson (Aus)	3–6 2–6 6–3 9–7 6–2	Laver	N A Fraser (Aus)	3–6 6–3 6–2 3–6 7–5
				Emerson	M Santana (Spa)	6–4 3–6 6–1 2–6 6–3
1963	R S Emerson (Aus)	P Darmon	3–6 6–1 6–4 6–4	Emerson	M J Sangster (GB)	8–6 6–3 6–4
				Darmon	M Santana (Spa)	6–3 4–6 2–6 9–7 6–2
1964	M Santana (Spa)	N Pietrangeli (Ita)	6–3 6–1 4–6 7–5	Santana	P Darmon	8–6 6–4 3–6 2–6 6–4
				Pietrangeli	J E Lundquist (Swe)	4–6 6–3 6–4 6–4
1965	F S Stolle (Aus)	A D Roche (Aus)	3–6 6–0 6–2 6–3	Stolle	E C Drysdale (SA)	6–8 6–4 6–1 4–6 6–4
				Roche	R S Emerson (Aus)	6–1 6–4 3–6 6–0
1966	A D Roche (Aus)	I Gulyas (Hun)	6–1 6–4 7–5	Roche	F Jauffret	6–3 6–4 6–4
				Gulyas	E C Drysdale (SA)	6–4 2–6 7–9 6–2 6–3
1967	R S Emerson (Aus)	A D Roche (Aus)	6–1 6–4 2–6 6–2	Emerson	I Gulyas (Hun)	6–3 6–4 6–2
				Roche	N Pilic (Yug)	3–6 6–3 6–4 2–6 6–4
1968	K R Rosewall (Aus)	R G Laver (Aus)	6–3 6–1 2–6 6–2	Rosewall	A Gimeno (Spa)	3–6 6–3 7–5 3–6 6–3
				Laver	R A Gonzales (USA)	6–3 6–3 6–1
1969	R G Laver (Aus)	K R Rosewall (Aus)	6–4 6–3 6–4	Laver	T S Okker (Hol)	4–6 6–0 6–2 6–4
				Rosewall	A D Roche (Aus)	7–5 6–2 6–2
1970	J Kodes (Cze)	Z Franulovic (Yug)	6–2 6–4 6–0	Kodes	G Goven	2–6 6–2 5–7 6–2 6–3
				Franulovic	C Richey (USA)	6–4 4–6 4–6 7–5 7–5
1971	J Kodes (Cze)	I Nastase (Rom)	8–6 6–2 2–6 7–5	Kodes	Z Franulovic (Yug)	6–4 6–2 7–5
				Nastase	F A Froehling (USA)	6–0 2–6 6–4 6–3
1972	A Gimeno (Spa)	P Proisy	4–6 6–3 6–1 6–1	Gimeno	A Metreveli (USSR)	4–6 6–3 6–1 2–6 6–3
				Proisy	M Orantes (Spa)	6–3 7–5 6–2
1973	I Nastase (Rom)	N Pilic (Yug)	6–3 6–3 6–0	Nastase	T W Gorman (USA)	6–3 6–4 6–1
				Pilic	A Panatta (Ita)	6–4 6–3 6–2
1974	B Borg (Swe)	M Orantes (Spa)	2–6 6–7 6–0 6–1 6–1	Borg	H Solomon (USA)	6–4 2–6 6–2 6–1
				Orantes	F Jauffret	6–2 6–4 6–4
1975	B Borg (Swe)	G Vilas (Arg)	6–2 6–3 6–4	Borg	A Panatta (Ita)	6–4 1–6 7–5 6–4
				Vilas	E Dibbs (USA)	6–1 6–4 1–6 6–1

Year	FINAL Winner	Loser	Score	SEMI-FINALS Winner	Loser	Score
1976	A Panatta (Ita)	H Solomon (USA)	6–1 6–4 4–6 7–6	Panatta	E Dibbs (USA)	6–3 6–2 6–4
				Solomon	R Ramirez (Mex)	6–7 6–0 4–6 6–4 6–4
1977	G Vilas (Arg)	B E Gottfried (USA)	6–0 6–3 6–0	Vilas	R Ramirez (Mex)	6–2 6–0 6–3
				Gottfried	P C Dent (Aus)	7–5 6–3 7–5
1978	B Borg (Swe)	G Vilas (Arg)	6–1 6–1 6–3	Borg	C Barazzutti (Ita)	6–0 6–1 6–0
				Vilas	R L Stockton (USA)	6–3 6–3 6–2
1979	B Borg (Swe)	V Pecci (Par)	6–3 6–1 6–7 6–4	Borg	V Gerulaitis (USA)	6–2 6–1 6–0
				Pecci	J S Connors (USA)	7–5 6–4 5–7 6–3
1980	B Borg (Swe)	V Gerulaitis (USA)	6–4 6–1 6–2	Borg	H Solomon (USA)	6–2 6–2 6–0
				Gerulaitis	J S Connors (USA)	6–1 3–6 6–7 6–2 6–4
1981	B Borg (Swe)	I Lendl (Cze)	6–1 4–6 6–2 3–6 6–1	Borg	V Pecci (Par)	6–4 6–4 7–5
				Lendl	J L Clerc (Arg)	3–6 6–4 4–6 7–6 6–2
1982	M Wilander (Swe)	G Vilas (Arg)	1–6 7–6 6–0 6–4	Wilander	J L Clerc (Arg)	7–5 6–2 1–6 7–5
				Vilas	J Higueras (Spa)	6–1 6–3 7–6

WOMEN'S SINGLES

Year	FINAL Winner	Loser	Score	SEMI-FINALS Winner	Loser	Score
Played at the Stade Francais, St Cloud.						
1925	Mlle S Lenglen	Miss K McKane (GB)	6–1 6–2	Mlle Lenglen	Mlle H Contosavlos	6–2 6–0
				Miss McKane	Mlle D Vlasto	6–2 6–2
Played at the Racing Club of France, Auteuil.						
1926	Mlle S Lenglen	Miss M K Browne (USA)	6–1 6–0	Mlle Lenglen	Miss J Fry (GB)	6–2 6–1
				Miss Browne	Miss K Bourman (Hol)	8–6 6–2
Played at the Stade Francais, St Cloud.						
1927	Miss K Bouman (Hol)	Mrs G Peacock (Ind)	6–2 6–4	Miss Bouman	Miss E L Heine (SA)	5–7 6–4 6–3
				Mrs Peacock	Miss E Bennett (GB)	5–7 6–1 9–7
Played at the Stade Roland Garros, Auteuil.						
1928	Miss H N Wills (USA)	Miss E Bennett (GB)	6–1 6–2	Miss Wills	Miss C Hardie (GB)	6–1 6–1
				Miss Bennett	Miss K Bouman (Hol)	6–2 8–6
1929	Miss H N Wills (USA)	Mme R Mathieu	6–3 6–4	Miss Wills	Miss E Bennett (GB)	6–2 7–5
				Mme Mathieu	Frl C Aussem (Ger)	8–6 2–6 6–2
1930	Mrs F S Moody (USA)	Miss H H Jacobs (USA)	6–2 6–1	Mrs Moody	Frl C Aussem (Ger)	6–2 6–1
				Miss Jacobs	Sta E de Alvarez (Spa)	6–1 6–0
1931	Frl C Aussem (Ger)	Miss B Nuthall (GB)	8–6 6–1	Frl Aussem	Sta E de Alvarez (Spa)	6–0 7–5
				Miss Nuthall	Frl H Krahwinkel (Ger)	6–1 6–2
1932	Mrs F S Moody (USA)	Mme R Mathieu	7–5 6–1	Mrs Moody	Frl H Krahwinkel (Ger)	6–3 10–8
				Mme Mathieu	Miss B Nuthall (GB)	6–2 6–4
1933	Miss M C Scriven (GB)	Mme R Mathieu	6–2 4–6 6–4	Miss Scriven	Miss B Nuthall (GB)	6–2 4–6 6–3
				Mme Mathieu	Miss H H Jacobs (USA)	8–6 6–3
1934	Miss M C Scriven (GB)	Miss H H Jacobs (USA)	7–5 4–6 6–1	Miss Scriven	Frl C Aussem (Ger)	7–5 6–3
				Miss Jacobs	Mme R Mathieu	6–2 6–2
1935	Fru S Sperling (Ger)	Mme R Mathieu	6–2 6–1	Fru Sperling	Miss H H Jacobs (USA)	7–5 6–3
				Mme Mathieu	Miss M C Scriven (GB)	6–2 6–1
1936	Fru S Sperling (Ger)	Mme R Mathieu	6–3 6–4	Fru Sperling	Countess de la Valdene (Spa)	6–2 6–1
				Mme Mathieu	Frl M Horn (Ger)	6–4 6–4
1937	Fru S Sperling (Ger)	Mme R Mathieu	6–2 6–4	Fru Sperling	Countess de la Valdene (Spa)	6–1 6–1
				Mme Mathieu	Miss J Jedrzejowska (Pol)	7–5 7–5
1938	Mme R Mathieu	Mme N Landry	6–0 6–3	Mme Mathieu	Mme A Halff	6–1 6–1
				Mme Landry	Miss M R Couquerque (Hol)	6–2 6–4
1939	Mme R Mathieu	Miss J Jedrzejowska (Pol)	6–3 8–6	Mme Mathieu	Mlle S Pannetier	6–2 6–2
				Miss Jedrzejowska	Mme M Lebailly	6–3 2–6 6–3
1940–1945 not held						
1946	Miss M E Osborne (USA)	Miss P M Betz (USA)	1–6 8–6 7–5	Miss Osborne	Miss A L Brough (USA)	7–5 6–3
				Miss Betz	Miss D M Bundy (USA)	6–3 6–4
1947	Mrs P C Todd (USA)	Miss D J Hart (USA)	6–3 3–6 6–4	Mrs Todd	Miss M E Osborne (USA)	2–6 6–3 6–4
				Miss Hart	Miss A L Brough (USA)	6–2 7–5
1948	Mme N Landry	Miss S J Fry (USA)	6–2 0–6 6–0	Mme Landry	Mrs P C Todd (USA)	w.o.
				Miss Fry	Miss D J Hart (USA)	6–3 4–6 11–9
1949	Mrs W du Pont (USA)	Mme N Adamson	7–5 6–2	Mrs du Pont	Mrs S P Summers (SA)	6–3 6–3
				Mme Adamson	Mrs A Bossi (Ita)	6–3 6–0

	FINAL			SEMI-FINALS		
Year	Winner	Loser	Score	Winner	Loser	Score
1950	Miss D J Hart (USA)	Mrs P C Todd (USA)	6–4 4–6 6–2	Miss Hart	Miss A L Brough (USA)	6–2 6–3
				Mrs Todd	Miss B Scofield (USA)	6–2 6–3
1951	Miss S J Fry (USA)	Miss D J Hart (USA)	6–3 3–6 6–3	Miss Fry	Mrs W du Pont (USA)	6–2 9–7
				Miss Hart	Mrs J J Walker-Smith (GB)	6–2 6–1
1952	Miss D J Hart (USA)	Miss S J Fry (USA)	6–4 6–4	Miss Hart	Miss D Head (USA)	6–2 8–6
				Miss Fry	Mrs H Redick-Smith (SA)	7–5 6–4
1953	Miss M C Connolly (USA)	Miss D J Hart (USA)	6–2 6–4	Miss Connolly	Mrs D P Knode (USA)	6–3 6–3
				Miss Hart	Miss S J Fry (USA)	8–6 6–4
1954	Miss M C Connolly (USA)	Mme G Bucaille	6–4 6–1	Miss Connolly	Miss S Lazzarino (Ita)	6–0 6–1
				Mme Bucaille	Mme N Adamson	6–2 6–4
1955	Miss A Mortimer (GB)	Mrs D P Knode (USA)	2–6 7–5 10–8	Miss Mortimer	Mrs H Brewer (Ber)	6–1 6–1
				Mrs Knode	Mrs J G Fleitz (USA)	6–2 6–3
1956	Miss A Gibson (USA)	Miss A Mortimer (GB)	6–0 12–10	Miss Gibson	Miss A Buxton (GB)	2–6 6–0 6–4
				Miss Mortimer	Mrs S Kormoczy (Hun)	6–4 6–3
1957	Miss S J Bloomer (GB)	Mrs D P Knode (USA)	6–1 6–3	Miss Bloomer	Miss V Puzejova (Cze)	6–4 2–6 6–4
				Mrs Knode	Miss A S Haydon (GB)	6–4 10–8
1958	Mrs S Kormoczy (Hun)	Miss S J Bloomer (GB)	6–4 1–6 6–2	Mrs Kormoczy	Mrs A Segal (Ber)	6–1 6–0
				Miss Bloomer	Miss M E Bueno (Bra)	2–6 6–1 6–2
1959	Miss C C Truman (GB)	Mrs S Kormoczy (Hun)	6–4 7–5	Miss Truman	Miss S Reynolds (SA)	4–6 8–6 6–2
				Mrs Kormoczy	Miss R M Reyes (Mex)	6–3 6–0
1960	Miss D R Hard (USA)	Miss Y Ramirez (Mex)	6–3 6–4	Miss Hard	Miss M E Bueno (Bra)	6–3 6–2
				Miss Ramirez	Miss S Reynolds (SA)	8–10 6–3 6–3
1961	Miss A S Haydon (GB)	Miss Y Ramirez (Mex)	6–2 6–1	Miss Haydon	Mrs S Kormoczy (Hun)	3–6 6–1 6–3
				Miss Ramirez	Frl E Buding (FRG)	6–4 4–6 6–3
1962	Miss M Smith (Aus)	Miss L R Turner (Aus)	6–3 3–6 7–5	Miss Smith	Miss R Schuurman (SA)	8–6 6–3
				Miss Turner	Miss A S Haydon (GB)	6–4 5–7 6–3
1963	Miss L R Turner (Aus)	Mrs P F Jones (GB)	2–6 6–3 7–5	Miss Turner	Miss C C Truman (GB)	11–9 6–2
				Mrs Jones	Mrs V Sukova (Cze)	6–0 6–1
1964	Miss M Smith (Aus)	Miss M E Bueno (Bra)	5–7 6–1 6–2	Miss Smith	Frl H Schultze (FRG)	6–3 4–6 6–2
				Miss Bueno	Miss L R Turner (Aus)	3–6 6–2 6–0
1965	Miss L R Turner (Aus)	Miss M Smith (Aus)	6–3 6–4	Miss Turner	Miss M E Bueno (Bra)	2–6 6–4 8–6
				Miss Smith	Miss N Richey (USA)	7–5 6–4
1966	Mrs P F Jones (GB)	Miss N Richey (USA)	6–3 6–1	Mrs Jones	Miss M E Bueno (Bra)	4–6 8–6 6–2
				Miss Richey	Miss M Smith (Aus)	6–1 6–3
1967	Mlle F Durr	Miss L R Turner (Aus)	4–6 6–3 6–4	Mlle Durr	Miss K Melville (Aus)	8–6 6–3
				Miss Turner	Miss A M Van Zyl (SA)	6–1 6–4
1968	Miss N Richey (USA)	Mrs P F Jones (GB)	5–7 6–4 6–1	Miss Richey	Mrs L W King (USA)	2–6 6–3 6–4
				Mrs Jones	Mrs A M Du Plooy (SA)	7–5 6–3
1969	Mrs B M Court (Aus)	Mrs P F Jones (GB)	6–1 4–6 6–3	Mrs Court	Miss N Richey (USA)	6–3 4–6 7–5
				Mrs Jones	Mrs W W Bowrey (Aus)	6–1 6–2
1970	Mrs B M Court (Aus)	Frl H Niessen (FDR)	6–2 6–4	Mrs Court	Miss J M Heldman (USA)	6–0 6–2
				Frl Niessen	Miss K M Krantzcke (Aus)	6–3 6–1
1971	Miss E F Goolagong (Aus)	Miss H Gourlay (Aus)	6–3 7–5	Miss Goolagong	Miss M Schaar (Hol)	6–4 6–1
				Miss Gourlay	Mrs K Gunter (USA)	6–2 6–3
1972	Mrs L W King (USA)	Miss E F Goolagong (Aus)	6–3 6–3	Mrs King	Frau H Masthoff (FRG)	6–4 6–4
				Miss Goolagong	Mlle F Durr	9–7 6–4
1973	Mrs B M Court (Aus)	Miss C M Evert (USA)	6–8 7–6 6–3	Mrs Court	Miss E F Goolagong (Aus)	6–3 7–6
				Miss Evert	Mlle F Durr	6–1 6–0
1974	Miss C M Evert (USA)	Mrs O Morozova (USSR)	6–1 6–2	Miss Evert	Frau H Masthoff (FRG)	7–5 6–4
				Mrs Morozova	Miss R Giscafre (Arg)	6–3 6–2
1975	Miss C M Evert (USA)	Miss M Navratilova (Cze)	2–6 6–2 6–1	Miss Evert	Mrs O Morozova (USSR)	6–4 6–0
				Miss Navratilova	Miss J Newberry (USA)	6–2 6–3
1976	Miss S Barker (GB)	Miss R Tomanova (Cze)	6–2 0–6 6–2	Miss Barker	Miss V Ruzici (Rom)	6–3 1–6 6–2
				Miss Tomanova	Miss F Mihai (Rom)	7–5 7–6
1977	Miss M Jausovec (Yug)	Miss F Mihai (Rom)	6–2 6–7 6–1	Miss Jausovec	Miss R Marsikova (Cze)	6–1 3–6 6–3
				Miss Mihai	Miss J Newberry (USA)	7–6 6–3
1978	Miss V Ruzici (Rom)	Miss M Jausovec (Yug)	6–2 6–2	Miss Ruzici	Mlle B Simon	6–3 6–0
				Miss Jausovec	Miss R Marsikova (Cze)	6–3 6–4
1979	Mrs J M Lloyd (USA)	Miss W M Turnbull (Aus)	6–2 6–0	Mrs Lloyd	Miss D Fromholtz (Aus)	6–1 6–3
				Miss Turnbull	Miss R Marsikova (Cze)	6–4 6–3
1980	Mrs J M Lloyd (USA)	Miss V Ruzici (Rom)	6–0 6–3	Mrs Lloyd	Miss H Mandlikova (Cze)	6–7 6–2 6–2
				Miss Rizici	Miss D Fromholtz (Aus)	7–6 6–1
1981	Miss H Mandlikova (Cze)	Frl S Hanika (FRG)	6–2 6–4	Miss Mandlikova	Mrs J M Lloyd (USA)	7–5 6–4
				Frl Hanika	Miss A Jaeger (USA)	4–6 6–1 6–4
1982	Miss M Navratilova (USA)	Miss A Jaeger (USA)	7–6 6–1	Miss Navratilova	Miss H Mandlikova (Cze)	6–0 6–2
				Miss Jaeger	Mrs J M Lloyd (USA)	6–3 6–1

MEN'S DOUBLES

	FINAL		
Year	Winners	Losers	Score

Played at the Stade Francais, St Cloud.

Year	Winners	Losers	Score
1925	J Borotra & R Lacoste	J Brugnon & H Cochet	7–5 4–6 6–3 2–6 6–3

Played at the Racing Club of France, Auteuil.

| 1926 | H Kinsey (USA) & V Richards (USA) | J Brugnon & H Cochet | 6–4 6–1 4–6 6–4 |

Played at the Stade Francais, St Cloud.

| 1927 | J Brugnon & H Cochet | J Borotra & R Lacoste | 2–6 6–2 6–0 1–6 6–4 |

Played at the Stade Roland Garros, Auteuil.

1928	J Borotra & J Brugnon	H Cochet & R de Buzelet	6–4 3–6 6–2 3–6 6–4
1929	J Borotra & R Lacoste	J Brugnon & H Cochet	6–3 3–6 6–3 3–6 8–6
1930	J Brugnon & H Cochet	H C Hopman (Aus) & J Willard (Aus)	6–3 9–7 6–3
1931	G M Lott (USA) & J Van Ryn (USA)	N G Farquharson (SA) & V G Kirby (SA)	6–4 6–3 6–4
1932	J Brugnon & H Cochet	M Bernard & C Boussus	6–4 3–6 7–5 6–3
1933	G P Hughes (GB) & F J Perry (GB)	V B McGrath (Aus) & A K Quist (Aus)	6–2 6–4 2–6 7–5
1934	J Borotra & J Brugnon	J H Crawford (Aus) & V B McGrath (Aus)	11–9 6–3 2–6 4–6 9–7
1935	J H Crawford (Aus) & A K Quist (Aus)	V B McGrath (Aus) & D P Turnbull (Aus)	6–1 6–4 6–2
1936	M Bernard & J Borotra	G P Hughes (GB) & C R D Tuckey (GB)	6–2 3–6 9–7 6–1
1937	H Henkel (Ger) & G von Cramm (Ger)	N G Farquharson (SA) & V G Kirby (SA)	6–4 7–5 3–6 6–1
1938	B Destremau & Y Petra	J D Budge (USA) & G Mako (USA)	3–6 6–3 9–7 6–1
1939	C Harris (USA) & W D McNeill (USA)	J Borotra & J Brugnon	4–6 6–4 6–0 2–6 10–8
1940–1945 not held			
1946	M Bernard & Y Petra	E Morea (Arg) & F Segura (USA)	7–5 6–3 0–6 1–6 10–8
1947	E Fannin (SA) & E W Sturgess (SA)	T P Brown (USA) & O W Sidwell (Aus)	6–4 4–6 4–6 6–3
1948	L Bergelin (Swe) & J Drobny (Cze)	H C Hopman (Aus) & F A Sedgman (Aus)	8–6 6–1 12–10
1949	R A Gonzales (USA) & F A Parker (USA)	E Fannin (SA) & E W Sturgess (SA)	6–3 8–6 5–7 6–3
1950	W F Talbert (USA) & M A Trabert (USA)	J Drobny (Egy) & E W Sturgess (SA)	6–2 1–6 10–8 6–2
1951	K McGregor (Aus) & F A Sedgman (Aus)	G Mulloy (USA) & R Savitt (USA)	6–2 2–6 9–7 7–5
1952	K McGregor (Aus) & F A Sedgman (Aus)	G Mulloy (USA) & R Savitt (USA)	6–3 6–4 6–4
1953	L A Hoad (Aus) & K R Rosewall (Aus)	M G Rose (Aus) & C Wilderspin (Aus)	6–2 6–1 6–1
1954	E V Seixas (USA) & M A Trabert (USA)	L A Hoad (Aus) & K R Rosewall (Aus)	6–4 6–2 6–1
1955	E V Seixas (USA) & M A Trabert (USA)	N Pietrangeli (Ita) & O Sirola (Ita)	6–1 4–6 6–2 6–4
1956	D W Candy (Aus) & R M Perry (USA)	A J Cooper (Aus) & L A Hoad (Aus)	7–5 6–3 6–3
1957	M J Anderson (Aus) & A J Cooper (Aus)	D W Candy (Aus) & M G Rose (Aus)	6–3 6–0 6–3
1958	A J Cooper (Aus) & N A Fraser (Aus)	R N Howe (Aus) & A Segal (SA)	3–6 8–6 6–3 7–5
1959	N Pietrangeli (Ita) & O Sirola (Ita)	R S Emerson (Aus) & N A Fraser (Aus)	6–3 6–2 14–12
1960	R S Emerson (Aus) & N A Fraser (Aus)	J L Arilla (Spa) & A Gimeno (Spa)	6–2 8–10 7–5 6–4
1961	R S Emerson (Aus) & R G Laver (Aus)	R N Howe (Aus) & R Mark (Aus)	3–6 6–1 6–1 6–4
1962	R S Emerson (Aus) & N A Fraser (Aus)	W P Bungert (FDR) & C Kuhnke (FDR)	6–3 6–4 7–5
1963	R S Emerson (Aus) & M Santana (Spa)	G L Forbes (SA) & A Segal (SA)	6–2 6–4 6–4
1964	R S Emerson (Aus) & K N Fletcher (Aus)	J D Newcombe (Aus) & A D Roche (Aus)	7–5 6–3 3–6 7–5
1965	R S Emerson (Aus) & F S Stolle (Aus)	K N Fletcher (Aus) & R A J Hewitt (Aus)	6–8 6–3 8–6 6–2
1966	C E Graebner (USA) & R D Ralston (USA)	I Nastase (Rom) & I Tiriac (Rom)	6–3 6–3 6–0
1967	J D Newcombe (Aus) & A D Roche (Aus)	R S Emerson (Aus) & K N Fletcher (Aus)	6–3 9–7 12–10
1968	K R Rosewall (Aus) & F S Stolle (Aus)	R S Emerson (Aus) & R G Laver (Aus)	6–3 6–4 6–3
1969	J D Newcombe (Aus) & A D Roche (Aus)	R S Emerson (Aus) & R G Laver (Aus)	4–6 6–1 3–6 6–4 6–4
1970	I Nastase (Rom) & I Tiriac (Rom)	A R Ashe (USA) & C M Pasarell (USA)	6–2 6–4 6–3
1971	A R Ashe (USA) & M C Riessen (USA)	T W Gorman (USA) & S R Smith (USA)	6–8 4–6 6–3 6–4 11–9
1972	R A J Hewitt (SA) & F D McMillan (SA)	P Cornejo (Chi) & J Fillol (Chi)	6–3 8–6 3–6 6–1
1973	J D Newcombe (Aus) & T S Okker (Hol)	J S Connors (USA) & I Nastase (Rom)	6–1 3–6 6–3 5–7 6–4
1974	R D Crealy (Aus) & O Parun (NZ)	R C Lutz (USA) & S R Smith (USA)	6–3 6–2 3–6 5–7 6–1
1975	B E Gottfried (USA) & R Ramirez (Mex)	J G Alexander (Aus) & P C Dent (Aus)	6–4 2–6 6–2 6–4
1976	F McNair (USA) & S E Stewart (USA)	B E Gottfried (USA) & S E Stewart (USA)	7–6 6–3 6–1
1977	B E Gottfried (USA) & R Ramirez (Mex)	W Fibak (Pol) & J Kodes (Cze)	7–6 4–6 6–3 6–4
1978	G Mayer (USA) & H Pfister (USA)	J Higueras (Spa) & M Orantes (Spa)	6–3 6–2 6–2
1979	A A Mayer (USA) & G Mayer (USA)	R L Case (Aus) & P C Dent (Aus)	6–4 6–4 6–4
1980	V Amaya (USA) & H Pfister (USA)	B E Gottfried (USA) & R Ramirez (Mex)	1–6 6–4 6–4 6–3
1981	H Gunthardt (Swe) & B Taroczy (Hun)	T Moor (USA) & E Teltscher (USA)	6–2 7–6 6–3
1982	S E Stewart (USA) & F Taygan (USA)	H Gildemeister (Chi) & B Prajoux (Chi)	7–5 6–3 1–1 ret'd

WOMEN'S DOUBLES

	FINAL		
Year	Winners	Losers	Score

Year	Winners	Losers	Score
Played at the Stade Francais, St Cloud.			
1925	Mlle S Lenglen & Mlle D Vlasto	Miss E Colyer (GB) & Miss K McKane (GB)	6–1 9–11 6–2
Played at the Racing Club of France, Auteuil.			
1926	Mlle S Lenglen & Mlle D Vlasto	Miss E Colyer (GB) & Mrs L A Godfree (GB)	6–1 6–1
Played at the Stade Francais, St Cloud.			
1927	Miss E L Heine (SA) & Mrs G Peacock (Ind)	Miss P Saunders (GB) & Mrs P H Watson (GB)	6–2 6–1
Played at the Stade Roland Garros, Auteuil.			
1928	Miss E Bennett (GB) & Mrs P H Watson (GB)	Mlle S Deve & Mme Lafaurie	6–0 6–2
1929	Miss K Bouman (Hol) & Sta E de Alvarez (Spa)	Miss E L Heine (SA) & Mrs A Neave (SA)	7–5 6–3
1930	Mrs F S Moody (USA) & Miss E Ryan (USA)	Mlle S Barbier & Mme R Mathieu	6–3 6–1
1931	Miss B Nuthall (GB) & Mrs E F Whittingstall (GB)	Frl C Aussem (Ger) & Miss E Ryan (USA)	9–7 6–2
1932	Mrs F S Moody (USA) & Miss E Ryan (USA)	Miss B Nuthall (GB) & Mrs E F Whittingstall (GB)	6–1 6–3
1933	Mme R Mathieu & Miss E Ryan (USA)	Mme S Henrotin & Mlle C Rosambert	6–1 6–3
1934	Mme R Mathieu & Miss E Ryan (USA)	Miss H H Jacobs (USA) & Miss S Palfrey (USA)	3–6 6–4 6–2
1935	Miss M C Scriven (GB) & Miss K E Stammers (GB)	Mlle I Adamoff & Fru S Sperling (Ger)	6–4 6–0
1936	Mme R Mathieu & Miss A M Yorke (GB)	Miss J Jedrzejowska (Pol) & Miss S Noel (GB)	2–6 6–4 6–4
1937	Mme R Mathieu & Miss A M Yorke (GB)	Mrs D B Andrus (USA) & Mme S Henrotin	3–6 6–2 6–2
1938	Mme R Mathieu & Miss A M Yorke (GB)	Mme A Halff & Mme N Landry	6–3 6–3
1939	Miss J Jedrzedjowska (Pol) & Mme R Mathieu	Mlle A Florian & Mlle H Kovac	7–5 7–5
1940–1945 not held			
1946	Miss A L Brough (USA) & Miss M E Osborne (USA)	Miss P M Betz (USA) & Miss D J Hart (USA)	6–4 0–6 6–1
1947	Miss A L Brough (USA) & Miss M E Osborne (USA)	Miss D J Hart (USA) & Mrs P C Todd (USA)	7–5 6–2
1948	Miss D J Hart (USA) & Mrs P C Todd (USA)	Miss S J Fry (USA) & Mrs M A Prentiss (USA)	6–4 6–2
1949	Miss A L Brough (USA) & Mrs W du Pont (USA)	Miss J Gannon (GB) & Mrs B E Hilton (GB)	7–5 6–1
1950	Miss S J Fry (USA) & Miss D J Hart (USA)	Miss A L Brough (USA) & Mrs W du Pont (USA)	1–6 7–5 6–2
1951	Miss S J Fry (USA) & Miss D J Hart (USA)	Mrs B Bartlett (SA) & Miss B Scofield (USA)	10–8 6–2
1952	Miss S J Fry (USA) & Miss D J Hart (USA)	Mrs H Redick-Smith (SA) & Mrs J Whipplinger (SA)	7–5 6–1
1953	Miss S J Fry (USA) & Miss D J Hart (USA)	Miss M C Connolly (USA) & Miss J Sampson (USA)	6–4 6–3
1954	Miss M C Connolly (USA) & Mrs H C Hopman (Aus)	Mme M Galtier & Mlle S Schmitt	7–5 4–6 6–0
1955	Mrs J G Fleitz (USA) & Miss D R Hard (USA)	Miss S J Bloomer (GB) & Miss P E Ward (GB)	7–5 6–8 13–11
1956	Miss A Buxton (GB) & Miss A Gibson (USA)	Miss D R Hard (USA) & Mrs D P Knode (USA)	6–8 8–6 6–1
1957	Miss S J Bloomer (GB) & Miss D R Hard (USA)	Miss Y Ramirez (Mex) & Miss R M Reyes (Mex)	7–5 4–6 7–5
1958	Miss Y Ramirez (Mex) & Miss R M Reyes (Mex)	Mrs M K Hawton (Aus) & Mrs T D Long (Aus)	6–4 7–5
1959	Miss S Reynolds (SA) & Miss R Schuurman (SA)	Miss Y Ramirez (Mex) & Miss R M Reyes (Mex)	2–6 6–0 6–1
1960	Miss M E Bueno (Bra) & Miss D R Hard (USA)	Mrs R Hales (GB) & Miss A S Haydon (GB)	6–2 7–5
1961	Miss S Reynolds (SA) & Miss R Schuurman (SA)	Miss M E Bueno (Bra) & Miss D R Hard (USA)	w.o.
1962	Mrs L E G Price (SA) & Miss R Schuurman (SA)	Miss J Bricka (USA) & Miss M Smith (Aus)	6–4 6–4
1963	Mrs P F Jones (GB) & Miss R Schuurman (SA)	Miss R A Ebbern (Aus) & Miss M Smith (Aus)	7–5 6–4
1964	Miss M Smith (Aus) & Miss L R Turner (Aus)	Miss N Baylon (Arg) & Frl H Schultze (FRG)	6–3 6–0
1965	Miss M Smith (Aus) & Miss L R Turner (Aus)	Mlle F Durr & Mlle J Lieffrig	6–3 6–1
1966	Miss M Smith (Aus) & Miss J A M Tegart (Aus)	Miss J Blackman (Aus) & Miss F Toyne (Aus)	4–6 6–1 6–1
1967	Mlle F Durr & Miss G Sherriff (Aus)	Miss A M Van Zyl (SA) & Miss P Walkden (SA)	6–2 6–2
1968	Mlle F Durr & Mrs P F Jones (GB)	Miss R Casals (USA) & Miss L W King (USA)	7–5 4–6 6–4
1969	Mlle F Durr & Mrs P F Jones (GB)	Mrs B M Court (Aus) & Miss N Richey (USA)	6–0 4–6 7–5
1970	Mme G Chanfreau & Mlle F Durr	Miss R Casals (USA) & Mrs L W King (USA)	6–3 1–6 6–3
1971	Mme G Chanfreau & Mlle F Durr	Miss H Gourlay (Aus) & Miss K Harris (Aus)	6–4 6–1
1972	Mrs L W King (USA) & Miss B F Stove (Hol)	Miss W M Shaw (GB) & Miss F E Truman (GB)	6–1 6–2
1973	Mrs B M Court (Aus) & Miss S V Wade (GB)	Miss B F Stove (Hol) & Mlle F Durr	6–2 6–3
1974	Miss C M Evert (USA) & Mrs O Morozova (USSR)	Mme G Chanfreau & Frl K Ebbinghaus (FRG)	6–4 2–6 6–1
1975	Miss C M Evert (USA) & Miss M Navratilova (Cze)	Miss J Anthony (USA) & Mrs O Morozova (USSR)	6–3 6–2
1976	Miss F Bonicelli (Uru) & Mme G Lovera	Miss K M Harter (USA) & Frau H Masthoff (FRG)	6–4 1–6 6–3
1977	Mrs R Marsikova (Cze) & Miss P Teeguarden (USA)	Miss R Fox (USA) & Miss H Gourlay (Aus)	5–7 6–4 6–2
1978	Miss M Jausovec (Yug) & Miss V Ruzici (Rom)	Mrs W W Bowrey (Aus) & Mme G Lovera	5–7 6–4 8–6
1979	Miss B F Stove (Hol) & Miss W M Turnbull (Aus)	Mlle F Durr & Miss S V Wade (GB)	3–6 7–5 6–4
1980	Miss K Jordan (USA) & Miss A E Smith (USA)	Miss I Madruga (Arg) & Miss A Villagran (Arg)	6–1 6–0
1981	Miss R Fairbank (SA) & Miss T Harford (SA)	Miss C Reynolds (USA) & Miss P G Smith (USA)	6–1 6–3
1982	Miss M Navratilova (USA) & Miss A E Smith (USA)	Miss R Casals (USA) & Miss W M Turnbull (Aus)	6–3 6–4

MIXED DOUBLES

Year	FINAL Winners	Losers	Score
	Played at the Stade Francais, St Cloud.		
1925	J Brugnon & Mlle S Lenglen	H Cochet & Mlle D Vlasto	6–2 6–2
	Played at the Racing Club of France, Auteuil.		
1926	J Brugnon & Mlle S Lenglen	J Borotra & Mme J R Le Besnerais	6–4 6–3
	Played at the Stade Francais, St Cloud.		
1927	J Borotra & Mme M Bordes	W T Tilden (USA) & Sta E de Alvarez (Spa)	6–4 2–6 6–2
	Played at the Stade Roland Garros, Auteuil.		
1928	H Cochet & Miss E Bennett (GB)	F T Hunter (USA) & Miss H N Wills (USA)	3–6 6–3 6–3
1929	H Cochet & Miss E Bennett (GB)	F T Hunter (USA) & Miss H N Wills (USA)	6–3 6–2
1930	W T Tilden (USA) & Frl C Aussem (Ger)	H Cochet & Mrs E F Whittingstall (GB)	6–4 6–4
1931	P D B Spence (SA) & Miss B Nuthall (GB)	H W Austin (GB) & Mrs D C Shepherd-Barron (GB)	6–3 5–7 6–3
1932	F J Perry (GB) & Miss B Nuthall (GB)	S B Wood (USA) & Mrs F S Moody (USA)	6–4 6–2
1933	J H Crawford (Aus) & Miss M C Scriven (GB)	F J Perry (GB) & Miss B Nuthall (GB)	6–2 6–3
1934	J Borotra & Mlle C Rosambert	A K Quist (Aus) & Miss E Ryan (USA)	6–2 6–4
1935	M Bernard & Miss L Payot (Swi)	A M Legeay & Mme S Henrotin	4–6 6–2 6–4
1936	M Bernard & Miss A M Yorke (GB)	A M Legeay & Mme S Henrotin	7–5 6–8 6–3
1937	Y Petra & Mme R Mathieu	R Journu & Frl M Horn (Ger)	7–5 7–5
1938	D Mitic (Yug) & Mme R Mathieu	C Boussus & Miss N Wynne (Aus)	2–6 6–3 6–4
1939	E T Cooke (USA) & Mrs M Fabyan (USA)	F Kukuljevic (Yug) & Mme R Mathieu	4–6 6–1 7–5
1940–1945 not held			
1946	J E Patty (USA) & Miss P M Betz (USA)	T P Brown (USA) & Miss D M Bundy (USA)	7–5 9–7
1947	E W Sturgess (SA) & Mrs S P Summers (SA)	C Caralulis (Rom) & Miss J Jedrzejowska (Pol)	6–0 6–0
1948	J Drobny (Cze) & Mrs P C Todd (USA)	F A Sedgman (Aus) & Miss D J Hart (USA)	6–3 3–6 6–3
1949	E W Sturgess (SA) & Mrs S P Summers (SA)	G D Oakley (GB) & Miss J Quertier (GB)	6–1 6–1
1950	E Morea (Arg) & Miss B Scofield (USA)	W F Talbert (USA) & Mrs P C Todd (USA)	w.o.
1951	F A Sedgman (Aus) & Miss D J Hart (USA)	M G Rose (Aus) & Mrs T D Long (Aus)	7–5 6–2
1952	F A Sedgman (Aus) & Miss D J Hart (USA)	E W Sturgess (SA) & Miss S J Fry (USA)	6–8 6–3 6–3
1953	E V Seixas (USA) & Miss D J Hart (USA)	M G Rose (Aus) & Miss M C Connolly (USA)	4–6 6–4 6–0
1954	L A Hoad (Aus) & Miss M C Connolly (USA)	R N Hartwig (Aus) & Mme J Patorni	6–4 6–3
1955	G L Forbes (SA) & Miss D R Hard (USA)	L Ayala (Chi) & Miss J Staley (Aus)	5–7 6–1 6–2
1956	L Ayala (Chi) & Mrs T D Long (Aus)	R N Howe (Aus) & Miss D R Hard (USA)	4–6 6–4 6–1
1957	J Javorsky (Cze) & Miss V Puzejova (Cze)	L Ayala (Chi) & Frl E Buding (FDR)	6–3 6–4
1958	N Pietrangeli (Ita) & Miss S J Bloomer (GB)	R N Howe (Aus) & Miss L Coghlan (Aus)	9–7 6–8 6–2
1959	W A Knight (GB) & Miss Y Ramirez (Mex)	R G Laver (Aus) & Miss R Schuurman (SA)	6–4 6–4
1960	R N Howe (Aus) & Miss M E Bueno (Bra)	R S Emerson (Aus) & Miss A S Haydon (GB)	1–6 6–1 6–2
1961	R G Laver (Aus) & Miss D R Hard (USA)	J Javorsky (Cze) & Miss V Puzejova (Cze)	6–0 2–6 6–3
1962	R N Howe (Aus) & Miss R Schuurman (SA)	F S Stolle (Aus) & Miss L R Turner (Aus)	3–6 6–4 6–4
1963	K N Fletcher (Aus) & Miss M Smith (Aus)	F S Stolle (Aus) & Miss L R Turner (Aus)	6–1 6–2
1964	K N Fletcher (Aus) & Miss M Smith (Aus)	F S Stolle (Aus) & Miss L R Turner (Aus)	6–3 6–4
1965	K N Fletcher (Aus) & Miss M Smith (Aus)	J D Newcombe (Aus) & Miss M E Bueno (Bra)	6–4 6–4
1966	F D McMillan (SA) & Miss A M Van Zyl (SA)	C E Graebner (USA) & Mrs P F Jones (GB)	1–6 6–3 6–2
1967	O K Davidson (Aus) & Mrs L W King (USA)	I Tiriac (Rom) & Mrs P F Jones (GB)	6–3 6–1
1968	J C Barclay & Mlle F Durr	O K Davidson (Aus) & Mrs L W King (USA)	6–1 6–4
1969	M C Riessen (USA) & Mrs B M Court (Aus)	J C Barclay & Mlle F Durr	7–5 6–4
1970	R A J Hewitt (SA) & Mrs L W King (USA)	J C Barclay & Mlle F Durr	3–6 6–3 6–2
1971	J C Barclay & Mlle F Durr	T Lejus (USSR) & Miss W M Shaw (GB)	6–2 6–4
1972	K Warwick (Aus) & Miss E F Goolagong (Aus)	J C Barclay & Mlle F Durr	6–2 6–4
1973	J C Barclay & Mlle F Durr	P Dominguez & Miss B F Stove (Hol)	6–1 6–4
1974	I Molina (Col) & Miss M Navratilova (Cze)	M Lara (Mex) & Mme P Darmon (Mex)	6–3 6–3
1975	T Koch (Bra) & Miss F Bonicelli (Uru)	J Fillol (Chi) & Miss P Teeguarden (USA)	6–4 7–6
1976	K Warwick & Miss I Kloss	C Dowdeswell (Rho) & Miss D A Boshoff (SA)	5–7 7–6 6–2
1977	J P McEnroe (USA) & Miss M Carillo (USA)	I Molina (Col) & Miss F Mihai (Rom)	7–6 6–3
1978	P Slozil (Cze) & Miss R Tomanova (Cze)	P Dominguez & Miss V Ruzici (Rom)	7–6 ret'd
1979	R A J Hewitt (SA) & Miss W M Turnbull (Aus)	I Tiriac (Rom) & Miss V Ruzici (Rom)	6–3 2–6 6–1
1980	W Martin (USA) & Miss A E Smith (USA)	S Birner (Cze) & Miss R Tomanova (Cze)	2–6 6–4 8–6
1981	J Arias (USA) & Miss A Jaeger (USA)	F McNair & Miss B F Stove (Hol)	7–6 6–4
1982	J M Lloyd (GB) & Miss W M Turnbull (Aus)	C Motta (Bra) & Miss C C Monteiro (Bra)	6–2 7–6

AUSTRALIA

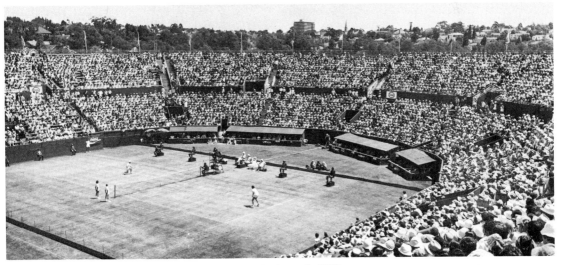

top **The South Australian Championships in Adelaide in the early 1900s.**

above **The Kooyong Stadium's main court in Melbourne.**

THE AUSTRALIAN CHAMPIONSHIPS

Australian lawn tennis is older than Australia as a state. The most venerable of the championships is that of Victoria and A F Robinson won the men's singles title as early as 1879. Miss Mackenzie must be held as the doyenne among women's champions as the Victorian winner in 1884.

The Australian Championships had to wait for the creation of Australia as a Commonwealth nation. The first national tournament was staged in 1905 in Melbourne. The organising body was the Australasian LTA and included New Zealand. Until 1925 the title was the Australasian Championships and New Zealand twice staged the tournament, in Christchurch in 1906 and in Hastings in 1912.

In Australia, Melbourne, Sydney, Adelaide, Brisbane and Perth have been venues, with Melbourne, where the championships have been held since 1972, the most constant. For 1980 and 1981 the men's and women's events were played as separate tournaments at different dates. The mixed doubles were last held in 1969.

The Australian season covered the turn of the year and it was customary to identify the championships by the forward year. In 1977, however, the Australian authorities, anxious to fit in the better with the Grand Prix Series, decreed that the meeting held in December 1977 should be classed as that year instead of 1978. Accordingly 1977 stands in the records as having a double set of champions.

The **most championships** were won by **Margaret Court** who, as Miss Margaret Smith, won first in 1960. Between then and 1975 she won the singles 11 times, the doubles 8 and the mixed twice—**21 titles** in all.

The **11 singles** championships by Mrs Court is a unique performance by a player in amassing singles in a major championship.

Nancye Wynne, later Mrs Nancye Bolton, won **20** Australian titles 1936 to 1952, with 6 singles, 10 women's doubles and 4 mixed doubles.

Mrs Thelma Long, formerly Thelma Coyne, won **18 titles**, comprising 2 singles, 12 women's doubles and 4 mixed doubles, 1936 to 1958.

The **greatest number of titles** won **by a man** was 13 with **Adrian Quist** singles champion 3 times and doubles winner 10 times 1936 to 1950. He was unbeaten in those years in the doubles, which he won twice with Don Turnbull and then with John Bromwich.

AUSTRALIAN SUPERLATIVES

The **longest final** was that of the **men's doubles** in Sydney in 1966 when Roy Emerson & Fred Stolle beat John Newcombe & Tony Roche 7–9 6–3 6–8 14–12 12–10—**87 games.**

The **longest men's singles final** was in Melbourne in 1927 when Gerald Patterson beat John Hawkes 3–6 6–4 3–6 18–16 6–3—**71 games.**

The **longest mixed doubles final** was in Melbourne in 1933 when Jack Crawford & Mrs Crawford beat Ellsworth Vines & Mrs J Van Ryn 3–6 7–5 13–11—**45 games.**

The **longest women's doubles final** was in 1926 in Adelaide. Miss E F Boyd & Mrs P O'Hara Wood beat Miss D Akhurst & Miss M Cox 6–3 6–8 8–6—**37 games.**

The **longest women's singles final** was in Brisbane in 1956. Miss M Carter beat Thelma Long 3–6 6–2 9–7—**33 games.**

The **shortest final** was that of the **women's doubles** in 1971 in Sydney. Margaret Court & Evonne Goolagong beat Lesley Hunt & Jill Emerson 6–0 6–0—**12 games.**

The **youngest singles champions** were Rodney Heath and Margaret Smith. Heath was 1? when he won the first title in 1905, his precise age unknown. Miss Smith was 17 years ? months old when she had her first success in 1960.

The **oldest singles champion** was **Ken Rosewall**. He won for the fourth time in 1972—his first having been 1953, 19 years earlier—at **37 years 2 months.**

The women's doubles was won by **Mrs T D Long** in 1956 at the age of **37 years 7 months.**

Norman Brookes (later Sir Norman Brookes) won the men's doubles in 1924 when he was aged **46 years 2 months.**

Margaret Court, formerly Miss Smith. The Australian who was one of the greatest women players of all time.

MULTIPLE CHAMPIONS
Players Winning Nine or more Titles

	Championships Won			
	Singles	Doubles	Mixed	Total
Mrs B M Court (Aus) (1960–73)	11	8	2	21
Mrs N Bolton (Aus) (1936–51)	6	10	4	20
Mrs T D Long (Aus) (1936–58)	2	12	4	18
Miss D Akhurst (Aus) (1924–30)	5	4	4	13
A K Quist (Aus) (1936–50)	3	10	–	13
J H Crawford (Aus) (1929–35)	4	4	3	11
J E Bromwich (Aus) (1938–50)	2	8	1	11
R S Emerson (Aus) (1961–69)	6	3	–	9
Mrs R A Cawley (Aus) (1971–77)	4	5	–	9

TRIPLE CHAMPIONS

Men	Women	Year
	Miss D Akhurst (Aus)	1925
J B Hawkes (Aus)		1926
J Borotra (Fra)	Miss D Akhurst (Aus)	1928
	Miss D Akhurst (Aus)	1929
J H Crawford (Aus)		1932
	Miss N Wynne (Aus)	1940
	Mrs N Bolton (Aus)	1947
	Mrs N Bolton (Aus)	1948
	Mrs T D Long (Aus)	1952
	Miss M Smith (Aus)	1963

(A mixed doubles championship has not been staged since 1968)

CHAMPIONSHIPS WON FROM MATCH POINT

1927 Men's singles*
Gerald Patterson in the final beat John Hawkes 3–6 6–4 3–6 18–16 6–3 after three match points in the fourth set.

1947 Men's singles*
Dinny Pails in the final beat John Bromwich 4–6 6–4 3–6 7–5 8–6 after a match point at 5–6 in the fifth set.

1956 Women's singles*
Miss M Carter in the final beat Thelma Long 3–6 6–2 9–7 after a match point in the third set.

1960 Men's singles*
Rod Laver in the final beat Neale Fraser 5–7 3–6 6–3 8–6 8–6 after a match point at 4–5 in the fourth set.

Jack Crawford, triple Australian champion 1932. He won the Wimbledon singles 1933.

1975 Men's singles
John Newcombe in the semi-final beat Tony Roche 6–4 4–6 6–4 2–6 11–9 after two match points at 2–5 and a third at 7–8 in the fifth set.

* Matches in which the losers, had they won, would have taken the title.

RESULTS

Year	Men's Singles	Women's Singles	Men's Doubles	Mixed Doubles
Australasian Championships				
1905	R W Heath		R Lycett (GB) & T Tachell	
1906	A F Wilding (NZ)		R W Heath & A F Wilding (NZ)	
1907	H M Rice		W A Gregg & H A Parker (NZ)	
1908	F B Alexander (USA)		F B Alexander (USA) & A W Dunlop	
1909	A F Wilding (NZ)		J P Keane & E F Parker	
1910	R W Heath		A Campbell & H M Rice	
1911	N E Brookes		R W Heath & R Lycett (GB)	
1912	J C Parke (GB)		C P Dixon (GB) & J C Parke (GB)	
1913	E F Parker		A H Hedemann & E F Parker	
1914	A O'Hara Wood		A Campbell & G L Patterson	

Year	Men's Singles	Women's Singles	Men's Doubles	Women's Doubles	Mixed Doubles
1915	F G Lowe (GB)		H M Rice & C V Todd		
1916–1918 not held					
1919	A R F Kingscote (GB)		P O'Hara Wood & R V Thomas		
1920	P O'Hara Wood		P O'Hara Wood & R V Thomas		
1921	R H Gemmell		S H Eaton & R H Gemmell		
1922	J O Anderson	Mrs M Molesworth	J B Hawkes & G L Patterson	Miss E F Boyd & Miss M Mountain	J B Hawkes & Miss E F Boyd
1923	P O'Hara Wood	Mrs M Molesworth	P O'Hara Wood & C B St John	Miss E F Boyd & Miss S Lance	H M Rice & Miss S Lance
1924	J O Anderson	Miss S Lance	J O Anderson & N E Brookes	Miss D Akhurst & Miss S Lance	J Willard & Miss D Akhurst
Australian Championships					
1925	J O Anderson	Miss D Akhurst	P O'Hara Wood & G L Patterson	Miss D Akhurst & Mrs R Harper	J Willard & Miss D Akhurst
1926	J B Hawkes	Miss D Akhurst	J B Hawkes & G L Patterson	Miss E F Boyd & Mrs P O'Hara Wood	J B Hawkes & Miss E F Boyd
1927	G L Patterson	Miss E F Boyd	J B Hawkes & G L Patterson	Miss L M Bickerton & Mrs P O'Hara Wood	J B Hawkes & Miss E F Boyd
1928	J Borotra (Fra)	Miss D Akhurst	J Borotra (Fra) & J Brugnon (Fra)	Miss D Akhurst & Miss E F Boyd	J Borotra (Fra) & Miss D Akhurst
1929	J C Gregory (GB)	Miss D Akhurst	J H Crawford & H C Hopman	Miss D Akhurst & Miss L M Bickerton	E F Moon & Miss D Akhurst
1930	E F Moon	Miss D Akhurst	J H Crawford & H C Hopman	Miss E Hood & Mrs M Molesworth	H C Hopman & Miss N Hall
1931	J H Crawford	Mrs C Buttsworth	C Donohoe & R Dunlop	Miss L M Bickerton & Mrs R Cozens	J H & Mrs Crawford
1932	J H Crawford	Mrs C Buttsworth	J H Crawford & E F Moon	Mrs C Buttsworth & Mrs J H Crawford	J H & Mrs Crawford
1933	J H Crawford	Miss J Hartigan	K Gledhill (USA) & H E Vines (USA)	Mrs M Molesworth & Mrs V Westacott	J H & Mrs Crawford
1934	F J Perry (GB)	Miss J Hartigan	G P Hughes (GB) & F J Perry (GB)	Mrs M Molesworth & Mrs V Westacott	E F Moon & Miss J Hartigan
1935	J H Crawford	Miss D E Round (GB)	J H Crawford & V B McGrath	Miss E M Dearman (GB) & Miss E M Lyle (GB)	C Boussus (Fra) & Miss L M Bickerton
1936	A K Quist	Miss J Hartigan	A K Quist & D P Turnbull	Miss T Coyne & Miss N Wynne	H C & Mrs Hopman
1937	V B McGrath	Miss N Wynne	A K Quist & D P Turnbull	Miss T Coyne & Miss N Wynne	H C & Mrs Hopman
1938	J D Budge	Miss D M Bundy (USA)	J E Bromwich & A K Quist	Miss T Coyne & Miss N Wynne	J E Bromwich & Miss M Wilson
1939	J E Bromwich	Mrs V Westacott	J E Bromwich & A K Quist	Miss T Coyne & Miss N Wynne	H C & Mrs Hopman
1940	A K Quist	Mrs N Bolton	J E Bromwich & A K Quist	Miss T Coyne & Mrs N Bolton	C Long & Mrs N Bolton
1941–1945 not held					
1946	J E Bromwich	Mrs N Bolton	J E Bromwich & A K Quist	Miss M Bevis & Miss J Fitch	C Long & Mrs N Bolton
1947	D Pails	Mrs N Bolton	J E Bromwich & A K Quist	Mrs N Bolton & Mrs T D Long	C Long & Mrs N Bolton
1948	A K Quist	Mrs N Bolton	J E Bromwich & A K Quist	Mrs N Bolton & Mrs T D Long	C Long & Mrs N Bolton
1949	F A Sedgman	Miss D J Hart (USA)	J E Bromwich & A K Quist	Mrs N Bolton & Mrs T D Long	F A Sedgman & Miss D J Hart (USA)
1950	F A Sedgman	Miss A L Brough (USA)	J E Bromwich & A K Quist	Miss A L Brough (USA) & Miss D J Hart (USA)	F A Sedgman & Miss D J Hart (USA)
1951	R Savitt (USA)	Mrs N Bolton	K McGregor & F A Sedgman	Mrs N Bolton & Mrs T D Long	G A Worthington & Mrs T D Long
1952	K McGregor	Mrs T D Long	K McGregor & F A Sedgman	Mrs N Bolton & Mrs T D Long	G A Worthington & Mrs T D Long
1953	K R Rosewall	Miss M Connolly (USA)	L A Hoad & K R Rosewall	Miss M Connolly (USA) & Miss J Sampson (USA)	R N Hartwig & Miss J Sampson (USA)

Year	Men's Singles	Women's Singles	Men's Doubles	Women's Doubles	Mixed Doubles
1954	M G Rose	Mrs T D Long	R N Hartwig & M G Rose	Mrs M K Hawton & Miss B Penrose	R N Hartwig & Mrs T D Long
1955	K R Rosewall	Miss B Penrose	E V Seixas & M A Trabert	Mrs M K Hawton & Miss B Penrose	G A Worthington & Mrs T D Long
1956	L A Hoad	Miss M Carter	L A Hoad & K R Rosewall	Mrs M K Hawton & Mrs T D Long	N A Fraser & Miss B Penrose
1957	A J Cooper	Miss S J Fry (USA)	N A Fraser & L A Hoad	Miss S J Fry (USA) & Miss A Gibson (USA)	M J Anderson & Miss F Muller
1958	A J Cooper	Miss A Mortimer (GB)	A J Cooper & N A Fraser	Mrs M K Hawton & Mrs T D Long	R N Howe & Mrs M K Hawton
1959	A Olmedo (USA)	Mrs M Reitano	R G Laver & R Mark	Miss S Reynolds (SA) & Miss R Schuurman (SA)	R Mark & Miss S Reynolds (SA)
1960	R G Laver	Miss M Smith	R G Laver & R Mark	Miss M E Bueno (Bra) & Miss C C Truman (GB)	T Fancutt (SA) & Miss J Lehane
1961	R S Emerson	Miss M Smith	R G Laver & R Mark	Mrs M Reitano & Miss M Smith	R A J Hewitt & Miss J Lehane
1962	R G Laver	Miss M Smith	R S Emerson & N A Fraser	Miss R A Ebbern & Miss M Smith	F S Stolle & Miss L R Turner
1963	R S Emerson	Miss M Smith	R A J Hewitt & F S Stolle	Miss R A Ebbern & Miss M Smith	K N Fletcher & Miss M Smith
1964	R S Emerson	Miss M Smith	R A J Hewitt & F S Stolle	Miss J A M Tegart & Miss L R Turner	K N Fletcher & Miss M Smith
1965	R S Emerson	Miss M Smith	J D Newcombe & A D Roche	Miss M Smith & Miss L R Turner	J D Newcombe & Miss M Smith div'd with O K Davidson & Miss R A Ebbern
1966	R S Emerson	Miss M Smith	R S Emerson & F S Stolle	Mrs C E Graebner (USA) & Miss N Richey (USA)	A D Roche & Miss J A M Tegart
1967	R S Emerson	Miss N Richey	J D Newcombe & A D Roche	Miss J A M Tegart & Miss L R Turner	O K Davidson & Miss L R Turner
1968	W W Bowrey	Mrs L W King (USA)	R D Crealy & A J Stone	Miss K Krantzcke & Miss K Melville	R D Crealy & Mrs L W King (USA)
1969	R G Laver	Mrs B M Court	R S Emerson & R G Laver	Mrs B M Court & Miss J A M Tegart	M C Riessen (USA) & Mrs B M Court div'd with F S Stolle & Mrs P F Jones (GB)
1970	A R Ashe (USA)	Mrs B M Court	R C Lutz (USA) & S R Smith (USA)	Mrs B M Court & Mrs D E Dalton	not held
1971	K R Rosewall	Mrs B M Court	J D Newcombe & A D Roche	Mrs B M Court & Miss E F Goolagong	not held
1972	K R Rosewall	Miss S V Wade (GB)	O K Davidson & K R Rosewall	Miss H Gourlay & Miss K Harris	not held
1973	J D Newcombe	Mrs B M Court	M J Anderson & J D Newcombe	Mrs B M Court & Miss S V Wade (GB)	not held
1974	J S Connors (USA)	Miss E F Goolagong	R Case & G Masters	Miss E F Goolagong & Miss M Michel (USA)	not held
1975	J D Newcombe	Miss E F Goolagong	J D Alexander & P Dent	Miss E F Goolagong & Miss M Michel (USA)	not held
1976	M R Edmondson	Mrs R A Cawley	J D Newcombe & A D Roche	Mrs R A Cawley & Miss H Gourlay	not held
1977 (Jan)	R Tanner (USA)	Mrs G E Reid	A R Ashe (USA) & A D Roche	Miss D Fromholtz & Miss H Gourlay	not held
1977 (Dec)	V Gerulaitis (USA)	Mrs R A Cawley	R O Ruffels & A J Stone	Mrs R A Cawley & Mrs R L Cawley div'd with Miss M Guerrant (USA) & Mrs G E Reid	not held
1978	G Vilas (Arg)	Miss C O'Neil	W Fibak (Pol) & K Warwick	Miss B Nagelsen (USA) & Miss R Tomanova (Cze)	not held
1979	G Vilas (Arg)	Miss B Jordan (USA)	P McNamara & P McNamee	Mrs D D Chaloner (NZ) & Miss D R Evers	not held
1980	B Teacher (USA)	Miss H Mandlikova (Cze)	M R Edmondson & K Warwick	Miss B Nagelsen (USA) & Miss M Navratilova (Cze)	not held
1981	J Kriek (SA)	Miss M Navratilova (Cze)	M R Edmondson & K Warwick	Miss K Jordan (USA) & Miss A E Smith (USA)	not held

ITALY

THE ITALIAN CHAMPIONSHIPS

An Italian Championship was first staged in 1894 and the men's singles winner was G de Martino. The game was played in Italy as early as 1878 when an English Club was founded in Bordighera. An Italian Lawn Tennis Association was founded in Rome in 1894 but lasted only 4 years. It was re-formed in Florence in 1910.

The Italian International Championships date from 1930 and until 1934 were held in Milan. They moved to the newly built Foro Italico in Rome in 1935 but were not held 1936 to 1949 because of the disturbance first of the Abyssinian War and then of World War II. In 1961 the meeting was staged in Turin as part of the centenary celebrations of the Risorgimento. The men's and women's events were held at different times in 1979. In 1980 the women moved to Perugia.

ITALIAN SUPERLATIVES

The **youngest men's singles** winner was Bjorn Borg (Swe) in 1974 at **17 years 361 days**.

The **youngest women's singles** winner was Maria Bueno (Bra) in 1958 at **18 years 214 days**.

The **oldest women's singles** champion was Elizabeth Ryan (USA) in 1933 at **41 years 130 days**.

The **oldest men's singles** champion was Bill Tilden (USA) in 1930 at **37 years 101 days**

The **longest men's singles** final was in 1979, when Vitas Gerulaitis (USA) beat Eddie Dibbs 6–7 7–6 6–7 6–4 6–2, a total of **57 games**.

The **longest women's singles** final was in 1962, when Margaret Smith (Aus) beat Maria Bueno (Bra) 8–6 5–7 6–4, a total of **36 games**.

The **shortest women's singles** finals were in 1959, when Christine Truman (GB) beat Sandra Reynolds (SA) 6–0 6–1, and in 1975, when Chris Evert (USA) beat Martina Navratilova (Cze) 6–1 6–0, a total of **13 games**.

The **shortest men's singles** final was in 1973. Ilie Nastase (Rom) beat Manuel Orantes (Spa) 6–1 6–1 6–1, a total of **21 games**.

The **longest men's doubles** final was 1958. A Jancso & Kurt Nielsen (Den) beat Luis Ayala (Chi) and Don Candy (Aus) 8–10 6–3 6–2 1–6 9–7, a total of **58 games**.

The **longest women's doubles** final was 1956 when Mary Hawton (Aus) and Thelma Long (Aus) beat Angela Buxton (GB) & Darlene Hard (USA) 6–4 6–8 9–7, a total of **40 games**.

The **longest mixed doubles** final was in 1951 Felicismo Ampon (Phi) & Shirley Fry (USA) beat Lennart Bergelin (Swe) & Doris Hart (USA) 8–6 3–6 6–4, a total of **33 games**.

The **shortest men's doubles** final over the best of five sets was in 1930 when W F Coen and Bill Tilden (USA) beat F Gaslini and H L de Morpurgo 6–0 6–3 6–3, a total of **24 games**.

The **shortest women's doubles** final was 1957. Mary Hawton and Thelma Long (both Aus) beat

Nicola Pietrangeli, Italian Champion 1957 and 1961, and one of the great artists of the game.

Yola Ramirez and Rosa Maria Reyes (both Mex) 6–1 6–1, a total of **14 games**.

The **shortest mixed doubles** final was 1931. Pat Hughes (GB) and Sga L Valerio (Ita) beat A del Bono (Ita) and Miss D Andrus (USA) 6–0 6–1, a total of **13 games**.

The final with the **longest duration** was the men's doubles of 1976. In Rome on 30 May Brian Gottfried and Raul Ramirez began against John Newcombe and Geoff Masters. Because of failing light play was suspended at two sets all. In

Houston, Texas, on 15 September Gottfried and his partner took the fifth set to win 7–6 5–7 6–3 3–6 6–3, the duration being **108 days**.

TRIPLE CHAMPIONS

Men	Women	Year
	Sen L de Alvarez (Spa)	1930
G P Hughes (GB)		1931
	Mrs B M Court (Aus)	1964

MULTIPLE CHAMPIONS
Players Winning Six or more Titles

	Championships Won			
	Singles	Doubles	Mixed	Total
Mrs B M Court (Aus) (1961–68)	3	3	3	9
J Drobny (Egy) (1950–56)	3	4	-	7
Mrs J M Lloyd (USA) (1974–82)	5	2	-	7

RESULTS

MEN'S SINGLES

Year	Winner	Runner-up	Score
1930	W T Tilden (USA)	H L de Morpurgo	6–1 6–1 6–2
1931	G P Hughes (GB)	H Cochet (Fra)	6–4 6–3 6–2
1932	A Merlin (Fra)	G P Hughes (GB)	6–1 5–7 6–0 8–6
1933	E Sertorio	A Martin Legeay (Fra)	6–3 6–1 6–3
1934	G Palmieri	G de Stefani	6–3 6–0 7–5
1935	W Hines (USA)	G Palmieri	6–3 10–8 9–7
1936–1949 not held			
1950	J Drobny (Egy)	W F Talbert (USA)	6–4 6–3 7–9 6–2
1951	J Drobny (Egy)	G Cucelli	6–3 10–8 6–1
1952	F A Sedgman (Aus)	J Drobny (Egy)	7–5 6–3 1–6 6–4
1953	J Drobny (Egy)	L A Hoad (Aus)	6–2 6–1 6–2
1954	J E Patty (USA)	E Morea (Arg)	11–9 6–4 6–4
1955	F Gardini	G Merlo	6–1 1–6 3–6 5–6 ret'd
1956	L A Hoad (Aus)	S Davidson (Swe)	7–5 6–2 6–0
1957	N Pietrangeli	G Merlo	8–6 6–2 6–4
1958	M G Rose (Aus)	N Pietrangeli	5–7 8–6 6–4 1–6 6–2
1959	L Ayala (Chi)	N A Fraser (Aus)	6–3 1–6 6–3 6–3
1960	B MacKay (USA)	L Ayala (Chi)	7–5 7–5 0–6 0–6 6–1
1961	N Pietrangeli	R G Laver (Aus)	6–8 6–1 6–1 6–2
1962	R G Laver (Aus)	R S Emerson (Aus)	6–1 1–6 3–6 6–3 6–1
1963	M F Mulligan (Aus)	B Jovanovic (Yug)	6–2 4–6 6–3 8–6
1964	J E Lundquist (Swe)	F S Stolle (Aus)	1–6 7–5 6–3 6–1
1965	M F Mulligan (Aus)	M Santana (Spa)	1–6 6–4 6–3 6–1
1966	A D Roche (Aus)	N Pietrangeli	11–9 6–1 6–2
1967	M F Mulligan (Aus)	A D Roche (Aus)	6–3 0–6 6–4 6–1
1968	T S Okker (Hol)	R A J Hewitt (SA)	10–8 6–8 6–1 1–6 6–0
1969	J D Newcombe (Aus)	A D Roche (Aus)	6–3 4–6 6–2 5–7 6–3
1970	I Nastase (Rom)	J Kodes (Cze)	6–3 1–6 6–3 8–6
1971	R G Laver (Aus)	J Kodes (Cze)	7–5 6–3 6–3
1972	M Orantes (Spa)	J Kodes (Cze)	4–6 6–1 7–5 6–2
1973	I Nastase (Rom)	M Orantes (Spa)	6–1 6–1 6–1
1974	B Borg (Swe)	I Nastase (Rom)	6–3 6–4 6–2
1975	R Ramirez (Mex)	M Orantes (Spa)	7–6 7–5 7–5
1976	A Panatta	G Vilas (Arg)	2–6 7–6 6–2 7–6
1977	V Gerulaitis (USA)	A Zugarelli	6–2 7–6 3–6 7–6
1978	B Borg (Swe)	A Panatta	1–6 6–3 6–1 4–6 6–3
1979	V Gerulaitis (USA)	E Dibbs (USA)	6–7 7–6 6–7 6–4 6–2
1980	G Vilas (Arg)	Y Noah (Fra)	6–0 6–4 6–4
1981	J L Clerc (Arg)	V Pecci (Por)	6–3 6–4 6–0
1982	A Gomez (Ecu)	E Teltscher (USA)	6–2 6–3 6–2

WOMEN'S SINGLES

Winner	Runner-up	Score
Sta E de Alvarez (Spa)	Sgna L Valerio	3–6 8–6 6–0
Sgna L Valerio	Mrs D Andrus (USA)	2–6 6–2 6–2
Mlle I Adamoff (Fra)	Sgna L Valerio	6–4 7–5
Miss E Ryan (USA)	Mlle I Adamoff (Fra)	6–1 6–1
Miss H Jacobs (USA)	Sgna L Valerio	6–3 6–0
Fru H Sperling (Ger)	Sgna L Valerio	6–4 6–1
Mrs A Bossi	Miss P J Curry (GB)	6–4 6–4
Miss D J Hart (USA)	Miss S J Fry (USA)	6–3 8–6
Miss S Partridge (GB)	Miss M P Harrison (GB)	6–3 7–5
Miss D J Hart (USA)	Miss M Connolly (USA)	4–6 9–7 6–3
Miss M Connolly (USA)	Miss P E Ward (GB)	6–3 6–0
Miss P E Ward (GB)	Frl E Vollmer (FRG)	6–4 6–3
Miss A Gibson (USA)	Mrs S Kormoczy (Hun)	6–3 7–5
Miss S J Bloomer (GB)	Mrs D P Knode (USA)	1–6 9–7 6–2
Miss M E Bueno (Bra)	Miss L Coghlan (Aus)	3–6 6–3 6–3
Miss C C Truman (GB)	Miss S Reynolds (SA)	6–0 6–1
Mrs S. Kormoczy (Hun)	Miss A S Haydon (GB)	6–4 4–6 6–1
Miss M E Bueno (Bra)	Miss L R Turner (Aus)	6–4 6–4
Miss M Smith (Aus)	Miss M E Bueno (Bra)	8–6 5–7 6–4
Miss M Smith (Aus)	Miss L R Turner (Aus)	6–3 6–4
Miss M Smith (Aus)	Miss L R Turner (Aus)	6–1 6–1
Miss M E Bueno (Bra)	Miss N Richey (USA)	6–1 1–6 6–3
Mrs P F Jones (GB)	Miss A Van Zyl (SA)	8–6 6–1
Miss L R Turner (Aus)	Miss M E Bueno (Bra)	6–3 6–3
Mrs W W Bowrey (Aus)	Mrs B M Court (Aus)	2–6 6–2 6–3
Miss J M Heldman (USA)	Miss K Melville (Aus)	7–5 6–4
Mrs L W King (USA)	Miss J M Heldman (USA)	6–1 6–3
Miss S V Wade (GB)	Frau H Masthoff (FRG)	6–4 6–4
Miss L Tuero (USA)	Mrs O Morozova (USSR)	6–4 6–3
Miss E F Goolagong (Aus)	Miss C M Evert (USA)	7–6 6–0
Miss C M Evert (USA)	Miss M Navratilova (Cze)	6–3 6–3
Miss C M Evert (USA)	Miss M Navratilova (Cze)	6–1 6–0
Miss M Jausovec (Yug)	Miss L Hunt (Aus)	6–1 6–3
Miss J Newberry (USA)	Miss R Tomanova (Cze)	6–3 7–6
Miss R Marsikova (Cze)	Miss V Ruzici (Rom)	7–5 7–5
Miss T A Austin (USA)	Frl S Hanika (FRG)	6–4 1–6 6–3
Mrs J M Lloyd (USA)	Miss V Ruzici (Rom)	5–7 6–2 6–2
Mrs J M Lloyd (USA)	Miss V Ruzici (Rom)	6–1 6–2
Mrs J M Lloyd (USA)	Miss H Mandlikova (Cze)	6–0 6–3

ITALIAN CHAMPIONSHIPS

Year	Men's Doubles Champions	Women's Doubles Champions	Mixed Doubles Champions
1930	W F Coen (USA) & W T Tilden (USA)	Sta E de Alvarez (Spa) & Sgna L Valerio	H L de Morpurgo & Sta E de Alvarez (Spa)
1931	A del Bono & G P Hughes (GB)	Sga Luzzatti & Sna Prouse	G P Hughes (GB) & Sga L Valerio
1932	G P Hughes (GB) & G de Stefini	Mlle L Payot (Swi) & Mlle C Rosambert (Fra)	J Bonte & Mlle L Payot (Swi)
1933	J Lesueur (Fra) & A Martin Legeay (Fra)	Mlle L Adamoff (Fra) & Mrs D Andrus Burke (USA)	A Martin Legeay (Fra) & Mrs D Andrus Burke (USA)
1934	G Palmieri & G L Rogers (Ire)	Miss H Jacobs (USA) & Miss E Ryan (USA)	H M Culley (USA) & Miss E Ryan (USA)
1935	J H Crawford (Aus) & V B McGrath (Aus)	Miss E M Dearman (GB) & Miss N M Lyle (GB)	H C Hopman (Aus) & Miss J Jedrzejowska (Pol)
1936–1949 not held			
1950	W F Talbert (USA) & M A Trabert (USA)	Miss J Quertier (GB) & Mrs J Walker-Smith (GB)	A K Quist (Aus) & Miss G Moran (USA) div'd with G Cucelli & Sna A Bossi
1951	J Drobny (Egy) & R Savitt (USA)	Miss S J Fry (USA) & Miss D J Hart (USA)	F Ampon (Phi) & Miss S J Fry (USA)
1952	J Drobny (Egy) & F A Sedgman (Aus)	Mrs H C Hopman (Aus) & Mrs T D Long (Aus)	K Nielsen (Den) & Miss A McGuire (USA)
1953	L A Hoad (Aus) & K R Rosewall (Aus)	Miss M Connolly (USA) & Miss J Sampson (USA)	E V Seixas (USA) & Miss D J Hart (USA)
1954	J Drobny (Egy) & E Morea (Arg)	Miss P E Ward (GB) & Miss E M Watson (GB)	E V Seixas (USA) & Miss M Connolly (USA) div'd with M A Trabert (USA) & Miss B M Kimbrell (USA)
1955	A Larsen (USA) & E Morea (Arg)	Mlle C Mercellis (Bel) & Miss P E Ward (GB)	E Morea (Arg) & Miss P E Ward (GB) div'd with M G Rose (Aus) & Miss B Penrose (Aus)
1956	J Drobny (Egy) & L A Hoad (Aus)	Mrs M Hawton (Aus) & Mrs T D Long (Aus)	L Ayala (Chi) & Mrs T D Long (Aus)
1957	N A Fraser (Aus) & L A Hoad (Aus)	Mrs M Hawton (Aus) & Mrs T D Long (Aus)	L Ayala (Chi) & Mrs T D Long (Aus)
1958	A Jancso (Hun) & K Nielsen (Den)	Miss S J Bloomer (GB) & Miss C C Truman (GB)	G Fachini & Miss S J Bloomer (GB)
1959	R S Emerson (Aus) & N A Fraser (Aus)	Sta Y Ramirez (Mex) & Sta R M Reyes (Mex)	F Contreras (Mex) & Sta R M Reyes (Mex)
1960	N Pietrangeli & O Sirola div'd with R S Emerson (Aus) & N A Fraser (Aus)	Miss M Hellyer (Aus) & Sta Y Ramirez (Mex)	not held
1961	R S Emerson (Aus) & N A Fraser (Aus)	Miss J Lehane (Aus) & Miss L R Turner (Aus)	R S Emerson (Aus) & Miss M Smith (Aus)
1962	N A Fraser (Aus) & R G Laver (Aus)	Miss M E Bueno (Bra) & Miss D R Hard (USA)	F S Stolle (Aus) & Miss L R Turner (Aus)
1963	R A J Hewitt (Aus) & F S Stolle (Aus)	Miss R Ebbern (Aus) & Miss M Smith (Aus)	not held
1964	R A J Hewitt (Aus) & F S Stolle (Aus)	Miss L R Turner (Aus) & Miss M Smith (Aus)	J D Newcombe (Aus) & Miss M Smith (Aus)
1965	J D Newcombe (Aus) & A D Roche (Aus) div'd with R W Barnes (Bra) & T Koch (Bra)	Miss M Schacht (Aus) & Miss A Van Zyl (SA)	J E Mandarino (Bra) & Sta M Coronado (Spa)
1966	R S Emerson (Aus) & F S Stolle (Aus)	Miss N Baylon (Arg) & Miss A Van Zyl (SA)	not held
1967	R A J Hewitt (SA) & F D McMillan (SA)	Miss R Casals (USA) & Miss L R Turner (Aus)	W W Bowrey (Aus) & Miss L R Turner (Aus)
1968	T S Okker (Hol) & M C Riessen (USA)	Mrs B M Court (Aus) & Miss S V Wade (GB)	M C Riessen (USA) & Mrs B M Court (Aus)
1969	J D Newcombe (Aus) & A D Roche (Aus) div'd with T S Okker (Hol) & M C Riessen (USA)	Mlle F Durr (Fra) & Mrs P F Jones (GB)	not held
1970	I Nastase (Rom) & I Tiriac (Rom)	Miss R Casals (USA) & Mrs L W King (USA)	not held
1971	J D Newcombe (Aus) & A D Roche (Aus)	Frl H Masthoff (Ger) & Miss S V Wade (GB)	not held
1972	I Nastase (Rom) & I Tiriac (Rom)	Miss L Hunt (Aus) & Miss O Morozova (USSR)	not held
1973	J D Newcombe (Aus) & T S Okker (Hol)	Miss O Morozova (USSR) & Miss S V Wade (GB)	not held

Year	Men's Doubles Champions	Women's Doubles Champions	Mixed Doubles Champions
1974	B E Gottfried (USA) & R Ramirez (Mex)	Miss C M Evert (USA) & Miss O Morozova (USSR)	not held
1975	B E Gottfried (USA) & R Ramirez (Mex)	Miss C M Evert (USA) & Miss M Navratilova (Cze)	not held
1976	B E Gottfried (USA) & R Ramirez (Mex)	Miss L Boshoff (SA) & Miss I Kloss (SA)	not held
1977	B E Gottfried (USA) & R Ramirez (Mex)	Miss B Cuypers (SA) & Miss M Kruger (SA)	not held
1978	V Pecci (Por) & B Prajoux (Chi)	Miss M Jausovec (Yug) & Miss V Ruzici (Rom)	not held
1979	P Fleming (USA) & T Smid (Cze)	Miss B Stove (Hol) & Miss W M Turnbull (Aus)	not held
1980	M R Edmondson (Aus) & K G Warwick (Aus)	Miss H Mandlikova (Cze) & Miss R Tomanova (Cze)	not held
1981	H Gildemeister (Chi) & A Gomez (Ecu)	Miss C Reynolds (USA) & Miss P G Smith (USA)	not held
1982	H Gunthardt (Swi) & B Taroczy (Hun)	Miss K Horvath (USA) & Miss Y Vermaak (SA)	not held

GERMANY

THE GERMAN CHAMPIONSHIPS

The German Championships, staged from 1892 in Hamburg, are older than the game as an organised sport, preceding by some 10 years the formation of the Deutscher Lawn Tennis Bund. The earliest known courts in Germany were laid at the English Club at Bad Homburg vor der Hohe in 1877. The first German club was founded at Baden Baden in 1881.

In its early days the German game was markedly dominated by aristocratic connections and moved slowly from being a pastime to a sport. In the late 1890's British players brought higher standards. The first overseas winner of the German title was the British George Hillyard when he won the men's singles in 1897 and that year Mrs Blanche Hillyard won the women's singles.

An American, Clarence Hobart, won the German title in 1899. The first American woman to take the singles was Dorothy Head in 1950.

The First World War disrupted the meeting for six years, 1914 to 1919, and the Second World War for eight, 1940 to 1947. Nor was it held in 1936 because of the Olympic Games being staged in Berlin.

In 1979 the women's events were staged as a separate tournament in Berlin. This entailed an interruption for 1980 when priority was given to the staging of the Federation Cup.

GERMAN SUPERLATIVES

The **youngest singles winner** was Fraulein **Cilly Aussem** in 1927 when she was **18 years 7 months** old. She was **17 years 7 months** old when she won the mixed doubles in 1926.

The **oldest singles winner** was **Gottfried von Cramm**. He won the men's singles in 1949 when **40 years 1 month** old.

Cilly Aussem, a precocious German champion, won Wimbledon in 1931.

MULTIPLE CHAMPIONS
Players Winning Six or more Titles

	Championships Won		
	Singles	Doubles	Mixed	Total
G von Cramm (1932–55)	6	5	3	14
O Froitzheim (1907–25)	7	4	–	11
Fru S Sperling (1932–39)	6	2	3	11
Mrs B M Court (Aus) (1964–66)	3	3	2	8
M J G Ritchie (GB) (1903–08)	5	2	–	7
H Schomburgk (1908–21)	1	3	3	7
R A J Hewitt (Aus & S A) (1961–77)	–	6	–	6

TRIPLE CHAMPIONS

Men	Women	Year
	Mrs N Bolton (Aus)	1951
M G Rose (Aus)		1957
	Miss S Reynolds (SA)	1961
	Mrs B M Court (Aus)	1965
	Mrs B M Court (Aus)	1966

RESULTS

Year	MEN'S SINGLES Winner	Runner-up	Score	WOMEN'S SINGLES Winner	Runner-up	Score
1892	W Bonne	R A Leers				
1893	C Winzer	W Bonne	6–4 6–0 3–6 6–3			
1894	V Voss	C Winzer	6–1 6–4 11–9			
1895	V Voss	C Winzer	6–2 6–1 6–2			
1896	V Voss	G Wantzelius	6–1 6–0 6–1	Frl M Thomsen	Frl Lantzius	6–3 6–2 7–5 (sic)
1897	G W Hillyard (GB)			Mrs G W Hillyard (GB)		
1898	H S Mahony (GB)	J Pim (GB)		Miss E Lane (GB)		
1899	C Hobart (USA)	H S Mahony (GB)	8–6 8–10 6–0 6–8 8–6	Miss C Cooper (GB)	Countess von Schulenberg	
1900	G W Hillyard (GB)	H L Doherty (GB)		Mrs G W Hillyard (GB)	Miss M E Robb (GB)	
1901	M Decugis (Fra)	F W Payn (GB)		Miss T Lowther (GB)	Frl Duddel	
1902	M Decugis (Fra)	J M Flavelle (GB)		Frl M Ross	Frl H Meyer	
1903	M J G Ritchie (GB)	M Decugis (Fra)	w.o.	Miss V Pinckney (GB)	Frl H Meyer	6–2 6–0
1904	M J G Ritchie (GB)	C von Wessely	6–4 6–0 10–8	Miss E Lane (GB)	Frl L Bergmann	6–3 6–0
1905	M J G Ritchie (GB)	A F Wilding (NZ)	8–6 7–5 8–6	Miss E Lane (GB)	Frl K Krug	6–0 6–1
1906	M J G Ritchie (GB)	F W Rahe	6–2 6–2 6–0	Frl L Berton	Miss M S Jewsbury (GB)	4–6 6–3 6–1
1907	O Froitzheim	M J G Ritchie (GB)	7–5 6–3 6–4	Frl M von Madarasz	Frau N Nerescheimer	7–5 0–6 6–2
1908	M J G Ritchie (GB)	G K Logie (GB)	6–1 6–1 6–3	Frl M von Madarasz	Miss R V Salusbury (GB)	2–6 6–4 6–0
1909	O Froitzheim	F W Rahe	6–0 6–2 6–3	Frl A Heimann	Frl M Rieck	6–4 3–6 6–4
1910	O Froitzheim	C Bergmann	w.o.	Frl M Rieck	Frl D Koring	6–1 6–3
1911	O Froitzheim	M Pipes	6–3 6–2 6–1	Frl M Rieck	Miss M Bjurdstedt (Nor)	6–1 4–6 6–1
1912	O von Muller	H Schomburgk	2–6 6–1 6–4 6–2	Frl D Koring	Frau A Lent	6–2 6–2
1913	H Schomburgk	O von Muller	6–2 6–4 7–5	Frl D Koring	Frau N von Satzger	6–4 6–4
1914–1919	not held					
1920	O Kreuzer	L M Heyden	6–0 6–0 6–2	Frau I Friedleben	Frau L Vormann	6–0 6–0
1921	O Froitzheim	R Kleinschroth	6–4 8–6 ret'd	Frau I Friedleben	Frau D Uhl	9–7 6–1
1922	O Froitzheim	F W Rahe	2–6 6–0 8–6 6–1	Frau I Friedleben	Frau N Neppach	6–2 6–1
1923	H Landmann	L M Heyden	6–2 6–3 7–5	Frau I Friedleben	Frau N Neppach	2–6 9–7 7–5
1924	B von Kehrling	L M Heyden	8–6 6–1 9–7	Frau I Friedleben	Frau N Neppach	6–2 1–6 6–3
1925	O Froitzheim	B von Kehrling (Hun)	6–4 6–1 4–6 6–1	Frau N Neppach	Frau I Friedleben	2–6 6–4 10–8
1926	H Moldenhauer	W Dessart	6–2 6–1 6–1	Frau I Friedleben	Frau N Neppach	6–8 6–4 6–2
1927	H Moldenhauer	W Hannemann	6–2 4–6 6–4 6–4	Frl C Aussem	Frau I Friedleben	6–3 6–3
1928	D Prenn	H Moldenhauer	6–1 6–4 6–3	Miss D Akhurst (Aus)	Frl C Aussem	2–6 6–0 6–4
1929	C Boussus (Fra)	O Froitzheim	6–1 4–6 6–1 6–8 6–1	Frau F von Reznicek	Miss M V Chamberlain (GB)	6–2 5–7 6–0
1930	C Boussus (Fra)	Y Ohta (Jap)	1–6 8–6 2–6 6–4 6–4	Frl C Aussem	Frl H Krahwinkel	6–1 6–2
1931	R Menzel (Cze)	G Jaenecke	6–2 6–2 6–1	Frl C Aussem	Frl J Rost	6–2 1–6 6–4
1932	G von Cramm	R Menzel (Cze)	3–6 6–2 6–2 6–3	Mlle L Payot (Swi)	Frl H Krahwinkel	6–4 4–6 6–3
1933	G von Cramm	R Menzel (Cze)	7–5 2–6 4–6 6–3 6–4	Frl H Krahwinkel	Mme S Henrotin (Fra)	6–2 6–1
1934	G von Cramm	C L Burwell (USA)	6–2 6–1 6–4	Fru H Sperling	Frl C Aussem	6–2 6–3
1935	G von Cramm	O Szigeti (Hun)	6–3 6–3 6–3	Fru H Sperling	Frl C Aussem	9–7 6–0
1936	not held					
1937	H Henkel	V B McGrath (Aus)	1–6 6–3 8–6 3–6 6–1	Fru H Sperling	Frl M L Horn	4–6 6–2 6–3
1938	O Szigeti (Hun)	B Destremau (Fra)	8–6 6–8 6–3 6–3	Fru H Sperling	Miss M E Lumb (GB)	6–1 6–0
1939	H Henkel	R Menzel	4–6 6–4 6–0 6–1	Fru H Sperling	Mlle H Kovacs (Fra)	6–0 6–1
1940–1947	not held					
1948	G von Cramm	H Gulcz	6–4 6–1 4–6 6–3	Frl U Rosenow	Frau I Pohmann	6–2 8–6
1949	G von Cramm	E Buchholz	7–5 6–1 6–0	Mrs M Weiss (Arg)	Frau I Pohmann	6–2 6–8 9–7
1950	J Drobny (Egy)	G von Cramm	6–3 6–4 6–4	Miss D Head (USA)	Frl U Heidtmann	6–3 6–0
1951	L Bergelin (Swe)	S Davidson (Swe)	4–6 6–3 4–6 6–4 7–5	Mrs N Bolton (Aus)	Mrs M Weiss (Arg)	6–3 6–0
1952	E W Sturgess (SA)	J Drobny (Egy)	6–3 6–2 6–3	Miss D Head (USA)	Frau E Vollmer	6–3 6–1
1953	J E Patty (USA)	F Gardini (Ita)	6–3 6–2 6–3	Mrs D P Knode (USA)	Mrs A J Mottram (GB)	6–0 4–6 6–4
1954	J E Patty (USA)	S Davidson (Swe)	6–1 6–1 7–5	Mrs A J Mottram (GB)	Frau I Pohmann	2–6 8–6 6–2
1955	A Larsen (USA)	V Skonecki (Pol)	3–6 6–3 7–5 6–8 6–3	Miss B Penrose (Aus)	Frau E Vollmer	6–4 6–4
1956	L A Hoad (Aus)	O Sirola (Ita)	6–2 5–7 6–4 8–6	Mrs T D Long (Aus)	Sga S Lazzarino (Ita)	7–5 6–2

	MEN'S SINGLES			WOMEN'S SINGLES		
Year	Winner	Runner-up	Score	Winner	Runner-up	Score
1957	M G Rose (Aus)	P Darmon (Fra)	6–3 6–0 6–1	Sta Y Ramirez (Mex)	Sta R M Reyes (Mex)	7–5 6–3
1958	S Davidson (Swe)	J Brichant (Bel)	5–7 6–4 0–6 9–7 6–3	Miss L Coghlan (Aus)	Miss S J Bloomer (GB)	6–4 7–5
1959	W A Knight (GB)	I C Vermaak (SA)	4–6 6–4 4–6 6–3 8–6	Frl E Buding	Mrs S Kormoczy (Hun)	w.o.
1960	N Pietrangeli (Ita)	J E Lundquist (Swe)	6–3 2–6 6–4 6–2	Miss S Reynolds (SA)	Miss M E Bueno (Bra)	7–5 8–6
1961	R G Laver (Aus)	L Ayala (Chi)	6–2 6–8 5–7 6–1 6–2	Miss S Reynolds (SA)	Sta Y Ramirez (Mex)	5–7 7–5 6–1
1962	R G Laver (Aus)	M Santana (Spa)	8–6 7–5 6–4	Mrs L E G Price (SA)	Miss A S Haydon (GB)	4–6 6–3 7–5
1963	M F Mulligan (Aus)	R A J Hewitt (Aus)	6–0 0–6 8–6 6–2	Miss R Schuurman (SA)	Miss L R Turner (Aus)	6–3 1–6 6–3
1964	W Bungert	C Kuhnke	0–6 4–6 7–5 6–2	Miss M Smith (Aus)	Miss M E Bueno (Bra)	6–1 6–1
1965	E C Drysdale (SA)	B Jovanovic (Yug)	6–2 6–4 3–6 6–3	Miss M Smith (Aus)	Frl E Buding	6–2 6–3
1966	F S Stolle (Aus)	I Gulyas (Hun)	2–6 7–6 6–1 6–2	Miss M Smith (Aus)	Miss M E Bueno (Bra)	8–6 6–3
1967	R S Emerson (Aus)	M Santana (Spa)	6–4 6–3 6–1	Mlle F Durr (Fra)	Miss L R Turner (Aus)	6–4 6–4
1968	J D Newcombe (Aus)	E C Drysdale (SA)	6–3 6–2 6–4	Mrs A Du Ploy (SA)	Miss J A M Tegart (Aus)	6–1 7–5
1969	A D Roche (Aus)	T S Okker (Hol)	6–1 5–7 7–5 8–6	Miss J A M Tegart (Aus)	Frl H Niessen	6–3 6–4
1970	T S Okker (Hol)	I Nastase (Rom)	4–6 6–3 6–3 6–4	Frau H Hoesl	Frl H Niessen	6–3 6–3
1971	A Gimeno (Spa)	P Szoke (Hun)	6–3 6–2 6–2	Mrs L W King (USA)	Frau H Masthoff	6–3 6–2
1972	M Orantes (Spa)	A Panatta (Ita)	6–3 9–8 6–0	Frau H Masthoff	Miss L Tuero (USA)	6–3 3–6 8–6
1973	E Dibbs (USA)	K Meiler	6–1 3–6 7–6 6–3	Frau H Masthoff	Mrs Q D Pretorius (SA)	6–4 6–1
1974	E Dibbs (USA)	H J Plotz	6–2 6–2 6–3	Frau H Masthoff	Miss M Navratilova (Cze)	6–4 5–7 6–3
1975	M Orantes (Spa)	J Kodes (Cze)	3–6 6–2 6–2 4–6 6–1	Miss R Tomanova (Cze)	Miss K Sawamatsu (Jap)	7–6 5–7 10–8
1976	E Dibbs (USA)	M Orantes (Spa)	6–4 4–6 6–1 2–6 6–1	Miss S Barker (GB)	Miss R Tomanova (Cze)	6–3 6–1
1977	P Bertolucci (Ita)	M Orantes (Spa)	6–3 4–6 6–2 6–3	Miss L Dupont (USA)	Frl H Esterlehner	6–1 6–4
1978	G Vilas (Arg)	W Fibak (Pol)	6–2 6–4 6–2	Miss M Jausovec (Yug)	Miss V Ruzici (Rom)	6–2 6–3
1979	J Higueras (Spa)	H Solomon (USA)	3–6 6–1 6–4 6–1	Miss C Stoll (USA)	Miss R Marsikova (Cze)	7–6 6–0
1980	H Solomon (USA)	G Vilas (Arg)	6–7 6–2 6–4 2–6 6–3	not held		
1981	P McNamara (Aus)	J S Connors (USA)	7–6 6–1 4–6 6–4	Miss R Marsikova (Cze)	Miss I Madruga (Arg)	6–2 6–1
1982	J Higueras (Spa)	P McNamara (Aus)	6–4 7–6 6–7 3–6 7–6	Miss B Bunge	Miss K Rinaldi (USA)	6–2 6–2

Year	Men's Doubles Winners	Women's Doubles Winners	Mixed Doubles Winners
1902	M Decugis (Fra) & M Germot (Fra)	not held	not held
1903	R Kinzel & C von Wessely	not held	not held
1904	W E Lane (GB) & M J G Ritchie (GB)	not held	not held
1905	E Spitz & A F Wilding (NZ)	not held	not held
1906	G F Adler & M J G Ritchie (GB)	not held	O Kreutzer & Frl N Schmoller
1907	O Froitzheim & L Transenster	not held	L Transenster & Frau N Neresheimer
1908	O von Muller & H Schomburgk	not held	L Transenster & Frl K von Csery
1909	C Bergmann & F W Rahe	not held	M Galvau & Frl M Rieck
1910	O von Muller & H Schomburgk	not held	C Uhl & Frau N Neresheimer
1911	O Froitzheim & F Pipes	not held	C Uhl & Frau N Neresheimer
1912	L M Heyden & L Transenster	not held	H Schomburgk & Frl D Koring
1913	R Kinzel & C von Wessely	not held	H Schomburgk & Frl D Koring
1914–1919 not held			
1920	O Kreuzer & L Slam	not held	O Kreuzer & Frau I Friedleben
1921	L M Heyden & H Schomburgk	not held	H Schomburgk & Frau Schomburgk
1922	O Froitzheim & O Kreuzer	not held	L M Heyden & Sta E de Alvarez (Spa)
1923	B von Kehrling (Hun) & F W Rahe	not held	L M Heyden & Sta E de Alvarez (Spa)
1924	B von Kehrling (Hun) & F W Rahe	not held	H Kleinschroth & Frau N Neppach
1925	O Froitzheim & O Kreuzer	Frl H Kaeber & Frau N Neppach	A Ludke & Frau N Neppach
1926	B von Kehrling (Hun) & F W Rahe	Frau M Galvau & Frl E Hoffman	H Moldenhauer & Frl C Aussem
1927	D M Grieg (GB) & M V Summerson (GB)	Frau N Neppach & Frl H von Petery	D M Grieg (GB) & Frl H Kallmeyer
1928	R O Cummings (Aus) & E F Moon (Aus)	Miss D Akhurst (Aus) & Miss E Boyd (Aus)	R Boyd (Aus) & Frl C Aussem
1929	C Boussus (Fra) & J Brugnon (Fra)	Miss E Colyer (GB) & Miss J Fry (GB)	H G N Lee (GB) & Miss E Colyer (GB)

Year	Men's Doubles Winners	Women's Doubles Winners	Mixed Doubles Winners
1930	J H Crawford (Aus) & E F Moon (Aus)	Mrs L A Godfree (GB) & Miss P Holcroft (GB)	J C Gregory (GB) & Mrs L A Godfree (GB)
1931	W Dessart & E Nourney	Mrs L A Godfree (GB) & Miss N Trentham (GB)	H C Fisher (NZ) & Mlle L Payot (Swi)
1932	J H Crawford (Aus) & H C Hopman (Aus)	Frl H Krahwinkel & Frl A Peitz	G von Cramm & Frl H Krahwinkel
1933	R Nunoi (Jap) & J Satoh (Jap)	Mrs J B Pittman (GB) & Miss K Stammers (GB)	G von Cramm & Frl H Krahwinkel
1934	E Maier (Spa) & A K Quist (Aus)	Miss E M Dearman (GB) & Miss N M Lyle (GB)	G von Cramm & Fru H Sperling
1935	H Denker & H Henkel	Mlle M R Couquerque (Hol) & Frau A Schneider	H Henkel & Frl C Aussem
1936	not held		
1937	J H Crawford (Aus) & V B McGrath (Aus)	Mlle M R Couquerque (Hol) & Fru H Sperling	H Denker & Frl M L Horn
1938	J Leseur (Fra) & Y Petra (Fra)	Miss T Coyne (Aus) & Miss N Wynne (Aus)	A Baworowski (Pol) & Miss J Jedrzejowska (Pol)
1939	H Henkel & R Menzel	Frau A Schneider & Fru H Sperling	E Smith (USA) & Miss G W Wheeler (USA)
1940–1947	not held		
1948	G von Cramm & J E Harper (Aus)	Frau T Dietz & Frl U Heidtmann	E Buchholz & Frl U Rosenow
1949	G von Cramm & J E Harper (Aus)	Frl A von Tarney & Frau T Zehden	E Koch & Frau I Pohmann
1950	A K Quist (Aus) & O W Sidwell (Aus)	Miss D Head (USA) & Frau I Pohmann	O W Sidwell (Aus) & Frau T Dietz
1951	K Nielsen (Den) & T Ulrich (Den)	Mrs N Bolton (Aus) & Miss C Proctor (Aus)	J Borotra (Fra) & Mrs N Bolton (Aus)
1952	I Ayre (Aus) & J Drobny (Egy)	Miss D Head (USA) & Mrs A J Mottram (GB)	E W Sturgess (SA) & Miss D Head (USA)
1953	G von Cramm & J E Patty (USA)	Mrs D P Knode (USA) & Mrs A J Mottram (GB)	A J Mottram (GB) & Miss P E Ward (GB)
1954	G von Cramm & J E Patty (USA)	Mrs A J Mottram (GB) & Frau E Vollmer	H Stewart (USA) & Frau E Vollmer
1955	G von Cramm & J E Patty (USA)	Miss M Carter (Aus) & Miss B Penrose (Aus)	H Stewart (USA) & Frau E Vollmer
1956	D Candy (Aus) & L A Hoad (USA)	Miss F Muller (Aus) & Miss D G Seeney (Aus)	L Ayala (Chi) & Mrs T D Long (Aus)
1957	D Candy (Aus) & M G Rose (Aus)	Miss A Mortimer (GB) & Miss P E Ward (GB)	M G Rose (Aus) & Frl E Buding
1958	F Contreras (Mex) & M Llamas (Mex)	Mrs K Hawton (Aus) & Mrs T D Long (Aus)	A Jancso (Yug) & Sta Y Ramirez (Mex)
1959	L Ayala (Chi) & D Candy (Aus)	Sta Y Ramirez (Mex) & Sta R M Reyes (Mex)	W A Knight (GB) & Sta Y Ramirez (Mex)
1960	R S Emerson (Aus) & N A Fraser (Aus)	Frl E Buding & Miss C C Truman (GB)	I Vermaak (SA) & Miss S Reynolds (SA)
1961	R A J Hewitt (Aus) & F S Stolle (Aus)	Miss S Reynolds (SA) & Miss R Schuurman (SA)	R A J Hewitt (Aus) & Miss S Reynolds (SA)
1962	R A J Hewitt (Aus) & M F Mulligan (Aus)	Miss J Lehane (Aus) & Miss L R Turner (Aus)	K Fletcher (Aus) & Miss L R Turner (Aus)
1963	R A J Hewitt (Aus) & F S Stolle (Aus)	Miss L Hunt (Aus) & Miss A Van Zyl (SA)	F S Stolle (Aus) & Miss L R Turner (Aus)
1964	J L Arilla (Spa) & M Santana (Spa)	Miss M Smith (Aus) & Miss L R Turner (Aus)	N Pilic (Yug) & Frl H Schultze
1965	I Buding & C Kuhnke	Miss M Smith (Aus) & Miss L R Turner (Aus)	N A Fraser (Aus) & Miss M Smith (Aus)
1966	F S Stolle (Aus) & J Ulrich (Den)	Mrs P F Jones (GB) & Miss M Smith (Aus)	J D Newcombe (Aus) & Miss M Smith (Aus)
1967	R A J Hewitt (SA) & F D McMillan (SA)	Miss J A M Tegart (Aus) & Miss L R Turner (Aus)	T S Okker (Hol) & Miss G Sherriff (Aus)
1968	T S Okker (Hol) & M C Riessen (USA)	Mrs J Du Ploy (SA) & Miss P Walkden (SA)	F D McMillan (SA) & Mrs J Du Ploy (SA)
1969	T S Okker (Hol) & M C Riessen (USA)	Frl H Niessen & Miss J A M Tegart (Aus)	M C Riessen (USA) & Miss J A M Tegart (Aus)
1970	R A J Hewitt (SA) & F D McMillan (SA)	Miss K Krantzcke (Aus) & Miss K Melville (Aus)	F D McMillan (SA) & Mrs D E Dalton (Aus)
1971	J G Alexander (Aus) & A Gimeno (Spa)	Miss R Casals (USA) & Mrs L W King (USA)	J Fassbender & Frau H Orth
1972	J Kodes (Cze) & I Nastase (Rom)	Frau H Masthoff & Frau H Orth	J Fassbender & Frau H Orth
1973	J Fassbender & H J Pohmann	Frau H Masthoff & Frau H Orth	H J Pohmann & Mrs Q Pretorius (SA)
1974	J Fassbender & H J Pohmann	Miss R Giscafre (Arg) & Frau H Hoesl	J Fassbender & Frau H Orth
1975	J Gisbert (Spa) & M Orantes (Spa)	Miss D Fromholtz (Aus) & Miss R Tomanova (Cze)	not held
1976	F McNair (USA) & S C Stewart (USA)	Miss L Boshoff (SA) & Miss I Kloss (SA)	not held
1977	R A J Hewitt (SA) & K Meiler	Miss L Boshoff (SA) & Miss I Kloss (SA)	not held
1978	W Fibak (Pol) & T S Okker (Hol)	Miss M Jausovec (Yug) & Miss V Ruzici (Rom)	not held
1979	J Kodes (Cze) & T Smid (Cze)	Miss R Casals (USA) & Miss W M Turnbull (Aus)	not held
1980	H Gildemeister (Chi) & A Gomez (Ecu)	Miss H Mandlikova (Cze) & Miss B F Stove (Hol)	not held
1981	H Gildemeister (Chi) & A Gomez (Ecu)	Miss T Harford (SA) & Miss R Fairbank (SA)	not held
1982	P Slozil (Cze) & T Smid (Cze)	Miss E Gordon (SA) & Miss B Mould (SA)	not held

International Team Championships

THE DAVIS CUP

top left **Dwight F. Davis, founder of the Davis Cup.**
above **The Davis Cup. The cup itself dates from 1900. The salver and wooden base were added later to give room for the inscription of the winners.**
right **Holcombe Ward. He partnered Davis in the US side 1900 and 1902.**
left **Arthur Gore, a three times Wimbledon champion, was the top British singles man in 1900.**

The Davis Cup, more properly the International Lawn Tennis Championship, had its origins in the rivalry between British and American players. An Englishman, O E Woodhouse, carried off the first so called Championship of America in 1880. American pride hardly swelled when in 1883 the brothers C M and J S Clark challenged the doubles skill of Ernest and William Renshaw as a representative US pair. They were well beaten in two matches, played 5 days apart, at the All England Club.

The next year, 1884, three American men took part without success in the Wimbledon Championships. The British E G Meers challenged for the American title at Newport in 1889 and reached the semi-finals. In 1894 another Briton, M F Goodbody, did better and won the All-Comers' final before losing in the challenge round to R D Wrenn.

In 1897 the Americans were even harder pressed to keep ahead in their own territory, From three British challengers, Harold Mahony, H A Nisbet and Willoughby Eaves the last two made for an all British final to the All-Comers' singles, with Eaves going through to challenge in vain against Wrenn.

In the meantime the British had initiated an international team event. England competed against Ireland in 1892, playing the best of nine rubbers, a format extended one year later to the best of 15.

The initiative for full scale international team competition came from America and was more ambitious and far reaching. In 1898 the British LTA had suggested the USA play the British Isles after the Wimbledon meeting but the

Americans, occupied with the Spanish–American war, were not able to raise a team. In 1899 Dwight F Davis, inspired by a trip to California, offered a challenge cup for an inter-national team championship. It was accepted by the US National Association on 9 February 1900 and made open to any nation with a recognised Lawn Tennis Association.

Dwight Davis was, like many other leading American players of that time, a Harvard graduate. He was 21 and subsequently had a distinguished public career. He was Secretary of State for War 1925 to 1929 and then Governor-General of the Philippines. He died in 1946.

Davis was made captain and member of the first US side. It comprised Davis, Malcolm Whitman and Holcombe Ward and was raised to meet the challenge of the British Isles. None other had been expected.

The British effort was less than one hundred per cent. Neither of the Doherty brothers could make the journey and the visiting enthusiasts were Herbert Roper Barrett, Ernest Black and Arthur Gore. The venue was the Longwood Cricket Club in Boston for Wednesday, Thursday and Friday, 8 to 10 August. The format of the tie had been agreed, two singles men playing against each other plus a doubles, allowing for two players at least and four at most. Each rubber was the best of five sets. It has not varied since.

The British trio arrived in New York on the *Campania* on the morning of 4 August. Instead of going straight to Boston for practice they went sightseeing to the Niagara Falls.

In the event the British found the heat—136°F *58°C*—exhausting, the courts uneven, the balls soft and uncontrollable and the American twist services a puzzling novelty. The USA built a winning 3-nil lead and when a thunderstorm interrupted the fourth rubber between Davis and Gore further play was abandoned. The only British glory to echo down the years is the fact that the first set played in the Davis Cup was won by Great Britain, since in the opening singles Davis beat Black 4–6 6–2 6–4 6–4.

The British Isles won in 1903, which meant that in 1904 the challenge could be made in Europe. It was simpler to travel to Wimbledon than to the US. In 1904 in fact the US did not face the Atlantic crossing. France and Belgium were the challengers, Austria doing so originally but withdrawing. Australia, then with New Zealand, came in the next year. By 1914 nine nations had taken part.

After the First World War it was expedient to split the challenging nations into zones, an

The Longwood Club at Boston in the early days.

American Zone and a European Zone. That was in 1923 and the inter-zone final became the equivalent of the old All-Comers' final in the earlier years of the individual national championships, the essential preliminary to the Challenge Round.

The disparity of standards brought the creation of qualifying rounds in the European Zone in 1933 and 1934. The weaker teams had to play-off among themselves to gain acceptance in the main draw the following season. It was unpopular and the system was not maintained. By 1939 there had been 41 participating nations, the peak being 1933 with 34 nations in action.

The growth after the Second World War brought worse congestion. An Eastern Zone was created in 1952, making for a semi-final and then a final at inter-zone level. The European Zone was seeded that year for the first time. Then from 1955 the European Zone had a drop out system whereby a nation could be made to stand down for a year if its standards were assessed as weak. The judgment of form was hardly perfect and in 1962 Yugoslavia, having been thus barred, had its doubles pair, Boro Jovanovic and Nikki Pilic reaching the Wimbledon final.

The European Zone was split into two sections in 1966, each section ranking as a zone for the inter-zone ties. The most radical change came in 1972. The Challenge Round was abolished and the cup holding nation was required to play through. The USA was the first nation involved. Not only did they play through successfully to the final but there they voluntarily surrendered their choice of ground to Romania, retaining the trophy after a brilliant win in Bucharest.

The following year, 1973, the logic which brought the abolition of the old Challenge Round brought a change in the administration of the competition. From the start the control of

John McEnroe, left-handed, determined, skilled and one of the many great Americans.

Kathy Rinaldi, another of the rich American crop of talented teenagers of the early 1980s.

any year's competition had been, technically, in the hands of the champion nation. This was now passed to a Committee of Management elected from among the competing nations.

Commercial sponsorship of the Davis Cup came about in 1980. In 1981 there was a marked change in the format of the competition as a whole. The best 16 nations were put into a non-zonal competition. The remainder still competed in zones, with each of the four zone winners earning promotion to the upper group for the year following. The four worst nations from the top group, found by staging a relegation round among the eight first round losers, fell back to the zonal rounds.

The entry of Tunisia in 1982 brought up the number of participating nations to 70.

Between 1900 and 1982 the Davis Cup, which is a massive silver punch bowl lined with gold, was played for 72 times. No challenge was made in 1901 and 1910 and the competition was in abeyance during the war years 1915 to 1918 and 1940 to 1945. By the end of 1982 the total number of ties played was 1989.

PEAK YEAR

In **1982** the highest number of nations played in the Davis Cup when **57** took part. This was from an original challenge from 59 nations.

MOST CONSTANT COMPETITOR

Great Britain has been **the most constant competitor** in the Davis Cup, taking part in all competitions from 1900, save only in 1901 and 1910 when she did not challenge.

The **USA** has been the **second most constant challenger.** She made no challenge only in 1904, 1910, 1912 and 1919. She did not, of course, play in 1901 when she was the unchallenged holder.

SEQUENTIAL SUCCESS IN TIES

The **longest run** of success as **Davis Cup holder** was by the **USA** 1920 to 1926 when they won **seven Challenge Rounds** in as many years.

The longest run of success in winning Davis Cup ties was also by the **USA.** Beginning on 5 May 1968 when they beat the British Caribbean in Richmond, Virginia, they won **17 consecutive ties** (and the trophy five times) before losing to Australia in Cleveland, Ohio, on an indoor court on 4 December 1973. The interval was 5 years 213 days.

The **USA** also won nine consecutive ties be-

tween beating France at Eastbourne on 10 July 1920 and losing to France in the Challenge Round in Philadelphia on 10 September 1927. In this case the interval between starting to win and being beaten was a record **7 years 62 days.**

Australia had a slightly longer tenure as an unbeaten Davis Cup nation between 1939 and their eventual loss in the Challenge Round of 1946 but there was no play in the war years 1940 to 1945. The greatest sequence of winning ties by **Australia** was **nine** between 1959 and 1962.

France achieved a sequence of **11 winning ties** and held the trophy for 6 years 1927 to 1932. Their interval between winning on 13 May 1927 against Romania in Paris and losing in the Challenge Round to Great Britain in Paris on 30 July 1927 was **6 years 78 days.**

Great Britain had **10 winning ties** when beating Spain in Barcelona on 23 April 1933 before the Challenge Round loss to the USA at Wimbledon on 26 July 1937, an interval of **4 years 95 days.** On the other occasion when Britain held the trophy for 4 years the run extended from 8 August 1903 to 23 July 1907, an interval of 3 years 349 days.

WINNING RUBBERS IN SEQUENCE

Australia accomplished the longest winning run of Davis Cup rubbers in 1955, 1956 and 1957 when, without a loss, the sequence was **27.**

It was initiated in the final of the American Zone when Ken Rosewall beat Bob Bedard in the course of a 5-nil win against Canada. Japan was beaten 4-nil (one rubber not being played) in the first of the inter-zone matches, then Italy 5-nil. In the Challenge Round at Forest Hills, Australia beat the USA 5-nil. In the 1956 Challenge Round in Adelaide, Australia again beat the USA 5-nil. Thus far 24 successive rubbers had been won by Rosewall, Lew Hoad and Rex Hartwig with only one, a doubles, going to five sets. In the Challenge Round of 1957 Ashley Cooper and Mervyn Rose won their opening singles. By taking the doubles Anderson and Mervyn Rose won Australia's 27th successive rubber. The sequence of invincibility by Australia did not end until the first of the dead singles when Barry MacKay beat Cooper.

The **USA** had a winning sequence of 23 rubbers in 1957 and 1958. It was, curiously, initiated with MacKay's win over Cooper which ended the Australian sequence. Vic Seixas also beat Anderson in the other dead rubber of that tie. In 1958 the USA won 5-nil successively against Venezuela, Canada, Argentina and Italy to create a sequence of 22 winning rubbers. The

23rd was achieved in the first rubber of the Challenge Round against Australia in Brisbane when Alex Olmedo beat Anderson. The sequence was ended in the next rubber with Barry MacKay losing to Ashley Cooper.

Great Britain also won **23** rubbers before being beaten. This was in 1931 when the players responsible were Bunny Austin, Fred Perry, Pat Hughes and Charles Kingsley. The first of the sequence was against Monaco at Plymouth with Austin losing only one game in the opening singles. Other 5-nil victories were then had against Belgium in Brussels, South Africa and Japan at Eastbourne. In Prague against Czechoslovakia the 23rd successive rubber was gained with the doubles victory of Hughes and Perry. The defeat of Austin by Ladislav Hecht on the third day ended the run.

The **USA** also had winning runs of **22** rubbers in 1946 and 1951 and a sequence of **21** in 1932.

GREATEST NUMBER OF TIES IN A YEAR

The highest number of ties played in one year was **eight** by **Spain** in 1965. The first was in the first round of the European Zone against Greece, starting on 30 April. The last, when she lost in the Challenge Round to Australia, ended on 29 December.

The sequence was:

v Greece, won 5–0 in Barcelona,
v Chile, won 5–0 in Barcelona,
v Germany, won 4–1 in Barcelona,
v Czechoslovakia, won 4–1 in Prague,
v South Africa, won 4–1 in Barcelona, final of European Zone,
v USA, won 4–1 in Barcelona, inter-zone semi-final,
v India, won 3–2 in Barcelona, inter-zone final,
v Australia, lost 1–4 in Sydney, Challenge Round.

Four players took part, Luis Arilla, Juan Couder, Juan Gisbert and Manuel Santana. Arilla played in all eight ties, winning three out of three singles, seven out of eight doubles. Santana won eleven out of twelve singles, six out of seven doubles. Gisbert won six out of thirteen singles. Couder won three out of four singles, one out of one doubles.

GREATEST NUMBER OF WINNING RUBBERS IN A YEAR

Spain, in winning seven out of eight ties in 1965,

equalled the record of Great Britain's seven winning ties in 1933. On that occasion Great Britain did not lose and her final tally was 28 rubbers won, 7 lost. In 1931 Great Britain lost in the Challenge Round and in winning six out of seven ties took 29 rubbers to six. Spain in 1935 won a record **30 rubbers**, losing 10.

OVER-ALL RECORDS

The greatest number of games in a tie was 327.
(1974. Eastern Zone final, Calcutta. India beat Australia 3–2. J Singh beat Bob Giltinan 11–9 9–11 12–10 8–6; Vijay Amritraj lost to John Alexander 12–14 15–17 8–6 2–6; Vijay and An Amritraj beat Alexander and Colin Dibley 17–15 6–8 6–3 16–18 6–4; Singh lost to Alexander 6–8 4–6 3–6; Vijay Amritraj beat Giltinan 6–1 5–7 6–4 6–4.)

The greatest number of games in a rubber was 122.
(1973. American Zone final, Arkansas. Stan Smith and Erik Van Dillen (USA) beat Jaime Fillol and Patricio Cornejo (Chi) 7–9 37–39 8–6 6–1 6–3.)

The greatest number of games in a set was 76.
(as above).

The greatest number of games in a singles was 100.
(1982. American Zone, North Section, first round, Caracas. H Fritz (Can) beat J Andrew (Ven) 16–14 11–9 9–11 4–6 11–9.)

The greatest number of games in a set in singles was 46.
(1975. American Zone, first round, Montreal, in 1976 competition. D Power (Can) beat A Betancur (Col) 6–4 22–24 2–6 6–3 7–5.)

The longest duration of a tie was 113 days.
(1976. Eastern Zone final. Australia beat New Zealand 3–1. In Brisbane 28, 29 February, 1 March, Ross Case lost to B Fairlie 6–3 8–10 1–6 6–2 4–6; John Newcombe beat Onny Parun 8–6 6–3 7–5; Newcombe and Tony Roche beat Fairlie and Parun 6–1 3–6 6–3 7–5; on 19 June in Nottingham, England, Newcombe beat Fairlie 8–6 5–7 11–9 6–3.)

The most decisive victory was for the loss of 4 games.
(1955. Eastern Zone, first round, Rangoon. Philippines led 3-nil against Burma when Felicismo Ampon beat Ko Ko 6–1 6–1 6–0, Reymundo Deyro beat Maung 6–0 6–0 6–2, Ampon and Deyro beat Maung and Thaung 6–0 6–0 6–0. Subsequently Deyro beat Thaung 6–1 6–2 6–2 and J M Jose beat Maung 6–3 6–4 6–2 for a win 5–nil with the loss of 18 games.)

The most decisive over-all victories were for the loss of 15 games.

(There were three such occasions: 1924 in the American Zone, first round, in New York, Australia beating China, taking a winning lead for the loss of 11 games; 1931 American Zone, first round, in Ascuncion with Argentina beating Paraguay and taking a winning lead also for the loss of 11 games; 1931 American Zone, second round, in Buenos Aires, Argentina this time beating Uruguay and taking a winning lead for the loss of 13 games.)

The youngest player in the Davis Cup was Haroon Rahim at 15 years 140 days.

(Rahim, born 12 November 1949, played for Pakistan against Viet Nam in Kuala Lumpur on 1 March 1965. Rahim beat Vo Van Bay 3–6 3–6 7–5 7–5 6–1 in the opening rubber. It was the only Pakistani success, Viet Nam winning 4–1.)

The second youngest was Bjorn Borg at 15 years 330 days.

(Borg, born 6 June 1956, played for Sweden against New Zealand in Baastad on 5 May 1972. Borg beat Onny Parun 4–6 3–6 6–3 6–4 6–4 in the opening rubber. Sweden won the tie 4–1.)

The oldest player in the Davis Cup, as far as is known, was Torben Ulrich at 48 years 11 months.

(Ulrich, born 4 October 1928, played for Denmark in Brussels in September in the preliminary round for the 1978 competition. In the second of his two singles he was beaten 3–6 1–6 3–6 by T Stevaux of Belgium, winners of the tie by 3–2.)

The second oldest was, as far as is known, Jean Borotra at 48 years 300 days.

(Borotra, born 13 August 1898, played for France against Czechoslovakia in Prague. In the doubles with Yvon Petra he lost, 8–10 12–14 3–6, to Jaroslav Drobny and Vladimir Cernik, on 13 June 1947, France losing the tie 1–4.)

The oldest player to win in the Davis Cup was, as far as is known, Colin Gregory at 48 years 295 days.

(Gregory, born 28 July 1903, played for Great Britain against Yugoslavia in Belgrade when he partnered Roger Becker to beat J Palada and S Laszlo 6–4 1–6 9–11 6–2 6–2 on 18 May 1952. Great Britain won the tie 3–2.)

Torben Ulrich, a left hander and the oldest Davis Cup player.

RESULTS

CHALLENGE/FINAL ROUNDS SUMMARY

Year	Number playing	Champion	Runner-up	Score	Winning Lead	Venue
1900	2	USA	British Isles	3–0	3–0	Boston
1901 not held						
1902	2	USA	British Isles	3–2	3–1	New York
1903	2	British Isles	USA	4–1	3–1	Boston
1904	3	British Isles	Belgium	5–0	3–0	Wimbledon
1905	5	British Isles	USA	5–0	3–0	Wimbledon
1906	3	British Isles	USA	5–0	3–0	Wimbledon
1907	3	Australasia	British Isles	3–2	3–2	Wimbledon
1908	3	Australasia	USA	3–2	3–2	Melbourne
1909	3	Australasia	USA	5–0	3–0	Sydney
1910 not held						
1911	3	Australasia	USA	5–0	3–0	Christchurch
1912	3	British Isles	Australasia	3–2	3–2	Melbourne
1913	8	USA	British Isles	3–2	3–1	Wimbledon
1914	7	Australasia	USA	3–2	3–1	New York
1915–1918 not held						
1919	5	Australasia	British Isles	4–1	3–1	Sydney
1920	6	USA	Australasia	5–0	3–0	Auckland
1921	11	USA	Japan	5–0	3–0	New York
1922	11	USA	Australasia	4–1	3–1	New York
1923	16	USA	Australia	4–1	3–1	New York
1924	22	USA	Australia	5–0	3–0	Philadelphia
1925	23	USA	France	5–0	3–0	Philadelphia
1926	24	USA	France	4–1	3–0	Philadelphia
1927	26	France	USA	3–2	3–2	Philadelphia
1928	33	France	USA	4–1	3–1	Paris
1929	29	France	USA	3–2	3–1	Paris
1930	28	France	USA	4–1	3–1	Paris
1931	30	France	Great Britain	3–2	3–1	Paris
1932	29	France	USA	3–2	3–1	Paris
1933	31	Great Britain	France	3–2	3–2	Paris
1934	27	Great Britain	USA	4–1	3–1	Wimbledon
1935	28	Great Britain	USA	5–0	3–0	Wimbledon
1936	23	Great Britain	Australia	3–2	3–2	Wimbledon
1937	25	USA	Great Britain	4–1	3–1	Wimbledon
1938	24	USA	Australia	3–2	3–1	Philadelphia
1939	25	Australia	USA	3–2	3–2	Philadelphia
1940–1945 not held						
1946	19	USA	Australia	5–0	3–0	Melbourne
1947	22	USA	Australia	4–1	3–1	New York
1948	29	USA	Australia	5–0	3–0	New York
1949	26	USA	Australia	4–1	3–1	New York
1950	25	Australia	USA	4–1	3–0	New York
1951	27	Australia	USA	3–2	3–2	Sydney
1952	29	Australia	USA	4–1	3–0	Adelaide
1953	30	Australia	USA	3–2	3–2	Melbourne
1954	31	USA	Australia	3–2	3–0	Sydney
1955	34	Australia	USA	5–0	3–0	New York
1956	33	Australia	USA	5–0	3–0	Adelaide
1957	36	Australia	USA	3–2	3–0	Melbourne
1958	37	USA	Australia	3–2	3–1	Brisbane
1959	39	Australia	USA	3–2	3–2	New York
1960	40	Australia	Italy	4–1	3–0	Sydney
1961	42	Australia	Italy	5–0	3–0	Melbourne
1962	42	Australia	Mexico	5–0	3–0	Brisbane
1963	48	USA	Australia	3–2	3–2	Adelaide
1964	46	Australia	USA	3–2	3–2	Cleveland
1965	44	Australia	Spain	4–1	3–0	Sydney
1966	46	Australia	India	4–1	3–1	Melbourne
1967	48	Australia	Spain	4–1	3–0	Brisbane
1968	49	USA	Australia	4–1	3–0	Adelaide
1969	51	USA	Romania	5–0	3–0	Cleveland

Year	Number playing	Champion	Runner-up	Score	Winning Lead	Venue
1970	50	USA	W Germany	5–0	3–0	Cleveland
1971	51	USA	Romania	3–2	3–1	Charlotte, NC
Challenge Round abolished						
1972	51	USA	Romania	3–2	3–1	Bucharest
1973	52	Australia	USA	5–0	3–0	Cleveland (indoors)
1974	55	South Africa	India	w.o.		
1975	54	Sweden	Czechoslovakia	3–2	3–1	Stockholm (indoors)
1976	53	Italy	Chile	4–1	3–0	Santiago
1977	55	Australia	Italy	3–1	3–1	Sydney
1978	50	USA	Great Britain	4–1	3–1	Palm Springs
1979	48	USA	Italy	5–0	3–0	San Francisco (indoors)
1980	50	Czechoslovakia	Italy	4–1	3–0	Prague (indoors)
1981	51	USA	Argentina	3–1	3–1	Cincinnati (indoors)
1982	57	USA	France	4–1	3–0	Grenoble, France

CHALLENGE ROUND SCORES

1900 USA beat British Isles 3–0, Boston

M D Whitman	beat	A W Gore	6–1 6–3 6–2
D F Davis	beat	E D Black	4–6 6–2 6–4 6–4
Davis & H Ward	beat	Black & H Roper Barrett	6–4 6–4 6–4
Davis	v	Gore	9–7 9–9 div'd

1901 not held

1902 USA beat British Isles 3–2, Brooklyn, New York

W A Larned	lost to	R F Doherty	6–2 6–3 3–6 4–6 4–6
M D Whitman	beat	J Pim	6–1 6–1 1–6 6–0
Larned	beat	Pim	6–3 6–2 6–3
Whitman	beat	R F Doherty	6–1 7–5 6–4
D F Davis & H Ward	lost to	R F & H L Doherty	6–3 8–10 3–6 4–6

1903 British Isles beat USA 4–1, Boston

H L Doherty	beat	R D Wrenn	6–0 6–3 6–4
R F Doherty	lost to	W A Larned	retired
R F & H L Doherty	beat	R D & G L Wrenn	7–5 9–7 2–6 6–3
H L Doherty	beat	Larned	6–3 6–8 6–0 2–6 7–5
R F Doherty	beat	R D Wrenn	6–4 3–6 6–3 6–8 6–4

1904 British Isles beat Belgium 5–0, Wimbledon

H L Doherty	beat	P de Borman	6–4 6–1 6–1
F L Riseley	beat	W Lemaire	6–1 6–4 6–2
R F & H L Doherty	beat	de Borman & Lemaire	6–0 6–1 6–3
H L Doherty	w.o.	Lemaire	scratched
Riseley	beat	de Borman	4–6 6–2 8–6 7–5

1905 British Isles beat USA 5–0, Wimbledon

H L Doherty	beat	H Ward	7–9 4–6 6–1 6–2 6–0
S H Smith	beat	W A Larned	6–4 6–4 5–7 6–4
R F & H L Doherty	beat	Ward & B Wright	8–10 6–2 6–2 4–6 8–6
Smith	beat	W J Clothier	4–6 6–1 6–4 6–3
H L Doherty	beat	Larned	6–4 2–6 6–8 6–4 6–2

1906 British Isles beat USA 5–0, Wimbledon

S H Smith	beat	R D Little	6–4 6–4 6–1
H L Doherty	beat	H Ward	6–2 8–6 6–3
R F & H L Doherty	beat	Little & Ward	3–6 11–9 9–7 6–1
Smith	beat	Ward	6–1 6–0 6–4
H L Doherty	beat	Little	3–6 6–3 6–8 6–1 6–3

1907 Australasia beat British Isles 3–2, Wimbledon

N E Brookes	beat	A W Gore	7–5 6–1 7–5
A F Wilding	beat	H Roper Barrett	1–6 6–4 6–3 7–5
Brookes & Wilding	lost to	Gore & Roper Barrett	6–3 6–4 5–7 2–6 11–13
Wilding	lost to	Gore	6–3 3–6 5–7 2–6
Brookes	beat	Roper Barrett	6–2 6–0 6–3

1908 Australasia beat USA 3–2, Melbourne

N E Brookes	beat	F B Alexander	5–7 9–7 6–2 4–6 6–3
A F Wilding	lost to	B Wright	6–3 5–7 3–6 1–6
Brookes & Wilding	beat	Alexander & Wright	6–4 6–2 5–7 1–6 6–4
Brookes	lost to	Wright	6–0 6–3 5–7 2–6 10–12
Wilding	beat	Alexander	6–3 6–4 6–1

1909 Australasia beat USA 5–0, Sydney

N E Brookes	beat	M E McLoughlin	6–2 6–2 6–4
A F Wilding	beat	M H Long	6–2 7–5 6–1
Brookes & Wilding	beat	Long & McLoughlin	12–10 9–7 6–3
Brookes	beat	Long	6–4 7–5 8–6
Wilding	beat	McLoughlin	3–6 8–6 6–2 6–3

1910 not held

1911 Australasia beat USA 5–0, Christchurch, NZ

N E Brookes	beat	B Wright	6–4 2–6 6–3 6–3
R W Heath	beat	W A Larned	2–6 6–1 7–5 6–2
Brookes & A W Dunlop	beat	Wright & M E McLoughlin	6–4 5–7 7–5 6–4
Brookes	beat	McLoughlin	6–4 3–6 4–6 6–3 6–4
Heath	w.o.	Wright	scratched

1912 British Isles beat Australasia 3–2, Melbourne

J C Parke	beat	N E Brookes	8–6 6–3 5–7 6–2
C P Dixon	beat	R W Heath	5–7 6–4 6–4 6–4
A E Beamish & Parke	lost to	Brookes & A W Dunlop	4–6 1–6 5–7
Dixon	lost to	Brookes	2–6 4–6 4–6
Parke	beat	Heath	6–2 6–4 6–4

1913 USA beat British Isles 3–2, Wimbledon

M E McLoughlin	lost to	J C Parke	10–8 5–7 4–6 6–1 5–7
R N Williams	beat	C P Dixon	8–6 3–6 6–2 1–6 7–5
H Hackett & McLoughlin	beat	Dixon & H Roper Barrett	5–7 6–1 2–6 7–5 6–4
McLoughlin	beat	Dixon	8–6 6–3 6–2
Williams	lost to	Parke	2–6 7–5 7–5 4–6 2–6

1914 Australasia beat USA 3–2, Forest Hills, NY

A F Wilding	beat	R N Williams	7–5 6–2 6–3
N E Brookes	lost to	M E McLoughlin	15–17 3–6 3–6
Brookes & Wilding	beat	T C Bundy and McLoughlin	6–3 8–6 9–7
Brookes	beat	Williams	6–1 6–2 8–10 6–3
Wilding	lost to	McLoughlin	2–6 3–6 6–2 2–6

1915–1918 not held

1919 Australasia beat British Isles 4–1, Sydney

G L Patterson	beat	A H Lowe	6–4 6–3 2–6 6–3
J O Anderson	lost to	A R F Kingscote	5–7 2–6 4–6
N E Brookes & Patterson	beat	A E Beamish & Kingscote	6–0 6–0 6–2
Patterson	beat	Kingscote	6–4 6–4 8–6
Anderson	beat	Lowe	6–4 5–7 6–3 4–6 12–10

1920 USA beat Australasia 5–0, Auckland

W T Tilden	beat	N E Brookes	10–8 6–4 1–6 6–4
W M Johnston	beat	G L Patterson	6–3 6–1 6–1

Johnston & Tilden	beat	Brookes & Patterson	4–6 6–4 6–0 6–4
Johnston	beat	Brookes	5–7 7–5 6–3 6–3
Tilden	beat	Patterson	5–7 6–2 6–3 6–3

1921 USA beat Japan 5–0, Forest Hills, NY

W M Johnston	beat	I Kumagae	6–2 6–4 6–2
W T Tilden	beat	Z Shimidzu	5–7 4–6 7–5 6–2 6–1
W Washburn & R N Williams	beat	Kumagae & Shimidzu	6–2 7–5 4–6 7–5
Tilden	beat	Kumagae	9–7 6–4 6–1
Johnston	beat	Shimidzu	6–3 5–7 6–2 6–4

1922 USA beat Australasia 4–1, Forest Hills, NY

W T Tilden	beat	G L Patterson	7–5 10–8 6–0
W M Johnston	beat	J O Anderson	6–1 6–2 6–3
V Richards & Tilden	lost to	P O'Hara Wood & Patterson	4–6 0–6 3–6
Johnston	beat	Patterson	6–2 6–2 6–1
Tilden	beat	Anderson	6–4 5–7 3–6 6–4 6–2

1923 USA beat Australia 4–1, Forest Hills, NY

W M Johnston	lost to	J O Anderson	6–4 2–6 6–2 5–7 2–6
W T Tilden	beat	J B Hawkes	6–4 6–2 6–1
Tilden & R N Williams	beat	Anderson & Hawkes	17–15 11–13 2–6 6–3 6–2
Johnston	beat	Hawkes	6–0 6–2 6–1
Tilden	beat	Anderson	6–2 6–3 1–6 7–5

1924 USA beat Australia 5–0, Philadelphia

W T Tilden	beat	G L Patterson	6–4 6–2 6–3
V Richards	beat	P O'Hara Wood	6–3 6–2 6–4
W M Johnston & Tilden	beat	O'Hara Wood & Patterson	5–7 6–3 6–4 6–1
Tilden	beat	O'Hara Wood	6–2 6–1 6–1
Richards	beat	Patterson	6–3 7–5 6–4

1925 USA beat France 5–0, Philadelphia

W T Tilden	beat	J Borotra	4–6 6–0 2–6 9–7 6–4
W M Johnston	beat	R Lacoste	6–1 6–1 6–8 6–3
V Richards & R N Williams	beat	Borotra & Lacoste	6–4 6–4 6–3
Tilden	beat	Lacoste	3–6 10–12 8–6 7–5 6–2
Johnston	beat	Borotra	6–1 6–4 6–0

1926 USA beat France 4–1, Philadelphia

W M Johnston	beat	R Lacoste	6–0 6–4 0–6 6–0
W T Tilden	beat	J Borotra	6–2 6–3 6–3
V Richards & R N Williams	beat	J Brugnon & H Cochet	6–4 6–4 6–2
Johnston	beat	Borotra	8–6 6–4 9–7
Tilden	lost to	Lacoste	6–4 4–6 6–8 6–8

1927 France beat USA 3–2, Philadelphia

R Lacoste	beat	W M Johnston	6–3 6–2 6–2
H Cochet	lost to	W T Tilden	4–6 6–2 2–6 6–8
J Borotra & J Brugnon	lost to	F Hunter & Tilden	6–3 3–6 3–6 6–4 0–6
Lacoste	beat	Tilden	6–4 4–6 6–3 6–3
Cochet	beat	Johnston	6–4 4–6 6–2 6–4

1928 France beat USA 4–1, Paris

R Lacoste	lost to	W T Tilden	6–1 4–6 4–6 6–2 3–6
H Cochet	beat	J Hennessey	5–7 9–7 6–3 6–0
J Borotra & Cochet	beat	F Hunter & Tilden	6–4 6–8 7–5 4–6 6–2
Lacoste	beat	Hennessey	4–6 6–1 7–5 6–3
Cochet	beat	Tilden	9–7 8–6 6–4

1929 France beat USA 3–2, Paris

H Cochet	beat	W T Tilden	6–3 6–1 6–2

J Borotra	beat	G M Lott	6–1 3–6 6–4 7–5
Borotra & Cochet	lost to	W Allison & J Van Ryn	1–6 6–8 4–6
Cochet	beat	Lott	6–1 3–6 6–0 6–3
Borotra	lost to	Tilden	6–4 1–6 4–6 5–7

1930 France beat USA 4–1, Paris

J Borotra	lost to	W T Tilden	6–2 5–7 4–6 5–7
H Cochet	beat	G M Lott	6–4 6–2 6–2
J Brugnon & Cochet	beat	W Allison & J Van Ryn	6–3 7–5 1–6 6–2
Borotra	beat	Lott	5–7 6–3 2–6 6–2 8–6
Cochet	beat	Tilden	4–6 6–3 6–1 7–5

1931 France beat Great Britain 3–2, Paris

H Cochet	beat	H W Austin	3–6 11–9 6–2 6–4
J Borotra	lost to	F J Perry	6–4 8–10 0–6 6–4 4–6
J Brugnon & Cochet	beat	G P Hughes & C H Kingsley	6–1 5–7 6–3 8–6
Cochet	beat	Perry	6–4 1–6 9–7 6–3
Borotra	lost to	Austin	5–7 3–6 6–3 5–7

1932 France beat USA 3–2, Paris

H Cochet	beat	W Allison	5–7 7–5 3–6 7–5 6–2
J Borotra	beat	H E Vines	6–4 6–2 2–6 6–4
J Brugnon & Cochet	lost to	Allison & J Van Ryn	3–6 13–11 5–7 6–4 4–6
Borotra	beat	Allison	1–6 3–6 6–4 6–2 7–5
Cochet	lost to	Vines	6–4 6–0 5–7 6–8 2–6

1933 Great Britain beat France 3–2, Paris

H W Austin	beat	A Merlin	6–3 6–4 6–0
F J Perry	beat	H Cochet	8–10 6–4 8–6 3–6 6–1
G P Hughes & H G N Lee	lost to	J Borotra & J Brugnon	3–6 6–8 2–6
Austin	lost to	Cochet	7–5 4–6 6–4 4–6 4–6
Perry	beat	Merlin	4–6 8–6 6–2 7–5

1934 Great Britain beat USA 4–1, Wimbledon

F J Perry	beat	S B Wood	6–1 4–6 5–7 6–0 6–3
H W Austin	beat	F X Shields	6–4 6–4 6–1
G P Hughes & H G N Lee	lost to	G M Lott & L Stoefen	5–7 0–6 6–4 7–9
Perry	beat	Shields	6–4 4–6 6–2 15–13
Austin	beat	Wood	6–4 6–0 6–8 6–3

1935 Great Britain beat USA 5–0, Wimbledon

F J Perry	beat	J D Budge	6–0 6–8 6–3 6–4
H W Austin	beat	W Allison	6–2 2–6 4–6 6–3 7–5
G P Hughes & C R D Tuckey	beat	Allison & J Van Ryn	6–2 1–6 6–8 6–3 6–3
Perry	beat	Allison	4–6 6–4 7–5 6–3
Austin	beat	Budge	6–2 6–4 6–8 7–5

1936 Great Britain beat Australia 3–2, Wimbledon

H W Austin	beat	J H Crawford	4–6 6–3 6–1 6–1
F J Perry	beat	A K Quist	6–1 4–6 7–5 6–2
G P Hughes & C R D Tuckey	lost to	Crawford & Quist	4–6 6–2 5–7 8–10
Austin	lost to	Quist	4–6 6–3 5–7 2–6
Perry	beat	Crawford	6–2 6–3 6–3

1937 USA beat Great Britain 4–1, Wimbledon

F A Parker	lost to	H W Austin	3–6 2–6 5–7
J D Budge	beat	C E Hare	15–13 6–1 6–2
Budge & G Mako	beat	C R D Tuckey & F H D Wilde	6–3 7–5 7–9 12–10
Parker	beat	Hare	6–2 6–4 6–2
Budge	beat	Austin	8–6 3–6 6–4 6–3

1938 USA beat Australia 3–2, Philadelphia

R L Riggs	beat	A K Quist	4–6 6–0 8–6 6–1
J D Budge	beat	J E Bromwich	6–2 6–3 4–6 7–5
Budge & G Mako	lost to	Bromwich & Quist	6–0 3–6 4–6 2–6
Budge	beat	Quist	8–6 6–1 6–2
Riggs	lost to	Bromwich	4–6 6–4 0–6 2–6

1939 Australia beat USA 3–2, Philadelphia

J E Bromwich	lost to	R L Riggs	4–6 0–6 5–7
A K Quist	lost to	F A Parker	3–6 6–2 4–6 6–1 5–7
Bromwich & Quist	beat	J R Hunt & J Kramer	5–7 6–2 7–5 6–2
Quist	beat	Riggs	6–1 6–4 3–6 3–6 6–4
Bromwich	beat	Parker	6–0 6–3 6–1

1940–1945 not held

1946 USA beat Australia 5–0, Melbourne

F R Schroeder	beat	J E Bromwich	3–6 6–1 6–2 0–6 6–3
J Kramer	beat	D Pails	8–6 6–2 9–7
Kramer & Schroeder	beat	Bromwich & A K Quist	6–2 7–5 6–4
Kramer	beat	Bromwich	8–6 6–4 6–4
G Mulloy	beat	Pails	6–3 6–3 6–4

1947 USA beat Australia 4–1, Forest Hills, NY

J Kramer	beat	D Pails	6–2 6–1 6–2
F R Schroeder	beat	J E Bromwich	6–4 5–7 6–3 6–3
Kramer & Schroeder	lost to	Bromwich & C F Long	4–6 6–2 2–6 4–6
Schroeder	beat	Pails	6–3 8–6 4–6 9–11 10–8
Kramer	beat	Bromwich	6–3 6–2 6–2

1948 USA beat Australia 5–0, Forest Hills, NY

F A Parker	beat	O W Sidwell	6–4 6–4 6–4
F R Schroeder	beat	A K Quist	6–3 4–6 6–0 6–0
G Mulloy & W F Talbert	beat	C F Long & Sidwell	8–6 9–7 2–6 7–5
Parker	beat	Quist	6–2 6–2 6–3
Schroeder	beat	Sidwell	6–2 6–1 6–1

1949 USA beat Australia 4–1, Forest Hills, NY

F R Schroeder	beat	O W Sidwell	6–1 5–7 4–6 6–2 6–3
R A Gonzales	beat	F A Sedgman	8–6 6–4 9–7
G Mulloy & W F Talbert	lost to	J E Bromwich & Sidwell	6–3 6–4 8–10 7–9 7–9
Schroeder	beat	Sedgman	6–4 6–3 6–3
Gonzales	beat	Sidwell	6–1 6–3 6–3

1950 Australia beat USA 4–1, Forest Hills, NY

F A Sedgman	beat	T Brown	6–0 8–6 9–7
K McGregor	beat	F R Schroeder	13–11 6–3 6–4
J E Bromwich & Sedgman	beat	G Mulloy & Schroeder	4–6 6–4 6–2 4–6 6–4
Sedgman	beat	Schroeder	6–2 6–2 6–2
McGregor	lost to	Brown	11–9 10–8 9–11 1–6 4–6

1951 Australia beat USA 3–2, Sydney

M G Rose	lost to	E V Seixas	3–6 4–6 7–9
F A Sedgman	beat	F R Schroeder	6–4 6–3 4–6 6–4
K McGregor & Sedgman	beat	Schroeder & M A Trabert	6–2 9–7 6–3
Rose	lost to	Schroeder	4–6 11–13 5–7
Sedgman	beat	Seixas	6–4 6–2 6–2

1952 Australia beat USA 4–1, Adelaide

F A Sedgman	beat	E V Seixas	6–3 6–4 6–3
K McGregor	beat	M A Trabert	11–9 6–4 6–1
McGregor & Sedgman	beat	Seixas & Trabert	6–3 6–4 1–6 6–3

Sedgman	beat	Trabert	7–5 6–4 10–8
McGregor	lost to	Seixas	3–6 6–8 8–6 3–6

1953 Australia beat USA 3–2, Melbourne

L A Hoad	beat	E V Seixas	6–4 6–2 6–3
K R Rosewall	lost to	M A Trabert	3–6 4–6 4–6
R Hartwig & Hoad	lost to	Seixas & Trabert	2–6 4–6 4–6
Hoad	beat	Trabert	13–11 6–3 2–6 3–6 7–5
Rosewall	beat	Seixas	6–2 2–6 6–3 6–4

1954 USA beat Australia 3–2, Sydney

M A Trabert	beat	L A Hoad	6–4 2–6 12–10 6–3
E V Seixas	beat	K R Rosewall	8–6 6–8 6–4 6–3
Seixas & Trabert	beat	Hoad & Rosewall	6–2 4–6 6–2 10–8
Trabert	lost to	Rosewall	7–9 5–7 3–6
Seixas	lost to	R Hartwig	6–4 3–6 2–6 3–6

1955 Australia beat USA 5–0, Forest Hills, NY

K R Rosewall	beat	E V Seixas	6–3 10–8 4–6 6–2
L A Hoad	beat	M A Trabert	4–6 6–3 6–3 8–6
R Hartwig & Hoad	beat	Seixas & Trabert	12–14 6–4 6–3 3–6 7–5
Rosewall	beat	H Richardson	6–4 3–6 6–1 6–4
Hoad	beat	Seixas	7–9 6–1 6–4 6–4

1956 Australia beat USA 5–0, Adelaide

L A Hoad	beat	H Flam	6–2 6–3 6–3
K R Rosewall	beat	E V Seixas	6–2 7–5 6–3
Hoad & Rosewall	beat	S Giammalva & Seixas	1–6 6–1 7–5 6–4
Hoad	beat	Seixas	6–2 7–5 6–3
Rosewall	beat	Giammalva	4–6 6–1 8–6 7–5

1957 Australia beat USA 3–2, Melbourne

A J Cooper	beat	E V Seixas	3–6 7–5 6–1 1–6 6–3
M J Anderson	beat	B MacKay	6–3 7–5 3–6 7–9 6–3
Anderson & M G Rose	beat	MacKay & Seixas	6–4 6–4 8–6
Cooper	lost to	MacKay	4–6 6–1 6–4 4–6 3–6
Anderson	lost to	Seixas	3–6 6–4 3–6 6–0 11–13

1958 USA beat Australia 3–2, Brisbane

A Olmedo	beat	M J Anderson	8–6 2–6 9–7 8–6
B MacKay	lost to	A J Cooper	6–4 3–6 2–6 4–6
Olmedo & H Richardson	beat	Anderson & N A Fraser	10–12 3–6 16–14 6–3 7–5
Olmedo	beat	Cooper	6–3 4–6 6–4 8–6
MacKay	lost to	Anderson	5–7 11–13 9–11

1959 Australia beat USA 3–2, Forest Hills, NY

N A Fraser	beat	A Olmedo	8–6 6–8 6–4 8–6
R G Laver	lost to	B MacKay	5–7 4–6 1–6
R S Emerson & Fraser	beat	E Buchholz & Olmedo	7–5 7–5 6–4
Laver	lost to	Olmedo	7–9 6–4 8–10 10–12
Fraser	beat	MacKay	8–6 3–6 6–2 6–4

1960 Australia beat Italy 4–1, Sydney

N A Fraser	beat	O Sirola	4–6 6–3 6–3 6–3
R G Laver	beat	N Pietrangeli	8–6 6–4 6–3
R S Emerson & Fraser	beat	Pietrangeli & Sirola	10–8 5–7 6–3 6–4
Laver	beat	Sirola	9–7 6–2 6–3
Fraser	lost to	Pietrangeli	9–11 3–6 6–1 2–6

1961 Australia beat Italy 5–0, Melbourne

R S Emerson	beat	N Pietrangeli	8–6 6–4 6–0
R G Laver	beat	O Sirola	6–1 6–4 6–3

Emerson & N A Fraser	beat	Pietrangeli & Sirola	6–2 6–3 6–4
Emerson	beat	Sirola	6–2 6–3 4–6 6–2
Laver	beat	Pietrangeli	6–3 3–6 4–6 6–3 8–6

1962 Australia beat Mexico 5–0, Brisbane

N A Fraser	beat	A Palafox	7–9 6–3 6–4 11–9
R G Laver	beat	R H Osuna	6–2 6–1 7–5
R S Emerson & Laver	beat	Osuna & Palafox	7–5 6–2 6–4
Fraser	beat	Osuna	3–6 11–9 6–1 3–6 6–4
Laver	beat	Palafox	6–1 4–6 6–4 8–6

1963 USA beat Australia 3–2, Adelaide

R D Ralston	beat	J D Newcombe	6–4 6–1 3–6 4–6 7–5
C R McKinley	lost to	R S Emerson	3–6 6–3 5–7 5–7
McKinley & Ralston	beat	Emerson & N A Fraser	6–3 4–6 11–9 11–9
Ralston	lost to	Emerson	2–6 3–6 6–3 2–6
McKinley	beat	Newcombe	10–12 6–2 9–7 6–2

1964 Australia beat USA 3–2, Cleveland, Ohio

F S Stolle	lost to	C R McKinley	1–6 7–9 6–4 2–6
R S Emerson	beat	R D Ralston	6–3 6–1 6–3
Emerson & Stolle	lost to	McKinley & Ralston	4–6 6–4 6–4 3–6 4–6
Stolle	beat	Ralston	7–5 6–3 3–6 9–11 6–4
Emerson	beat	McKinley	3–6 6–2 6–4 6–4

1965 Australia beat Spain 4–1, Sydney

F S Stolle	beat	M Santana	10–12 3–6 6–1 6–4 7–5
R S Emerson	beat	J Gisbert	6–3 6–2 6–2
J D Newcombe & A D Roche	beat	J L Arilla & Santana	6–3 4–6 7–5 6–2
Emerson	lost to	Santana	6–2 3–6 4–6 13–15
Stolle	beat	Gisbert	6–2 6–4 8–6

1966 Australia beat India 4–1, Melbourne

F S Stolle	beat	R Krishnan	6–3 6–2 6–4
R S Emerson	beat	J Mukerjea	7–5 6–4 6–2
J D Newcombe & A D Roche	lost to	Krishnan & Mukerjea	6–4 5–7 4–6 4–6
Emerson	beat	Krishnan	6–0 6–2 10–8
Stolle	beat	Mukerjea	7–5 6–8 6–3 5–7 6–3

1967 Australia beat Spain 4–1, Brisbane

R S Emerson	beat	M Santana	6–4 6–1 6–1
J D Newcombe	beat	M Orantes	6–3 6–3 6–2
Newcombe & A D Roche	beat	Orantes & Santana	6–4 6–4 6–4
Newcombe	lost to	Santana	5–7 4–6 2–6
Emerson	beat	Orantes	6–1 6–1 2–6 6–4

1968 USA beat Australia 4–1, Adelaide

C Graebner	beat	W W Bowrey	8–10 6–4 8–6 3–6 6–1
A R Ashe	beat	R O Ruffels	6–8 7–5 6–3 6–3
R C Lutz & S R Smith	beat	J G Alexander & Ruffels	6–4 6–4 6–2
Graebner	beat	Ruffels	3–6 8–6 2–6 6–3 6–1
Ashe	lost to	Bowrey	6–2 3–6 9–11 6–8

1969 USA beat Romania 5–0, Cleveland, Ohio

A R Ashe	beat	I Nastase	6–2 15–13 7–5
S R Smith	beat	I Tiriac	6–8 6–3 5–7 6–4 6–4
R C Lutz & Smith	beat	Nastase & Tiriac	8–6 6–1 11–9
Smith	beat	Nastase	4–6 4–6 6–4 6–1 11–9
Ashe	beat	Tiriac	6–3 8–6 3–6 4–0 ret'd

1970 USA beat West Germany 5–0, Cleveland, Ohio

A R Ashe	beat	W Bungert	6–2 10–8 6–2

C Richey	beat	C Kuhnke	6–3 6–4 6–2
R C Lutz & S R Smith	beat	Bungert & Kuhnke	6–3 7–5 6–4
Richey	beat	Bungert	6–4 6–4 7–5
Ashe	beat	Kuhnke	6–8 10–12 9–7 13–11 6–4

1971 USA beat Romania 3–2, Charlotte, NC

S R Smith	beat	I Nastase	7–5 6–3 6–1
F A Froehling	beat	I Tiriac	3–6 1–6 6–1 6–3 8–6
Smith & E Van Dillen	lost to	Nastase & Tiriac	5–7 4–6 8–6
Smith	beat	Tiriac	8–6 6–3 6–0
Froehling	lost to	Nastase	3–6 1–6 6–1 4–6

Challenge Round abolished.

FINAL ROUND SCORES

1972 USA beat Romania 3–2, Bucharest

S R Smith	beat	I Nastase	11–9 6–2 6–3
T Gorman	lost to	I Tiriac	6–4 6–2 4–6 3–6 2–6
Smith & E Van Dillen	beat	Nastase & Tiriac	6–2 6–0 6–3
Smith	beat	Tiriac	4–6 6–2 6–4 2–6 6–0
Gorman	lost to	Nastase	1–6 2–6 7–5 8–10

1973 Australia beat USA 5–0, Cleveland, Ohio (indoors)

J D Newcombe	beat	S R Smith	6–1 3–6 6–3 3–6 6–4
R G Laver	beat	T Gorman	8–10 8–6 6–8 6–3 6–1
Laver & Newcombe	beat	Smith & E Van Dillen	6–1 6–2 6–4
Newcombe	beat	Gorman	6–2 6–1 6–3
Laver	beat	Smith	6–3 6–4 3–6 6–2

1974 South Africa walked over India

1975 Sweden beat Czechoslovakia 3–2, Stockholm (indoors)

O Bengtson	lost to	J Kodes	4–6 6–2 5–7 4–6
B Borg	beat	J Hrebec	6–1 6–3 6–0
Bengtson & Borg	beat	Kodes & V Zednik	6–4 6–4 6–4
Borg	beat	Kodes	6–4 6–2 6–2
Bengtson	lost to	Hrebec	6–1 3–6 1–6 4–6

1976 Italy beat Chile 4–1, Santiago

C Barazzutti	beat	J Fillol	7–5 4–6 7–5 6–1
A Panatta	beat	P Cornejo	6–3 6–1 6–3
P Bertolucci & Panatta	beat	Cornejo & Fillol	3–6 6–2 9–7 6–3
Panatta	beat	Fillol	8–6 6–4 3–6 10–8
A Zugarelli	lost to	B Prajoux	4–6 4–6 2–6

1977 Australia beat Italy 3–1, Sydney

A D Roche	beat	A Panatta	6–3 6–4 6–4
J G Alexander	beat	C Barazzutti	6–2 8–6 4–6 6–2
Alexander & P Dent	lost to	P Bertolucci & Panatta	4–6 4–6 5–7
Alexander	beat	Panatta	6–4 4–6 2–6 8–6 11–9
Roche	v	Barazzutti	12–12 div'd

1978 USA beat Great Britain 4–1, Palm Springs, California

J P McEnroe	beat	J M Lloyd	6–1 6–2 6–2
B E Gottfried	lost to	C J Mottram	6–4 6–2 8–10 4–6 3–6
R C Lutz & S R Smith	beat	M Cox & D A Lloyd	6–2 6–2 6–3
McEnroe	beat	Mottram	6–2 6–2 6–1
Gottfried	beat	J M Lloyd	6–1 6–2 6–4

1979 USA beat Italy 5–0, San Francisco (indoors)

| V Gerulaitis | beat | C Barazzutti | 6–3 3–2 ret'd |

J P McEnroe	beat	A Panatta	6–2 6–3 6–4
R C Lutz & S R Smith	beat	P Bertolucci & Panatta	6–4 12–10 6–2
McEnroe	beat	A Zugarelli	6–4 6–3 6–1
Gerulaitis	beat	Panatta	6–1 6–3 6–3

1980 Czechoslovakia beat Italy 4–1, Prague (indoors)

T Smid	beat	A Panatta	3–6 3–6 6–3 6–4 6–4
I Lendl	beat	C Barazzutti	4–6 6–1 6–1 6–2
Lendl & Smid	beat	P Bertolucci & Panatta	3–6 6–3 3–6 6–3 6–4
Smid	lost to	Barazzutti	6–3 3–6 2–6
Lendl	beat	G Ocleppo	6–3 6–3

1981 USA beat Argentina 3–1, Cincinnati (indoors)

J P McEnroe	beat	G Vilas	6–3 6–2 6–2
R Tanner	lost to	J L Clerc	5–7 3–6 6–8
P Fleming & McEnroe	beat	Clerc & Vilas	6–3 4–6 6–4 4–6 11–9
McEnroe	beat	Clerc	7–5 5–7 6–3 3–6 6–3
Tanner	div'd	with Vilas	11–10 unfinished.

1982 USA beat France 4–1, Grenoble (indoors)

J P McEnroe	beat	Y Noah	12–10 1–6 3–6 6–2 6–3
G Mayer	beat	H Leconte	6–2 6–2 7–9 6–4
P Fleming & McEnroe	beat	Leconte & Noah	6–3 6–4 9–7
Mayer	lost to	Noah	1–6 0–6
McEnroe	beat	Leconte	6–2 6–3

CHALLENGE AND FINAL ROUND SUPERLATIVES

The greatest number of games was played in the Challenge Round at Brisbane in 1958 when the USA beat Australia 3–2 after a total of 270 games.

The hardest tie was in Adelaide in 1963 when the USA beat Australia 3–2 in the fifth rubber after a total of 237 games.

The longest opening singles was in Sydney in 1965 when Fred Stolle (Aus) beat Manuel Santana (Spa) 10–12 3–6 6–1 6–4 7–5, a total of 60 games.

The longest second singles was in 1973 at the Public Auditorium, Cleveland, Ohio, when Rod Laver (Aus) beat Tom Gorman (USA) 8–10 8–6 6–8 6–3 6–1, a total of 62 games.

The longest doubles was at Brisbane in 1958 when Alex Olmedo and Ham Richardson (USA) beat Mal Anderson and Neale Fraser (Aus) by 10–12 3–6 16–14 6–3 7–5, a total of 82 games.

The longest third singles was in 1947 at Forest Hills, New York, when Ted Schroeder (USA) made a winning 3–1 lead by beating Dinny Pails (Aus) 6–3 8–6 4–6 9–11 10–8, a total of 71 games.

The longest fourth singles in a live tie was in 1963 in Adelaide when Chuck McKinley (USA) beat John Newcombe (Aus) 10–12 6–2 9–7 6–2, a total of 54 games.

The longest fourth singles, albeit when the tie was dead was at the Clark Stadium, Cleveland, Ohio, when Arthur Ashe (USA) beat Christian Kuhnke (FRG) 6–8 10–12 9–7 13–11 6–4, a total of 86 games.

The most one sided outcome in the Challenge or Final round was by the British Isles against Belgium at Wimbledon in 1904 when a winning 3–nil lead was built 19 sets to nil and by 54 games to 17.

(A winning 3-nil lead without the loss of a set was achieved on five other occasions:

1909 Australasia against USA
1961 Australia against Italy
1967 Australia against Spain
1970 USA against Germany
1979 USA against Italy)

The most decisive opening singles were in 1947, when at Forest Hills Jack Kramer (USA) beat Dinny Pails (Aus) 6–2 6–1 6–2, and in 1978, when in Palm Springs John McEnroe (USA) beat John Lloyd (GB) 6–1 6–2 6–2, a loss in each case of 5 games. In 1979 in San Francisco Vitas Gerulaitis (USA) beat Corrado Barazzutti (Ita) 6–3 6–2 retired, winning after a total of 14 games.

The most decisive second singles was indoors at Stockholm in 1973 when Bjorn Borg (Swe) beat Jiri Hrebec (Cze) 6–1 6–3 6–0, a loss of 4 games.

The most decisive doubles was in 1919 in Sydney when Norman Brookes and Gerald Patterson (Aus) beat Arthur Beamish and Archibald Kingscote (GB) 6–0 6–0 6–2, a loss of **2 games**.

The **most decisive third singles** occurred in 1923 at Forest Hills when in a live rubber William Johnston (USA) beat John Hawkes (Aus) 6–0 6–2 6–1, a loss of **3 games**. This was the **most one sided rubber settling the destiny of the trophy**.

The **most decisive fourth singles** was at the Merion Cricket Club, Philadelphia, in 1939 when John Bromwich (Aus) beat Frank Parker (USA) 6–0 6–3 6–1, a loss of **4 games**. With this one sided rubber Australia completed their recovery from their 0–2 deficit, taking the cup 3–2.

The **youngest** to play in the Challenge or Final Round was **Manuel Orantes**. He played in the singles and doubles for Spain against Australia at Brisbane in 1967. His age on the first day was **18 years 320 days**.

The **youngest to win** was **Lew Hoad**. In December 1953 in the opening singles at Melbourne against the USA he paved the way for the Australian 3–2 success by beating Vic Seixas, then **19 years 33 days** old.

Ken Rosewall, aged **19 years 54 days**, also played for Australia in 1953, winning the decisive fifth rubber.

Vincent Richards, aged **19 years 183 days**, was the youngest to **play for the USA**. He was in the doubles with William Tilden against Australasia in 1922.

Bjorn Borg won two singles and a doubles for Sweden against Czechoslovakia in Stockholm in 1975, at **19 years 196 days old**.

John Newcombe was number two in singles for Australia against the USA at Adelaide in 1963, aged **19 years 217 days**.

John McEnroe played the singles for the USA in their win against Great Britain at Palm Springs in 1978, aged **19 years 295 days old**.

The **oldest player** in the Challenge or Final Round was the Australian **Norman Brookes**. When he played for the last time for Australasia in 1920, in the doubles against the USA at Auckland, New Zealand, he was **43 years 47 days old**. In 1919 Brookes won the doubles in Sydney against the British Isles. He was the **oldest winner** in the Challenge Round at the age of **42 years 66 days**.

The **oldest British man** was **Charles Dixon** in 1913 in the side beaten by the USA at Wimbledon. Dixon, who lost a vital third singles to Maurice McLoughlin, was then **40 years 171 days old**.

(The British side comprised Dixon, Cecil Parke and Herbert Roper Barrett. **Barrett**, who played in the doubles, was **39 years 245 days old**. Parke on the last day was 32 years 2 days old. The total age of the three man team was 112 years 55 days.)

The oldest American was **William Larned**. In 1911 he played against Australasia at Christchurch, New Zealand, losing the second singles to Rodney Heath. His age was **39 years 4 days**.

The **longest gap**, 14 years 98 days, between first and last appearances in the Challenge or Final Round was by the Australian **Rod Laver**. His initial match at that stage of the competition was against Barry MacKay (USA), to whom he lost, on 28 August 1959 in the second singles at Forest Hills, New York. His last was indoors against the USA at the Public Auditorium, Cleveland, Ohio when, having already won a singles and a doubles, he polished a 5-nil victory by beating Stan Smith on 4 December 1973.

Norman Brookes, for Australasia, first played in the Challenge Round at Wimbledon on 13 July 1907, last at Auckland, New Zealand, 1 January 1921, a gap of **13 years 171 days**.

Herbert Roper Barrett, for the British Isles, played in the first tie of all, at Boston in 1900 on 9 August. His last was at Wimbledon on 26 July 1913, the gap being **12 years 351 days**.

NATIONAL ACHIEVEMENT

DAVIS CUP NATIONS 1900–82

Nation	Ties Played	Ties Won	Year First Played
Algeria	5	0	1977
Argentina	62	34	1923
Australia/Australasia	159	120	1905
Austria	80	32	1905
Belgium	113	54	1904
Bolivia	8	2	1971
Brazil	78	44	1932
Bulgaria	23	8	1964
Burma	2	0	1955
Canada	76	23	1913
Chile	74	40	1928
China	8	1	1924
Colombia	30	15	1959
Commonwealth, Caribbean/ British West Indies	30	1	1953
Cuba	25	4	1924
Czechoslovakia	126	80	1921
Denmark	104	51	1921
Ecuador	29	12	1961
Egypt	60	21	1929
Estonia	1	0	1934
Finland	52	14	1928
France	162	105	1904
Germany/West Germany	139	91	1913
Great Britain/British Isles	172	111	1900

Nation	Ties Played	Ties Won	Year First Played
Greece	43	10	1927
Hawaii	1	0	1923
Hong Kong	6	0	1970
Hungary	84	36	1924
India	112	68	1921
Indonesia	25	10	1961
Iran	26	9	1962
Ireland	72	21	1923
Israel	39	10	1949
Italy	169	118	1922
Japan	113	63	1921
Kenya	1	0	1975
Lebanon	8	0	1957
Luxembourg	37	3	1947
Malaysia	22	1	1957
Mexico	92	42	1924
Monaco	59	17	1929
Morocco	19	8	1961
Netherlands	89	35	1920
New Zealand	54	22	1924
Nigeria	3	1	1974
Norway	57	10	1928
Pakistan	26	10	1948
Paraguay	5	4	1931
Peru	10	1	1968
Philippines	60	32	1926
Poland	76	33	1925
Portugal	32	5	1925
Rhodesia	8	2	1963
Romania	80	41	1922
South Africa	81	48	1913
South Korea	27	5	1960
South Viet Nam	18	10	1964
Spain	116	69	1921
Sri Lanka/Ceylon	27	4	1953
Sweden	132	84	1925
Switzerland	86	32	1923
Taiwan	10	1	1972
Thailand	14	4	1958
Tunisia	1	0	1982
Turkey	28	4	1948
Uruguay	19	4	1931
USA	193	153	1900
USSR	50	34	1962
Venezuela	27	8	1957
Yugoslavia	103	53	1927

NATIONS BY SENIORITY

Year First Played	Nations	
1900	USA	British Isles (as England 1922–28, Great Britain 1929 et seq.)
1904	France	Belgium

Year First Played	Nations	
1905	Austria (challenged first in 1904)	
	Australasia (including New Zealand. Australia 1923 et seq)	
1913	Canada	Germany
	South Africa (challenged first in 1911)	
1920	Netherlands	
1921	Czechoslovakia	Denmark
	India	Japan
	Spain	
1922	Italy	Romania
1923	Argentina	Hawaii (challenged first in 1922)
	Ireland	Switzerland
1924	China	Cuba
	Hungary	Mexico
	New Zealand	
1925	Poland	Portugal
	Sweden	
1926	Philippines (challenged first in 1921, 1922)	
1927	Greece	Yugoslavia
1928	Chile	Finland
	Norway	
1929	Egypt	Monaco
1931	Paraguay	Uruguay
1932	Brazil (challenged first in 1931)	
1934	Estonia (in qualifying round for 1935)	
1947	Luxembourg	
1948	Pakistan	Turkey (challenged first in 1946)
1949	Israel	
1953	British West Indies (as British Caribbean 1961–69, Commonwealth Caribbean 1970 et seq.)	
	Ceylon (as Sri Lanka 1973 et seq)	
1955	Burma	
1957	Lebanon	Malaysia
	Venezuela	
1958	Thailand	
1959	Colombia	
1960	South Korea (challenged first in 1959)	
1961	Ecuador	Indonesia
	Morocco	
1962	Iran (challenged first in 1959)	
	USSR	
1963	Rhodesia	
1964	Bulgaria	South Vietnam
1968	Peru (challenged first in 1933, 1934)	
1970	Hong Kong	
1971	Bolivia	
1972	Taiwan	
1974	Nigeria	
1975	Kenya	
1977	Algeria	
1982	Tunisia	

Total number of nations playing 1900 to 1982 = 70.

ORDER OF ACHIEVEMENT 1900–81

Nation	Times Champion	Times Loser Final/ Challenge Rd	Year First Entered	No. Years Played	No. of Ties Played	Won
USA	28	25	1900	68	193	153
Australasia/Australia	24	15	1905	73	159	120
British Isles/Great Britain	9	8	1900	71	172	111
France	6	3	1904	63	162	105
Italy	1	5	1922	52	169	118
Czechoslovakia	1	1	1921	49	126	80
Sweden	1	—	1925	49	132	84
South Africa	1	—	1913	34	81	48
Romania	—	3	1922	39	78	41
Spain	—	2	1921	47	116	69
India	—	2	1921	45	112	68
Germany	—	1	1913	47	139	91
Belgium	—	1	1904	60	113	54
Japan	—	1	1921	47	113	63
Mexico	—	1	1924	51	92	42
Chile	—	1	1928	35	74	40
Argentina	—	1	1923	28	62	33

The competition was played 70 times 1900 to 1981.

AUSTRALIA IN THE DAVIS CUP

The most decisive Australian victory in the Challenge/Final Round was for the loss of 26 games.

(1967. Australia beat Spain 4–1, Brisbane. Roy Emerson beat Manuel Santana 6–4 6–1 6–1; John Newcombe beat Manuel Orantes 6–3 6–3 6–2; Newcombe and Tony Roche beat Orantes and Santana 6–4 6–4 6–4; subsequently Newcombe lost to Santana 5–7 4–6 2–6; Emerson beat Orantes 6–1 6–1 2–6 6–4.)

The most decisive Australian victory was for the loss of 11 games and an over-all loss of 15 games.

(1924. American zone, first round, New York. Australia beat China 5–0. Gerald Patterson beat W. Lock Wei 6–1 6–2 6–2; Pat O'Hara Wood beat P Kong 6–0 6–1 6–2; Patterson and O'Hara Wood beat Lock Wei and C K Huang 6–1 6–2 6–0; subsequently Patterson beat Kong 6–0 6–0 6–2; O'Hara Wood beat Lock Wei 6–0 6–0 6–2.)

The highest number of games in an Australian tie was 327, the highest by any nation.

(1974. Eastern zone, final, Calcutta. India beat Australia 3–2. J Singh beat Bob Giltinan 11–9 9–11 12–10 8–6; Vijay Amritraj lost to John Alexander 12–14 15–17 8–6 2–6; V and An Amritraj beat Alexander and Colin Dibley 17–15 6–8 6–3 16–18 6–4; Singh lost to Alexander 6–8 4–6 3–6; V Amritraj beat Giltinan 6–1 5–7 6–4 6–4.)

The longest Australian rubber was a doubles of 99 games.

(1974. Eastern zone final, Calcutta. Vijay and An Amritraj (Ind) beat John Alexander and Colin Dibley (Aus) 17–15 6–8 6–3 16–18 6–4.)

The longest Australian singles was 80 games, on two occasions.

(1974. Eastern zone final, Calcutta. John Alexander (Aus) beat Vijay Amritraj (Ind) 14–12 17–15 6–8 6–2 in the second rubber. 1979. Inter-zone, semi-final, Sydney. Vitas Gerulaitis (USA) beat Mark Edmondson (Aus) 6–8 14–16 10–8 6–3 6–3 in the first rubber.)

AUSTRALIAN RESULTS 1905–82

Australia and New Zealand played jointly as Australasia 1905 to 1922, with New Zealand challenging independently for the first time in 1924.

Year	Opponent	Won/Lost	Score	Venue	
1905	Austria	W	5–0	Queen's Club	
	USA	L	0–5	Queen's Club	
1906	USA	L	2–3	Newport, Mon	
1907	USA	W	3–2	Wimbledon	
	British Isles	W	3–2	Wimbledon	Challenge Round **Champions**
1908	USA	W	3–2	Melbourne	Challenge Round **Champions**
1909	USA	W	5–0	Sydney	Challenge Round **Champions**
1910	no challenge				
1911	USA	W	5–0	Christchurch	Challenge Round **Champions**
1912	British Isles	L	2–3	Melbourne	Challenge Round
1913	USA	L	1–4	New York	
1914	Canada	W	5–0	Chicago	
	Germany	W	5–0	Pittsburgh	
	British Isles	W	3–0	Boston	
	USA	W	3–2	New York	Challenge Round **Champions**
1915–1918 not held					
1919	British Isles	W	4–1	Sydney	Challenge Round **Champions**
1920	USA	L	0–5	Auckland	Challenge Round
1921	Canada	W	5–0	Toronto	
	British Isles	W	3–2	Pittsburgh	
	Denmark	W	5–0	Cleveland	
	Japan	L	1–4	Newport, RI	
1922	Belgium	W	4–0	Scarborough	
	Czechoslovakia	W	5–0	Roehampton	
	France	W	4–1	Boston	
	Spain	W	4–1	Philadelphia	
	USA	L	1–4	New York	Challenge Round
1923	Hawaii	W	4–1	Orange, NJ	
	Japan	W	4–1	Chicago	
	France	W	4–1	Boston	
	USA	L	1–4	New York	Challenge Round
1924	China	W	5–0	New York	
	Mexico	W	5–0	Baltimore	
	Japan	W	5–0	Providence, RI	
	France	W	3–2	Boston	
	USA	L	0–5	Philadelphia	Challenge Round
1925	Canada	W	5–0	Montreal	
	Japan	W	4–1	Boston	
	France	L	1–3	New York	Inter-zone Final
1926, 1927 did not play					
1928	Italy	L	1–4	Genoa	
1929	did not play				
1930	Switzerland	W	5–0	Zurich	
	Ireland	W	4–1	Dublin	
	Great Britain	W	4–1	Eastbourne	
	Italy	L	2–3	Milan	
1931	did not play				
1932	Cuba	W	5–0	Havana	
	USA	L	0–5	Philadelphia	
1933	Norway	W	5–0	Oslo	
	S Africa	W	3–2	Queen's Club	
	Japan	W	3–2	Paris	
	Great Britain	L	2–3	Wimbledon	
1934	Japan	W	4–1	Eastbourne	
	France	W	3–2	Paris	

Year	Opponent	Won/Lost	Score	Venue	
	Czechoslovakia	W	3–2	Prague	
	USA	L	2–3	Wimbledon	Inter-zone Final
1935	New Zealand	W	3–0	Eastbourne	
	France	W	3–2	Paris	
	Germany	L	1–4	Berlin	
1936	USA	W	3–2	Philadelphia	
	Germany	W	4–1	Wimbledon	Inter-zone Final
	Great Britain	L	2–3	Wimbledon	Challenge Round
1937	Mexico	W	5–0	Mexico City	
	USA	L	0–5	New York	
1938	Mexico	W	5–0	Kansas City	
	Japan	W	3–2	Montreal	
	Germany	W	5–0	Boston	Inter-zone Final
	USA	L	2–3	Philadelphia	Challenge Round
1939	Mexico	W	5–0	Mexico City	
	Philippines	W	5–0	Long Beach	
	Cuba	W	5–0	Havana	
	Yugoslavia	W	4–1	New York	Inter-zone Final
	USA	W	3–2	Philadelphia	Challenge Round **Champions**
1940–1945 not held					
1946	USA	L	0–5	Melbourne	Challenge Round
1947	Canada	W	5–0	Montreal	
	Czechoslovakia	W	4–1	Montreal	Inter-zone Final
	USA	L	1–4	New York	Challenge Round
1948	Cuba	W	4–1	Havana	
	Mexico	W	4–1	Mexico City	
	Czechoslovakia	W	3–2	Boston	Inter-zone Final
	USA	L	0–5	New York	Challenge Round
1949	Canada	W	4–1	Montreal	
	Mexico	W	5–0	Wilmington	
	Italy	W	5–0	New York	Inter-zone Final
	USA	L	1–4	New York	Challenge Round
1950	Canada	W	5–0	Montreal	
	Mexico	W	4–1	Mexico City	
	Sweden	W	3–2	Rye, NY	Inter-zone Final
	USA	W	4–1	New York	Challenge Round **Champions**
1951	USA	W	3–2	Sydney	Challenge Round **Champions**
1952	USA	W	4–1	Adelaide	Challenge Round **Champions**
1953	USA	W	3–2	Melbourne	Challenge Round **Champions**
1954	USA	L	2–3	Sydney	Challenge Round
1955	Mexico	W	3–0	Chicago	
	Brazil	W	4–1	Louisville	
	Canada	W	5–0	Montreal	
	Japan	W	4–0	New York	
	Italy	W	5–0	Philadelphia	Inter-zone Final
	USA	W	5–0	New York	Challenge Round **Champions**
1956	USA	W	5–0	Adelaide	Challenge Round **Champions**
1957	USA	W	3–2	Melbourne	Challenge Round **Champions**
1958	USA	L	2–3	Brisbane	Challenge Round
1959	Mexico	W	4–1	Mexico City	
	Canada	W	5–0	Montreal	
	Cuba	W	5–0	Montreal	
	Italy	W	4–1	Philadelphia	
	India	W	4–1	Boston	Inter-zone Final
	USA	W	3–2	New York	Challenge Round **Champions**
1960	Italy	W	4–1	Sydney	Challenge Round **Champions**
1961	Italy	W	5–0	Melbourne	Challenge Round **Champions**
1962	Mexico	W	5–0	Brisbane	Challenge Round **Champions**
1963	USA	L	2–3	Adelaide	Challenge Round

Year	Opponent	Won/Lost	Score	Venue	
1964	Canada	W	5–0	Montreal	
	Mexico	W	4–1	Mexico City	
	Chile	W	5–0	Minneapolis	
	Sweden	W	5–0	Baastad	Inter-zone Final
	USA	W	3–2	Cleveland	Challenge Round **Champions**
1965	Spain	W	4–1	Sydney	Challenge Round **Champions**
1966	India	W	4–1	Melbourne	Challenge Round **Champions**
1967	Spain	W	4–1	Brisbane	Challenge Round **Champions**
1968	USA	L	1–4	Adelaide	Challenge Round
1969	Mexico	L	2–3	Mexico City	
1970	Philippines	W	5–0	Manila	
	Japan	W	5–0	Tokyo	
	India	L	1–3	Bangalore	
1971	Hong Kong	W	5–0	Hong Kong	
	Indonesia	W	3–2	Jakarta	
	Japan	L	2–3	Tokyo	
1972	Korea	W	5–0	Seoul	
	Japan	W	4–1	Tokyo	
	India	W	5–0	Bangalore	
	Romania	L	1–4	Bucharest	
1973	Japan	W	4–1	Tokyo	
	India	W	4–0	Madras	
	Czechoslovakia	W	4–1	Melbourne	
	USA	W	5–0	Cleveland	Final Round **Champions**
1974	Pakistan	W	3–0	Rawalpindi	
	India	L	2–3	Calcutta	
1975	Japan	W	4–1	Adelaide	
	New Zealand	W	4–0	Auckland	
	Czechoslovakia	L	1–3	Prague	
1976	Indonesia	W	5–0	Hobart	
	New Zealand	W	3–1	Brisbane/Nottingham	
	Italy	L	2–3	Rome	
1977	India	W	5–0	Perth	
	New Zealand	W	4–0	Auckland	
	Argentina	W	3–2	Buenos Aires	
	Italy	W	3–1	Sydney	Final Round **Champions**
1978	Japan	W	5–0	Tokyo	
	New Zealand	W	4–0	Adelaide	
	Great Britain	L	2–3	Crystal Palace	
1979	India	W	3–2	Madras	
	New Zealand	W	3–2	Christchurch	
	USA	L	1–4	Sydney	
1980	Japan	W	5–0	Hobart	
	New Zealand	W	4–1	Brisbane	
	Italy	L	2–3	Rome	
1981	France	W	3–2	Lyons	
	Sweden	W	3–1	Baastad	
	USA	L	0–5	Portland, Oregon	
1982	Mexico	W	3–2	Mexico City	
	Chile	W	4–1	Brisbane	
	USA	L	0–5	Perth	

AUSTRALIAN PLAYERS 1905–82

	Total Rubbers		(Singles)		(Doubles)			
	Pl'd	Won	Pl'd	Won	Pl'd	Won	Ties	Years
N E Brookes	39	28	25	18	14	10	14	1905, 07–09, 11, 12, 14, 19, 20
A F Wilding†	30	21	21	15	9	6	11	1905–09, 14
A W Dunlop	4	3			4	3	4	1905, 11
L O S Poideven	3	0	2	0	1	0	1	1906
R W Heath	3	1	3	1			2	1911, 12
H Rice	2	0	2	0			1	1913
S N Doust	3	1	2	0	1	1	1	1913
A B Jones	1	1			1	1	1	1913
G L Patterson	46	32	31	21	15	11	16	1919, 20, 22, 24, 25, 28
J O Anderson	36	28	27	20	9	8	15	1919, 21–23, 25
J B Hawkes	20	11	13	6	7	5	10	1921, 23, 25
C V Todd	5	5	1	1	4	4	4	1921
N Peach	2	2	2	2			1	1921
P O'Hara Wood	23	17	14	9	9	8	9	1922, 24
R Wertheim	1	1			1	1	1	1922
R Schlesinger	1	0	1	0			1	1923
I McInnes	1	0	1	0			1	1923
J H Crawford	*58	36	*40	23	18	13	23	1928, 30, 32–37
H C Hopman	16	8	9	4	7	4	7	1928, 30, 32
E F Moon	4	4	4	4			2	1930
J Willard	3	3			3	3	3	1930
C Sproule	1	1	1	1			1	1932
V B McGrath	26	12	23	11	3	1	14	1933–37
A K Quist	55	42	33	23	22	19	28	1933–39, 46, 48
D P Turnbull	3	1	1	1	2	1	3	1933, 34
J E Bromwich	52	39	31	19	21	20	23	1937–39, 46, 47, 49, 50
L Schwartz	1	1	1	1			1	1938
D Pails	8	3	8	3			4	1946, 47
G E Brown	4	3	2	2	2	1	3	1947, 48
C Long	7	5			7	5	7	1947, 48
O W Sidwell	17	11	14	9	3	2	8	1948, 49
F A Sedgman	28	25	19	16	9	9	10	1949–52
K McGregor	9	6	7	4	2	2	5	1950–52
M G Rose	3	1	2	0	1	1	2	1951, 57
L A Hoad	22	18	13	11	9	7	9	1953–56
K R Rosewall	22	19	19	17	3	2	11	1953–56, 73, 75
R N Hartwig	13	12	6	6	7	6	8	1953–55
M J Anderson	19	13	14	11	5	2	8	1957, 58, 72, 73
A J Cooper	4	2	4	2			2	1957, 58
N A Fraser	21	18	12	11	9	7	11	1958–63
R G Laver	24	20	20	16	4	4	11	1959–62, 73
R S Emerson	35	31	21	19	14	12	17	1959–67
R Mark	1	1	1	1			1	1959
J D Newcombe	*35	26	*24	16	11	10	15	1963–67, 73, 75, 76
A D Roche	*20	14	*11	7	9	7	11	1964–67, 74–78
F S Stolle	16	13	12	10	4	3	6	1964–66
W W Bowrey	4	2	4	2			2	1968, 69
R O Ruffels	*11	5	*9	4	2	1	5	1968–70
J G Alexander	39	27	25	17	14	10	18	1968–70, 74–80
P Dent	18	13	8	6	10	7	12	1969, 75, 77–81
R D Crealy	6	4	5	3	1	1	3	1970
A J Stone	*7	6	*3	2	4	4	5	1970, 78
C Dibley	19	13	12	8	7	5	9	1971, 72, 74
J Cooper	7	4	6	3	1	1	4	1971, 73
R Giltinan	5	3	3	1	2	2		1971, 74
R Case	7	3	5	3	2	0	5	1971, 72, 76, 78, 79
G Masters	*12	8	*3	2	9	6	9	1972, 73, 75, 78, 79
S Ball	1	1	1	1			1	1974
M Edmondson	*19	11	*17	9	2	2	9	1977, 79, 81, 82
K G Warwick	4	2	3	1	1	1	2	1978, 81
P McNamara	*18	8	*13	7	5	1	8	1980–82
B Drewett	2	2			2	2	2	1980

	Total Rubbers		(Singles)		(Doubles)			
	Pl'd	Won	Pl'd	Won	Pl'd	Won	Ties	Years
P McNamee	7	3	3	2	4	1	4	1980, 82
J Fitzgerald	2	2	2	2			1	1982

† Wilding was a New Zealander. Australia and New Zealand were a lawn tennis entity as Australasia until 1923.
* Including one unfinished rubber.

FRANCE IN THE DAVIS CUP

The most decisive French victory in the Challenge/Final Round was winning in the 4th rubber, having lost 5 sets.

(1929. France beat USA 3–2, Paris. Henri Cochet beat Bill Tilden 6–3 6–1 6–2; Jean Borotra beat George Lott 6–1 3–6 6–4 7–5; Borotra and Cochet lost to Wilmer Allison and John Van Ryn 1–6 6–8 4–6; Cochet beat Lott 6–1 3–6 6–0 6–3; subsequently Borotra lost to Tilden 6–4 1–6 4–6 5–7.)

The most decisive French victory was for the loss of 12 games and an over-all loss of 23 games.

(1947. European zone, third round, Paris. France beat Monaco 5–0. M Bernard beat A Noghes 6–1 6–2 6–0; B Destremau beat V Landau 6–3 6–2 6–1; P Pelizza and R Abdesselam beat Landau and G Medecin 6–2 6–1 6–0; subsequently Destremau beat Noghes 7–5 6–2 6–1; Abdesselam beat Landau 6–2 6–1 6–0.)

The highest number of games in a French tie was 259.

(1946. European zone, semi-final, Paris. Yugoslavia beat France 3–2. D Mitic lost to Y Petra 6–2 6–8 4–6 6–3 6–8; F Puncec lost to M Bernard 6–2 1–6 6–0 5–7 3–6; Mitic and Puncec beat B Destremau and P Pelizza 8–10 8–6 6–3 5–7 10–8; Mitic beat Bernard 6–3 4–6 3–6 6–0 6–3; Puncec beat Petra 6–3 3–6 6–4 7–9 6–0.)

The longest rubber for France was a doubles of 71 games.

(1946. European zone, semi-final, Paris, D Mitic and F Puncec (Yug) beat B Destremau and P Pelizza (Fra) 8–10 8–6 6–3 5–7 10–8.)

The longest singles for France was 66 games.

(1979. European zone B, quarter-final, Paris. D Bedel (Fra) beat H Gunthardt 2–6 6–4 4–6 14–12 7–5 in fifth and dead rubber.)

THE FOUR MUSKETEERS

The spectacular success of the 'Four Musketeers' as a Davis Cup side for France in the period 1922 to 1934 merits analysis. The team comprised Jacques Brugnon (11 May 1895–20 March 1978), Henri Cochet (born 14 December

The 'Four Musketeers'—Henri Cochet, Jean Borotra (captain Pierre Gillou), Rene Lacoste and Jacques Brugnon.

1901), Jean Borotra (born 13 August 1898) and Jean Rene Lacoste (born 2 July 1904).

The team building began in 1922 when Cochet and Borotra were members of the French side that beat Denmark. All four played in the tie against Ireland in 1923. Their last appearance as a team was when Borotra and Brugnon played the doubles against Australia in 1934.

Their individual performances, taking into account only those when they were sharing responsibility with at least one other team member, were:

	Rubbers		Singles		Doubles			
	Pl'd	Won	Pl'd	Won	Pl'd	Won	Ties	Years
Borotra	47	31	30	18	17	13	26	1922–34
Cochet	53	42	38	32	15	10	24	1922–33
Lacoste	52	41	41	33	11	8	26	1923–28
Brugnon	33	25	3	3	30	22	30	1923–34
Team totals	149	113	112	86	37	27	37	1922–34

As can be seen all played singles and all played doubles, with Brugnon the doubles specialist. Every possible doubles combination was used, except for Cochet and Lacoste. The records were:

	Pl'd	Won
Brugnon and Lacoste	8	6
Brugnon and Cochet	11	7
Brugnon and Borotra	11	9
Cochet and Borotra	3	2
Lacoste and Borotra	3	2

All played singles and doubles at various times in the Challenge Round, except Brugnon, who played only doubles. Cochet played the most at that level, taking part in 20 rubbers and winning 14. This was in eight Challenge Round ties. Borotra played in more Challenge Round ties, all nine, but participated in 17 rubbers, of which he won six. Lacoste retired after 1928 through ill health, having won four out of nine Challenge Round rubbers in four ties. Brugnon won three out of six doubles rubbers in six Challenge Rounds.

FRENCH RESULTS 1904–82

Year	Opponent	Won/Lost	Score	Venue	
1904	Belgium	L	2–3	Wimbledon	
1905	USA	L	0–5	Queen's Club	
1906 to 1911 did not play					
1912	British Isles	L	1–4	Folkestone	
1913	Germany	L	1–4	Wiesbaden	
1914	British Isles	L	1–4	Wimbledon	
1915 to 1918 not held					
1919	Belgium	W	3–0	Brussels	
	British Isles	L	2–3	Deauville	
1920	USA	L	0–3	Eastbourne	
1921	India	L	1–4	Paris	
1922	Denmark	W	4–1	Copenhagen	
	Australasia	L	1–4	Boston	
1923	Denmark	W	4–1	Bordeaux	
	Ireland	W	4–1	Dublin	
	Switzerland	W	3–2	Lyons	
	Spain	W	3–2	Deauville	
	Australia	L	1–4	Boston	Inter-zone Final
1924	Ireland	W	5–0	Dublin	
	India	W	4–0	Paris	
	Great Britain	W	4–1	Eastbourne	
	Czechoslovakia	W	5–0	Evian-les-Bains	
	Australia	L	2–3	Boston	Inter-zone Final
1925	Hungary	W	4–1	Budapest	
	Italy	W	5–0	Paris	
	Great Britain	W	4–0	Eastbourne	
	Netherlands	W	4–0	Noordwijk	
	Australia	W	3–1	New York	Inter-zone Final
	USA	L	0–5	Philadelphia	Challenge Round
1926	Denmark	W	5–0	Copenhagen	
	Czechoslovakia	W	3–0	Prague	
	Sweden	W	5–0	Stockholm	
	Great Britain	W	4–0	Cabourg	
	Japan	W	3–2	New York	Inter-zone Final
	USA	L	1–4	Philadelphia	Challenge Round
1927	Romania	W	5–0	Paris	
	Italy	W	3–2	Rome	
	S Africa	W	5–0	Eastbourne	
	Denmark	W	3–0	Copenhagen	
	Japan	W	3–0	Boston	Inter-zone Final
	USA	W	3–2	Philadelphia	Challenge Round **Champions**
1928	USA	W	4–1	Paris	Challenge Round **Champions**
1929	USA	W	3–2	Paris	Challenge Round **Champions**
1930	USA	W	4–1	Paris	Challenge Round **Champions**
1931	Great Britain	W	3–2	Paris	Challenge Round **Champions**

Year	Opponent	Won/Lost		Score	Venue	
1932	USA	W		3–2	Paris	Challenge Round **Champions**
1933	Great Britain		L	2–3	Paris	Challenge Round
1934	Austria	W		5–0	Paris	
	Germany	W		3–2	Paris	
	Australia		L	2–3	Paris	
1935	Australia		L	2–3	Paris	
1936	China	W		5–0	Paris	
	Netherlands	W		4–1	The Hague	
	Yugoslavia		L	2–3	Paris	
1937	Norway	W		5–0	Paris	
	Czechoslovakia		L	1–4	Prague	
1938	Netherlands	W		3–2	Scheveningen	
	Monaco	W		5–0	Marseille	
	Italy	W		4–1	Paris	
	Germany		L	2–3	Berlin	
1939	China	W		4–1	Paris	
	Great Britain		L	2–3	Wimbledon	
1940 to 1945 not held						
1946	Great Britain	W		5–0	Paris	
	Switzerland	W		3–2	Montreux	
	Yugoslavia		L	2–3	Paris	
1947	India	W		5–0	Paris	
	Monaco	W		5–0	Paris	
	Czechoslovakia		L	1–4	Prague	
1948	Romania	W		3–2	Bucharest	
	Hungary		L	1–4	Paris	
1949	Luxembourg	W		5–0	Mondorf-les-Bains	
	Denmark	W		4–1	Paris	
	Czechoslovakia	W		3–2	Paris	
	Hungary	W		3–2	Budapest	
	Italy		L	2–3	Paris	
1950	Switzerland	W		4–0	Paris	
	Denmark		L	2–3	Copenhagen	
1951	Great Britain		L	2–3	Wimbledon	
1952	Norway	W		5–0	Oslo	
	Netherlands	W		4–1	Paris	
	Argentina	W		3–2	Paris	
	Belgium		L	2–3	Paris	
1953	Yugoslavia	W		4–1	Zagreb	
	West Germany	W		4–1	Paris	
	Denmark		L	1–4	Paris	
1954	Norway	W		5–0	Oslo	
	India	W		4–1	Paris	
	Denmark	W		4–1	Copenhagen	
	Sweden		L	0–5	Paris	
1955	Argentina	W		3–2	Paris	
	Sweden		L	2–3	Stockholm	
1956	Switzerland	W		5–0	Laussanne	
	West Germany	W		4–1	Duisburg	
	Italy		L	2–3	Paris	
1957	Czechoslovakia	W		4–0	Lyons	
	Great Britain		L	2–3	Paris	
1958	Chile	W		4–1	Paris	
	Sweden	W		3–2	Paris	
	Great Britain		L	0–5	Manchester	
1959	Denmark	W		5–0	Copenhagen	
	Romania	W		5–0	Paris	
	Italy		L	1–4	San Remo	
1960	Argentina	W		5–0	Paris	
	Denmark	W		5–0	Paris	

Year	Opponent	Won/Lost		Score	Venue	
	Sweden		L	2–3	Baastad	
1961	Brazil	W		4–1	Paris	
	Poland	W		5–0	Warsaw	
	Italy		L	1–4	Paris	
1962	S Africa		L	2–3	Paris	
1963	Poland	W		5–0	Paris	
	Brazil	W		4–1	Paris	
	Spain		L	1–4	Barcelona	
1964	Bulgaria	W		5–0	Dijon	
	Netherlands	W		5–0	Paris	
	S Africa	W		3–2	Paris	
	Great Britain	W		3–2	Bristol	
	Sweden		L	1–4	Baastad	
1965	Austria	W		5–0	Vienna	
	Yugoslavia	W		5–0	Paris	
	S Africa		L	1–4	Paris	
1966	Romania	W		4–1	Paris	
	Canada	W		5–0	Paris	
	Czechoslovakia	W		4–1	Paris	
	Brazil		L	1–4	Paris	
1967	Norway	W		5–0	Paris	
	Hungary	W		5–0	Paris	
	S Africa		L	0–5	Paris	
1968	Great Britain		L	0–3	Bournemouth	
1969	Yugoslavia		L	2–3	Maribor	
1970	Switzerland	W		4–1	Geneva	
	Austria	W		5–0	Paris	
	Spain		L	0–5	Paris	
1971	Sweden	W		5–0	Baastad	
	Finland	W		3–0	Paris	
	Spain		L	1–4	Barcelona	
1972	Great Britain	W		4–1	Paris	
	Spain		L	2–3	Paris	
1973	Norway	W		5–0	Oslo	
	USSR		L	2–3	Moscow	
1974	Portugal	W		5–0	Porto	
	Austria	W		3–1	Vienna	
	Romania		L	2–3	Bucharest	
1975	Belgium	W		4–1	Paris	
	Yugoslavia	W		3–0	Paris	
	Italy	W		3–2	Paris	
	Czechoslovakia		L	2–3	Prague	
1976	Great Britain		L	1–4	Eastbourne	
1977	Switzerland	W		3–2	Zurich	
	Poland	W		5–0	Warsaw	
	Romania	W		3–2	Paris	
	Italy		L	1–4	Rome	
1978	Great Britain		L	2–3	Paris	
1979	Netherlands	W		3–2	Amsterdam	
	Switzerland	W		5–0	Paris	
	Czechoslovakia		L	1–4	Paris	
1980	USSR	W		3–2	Montpelier	
	Finland	W		3–2	Toulouse	
	Czechoslovakia		L	0–5	Prague	
1981	Australia		L	2–3	Lyons	
	Japan	W		4–1	Paris	
1982	Argentina	W		3–2	Buenos Aires	
	Czechoslovakia	W		3–1	Paris	
	New Zealand	W		3–2	Aix-en-Provence	
	USA		L	1–4	Grenoble	Final Round

FRENCH PLAYERS 1904–82

	Total Rubbers Pl'd	Won	(Singles) Pl'd	Won	(Doubles) Pl'd	Won	Ties	Years
M Decugis	15	6	10	3	5	3	6	1904, 05, 12–14, 19
P Ayme	3	1	2	0	1	1	1	1904
M Germot	7	1	4	0	3	1	3	1905, 13, 14
A H Gobert	13	3	9	2	4	1	5	1912, 13, 19, 20, 22
W H Laurentz	10	3	5	1	5	2	5	1912, 19–21
J Samezeuilh	5	3	3	2	2	1	3	1921, 23
J Brugnon	37	26	6	4	31	22	31	1921, 23–27, 30–34
J Borotra	54	36	31	19	23	17	32	1922–37, 47
J Couiteas	3	2	3	2			2	1922, 24
H Cochet	58	44	42	34	16	10	26	1922–24, 26–33
R Lacoste	51	40	40	32	11	8	26	1923–28
J Blanchy	5	3	4	3	1	0	2	1923
P Hirsch	1	0	1	0			1	1923
P Feret	2	2	2	2			2	1925
A Merlin	10	6	10	6			5	1933–35
C Boussus	19	10	19	10			10	1934–37, 39
M Bernard	42	29	21	13	21	16	25	1935–37, 45–50, 52, 53, 55, 56
B Destremeau	42	26	39	25	3	1	24	1936–39, 46–48, 50–52
Y Petra	22	15	14	11	8	4	12	1937–39, 46, 47
H Bolelli	11	8	2	2	9	6	9	1938, 48, 49
P Pelizza	14	10	7	5	7	5	9	1938, 39, 46, 47
J Lesueur	1	0			1	0	1	1938
R Abdesselam	21	11	15	6	6	5	14	1947–53
P Remy	53	33	29	16	24	17	25	1949–58
J Thomas	4	3	3	3	1	0	3	1949, 50
R Haillet	43	30	42	29	1	1	23	1952–60
J D de la Haille	5	3			5	3	5	1953, 54
J C Molinari	12	8	4	3	8	5	9	1954, 57–60
P Darmon	69	47	62	44	7	3	34	1956–67
J N Grinda	13	7	3	2	10	5	10	1959–61, 64
G Pilet	9	6	9	6			6	1959–62
D Contet	21	9	2	1	19	8	16	1961, 63, 64, 66–69
J Renavand	5	3	2	2	3	1	4	1961, 62
J C Barclay	7	3	6	3	1	0	4	1962, 63
P Beust	13	7			13	7	13	1963, 64, 66–69
P Barthes	33	19	23	14	10	5	15	1964, 65, 71–74
F Jauffret	69	42	50	33	19	9	35	1964–71, 73–78
G Goven	*16	9	*15	9	1	0	9	1967–70, 72, 74
J B Chanfreau	4	3			4	3	4	1970–73
J P Rouyer	3	2			3	2	3	1970
P Proisy	*22	12	*18	10	4	2	10	1971–73, 75–77
P Dominguez	*25	15	*15	10	10	5	11	1971, 72, 75, 77, 79
W N'Godrella	2	2			2	2	2	1973, 74
F Caujolle	1	1			1	1	1	1974
J L Haillet	6	4	4	2	2	2	2	1977, 80
Y Noah	30	20	20	14	10	6	11	1978–82
E Deblicker	2	1	2	1			1	1978
P Portes	13	5	10	4	3	1	5	1979–81
G Moretton	8	3	3	0	5	3	6	1979–82
D Bedel	3	2	2	2	1	0	2	1979, 80
C Roger-Vasselin	4	2	3	1	1	1	2	1980, 81
T Tulasne	7	4	7	4			4	1981, 82
H Leconte	5	1	2	0	3	1	3	1982

* Including unfinished rubber.

GREAT BRITAIN IN THE DAVIS CUP

The most decisive British victory in the Challenge/Final Round was for the loss of 17 games and the most one sided at that level.

(1904. British Isles beat Belgium 5–0 at Wimbledon. Laurie Doherty beat Paul de Borman 6–4 6–1 6–1; Frank Riseley beat W Lemaire 6–1 6–4 6–2; Reggie and Laurie Doherty beat de Borman and Lemaire 6–0 6–1 6–3; subsequently Laurie Doherty beat Lemaire w.o.; Riseley beat de Borman 4–6 6–2 8–6 7–5.)

The most decisive British victory was a winning lead for the loss of 13 games and an over-all loss of 16 games.

(1925. European zone, first round, Warsaw. Great Britain beat Poland 5-nil. Gordon Lowe beat M Sjwede 6–0 6–0 6–1; Patrick Wheatley beat M Soerster 6–1 6–2 6–1; Charles Kingsley and Leslie Godfree beat M Kuchar and M Steinert 6–4 6–2 6–2; subsequently Lowe beat Soerster 6–0 6–0 6–1; Wheatley beat Sjwede 6–2 6–0 6–0.)

The highest number of games in a British tie was 274.

(1963. European zone, final, Wimbledon. Great Britain beat Sweden 3–2. Mike Sangster beat Jon Erik Lundquist 3–6 6–2 4–6 12–10 9–7; Bobby Wilson lost to Ulf Schmidt 4–6 6–4 4–6 6–4 4–6; Sangster and Wilson beat Lundquist and Schmidt 22–20 6–4 6–3; Wilson lost to Lundquist 6–3 6–2 2–6 2–6 1–6; Sangster beat Schmidt 7–5 6–2 9–11 3–6 6–3.)

The longest rubber by a Briton was over 95 games, a doubles.

(1969. European zone, 3rd round, Birmingham. Wilhelm Bungert and Christian Kuhnke (FRG) beat Mark Cox and Peter Curtis (GB) 10–8 17–19 13–11 3–6 6–2.)

The longest singles rubber by a Briton was over 71 games.

(1969. Inter-zone, semi-final, Wimbledon. Thomas Koch (Bra) beat Mark Cox (GB) 4–6 11–13 6–3 8–6 8–6 in the second rubber.)

The worst defeat suffered **by a British side** was in the semi-final of the European Zone in June 1939 in Berlin. Germany built a winning lead on the outcome of the first three rubbers with the British players having won no set and a total of only **15 games.** Henner Henkel beat Ronald Shayes 6–2 6–3 6–1, Roderick Menzel beat Charles Hare, who hurt his back, 6–0 6–1 retired and Henkel and G von Metaxa beat Laurie Shaffi and Frank Wilde 6–4 6–2 6–2. Subsequently Menzel beat Shayes 6–1 6–1 6–0 and von Metaxa beat Wilde 3–6 6–0 6–2 6–3.

The only other occasion a British side was beaten without taking a set was in the semi-final of 1981. In Buenos Aires the Argentine took a winning lead when Jose Luis Clerc beat Richard Lewis 6–4 6–4 6–0, Guillermo Vilas beat Christopher Mottram 6–3 6–1 6–1 and Clerc and Vilas beat Andrew Jarrett and Jonathon Smith 8–6 8–6 6–2. On this occasion Britain had won **27 games.**

BRITISH RESULTS 1900–82

Year	Opponent	Won/Lost	Score	Venue	
1900	USA	L	0–3	Boston	Challenge Round
1901	did not challenge				
1902	USA	L	2–3	New York	Challenge Round
1903	USA	W	4–1	Boston	Challenge Round **Champions**
1904	Belgium	W	5–0	Wimbledon	Challenge Round **Champions**
1905	USA	W	5–5	Wimbledon	Challenge Round **Champions**
1906	USA	W	5–0	Wimbledon	Challenge Round **Champions**
1907	Australasia	L	2–3	Wimbledon	Challenge Round
1908	USA	L	1–4	Boston	
1909	USA	L	0–5	Philadelphia	
1910	did not challenge				
1911	USA	L	1–4	New York	
1912	France	W	4–1	Folkestone	
	Australasia	W	3–2	Melbourne	Challenge Round **Champions**
1913	USA	L	2–3	Wimbledon	Challenge Round
1914	Belgium	W	5–0	Folkestone	
	France	W	4–1	Wimbledon	
	Australasia	L	0–3	Boston	
1915–1918	no competition				

Year	Opponent	Won/Lost	Score	Venue	
1919	S Africa	W	4–1	Eastbourne	
	France	W	3–2	Deauville	
	Australasia	L	1–4	Sydney	Challenge Round
1920	USA	L	0–5	Wimbledon	
1921	Spain	W	4–1	Hendon	
	Australasia	L	2–3	Pittsburgh	
1922	Italy	W	5–0	Roehampton	
	Spain	scratched			
1923	Belgium	W	3–2	Brussels	
	Spain	L	2–3	Manchester	
1924	Belgium	W	3–2	Torquay	
	Spain	W	3–2	Birmingham	
	S Africa	W	4–1	Scarborough	
	France	L	1–4	Eastbourne	
1925	Poland	W	5–0	Warsaw	
	Denmark	W	3–0	Copenhagen	
	France	L	0–4	Eastbourne	
1926	Poland	W	5–0	Harrogate	
	Italy	W	3–2	Rome	
	Spain	W	4–1	Barcelona	
	France	L	0–4	Corbourg	European Zone Final
1927	Sweden	W	4–1	Birmingham	
	Denmark	L	2–3	Harrogate	
1928	Argentina	W	4–1	Torquay	
	Finland	W	5–0	Helsinki	
	Germany	W	4–1	Birmingham	
	Italy	L	1–4	Felixstowe	
1929	Poland	W	5–0	Warsaw	
	S Africa	W	5–0	Bournemouth	
	Hungary	W	3–2	Budapest	
	Germany	L	2–3	Berlin	European Zone Final
1930	Germany	W	3–2	Queen's Club	
	Poland	W	5–0	Torquay	
	Australia	L	1–4	Eastbourne	
1931	Monaco	W	5–0	Plymouth	
	Belgium	W	5–0	Brussels	
	S Africa	W	5–0	Eastbourne	
	Japan	W	5–0	Eastbourne	
	Czechoslavakia	W	4–1	Prague	European Zone Final
	USA	W	3–2	Paris	Inter-Zone Final
	France	L	2–3	Paris	Challenge Round
1932	Romania	W	5–0	Torquay	
	Poland	W	4–1	Warsaw	
	Germany	L	2–3	Berlin	
1933	Spain	W	4–1	Barcelona	
	Finland	W	5–0	Queen's Club	
	Italy	W	4–1	Eastbourne	
	Czechoslavakia	W	5–0	Eastbourne	
	Australia	W	3–2	Wimbledon	European Zone Final
	USA	W	4–1	Paris	Inter-Zone Final
	France	W	3–2	Paris	Challenge Round **Champions**
1934	USA	W	4–1	Wimbledon	Challenge Round **Champions**
1935	USA	W	5–0	Wimbledon	Challenge Round **Champions**
1936	Australia	W	3–2	Wimbledon	Challenge Round **Champions**
1937	USA	L	1–4	Wimbledon	Challenge Round
1938	Romania	W	3–2	Harrogate	
	Yugoslavia	L	0–5	Zagreb	
1939	New Zealand	W	3–2	Brighton	
	France	W	3–2	Wimbledon	
	Germany	L	0–5	Berlin	

Year	Opponent	Won/Lost	Score	Venue	
1940-1945 no competition					
1946	France	L	0–5	Paris	
1947	Poland	W	3–2	Warsaw	
	S Africa	L	1–4	Scarborough	
1948	India	W	3–2	Harrogate	
	Norway	W	4–1	Oslo	
	Netherlands	W	4–1	Birmingham	
	Sweden	L	1–4	Stockholm	
1949	Portugal	W	5–0	Lisbon	
	Czechoslovakia	L	1–4	Wimbledon	
1950	Italy	L	2–3	Eastbourne	
1951	France	W	3–2	Wimbledon	
	Sweden	L	0–5	Scarborough	
1952	Yugoslavia	W	3–2	Belgrade	
	Italy	L	1–4	Bologna	
1953	Norway	W	5–0	Oslo	
	Belgium	L	1–4	Brussels	
1954	Brazil	W	4–1	Eastbourne	
	Belgium	L	2–3	Scarborough	
1955	Austria	W	4–1	Vienna	
	India	W	3–2	Manchester	
	Italy	L	0–5	Birmingham	
1956	Yugoslavia	W	5–0	Belgrade	
	Chile	W	3–2	Bristol	
	Sweden	L	1–4	Stockholm	
1957	New Zealand	W	5–0	Eastbourne	
	France	W	3–2	Paris	
	Belgium	L	2–3	Brussels	
1958	Brazil	W	5–0	Eastbourne	
	West Germany	W	5–0	Scarborough	
	France	W	5–0	Manchester	
	Italy	L	1–4	Milan	European Zone Final
1959	Luxembourg	W	5–0	Mondorf-les-Bains	
	Chile	W	3–2	Eastbourne	
	Spain	L	2–3	Barcelona	
1960	Netherlands	W	5–0	Scheveningen	
	Belgium	W	5–0	Scarborough	
	Italy	L	1–4	Wimbledon	
1961	Austria	W	3–2	Vienna	
	S Africa	W	3–2	Birmingham	
	Sweden	L	1–4	Baastad	
1962	Austria	W	4–1	Vienna	
	Brazil	W	4–1	Eastbourne	
	Italy	L	0–5	Milan	
1963	Belgium	W	5–0	Brussels	
	USSR	W	4–1	Eastbourne	
	Spain	W	4–1	Bristol	
	Sweden	W	3–2	Wimbledon	European Zone Final
	USA	L	0–5	Bournemouth	Inter-Zone Semi-Final
1964	Austria	W	5–0	Birmingham	
	Ireland	W	5–0	Eastbourne	
	Yugoslavia	W	3–2	Manchester	
	France	L	2–3	Bristol	
1965	Israel	W	4–1	Hampstead, London	
	Denmark	W	3–1	Copenhagen	
	S Africa	L	2–3	Eastbourne	
1966	New Zealand	W	4–1	Queen's Club	
	Hungary	W	3–2	Budapest	
	West Germany	L	2–3	Hanover	
1967	Canada	W	4–1	Bournemouth	

Year	Opponent	Won/Lost	Score	Venue	
	Bulgaria	W	5–0	Sofia	
	Spain	L	2–3	Eastbourne	
1968	France	W	3–0	Bournemouth	
	Finland	W	5–0	Queen's Club	
	Spain	L	1–4	Barcelona	
1969	Switzerland	W	5–0	Zurich	
	Ireland	W	5–0	Eastbourne	
	Germany	W	3–2	Birmingham	
	S Africa	W	3–2	Bristol	European Zone "A" Final
	Brazil	W	3–2	Wimbledon	Inter-Zone Semi-Final
	Romania	L	2–3	Wimbledon	Inter-Zone Final
1970	Austria	L	2–3	Edinburgh	
1971	Yugoslavia	L	0–3	Zagreb	
1972	France	L	1–4	Paris	
1973	West Germany	L	1–4	Munich	
1974	Egypt	L	0–5	Cairo	
1975	Iran	W	5–0	Queen's Club (Indoors), played 1974	
	Austria	W	4–0	Vienna	
	Spain	L	2–3	Barcelona	
1976	Switzerland	W	4–1	Zurich	
	Romania	W	5–0	Eastbourne	
	France	W	4–1	Eastbourne	
	Italy	L	1–4	Wimbledon	European Zone "B" Final
1977	Romania	L	1–4	Bucharest	
1978	Monaco	W	5–0	Monte Carlo	
	Austria	W	5–0	Bristol	
	France	W	3–2	Paris	
	Czechoslovakia	W	5–0	Eastbourne	European Zone "A" Final
	Australia	W	3–2	Crystal Palace (Indoors)	Inter-Zone Semi-Final
	USA	L	1–4	Palm Springs	Final Round
1979	Spain	W	4–1	Eastbourne	
	Italy	L	1–4	Rome	
1980	Romania	L	2–3	Bristol	
1981	Italy	W	3–2	Brighton (Indoors)	
	New Zealand	W	4–1	Christchurch (Indoors)	
	Argentina	L	0–5	Buenos Aires	
1982	Italy	L	2–3	Rome	
	Spain	W	3–2	Barcelona	Relegation tie

BRITISH PLAYERS 1900–82

	Total Rubbers		(Singles)		(Doubles)		Ties	Years
	Pl'd	Won	Pl'd	Won	Pl'd	Won		
A W Gore	*7	3	*6	2	1	1	3	1900, 07, 12
E D Black	2	0	1	0	1	0	1	1900
H Roper Barrett	10	4	2	0	8	4	8	1900, 07, 12–14, 19
J Pim	2	0	2	0			1	1902
R F Doherty	8	7	3	2	5	5	5	1902–06
H L Doherty	12	12	7	7	5	5	5	1902–06
F L Riseley	3	3	2	2	1	1	2	1904, 22
S H Smith	4	4	4	4			2	1905, 06
M J G Ritchie	3	1	2	1	1	0	1	1908
J C Parke	20	8	15	8	5	0	8	1908, 09, 12–14, 20
C P Dixon	13	5	10	3	3	2	5	1909, 11–13
W C Crawley	1	0			1	0	1	1909
A H Lowe	5	0	5	0			3	1911, 14, 19
A E Beamish	3	1			3	1	3	1911, 12, 19

	Total Rubbers		(Singles)		(Doubles)		Ties	Years
	Pl'd	Won	Pl'd	Won	Pl'd	Won		
T M Mavrogordato	9	6	6	5	3	1	4	1914, 19
A R F Kingscote	17	9	13	7	4	2	7	1919, 20, 22, 24
P M Davson	2	1	2	1			1	1919
O G N Turnbull	9	3	7	3	2	0	6	1919, 21, 25, 26
F G Lowe	8	6	8	6			3	1921, 22, 25
R Lycett	9	6	8	4	3	2	3	1921, 23
M Woosnam	8	4	2	1	6	3	6	1921, 24
J B Gilbert	11	7	11	7			6	1923–25
L A Godfree	11	6			11	6	11	1923–25, 27
J D P Wheatley	14	10	13	10	1	0	8	1923–26
C H Kingsley	12	9	4	3	8	6	9	1925–27, 31
C R O Crole-Rees	11	7	2	0	9	7	10	1925, 26, 28, 29
J C Gregory	30	21	21	13	9	8	15	1926–30, 52
H K Lester	1	0	1	0			1	1926
E Higgs	12	8	12	8			6	1927, 28
C G Eames	5	4			5	4	5	1928, 29
H W Austin	48	36	48	36			24	1929–37
G P Hughes	22	15	2	2	20	13	21	1929, 31–36
I G Collins	6	6			6	6	6	1929, 30
H G N Lee	11	4	9	4	2	0	7	1930, 32–34
N Sharpe	2	2	2	2			1	1930
F J Perry	52	45	38	34	14	11	20	1931–36
H F David	2	2	2	2			1	1932
C R D Tuckey	3	1			3	1	3	1935–37
C E Hare	8	4	6	3	2	1	4	1937, 39
F H D Wilde	7	2	1	0	6	2	6	1937–39
C M Jones	2	0	2	0			1	1938
R A Shayes	10	4	10	4			5	1938, 39
D W Butler	7	2	4	0	3	2	4	1938, 47
L Shaffi	2	0	1	0	1	0	2	1939
D W Barton	4	0	4	0			2	1946, 47
D McPhail	2	0	2	0			1	1946
J S Olliff	1	0			1	0	1	1946
H Billington	2	1			2	1	2	1946, 48
A J Mottram	56	36	38	25	18	11	19	1947–55
G L Paish	40	17	23	7	17	10	19	1947–55
H F Walton	2	0	2	0			1	1948
N R Lewis	1	1	1	1			1	1949
A G Roberts	1	0	1	0			1	1951
R Becker	18	11	16	10	2	1	10	1952, 55, 56, 58, 60
G D Oakley	2	2	2	2			2	1953, 54
W A Knight	43	27	34	21	9	6	21	1955, 56, 58–60
R K Wilson	*62	41	*29	16	33	25	34	1955, 57–61, 63–68
M G Davies	37	24	22	15	15	9	16	1955–60
J E Barrett	1	1	1	1			1	1956
A R Mills	4	3	3	2	1	1	3	1959, 61, 64
M J Sangster	65	43	48	29	17	14	26	1960–68
J A Pickard	6	3	1	0	5	3	5	1961–63
R Taylor	*41	29	*36	26	5	3	18	1964–67, 73, 75, 76
M Cox	35	23	21	15	14	8	16	1967–69, 73, 78, 79
P Hutchins	3	1	2	0	1	1	2	1968
G R Stilwell	13	10	12	10	1	0	6	1969
P W Curtis	6	4			6	4	6	1969, 70
G D Battrick	5	2	3	1	2	1	2	1970, 71
J G Clifton	2	0	2	0			1	1970
S J Matthews	2	0	1	0	1	0	1	1971
D A Lloyd	19	9	4	0	15	9	15	1972–74, 76–80
J G Paish	3	1	2	0	1	1	1	1972
J M Lloyd	33	15	24	10	9	5	16	1974–80
M J Farrell	1	1			1	1	1	1975
C J Mottram	36	27	31	24	5	3	17	1975, 76, 78–82
J W Feaver	4	0	4	0			2	1977, 80
R A Lewis	12	6	12	6			7	1977, 78, 81, 82
J R Smith	6	2	1	0	5	2	5	1981, 82
A M Jarrett	7	3	2	1	5	2	5	1981, 82

* Including unfinished rubber.

GREAT BRITAIN'S FIFTH RUBBER DECISIONS
Ties won or lost 3–2 on the outcome of the last rubber

Year	Opponent	Vital result		
1907	Australasia	N E Brookes d. H Roper Barrett	6–2 6–0 6–3	LOST
1912	Australasia	J C Parke d. R W Heath	6–2 6–4 6–4	WON
1919	France	A R F Kingscote d. A H Gobert	6–4 6–4 7–5	WON
1924	Belgium	J B Gilbert d. G Watson	6–4 6–3 6–1	WON
	Spain	J B Gilbert d. J M Alonso	6–0 6–4 6–0	WON
1927	Denmark	E Ulrich d. E Higgs	1–6 3–6 6–2 6–2 6–4	LOST
1929	Hungary	H W Austin d. I de Takacs	6–4 6–2 6–2	WON
	Germany	D Prenn d. H W Austin	4–6 6–2 6–4 4–6 5–1 ret'd	LOST
1930	Germany	H G N Lee d. H Landmann	5–7 6–3 6–2 6–3	WON
1931	USA	H W Austin d. F X Shields	8–6 6–3 7–5	WON
	France	H Cochet d. F J Perry	6–4 1–6 9–7 6–3	LOST
1933	France	F J Perry d. A Merlin	4–6 8–6 6–2 7–5	WON
1936	Australia	F J Perry d. J H Crawford	6–2 6–3 6–3	WON
1938	Romania	R A Shayes d. C Caralulis	6–3 6–0 6–3	WON
1939	New Zealand	C E Hare d. C E Malfroy	7–5 6–4 6–4	WON
1950	Italy	G Cucelli d. G L Paish	1–6 6–2 4–6 6–4 8–6	LOST
1954	Belgium	P Washer d. A J Mottram	7–5 6–4 6–4	LOST
1955	India	A J Mottram d. N Kumar	2–6 9–7 4–6 7–5 6–3	WON
1956	Chile	R Becker d. A Hammersley	6–4 6–1 6–1	WON
1957	France	M G Davies d. R Haillet	6–8 5–7 6–4 6–1 6–4	WON
	Belgium	J Brichant d. M G Davies	1–6 4–6 6–3 6–4 6–2	LOST
1959	Spain	M Santana d. M G Davies	6–2 3–6 4–6 6–0 6–1	LOST
1963	Sweden	M J Sangster d. U Schmidt	7–5 6–2 9–11 3–6 6–3	WON
1964	Yugoslavia	R K Wilson d. B Jovanovic	6–4 7–5 0–6 3–6 6–2	WON
	France	P Barthes d. W A Knight	6–4 6–4 6–1	LOST
1966	Hungary	R Taylor d. I Gulyas	16–18 6–3 6–1 6–4	WON
1969	West Germany	M Cox d. W Bungert	6–3 2–6 8–10 7–5 6–2	WON
	Brazil	M Cox d. J E Mandarino	6–3 18–16 3–6 6–2	WON
	Romania	I Nastase d. M Cox	3–6 6–1 6–4 6–4	LOST
1970	Austria	H Kary d. J G Clifton	6–3 6–2 6–4	LOST
1975	Spain	M Orantes d. R Taylor	6–3 3–6 7–5 6–8 7–5	LOST
1980	Romania	I Nastase d. J W Feaver	7–5 8–6 2–6 2–6 6–4	LOST
1982	Italy	A Panatta d. R A Lewis	8–6 6–4 6–2	LOST
	Spain	C J Mottram d. F Luna	8–6 8–6 6–2	WON

BRITISH CAPTAINS

H Roper Barrett	1900, 1919, 1926–39	F T Stowe	1946–48
W H Collins	1902–06	J C Gregory	1949–52
S A E Hickson	1907, 1914	H F David	1953–58
J C Parke	1908, 1909, 1914	G L Paish	1957–58
C P Dixon	1911, 1912	J E Barrett	1959–62
R J McNair	1912, 1913, 1919, 1920	A D C Macaulay	1963, 1964
A R F Kingscote	1919	H T Baxter	1964–66, 1968–71, 1975
M Woosnam	1921	P E Hare	1967
F L Riseley	1922, 1924, 1925	J K Jarvis	1972
J A Batley	1923	J A Pickard	1973, 1974
L A Godfree	1924	P R Hutchins	1976–82
A D Prebble	1926		

USA IN THE DAVIS CUP

The most decisive American victory in the Challenge/Final Round was for the loss of 30 games.

(1979. San Francisco, indoors, USA beat Italy 5–0. Vitas Gerulaitis beat Corrado Barazzutti 6–3 3–2 ret'd; John McEnroe beat Adriano Panatta 6–2 6–3 6–4; Bob Lutz and Stan Smith beat Panatta and Paola Bertolucci 6–4 12–10 6–2; subsequently McEnroe beat Toni Zugarelli 6–4 6–3 6–1; Gerulaitis beat Panatta 6–1 6–3 6–3.)

The most decisive American victory at any stage was for the loss of 8 games.

(1957. American Zone, first round, Port of Spain. USA beat British West Indies 5–0. Vic Seixas beat B Phillips 6–0 6–2 6–0; Tut Bartzen beat Ian McDonald 6–1 6–0 6–1; Seixas and Grant Golden beat Phillips and McDonald 6–4 6–0 6–0; subsequently Bartzen beat P Valdez 6–1 6–1 6–1; Golden beat McDonald 8–6 6–4 4–6 6–2.)

The widest over-all American victory was for the loss of 18 games.

(1954. American Zone, first round, Port of Spain. USA beat British West Indies 5–0. Ham Richardson beat G Inglefield 6–2 6–2 6–0; Streight Clark beat R Segall 6–2 6–0 6–3; Clark and Hal Burrows beat H Nothnage and Segall 6–0 6–1 6–3; Richardson beat L Phang 6–0 6–0 6–2; Burrows beat Inglefield 6–0 6–0 6–3.)

The highest number of games in an American tie was 281.

(1960. Inter-zone final, Perth, Italy beat USA 3–2. Nicola Pietrangeli lost to Barry MacKay 6–8 6–3 10–8 6–8 11–13; Orlando Sirola lost to Earl Buchholz 8–6 5–7 9–11 2–6 Pietrangeli and Sirola beat Buchholz and Chuck McKinley 3–6 10–8 6–4 6–8 6–4 Pietrangeli beat Buchholz 6–1 6–2 6–8 3–6 6–4; Sirola beat MacKay 9–7 6–3 8–6.)

The longest rubber by an American extended for 122 games.

(1973. American zone final, Arkansas, doubles. Stan Smith and Erik Van Dillen (USA) beat Jaime Fillol and Patricio Conejo (Chi) 7–9 37–39 8–6 6–1 6–3. The longest rubber played.)

The longest singles by an American extended for 86 games.

(1970. Challenge Round, Cleveland. Fifth and dead rubber. Arthur Ashe (USA) beat Christian Kuhnke (FRG) 6–8 10–12 9–7 13–11 6–4. The longest singles played.)

US RESULTS 1900–82

Year	Opponent	Won/Lost		Score	Venue	
1900	British Isles	W		3–0	Boston	Challenge Round **Champions**
1901	no challenge					
1902	British Isles	W		3–2	New York	Challenge Round **Champions**
1903	British Isles		L	1–4	Boston	Challenge Round
1904	did not play					
1905	France	W		5–0	Queen's Club	
	Australasia	W		5–0	Queen's Club	
	British Isles		L	0–5	Wimbledon	Challenge Round
1906	Australasia	W		3–2	Newport, Mon.	
	British Isles		L	0–5	Wimbledon	Challenge Round
1907	Australasia		L	2–3	Wimbledon	
1908	British Isles	W		4–1	Boston	
	Australasia		L	2–3	Melbourne	Challenge Round
1909	British Isles	W		5–0	Philadelphia	
	Australasia		L	0–5	Sydney	Challenge Round
1910	did not play					
1911	British Isles	W		4–1	New York	
	Australasia		L	0–5	Christchurch	Challenge Round
1912	did not play					
1913	Australasia	W		4–1	New York	
	Germany	W		5–0	Nottingham	
	Canada	W		3–0	Wimbledon	
	British Isles	W		3–2	Wimbledon	Challenge Round **Champions**
1914	Australasia		L	2–3	New York	Challenge Round
1915–1918	no competition					
1919	did not play					

Wimbledon 1981. The gangway between courts 3 and 4 during the year of record attendance.

Vitas Gerulaitis of New York. A player of some great matches.

Yannick Noah who came from the Cameroons to become the top player of France in 1982.

Andrea Jaeger, one of America's precocious double handers.

Year	Opponent	Won/Lost	Score	Venue	
1920	France	W	3–0	Eastbourne	
	British Isles	W	5–0	Wimbledon	
	Australasia	W	5–0	Auckland	Challenge Round **Champions**
1921	Japan	W	5–0	New York	Challenge Round **Champions**
1922	Australasia	W	4–1	New York	Challenge Round **Champions**
1923	Australia	W	4–1	New York	Challenge Round **Champions**
1924	Australia	W	5–0	Philadelphia	Challenge Round **Champions**
1925	France	W	5–0	Philadelphia	Challenge Round **Champions**
1926	France	W	4–1	Philadelphia	Challenge Round **Champions**
1927	France	L	2–3	Philadelphia	Challenge Round
1928	Mexico	W	3–0	Mexico City	
	China	W	5–0	Kansas City	
	Japan	W	5–0	Chicago	
	Italy	W	4–1	Paris	Inter-zone Final
	France	L	1–4	Paris	Challenge Round
1929	Canada	W	5–0	Montreal	
	Japan	W	4–1	Washington	
	Cuba	W	3–1	Detroit	
	Germany	W	5–0	Berlin	Inter-zone Final
	France	L	2–3	Paris	Challenge Round
1930	Canada	W	5–0	Philadelphia	
	Mexico	W	5–0	Washington	
	Italy	W	4–1	Paris	Inter-zone Final
	France	L	1–4	Paris	Challenge Round
1931	Mexico	W	5–0	Mexico City	
	Canada	W	4–1	Montreal	
	Argentina	W	5–0	Washington	
	Great Britain	L	2–3	Paris	Inter-zone Final
1932	Canada	W	5–0	Washington	
	Mexico	W	5–0	New Orleans	
	Australia	W	5–0	Philadelphia	
	Brazil	W	5–0	New York	
	Germany	W	3–2	Paris	Inter-zone Final
	France	L	2–3	Paris	Challenge Round
1933	Mexico	W	5–0	Mexico City	
	Canada	W	5–0	Montreal	
	Argentina	W	4–0	Washington	
	Great Britain	L	1–4	Paris	Inter-zone Final
1934	Canada	W	5–0	Wilmington	
	Mexico	W	5–0	Baltimore	
	Australia	W	3–2	Wimbledon	Inter-zone Final
	Great Britain	L	1–4	Wimbledon	Challenge Round
1935	China	W	5–0	Mexico City	
	Mexico	W	5–0	Mexico City	
	Germany	W	4–1	Wimbledon	Inter-zone Final
	Great Britain	L	0–5	Wimbledon	Challenge Round
1936	Mexico	W	5–0	Houston	
	Australia	L	2–3	Philadelphia	
1937	Japan	W	5–0	San Francisco	
	Australia	W	5–0	New York	
	Germany	W	3–2	Wimbledon	Inter-zone Final
	Great Britain	W	4–1	Wimbledon	Challenge Round **Champions**
1938	Australia	W	3–2	Philadelphia	Challenge Round **Champions**
1939	Australia	L	2–3	Philadelphia	Challenge Round
1940–1945 not held					
1946	Philippines	W	5–0	St Louis	
	Mexico	W	5–0	Orange, NJ	
	Sweden	W	5–0	New York	Inter-zone Final
	Australia	W	5–0	Melbourne	Challenge Round **Champions**
1947	Australia	W	4–1	New York	Challenge Round **Champions**

Year	Opponent	Won/Lost		Score	Venue	
1948	Australia	W		5–0	New York	Challenge Round **Champions**
1949	Australia	W		4–1	New York	Challenge Round **Champions**
1950	Australia		L	1–4	New York	Challenge Round
1951	Japan	W		5–0	Louisville	
	Mexico	W		5–0	New York	
	Canada	W		5–0	Montreal	
	Sweden	W		5–0	Melbourne	Inter-zone Final
	Australia		L	2–3	Sydney	Challenge Round
1952	Japan	W		5–0	Cincinnati	
	Cuba	W		5–0	Havana	
	Canada	W		4–1	Montreal	
	Italy	W		5–0	Sydney	Inter-zone Final
	Australia		L	1–4	Adelaide	Challenge Round
1953	Japan	W		5–0	Vancouver	
	West Indies	W		5–0	Kingston	
	Canada	W		5–0	Montreal	
	Belgium	W		4–1	Brisbane	Inter-zone Final
	Australia		L	2–3	Melbourne	Challenge Round
1954	West Indies	W		5–0	Trinidad	
	Cuba	W		5–0	St Petersburg	
	Mexico	W		4–1	Mexico City	
	Sweden	W		5–0	Brisbane	Inter-zone Final
	Australia	W		3–2	Sydney	Challenge Round **Champions**
1955	Australia		L	0–5	New York	Challenge Round
1956	Canada	W		4–1	Victoria	
	Mexico	W		4–1	New York	
	Italy	W		4–1	New York	
	India	W		4–1	Perth	Inter-zone Final
	Australia		L	0–5	Adelaide	Challenge Round
1957	West Indies	W		5–0	Trinidad	
	Venezuela	W		4–1	Caracas	
	Brazil	W		5–0	Boston	
	Philippines	W		5–0	Adelaide	
	Belgium	W		3–2	Brisbane	Inter-zone Final
	Australia		L	2–3	Melbourne	Challenge Round
1958	Venezuela	W		5–0	Caracas	
	Canada	W		5–0	Toronto	
	Argentina	W		5–0	Rye, NY	
	Italy	W		5–0	Perth	Inter-zone Final
	Australia	W		3–2	Brisbane	Challenge Round **Champions**
1959	Australia		L	2–3	New York	Challenge Round
1960	Canada	W		5–0	Quebec	
	Mexico	W		3–2	Mexico City	
	Venezuela	W		5–0	Cleveland	
	Philippines	W		5–0	Perth	
	Italy		L	2–3	Perth	Inter-zone Final
1961	British Caribbean	W		5–0	Barbados	
	Ecuador	W		5–0	St Louis	
	Mexico	W		3–2	Cleveland	
	India	W		3–2	New Delhi	
	Italy		L	1–4	Rome	Inter-zone Final
1962	Canada	W		5–0	Cleveland	
	Mexico		L	2–3	Mexico City	
1963	Iran	W		5–0	Teheran	
	Mexico	W		4–1	Los Angeles	
	Venezuela	W		5–0	Denver	
	Great Britain	W		5–0	Bournemouth	
	India	W		5–0	Bombay	Inter-zone Final
	Australia	W		3–2	Adelaide	Challenge Round **Champions**
1964	Australia		L	2–3	Cleveland	Challenge Round

Year	Opponent	Won/Lost	Score	Venue	
1965	Canada	W	5–0	Bakersfield	
	Mexico	W	4–1	Dallas	
	Spain	L	1–4	Barcelona	
1966	British Caribbean	W	4–1	Kingston, Jamaica	
	Mexico	W	5–0	Cleveland	
	Brazil	L	2–3	Porto Alegre	
1967	British Caribbean	W	5–0	Trinidad	
	Mexico	W	4–1	Mexico City	
	Ecuador	L	2–3	Guayaquil	
1968	British Caribbean	W	5–0	Richmond, Va	
	Mexico	W	5–0	Berkeley	
	Ecuador	W	5–0	Charlotte, NC	
	Spain	W	4–1	Cleveland	
	India	W	4–1	San Juan	Inter-zone Final
	Australia	W	4–1	Adelaide	Challenge Round **Champions**
1969	Romania	W	5–0	Cleveland	Challenge Round **Champions**
1970	West Germany	W	5–0	Cleveland	Challenge Round **Champions**
1971	Romania	W	3–2	Charlotte, NC	Challenge Round **Champions**
1972	Commonwealth Caribbean	W	4–1	Kingston, Jamaica	
	Mexico	W	5–0	Mexico City	
	Chile	W	5–0	Santiago	
	Spain	W	3–2	Barcelona	
	Romania	W	3–2	Bucharest	Final Round **Champions**
1973	Mexico	W	4–1	Mexico City	
	Chile	W	4–1	Little Rock, Ark	
	Romania	W	4–1	Alamo, Cal.	
	Australia	L	0–5	Cleveland	Final Round
1974	Colombia	L	1–4	Bogota	
1975	Commonwealth Caribbean	W	5–0	Nassau	
	Mexico	L	2–3	Palm Springs	
1976	Venezuela	W	5–0	Tucson	
	Mexico	L	2–3	Mexico City	
1977	Venezuela	W	4–1	Caracas	
	Mexico	W	4–1	Tucson	
	S Africa	W	4–1	Newport Beach	
	Argentina	L	2–3	Buenos Aires	
1978	S Africa	W	4–1	Nashville	
	Chile	W	3–2	Santiago	
	Sweden	W	3–2	Gothenberg	
	Great Britain	W	4–1	Palm Springs	Final Round **Champions**
1979	Colombia	W	5–0	Cleveland	
	Argentina	W	4–1	Memphis	
	Australia	W	4–1	Sydney	
	Italy	W	5–0	San Francisco	Final Round **Champions**
1980	Mexico	W	3–2	Mexico City	
	Argentina	L	1–4	Buenos Aires	
1981	Mexico	W	3–2	Carlsbad, Cal	
	Czechoslovakia	W	4–1	New York	
	Australia	W	5–0	Portland, Oregon	
	Argentina	W	3–1	Cincinnati	Final Round **Champions**
1982	India	W	4–1	Carlsbad, Cal	
	Sweden	W	3–2	St Louis	
	Australia	W	5–0	Perth	
	France	W	4–1	Grenoble	Final Round **Champions**

US PLAYERS 1900–82

	Total Rubbers Pl'd	Won	(Singles) Pl'd	Won	(Doubles) Pl'd	Won	Ties	Years
D F Davis	*4	2	*2	1	2	1	2	1900, 02
M D Whitman	3	3	3	3			2	1900, 02
H Ward	14	7	7	3	7	4	7	1900, 02, 05, 06
W A Larned	14	9	14	9			8	1902, 03, 05, 08, 09, 11
R D Wrenn	3	0	2	0	1	0	1	1903
G L Wrenn	1	0			1	0	1	1903
W J Clothier	5	4	5	4			3	1905, 09
B C Wright	15	9	9	6	6	3	7	1905, 07, 08, 11
R D Little	8	3	4	1	4	2	4	1906, 09, 11
K Behr	3	1	2	0	1	1	1	1907
F B Alexander	4	1	2	0	2	1	2	1908
H H Hackett	6	5			6	5	6	1908, 09, 13
M C McLoughlin	20	12	13	9	7	3	8	1909, 11, 13, 14
M H Long	3	0	2	0	1	0	1	1909
T C Bundy	2	0			2	0	2	1911, 14
W F Johnson	1	0	1	0			1	1913
R N Williams	13	10	9	6	4	4	9	1913, 14, 21, 23, 25, 26
W M Johnston	21	18	17	14	4	4	10	1920–27
W T Tilden	41	34	30	25	11	9	17	1920–30
W M Washburn	1	1			1	1	1	1921
V Richards	5	4	2	2	3	2	4	1922, 24–26
F T Hunter	6	4	4	3	2	1	4	1927–29
J F Hennessey	15	13	12	10	3	3	8	1928, 29
A Jones	1	1			1	1	1	1928
G M Lott	22	18	11	7	11	11	18	1928–31, 33, 34
W F Coen	2	2	1	1	1	1	2	1928
J Van Ryn	32	29	8	7	24	22	24	1929–36
W L Allison	*45	32	*29	18	16	14	20	1929–33, 35, 36
J H Doeg	2	2	2	2			2	1930
F X Shields	24	18	21	15	3	3	12	1931, 32, 34
S B Wood	14	8	11	5	3	3	7	1931, 34
C S Sutter	3	3	3	3			2	1931, 33
H E Vines	16	13	16	13			8	1932, 33
L R Stoefen	6	6	3	3	3	3	4	1934
B M Grant	10	8	10	8			5	1935–37
J D Budge	29	25	21	19	8	6	11	1935–38
C G Mako	9	6	1	0	8	6	8	1935–38
F A Parker	14	12	14	12			7	1937, 39, 46, 48
R L Riggs	4	2	4	2			2	1938, 39
J A Kramer	9	8	6	6	3	2	4	1939, 46, 47
J Hunt	1	0			1	0	1	1939
W F Talbert	10	9	2	2	8	7	8	1946, 48, 49, 51–53
F R Schroeder	19	13	14	11	5	2	8	1946–51
G Mulloy	14	11	3	3	11	8	12	1946, 48–50, 52, 53, 57
R A Gonzales	2	2	2	2			1	1949
T P Brown	4	3	3	2	1	1	2	1950, 53
R Savitt	3	3	3	3			3	1951
H Flam	14	12	12	10	2	2	8	1951, 52, 56, 57
M A Trabert	35	27	21	16	14	11	14	1951–55
A Larsen	4	4	4	4			3	1951, 52
E V Seixas	55	38	36	24	19	14	19	1951–57
J E Patty	2	2	1	1	1	1	1	1951
B Bartzen	14	14	13	13	1	1	8	1952, 53, 57, 60, 61
H Stewart	4	4	2	2	2	2	2	1952, 61
R Perry	3	2	2	1	1	1	2	1952, 53
H Richardson	22	20	18	17	4	3	14	1952–56, 58, 65
S Clark	5	5	3	3	2	2	3	1953, 54
H Burrows	4	4	2	2	2	2	2	1954
R Holmberg	1	1			1	1	1	1956
B MacKay	29	20	23	16	6	4	14	1956–60
S Giammalva	10	7	5	4	5	3	6	1956–58
M Green	3	0	3	0			2	1956, 57
G Golden	3	2	2	1	1	1	2	1957

	Total Rubbers Pl'd	Won	(Singles) Pl'd	Won	(Doubles) Pl'd	Won	Ties	Years
W Quillian	2	2	1	1	1	1	1	1958
W Reed	4	1	3	1	1	0	2	1958, 61
J Douglas	9	6	8	5	1	1	5	1958, 61, 62
A Olmedo	9	7	6	5	3	2	3	1958, 59
E Buchholtz	7	5	4	3	3	2	5	1959, 60
C R McKinley	38	30	22	17	16	13	16	1960–65
R D Ralston	35	25	20	14	15	11	15	1960–66
C Crawford	2	2	2	2			1	1961
D Dell	3	2	1	1	2	1	2	1961, 63
E L Scott	4	4	3	3	1	1	2	1963, 65
A Fox	2	2	2	2			1	1963
M C Riessen	10	7	4	3	6	4	8	1963, 65–70, 75, 77, 78, 81
A R Ashe	34	28	32	27	2	1	18	1963, 65–70, 75, 77, 78
F A Froehling	6	3	6	3			3	1963, 65, 71
C Graebner	20	16	13	11	7	5	11	1965–68
C Richey	13	10	13	10			7	1966, 67, 70
C Pasarell	7	6	3	3	4	3	5	1966–68, 74
S R Smith	41	34	19	15	22	19	23	1968–73, 75, 77–79
R C Lutz	16	14	1	1	15	13	15	1968–70, 75, 77–79
E Van Dillen	18	12	4	1	14	11	14	1971–76
T W Gorman	13	8	12	7	1	1	7	1972, 73, 75
H Solomon	13	9	13	9			7	1972–74, 78
R L Stockton	10	5	7	4	3	1	7	1973, 75–77, 79
R Tanner	*14	9	*14	9			7	1975–77, 81
J S Connors	4	3	4	3			2	1976
B E Gottfried	14	7	13	6	1	1	7	1976–78, 80, 82
V Gerulaitis	12	10	12	10			6	1977–80
F McNair	3	2			3	2	3	1977, 78
S Stewart	4	2			4	2	4	1977, 78, 81
J P McEnroe	39	36	29	26	10	10	16	1978–82
P Fleming	9	9			9	9	9	1979–82
S Davis	1	0	1	0			1	1980
E Teltscher	3	1	3	1			2	1982
G Mayer	4	3	4	3			2	1982

* Including unfinished rubber.

US CAPTAINS

D F Davis	1900	A Man	1947–50
M D Whitman	1902	F X Shields	1951
W A Larned	1903, 1909, 1911	W F Talbert	1952–57
P Dashiell	1905	G Mulloy	1952–53
B C Wright	1906, 1913, 1914	E V Seixas	1952, 1957, 1964
M C McLoughlin	1909, 1913, 1914	M A Trabert	1953, 1976–79
H H Hackett	1913	L Baker	1953
S Hardy	1920, 1931	H Richardson	1954
R N Williams	1921–26, 1934	P Jones	1958, 1959
C Garland	1927	D Freed	1960, 1961
W T Tilden	1928	R Kelleher	1962, 1963
J Wear	1928, 1935	C Alphonse Smith	1963
F E Dixon	1929, 1930, 1932	G McCall	1965–67
B Prentice	1931–33	D Dell	1968, 1969
W L Allison	1933, 1936	E Turville	1970, 1971
W Pate	1935–39, 1946	R D Ralston	1972–75
W Chandler	1937	A R Ashe	1981, 82

MOST GALLANT LOSER

The palm as the most gallant and persistent loser must be awarded to Luxembourg. This tiny nation first bravely challenged in 1947.

1947	lost Belgium	0–5
1948	lost Ireland	0–5
1949	lost France	0–5
1950	lost Italy	0–5
1951	lost Switzerland	0–5
1952	lost Egypt	0–5
1953	lost Norway	0–5
1954	lost Denmark	0–5
1955	not accepted	
1956	lost Switzerland	2–3
1957	lost Poland	0–5
1958	lost Finland	0–5
1959	lost Great Britain	0–5
1960	lost Monaco	2–3
1961	lost Monaco	2–3
1962	lost Hungary	0–5
1963	lost Portugal	2–3
1964	lost Yugoslavia	0–3
1965	**beat Turkey**	**3–2**
		(won from 1–2)
	lost Germany	0–5
1966	lost Switzerland	0–5
1967	**beat Ireland**	**3–2**
		(won from 1–2)
	lost Italy	0–5
1968	lost Norway	1–4
1969	lost Ireland	0–5
1970	lost Ireland	0–3
1971	**beat Monaco**	**5–0**
	lost Hungary	0–5
1972	lost Monaco	2–3
1973	lost Morocco	0–5
1974	lost Turkey	0–5
1975	lost Israel	0–5
1976	lost Portugal	0–5
1977	lost Finland	0–5
1978	lost Monaco	0–5
1979	did not play	
1980	lost Turkey	1–4
1981	lost Bulgaria	0–5

ACHIEVEMENT BY INDIVIDUALS

Roy Emerson is unique in having been on a side winning the Davis Cup on **eight occasions.** He was a member of the victorious Australian team in 1959, 1960, 1961, 1962, 1964, 1965, 1966 and 1967. His stint as a Challenge Round player was over 9 consecutive years, since he was on the losing side in 1963. On that occasion he won both his singles. In vital rubbers his record was 13 wins out of 18, that is 72·22 per cent.

Big Bill Tilden played in the Challenge Round for the USA for 11 successive years,

1920 to 1930, an unrivalled record. He was on the winning side 7 years running, 1920 to 1926. His personal achievement was 13 single wins in sequence. In vital rubbers he won 14 out of 18, that is 77·77 per cent.

Norman Brookes represented Australasia in the Challenge Round eight times, in six of which they were winners, 1907–1920. Uniquely he **played 19 vital rubbers,** winning 13, a winning proportion of 68·42 per cent.

Bjorn Borg won the highest number of Davis Cup singles in sequence, going from 1973 to 1980 and taking **33 singles** without loss. In 1975, the year Sweden took the trophy, Borg won 12 singles in sequence.

Neale Fraser, for Australia, had the best winning run without loss, in singles and doubles, in 1959 and 1960, with a total of **13.** Counting only live rubbers his run from 1959 to 1962 extended to **13 sequential vital rubbers** before being beaten in the Challenge Round doubles of 1963.

Ilie Nastase of Romania, a notable Davis Cup competitor.

Ilie Nastase won an unrivalled **18 rubbers** in one year in 1971. He played 20 in all as Romania reached the last of the Challenge Rounds. Nastase won 13 out of his 14 singles, five out of his six doubles.

Manuel Santana for Spain played most rubbers in a year in 1967. With Spain reaching the Challenge Round Santana played two singles and a doubles in all seven ties, that is **21** in all. He won 17, 13 out of 14 singles, six out of seven doubles.

THE CENTURIONS

No Davis Cup player can match the figures of the Italian Nicola Pietrangeli. Between 1954 and 1972 he played more rubbers and won more in more rubbers than any other man.

Between 1900 and 1982 there were 13 players who had taken part in 100 or more Davis Cup rubbers for their country.

	Rubbers Pl'd	Won	(Singles) Pl'd	Won	(Doubles) Pl'd	Won	Ties	Years
N Pietrangeli (Ita)	164	120	110	78	54	42	66	1954–72
I Nastase (Rom)	136	107	90	72	46	35	48	1966–82
J Brichant (Bel)	120	71	79	52	41	19	42	1949–65
M Santana (Spa)	119	91	85	69	34	22	46	1958–73
T Koch (Bra)	118	75	77	46	41	29	44	1962–81
J E Mandarino (Bra)	109	67	73*	41	36	26	42	1961–76
I Tiriac (Rom)	109	70	68	40	41	30	43	1959–77
G von Cramm (Ger)	102	82	69	58	33	24	37	1932–53
W Bungert (Ger)	102**	66	79**	52	23	14	43	1958–71
U Schmidt (Swe)	102	66	69	44	33	22	38	1955–64
P Washer (Bel)	102	66	64	46	38	20	39	1946–61
T Ulrich (Den)	101	45	65	31	36	14	40	1948–77
A Metreveli (USSR)	100**	73	67**	51	33	22	36	1963–79
A Panatta (Ita)	100	64	64	38	36	26	37	1970–82

* one rubber unfinished.
** two rubbers unfinished.

In percentage terms Gottfried von Cramm has the best record among the centurions. He won 80·39 per cent of his total rubbers, 84·05 per cent of his singles. Pietrangeli had the best in doubles, 77·77 per cent.

Torben Ulrich has the lowest percentage of success, with 45·55 per cent over-all, 47·69 per cent in singles, 38·88 per cent in doubles. The span of years of his performance is unequalled—29 years, 8 more than von Cramm with 21.

DAVIS CUP STALWARTS 1900–82

A record of players who have *won* 50 or more rubbers.

	Rubbers Won	Pl'd	(Singles) Won	Pl'd	(Doubles) Won	Pl'd	Ties	Years
N Pietrangeli (Ita)	120	164	78	110	42	54	66	1954–72
I Nastase (Rom)	107	136	72	90	35	46	48	1966–82
M Santana (Spa)	91	119	69	85	22	34	46	1958–73
G von Cramm (Ger)	82	102	58	69	24	33	37	1932–53
T Koch (Bra)	75	118	46	77	29	41	44	1962–81
A Metreveli (USSR)	73	100**	51	67**	22	33	36	1963–79
J Brichant (Bel)	71	120	52	79	19	41	42	1949–65
I Tiriac (Rom)	70	109	40	68	30	41	43	1959–77
R Krishnan (Ind)	69	97	50	69	19	28	42	1953–69
J E Mandarino (Bra)	67	109*	41	73*	26	36	42	1961–76
W Bungert (FRG)	66	102**	52	79**	14	23	43	1958–71
P Washer (Bel)	66	102	46	64	20	38	39	1946–61
U Schmidt (Swe)	66	102	44	69	22	33	38	1955–64
J E Lundquist (Swe)	64	89	47	61	17	28	34	1957–69
A Panatta (Ita)	64	100	38	64	26	36	37	1970–82
R Menzel (Ger & Cze)	62	85	48	61	14	24	35	1928–39
L Bergelin (Swe)	62	88	43	60	19	28	36	1946–65
J Mukerjea (Ind)	62	98*	39	63*	23	35	43	1960–72
S Davidson (Swe)	61	83	40	53	21	30	34	1950–60
M Orantes (Spa)	60	87	39	58	21	29	38	1967–80
J Kodes (Cze)	60	97*	39	61*	21	36	39	1966–80

* one rubber unfinished.
** two rubbers unfinished.

	Rubbers Won	Pl'd	(Singles) Won	Pl'd	(Doubles) Won	Pl'd	Ties	Years
P Lall (Ind)	58	91*	34	55*	24	36	40	1959–73
O Sirola (Ita)	56	89	21	46	35	43	46	1953–63
H L Morpurgo (Ita)	55	79	39	53	16	26	28	1923–33
K Nielsen (Den)	53	96	42	65	11	31	33	1948–60
C Kuhnke (FRG)	53	75	36	51	17	24	32	1960–72
T Johansson (Swe)	52	73	33	46	19	27	32	1946–60

* one rubber unfinished.
** two rubbers unfinished.
Among the above Gottfried von Cramm's percentage of success is the best. He won 80.39 per cent of his rubbers overall and 84.05 per cent of his singles. The best in doubles is Orlando Sirola, winning 81.39 per cent.

CHALLENGE/FINAL ROUND PLAYERS 1900–82

Player	Total Rubbers Pl'd	Won	Live Rubbers Singles Pl'd	Won	Doubles Pl'd	Won	No. Ties	Nation	Years
D F Davis	4	2	1	1	1	1	2	USA	1900, 02
M D Whitman	3	3	3	3			2	USA	1900, 02
H Ward	7	1	2	0	3	1	4	USA	1900, 02, 05, 06
A W Gore	5*	2	3	1	1	1	2	Brit. Isles	1900, 07
E D Black	2	0	1	0	1	0	1	Brit. Isles	1900
H Roper Barrett	5	1	2	0	3	1	3	Brit. Isles	1900, 07, 13
W A Larned	6	1	5	1			4	USA	1902, 03, 05, 11
R F Doherty	8	7	3	2	4	4	5	Brit. Isles	1902–06
H L Doherty	12	12	5	5	4	4	5	Brit. Isles	1902–06
J Pim	2	0	2	0			1	Brit. Isles	1902
R D Wrenn	3	0	2	0	1	0	1	USA	1903
G L Wrenn	1	0			1	0	1	USA	1903
P de Borman	3	0	1	0	1	0	1	Belgium	1904
W Lemaire	2	0	1	0	1	0	1	Belgium	1904
F L Riseley	2	2	1	1			1	Brit. Isles	1904
S H Smith	4	4	2	2			2	Brit. Isles	1905, 06
B C Wright	6	2	3	2	3	0	3	USA	1905, 08, 11
W J Clothier	1	0					1	USA	1905
R D Little	3	0	1	0	1	0	1	USA	1906
N E Brookes	22	15	11	7	8	6	8	Australasia	1907–09, 11, 12, 14, 19, 20
A F Wilding	12	8	6	4	4	3	4	Australasia	1907–09, 14
F B Alexander	3	0	2	0	1	0	1	USA	1908
M McLoughlin	11	4	4	2	4	1	4	USA	1909, 11, 13, 14
M H Long	3	0	1	0	1	0	1	USA	1909
R W Heath	3	1	3	1			2	Australasia	1911, 12
A W Dunlop	2	2			2	2	2	Australasia	1911, 12
J C Parke	5	4	3	3	1	0	2	Brit. Isles	1912, 13
C P Dixon	5	1	4	1	1	0	2	Brit. Isles	1912, 13
A E Beamish	2	0			2	0	2	Brit. Isles	1912, 19
R N Williams	8	5	3	1	4	4	6	USA	1913, 14, 21, 23, 25, 26
H Hackett	1	1			1	1	1	USA	1913
T C Bundy	1	0			1	0	1	USA	1914
G L Patterson	12	4	6	2	4	2	4	Australasia	1919, 20, 22, 24
J O Anderson	7	2	3	1	1	0	3	USA	1919, 22, 23
A H Lowe	2	0	1	0			1	Brit. Isles	1919
A R F Kingscote	3	1	2	1	1	0	1	Brit. Isles	1919
W T Tilden	28	21	12	10	6	4	11	USA	1920–30
W M Johnston	16	13	10	7	2	2	8	USA	1920–27
I Kumagae	3	0	1	0	1	0	1	Japan	1921
Z Shimizu	3	0	1	0	1	0	1	USA	1921
W Washburn	1	1			1	1	1	USA	1921
V Richards	5	4	1	1	3	2	4	USA	1922, 24–26
P O'Hara Wood	4	1	1	0	2	1	2	Australasia	1922, 24
J B Hawkes	3	0	2	0	1	0	1	Australasia	1923
J Borotra	17	6	8	4	5	2	9	France	1925–33

Player	Total Rubbers Pl'd	Won	Live Rubbers Singles Pl'd	Won	Doubles Pl'd	Won	No. Ties	Nation	Years
R Lacoste	9	4	6	3	1	0	4	France	1925–28
H Cochet	20	14	11	9	6	3	8	France	1926–33
J Brugnon	6	3			6	3	6	France	1926, 27, 30–33
F T Hunter	2	1			2	1	2	USA	1927, 28
J Hennessey	2	0	2	0			1	USA	1928
G M Lott	5	1	4	0	1	1	3	USA	1929, 30, 34
W L Allison	8	2	3	0	4	2	4	USA	1929, 30, 32, 35
J Van Ryn	4	2			4	2	4	USA	1929, 30, 32, 35
H W Austin	12	8	8	5			6	Great Britain	1931, 33–37
F J Perry	10	9	9	8			5	Great Britain	1931, 33–36
G P Hughes	5	1			5	1	5	Great Britain	1931, 33–36
C H Kingsley	1	0			1	0	1	Great Britain	1931
H E Vines	2	1	1	0			1	USA	1932
A Merlin	2	0	2	0			1	France	1933
H G N Lee	2	0			2	0	2	Great Britain	1933, 34
S B Wood	2	0	1	0			1	USA	1934
F X Shields	2	0	2	0			1	USA	1934
L R Stoefen	1	1			1	1	1	USA	1934
J D Budge	8	5	4	3	2	1	3	USA	1935, 37, 38
C R D Tuckey	3	1			3	1	3	Great Britain	1935–37
J H Crawford	3	1	2	0	1	1	1	Australia	1936
A K Quist	12	5	7	2	4	3	5	Australia	1936, 38, 39, 46, 48
F A Parker	6	4	5	3			3	USA	1937, 39, 48
G Mako	2	1			2	1	2	USA	1937, 38
C E Hare	2	0	2	0			1	Great Britain	1937
F H D Wilde	1	0			1	0	1	Great Britain	1937
J H Bromwich	14	7	5	1	6	5	6	Australia	1938,39,46,47,49,50
R L Riggs	4	2	3	2			2	USA	1938, 39
J A Kramer	7	5	2	2	3	1	3	USA	1939, 46, 47
J R Hunt	1	0			1	0	1	USA	1939
F R Schroeder	15	9	9	7	4	1	6	USA	1946–51
G Mulloy	4	2			3	1	4	USA	1946, 48–50
D Pails	4	0	3	0			2	Australia	1946, 47
C Long	2	1			2	1	2	Australia	1947, 48
O W Sidwell	6	1	2	0	2	1	2	Australia	1948, 49
W F Talbert	2	1			2	1	2	USA	1948, 49
R A Gonzales	2	2	1	1			1	USA	1949
F A Sedgman	11	9	6	2	3	3	4	Australia	1949–52
K McGregor	6	4	2	2	2	2	3	Australia	1950–52
T P Brown	2	1	1	0			1	USA	1950
E V Seixas	20	6	9	2	6	2	7	USA	1951–57
M A Trabert	12	4	5	2	5	2	5	USA	1951–55
M G Rose	3	1	2	0	1	1	2	Australia	1951, 57
L A Hoad	11	8	5	4	4	2	4	Australia	1953–56
K R Rosewall	10	7	5	3	2	1	4	Australia	1953–56
R N Hartwig	3	2			2	1	3	Australia	1953–55
H Richardson	2	1			2	1	2	USA	1955, 58
H Flam	1	0	1	0			1	USA	1956
S Giammalva	2	0			1	0	1	USA	1956
M J Anderson	6	3	2	1	2	1	2	Australia	1957, 58
A J Cooper	4	2	3	2			2	Australia	1957, 58
B MacKay	7	2	4	1	1	0	2	USA	1957–59
A Olmedo	6	4	4	3	2	1	2	USA	1958, 59
N A Fraser	11	8	4	4	5	3	6	Australia	1958–63
R G Laver	12	10	6	4	2	2	5	Australia	1959–62, 73
R S Emerson	18	15	9	9	6	4	9	Australia	1959–67
E Buchholz	1	0			1	0	1	USA	1959
N Pietrangeli	6	1	2	0	2	0	2	Italy	1960, 61
O Sirola	6	0	2	0	2	0	2	Italy	1960, 61
R H Osuna	3	0	1	0	1	0	1	Mexico	1962
A Palafox	3	0	1	0	1	0	1	Mexico	1962
C R McKinley	6	4	4	2	2	2	2	USA	1963, 64
R D Ralston	6	3	4	1	2	2	2	USA	1963, 64
J D Newcombe	10	6	4	2	4	3	5	Australia	1963, 65–67, 73
F S Stolle	7	5	4	3	1	0	3	Australia	1964–66
A D Roche	5*	3	1	1	3	2	4	Australia	1965–67, 77

Player	Total Rubbers Pl'd	Won	Live Rubbers Singles Pl'd	Won	Doubles Pl'd	Won	No. Ties	Nation	Years
M Santana	6	2	2	0	2	0	2	Spain	1965, 67
J Gisbert	2	0	1	0			1	Spain	1965
J L Arilla	1	0			1	0	1	Spain	1965
R Krishnan	3	1	2	0	1	1	1	India	1966
J Mukerjea	3	1	1	0	1	1	1	India	1966
M Orantes	3	0	1	0	1	0	1	Spain	1967
C E Graebner	2	2	1	1			1	USA	1968
A R Ashe	6	5	3	3			3	USA	1968–70
R C Lutz	5	5			5	5	5	USA	1968–70, 78, 79
S R Smith	16	12	6	5	8	6	8	USA	1968–73, 78, 79
W W Bowrey	2	1	1	0			1	Australia	1968
R O Ruffels	3	0	1	0	1	0	1	Australia	1968
J G Alexander	4	2	2	2	2	0	2	Australia	1968, 77
I Tiriac	9	2	5	1	3	1	3	Romania	1969, 71, 72
I Nastase	9	3	3	0	3	1	3	Romania	1969, 71, 72
C Richey	2	2	1	1			1	USA	1970
W P Bungert	3	0	1	0	1	0	1	Germany	1970
C Kuhnke	3	0	1	0	1	0	1	Germany	1970
E Van Dillen	3	1			3	1	3	USA	1971–73
F A Froehling	2	1	1	1			1	USA	1971
T S Gorman	4	0	2	0			2	USA	1972, 73
O Bengtson	3	1	1	0	1	1	1	Sweden	1975
B Borg	3	3	2	2	1	1	1	Sweden	1975
J Kodes	3	1	2	1	1	0	1	Czechoslovakia	1975
J Hrebec	2	1	1	0			1	Czechoslovakia	1975
V Zednik	1	0			1	0	1	Czechoslovakia	1975
A Panatta	11	4	5	1	4	2	4	Italy	1976, 77, 79, 80
C Barazzutti	7*	2	4	1			4	Italy	1976, 77, 79, 80
P Bertolucci	4	2			4	2	4	Italy	1976, 77, 79, 80
A Zugarelli	1	0					1	Italy	1976
J Fillol	3	0	1	0	1	0	1	Chile	1976
P Cornejo	2	0	1	0	1	0	1	Chile	1976
B Prajoux	1	1					1	Chile	1976
P Dent	1	0			1	0	1	Australia	1977
J M Lloyd	2	0	1	0			1	Great Britain	1978
C J Mottram	2	1	2	1			1	Great Britain	1978
M Cox	1	0			1	0	1	Great Britain	1978
D A Lloyd	1	0			1	0	1	Great Britain	1978
B E Gottfried	2	1	1	0			1	USA	1978
J P McEnroe	10	10	8	8	2	2	4	USA	1978, 79, 81, 82
V Gerulaitis	2	2	2	2			1	USA	1979
I Lendl	3	3	1	1	1	1	1	Czechoslovakia	1980
T Smid	3	2	1	1	1	1	1	Czechoslovakia	1980
G Oleppo	1	0					1	Italy	1980
G Vilas	3*	0	2*	0	1	0	1	Argentina	1981
J L Clerc	3	1	2	1	1	0	1	Argentina	1981
P Fleming	2	2			2	2	2	USA	1981, 82
R Tanner	2*	0	2*	0			1	USA	1981
Y Noah	3	1	2	1	1	0	1	France	1982
H Leconte	3	0	2	0	1	0	1	France	1982
G Mayer	2	1	2	1			1	USA	1982

* Including unfinished rubber.

DAVIS CUP ELITE

There were twelve occasions when the Davis Cup competition was taken to its ultimate dramatic climax, the destiny of the trophy turning on the outcome of the fifth rubber in the challenge round.

In nine of those years the winning side surged ahead to victory having already led by 2-nil or 2–1 before being pulled back to 2 all. In both 1964 and 1953 Australia recovered from trailing 1–2. In 1939 Australia uniquely came back from a 2–nil deficit against the US.

Those players who thus won rubbers when to have lost would have meant the Cup going to the opposition must be ranked among the elite. They were:

Victor	Loser	Score	Rubber	Venue	Year
Norman Brookes (Aus)	H Roper Barrett (British Isles)	6–2 6–0 6–3	5th	Wimbledon	1907
Tony Wilding (Aus)	Fred Alexander (USA)	6–3 6–4 6–1	5th	Melbourne	1908
James Parke (British Isles)	Rodney Heath (Aus)	6–2 6–4 6–4	5th	Melbourne	1912
Henri Cochet (Fra)	William Johnston (USA)	6–4 4–6 6–2 6–4	5th	Philadelphia	1927
Fred Perry (GB)	Andre Merlin (Fra)	4–6 8–6 6–2 7–5	5th	Paris	1933
Fred Perry (GB)	Jack Crawford (Aus)	6–2 6–3 6–3	5th	Wimbledon	1936
Adrian Quist & John Bromwich (Aus)	Jack Kramer & Joe Hunt (USA)	5–7 6–2 7–5 6–2	3rd	Philadelphia	1939
Quist (Aus)	Bobby Riggs (USA)	6–1 6–4 3–6 3–6 6–4	4th	Philadelphia	1939
Bromwich (Aus)	Frank Parker (USA)	6–0 6–3 6–1	5th	Philadelphia	1939
Frank Sedgman (Aus)	Vic Seixas (USA)	6–4 6–2 6–2	5th	Sydney	1951
Lew Hoad (Aus)	Tony Trabert (USA)	13–11 6–3 2–6 3–6 7–5	4th	Melbourne	1953
Ken Rosewall (Aus)	Vic Seixas (USA)	6–2 2–6 6–3 6–4	5th	Melbourne	1953
Neale Fraser (Aus)	Barry MacKay (USA)	8–6 3–6 6–2	5th	New York	1959
Chuck McKinley (USA)	John Newcombe (Aus)	10–12 6–2 9–7 6–2	5th	Adelaide	1963
Fred Stolle (Aus)	Dennis Ralston (USA)	7–5 6–3 3–6 9–11 6–4	4th	Cleveland	1964
Roy Emerson (Aus)	Chuck McKinley (USA)	3–6 6–2 6–4 6–4	5th	Cleveland	1964

OUTSTANDING TEAMS

Even if individual performance has counted for much team work has always been the essence in the Davis Cup, where there must be at least two players in a side and at the most four. Outstanding not only for its success but for its personalities and the way it caught the public imagination was the team known as the 'Four Musketeers'. Comprising the four Frenchmen, Jacques Brugnon, Henri Cochet, Jean Borotra and René Lacoste, it thrived between 1922 and 1934 and won the trophy for France on six occasions, 1927 to 1932. Even more successful as a winning side was that made up by 'Big Bill' Tilden and 'Little Bill' Johnston, the architects of the seven victories of the USA 1920 to 1926.

The following table records the outstanding teams. It is essentially a measure of success as a team and ties that took place in the relevant period are ignored unless at least two members participated.

	Ch'ge Rd Pl'd	Won	Ties Pl'd	Won	Rubbers Pl'd	Won	(Singles) Pl'd	Won	(Doubles) Pl'd	Won	Years
H L Doherty / R F Doherty (British Isles)	5	4	5	4	15	14	10	9	5	5	1902–06
N E Brookes / A F Wilding (Australasia)	4	4	10	9	48	35	38	28	10	7	1905–14
W T Tilden / W M Johnston (USA)	8	7	10	9	43	37	36	31	7	6	1920–27
J Brugnon / H Cochet / J Borotra / R Lacoste (France)	9	6	37	31	149	113	112	86	37	27	1922–34
F J Perry / *H W Austin (Great Britain)	5	4	18	16	82	68	70	59	12	9	1931–36

* Austin played no doubles.

	Ch'ge Rd Pl'd	Won	Ties Pl'd	Won	Rubbers Pl'd	Won	(Singles) Pl'd	Won	(Doubles) Pl'd	Won	Years
R S Emerson N A Fraser R G Laver (Australia)	5	4	10	9	48	41	38	32	10	9	1959–63

DOUBLES PAIRS

Nicola Pietrangeli and Orlando Sirola played the **highest number of Davis Cup doubles rubbers** as a partnership. In an unbroken sequence for Italy 1955 to 1963 they won **34 out of 42 matches**. In 1958, 1960 and 1961 they won **5 out of 6** and in 1957/58 won 9 in succession. They twice took Italy to the Challenge Round.

Bob Lutz and Stan Smith were the **most successful** pairing in the Challenge and Final Rounds. Their joint record at that level was **Played 5, Won 5**.

They played for the USA in 1968, 1969, 1970, 1978 and 1979, the USA taking the trophy each time. Moreover their record was **Sets played 15, sets won 15, sets lost nil**.

This one hundred per cent success in sets puts them above Laurie and Reggie Doherty, who played in the Challenge Round for the British Isles 1902 to 1906 and who also achieved a record of **Played 5, Won 5**. However their tally in sets was **Sets played 20, sets won 15, sets lost 5**.

Their first joint rubber, in 1902, was, uniquely, a 'dead' match, with all four singles already played and the USA established as winners of the tie.

No other pair, as a pair, played as many as five times in the ultimate round. For Australasia Norman Brookes and Tony Wilding won three times out of four, for Australia Roy Emerson and Neale Fraser won three times out of four also while for the USA Vic Seixas and Tony Trabert won two times out of four.

THE ULRICH FAMILY

The Ulrichs of Denmark, comprising Einer Ulrich and his two sons, Torben Ulrich (born 4 October 1928) and Jorgen Ulrich (born 21 August 1935), played most Davis Cup matches as a family.

Their joint careers stretched from 1924 to 1977, covered 80 ties and a total of **226 rubbers**.

The figures are:

	Total Pl'd	Won	Singles Pl'd	Won	Doubles Pl'd	Won	Ties	Years
Einer Ulrich	74	39	46	23	28	16	28	1924–38
Torben Ulrich	101	45	65	31	36	14	40	1948–61, 64–68, 77
Jorgen Ulrich	57	25	38	17	19	8	24	1955, 58–71
Composite totals, allowing for 12 ties in common and six doubles Torben and Jorgen played together	226	106	149	71	77	35	80	

THE RUTHLESS VICTORS
Players winning Davis Cup rubbers 6–0 6–0 6–0

Year	Winner	Loser	Occasion and venue
1928	G M Lott (USA)	P Kong (Chn)	American zone, s/f. Kansas City
1930	J C Gregory & I G Collins (GB)	I Tloczynski & P Warminski (Pol)	European zone, 2nd rd. Torquay
1930	G M Lott (USA)	I de la Bordolla (Mex)	American zone, final. Washington, DC
1939	J E Bromwich (Aus)	D Hernandez (Mex)	American zone, 1st rd. Mexico City
1946	F A Parker (USA)	F Ampon (Phi)	American zone, 1st rd. St Louis
1955	F Ampon & R Deyro (Phi)	Maung & Thaung (Bur)	Eastern zone, 1st rd. Rangoon
1957	A Licis (Pol)	G Wertheim (Lux)	European zone, 1st rd. Mondorf-les-Bains

Year	Winner	Loser	Occasion and venue
1959	A R Mills (GB)	J Offenheim (Lux)	European zone, 2nd rd. Mondorf-les-Bains
1960	M Otway (NZ)	L Price (Brit WI)	American zone, 1st rd. Trinidad
1966	J Javorsky (Cze)	J Shalem (Isr)	European zone A, 2nd rd. Prague
1967	M Cox & R K Wilson (GB)	B Pampulov & S Velov (Bul)	European zone A, 2nd rd. Sofia
1967	R A J Hewitt (SA)	A Viviani (Mon)	European zone B, 2nd rd. Monte Carlo
1968	M F Mulligan (Ita)	A Manigley (Mon)	European zone A, 2nd rd. Monte Carlo
1969	Luu Hoang Duc & Vo Van Bay (Vnm)	T K Kim & Y H Chung (Kor)	Eastern zone, 2nd rd. Seoul
1970	V Korotkov (USSR)	A Vatrican (Mon)	European zone B, 2nd rd. Monte Carlo
1971	I Tiriac (Rom)	Y Stabholts (Isr)	European zone B, 2nd rd. Tel Aviv
1972	Vo Van Bay (Vnm)	Lin Chu Yuan (Tai)	Eastern zone, 1st rd. Saigon
1973	G Widjojo (Ina)	Tao Po (HK)	Eastern zone, 1st rd. Hong Kong
1974	R A J Hewitt (SA)	E Andrade (Ecu)	American zone, 1st rd. Guayaquil
1975	C Kirmayr (Bra)	A Acuna (Peru)	American zone, 1st rd. Brasilia
1976	A D Roche (Aus)	A Wijono (Ina)	Eastern zone, s/f. Hobart
1976	W Fibak (Pol)	O Foss Abrehamson (Nor)	European zone A, 1st rd. Posnan
1977	M Mohammad (Pak)	A Cheah (Mal)	Eastern zone, 1st rd. Rawalpindi
1978	K Johansson (Swe)	K Newton (Ire)	European zone B, 2nd rd. Dublin
1981	T Tulasne (Fra)	Shin-ichi Sakamoto (Jap)	Relegation round, Paris

WHO PLAYED FOR WHOM?

Davis Cup Qualification—1939 Style

Events in the Davis Cup in 1939 echoed less resoundingly through the pages of lawn tennis history because of the more fateful happenings of that year. In the second round of the European Zone, in Warsaw on 19, 20 and 21 May, Germany beat Poland 3–2. The winners went on to beat Sweden and Great Britain before losing to Yugoslavia in the Zone final. Its ultimate effect on the competition, which ended in Australia retrieving a 2–0 deficit in the Challenge Round, unique at that stage, to beat the USA, was not great.

None the less the tie had features all its own. The details were:

Henner Henkel (Ger) beat Adam Bawarowski (Pol) 6–4 6–2 6–3;
Roderick Menzel (Ger) lost to Ignacy Tloczynski (Pol) 6–2 1–6 7–5 2–6 7–9;
Henkel & Count George von Metaxa (Ger) beat Josef Hebda & Bawarowski (Pol) 5–7 6–4 6–2 6–2;
Henkel (Ger) lost to Tloczynski (Pol) 4–6 8–6 4–6 6–3 3–6;
Menzel (Ger) beat Bawarowski (Pol) 7–5 6–3 2–6 2–6 6–4.

Bawarowski can hardly have been surprised by his opening loss against Henkel. He went down to the same man in another Davis Cup tie two years before in Munich. It can be found in the record of the 1937 event, Germany beat **Austria** 3–2.

If Bawarowski played as the number one for Poland, with Tloczynski as number two, that was only logical. Had not Bawarowski proved himself the better player in a Davis Cup singles? In 1936 **Austria** beat Poland 3–2 in Vienna and Bawarowski beat Tloczynski 6–4 6–3 6–3.

The key to victory in that tie was the doubles. The Poles, Hebda and K Tarlowski, were beaten 6–1 6–2 6–4. By whom? It was by Hebda's current (1939) partner, Bawarowski, in liaison with von Metaxa.

As for von Metaxa he can hardly have failed on that day in Warsaw in 1939 to recall, as he looked to his partner Henkel, that this was the man who had joined Baron Gottfried von Cramm in Munich in 1937, on the occasion of Germany beating Austria 3–2, to defeat him and Bawarowski 11–9 8–6 7–5. If he wished to reminisce about it he had only to talk across the net to his erstwhile partner.

Bawarowski, now a Pole, and von Metaxa, now a German, had shared Austrian Davis Cup loyalties as doubles partners in 1936 and 1937. But the complications did not end there.

Menzel, now a German colleague of von Metaxa, had in 1935 as a Czech beaten his other team mate, Henkel, in the only rubber gained as Germany beat Czechoslovakia 4–1 in Prague.

The national qualifications of the three players concerned were:

Bawarowski—Austria 1933, 1936, 1937; Poland 1939.
Von Metaxa—Austria 1934, 1936, 1937; Germany 1939.
Menzel—Czechoslovakia 1928–1934, 1937, 1938; Germany 1939.

The involved tapestry of Davis Cup loyalties reflects the history of those times. The Davis Cup regulations, under which it was woven, had in 1939 just been amended and regulation 33 said:

'If a player shall have represented a Nation, and such Nation shall be absorbed in whole or in part by another Nation, he shall, if belonging to the whole or part absorbed, be deemed for the purpose of these Regulations not to have previously represented any Nation.'

THE RETURN OF HANS REDL

Another player to experience the vagaries of changing frontiers was Hans Redl of Austria. He first played for Austria in 1937 and took part in the tie against Germany. In 1938 and 1939 he found himself playing for Germany against France, Yugoslavia and Switzerland.

In 1948 and for 7 subsequent years Redl again played for Austria. He had the experience of playing against Yugoslavia as a German in 1938 and as an Austrian in 1949 and 1950.

Redl was unique in playing his post-war tennis with only one arm. He lost his left arm whilst on active service. It was because of his handicap that the service rule was amended with the addition of the clause 'A player with the use of only one arm may utilize the racket for the projection'.

THE FEDERATION CUP

The Federation Cup, the women's international team championship, was inaugurated in 1963 to mark the 50th anniversary of the International Tennis Federation. It is staged at various venues on a knock-out basis within a period of a week. Each tie comprises two singles and a doubles. The tie break has been used since 1976.

The first event was held at Queen's Club, London, on grass, though bad weather caused many rubbers to be played indoors on wood. The original challenging nations were Australia, Austria, Belgium, Canada, Czechoslovakia, Denmark, France, Great Britain, Hungary, Italy, Netherlands, Norway, Switzerland, South Africa, USA and West Germany. Fifty nations have participated 1963 to 1982.

The **most arduous final** was the first. The US beat Australia 2–1, 4 sets all, 44 games to 40, on the outcome of the last rubber when Darlene Hard and Billie Jean Moffitt beat Margaret Smith and Lesley Turner 3–6 13–11 6–3.

The **most number of games in a rubber** was **51.** In Paris in 1968 Margaret Court and Kerry Melville (Aus) beat Winnie Shaw and Virginia Wade (GB) 9–7 3–6 14–12 to complete a 3–nil victory.

The Federation Cup.

The **most number of games in a set was 28.** In Johannesburg in 1972 Betty Stove and Trudy Walhof (Hol) beat Marylin Pryde and Ruia Hunt (NZ) **15–13** 10–8.

The **easiest victory** was had by the USA in 1981. In beating, in sequence, South Korea, Spain, Romania, Switzerland and Great Britain the Federation Cup was won by the Americans 15 rubbers to nil, 30 sets to one, 187 games to 65.

The **easiest final win,** as measured by the fewest number of games lost, was by Australia beating South Africa at Bad Homburg in 1973. Australia won 3 rubbers to nil, six sets to nil, 40 games to **13.**

The **least number of games lost in a tie was one.** In 1977 at Eastbourne, Brazil beat Taiwan 3–nil, 6 sets to nil, 36 games to 1. In 1972 in Johannesburg the USA beat Uruguay with the loss of only one game but the doubles was not played. In 1977 also France beat Luxembourg 3–nil, 6 sets to nil, 36 games to 2. In 1978 at Melbourne Czechoslovakia beat Portugal 3–nil, 6 sets to nil, 36 games to 3.

In individual rubbers the punishing score 6–0 6–0 has been inflicted on at least 38 occasions. Chris Lloyd (USA) is unique in having won by this score three times in singles, against Switzerland in 1977, against France in 1979, against Thailand in 1980, and once in doubles against Indonesia in 1982.

The **USA,** winning for the seventh successive year in 1982 took their **sequence of success to 34 ties** and won their **48th rubber** without loss.

The **most experienced Federation Cup player** was Virginia Wade of Great Britain. By 1982 she had achieved every possible record, except that of percentage success. In competing 1967 to 1982 without missing a year she played for **16 years**. In that time she played **54 ties**. She played **97 rubbers**. She *won* **64**. In singles she **played 53** rubbers, **winning 34**. In doubles she **played 44, winning 30**.

The **most successful** player was Chris Lloyd of the US. In playing 28 ties 1977 to 1982 she **won 42 out of 43**, 28 out of 28 singles, 14 out of 15 doubles.

For Australia 1963 to 1971 Margaret Court competed in 20 ties and **won 35 out of 40 rub-** **bers,** 20 out of 20 singles, and 15 out of 20 doubles.

For the USA 1963 to 1979 Billie Jean King played 36 ties. She won 52 from 58 rubbers, 25 out of 29 singles, 27 out of 29 doubles. One of her two non-winning doubles was not a loss but an unfinished contest.

Uniquely Martina Navratilova played number one for Czechoslovakia, champion nation in 1975, and number one for the USA, champion nation in 1982.

RESULTS IN SUMMARY

Year	Venue	Number playing	Champion	Finalist
1963	Queen's Club, London	16	USA	Australia
1964	Philadelphia (Germantown CC)	20	Australia	USA
1965	Melbourne	11	Australia	USA
1966	Turin	20	USA	W Germany
1967	Berlin	15	USA	Great Britain
1968	Paris	22	Australia	Netherlands
1969	Athens	18	USA	Australia
1970	Freiburg	19	Australia	W Germany
1971	Perth (played Dec. 1970)	12	Australia	Great Britain
1972	Johannesburg	31	S Africa	Great Britain
1973	Bad Homburg	30	Australia	S Africa
1974	Naples	27	Australia	USA
1975	Aix-en-Provence	30	Czechoslovakia	Australia
1976	Philadelphia (Spectrum)	36	USA	Australia
1977	Eastbourne	32	USA	Australia
1978	Melbourne	35	USA	Australia
1979	Madrid	29	USA	Australia
1980	Berlin	32	USA	Australia
1981	Tokyo	32	USA	Great Britain
1982	Santa Clara, Cal	32	USA	W Germany

FINALS RESULTS

1963 **USA 2 Australia 1** (Miss D R Hard lost to Miss M Smith 3–6 0–6; Miss B J Moffitt beat Miss L R Turner 5–7 6–0 6–3; Miss Hard & Miss Moffitt beat Miss Smith & Miss Turner 3–6 13–11 6–3.)

1964 **Australia 2, USA 1** (Miss Smith beat Miss Moffitt 6–2 6–3; Miss Turner beat Miss N Richey 7–5 6–1; Miss Smith & Miss Turner lost to Miss Moffitt & Mrs J R Susman 6–4 5–7 1–6.)

1965 **Australia 2, USA 1** (Miss Turner beat Mrs C Graebner 6–3 2–6 6–3; Miss Smith beat Miss Moffitt 6–4 8–6; Miss Smith & Miss J M Tegart lost to Mrs Graebner & Miss Moffitt 5–7 6–4 4–6.)

1966 **USA 3, W Germany 0** (Miss J M Heldman beat Frl H Niessen 4–6 7–5 6–1; Mrs L W King beat Frl E Buding 6–3 3–6 6–1; Mrs Graebner & Mrs King beat Frl Buding &

Frl H Schultze 6–4 6–2)

1967 **USA 2, Great Britain 0** (Miss R Casals beat Miss S V Wade 9–7 8–6; Mrs King beat Mrs P F Jones 6–3 6–4; Miss Casals & Mrs King divided with Mrs Jones & Miss Wade 6–8 9–7.)

1968 **Australia 3, Netherlands 0** (Miss K A Melville beat Miss M Jansen 4–6 7–5 6–3; Mrs B M Court beat Miss A Suurbeck 6–1 6–3; Mrs Court & Miss Melville beat Miss Suurbeck and Miss L Vennboer 6–3 6–8 7–5.)

1969 **USA 2, Australia 1** (Miss Richey beat Miss Melville 6–4 6–3; Miss Heldman lost to Mrs Court 1–6 6–8; Miss J Bartkowicz & Miss Richey beat Mrs Court & Miss Tegart 6–4 6–4.)

1970 **Australia 3, W Germany 0** (Miss K M Krantzcke beat Frau B Hoesl 6–2 6–3; Mrs D E Dalton beat Frl Niessen 4–6 6–3 6–3; Mrs Dalton & Miss Krantzcke beat Frl

Hoesl & Frl Niessen 6–2 7–5.)

1971 **Australia 3, Great Britain 0** (Mrs Court beat Mrs Jones 6–8 6–3 6–2; Miss E F Goolagong beat Miss Wade 6–4 6–1; Mrs Court & Miss L Hunt beat Miss W M Shaw & Miss Wade 6–4 6–4.)

1972 **South Africa 2, Great Britain 1** (Mrs Q C Pretorius lost to Miss Wade 3–6 2–6; Miss B Kirk beat Miss Shaw 4–6 7–5 6–0; Miss Kirk & Mrs Pretorius beat Miss Wade & Mrs G M Williams 6–1 7–5.)

1973 **Australia 3, South Africa 0** (Miss Goolagong beat Mrs Pretorius 6–0 6–2; Miss P Coleman beat Miss Kirk 10–8 6–0; Miss Goolagong & Miss J Young beat Miss Kirk & Mrs Pretorius 6–1 6–2.)

1974 **Australia 2, USA 1** (Miss Goolagong beat Miss Heldman 6–1 7–5; Miss D L Fromholtz lost to Miss C M Evert 6–2 5–7 3–6; Miss Goolagong & Miss Young beat Miss Heldman & Miss S A Walsh 7–5 8–6.)

1975 **Czechoslovakia 3, Australia 0** (Miss M Navratilova* beat Miss Goolagong 6–3 6–4; Miss R Tomanova beat Miss H Gourlay 6–4 6–2; Miss Navratilova & Miss Tomanova beat Miss Fromholtz & Miss Gourlay 6–3 6–1.)

1976 **USA 2, Australia 1** (Miss Casals lost to Mrs G E Reid 6–1 3–6 5–7; Mrs King beat Mrs R A Cawley 7–6 6–4; Miss Casals & Mrs King beat Mrs Cawley & Mrs Reid 7–5 6–3.)

1977 **USA 2, Australia 1** (Mrs King beat Miss Fromholtz 6–1 2–6 6–2; Miss Evert beat Mrs Reid 7–5 6–3; Miss Casals & Miss Evert lost to Mrs Reid & Miss W M Turnbull 3–6 3–6.)

1978 **USA 2, Australia 1** (Miss T A Austin lost to Mrs Reid 3–6 3–6; Miss Evert beat Miss Turnbull 3–6 6–1 6–1; Miss Evert & Mrs King beat Mrs Reid & Miss Turnbull 4–6 6–1 6–4)

1979 **USA 3, Australia 0** (Miss Austin beat Mrs Reid 6–3 6–0; Mrs J M Lloyd beat Miss Fromholtz 2–6 6–3 8–6; Miss Casals & Mrs King beat Mrs Reid & Miss Turnbull 3–6 6–3 8–6.)

1980 **USA 3 Australia 0** (Mrs Lloyd beat Miss Fromholtz 4–6 6–1 6–1; Miss Austin beat Miss Turnbull 6–2 6–3; Miss Casals & Miss K Jordan beat Miss Fromholtz & Miss S Leo 2–6 6–4 6–4.)

1981 **USA 3, Great Britain 0** (Miss A Jaeger beat Miss Wade 6–3 6–1; Mrs Lloyd beat Miss S Barker 6–2 6–1; Miss Casals & Miss Jordan

Virginia Wade, outstanding player in the Federation Cup, seen here in the match Great Britain v West Germany in 1980 in Berlin.

ORDER OF ACHIEVEMENT 1963–82

Nation	No. of Times Champion	No. of Times Runner-up	No. of Times Losing Semi-Finalist	No. of Times Played
USA	11	3	5	20
Australia	7	8	5	20
South Africa	1	1	2	15
Czechoslovakia	1	–	3	12
Great Britain	–	4	11	20
West Germany	–	3	4	18
Netherlands	–	1	2	19
France	–	–	4	20
USSR	–	–	2	6
Romania	–	–	1	8
Switzerland	–	–	1	18

beat Miss J M Durie & Miss Wade 6–4 7–5.)

1982 USA 3, West Germany 0 (Mrs Lloyd beat Frl C Kohde 2–6 6–1 6–3; Miss Navratilova* beat Frl B Bunge 6–4 6–4; Mrs Lloyd & Miss Navratilova beat Frl Bunge & Frl Kohde 3–6 6–1 6–2)

* Miss M Navratilova adopted USA nationality in 1981.

FEDERATION CUP NATIONS 1963–82

Nation	Year First Played	No. of Years Played	No. of Ties Pl'd	Won
Argentina	1964	14	21	7
Australia	1963	20	73	60
Austria	1963	11	13	2
Belgium	1963	18	22	4
Brazil	1965	10	15	5
Bulgaria	1966	4	5	1
Canada	1963	19	26	7
Chile	1968	4	5	1
China	1981	2	4	2
Colombia	1972	1	2	1
Czechoslovakia	1963	12	32	21
Denmark	1963	14	17	3
Ecuador	1972	1	2	1
Finland	1968	4	4	0
France	1963	20	47	27
Great Britain	1963	20	67	47
Greece	1968	7	8	1
Hong Kong	1981	2	3	1
Hungary	1963	8	11	4
Indonesia	1969	13	18	5
Iran	1972	1	1	0
Ireland	1964	10	12	2
Israel	1972	10	13	3
Italy	1963	20	36	16
Japan	1964	15	20	5
Luxembourg	1972	8	9	1
Mexico	1964	12	14	2
Morocco	1966	1	1	0
Netherlands	1963	19	49	30
New Zealand	1965	14	20	5
Norway	1963	14	16	2
Peru	1982	1	2	1
Philippines	1974	5	7	2
Poland	1966	4	6	2
Portugal	1968	5	5	0
Rhodesia	1966	4	5	1
Romania	1973	8	21	13
Senegal	1982	1	1	0
South Africa	1963	15	38	24
South Korea	1973	8	11	3
Spain	1972	11	15	4
Sweden	1964	15	26	11
Switzerland	1963	18	32	14
Taiwan	1972	6	7	1
Thailand	1978	3	3	0
Uruguay	1972	5	6	1
USA	1963	20	81	72
USSR	1968	6	20	14
West Germany	1963	18	52	34
Yugoslavia	1969	9	13	4

NATIONS BY SENIORITY

	Year First Played
Australia, Austria, Belgium, Canada, Czechoslovakia, Denmark, France, Great Britain, Hungary, Italy, Netherlands, Norway, South Africa, Switzerland, West Germany, USA	1963
Argentina, Ireland, Japan, Mexico, Sweden	1964
Brazil, New Zealand	1965
Bulgaria, Morocco, Poland, Rhodesia	1966
Chile, Finland, Greece, Portugal, USSR	1968
Indonesia, Yugoslavia	1969
Colombia, Ecuador, Iran, Israel, Luxembourg, Spain, Taiwan, Uruguay	1972
Romania, South Korea	1973
Philippines	1974
Thailand	1978
China, Hong Kong	1981
Peru, Senegal	1982

(50 nations played 1963–1982. East Germany challenged in 1966, Sudan in 1974, India in 1976 & 1977, Jamaica in 1976 but did not compete.)

RECORD OF THE CHAMPION NATIONS

USA, Australia, South Africa and Czechoslovakia, together with that of Great Britain.

USA

1963	beat Italy	3–0
	beat Netherlands	3–0
	beat Great Britain	3–0
	beat Australia	2–1 **Champions**
1964	beat Ireland	3–0
	beat Argentina	3–0
	beat Great Britain	3–0
	lost to Australia	1–2 Runners-up
1965	beat Italy	3–0
	beat Great Britain	3–0
	lost to Australia	1–2 Runners-up
1966	beat Sweden	3–0
	beat France	2–1
	beat Great Britain	2–1
	beat West Germany	3–0 **Champions**
1967	beat Rhodesia	3–0
	beat South Africa	3–0
	beat Germany	3–0
	beat Great Britain	2–0 **Champions**
1968	beat Switzerland	3–0

	beat France	2–1
	lost to Netherlands	1–2 semi-final
1969	beat Yugoslavia	3–0
	beat Italy	3–0
	beat Netherlands	3–0
	beat Australia	2–1 **Champions**
1970	beat Yugoslavia	3–0
	beat South Africa	3–0
	lost to West Germany	1–2 semi-final
1971	beat Italy	3–0
	beat South Africa	2–1
	lost to Great Britain	0–3 semi-final
1972	beat Rhodesia	3–0
	beat Uruguay	2–0
	beat Netherlands	3–0
	lost to South Africa	1–2 semi-final
1973	beat Italy	3–0
	beat Korea	2–1
	lost to Germany	0–3 quarter-final
1974	beat Poland	3–0
	beat France	3–0
	beat West Germany	2–1
	lost to Australia	1–2 Runners-up
1975	beat Switzerland	3–0
	beat Sweden	2–1
	beat South Africa	2–1
	lost to Australia	1–2 semi-final
1976	beat Israel	3–0
	beat Yugoslavia	3–0
	beat Switzerland	3–0
	beat Netherlands	3–0
	beat Australia	2–1 **Champions**
1977	beat Austria	3–0
	beat Switzerland	3–0
	beat France	3–0
	beat South Africa	3–0
	beat Australia	2–1 **Champions**
1978	beat Korea	3–0
	beat New Zealand	3–0
	beat France	3–0
	beat Great Britain	3–0
	beat Australia	2–1 **Champions**
1979	beat Philippines	w.o.
	beat West Germany	3–0
	beat France	3–0
	beat USSR	2–0
	beat Australia	3–0 **Champions**
1980	beat Poland	3–0
	beat New Zealand	3–0
	beat USSR	3–0
	beat Czechoslovakia	3–0
	beat Australia	3–0 **Champions**
1981	beat South Korea	3–0
	beat Spain	3–0
	beat Romania	3–0
	beat Switzerland	3–0
	beat Great Britain	3–0 **Champions**
1982	beat Indonesia	3–0
	beat Mexico	3–0
	beat Brazil	3–0
	beat Czechoslovakia	3–0
	beat West Germany	3–0 **Champions**

AUSTRALIA

1963	beat Belgium	3–0
	beat Hungary	3–0
	beat South Africa	3–0
	lost to USA	1–2 Runners-up
1964	beat Denmark	3–0
	beat Canada	3–0
	beat France	3–0
	beat USA	2–1 **Champions**
1965	beat New Zealand	3–0
	beat France	3–0
	beat USA	2–1 **Champions**
1966	beat Switzerland	3–0
	beat Netherlands	2–1
	lost to Germany	1–2 semi-final
1967	beat Czechoslovakia	w.o.
	beat France	2–1
	lost to Great Britain	0–3 semi-final
1968	beat Brazil	3–0
	beat South Africa	2–1
	beat Great Britain	3–0
	beat Netherlands	3–0 **Champions**
1969	beat Poland	w.o.
	beat France	3–0
	beat Great Britain	3–0
	lost to USA	1–2 Runners-up
1970	beat Czechoslovakia	3–0
	beat Sweden	3–0
	beat Great Britain	3–0
	beat West Germany	3–0 **Champions**
1971	beat France	3–0
	beat Great Britain	3–0 **Champions**
1972	beat Canada	2–0
	beat Italy	3–0
	lost to Great Britain	1–2 semi-final
1973	beat Japan	3–0
	beat Indonesia	3–0
	beat Germany	3–0
	beat South Africa	3–0 **Champions**
1974	beat Japan	2–0
	beat Italy	3–0
	beat Great Britain	3–0
	beat USA	2–1 **Champions**
1975	beat Belgium	2–0
	beat Italy	3–0
	beat USA	2–1
	lost to Czechoslovakia	0–3 Runners-up
1976	beat Romania	3–0
	beat Belgium	3–0
	beat West Germany	3–0
	beat Great Britain	3–0
	lost to USA	1–2 Runners-up
1977	beat Indonesia	3–0
	beat Brazil	3–0
	beat West Germany	2–1
	beat Great Britain	2–1
	lost to USA	1–2 Runners-up
1978	beat Belgium	3–0
	beat Japan	3–0
	beat Netherlands	3–0
	beat USSR	2–1

	lost to USA	1–2 Runners-up
1979	beat Canada	3–0
	beat Yugoslavia	3–0
	beat Netherlands	2–1
	beat Czechoslovakia	3–0
	lost to USA	0–3 Runners-up
1980	beat Norway	3–0
	beat Indonesia	3–0
	beat Sweden	2–1
	beat Germany	2–1
	lost to USA	0–3 Runners-up
1981	beat Philippines	3–0
	beat China	3–0
	beat Netherlands	3–0
	lost to Great Britain	1–2 semi-final
1982	beat South Korea	3–0
	beat Netherlands	3–0
	beat USSR	3–0
	lost to West Germany	0–3 semi-final

SOUTH AFRICA

1963	beat Czechoslovakia	2–1
	beat France	3–0
	lost to Australia	0–3 semi-final
1964	beat Japan	3–0
	beat Czechoslovakia	2–1
	lost to Great Britain	1–2 quarter-final
1965	lost to Great Britain	1–2 quarter-final
1966	lost to Netherlands	1–2 second round
1967	beat Norway	3–0
	lost to USA	0–3 quarter-final
1968	beat Canada	3–0
	lost to Australia	1–2 quarter-final
1969	lost to France	1–2 second round
1970	beat Hungary	w.o.
	lost to USA	0–3 quarter-final
1971	beat Indonesia	3–0
	lost to USA	1–2 quarter-final
1972	beat Belgium	3–0
	beat Brazil	2–0
	beat France	2–1
	beat USA	2–1
	beat Great Britain	2–1 **Champions**
1973	beat Greece	3–0
	beat Belgium	3–0
	beat Netherlands	3–0
	beat Romania	2–1
	lost to Australia	0–3 Runners-up
1974	beat Sudan	w.o.
	beat Switzerland	3–0
	lost to Great Britain	1–2 quarter-final
1975	beat Norway	2–0
	beat Japan	2–1
	lost to USA	1–2 quarter-final
1976	beat Korea	3–0
	beat Sweden	3–0
	lost to Great Britain	1–2 quarter-final
1977	beat Japan	2–1
	beat New Zealand	3–0
	beat Netherlands	2–1
	lost to USA	0–3 semi-final
1978	et seq not played	

CZECHOSLOVAKIA

1963	lost to South Africa	1–2 first round
1964	beat Mexico	3–0
	lost to South Africa	1–2 second round
1965	did not play	
1966	beat Poland	3–0
	lost to Great Britain	0–3 quarter-final
1967	lost to Australia	default
1968	beat Norway	2–1
	lost to Great Britain	1–2 second round
1969	beat Switzerland	3–0
	lost to Netherlands	1–2 quarter-final
1970	lost to Australia	0–3 second round
1971–1974	did not play	
1975	beat Ireland	3–0
	beat Norway	2–0
	beat Germany	2–1
	beat France	3–0
	beat Australia	3–0 **Champions**
1976	lost to Canada	default
1977	did not play	
1978	beat Portugal	3–0
	beat Indonesia	3–0
	lost to Great Britain	1–2 quarter-final
1979	beat Hungary	3–0
	beat Sweden	2–1
	beat Great Britain	3–0
	lost to Australia	0–3 semi-final
1980	beat Hungary	2–0
	beat Yugoslavia	3–0
	beat Romania	2–1
	lost to USA	0–3 semi-final
1981	beat Sweden	3–0
	lost to USSR	1–2 second round
1982	beat Canada	2–1
	beat Philippines	3–0
	beat Great Britain	2–1
	lost to USA	0–3 semi-final

GREAT BRITAIN

1963	beat Canada	3–0
	beat Austria	3–0
	lost to USA	0–3 semi-final
1964	beat Norway	3–0
	beat South Africa	2–1
	lost to USA	0–3 semi-final
1965	beat South Africa	2–1
	lost to USA	0–3 semi-final
1966	beat Canada	3–0
	beat Czechoslovakia	3–0
	lost to USA	1–2 semi-final
1967	beat Sweden	3–0
	beat Italy	2–1
	beat Australia	3–0
	lost to USA	1–2 Runners-up
1968	beat Sweden	3–0
	beat Czechoslovakia	2–1
	beat USSR	3–0
	lost to Australia	0–3 semi-final

1969	beat Belgium	3–0
	beat West Germany	2–1
	lost to Australia	0–3 semi-final
1970	beat New Zealand	3–0
	beat Netherlands	2–1
	lost to Australia	0–3 semi-final
1971	beat New Zealand	3–0
	beat USA	3–0
	lost to Australia	0–3 Runners-up
1972	beat Japan	3–0
	beat Argentina	2–1
	beat Germany	2–1
	beat Australia	2–1
	lost to South Africa	1–2 Runners-up
1973	beat Mexico	3–0
	lost to Romania	1–2 quarter-final
1974	beat Ireland	3–0
	beat Norway	3–0
	beat South Africa	2–1
	lost to Australia	0–3 semi-final
1975	beat Austria	3–0
	beat Spain	3–0
	lost to France	1–2 quarter-final
1976	beat France	3–0
	beat Hungary	w.o.

	beat South Africa	2–1
	lost to Australia	0–3 semi-final
1977	beat Denmark	3–0
	beat Korea	3–0
	beat Sweden	3–0
	lost to Australia	1–2 semi-final
1978	beat Spain	3–0
	beat West Germany	2–1
	beat Czechoslovakia	2–1
	lost to USA	0–3 semi-final
1979	beat New Zealand	3–0
	beat Belgium	3–0
	lost to Czechoslovakia	0–3 quarter-final
1980	beat Israel	3–0
	beat Argentina	2–1
	lost to Germany	0–3 quarter-final
1981	beat Belgium	3–0
	beat France	3–0
	beat USSR	2–1
	beat Australia	2–1
	lost to USA	0–3 final
1982	beat Italy	2–1
	beat Israel	3–0
	lost to Czechoslovakia	1–2 quarter-final

US PLAYERS 1963–82

	Total Rubbers Pl'd	Won	Singles Pl'd	Won	Doubles Pl'd	Won	No. of Ties	Years
Miss D R Hard	7	6	4	3	3	3	4	1963
Mrs L W King	58*	52	29	25	29*	27	36	1963, 67, 76–79
Mrs C Graebner	13	12	3	2	10	10	10	1963, 65, 66
Mrs N Richey-Gunter	17	15	11	10	6	5	11	1964, 66, 69
Mrs J R Susman	4	4			4	4	4	1964
Mrs J M Heldman	30	21	19	13	11	8	19	1966, 69, 70, 74, 75
Miss R Casals	38*	34	9	8	29*	26	29	1967, 76–81
Miss M A Eisel	9	5	3	1	6	4	6	1968, 70
Miss K M Harter	1	1			1	1	1	1968
Miss J Bartkowicz	7	7	3	3	4	4	7	1969, 70
Miss S A Walsh	16	10	3	1	13	9	13	1971–74
Miss P S A Hogan	11	7	6	3	5	4	6	1971–73
Miss V Ziegenfuss	7	6	4	4	3	2	4	1972
Miss L Tuero	7	5	7	5			7	1972, 73
Miss J Metcalf	1	0			1	0	1	1973
Miss J Evert	4	4	4	4			4	1974
Miss K Kuykendall	4	3	4	3			4	1975
Miss J Newberry	4	3			4	3	4	1975
Mrs J M Lloyd	43	42	28	28	15	14	28	1977–82
Miss T A Austin	14	13	14	13			14	1978–80
Miss K Jordan	11	11	1	1	10	10	10	1980, 81
Miss A Jaeger	5	5	5	5			5	1981
Miss M Navratilova	10	10	5	5	5	5	5	1982
Miss A Leand	1	1			1	1	1	1982

* Including one unfinished rubber.

AUSTRALIAN PLAYERS 1963–82

	Total Rubbers Pl'd	Won	Singles Pl'd	Won	Doubles Pl'd	Won	No. of Ties	Years
Mrs B M Court	40	35	20	20	20	15	20	1963–65, 68, 69, 71
Miss L R Turner	21	14	10	7	11	7	13	1963–65, 67
Miss J Lehane	3	3	3	3			3	1963
Miss R A Ebbern	1	1			1	1	1	1964
Mrs D E Dalton	20	17	7	6	13	11	13	1965–67, 69, 70
Miss G Sherriff	2	1	2	1			2	1966
Miss K M Krantzcke	12	11	5	4	7	7	7	1966, 70
Mrs G E Reid	45	35	23	19	22	16	28	1967–69, 76–79
Mrs R A Cawley	38	33	24	21	14	12	24	1971–76, 82
Miss L Hunt	2	2	1	1	1	1	2	1971, 72
Mrs H Gourlay	11	6	6	3	5	3	6	1972, 75
Miss P Coleman	4	4	4	4			4	1973
Miss J Young	5	5			5	5	5	1973, 75
Miss D M Fromholtz	39	29	30	22	9	7	33	1974–82
Miss W M Turnbull	39	29	15	11	24	18	27	1977–82
Miss S Leo	11	8	2	2	9	6	10	1980–82
Miss A Minter	1	1			1	1	1	1981

BRITISH PLAYERS 1963–82

	Total Rubbers Pl'd	Won	Singles Pl'd	Won	Doubles Pl'd	Won	No. of Ties	Years
Mrs P F Jones	34*	21	17	10	17*	11	18	1963–67, 71
Mrs G T Janes	13	8	9	6	4	2	9	1963, 65, 68
Miss D M Catt	8	6	4	3	4	3	5	1963–65
Miss D M Starkie	3	2			3	2	3	1966
Miss W M Shaw	24	15	13	9	11	6	19	1966, 68–72
Miss S V Wade	97*	64	53	34	44*	30	54	1967–82
Mrs G M Williams	11	6	3	1	8	5	9	1969, 70, 72, 73
Miss G L Coles	13	9	6	4	7	5	9	1974, 75, 80
Miss S Barker	45	32	24	16	21	16	27	1974–82
Miss M Tyler	5	2	2	1	3	1	5	1976, 78, 79
Miss A E Hobbs	6	4			6	4	6	1978, 79, 82
Miss J M Durie	8	5	4	2	4	3	5	1981, 82

* Including one unfinished rubber.

THE KING'S CUP

The King of Sweden's Cup, an international men's indoor team championships, was originally played on a challenge round basis and then, from 1952, as a straight knock-out competition. The ties in the early rounds comprised two reverse singles and a doubles, shortening to two singles and a doubles for the semi-finals and final. The European Tennis Association took control in 1975 and the competition has been on a league basis, with home and away ties, each comprising two singles and a doubles, since 1976.

WINNERS

1936	France	1965	Great Britain
1937	France	1966	Great Britain
1938	Germany	1967	Great Britain
1939-1951	not held	1968	Sweden
1952	Denmark	1969	Czechoslovakia
1953	Denmark	1970	France
1954	Denmark	1971	Italy
1955	Sweden	1972	Spain
1956	Sweden	1973	Sweden
1957	Sweden	1974	Italy
1958	Sweden	1975	not held
1959	Denmark	1976	Hungary
1960	Denmark	1977	Sweden
1961	Sweden	1978	Sweden
1962	Denmark	1979	Czechoslovakia
1963	Yugoslavia	1980	Czechoslovakia
1964	Great Britain	1981	West Germany
		1982	West Germany

LONGEST TIE

The **greatest number of games in a singles**, 126, were played in 1966 on the nights of 5 and 6 November when Great Britain beat Poland 5–0 in Warsaw in the first round. The tie was on very fast wood with very poor lighting.

Roger Taylor (GB) beat W Gasoriek (Pol) 27–29 31–29 6–4 (126 games)

Mike Sangster (GB) beat T Nowicki (Pol) 6–4 22–20 (52 games)

Sangster beat Gasoriek 15–17 19–17 6–4 (78 games)

Taylor beat Nowicki 33–31 6–3 (73 games)

Taylor and Bobby Wilson beat Nowicki and B Lewandowski 10–10 ret'd (20 games)

Total number of games 349.

GREAT BRITAIN IN THE KING'S CUP 1962–82

		Score	Venue	
1962	beat Norway	4–1	Oslo	
	lost to Yugoslavia	2–3	Queen's Club	
1963	beat Poland	5–0	Warsaw	
	lost to Sweden	2–3	Stockholm	
1964	beat West Germany	4–1	Bremen	
	beat Denmark	3–2	Copenhagen	
	beat Belgium	3–0	Stockholm	
	beat Sweden	3–0	Stockholm	Won King's Cup
1965	beat Norway	5–0	Oslo	
	beat France	2–1	Torquay	
	beat Denmark	2–1	Torquay	Won King's Cup
1966	beat Poland	5–0	Warsaw	
	beat Finland	5–0	Helsinki	
	beat Czechoslovakia	3–0	Milan	
	beat Italy	3–0	Milan	Won King's Cup
1967	beat West Germany	3–2	Cologne	
	beat Yugoslavia	4–1	Lublijana	
	beat Spain	2–1	Stockholm	
	beat Sweden	2–1	Stockholm	Won King's Cup
1968	beat Italy	5–0	Padua	
	lost to Denmark	1–4	Crystal Palace	
1969	beat Switzerland	4–1	Bracknell	
	beat Yugoslavia	4–1	Lublijana	
	lost to Czechoslovakia	1–2	Cologne	
	beat West Germany	3–0	Cologne	for 3rd place
1970	lost to Hungary	1–4	Budapest	
1971	beat France	3–2	Paris	
	beat Finland	3–2	Helsinki	
	lost to Czechoslovakia	1–4	Basingstoke	
1972	lost to West Germany	2–3	Hanover	
1973	beat Switzerland	3–2	Queen's Club	
	lost to Sweden	2–3	Stockholm	
1974	lost to Czechoslovakia	1–4	Plzen	
1975	not held			

In 1976 the competition was resumed on a league basis with nations playing against each other both home and away.

1976 v. Spain	won 2–1 home	won 2–1 away
v. Yugoslavia	won 3–0 home	won 2–1 away
v. Italy	won 3–0 home	won 2–1 away
v. Hungary	won 3–0 home	lost 1–2 away
v. West Germany	won 3–0 home	lost 1–2 away
v. France	won 2–1 home	lost 1–2 away
v. Sweden	won 3–0 home	lost 0–3 away

Final position: Great Britain 2nd

1977 v. Spain	won 2–1 home	won 3–0 away
v. West Germany	lost 1–2 home	lost 1–2 away
v. Yugoslavia	won 3–0 home	won 3–0 away
v. Hungary	won 2–1 home	lost 1–2 away

Final position: Great Britain 3rd

1978 v. Sweden	lost 1–2 home	lost 1–2 away
v. Austria	lost 1–2 home	lost 1–2 away
v. Spain	won 3–0 home	lost 1–2 away
v. Yugoslavia	won 3–0 home	lost 1–2 away

Final position: Great Britain 7th

1979 v. Hungary	lost 0–3 home	lost 0–3 away
v. Spain	won 3–0 home	won 2–1 away
v. Germany	won 3–0 home	won 2–1 away
v. Sweden	won 2–1 home	won 2–1 away

Final position: Great Britain 3rd

1980 v. Czechoslovakia	lost 1–2 home	lost 0–3 away
v. West Germany	won 2–1 home	lost 0–3 away
v. Sweden	lost 1–2 home	lost 0–3 away
v. France	lost 1–2 home	won 3–0 away

Final position: Great Britain 7th

1981 v. Hungary	won 3–0 home	lost 1–2 away
v. Sweden	lost 1–2 home	lost 1–2 away
v. USSR	lost 1–2 home	lost 0–3 away
v. Czechoslovakia	won 2–1 home	won 2–1 away

Final position: Great Britain 5th

1982 v. West Germany	won 3–0 home	lost 1–2 away
v. Netherlands	won 2–1 home	lost 1–2 away
v. Sweden	lost 1–2 home	lost 0–3 away

Final position: Great Britain equal 5th

BRITISH PLAYERS

	Rubbers Pl'd	Won	Singles Pl'd	Won	Doubles Pl'd	Won	No. of Ties	Years
J E Barrett	2	2	1	1	1	1	1	1962
M P Hann	3	3	2	2	1	1	1	1962
J A Pickard	4	1	3	1	1	0	2	1962
M J Sangster	22	18	14	12	8	6	9	1962, 64, 66
R K Wilson	26	20	14	10	12	10	17	1963–67
M Cox	57	40	41	32	16	8	34	1963, 65, 67–69, 73, 76–79
H Matheson	1	1			1	1	1	1963
A R Mills	5	4	2	1	3	3	3	1963, 65
R Taylor	17	14	14	13	3	1	10	1964, 66, 67, 76
G R Stilwell	7	5	5	3	2	2	5	1965, 69
P R Hutchins	2	1			2	1	2	1967
G D Battrick	17	10	12	7	5	3	8	1968–71
P W Curtis	6	3			6	3	6	1968
J G Clifton	1	1	1	1			1	1969
D A Lloyd	33	19	2	0	31	19	32	1970, 73, 77–81
J G Paish	9	4	6	3	3	1	4	1971, 73
S J Matthews	1	0			1	0	1	1971
S A Warboys	7	3	4	2	2	1	3	1971–73
J M Lloyd	56	34	25	13	31	21	31	1972, 74, 76–78
C J Mottram	45	31	29	23	16	8	27	1973, 76, 79–82
M J Farrell	3	1	2	0	1	1	1	1974
J W Feaver	19	7	14	5	5	2	15	1978, 81, 82
R W Drysdale	20	8	13	4	7	4	13	1979, 80
C Bradnam	1	1			1	1	1	1979
A M Jarrett	21	8	9	2	12	6	15	1980, 81
R H Beven	3	0	2	0	1	0	3	1980
R A Lewis	12	6	9	6	3	0	9	1981, 82
M J Bates	3	0	1	0	2	0	3	1981
J R Smith	3	1			3	1	3	1981
J Dier	3	0	2	0	1	0	3	1982
J Whiteford	2	1			2	1	2	1982

THE NATIONS CUP

The men's international team championship organised by the Association of Tennis Professionals. The format of each tie comprises two singles and a doubles. The competition is restricted to eight teams, the eligibility of the first seven being governed by the relative standing of the nation's two best players on the ATP ranking list. The eighth nation may be nominated by the promoting country.

Date Final Tie	Other qualifying nations
Held in Kingston, Jamaica	
1975 USA beat Great Britain 2–1	Australia
	Commonwealth
	Caribbean
	India
	Chile
	West Germany
	Mexico
(1976–1977 not held)	
Held in Dusseldorf, Germany	
1978 Spain beat Australia 2–1	Chile
	Great Britain
	Poland
	West Germany
	Italy
	USA
1979 Australia beat Italy 2–1	Argentina
	Great Britain
	Spain
	West Germany
	Mexico
	USA
1980 Argentina beat Italy 3–0	Australia
	West Germany
	Sweden
	Czechoslovakia
	Spain
	USA
1981 Czechoslovakia beat Australia 2–1	Argentina
	Italy
	Sweden
	West Germany
	Spain
	USA
1982 USA beat Australia 2–1	Argentina
	West Germany
	Spain
	France
	Italy
	Sweden

THE GALEA CUP

International team championship for men under 21. Match format four singles among two players, one doubles.

Played at Deauville

1950	Italy	beat France	4–1
1951	France	beat W Germany	5–0

Played at Vichy

1952	Italy	beat France	4–1
1953	France	beat Italy	4–1
1954	Italy	beat Yugoslavia	3–2
1955	Italy	beat Spain	5–0
1956	Spain	beat Italy	4–1
1957	Spain	beat Italy	4–1
1958	Spain	beat W Germany	3–2
1959	W Germany	beat USSR	4–1
1960	France	beat USSR	3–2
1961	France	beat Spain	3–2
1962	France	beat USSR	3–2
1963	Czechoslovakia	beat Italy	3–2
1964	USSR	beat Czechoslovakia	3–2
1965	Czechoslovakia	beat USSR	3–2
1966	Czechoslovakia	beat USSR	4–1
1967	France	beat Great Britain	3–1
1968	Spain	beat France	3–2
1969	Spain	beat Czechoslovakia	3–2
1970	Czechoslovakia	beat Spain	3–2
1971	Sweden	beat France	5–0
1972	Great Britain	beat Spain	4–1
1973	Spain	beat Great Britain	4–1
1974	Czechoslovakia	beat Spain	4–1
1975	Czechoslovakia	beat Spain	3–2
1976	W Germany	beat Italy	3–2
1977	Argentina	beat France	3–2
1978	France	beat Czechoslovakia	4–1
1979	France	beat Czechoslovakia	3–2
1980	France	beat Spain	3–2
1981	W Germany	beat Australia	5–0
1982	Australia	beat Spain	5–0

GREAT BRITAIN IN THE GALEA CUP

Year	Venue		Opponent	Score	
1966	Le Zoute	beat	Belgium	3–2	
		beat	Poland	3–2	
	Vichy	lost to	Czechoslovakia	1–4	
		beat	France	3–2	
1967	Vught	beat	Netherlands	4–1	
		beat	Belgium	4–1	
	Vichy	beat	West Germany	4–1	
		lost to	France	1–3	
1968	Palma	lost to	Spain	2–3	
		lost to	Yugoslavia	2–3	
1969	Prague	lost to	France	1–4	
1970	Barcelona	beat	Switzerland	4–1	
		lost to	Spain	2–3	
1971	Budapest	lost to	Hungary	2–3	
1972	Germany	beat	West Germany	4–1	
		beat	Sweden	4–1	
	Vichy	beat	Czechoslovakia	4–1	
		beat	Spain	4–1	Won Trophy
1973	West Germany	beat	Finland	5–0	
		beat	West Germany	3–2	

Year	Venue		Opponent	Score
	Vichy	beat	Czechoslovakia	3–1
		lost to	Spain	1–4
1974	Budapest	beat	New Zealand	4–1
		lost to	Hungary	1–4
1975	Prague	beat	India	4–1
		lost to	Czechoslovakia	0–5
1976	Murcia	beat	Israel	3–2
		lost to	Spain	0–5
1977	Kiel	lost to	France	1–4
		beat	Hungary	2–1 Place match
		beat	Netherlands	3–0 Place match
1978	Bournemouth	beat	Israel	3–2
		beat	USSR	3–2
		beat	Australia	3–2
	Vichy	lost to	France	1–4
		beat	Sweden	3–1
1979	Pamplona	lost to	West Germany	2–3
1980	Monte Catini	lost to	Italy	1–4
		beat	Hungary	4–0
1981	Lee-on-Solent	beat	Morocco	5–0
		beat	Monaco	5–0
	Kiel	lost to	Egypt	2–3
1982	Oporto	beat	Morocco	3–2
		beat	Portugal	4–1
	Vich, Spain	lost to	Spain	0–5

The **most appearances** in the Galea Cup were made by **Stephen Warboys**, born 25 October 1953. He first played for Great Britain in 1968 and then every year until 1973, six in all. He took part in 12 ties, He played 29 rubbers, winning 16, taking 11 from 19 singles and 5 from 10 doubles.

BRITISH PLAYERS

Years Played

G D Battrick	1966, 1967
J G Clifton	1966
D A Lloyd	1966, 1967, 1968
J G Paish	1967
S A Warboys*	1968, 1969, 1970, 1971, 1972, 1973
J de Mendoza	1968
W E Dickson	1969
R A V Walker	1970
A F Whittaker	1970
C J Mottram*	1971, 1972, 1973
J M Lloyd*	1972, 1973
J W Feaver	1972
M J Farrell	1973
C M Robinson	1974, 1975
R A Lewis	1974
J R Smith	1974, 1975
A H Lloyd	1975, 1976
C S Wells	1975
N Sears	1976
C J Kaskow	1976, 1977
A M Jarrett	1977, 1978
C Bradnam	1977, 1978
R Beven	1977

Years Played

M R E Appleton	1978, 1979
J Dier	1978, 1979
M J Bates	1980, 1981
S M Shaw	1980, 1981, 1982
K Gilbert	1980
P S J Farrell	1980
N Brown	1981
S Bale	1982
P Heath	1982
D Felgate	1982

* member of team winning final tie.

THE ANNIE SOISBAULT CUP

International team competition for women under 21. Match format 2 singles, 1 doubles.

Played at Le Touquet

1965	Netherlands	beat France	2–1
1966	France	beat Netherlands	2–1
1967	Netherlands	beat France	2–1
1968	USSR	beat Czechoslovakia	3–0
1969	USSR	beat Hungary	3–0
1970	USSR	beat France	3–0
1971	France	beat Czechoslovakia	2–1
1972	USSR	beat Great Britain	2–1
1973	Great Britain	beat USSR	2–1
1974	Czechoslovakia	beat Great Britain	2–1
1975	Great Britain	beat Romania	2–1
1976	Czechoslovakia	beat Great Britain	2–1
1977	Czechoslovakia	beat Switzerland	3–0
1978	USSR	beat Switzerland	3–0
1979	Great Britain	beat Czechoslovakia	2–1
1980	Czechoslovakia	beat Australia	2–1
1981	Netherlands	beat USSR	3–0
1982	USSR	beat Great Britain	2–1

GREAT BRITAIN IN THE ANNIE SOISBAULT CUP

Year	Venue		Opponent	Score
1972	Valencia	beat	Spain	2–1
		beat	Netherlands	3–0
	Le Touquet	beat	Sweden	2–1
		beat	France	2–1
		lost to	USSR	1–2
1973	Le Touquet	beat	Hungary	2–0
		beat	Czechoslovakia	2–1
		beat	USSR	2–1 Won Trophy
1974	Le Touquet	beat	Sweden	3–0
		beat	West Germany	3–0
		lost to	Czechoslovakia	1–2
1975	Le Touquet	beat	France	3–0
		beat	Italy	2–0
		beat	Romania	3–0 Won Trophy

Year	Venue		Opponent	Score	
1976	Le Touquet	beat	Australia	3–0	
		beat	Sweden	3–0	
		lost to	Czechoslovakia	1–2	
1977	Varga	beat	Netherlands	2–1	
		lost to	Hungary	1–2	
	Le Touquet	lost to	Czechoslovakia	0–3	
		beat	Romania	3–0	
		beat	Australia	3–0	
1978	Oslo	beat	Sweden	2–1	
		beat	Romania	3–0	
		lost to	USSR	1–2	
		lost to	Australia	0–3	
1979	Karlovy Vary	beat	Italy	2–1	
		lost to	Czechoslovakia	1–2	
	Le Touquet	beat	Australia	2–1	
		beat	Switzerland	3–0	
		beat	Czechoslovakia	2–1	Won Trophy
1980	Bournemouth	beat	Canada	3–0	
		beat	West Germany	3–0	
	Le Touquet	lost to	USSR	1–2	
		lost to	West Germany	1–2	
1981	Maribor	lost to	Poland	1–2	
1982	Spain	beat	Belgium	3–0	
		beat	USSR	2–1	
	Le Touquet	beat	Australia	2–1	
		beat	Yugoslavia	3–0	
		lost to	USSR	1–2	

BRITISH PLAYERS

	Years Played
Miss V Burton	1972
Miss G L Coles*	1972, 1973, 1974
Miss L J Charles	1972
Miss S Barker*	1973, 1974, 1975
Miss L J Mottram*	1974, 1975, 1976
Miss M Tyler	1976, 1977, 1978
Miss B R L Thompson	1976
Miss A E Hobbs	1977, 1978, 1979
Miss J M Durie*	1977, 1978, 1979, 1980
Miss D A Jevans*	1979, 1980
Miss E Jones	1980, 1981
Miss K Brasher	1980, 1981
Miss S Gomer	1981
Miss S Walpole	1982
Miss A Brown	1982
Miss J Salmon	1982

* playing member of team winning final match.

THE WIGHTMAN CUP

The Wightman Cup is named after the donor of the trophy, Hazel Hotchkiss Wightman, born in California 20 December 1886, died in Boston 5 December 1974, one of the most successful players in the years before and after the First World War. She bought the silver cup in the first instance when, around 1920, moves were being made to start an international team competition for women on the same lines as the Davis Cup. This came to naught but in 1923 a contest was arranged between the women of the USA and Great Britain to mark the opening of the Stadium Court at the West Side Club, Forest Hills, New York. Mrs Wightman donated her cup and it has been played for year by year since that time.

The Wightman Cup.

Its format has always comprised five singles rubbers (with the top two players meeting each other) and two doubles. Originally two singles and a doubles were played on the first day with three singles and the other doubles on the second. Since 1969 in the USA and since 1974 in Great Britain it has been staged as a 3–day contest with two singles on the first day, a singles and a doubles on the second with two singles and a doubles on the third.

WIGHTMAN CUP SUPERLATIVES

The **quickest result** was achieved when the USA won at the Merion Cricket Club, Philadelphia, in 1949. A winning lead of 4–nil was built when Doris Hart beat Jean Walker-Smith 6–3 6–1, Margaret du Pont beat Betty Hilton 6–1 6–3, Miss Hart and Shirley Fry beat Jean Quertier and Molly Lincoln 6–1 6–2 and Miss Hart beat Mrs Hilton 6–1 6–3. At that stage the Americans had won **48 games to 15**.

The **quickest result in Great Britain** was the USA win on Court One at Wimbledon in 1950. The winning 4–nil lead was built when Louise Brough (USA) beat Jean Walker-Smith 6–0, 6–0, Margaret du Pont beat Betty Hilton 6–3 6–4, Doris Hart and Pat Todd beat Jean Quertier and Mrs Walker-Smith 6–2 6–3, Mrs du Pont beat Mrs Walker-Smith 6–2 6–3. The Americans ensured victory by **48 games to 17**.

The **most one-sided contests** were at the Westchester Country Club, Rye, New York, in 1953, and indoors in the International Amphitheatre, Chicago, in 1981, when in each case the USA beat Great Britain by an overall score of 7 rubbers to nil, 14 sets to nil and by **85 games to 29**. The 1981 result was the more devastating since the winning lead was made by 49 games to 16 compared with 49 games to 22 in 1953.

The **easiest and quickest win by Great Britain** was at Wimbledon in 1924. Great Britain won 6–1, 13 sets to 4 and achieved a winning lead by 4–nil, 8 sets to nil, 48 games to 20.

The **shortest singles** were at Wimbledon 1950, when Louise Brough (USA) beat Jean Walker-Smith, and in Chicago 1981 when Andrea Jaeger (USA) beat Anne Hobbs. On each occasion the score was 6–0 6–0.

The **shortest doubles** was at Wimbledon 1960. Karen Hantze and Darlene Hard (USA) beat Ann Haydon and Angela Mortimer **6–0 6–0** in a live rubber. Nevertheless Great Britain won the contest 4–3.

Hazel Hotchkiss Wightman who gave the cup named after her in 1923.

The **longest singles** was at the Cleveland Skating Club, Cleveland, in 1963. Billie Jean Moffitt (USA) beat Christine Truman 6–4 19–17 **46 games**.

The **longest set** was in the singles above, 19–17 **36 games**.

The **longest doubles** was at Forest Hills in 1927. Gwen Sterry and Mrs John Hill (GB) beat Eleanor Goss and Mrs Alfred H Chapin 5–7 7–5 7–5 **36 games**.

YOUNGEST PLAYERS

Player	Born	First played	Age
(British in italics)			
Andrea Jaeger	4 June 1965	31 October 1980 Royal Albert Hall, London	15 years 149 days
(Miss Jaeger played number two singles and in her first rubber beat the British number one, Virginia Wade, 3–6 6–3 6–2.)			
Jeanne Evert	5 October 1957	26 August 1973 Boston	15 years 325 days
Tracy Austin	12 December 1962	3 November 1978 Royal Albert Hall, London	15 years 326 days

Player	Born	First played	Age
Betty Nuthall	25 May 1911	13 August 1927 Forest Hills	16 years 80 days
Pam Shriver	4 July 1962	2 November 1978 Royal Albert Hall, London	16 years 121 days
Christine Truman (Mrs Janes)	16 January 1941	10 August 1957 Sewickley, Pa	16 years 206 days
Chris Evert (Mrs Lloyd)	21 December 1954	21 August 1971 Cleveland	16 years 243 days
Maureen Connolly	17 September 1934	25 August 1951 Boston	16 years 342 days
Karen Hantze	11 December 1942	12 June 1960 Wimbledon	17 years 184 days
Sarah Palfrey (Mrs Fabyan)	28 September 1912	13 June 1930 Wimbledon	17 years 258 days
Billie Jean Moffitt (Mrs King)	22 November 1943	11 August 1961 Chicago	17 years 262 days
Helen Wills	6 October 1905	11 August 1923 Forest Hills	17 years 309 days

OLDEST PLAYERS

Player	Born	Last played	Age
Dorothea Lambert Chambers	3 September 1878	17 June 1926 Wimbledon	47 years 287 days
Hazel Wightman	20 December 1886	8 August 1931 Forest Hills	44 years 231 days
Margaret du Pont	4 March 1918	15 June 1962 Wimbledon	44 years 103 days
May Bundy	25 September 1887	14 August 1925 Wimbledon	37 years 324 days
Kitty Godfree	7 May 1897	15 June 1934 Wimbledon	37 years 39 days

The **most successful competitor,** as measured by her actual number of victories, was Chris Lloyd. Between 1971 and 1982 she won **28 rubbers.** She won 22 singles (out of 22 played) and 6 doubles (out of 10 played).

Her fellow American, Louise Brough, won 22 rubbers, as did Doris Hart. Miss Brough was invincible in 10 ties 1946 to 1957, winning 12 out of 12 singles and 10 out of 10 doubles. Miss Hart, in 10 consecutive ties 1946 to 1955, won 14 out of 15 singles, 8 out of 9 doubles.

The **most successful British player,** as measured by the number of rubbers won, was Virginia Wade in 17 consecutive contests 1965 to 1981. She won a total of 18 rubbers, 12 out of 33 singles, 6 out of 17 doubles. Her total of **50 rubbers played** makes her the **most experienced** player on either side.

The **widest span** between first and last appearances was by Ann Jones (GB). She played first in 1957 and made her 13th appearance in 1975, a span of **18 years.**

Billie Jean Moffitt first played for the USA in 1961 and, as Mrs King, for the 10th time in 1978, a span of **17 years.**

LAST RUBBER DECISIONS

The following were the critical results when the destiny of the trophy turned on the closing rubber:

1925 Forest Hills. *Great Britain won 4–3* when Kitty McKane and Evelyn Colyer beat Helen Wills and Mary Brown 6–0 6–3.

1926 Wimbledon. *USA won 4–3* after Marion Jessup beat Dorothy Shepherd-Barron 6–1 5–7 6–4 and when Mary Browne and Elizabeth Ryan beat Kitty McKane and Evelyn Colyer 2–6 6–2 6–4.

1928 Wimbledon. *Great Britain won 4–3* when Phoebe Watson and Eileen Bennett beat Helen Wills and Penelope Anderson 6–2 6–1.

1930 Wimbledon. *Great Britain won 4–3* after Phylis Mudford beat Sarah Palfrey 6–0 6–2 and when Kitty McKane and Phoebe Watson beat Helen Wills and Helen Jacobs 7–5 1–6 6–4.

1936 Wimbledon. USA won 4–3 after Caroline Babcock beat Mary Hardwick 6–4 4–6 6–2 and when Helen Jacobs and Sarah Fabyan beat Kay Stammers and Freda James 1–6 6–3 7–5.

1960 Wimbledon. Great Britain won 4–3 after Angela Mortimer beat Janet Hopps 6–8 6–4 6–1 and when Shirley Brasher and Christine Truman beat Janet Hopps and Dorothy Knode 6–4 9–7.

1966 Wimbledon. USA won 4–3 after Nancy Richey beat Virginia Wade 2–6 6–2 7–5 and when Billie Jean King beat Ann Jones 5–7 6–2

6–3 and when Nancy Richey and Mary Ann Eisel beat Elizabeth Starkie and Rita Bentley 6–1 6–2.

1968 Wimbledon. Great Britain won 4–3 after Virginia Wade beat Nancy Richey 6–4 2–6 6–3 and when Nell Truman and Christine Janes beat Stephanie de Fina and Kathy Harter 6–3 2–6 6–3.

1970 Wimbledon. USA won 4–3 when Billie Jean King and Jane Bartkowicz beat Winnie Shaw and Virginia Wade 7–5 6–8 6–2.

1978 Royal Albert Hall, London. Great Britain won 4–3 after Sue Barker beat Tracy Austin 6–3 3–6 6–0 and when Virginia Wade and Sue Barker beat Chris Evert and Pam Shriver 6–0 5–7 6–4.

BRITISH PLAYERS 1923–82

	Total Rubbers Pl'd	Won	Singles Pl'd	Won	Doubles Pl'd	Won	Contests	Years
Mrs L A Godfree	12	7	10	5	7	2	7	1923–27, 30, 34
Mrs A Clayton	3	0	2	0	1	0	2	1923, 24
Mrs A E Beamish	3	1	2	1	1	0	2	1923, 24
Mrs B C Covell	5	4	2	2	3	2	3	1923, 24, 29
Miss E L Colyer	3	1			3	1	3	1924–26
Mrs D C Shepherd-Barron	5	3	1	0	4	3	4	1924, 26, 29, 31
Miss J Fry	9	2	8	1	1	1	4	1925–27, 30
Mrs R Lambert Chambers	3	2	1	1	2	1	2	1925, 26
Miss E H Harvey	4	3			4	3	4	1925, 27, 28, 30
Miss B Nuthall	13	6	8	3	5	3	8	1927–29, 31–34, 39
Mrs J Hill	1	1			1	1	1	1927
Miss G E Sterry	1	1			1	1	1	1927
Mrs E F Whittingstall	7	5	4	2	3	3	3	1928, 31, 32
Mrs P H Watson	9	6	6	3	3	3	3	1928–30
Mrs L R C Michell	4	2	1	0	3	2	3	1928, 29, 32
Mrs M R King	6	3	5	2	1	1	4	1930–32, 35
Miss D E Round	13	4	11	4	2	0	6	1931–36
Miss M C Scriven	6	0	6	0			3	1933, 34, 38
Miss M Heeley	1	0			1	0	1	1933
Mrs S H Hammersley	6	2			6	2	6	1933, 35–39
Miss N M Lyle	3	2			3	2	3	1934–36
Miss E M Dearman	5	3			5	3	5	1934–38
Mrs M Menzies	19	5	14	4	5	1	8	1935–39, 46–48
Miss R M Hardwick	5	0	5	0			3	1936, 37, 39
Miss M E Lumb	3	0	2	0	1	0	2	1937, 38
Miss J Ingram	2	1			2	1	2	1937, 38
Miss V E Scott	1	1	1	1			1	1939
Miss N B Brown	1	0			1	0	1	1939
Mrs E W A Bostock	8	1	6	0	2	1	3	1946–48
Miss J Curry	2	0	2	0			2	1946, 50
Mrs W C J Halford	1	0			1	0	1	1946
Mrs N Passingham	1	0			1	0	1	1946
Mrs N W Blair	3	1			3	1	3	1946, 48, 49
Mrs B E Hilton	10	0	7	0	3	0	4	1947–50
Mrs A J Mottram	4	0	1	0	3	0	4	1947, 48, 51, 52
Mrs J Rinkel-Quertier	12	1	6	1	6	0	6	1947, 49–53
Mrs J Walker-Smith	9	0	8	0	1	0	4	1949–52
Miss K L A Tuckey	4	0	1	0	3	0	3	1949–51
Miss P E Ward	5	0			5	0	5	1951, 52, 55, 56, 58
Miss J S V Partridge	1	0	1	0			1	1952
Miss H M Fletcher	6	0	4	0	2	0	3	1952–54
Miss A Mortimer	16	5	10	3	6	2	7	1953, 55, 56, 59–61, 64
Miss J A Shilcock	5	0	2	0	3	0	4	1953, 54, 57, 58

	Total Rubbers Pl'd	Won	Singles Pl'd	Won	Doubles Pl'd	Won	Contests	Years
Miss A Buxton	7	0	4	0	3	0	3	1954–56
Miss P A Hird	1	0			1	0	1	1954
Mrs C W Brasher	13	3	7	1	6	2	6	1955–60
Mrs G T Janes	27	12	18	7	9	5	11	1957–63, 67–69, 71
Mrs P F Jones	32	16	21	10	11	6	13	1957–67, 70, 75
Miss S M Armstrong	1	0			1	0	1	1957
Miss D M Catt	8	2	4	1	4	1	4	1961–64
Miss D E Starkie	8	1	3	0	5	1	5	1962–66
Miss S V Wade	52	18	34	12	18	6	18	1965–82
Miss F E Truman	5	2			5	2	5	1965, 68, 69, 71, 72
Miss W M Shaw	11	2	6	1	5	1	7	1966–72
Miss R H Bentley	1	0			1	0	1	1966
Mrs G M Williams	8	4	4	2	4	2	4	1967, 70–72
Miss C Molesworth	1	0	1	0			1	1972
Miss V Burton	2	0	2	0			1	1973
Miss G L Coles							7	1973–76, 80, 81
Miss L J Charles	4	1			4	1	4	1973, 74, 76, 77
Miss L Beaven	1	0			1	0	1	1973
Miss S Barker	24	8	16	5	8	3	9	1974–82
Miss S Mappin	4	1			4	1	4	1974, 76–78
Miss M Tyler	2	1	2	1			2	1977, 78
Miss A E Hobbs	7	2	3	1	4	1	5	1978–82
Miss J M Durie	5	1	2	0	3	1	3	1979, 81, 82
Miss D A Jevans	1	0			1	0	1	1979

US PLAYERS 1923–82

	Total Rubbers Pl'd	Won	Singles Pl'd	Won	Doubles Pl'd	Won	Contests	Years
Mrs H Wills Moody	30	21	20	18	10	3	10	1923–25, 27, 29–32, 38
Mrs F Mallory	12	6	10	5	2	1	5	1923–25, 27, 28
Miss E Goss	8	3	3	1	5	2	6	1923–28
Mrs G W Wightman	5	3			5	3	5	1923, 24, 27, 29, 31
Mrs M Z Jessup	3	2	1	1	2	1	2	1924, 26
Mrs T C Bundy	1	0			1	0	1	1925
Miss M K Browne	4	1	2	0	2	1	2	1925, 26
Miss E Ryan	3	2	2	1	1	1	1	1926
Miss H H Jacobs	30	19	22	14	8	5	12	1927–37, 39
Mrs A H Chapin	1	0			1	0	1	1927
Miss P Anderson	1	0			1	0	1	1928
Miss E Cross	3	1	1	1	2	1	2	1929, 30
Mrs M Fabyan	21	14	11	7	10	7	10	1930–39
Mrs A M Harper	4	2	2	1	2	1	2	1931, 32
Miss C Babcock	6	2	3	1	3	1	4	1933–36
Miss A Marble	10	8	6	5	4	3	4	1933, 37–39
Mrs J Van Ryn	3	1			3	1	3	1933, 36, 37
Miss J Cruickshank	1	0			1	0	1	1934
Mrs E B Arnold	2	1	2	1			1	1935
Mrs D Andrus	1	0			1	0	1	1935
Miss D M Bundy	3	1			3	1	3	1937–39
Miss M Arnold	1	0			1	0	1	1939
Miss P M Betz	3	3	2	2	1	1	1	1946
Mrs W du Pont	18	18	10	10	8	8	9	1946–50, 54, 55, 57, 62
Miss A L Brough	22	22	12	12	10	10	10	1946–48, 50, 52–57
Miss D J Hart	24	22	15	14	9	8	10	1946–55
Mrs P C Todd	5	4			5	4	5	1947–51
Mrs J G Fleitz	4	4	3	3	1	1	3	1949, 56, 59
Miss S J Fry	12	10	6	4	6	6	6	1949, 51–53, 55, 56
Miss G Moran	1	1			1	1	1	1949
Miss M C Connolly	9	9	7	7	2	2	4	1951–54
Miss N Chaffee	1	1			1	1	1	1951

	Total Rubbers Pl'd	Won	Singles Pl'd	Won	Doubles Pl'd	Won	Contests	Years
Mrs D P Knode	9	5	6	4	3	1	5	1955–58, 60
Miss A Gibson	6	5	4	3	2	2	2	1957, 58
Miss D R Hard	14	10	9	6	5	4	5	1957, 59, 60, 62, 63
Miss Mimi Arnold	1	0	1	0			1	1958
Miss K Fageros	1	0			1	0	1	1958
Miss J S Hopps	4	1	1	0	3	1	3	1958–60
Miss S Moore	2	0	1	0	1	0	1	1959
Miss J Arth	1	1			1	1	1	1959
Mrs J R Susman	9	6	6	3	3	3	4	1960–62, 65
Mrs L W King	26	21	16	14	10	7	10	1961–67, 70, 77, 78
Miss J Bricka	1	1	1	1			1	1961
Miss N Richey	21	12	16	9	5	3	9	1962–70
Miss M Varner	2	2			2	2	2	1961, 62
Mrs D Fales	2	1			2	1	2	1963, 64
Mrs C Graebner	6	4	2	2	4	2	4	1964, 65, 67, 71
Miss M A Eisel	9	4	3	1	6	3	6	1966–71
Miss J Albert	1	0			1	0	1	1966
Miss R Casals	11	7	4	1	7	6	7	1967, 76, 77, 79–82
Miss J Bartkowicz	4	4	2	2	2	2	3	1968–70
Mrs S D Johnson	1	0			1	0	1	1968
Miss K Harter	1	0			1	0	1	1968
Miss J M Heldman	9	5	6	3	3	2	4	1969–71, 74
Miss V Ziegenfuss	4	3	1	1	3	2	3	1969, 71, 72
Mrs J M Lloyd	32	28	22	22	10	6	11	1971–73, 75–82
Miss W Overton	3	1	2	0	1	1	1	1972
Miss P S A Hogan	5	4	3	2	2	2	2	1972, 73
Miss L Tuero	1	1	1	1			1	1973
Miss M Redondo	1	0			1	0	1	1973
Miss J Evert	2	1	1	0	1	1	2	1973, 74
Miss J Newberry	5	0	3	0	2	0	2	1974, 75
Miss B Nagelsen	1	0			1	0	1	1974
Miss M Schallau	5	2	2	0	3	2	3	1974–76
Miss J Anthony	1	0			1	0	1	1975
Miss T Holladay	1	1	1	1			1	1976
Miss A K Kiyomura	2	2			2	2	2	1976, 79
Miss J Russell	1	1			1	1	1	1977
Miss T A Austin	8	6	6	4	2	2	3	1978, 79, 81
Miss P M Shriver	3	1	1	0	2	1	2	1978, 81
Miss K Jordan	3	2	2	1	1	1	2	1979, 80
Miss A Jaeger	4	3	3	2	1	1	2	1980, 81
Miss A E Smith	3	2	1	1	2	1	2	1980, 82
Miss B Potter	3	3	2	2	1	1	1	1982
Miss S A Walsh	1	1			1	1	1	1982

CAPTAINS

GREAT BRITAIN	Years of captaincy	USA	Years of captaincy
Mr H A Sabelli	1923	Mrs G W Wightman	1923, 24, 27, 29, 31, 33, 35, 37–39, 46–48
Mrs R Lambert Chambers	1924–26	Miss M K Browne	1925, 26
Mrs D R Larcombe	1927	Miss E Goss	1928
Miss E H Harvey	1928	Mrs F S Moody	1930, 32
Mrs B C Covell	1929	Mr J Cushman	1934, 36
Mrs P H Watson	1930	Mrs M G Buck	1949–52
Mrs D C Shepherd-Barron	1931, 32, 50, 51	Mrs W du Pont	1953–55, 57, 58, 61–63, 65
Mr M D Horn	1933–37	Miss A L Brough	1955
Mrs M R King	1938	Miss J S Hopps	1959, 60
Miss B Nuthall	1939	Mrs D Fales	1964
Mrs P F Glover	1946	Miss M Varner	1966
Mr E R Avory	1947	Mrs B Pratt	1967–69
Mrs M Menzies	1948, 49	Miss D J Hart	1970
Col D C Macaulay	1952, 53		

GREAT BRITAIN	Years of captaincy	USA	Years of captaincy
Mrs W C J Halford	1954–58	Mrs C Graebner	1971
Mrs B Walter	1959–63	Mrs E McGoldrick	1972, 73
Miss A Mortimer	1964–70	Miss J M Heldman	1974, 75
Mrs P F Jones	1971, 72	Miss V Berner	1976–79
Miss S V Wade	1973–82	Mrs J M Lloyd	1980, 82

RESULTS IN SUMMARY

Year	Winner	Score	Winning Lead	Venue
1923	USA	7–0	4–0	Forest Hills, NY
1924	Great Britain	6–1	4–0	Wimbledon (Centre Court)
1925	Great Britain	4–3	4–3	Forest Hills, NY
1926	USA	4–3	4–3	Wimbledon (Centre Court)
1927	USA	5–2	4–2	Forest Hills, NY
1928	Great Britain	4–3	4–3	Wimbledon (Centre Court)
1929	USA	4–3	4–2	Forest Hills, NY
1930	Great Britain	4–3	4–3	Wimbledon (Centre Court)
1931	USA	5–2	4–1	Forest Hills, NY
1932	USA	4–3	4–0	Wimbledon (Court One)
1933	USA	4–3	4–2	Forest Hills, NY
1934	USA	5–2	4–1	Wimbledon (Centre Court)
1935	USA	4–3	4–2	Forest Hills, NY
1936	USA	4–3	4–3	Wimbledon (Centre Court)
1937	USA	6–1	4–0	Forest Hills, NY
1938	USA	5–2	4–1	Wimbledon (Centre Court)
1939	USA	5–2	4–1	Forest Hills, NY
1940–1945 not held				
1946	USA	7–0	4–0	Wimbledon (Court One)
1947	USA	7–0	4–0	Forest Hills, NY
1948	USA	6–1	4–1	Wimbledon (Court One)
1949	USA	7–0	4–0	Merion Club, Philadelphia
1950	USA	7–0	4–0	Wimbledon (Court One)
1951	USA	6–1	4–0	Longwood Club, Boston
1952	USA	7–0	4–0	Wimbledon (Court One)
1953	USA	7–0	4–0	Rye, NY
1954	USA	6–0*	4–0	Wimbledon (Court One),
1955	USA	6–1	4–1	Rye, NY
1956	USA	5–2	4–1	Wimbledon (Court One)
1957	USA	6–1	4–1	Sewickley, Pa.
1958	Great Britain	4–3	4–2	Wimbledon (Court One)
1959	USA	4–3	4–2	Sewickley, Pa.
1960	Great Britain	4–3	4–3	Wimbledon (Court One)
1961	USA	6–1	4–1	Chicago (Saddle & Cycle Club)
1962	USA	4–3	4–2	Wimbledon (Court One)
1963	USA	6–1	4–1	Cleveland (Skating Club)
1964	USA	5–2	4–1	Wimbledon (Court One)
1965	USA	5–2	4–1	Cleveland (Clark Stadium)
1966	USA	4–3	4–3	Wimbledon (Court One)
1967	USA	6–1	4–1	Cleveland (Clark Stadium)
1968	Great Britain	4–3	4–3	Wimbledon (Court One)
1969	USA	5–2	4–2	Cleveland (Clark Stadium)
1970	USA	4–3	4–3	Wimbledon (Court One)
1971	USA	4–3	4–2	Cleveland (Clark Stadium)
1972	USA	5–2	4–1	Wimbledon (Court One)
1973	USA	5–2	4–1	Longwood Club, Boston
1974†	Great Britain	6–1	4–0	Deeside, N Wales (indoors)

Ivan Lendl, one of the great Czechs and with a capacity to hit the ball as hard as anyone in the history of the game.

John Newcombe of Australia. Three times Wimbledon singles champion.

Virginia Ruzici, the most successful woman player to come from Romania.

Roger Taylor, the British leader in the 1970s. Thrice a Wimbledon semi-finalist. *below left.*

Tony Roche, a noted left hander from Australia. A great doubles player. *below.*

Year	Winner	Score	Winning Lead	Venue
1975	Great Britain	5–2	4–2	Cleveland (Public Auditorium)
1976	USA	5–2	4–2	Crystal Palace, London (indoors)
1977	USA	7–0	4–0	Oakland, Cal (indoors)
1978	Great Britain	4–3	4–3	Albert Hall, London
1979	USA	7–0	4–0	West Palm Beach, Florida
1980	USA	5–2	4–2	Albert Hall, London
1981	USA	7–0	4–0	Chicago (indoors)
1982	USA	6–1	4–1	Albert Hall, London

* one rubber not played.
† the match has been sponsored since this year.

MAUREEN CONNOLLY CUP

USA versus Great Britain, women under 21, maximum of 5 players each side.

Year	Venue	Winner	Score
1973	La Jolla, Cal	USA	6–0
1974	Little Rock, Ark	USA	6–0
1975	Torquay	Great Britain	6–4
1976	Naples, Fla	USA	6–5
1977	Torquay	USA	10–1
1978	Deer Creek, Fla	USA	10–1
1979	Bradford	USA	8–3
1980	Houston	USA	9–2
1981	Cambridge, England	USA	8–3
1982	Dallas, Texas	USA	6–5

BRITISH PLAYERS

	Years Played
Miss S Barker	1973, 1974, 1975
Miss V Burton	1973
Miss L J Charles	1973
Miss G L Coles	1973, 1974, 1975
Miss L Blachford	1974
Miss L J Mottram	1974, 1975, 1976
Miss M Tyler	1975, 1976, 1977
Miss J M Durie	1976, 1977, 1978, 1979, 1981
Miss A E Hobbs	1976, 1977, 1978, 1979, 1980
Miss B R L Thompson	1976, 1977
Miss D A Jevans	1977, 1979, 1980, 1981
Miss A Cooper	1978, 1980
Miss C Drury	1978, 1981
Miss K Glancy	1978
Miss K Brasher	1979, 1981, 1982
Miss S Davies	1979
Miss E Jones	1980, 1981, 1982
Miss L Pennington	1980
Miss A Brown	1982
Miss S Gomer	1982
Miss S Walpole	1982

Series Events of the Open Era

The Grand Prix Series, an integrated tournament circuit, was envisaged by Jack Kramer and inaugurated in 1970 under the direction of the International Federation. In the first year all open tournaments were eligible for Grand Prix status provided they fulfilled the primary condition of not paying expenses to commercial enterprises with players under contract.

The first Grand Prix event was the British Hard Court Championships at Bournemouth in 1970. Mark Cox of Great Britain was the singles winner.

A total of 20 tournaments were classed as Grand Prix events in 1970. The total prize money made available, over and above that in the individual tournaments, was $150 000, ranging from a first prize of $25 000 to a twentieth of $1000. Three different categories of tournaments awarded varying points and only men were involved.

A Grand Prix Masters' Tournament provides the climax. The eight top players qualify, though in the first 6 years the qualifying number was seven, with the organisers having the right to nominate an eighth.

Women had their own Grand Prix Series in 1971, 1972 and 1973 but without the closing tournament to provide a climax. A separate International Series under different sponsorhip was organised in 1977 with the eight leading players qualifying for the final championship event.

Both men and women play the concluding tournament on a round-robin basis, though with different rules. Each is brought down to a knock-out semi-final stage. The first two men's Masters' tournaments were conducted on a round-robin basis throughout.

A record for consistency was established by Jimmy Connors (USA). He qualified for the Masters' event every year 1972–1982. He did not take up his qualification in 1974, 1975 or 1976.

Most success was had by Ilie Nastase (Rom). He won the Grand Prix Series 1972, 1973 and the Masters' Tournaments 1971, 1972, 1973 and 1975. In Stockholm in 1975 he had a bizarre triumph. In the round-robin series he was disqualified against Arthur Ashe (USA) but none the less qualified for the knock-out stages and won.

THE GRAND PRIX

Year	No. of Tournaments	Singles Winner	Bonus	Doubles Winners	Sponsor
1970	20	C Richey (USA)	$25 000	—	Pepsi-Cola
1971	31	S R Smith (USA)	$25 000	—	Pepsi-Cola
1972	33	I Nastase (Rom)	$50 000	—	Commercial Union
1973	50	I Nastase (Rom)	$50 000	—	Commercial Union
1974	48	G Vilas (Arg)	$100 000	—	Commercial Union
1975	42	G Vilas (Arg)	$100 000	J Gisbert (Spa) & M Orantes (Spa)	Commercial Union
1976	47	R Ramirez (Mex)	$150 000	B E Gottfried (USA) & R Ramirez (Mex)	Commercial Union
1977	76	G Vilas (Arg)	$300 000	R A J Hewitt (SA) & F D McMillan (SA)	Colgate
1978	86	J S Connors* (USA)	$300 000	R A J Hewitt (SA) & F D McMillan (SA)	Colgate
1979	87	J P McEnroe (USA)	$300 000	P Fleming (USA) & J P McEnroe (USA)	Colgate
1980	91	J P McEnroe (USA)	$300 000	R C Lutz (USA) & S R Smith (USA)	Volvo
1981	89	I Lendl (Cze)	$300 000	P Fleming (USA) & J P McEnroe (USA)	Volvo

* The bonus was awarded to third placed E Dibbs. Neither Connors nor the second placed B Borg had played enough tournaments to qualify for the bonus earnings.

THE GRAND PRIX MASTERS' TOURNAMENT

Year	Venue	Winner	Runner-up	Score	Doubles Winners	Singles Qualifiers (in merit order)
1970	Tokyo	S R Smith (USA)	R G Laver (Aus)	round robin	J Kodes (Cze) & R G Laver (Aus)	C Richey* (USA); S R Smith (USA); A R Ashe (USA); Z Franulovic (Yug); K R Rosewall (Aus); J D Newcombe* (Aus); R G Laver (Aus); J Kodes (Cze)
1971	Paris	I Nastase (Rom)	S R Smith (USA)	round robin	—	S R Smith (USA); J D Newcombe* (Aus); I Nastase (Rom); P Barthes (Fra); Z Franulovic (Yug); K R Rosewall* (Aus); J Kodes (Cze); C Graebner (USA); C Richey (USA); T S Gorman (USA)
1972	Barcelona	I Nastase (Rom)	S R Smith (USA)	6–3 6–2 3–6 2–6 6–3	—	I Nastase (Rom); A Gimeno (Spa); S R Smith (USA); R A J Hewitt (SA); M Orantes (Spa); J S Connors (USA); J Kodes (Cze); T S Gorman (USA)
1973	Boston	I Nastase (Rom)	T S Okker (Hol)	6–3 7–5 4–6 6–3	—	I Nastase (Rom); M Orantes (Spa); J D Newcombe (Aus); J Kodes (Cze); T S Okker (Hol); S R Smith (USA); J S Connors (USA); T S Gorman (USA)
1974	Melbourne	G Vilas (Arg)	I Nastase (Rom)	7–6 6–2 3–6 3–6 6–4	—	G Vilas (Arg); I Nastase (Rom); J S Connors* (USA); O Parun (NZ); M Orantes (Spa); H Solomon (USA); B Borg (Swe); J D Newcombe (Aus); R Ramirez (Mex)
1975	Stockholm	I Nastase (Rom)	B Borg (Swe)	6–2 6–2 6–1	J Gisbert (Spa) & M Orantes (Spa)	G Vilas (Arg); J S Connors* (USA); M Orantes (Spa); R Ramirez (Mex); B Borg (Swe); A Panatta (Ita); A R Ashe (USA); H Solomon (USA); I Nastase (Rom)
1976	Houston	M Orantes (Spa)	W Fibak (Pol)	5–7 6–2 0–6 7–6 6–1	F McNair (USA) & S E Stewart (USA)	R Ramirez (Mex); G Vilas (Arg); M Orantes (Spa); R Tanner (USA); J S Connors* (USA); W Fibak (Pol); E Dibbs (USA); B E Gottfried (USA); H Solomon (USA)
1977	New York (Madison Sq Garden) (played Jan 1978)	J S Connors (USA)	B Borg (Swe)	6–4 1–6 6–4	R A J Hewitt (SA) & F D McMillan (SA)	G Vilas (Arg); E Dibbs (USA); B E Gottfried (USA); R Tanner (USA); B Borg (Swe); R Ramirez (Mex); M Orantes (Spa); J S Connors (USA)
1978	New York (Madison Sq Garden) (played Jan 1979)	J P McEnroe (USA)	A R Ashe (USA)	6–7 6–3 7–5	P Fleming (USA) & J P McEnroe (USA)	J S Connors (USA); J P McEnroe (USA); B Borg* (Swe); G Vilas* (Arg); E Dibbs (USA); B E Gottfried (USA); R Ramirez (Mex); C Barazzutti (Ita); H Solomon (USA); A R Ashe (USA)
1979	New York (Madison Sq Garden) (played Jan 1980)	B Borg (Swe)	V Gerulaitis (USA)	6–2 6–2	P Fleming (USA) & J P McEnroe (USA)	J P McEnroe (USA); V Gerulaitis (USA); B Borg (Swe); R Tanner (USA); J S Connors (USA); J Higueras (Spa); G Vilas (Arg); H Solomon (USA)
1980	New York (Madison Sq Garden) (played Jan 1981)	B Borg (Swe)	I Lendl (Cze)	6–4 6–2 6–2	P Fleming (USA) & J P McEnroe (USA)	J P McEnroe (USA); G Mayer (USA); I Lendl (Cze); H Solomon (USA); J S Connors (USA); G Vilas (Arg); B Borg (Swe); J L Clerc (Arg)
1981	New York (Madison Sq Garden) (played Jan 1982)	I Lendl (Cze)	V Gerulaitis (USA)	6–7 2–6 7–6 6–2 6–4	P Fleming (USA) & J P McEnroe (USA)	I Lendl (Cze); G Vilas (Arg); J P McEnroe (USA); B Borg* (Swe); J S Connors (USA); R Tanner (USA); J L Clerc (Arg); E Teltscher (USA); V Gerulaitis (USA)

* Qualified but did not compete.

WOMEN'S INTERNATIONAL SERIES

Year	No. of Tourna- ments	Singles Winner	Bonus	Doubles Winners	Sponsor
1971	17	Mrs L W King (USA)	$10 000	—	Pepsi-Cola
1972	30	Mrs L W King (USA)	$20 000	—	Commercial Union
1973	27	Miss C M Evert (USA)	$23 750	—	Commercial Union
1974	not held				
1975	not held				
1976	not held				
1977	24	Miss C M Evert (USA)	$100 000	Miss M Navratilova (Cze) & Miss B F Stove (Hol)	Colgate
1978	29	Miss C M Evert (USA)	$100 000	Mrs G E Reid (Aus) & Miss W M Turnbull (Aus)	Colgate
1979	33	Mrs J M Lloyd (USA)	$115 000	Miss B F Stove (Hol) & Miss W M Turnbull (Aus)	Colgate
1980	39	Miss H Mandlikova (Cze)	$115 000	Miss K Jordan (USA) & Miss A E Smith (USA)	Colgate
1981	31	Miss M Navratilova (USA)	$125 000	Miss R Casals (USA) & Miss W M Turnbull (Aus)	Toyota

WOMEN'S INTERNATIONAL SERIES CHAMPIONSHIPS

Year	Venue	Singles Winner	Runner-up	Score	Doubles Winners	Singles Qualifiers (in merit order)
1977	Palm Springs	Miss C M Evert (USA)	Mrs L W King (USA)	6–2 6–2	Miss F Durr (Fra) & Miss S V Wade (GB)	Miss C M Evert (USA) Miss B F Stove (Hol) Mrs L W King (USA) Miss M Navratilova (Cze) Miss S V Wade (GB) Mrs G E Reid (Aus) Miss W M Turnbull (Aus) Miss D Fromholtz (Aus)
1978	Palm Springs	Miss C M Evert (USA)	Miss M Navratilova (Cze)	6–3 6–3	Mrs L W King (USA) & Miss M Navratilova (Cze)	Miss C M Evert (USA) Miss M Navratilova (Cze) Miss S V Wade (GB) Miss V Ruzici (Rom) Miss B F Stove (Hol) Mrs G E Reid (Aus) Miss W M Turnbull (Aus) Miss R Marsikova (Cze)
1979	Landover, Md (played Jan 1980)	Miss M Navratilova (Cze)	Miss T A Austin (USA)	6–2 6–1	Mrs L W King (USA) & Miss M Navratilova (Cze)	Mrs J M Lloyd (USA) Miss M Navratilova (Cze) Miss T A Austin (USA) Mrs R A Cawley (Aus) Miss W M Turnbull (Aus) Mrs G E Reid (Aus) Miss D Fromholtz (Aus) Miss R Marsikova (Cze)
1980	Landover, Md (played Jan 1980)	Miss T A Austin (USA)	Miss A Jaeger (USA)	6–2 6–2	Miss R Casals (USA) & Miss W M Turnbull (Aus)	Miss H Mandlikova (Cze) Mrs J M Lloyd (USA) Miss T A Austin (USA) Miss W M Turnbull (Aus) Miss M Navratilova (Cze) Miss V Ruzici (Rom) Miss A Jaeger (USA) Miss P H Shriver (USA)
1981	E Rutherford, NJ	Miss T A Austin (USA)	Miss M Navratilova (USA)	2–6 6–4 6–2	Miss M Navratilova (USA) & Miss P H Shriver (USA)	Miss M Navratilova (USA) Mrs J M Lloyd (USA) Miss T A Austin (USA) Miss A Jaeger (USA) Miss P H Shriver (USA) Miss H Mandlikova (Cze) Miss M Jausovec (Yug) Miss V Ruzici (Rom)

INDEPENDENT WOMEN

Up to September 1970 events for individual women were almost always held in association with those for men. At that time the prize money offered by the Los Angeles tournament was so paltry compared with that for the men that Gladys Heldman, then owner and editor of the magazine *World Tennis*, was moved to look for independence.

The solution she found was to persuade Joe Culman, the head of Philip Morris Incorporated, to sponsor a tournament exclusively for women. She put leading players under a professional contract for a nominal sum of one dollar and with total prize money of $7500 the event took place at Houston, Texas, under the banner of 'Virginia Slims'.

The eight contracted participants were Rosemary Casals, Valerie Ziegenfuss, Kristy Pigeon, Billie Jean King, Nancy Richey, Jane Bartkowicz (all USA), Kerry Reid and Judy Dalton (both Aus). Miss Casals beat Mrs Dalton 5–7 6–1 7–5 in the final to win the tournament.

In 1971 there was a circuit of Virginia Slims tournaments. The Virginia Slims Championships were at Houston but were staged before the end of the series.

In 1972 the 'Virginia Slims Championships' came as a climax event at the end of the series. From 1974 the circuit was played mainly on indoor courts and confined to the earlier part of the year.

In 1977 the 'Avon Futures' circuit was initiated as a series of subsidiary tournaments for lesser players who could qualify for the main events. When Virginia Slims ceased their sponsorship Avon Products took on both series. This was in 1979.

VIRGINIA SLIMS/AVON SERIES CHAMPIONSHIPS

Year	Venue	Singles Winner	Runner-up	Score	Doubles Winners	Qualifiers (last eight 1971–74)	
1971	Houston	Mrs L W King (USA)	Miss K Melville (Aus)	6–4 4–6 6–1	Miss R Casals (USA) & Mrs L W King (USA)	Mrs L W King (USA) Miss K Melville Mrs N Gunter (USA) Mrs D E Dalton (Aus)	Mrs P W Curtis (USA) Miss J M Heldman (USA) Miss F Durr (Fra) Miss R Casals (USA)
1972	Boca Raton	Miss C M Evert (USA)	Miss K Melville (Aus)	7–5 6–4	not played	Miss C M Evert (USA) Miss K Melville (Aus) Mrs L W King (USA) Miss F Durr (Fra)	Miss K Krantzcke (Aus) Miss W Overton (USA) Miss J Evert (USA) Miss B F Stove (Hol)
1973	Boca Raton	Miss C M Evert (USA)	Mrs N Gunter (USA)	6–3 6–3	Miss R Casals (USA) & Mrs B M Court (Aus)	Miss C M Evert (USA) Mrs N Gunter (USA) Miss F Durr (Fra) Miss K Melville (Aus)	Miss J Newberry (USA) Miss S V Wade (GB) Miss M Schallau (USA) Miss J M Heldman (USA)
1974	Los Angeles	Miss E Goolagong (Aus)	Miss C M Evert (USA)	6–3 6–4	Miss R Casals (USA) & Mrs L W King (USA)	Miss E Goolagong (Aus) Miss C M Evert (USA) Mrs L W King (USA) Miss S V Wade (GB)	Miss H Gourlay (Aus) Miss L Hunt (Aus) Miss M Navratilova (Cze) Miss R Casals (USA)
1975	Los Angeles	Miss C M Evert (USA)	Miss M Navratilova (Cze)	6–4 6–2	not played	Miss C M Evert (USA) Miss M Navratilova (Cze) Miss S V Wade (GB) Miss E Goolagong (Aus)	Miss O Morozova (USSR) Miss J M Heldman (USA) Miss M Schallau (USA) Miss Marcie Louie (USA)
1976	Los Angeles	Mrs R A Cawley (Aus)	Miss C M Evert (USA)	6–4 5–7 6–3	not played	Mrs R A Cawley (Aus)	Miss S Barker (GB)

Year	Venue	Singles Winner	Runner-up	Score	Doubles Winners	Qualifiers (last eight 1971–74)	
						Miss C M Evert (USA)	Miss M Redondo (USA)
						Miss R Casals (USA)	Miss S V Wade (GB)
						Miss M Navratilova (Cze)	Miss F Durr (Fra)
1977	New York	Miss C M Evert (USA)	Miss S Barker (GB)	2–6 6–1 6–1	not played	Miss C M Evert (USA)	Miss M Jausovec (Yug)
						Miss S Barker (GB)	Miss S V Wade (GB)
						Miss M Navratilova (Cze)	Miss B F Stove (Hol)
						Miss R Casals (USA)	Mrs K Shaw (USA)
1978	Oakland	Miss M Navratilova (Cze)	Mrs R A Cawley (Aus)	7–6 6–4	not played	Miss M Navratilova (Cze)	Miss S V Wade (GB)
						Mrs R A Cawley (Aus)	Mrs L W King (USA)
						Miss W M Turnbull (Aus)	Miss B F Stove (Hol)
						Miss R Casals (USA)	Mrs G E Reid (Aus)

Virginia Slims series ceased, Avon series started.

Year	Venue	Singles Winner	Runner-up	Score	Doubles Winners	Qualifiers (last eight 1971–74)	
1979	New York	Miss M Navratilova (Cze)	Miss T A Austin (USA)	6–3 3–6 6–2	Miss F Durr (Fra) & Miss B F Stove (Hol)	Miss M Navratilova (Cze)	Miss G Stevens (SA)
						Miss T A Austin (USA)	Miss S V Wade (GB)
						Miss S Barker (GB)	Miss W M Turnbull (Aus)
						Miss D Fromholtz (Aus)	Miss C M Evert (USA)
1980	New York	Miss T A Austin (USA)	Miss M Navratilova (Cze)	6–2 2–6 6–2	Mrs L W King (USA) & Miss M Navratilova (Cze)	Miss T A Austin (USA)	Miss K Jordan (USA)
						Miss M Navratilova (Cze)	Miss S V Wade (GB)
						Mrs R A Cawley (Aus)	Miss W M Turnbull (Aus)
						Mrs L W King (USA)	Miss G Stevens (SA)
1981	New York	Miss M Navratilova (Cze)	Miss A Jaeger (USA)	6–3 7–6	Miss M Navratilova (Cze) & Miss P H Shriver (USA)	Miss M Navratilova (Cze)	Miss H Mandlikova (Cze)
						Miss A Jaeger (USA)	Miss L Allen (USA)
						Miss S Hanika (FRG)	Miss P H Shriver (USA)
						Miss B Bunge (USA)	Miss B Potter (USA)
1982	New York	Frl S Hanika (FRG)	Miss M Navratilova (USA)	1–6 6–3 6–4	Miss M Navratilova (USA) & Miss P H Shriver (USA)	Miss M Navratilova (USA)	Miss B Bunge (USA)
						Miss M Jausovec (Yug)	Miss W M Turnbill (Aus)
						Miss B Potter (USA)	Miss A E Smith (USA)
						Frl S Hanika (FRG)	Miss K Jordan (USA)

WORLD CHAMPIONSHIP TENNIS

World Championship Tennis Incorporated was founded in Dallas, Texas, in 1967 to promote professional lawn tennis. It made contracts with eight players, the Australians Tony Roche and John Newcombe, the Americans Dennis Ralston and Earl Buchholz, the South African Cliff Drysdale, the Yugoslav Nikki Pilic, the French Pierre Barthes and the British Roger Taylor, who began professional careers in January 1968. An attempt to reform the scoring system and to involve crowds in noisy participation failed. WCT moved into the sphere of more orthodox tournament promotion.

The WCT formula of organising a series of tournaments from which the most successful participants qualified for a climax event was devised first in 1971. The WCT Finals in Dallas became one of the leading events in the world game.

The number and place of the qualifying tournaments has varied but the format of the final event, eight qualifiers playing a knock-out tournament the best of five sets throughout, has not. Not all qualifying players have taken part in the Finals because of injury or other reasons.

The **youngest winner** was Bjorn Borg (Swe) in

1976 when he was **19**. Borg was the **youngest finalist** and also the **youngest participant** in 1974 at the age of **17**.

The **oldest winner** and **oldest finalist** was Ken Rosewall in 1972 when he was **37**. He was the **oldest participant** in 1973 at the age of **38**.

The WCT Series retained its identity but functioned as part of the Grand Prix Series 1978 to 1981, after which year it again became a separate entity.

WORLD CHAMPIONSHIP TENNIS FINALS

(The number of qualifying tournaments varied from year to year. In the inaugural year, 1971, the early rounds in the Finals were staged in Houston and only the last match at the Moody Stadium in Dallas. The Dallas venue was switched from the Moody Stadium to the Reunion Arena in 1980.)

Year	Winner	Runner-up	Score	Other Qualifiers	
1971	K R Rosewall (Aus)	R G Laver (Aus)	6–4 1–6 7–6 7–6	A R Ashe R C Lutz T S Okker	E C Drysdale J D Newcombe M C Riessen
1972	K R Rosewall (Aus)	R G Laver (Aus)	4–6 6–0 6–3 6–7 7–6	A R Ashe R C Lutz T S Okker	E C Drysdale J D Newcombe M C Riessen
1973	S R Smith (USA)	A R Ashe (USA)	6–3 6–4 4–6 6–4	J Alexander R G Laver K R Rosewall	R S Emerson M C Riessen R Taylor
1974	J D Newcombe (Aus)	B Borg (Swe)	4–6 6–3 6–3 6–2	A R Ashe R G Laver T S Okker	J Kodes I Nastase S R Smith
1975	A R Ashe (USA)	B Borg (Swe)	3–6 6–4 6–4 6–0	J Alexander R G Laver H Solomon	M Cox R Ramirez R Tanner
1976	B Borg (Swe)	G Vilas (Arg)	1–6 6–1 7–5 6–1	A R Ashe R C Lutz H Solomon	E Dibbs R Ramirez R L Stockton
1977	J S Connors (USA)	R L Stockton (USA)	6–7 6–1 6–4 6–3	E Dibbs W Fibak I Nastase	E C Drysdale V Gerulaitis A Panatta
1978	V Gerulaitis (USA)	E Dibbs (USA)	6–3 6–2 6–1	C Barazzutti B Gottfried R Ramirez	B Borg I Nastase R L Stockton
1979	J P McEnroe (USA)	B Borg (Swe)	7–5 4–6 6–2 7–6	J Alexander V Gerulaitis G Masters	J S Connors B Gottfried G Mayer
1980	J S Connors (USA)	J P McEnroe (USA)	2–6 7–6 6–1 6–2	V Amritraj J Kriek J Sadri	H Gunthardt I Lendl W Scanlon
1981	J P McEnroe (USA)	J Kriek (SA)	6–1 6–2 6–4	V Amritraj B Gottfried A A Mayer	W Fibak S Giammalva R Tanner
1982	I Lendl (Cze)	J P McEnroe (USA)	6–2 3–6 6–3 6–3	V Amritraj E Dibbs W Scanlon	J L Clerc W Fibak T Smid

British Domestic Events

British Hard Court Championships
The County Championships
The Wembley Tournament
British Junior Championships
British Covered Court Championships
All England Championships
Dewar Cup

(Note: for Great Britain in the Davis Cup, Federation Cup, King's Cup, Galea Cup, Annie Soisbault Cup, Wightman Cup, Maureen Connolly Cup and for Wimbledon Championships see under the separate sections.)

BRITISH HARD COURT CHAMPIONSHIPS

The British Hard Court Championships were first held in 1924 in Torquay, Devon. The venue was changed to the West Hants Lawn Tennis Club, Bournemouth, in 1927.

Notably the tournament was the first in the world to become open to professionals and amateurs. This historic meeting was staged April 22 to 27 1968.

The first match between an amateur and professional under the new conditions was John Clifton of Great Britain against the Australian Owen Davidson. The professional won with Davidson's victory by 6–2 6–3 4–6 8–6.

The eight men's singles seeds in the field of 32 were Rod Laver, Ken Rosewall, Ricardo Gonzales, Andres Gimeno, Roy Emerson, Fred Stolle and Davidson, with Bobby Wilson the only 'amateur'.

All except Gonzales reached their allotted quarter-final places. Gonzales was beaten by the British Mark Cox, who also beat Emerson to reach the semi-final.

In the semi-finals Laver beat Cox 6–4 6–1 6–0 and Rosewall beat Gimeno 6–2 6–1 6–3. In the final Rosewall beat Laver 3–6 6–2 6–0 6–3 and

thus became the first open champion in the history of the game.

The prize money was: winner £1000; runner-up £500; semi-finalists £250; quarter-finalists £100; second round losers £40; first round losers £20.

Prize money for the women's singles was: winner £300; runner-up £120; semi-finalists £60; quarter-finalists £30; third round losers £20; second round losers £10 (in a field of 39).

Prize money in the men's doubles was: winners £250; runners-up £125; semi-finalists £75 (in a field of 15 pairs).

Prize money in the women's doubles was: winners £50; runners-up £25; semi-finalists £15 (in a field of 19 pairs).

Prize money in the mixed doubles was: winners £40; runners-up £20; semi-finalists £10 (in a field of 22).

TRIPLE CHAMPIONS

All three championships, singles, doubles and mixed doubles, were won in

	Men	Women
1924		Miss E Ryan (USA)
1930		Miss J Fry
1946		Mrs E W A Bostock
1947	E W Sturgess (SA)	
1948	E W Sturgess (SA)	
1949	P Masip (Spa)	
1951		Miss D J Hart (USA)
1954		Miss D J Hart (USA)
1967		Miss S V Wade

SINGLES CHAMPIONS AT FIRST ATTEMPT

	Men	Women
1924	R Lycett	Miss E Ryan (USA) (inaugural year)

Men	Women
1925 P D B Spence (SA)	
1926 J Brugnon (Fra)	
1927 R Lacoste (Fra)	
1929	Miss E L Heine (SA)
1930 H G N Lee	
1931 C Boussus (Fra)	Mme R Mathieu (Fra)
1938 Kho Sin Kie (Chn)	
1946 J E Harper (Aus)	
1947 E W Sturgess (SA)	
1949 P Masip (Spa)	
1950 J Drobny (Egy)	
1951	Miss D J Hart (USA)
1953 E Morea (Arg)	
1955 S Davidson (Swe)	
1956 J E Patty (USA)	
1959 L A Gerard (NZ)	
1961 R Emerson (Aus)	
1962	Miss R Schuurman (SA)
1965 J E Lundquist (Swe)	
1966 K N Fletcher (Aus)	
1968 K R Rosewall (Aus)	
1969 J D Newcombe (Aus)	Mrs B M Court (Aus)
1973 A Panatta (Ita)	
1975 M Orantes (Spa)	Miss J Newberry (USA)
1976 W Fibak (Pol)	
1978	Frl I Riedel (FRG)
1989 A Gimenez (Spa)	
1981 V Pecci (Por)	

The **longest men's singles** final was in 1969 when John Newcombe (Aus) beat Bob Hewitt (SA) 6–8 6–3 5–7 6–4 6–4, a total of **55 games.**

The **longest women's singles** final was in 1975 when Janet Newberry (USA) beat Terry Holladay (USA) 7–9 7–5 6–3, a total of **37 games.**

The **youngest champion** was Betty Nuthall (GB), women's doubles winner in 1926 at the age of **14 years 329 days.**

The youngest singles champion was Miss Nuthall, women's singles winner in 1927 at the age of **15 years 342 days.**

MOST PERILOUS TITLE DEFENCE

Angel Gimenez, defending his singles title in 1982, reached the final in four rounds. In the first he saved two match points in beating John Feaver 6–3 7–6 8–6, walked over P Rebolledo, beat Paul McNamee 3–6 7–6 6–2 after saving two match points and then beat J L Damiani 5–7 6–2 7–5 after saving a match point, thus hauling three successive matches back from the brink.

CHAMPIONSHIPS WON FROM MATCH POINT

1929 Women's Singles
Bobbie Heine (SA) beat Joan Ridley (GB) in the final 6–4 3–6 8–6, saving two match points at 5–6 in the third set.

1934 Women's Singles
Dorothy Round (GB) beat Peggy Scriven (GB) in the final 6–2 2–6 8–6, saving five match points in the third set.

1949 Women's Singles
Joan Curry (GB) beat Jean Quertier (GB) in the final 3–6 7–5 7–5, saving a match point at 4–5 in the second set.

1959 Men's Singles
Lew Gerard (NZ) beat Billy Knight (GB) in the final 3–6 2–6 6–2 7–5 9–7, saving two match points at 3–5 in the fifth set.

MOST PROLIFIC CHAMPIONS

Doris Hart (USA) and Virginia Wade (GB) each won **10 championships.**

Miss Hart, 1951 to 1954, won 4 singles, 4 doubles and 2 mixed doubles.

Miss Wade, 1967 to 1974, won 4 singles, 2 doubles and 4 mixed doubles.

Ann Jones (GB) won **9 championships,** 1960 to 1967 (4 singles, 5 doubles).

Betty Nuthall (GB) and Eric Sturgess (SA) won **8 championships.**

Miss Nuthall, 1927 to 1939, won 1 singles, 5 doubles and 2 mixed doubles.

Sturgess, the most prolific man, 1947 to 1951, won 2 singles, 3 doubles and 3 mixed doubles.

Fred Perry (GB), Jaroslav Drobny (Egy), Billy Knight (GB), Angela Mortimer (GB) and Shirley Brasher (GB) won **7 championships.** Perry, 1932 to 1936, won 5 singles, 1 doubles, 1 mixed. Drobny, 1950 to 1962, won 4 singles, 3 doubles. Knight, 1958 to 1964, won 3 singles, 1 doubles, 3 mixed. Miss Mortimer, 1955 to 1963, won 4 singles, 3 doubles. Mrs Brasher, 1955 to 1960, won 2 singles, 2 doubles, 3 mixed.

RESULTS

MEN'S SINGLES

Year	Winner	Runner-up	Final Score
1924	R Lycett	C van Lennep (Hol)	6–1 3–6 6–4 6–3
1925	P D B Spence (SA)	C H Kingsley	6–1 6–4 9–7
1926	J Brugnon (Fra)	H W Austin	7–5 4–6 3–6 8–6 6–3
1927	R Lacoste (Fra)	P D B Spence (SA)	6–1 6–2 6–2
1928	R Lacoste (Fra)	P D B Spence (SA)	6–2 6–2 6–2
1929	H W Austin	L Raymond (SA)	6–3 6–2 1–6 6–4
1930	H G N Lee	E C Peters	6–3 2–6 6–4 6–4
1931	C Boussus (Fra)	G P Hughes	8–6 6–4 4–6 6–2
1932	F J Perry	G L Rogers (Ire)	4–6 7–9 6–3 6–0 6–2
1933	F J Perry	H W Austin	2–6 7–5 7–5 6–2
1934	F J Perry	J H Crawford (Aus)	8–6 7–5 6–1
1935	F J Perry	H W Austin	0–6 6–4 3–6 6–2 6–0
1936	F J Perry	H W Austin	6–2 8–6 6–3
1937	H W Austin	H G N Lee	6–2 6–2 6–0
1938	Kho Sin Kie (Chn)	H W Austin	6–4 6–4 3–6 6–3
1939	Kho Sin Kie (Chn)	W C Choy (Chn)	7–5 6–1 6–4
1940–1945 not held			
1946	J E Harper (Aus)	D W Barton	7–5 6–2 6–1
1947	E W Sturgess (SA)	I Tloczynski (Pol)	11–9 6–1 6–4
1948	E W Sturgess (SA)	I Tloczynski (Pol)	6–2 6–3 6–1
1949	P Masip (Spa)	H Cochet (Fra)	6–3 4–6 6–2 9–7
1950	J Drobny (Egy)	G E Brown (Aus)	7–5 6–0 6–4
1951	J Drobny (Egy)	F Ampon (Phi)	6–4 6–2 6–0
1952	J Drobny (Egy)	F A Sedgman (Aus)	6–2 6–4 1–6 6–4
1953	E Morea (Arg)	F Ampon (Phi)	6–3 6–2 6–1
1954	A J Mottram	G L Paish	6–4 6–3 7–5
1955	S Davidson (Swe)	R Becker	11–9 6–3 6–1
1956	J E Patty (USA)	H Richardson (USA)	1–6 6–3 6–3 6–3
1957	J Drobny (Egy)	L A Hoad (Aus)	6–4 6–4 6–4
1958	W A Knight	G Merlo (Ita)	5–7 6–0 6–2 6–3
1959	L A Gerard (NZ)	W A Knight	3–6 2–6 6–2 7–5 9–7
1960	M G Davies	W A Knight	6–2 4–6 6–2 6–1
1961	R Emerson (Aus)	R Laver (Aus)	8–6 6–4 6–0
1962	R Laver (Aus)	I Crookenden (NZ)	6–3 6–3 6–3
1963	W A Knight	M F Mulligan (Aus)	5–7 6–3 6–1 6–3
1964	W A Knight	E C Drysdale (SA)	6–3 1–6 6–1 5–7 7–5
1965	J E Lundquist (Swe)	E C Drysdale (SA)	3–6 6–4 8–6 6–1
1966	K N Fletcher (Aus)	T S Okker (Hol)	7–5 6–4 (sic)
1967	J E Lundquist (Swe)	R A J Hewitt (Aus)	6–1 6–8 6–3 6–2
1968	K R Rosewall (Aus)	R Laver (Aus)	3–6 6–2 6–0 6–3
1969	J D Newcombe (Aus)	R A J Hewitt (SA)	6–8 6–3 5–7 6–4 6–4
1970	M Cox	R A J Hewitt (SA)	6–1 6–2 6–3
1971	G Battrick	Z Franulovic (Yug)	6–3 6–2 5–7 6–0
1972	R A J Hewitt (SA)	P Barthes (Fra)	6–2 6–4 6–3
1973	A Panatta (Ita)	I Nastase (Rom)	6–8 7–5 6–3 8–6
1974	I Nastase (Rom)	P Bertolucci (Ita)	6–1 6–3 6–2
1975	M Orantes (Spa)	P Proisy (Fra)	6–4 4–6 6–2 7–5
1976	W Fibak (Pol)	M Orantes (Spa)	6–2 7–9 6–2 6–2
1977	not held		
1978	J Higueras (Spa)	P Bertolucci (Ita)	6–2 6–1 6–3
1979	not held		
1980	A Gimenez (Spa)	S Glickstein (Isr)	3–6 6–3 6–3
1981	V Pecci (Por)	B Taroczy (Hun)	6–3 6–4
1982	M Orantes (Spa)	A Gimenez (Spa)	6–2 6–0

WOMEN'S SINGLES

Year	Winner	Runner-up	Final Score
1924	Miss E Ryan (USA)	Mrs A E Beamish	6–2 6–2
1925	Miss E Ryan (USA)	Miss J Fry	6–2 6–2
1926	Miss J Fry	Mrs P H Watson	6–1 7–9 6–1
1927	Miss B Nuthall	Miss E R Clarke	8–6 6–2
1928	Miss E A Goldsack	Miss J C Ridley	8–6 6–4
1929	Miss E L Heine (SA)	Miss J C Ridley	6–4 3–6 8–6
1930	Miss J Fry	Mrs W D List	6–1 2–6 6–2
1931	Mme R Mathieu (Fra)	Miss M Heeley	6–4 6–4
1932	Mme R Mathieu (Fra)	Miss D E Round	6–1 6–2
1933	Miss D E Round	Miss H Jacobs (USA)	3–6 6–2 6–3
1934	Miss D E Round	Miss M C Scriven	6–2 2–6 8–6
1935	Miss K E Stammers	Miss M C Scriven	6–2 6–2
1936	Miss K E Stammers	Sta A Lizana (Chi)	7–5 7–5
1937	Sta A Lizana (Chi)	Miss M C Scriven	7–5 6–3
1938	Miss M C Scriven	Miss N Wynne (Aus)	7–5 6–2
1939	Miss K E Stammers	Mrs R Ellis (Chi)	6–3 6–3
1940–1945 not held			
1946	Mrs E W A Bostock	Mrs M Menzies	6–3 6–4
1947	Mrs N Bolton	Miss P J Curry	7–5 6–3
1948	Mrs B E Hilton	Mrs D R Bocquet	6–1 6–4
1949	Miss P J Curry	Miss J Quertier	3–6 7–5 7–5
1950	Miss P J Curry	Mrs H Weiss (Arg)	8–6 8–6
1951	Miss D J Hart (USA)	Mrs J J Walker-Smith	6–4 8–6
1952	Miss D J Hart (USA)	Miss S J Fry (USA)	6–4 6–3
1953	Miss D J Hart (USA)	Miss S J Fry (USA)	6–3 4–6 6–4
1954	Miss D J Hart (USA)	Mrs A J Mottram	6–1 6–3
1955	Miss A Mortimer	Miss A Buxton	6–1 6–1
1956	Miss A Mortimer	Miss S J Bloomer	7–5 5–7 6–1
1957	Miss S J Bloomer	Miss P E Ward	3–6 6–2 6–3
1958	Miss S J Bloomer	Miss A S Haydon	6–4 6–4
1959	Miss A Mortimer	Miss C C Truman	6–4 2–6 6–4
1960	Miss C C Truman	Miss A S Haydon	6–2 6–2
1961	Miss A Mortimer	Miss D M Catt	6–2 6–3
1962	Miss R Schuurman (SA)	Miss A Mortimer	5–7 6–2 6–4
1963	Mrs P F Jones	Miss N Baylon (Arg)	6–0 1–6 9–7
1964	Mrs P F Jones	Miss J Lehane (Aus)	6–2 12–10
1965	Mrs P F Jones	Miss A M Van Zyl (SA)	7–5 6–1
1966	Mrs P F Jones	Miss S V Wade	6–3 6–1
1967	Miss S V Wade	Mrs P F Jones	6–1 10–8
1968	Miss S V Wade	Miss W M Shaw	6–4 6–1
1969	Mrs B M Court (Aus)	Miss W M Shaw	5–7 6–4 6–4
1970	Mrs B M Court (Aus)	Miss S V Wade	6–2 6–4
1971	Mrs B M Court (Aus)	Miss E Goolagong (Aus)	7–5 6–1
1972	Miss E Goolagong (Aus)	Frl H Masthoff (FGR)	6–0 6–4
1973	Miss S V Wade	Miss E Goolagong (Aus)	6–4 6–4
1974	Miss S V Wade	Miss J M Heldman (USA)	6–1 3–6 6–1
1975	Miss J Newberry (USA)	Miss T Holladay (USA)	7–9 7–5 6–3
1976	Frl H Masthoff (FRG)	Miss S Barker	5–7 6–3 6–2
1977 not held			
1978	Frl I Riedel (FRG)	Miss B R Thompson	6–2 6–1
1979, 1980 not held			
1981	Miss J M Durie	Mlle S Amiach (Fra)	7–5 1–6 6–3
1982 not held			

DOUBLES CHAMPIONS

Year	Men's Doubles	Women's Doubles	Mixed Doubles
1924	F L Riseley & J D P Wheatley	Mrs D C Shepherd-Barron & Miss E Ryan (USA)	R Lycett & Miss E Ryan (USA)
1925	C H Kingsley & H S Lewis-Barclay	Miss E L Colyer & Miss E Ryan (USA)	P D B Spence (SA) & Miss E L Colyer
1926	G R O Crole-Rees & C G Eames	Miss B Nuthall & Miss G R Sterry	D A Hodges & Miss J Fry
1927	J Brugnon (Fra) & R Lacoste (Fra)	Miss M V Chamberlain & Mrs C O Tuckey	P D B Spence (SA) & Miss B Nuthall
1928	C H Kingsley & P D B Spence (SA)	Miss B Nuthall & Mrs P H Watson	H Cochet (Fra) & Miss E Bennett
1929	G R O Crole-Rees & C G Eames	Miss E A Goldsack & Miss J C Ridley	G P Hughes & Miss J Fry
1930	H W Austin & J S Olliff	Miss J Fry & Miss E H Harvey	C H Kingsley & Miss J Fry
1931	H W Austin & C H Kingsley	Miss B Nuthall & Miss E Ryan (USA)	F J Perry & Miss M Heeley
1932	J S Olliff & F J Perry	Miss B Nuthall & Mrs E F Whittingstall	A Martin Legeay (Fra) & Mme R Mathieu (Fra)
1933	J H Crawford (Aus) & D P Turnbull (Aus)	Miss M Heeley & Miss D E Round	H G N Lee & Miss F James
1934	J H Crawford (Aus) & V B McGrath (Aus)	Mrs L A Godfree & Miss S Noel	R Miki (Jap) & Miss D E Round
1935	C E Malfroy (NZ) & A C Stedman (NZ)	Mrs J B Pittman & Miss A M Yorke	C R D Tuckey & Miss M C Scriven
1936	G P Hughes & C R D Tuckey	Miss F James & Miss K E Stammers	F J Perry & Miss D E Round
1937	C E Hare & F H D Wilde	Miss E M Dearman & Miss J Ingram	F H D Wilde & Miss M Whitmarsh
1938	Kho Sin Kie (Chn) & G L Rogers (Ire)	Miss E M Dearman & Miss J Ingram	C Boussus (Fra) & Miss N Wynne (Aus)
1939	H Billington & J S Olliff	Miss J Nicoll & Miss B Nuthall	C E Malfroy (NZ) & Miss B Nuthall
1940–1945	not held		
1946	J E Harper & C E Malfroy (NZ)	Mrs E W A Bostock & Mrs M Menzies	D W Butler & Mrs E W A Bostock
1947	E Fannin (SA) & E W Sturgess (SA)	Mrs N Bolton (Aus) & Mrs H C Hopman (Aus)	E W Sturgess (SA) & Mrs S P Summers (SA)
1948	E W Sturgess (SA) & R van Meegeren (Hol)	Mrs B E Hilton & Mrs M Menzies	E W Sturgess (SA) & Miss J Quertier
1949	J Bartroli (Spa) & P Masip (Spa)	Mrs W C J Halford & Mrs B E Hilton	P Masip (Spa) & Miss J Gannon
1950	V Cernik (Cze) & J Drobny (Egy)	Mrs B E Hilton & Miss K L A Tuckey	G E Brown (Aus) & Mrs B E Hilton
1951	L Norgarb (SA) & E W Sturgess (SA)	Miss S J Fry (USA) & Miss D J Hart (USA)	E W Sturgess (SA) & Miss D J Hart (USA)
1952	J Drobny (Egy) & F A Sedgman (Aus)	Miss S J Fry (USA) & Miss D J Hart (USA)	G L Paish & Mrs I Rinkel-Quertier
1953	F Ampon (Phi) & J Deyro (Phi)	Miss S J Fry (USA) & Miss D J Hart (USA)	G L Paish & Mrs I Rinkel-Quertier
1954	K Nielsen (Den) & T Ulrich (Den)	Miss D J Hart (USA) & Mrs A J Mottram	K Nielsen (Den) & Miss D J Hart (USA)
1955	A J Mottram & G L Paish	Miss S J Bloomer & Miss P E Ward	R N Howe (Aus) & Miss J A Shilcock
1956	R N Howe (Aus) & U Schmidt (Swe)	Miss A Buxton & Miss D R Hard (USA)	R N Howe (Aus) & Miss P E Ward
1957	G L Forbes (SA) & A Segal (SA)	Miss S J Bloomer & Miss D R Hard (USA)	R N Howe (Aus) & Miss D R Hard (USA)
1958	M G Davies & R K Wilson	Miss J A Shilcock & Miss P E Ward	W A Knight & Miss S J Bloomer
1959	G L Forbes (SA) & A Segal (SA)	Miss A Mortimer & Miss P E Ward	W A Knight & Miss S J Bloomer
1960	M G Davies & W A Knight	Miss A S Haydon & Miss A Mortimer	W A Knight & Mrs C W Brasher
1961	R Emerson (Aus) & R Laver (Aus)	Miss A S Haydon & Miss Y Ramirez (Mex)	A R Mills & Mrs A R Mills
1962	J Drobny (Egy) & R Laver (Aus)	Miss R Schuurman (SA) & Miss D E Starkie	M P Hann & Miss C Yates-Bell
1963	R A J Hewitt (Aus) & F S Stolle (Aus)	Mrs P F Jones & Miss A Mortimer	A R Mills & Mrs A R Mills
1964	K Diepraam (SA) & E C Drysdale (SA)	Miss J Lehane (Aus) & Frl H Schultze (FGR)	R N Howe (Aus) & Miss J Lehane (Aus)
1965	I Buding (FRG) & A R Mills	Miss D E Starkie & Miss A M Van Zyl (SA)	R Maud (SA) & Miss G Swan (SA)
1966	R Taylor & R K Wilson	Mrs P F Jones & Miss D E Starkie	P Van Lingen (Hol) & Miss F Urban (Can)
1967	R A J Hewitt (SA) & F D McMillan (SA)	Mrs P F Jones & Miss S V Wade	R Maud (SA) & Miss S V Wade
1968	R Emerson (Aus) & R Laver (Aus)	Mrs G T Janes & Miss F E Truman	R N Howe (Aus) & Miss S V Wade
1969	R A J Hewitt (SA) & F D McMillan (SA)	Mrs B M Court (Aus) & Miss J A Tegart (Aus)	R Maud (SA) & Miss S V Wade
1970	T S Okker (Hol) & A D Roche (Aus)	Mrs B M Court (Aus) & Mrs D E Dalton (Aus)	R A J Hewitt (SA) & Mrs L W King (USA)
1971	W W Bowrey (Aus) & O K Davidson (Aus)	Mrs P W Curtis (USA) & Mlle F Durr (Fra)	F D McMillan (SA) & Mrs D E Dalton (Aus)
1972	R A J Hewitt (SA) & F D McMillan (SA)	Miss E Goolagong (Aus) & Miss H F Gourlay (Aus)	F D McMillan (SA) & Mme J B Chanfreau (Fra)
1973	J Gisbert (Spa) & I Nastase (Rom)	Miss P Coleman (Aus) & Miss W Turnbull (Aus)	F D McMillan (SA) & Miss S V Wade
1974	J Gisbert (Spa) & I Nastase (Rom)	Miss J M Heldman & Miss S V Wade	M J Farrell & Miss L J Charles
1975	J Gisbert (Spa) & M Orantes (Spa)	Miss L J Charles & Miss S Mappin	D A Lloyd & Miss S A Walsh (USA)
1976	W Fibak (Pol) & F McNair (USA)	Miss L Boshoff (SA) & Miss I S Kloss (SA)	C Dowdeswell (Rho) & Miss L Boshoff (SA)
1977	not held	not held	not held
1978	L Sanders (Hol) & R Thung (Hol)	Miss J M Durie & Miss A E Hobbs	R A Lewis & Miss L J Charles
1979	not held	not held	not held
1980	C Edwards & E Edwards	not held	not held
1981	R Cano (Arg) & V Pecci (Per)	Miss J M Durie & Miss D A Jevans	not held
1982	P McNamee (Aus) & C J Mottram	not held	not held

THE COUNTY CHAMPIONSHIPS

The Inter-County Championship was instituted for men's teams in 1895 and played as a knock-out competition on grass courts. A similar competition for women was begun in 1899. The format comprises six players a side with three doubles pairs playing each other. In 1925 both events were changed to a league system, divided in groups of six counties with each team playing all others in the same group in the course of one week. Two teams earn promotion or suffer relegation.

The Inter-County Championship on Hard Court began for both men and women's teams in 1920 and has been a knock-out event throughout. Six players comprise each team. The men play only singles, twelve in all. Women play six singles and three doubles.

	Number of Times Champion (to 1981)		
	Grass Courts	Hard Courts	Total

MEN'S CHAMPIONSHIPS

Middlesex	35	19	54
Surrey	14	17	31
Essex	5	7	12
Warwickshire	5	6	11
Gloucestershire	9	–	9
Lancashire	4	3	7
Yorkshire	2	1	3
Staffordshire	1	–	1

WOMEN'S CHAMPIONSHIPS

Surrey	36	27	63
Middlesex	21	19	40
Warwickshire	4	2	6
Yorkshire	2	3	5
Devonshire	3	1	4
Kent	2	1	3
Cheshire	1	–	1
Durham	1	–	1
Sussex	1	–	1

The longest sequence of victories was had by **Middlesex** in the men's grass championship with **9 consecutive wins** 1924 to 1932.

Middlesex also had the longest sequence in the men's hard court championship with **7 consecutive wins** 1956 to 1962.

In the **women's hard court** championship **Middlesex** won **6 years** 1952 to 1957 and **Surrey 6 years** also 1965 to 1970. In the **women's**

grass championship the highest sequential success was **4 years,** by **Surrey** on two occasions, 1959 to 1962 and 1968 to 1971.

Somerset men, languishing in the bottom Group VII in 1972, earned promotion every subsequent year until they joined the top championship group at Eastbourne in 1978.

The same feat was also accomplished by **Surrey and Yorkshire men** who, with Surrey first and Yorkshire second, climbed from Group VII in 1933 to join the championship group 6 years later in 1939. In their case, however, their sojourn in the bottom group had been occasioned not by lack of form but because a dispute had made them withdraw from the competition in 1928.

The **most one sided** success in the grass court championship was achieved by **Middlesex women** in 1951. They won the championship group at Bournemouth by beating Sussex, Surrey, Kent, Yorkshire and Hampshire and winning **43 rubbers** out of a possible 45. Their sets totalled 87.

The **most one sided success among the men** was in Group VII at Minehead in 1974 when the **North of Scotland** won with **41 rubbers.**

The **most one sided men's championship win** was by **Surrey** in 1971. At Eastbourne they won a total of **40 rubbers, 83 sets.** This was one set better than their victory with 40 rubbers, 82 sets the following year.

The **worst** result at 'County Week' was by **Westmorland** in Group VII in the women's championship. In 1957, 1967 and 1969 they won nil rubbers and only 2 sets.

Westmorland also endured the worst result among the men. In 1964 in Group VII they won **1 rubber** and **2 sets.**

The **most one sided** defeat inflicted by one county on another was in Group VI in 1924 when Surrey men beat Cornwall men **9 rubbers to 0, 18 sets to 0, 109 games to 21.**

THE WEMBLEY TOURNAMENT

The Empire Pool and Sports Arena at Wembley was from the first the major centre in Great Britain for professional lawn tennis. On boards laid over the skating rink and swimming pool, the original functions of the new sports centre, a round robin tournament was played during the week beginning 19 November 1934. Ellsworth Vines (USA), Hans Nusslein (Ger), Bill Tilden (USA), Martin Plaa (Fra), Bruce Barnes (USA) and Dan Maskell (GB) were the competitors, finishing in that order.

In 1951 the event was officially recognised by the British Lawn Tennis Association and renamed the London Indoor Professional Championships. It became arguably the leading event on the professional calendar and increasingly flourished until, in 1968, the onset of open lawn tennis removed its special status.

The **longest final,** and a match often listed when matches of outstanding quality are recorded, was in 1956 when Ricardo Gonzales (USA) beat Frank Sedgman (Aus) 4–6 11–9 11–9 9–7, a total of **66 games.**

Ken Rosewall (Aus) was historically the **outstanding competitor** at Wembley. He competed 14 times in 15 years 1957 to 1971 and won the singles **6 times,** the doubles **9 times.**

The indoor court at Wembley. The American John McEnroe is arguing with the umpire during his final against Jimmy Connors in 1981.

RESULTS

Year	Event	Winner's Prize	Winner	Runner-up	Score	Doubles Winners
1934			E Vines (USA)	H Nusslein (Ger)	Round Robin	
1935			E Vines (USA)	W T Tilden (USA)	6–1 6–3 5–7 3–6 6–3	W T Tilden & E Vines (USA)
1936			E Vines (USA)	H Nusslein (Ger)	6–4 6–4 6–2	
1937			H Nusslein (Ger)	W T Tilden (USA)	6–4 3–6 6–3 2–6 6–3	
1938			H Nusslein (Ger)	W T Tilden (USA)	7–5 3–6 6–3 6–3 6–2	
1939			J D Budge (USA)	H Nusslein (Ger)	13–11 2–6 6–4	
1940–1948 not held						
1949		£350	J A Kramer (USA)	R L Riggs (USA)	6–4 6–2 6–3	J A Kramer (USA) & R L Riggs (USA)
1950		£350	R A Gonzales (USA)	W Van Horn (USA)	6–3 6–2 6–4	J D Budge (USA) & R A Gonzales (USA)

Year	Event	Winner's Prize	Winner	Runner-up	Score	Doubles Winners
1951	London Indoor Professional Champs	£350	R A Gonzales (USA)	F Segura (USA)	6–2 6–2 2–6 6–4	R A Gonzales (USA) & F Segura (USA)
1952	London Indoor Professional Champs	£350	R A Gonzales (USA)	J A Kramer (USA)	3–6 3–6 6–2 6–4 7–5	R A Gonzales (USA) & F Segura (USA)
1953	London Indoor Professional Champs	£350	F A Sedgman (Aus)	R A Gonzales (USA)	6–1 6–2 6–2	J D Budge (USA) & F A Sedgman (Aus)
1954, 1955 not held						
1956	London Indoor Professional Champs	£425	R A Gonzales (USA)	F A Sedgman (Aus)	4–6 11–9 11–9 9–7	R A Gonzales (USA) & M A Trabert (USA)
1957	London Indoor Professional Champs	£425	K R Rosewall (Aus)	F Segura (USA)	1–6 6–3 6–4 3–6 6–4	L A Hoad (Aus) & K R Rosewall (Aus)
1958	London Indoor Professional Champs	£1000	F A Sedgman (Aus)	M A Trabert (USA)	6–4 6–3 6–4	R A Gonzales (USA) & K R Rosewall (Aus)
1959	London Indoor Professional Champs	£1000	M J Anderson (Aus)	F Segura (USA)	4–6 6–4 3–6 6–3 8–6	L A Hoad (Aus) & K R Rosewall (Aus)
1960	London Indoor Professional Champs	£1000	K R Rosewall (Aus)	F Segura (USA)	5–7 8–6 6–1 6–3	K R Rosewall (Aus) & F A Sedgman (Aus)
1961	London Indoor Professional Champs	£1000	K R Rosewall (Aus)	L A Hoad (Aus)	6–3 3–6 6–2 6–3	L A Hoad (Aus) & K R Rosewall (Aus)
1962	London Indoor Professional Champs	£1000	K R Rosewall (Aus)	L A Hoad (Aus)	6–4 5–7 15–13 7–5	L A Hoad (Aus) & K R Rosewall (Aus)
1963	London Indoor Professional Champs	£1000	K R Rosewall (Aus)	L A Hoad (Aus)	6–4 6–2 4–6 6–3	A Olmedo (USA) & F A Sedgman (Aus)
1964	London Indoor Professional Champs	£1000	R G Laver (Aus)	K R Rosewall (Aus)	7–5 4–6 5–7 8–6 8–6	L A Hoad (Aus) & K R Rosewall (Aus)
1965	London Indoor Professional Champs	£1000	R G Laver (Aus)	A Gimeno (Spa)	6–2 6–3 6–4	E Buchholtz (USA) & R G Laver (Aus)
1966	London Indoor Professional Champs	£1000	R G Laver (Aus)	K R Rosewall (Aus)	6–2 6–2 6–3	L A Hoad (Aus) & K R Rosewall (Aus)
1967	London Indoor Professional Champs	£1000	R G Laver (Aus)	K R Rosewall (Aus)	2–6 6–1 1–6 8–6 6–2	R G Laver (Aus) & F S Stolle (Aus)
1968	Kramer Tournaments of Champions	£5000	K R Rosewall (Aus)	J D Newcombe (Aus)	6–4 4–6 7–5 6–4	J D Newcombe (Aus) & A D Roche (Aus)
1969	British Covered Court Champs*	£3000	R G Laver (Aus)	A D Roche (Aus)	6–4 6–1 6–3	R S Emerson (Aus) & R G Laver (Aus)
1970	British Covered Court Champs*	£3000	R G Laver (Aus)	C Richey (USA)	6–3 6–4 7–5	K R Rosewall (Aus) & S R Smith (USA)
1971	British Covered Court Champs*	£3000	I Nastase (Rom)	R G Laver (Aus)	3–6 6–3 3–6 6–4 6–4	R A J Hewitt (SA) & F D McMillan (SA)
1972–1975 not held						
1976	Benson & Hedges Tournament	£12 500	J S Connors (USA)	R Tanner (USA)	3–6 7–6 6–4	S R Smith (USA) & R Tanner (USA)
1977	Benson & Hedges Tournament	£15 000	B Borg (Swe)	J M Lloyd	6–4 6–4 6–3	A A Mayer (USA) & F D McMillan (SA)
1978	Benson & Hedges Tournament	£18 200	J P McEnroe (USA)	Tim Gullikson (USA)	6–7 6–4 7–6 6–2	P Fleming (USA) & J P McEnroe (USA)
1979	Benson & Hedges Tournament	£17 238	J P McEnroe (USA)	H Solomon (USA)	6–3 6–3 7–5	P Fleming (USA) & J P McEnroe (USA)
1980	Benson & Hedges Tournament	£15 000	J P McEnroe (USA)	G Mayer (USA)	6–4 6–3 6–3	P Fleming (USA) & J P McEnroe (USA)
1981	Benson & Hedges Tournament	£17 000	J S Connors (USA)	J P McEnroe (USA)	3–6 2–6 6–3 6–4 6–2	S E Stewart (USA) & F Taygan (USA)

* Women's events were also played. 1969 Singles, Final: Mrs P F Jones beat Mrs L W King (USA) 9–11 6–2 9–7.
Doubles: Mrs P F Jones & Miss S V Wade.
1970 Singles, Final: Mrs L W King (USA) beat Mrs P F Jones 8–6 3–6 6–1.
Doubles: Miss R Casals (USA) & Mrs L W King (USA).
1971 Singles, Final: Mrs L W King (USA) beat Mlle F Durr (Fra) 7–1 5–7 7–5.
Doubles: Mlle F Durr (Fra) & Miss S V Wade.

BRITISH JUNIOR CHAMPIONSHIPS

Junior Championships of Great Britain for both boys and girls are staged on three different surfaces, hard courts, wood and grass. The limiting age is 18 on the last day of the preceding year with separate Under 16, Under 14 and Under 12 events being staged on hard courts and grass since 1982.

The oldest of the events is the hard court championship. It was first staged at Ventnor in 1908. Singles only were played with an entry of 13 boys and 5 girls. Doubles events started in 1921 at Surbiton. It remained a peripatetic tournament until 1924 when it settled as a hard court event at the All England Club, Wimbledon.

The Junior Covered Court Championships were initiated at Queen's Club, London, December 1955/January 1956. The Junior Grass Court Championships began in 1970 at Devonshire Park, Eastbourne.

The **youngest champion** was **Betty Nuthall**. She won the first of seven titles in 1924 at the age of **13 years 113 days**. She was unbeaten in all events for three years, 1924 to 1926. The mixed title was divided in 1924 and not played in 1925.

The **youngest boy champion** was **Stanley Matthews**, first winner of the singles in 1960 at Wimbledon when **14 years 287 days old**. He won 8 titles at Wimbledon and, with three covered court titles, **11 in all**. He won the Wimbledon hard court singles for three consecutive years, 1960, 1961 and 1962 and was beaten by Graham Stilwell in his fourth final in 1963.

Most junior titles in Great Britain were won by **Sue Barker**. Indoors she won the singles 1972, doubles 1972 and 1973. On grass she won the singles three times, 1972, 1973 and 1974 (after being the losing finalist in 1971) and the doubles twice, 1973, 1974. On hard courts she was singles champion 1973, doubles champion 1973, 1974 and mixed winner 1972, 1973—a total of **13 titles**. To this can be added her success as winner of the National Age Group Under 16 singles in 1972.

Three players have been junior singles champion on all three surfaces at the same time. Glynis Coles (in 1971) and Jo Durie (1976) were winners in the one year. Kate Brasher was hard court champion in 1978 and still the holder when she took the indoor and grass titles in 1979.

BRITISH COVERED COURT CHAMPIONSHIPS

The British Covered Court Championships were first played at the Hyde Park Club in Maida Vale, London, in 1885 and moved to its better known home at Queen's Club in 1895. The playing surface was wood. For many years it ranked as the second most important British event after the Wimbledon Championships.

It was not until 1935 that the British Lawn Tennis Association granted recognition as an official championship. Financial problems caused its abandonment in 1958 and it did not take place in 1966 and 1967. There was a revival as a leg of the Dewar Cup series in 1968. In 1969 it became a fully sponsored event and was moved to the Wembley Arena. There the championship made its last appearance in 1971.

The **most frequent winner** of the British Covered Court Championship was **Laurie Doherty**. Between 1898 and 1906 he won the men's doubles 9 times, the men's singles 6 times and the mixed doubles twice—that is **17 titles**.

Laurie Doherty and **Jean Borotra** both won the singles for six successive years. **Borotra** won the **record number** of singles, **11 in all between 1926 and 1949**. In the latter year he was 51 years old. He reached the singles final in 8 successive years, 1928 to 1935. With 5 wins in the mixed doubles Borotra's titles numbered 16.

Among women the greatest number of titles was won by **Dorothea Lambert Chambers**. Between 1904 and 1919 she won the women's singles 7 times and the mixed 3—that is **10 titles** in all.

Two men and two women have been **triple champions**. **Laurie Doherty** won all three events twice, 1902 and 1903 and **Anthony Wilding** did so in 1907. The feat did not become possible for women until the start of the women's doubles in 1929. **Anne Shilcock** was triple champion in 1955, **Ann Jones** in 1965.

The championships filled a double role in 1908 when the events were part of the Olympic Games. In 1968 it was one of the legs in the Dewar Cup series.

The **first overseas winner** was **E L Williams** of South Africa taking the men's singles in **1886**. **Elizabeth Ryan (USA)** was the first overseas winner of the women's singles in **1920**.

The **most precarious match** was arguably the semi-final of the mixed doubles in 1928 when J D P Wheatley and Eileen Bennett beat Pat Spence and Betty Nuthall 7–9 7–5 16–14 after saving **17 match points**.

RESULTS

Year	Men's Singles	Women's Singles	Men's Doubles	Women's Doubles	Mixed Doubles
WINNERS					

Played at the Hyde Park Club:

Year	Men's Singles	Women's Singles	Men's Doubles	Women's Doubles	Mixed Doubles
1885	H F Lawford				
1886	E L Williams				
1887	E W Lewis				
1888	E W Lewis				
1889	E W Lewis				
1890	E W Lewis	Miss L Jacks	G W Hillyard & H S Scrivener		
1891	E W Lewis	Miss M Shackle	G W Hillyard & H S Scrivener		
1892	E G Meers	Miss M Shackle	H S Mahony & E G Meers		
1893	H S Mahony	Miss M Shackle	H S Mahony & E G Meers		
1894	H S Mahony	Miss L Austin	H S Mahony & E G Meers		

Played at Queen's Club.

Year	Men's Singles	Women's Singles	Men's Doubles	Women's Doubles	Mixed Doubles
1895	E W Lewis	Miss C Cooper	W V Eaves & C H Martin		
1896	E W Lewis	Miss L Austin	W V Eaves & C H Martin		
1897	W V Eaves	Miss L Austin	G Greville & H A Nisbet		
1898	W V Eaves	Miss L Austin	H L Doherty & R F Doherty		R F Doherty & Miss C Cooper
1899	W V Eaves	Miss L Austin	H L Doherty & R F Doherty		R F Doherty & Miss C Cooper
1900	A W Gore	Miss T Lowther			R F Doherty & Miss C Cooper
1901	H L Doherty	Mrs G W Hillyard	H L Doherty & R F Doherty		G W Hillyard & Mrs Hillyard
1902	H L Doherty	Miss T Lowther	H L Doherty & R F Doherty		H L Doherty & Miss T Lowther
1903	H L Doherty	Miss T Lowther	H L Doherty & R F Doherty		
1904	H L Doherty	Miss D K Douglass	H L Doherty & G W Hillyard		C Greville & Mrs Greville
1905	H L Doherty	Miss H Lane	H L Doherty & G W Hillyard		R F Doherty & Miss G Eastlake Smith
1906	H L Doherty	Miss D K Douglass	H L Doherty & R F Doherty		A F Wilding (NZ) & Miss D K Douglass
1907	A F Wilding	Miss G Eastlake Smith	M J G Ritchie & A F Wilding (NZ)		A F Wilding (NZ) & Miss G Eastlake Smith
1908	A W Gore	Mrs R Lambert Chambers	M J G Ritchie & A F Wilding		A F Wilding & Miss G Eastlake-Smith
1909	M J G Ritchie	Miss D Boothby	A W Gore & H Roper Barrett		F W Rahe (Ger) & Miss E L Bosworth
1910	F G Lowe	Mrs R Lambert Chambers	S N Doust (Aus) & L O S Poidevin (USA)		H Roper Barrett & Mrs O'Neill
1911	A H Gobert (Fra)	Mrs R Lambert Chambers	A H Gobert (Fra) & M J G Ritchie		A F Wilding (NZ) & Mrs R Lambert Chambers
1912	A H Gobert (Fra)	Miss E D Holman	S N Doust (Aus) & A F Wilding (NZ)		A H Gobert (Fra) & Mrs O'Neill
1913	P M Davson	Mrs R Lambert Chambers	S N Doust (Aus) & A F Wilding (NZ)		S N Doust (Aus) & Mrs R Lambert Chambers
1914	M J G Ritchie	Miss E D Holman	P M Davson & T M Mavrogordato		E Gwynne Evans & Miss E D Holman
1915–1918 not held					
1919	P M Davson	Mrs R Lambert Chambers	R W Heath (Aus) & R Lycett		R Lycett & Miss E Ryan (USA)
1920	A H Gobert (Fra)	Miss E Ryan (USA)	A H Gobert (Fra) & R Lycett		R Lycett & Miss E Ryan (USA)
1921	A H Gobert (Fra)	Miss E D Holman	P M Davson & T M Mavrogordato		F M B Fisher (NZ) & Mrs G Peacock (Ind)
1922	A H Gobert (Fra)	Miss E D Holman	S N Doust (Aus) & R Lycett		R Lycett & Miss K McKane
1923	J D P Wheatley	Mrs R C Clayton	A W Asthalter & S N Doust (Aus)		A W Asthalter & Mrs H Edgington
1924	P D B Spence (SA)	Mrs A E Beamish	C H Kingsley & P D B Spence (SA)		C G Eames & Mrs A E Beamish
1925	S M Jacob (Ind)	Miss J Reid-Thomas	C H Kingsley & P D B Spence (SA)		P D B Spence (SA) & Miss E L Colyer
1926	J Borotra (Fra)	Miss P Saunders	G R O Crole-Rees & C G Eames		S N Doust & Miss J C Ridley
1927	E Higgs	Miss E Bennett	G R O Crole Rees & C G Eames		G R O Crole-Rees & Mrs J Hill
1928	J Borotra (Fra)	Mrs L A Godfree	C H Kingsley & J D P Wheatley		G R O Crole-Rees & Mrs L R C Michell

Year	WINNERS Men's Singles	Women's Singles	Men's Doubles	Women's Doubles	Mixed Doubles
1929	J Borotra (Fra)	Mrs L R C Michell	G R O Crole-Rees & C G Eames	Mrs L R C Michell & Miss M E Dix	G R O Crole-Rees & Mrs L R C Michell
1930	J Borotra (Fra)	Miss J C Ridley	H W Austin & J S Olliff	not held	C H Kingsley & Miss J C Ridley
1931	J Borotra (Fra)	Miss M Heeley	H W Austin & J S Olliff	Mrs L R C Michell & Miss E H Harvey	J S Olliff & Miss P G Brazier
1932	J Borotra (Fra)	Miss M C Scriven	H G N Lee & G L Tuckett	Mrs L R C Michell & Miss D E Round	J Borotra (Fra) & Miss B Nuthall
1933	J Borotra (Fra)	Mrs M R King	V G Kirby (SA) & & G L Rogers (Ire)	Mrs L R C Michell & Miss M C Scriven	J Borotra (Fra) & Miss B Nuthall
1934	H W Austin	Mrs M R King	J S Olliff & D Prenn (Ger)	Mrs J B Pittman & Miss A M Yorke	J Borotra (Fra) & Miss M C Scriven
1935	J Borotra (Fra)	Miss M C Scriven	D N Jones (USA) & D Prenn (Ger)	Mrs J B Pittman & Miss A M Yorke	J Borotra (Fra) & Miss M C Scriven
1936	K Schroeder (Swe)	Sen. A Lizana (Chi)	C E Hare & F H D Wilde	Miss M Whitmarsh & Miss A M Yorke	J S Olliff & Miss F James
1937	H W Austin	Miss M C Scriven	D W Butler & F H D Wilde	Miss J Saunders & Miss V E Scott	K Schroeder (Swe) & Miss J Saunders
1938	J Borotra (Fra)	Miss M C Scriven	H Billington & J S Olliff	Miss E M Dearman & Miss J Ingram	C M Jones & Miss E H Harvey
1939–1947 not held					
1948	J Borotra (Fra)	Miss G C Hoahing	C J Hovell & C M Jones	Miss P J Curry & Miss J Quertier	J Borotra (Fra) & Mrs G Walter
1949	J Borotra (Fra)	Miss P J Curry	H Billington & G L Paish	Mrs W C J Halford & Miss P A O'Connell	G L Paish & Miss J Quertier
1950	J Drobny (Egy)	Miss J Quertier	H Cochet (Fra) & J Drobny (Egy)	Mrs R Anderson & Miss P J Curry	G L Paish & Miss J Quertier
1951	G L Paish	Miss J S V Partridge	A J Mottram & G L Paish	Mrs E W Dawson Scott & Miss E M Wilford	G L Paish & Miss J Quertier
1952	J Drobny (Egy)	Miss A Mortimer	A J Mottram & G L Paish	Miss H M Fletcher & Mrs J Rinkel-Quertier	G L Paish & Mrs Rinkel-Quertier
1953	J Drobny (Egy)	Miss A Mortimer	J E Barrett & D L M Black (Rho)	Mme P Chatrier (Fra) & Miss J A Shilcock	G D Oakley & Mme P Chatrier (Fra)
1954	J Drobny (Egy)	Miss A Mortimer	J Drobny (Egy) & R K Wilson	Miss R J R Bulleid & Miss A Mortimer	M G Davies & Miss D Spiers
1955	W Skonecki (Pol)	Miss J A Shilcock	R N Howe (Aus) & W Skonecki (Pol)	Miss J Shilcock & Miss P E Ward	W A Knight & Miss J A Shilcock
1956	A Huber	Miss A Buxton	G L Paish & A R Mills	G L Paish & J A Pickard	not held
1960	W A Knight	Miss A Mortimer	M J Sangster & R K Wilson	Miss S M Armstrong & Mrs C W Brasher	W A Knight & Mrs C W Brasher
1961	J A Pickard	Miss A Mortimer	M P Coni & M A Otway (NZ)	Miss D M Catt & Miss A Mortimer	J R McDonald (NZ) & Miss D M Catt
1962	R K Wilson	Miss A S Haydon	A R Mills & R K Wilson	Miss A S Haydon & Miss C C Truman	P Damon (Fra) & Mme Darmon (Mex)
1963	R K Wilson	Miss D M Catt	B Jovanovic (Yug) & N Pilic (Yug)	Mrs P F Jones & Miss R Schuurman (SA)	G D Oakley & Miss C C Truman
1964	M J Sangster	Mrs P F Jones	R Taylor & R K Wilson	Miss P R McClenaughan (Aus) & Miss F M E Toyne (Aus)	R N Howe (Aus) & Miss P R McClenaughan (Aus)
1965	R K Wilson		A R Mills & R K Wilson	Mrs P F Jones & Miss S V Wade	R Carmichael (Aus) & Mrs P F Jones
1966, 1967 not held					
1968	R A J Hewitt (SA)	Mrs B M Court (Aus)	R C Lutz (USA) & S R Smith (USA)	Miss M A Eisel (USA) & Miss W M Shaw	S R Smith (USA) & Mrs B M Court (Aus)
Venue changed from Queen's Club to Wembley Arena.					
1969	R G Laver (Aus)	Mrs P F Jones	R S Emerson (Aus) & R G Laver (Aus)	Mrs P F Jones & Miss S V Wade	not held
1970	R G Laver (Aus)	Mrs L W King (USA)	K R Rosewall (Aus) & S R Smith (USA)	Miss R Casals (USA) & Mrs L W King (USA)	not held
1971	I Nastase (Rom)	Mrs L W King (USA)	R A J Hewitt (SA) & F D McMillan (SA)	Mlle F Durr (Fra) & Miss S V Wade	not held
1972 et seq not held					

THE ALL ENGLAND CHAMPIONSHIPS

In the early days of the game the title 'All England Championship' was sometimes affixed to events at Wimbledon because of the promotion of the more properly named 'The Lawn Tennis Championships' by the All England Club. This applied to the men's and women's singles and the men's doubles. However, a clear distinction always pertained with the All England women's doubles and the All England mixed doubles championships which, from an early stage, were staged elsewhere. The women's doubles were always held in conjunction with the Buxton tournament. The mixed doubles alternated with the Northern Championships between Liverpool and Manchester.

The 'All England' Champions were:

ALL ENGLAND WOMEN'S DOUBLES CHAMPIONS

1884 Miss Noon & Mrs F Watts
1885 Miss G Bracewell & Mrs F Watts
1886/87/88 Miss C Dodd & Miss M Langrishe
1889/90 Miss B Steedman & Miss M Steedman
1891 Miss L Marriott & Miss M Marriott
1892 Miss Crofton & Miss H Jackson
1893/94/95/96 Mrs G W Hillyard
    & Miss B Steedman
1897 Mrs G W Hillyard & Mrs W H Pickering
1898 Mrs R Dyas & Miss B Steedman
1899 Mrs N Durlacher & Miss B Steedman
1900/01/02 Mrs W H Pickering
    & Miss M E Robb
1903/04 Miss D K Douglass
    & Miss E W Thomson
1905 Miss H Lane & Miss C M Wilson
1906/07 Mrs G W Hillyard & Miss C Meyer
1908 Miss H M Garfitt & Mrs A Sterry
1909 Miss H Aitchison & Mrs C O Tuckey
1910 Miss H M Garfitt & Mrs W E Hudleston
1911/12/13 Mrs D R Larcombe
    & Miss W A Longhurst
1914–1918 not held
1919/20/21 Mrs D R Larcombe
    & Miss E Ryan (USA)
1922 Miss K McKane & Mrs G Peacock (Ind)
1923 Miss C Beckingham
    & Miss E M Beckingham
1924 Mrs A Clayton & Miss E D Holman
1925 Mrs P Satterthwaite & Miss M Valentine
1926 Miss D Gordon & Mrs G Hawkins
1927 Miss E A Goldsack & Miss P Saunders

1928 Miss B Faltham & Miss E Hemmant
1929 Miss J C Boucher & Miss M Howes
1930 Miss M Heeley & Miss G Vaughton
1931/32/33 Miss J Ingram & Miss F K Scott
1934 Miss J McAlpine & Miss A M Yorke
1935 Mrs C P Bruton & Miss A M Yorke
1936 Mrs V Burr & Miss M Heeley
1937 Mrs V Burr & Miss M Heeley divided with
    Miss S Noel & Miss J Saunders
1938 Miss V E Scott & Miss M Whitmarsh
1939 Miss R Jarvis & Mrs R D McKelvie
1940–1945 not held
1946 Mrs B Carris & Miss E H Harvey
1947/48/49 Miss G C Hoahing
    & Miss E A Middleton
1950 Mrs D L Wedderburn (SA)
    & Miss G E Woodgate
1951 Mrs S Van Coller (SA)
    & Miss R F Woodgate
1952 Mrs J M E Wallace & Miss R F Woodgate
    divided with Miss B Penrose (Aus)
    & Miss D Spiers
1953 Miss K Nevill Smith & Miss R Walsh
    divided with Miss R H Bentley
    & Miss P A Hird
Tournament and title ceased.

ALL ENGLAND MIXED DOUBLES CHAMPIONS

1888 E Renshaw & Mrs G W Hillyard
1889 J C Kay & Miss C Dod
1890* J Baldwin & Miss K Hill
1891* J C Kay & Miss H Jackson
1892* A Dod & Miss C Dod
1893 W Baddeley & Mrs G W Hillyard
1894/95/96/97/98 H S Mahony & Miss C Cooper
1899 C H L Cazalet & Miss M E Robb
1900 H L Doherty & Miss C Cooper
1901*/02 S H Smith & Miss L Martin
1903 F L Riseley & Miss D K Douglass
1904/05 S H Smith & Miss E W Thomson
1906 F L Riseley & Miss D K Douglass
1907* N E Brookes (Aus) & Mrs G W Hillyard
1908* X A Casdagli & Mrs A Sterry
1909* X A Casdagli & Miss H M Garfitt
1910 J C Parke & Mrs J F Luard
1911* T M Mavrogordato & Mrs E G Parton
1912/13/14 J C Parke & Mrs D R Larcombe
1915–1918 not held
1919 F L Riseley & Mrs R Lambert Chambers
1920*/21/22 R Lycett & Miss E Ryan (USA)
1923 M Woosnam & Miss E Ryan
1924 W Radcliffe & Miss E M Beckingham
1925 M Woosnam & Miss E Ryan (USA)

1926 W Radcliffe & Mrs F M Strawson
1927 D A Hodges & Mrs C Beckingham
1928 H C Hopman (Aus) & Miss V B Southam
1929/30 D M Grieg & Mrs F M Strawson
1931 D A Hodges & Mrs P H Watson divided
     with J S Olliff & Miss J McAlpine
1932 H Timmer (Hol) & Miss J McAlpine
1933 J H Booth & Miss E Goldsworth
1934 G Kirby (SA) & Mrs F M Strawson
1935 W Hines (USA) & Miss M Whitmarsh
1936 J L Chamberlain & Mrs F M Strawson
1937 A C Stedman (NZ) & Mme R Mathieu (Fra)
1938 C E Malfron (NZ) & Fru S Sperling (Ger)
Championship ceased.

* Holders did not defend; from 1889 to 1922 the event was played on the challenge round system. From 1928 the event was held in Liverpool except for 1933 when it reverted to Manchester.

ALL ENGLAND MARRIED COUPLES CHAMPIONSHIPS

This, the most ephemeral of the 'All England' titles, was held at the Nottingham tournament. At no time was there an entry of more than five pairs. The champions were:

1910/11/12 Mr & Mrs G W Hillyard
1913 Dr and Mrs Lamplough
1914 Mr & Mrs G W Hillyard
1915–1919 not held
1920 Mr & Mrs C L Winslow (SA)
1921/22/23 Mr & Mrs F T Walker
Championship ceased.

Ann Jones was the only British woman other than Virginia Wade to win a Dewar Cup singles.

THE DEWAR CUP

The Dewar Cup, sponsored by the whisky firm of Dewar, flourished 1968 to 1976. It was an integrated circuit of British indoor tournaments staged in a continuous series of weeks in the autumn, each event being complete in itself but giving qualifying points for the climax. This was always staged in London, at the Crystal Palace in the first 2 years, subsequently at the Royal Albert Hall.

The growth of open lawn tennis brought increasing difficulties to the staging of the provincial tournaments and the circuit had

The Dewar Cup seen here with the winner of the men's singles in 1973, Jimmy Connors.

declined to the one main event for 1975 and 1976.

During the 9 years the Dewar Cup lasted, 35 tournaments were staged. An outstanding personal record was set by the leading British player Virginia Wade. She competed in every tournament except one. (The exception was the Cardiff event of 1974.) In singles she played 33 semi-finals. She played 27 finals. She won 18 singles trophies.

Margaret Court of Australia played in 1968 and 1972, competing in a total of 11 tournaments. She won the singles in 10. Her only singles defeat was in the Crystal Palace final 1968 when Miss Wade beat her.

Miss Wade also participated in 24 doubles finals winning 21, of which 20 were women's doubles.

RESULTS

Venue	Men's Singles Winner	Women's Singles Winner
1968 Stalybridge	R A J Hewitt (SA)	Mrs B M Court (Aus)
Perth	M Cox (GB)	Mrs B M Court (Aus)
Aberavon	R A J Hewitt (SA)	Mrs B M Court (Aus)
Torquay	R A J Hewitt (SA)	Mrs B M Court (Aus)
Queen's Club	R A J Hewitt (SA)	Mrs B M Court (Aus)
Crystal Palace	S R Smith (USA)	Miss S V Wade (GB)
1969 Perth	I El Shafei (Egy)	Miss S V Wade (GB)
Stalybridge	M Cox (GB)	Miss S V Wade (GB)
Aberavon	L A Hoad (Aus)	Miss S V Wade (GB)
Torquay	M Cox (GB)	Miss J M Heldman (USA)
Crystal Palace	M Cox (GB)	Miss S V Wade (GB)
1970 Edinburgh	T W Gorman (USA)	Miss S Walsh (USA)
Stalybridge	I Tiriac (Rom)	Miss S V Wade (GB)
Aberavon	G D Battrick (GB)	Miss S V Wade (GB)
Torquay	V Zednik (Cze)	Mrs P F Jones (GB)
R Albert Hall	J G Alexander (Aus)	Mlle F Durr (Fra)
1971 Edinburgh	R A J Hewitt (SA)	Miss E Goolagong (Aus)
Billingham	J Fillol (Chi)	Miss S V Wade (GB)
Aberavon	R A J Hewitt (SA)	Miss S V Wade (GB)
Torquay	R A J Hewitt (SA)	Miss E Goolagong (Aus)
R Albert Hall	G D Battrick (GB)	Miss S V Wade (GB)
1972 Billingham	J M Lloyd (GB)	Mrs B M Court (Aus)
Edinburgh	R J Moore (SA)	Mrs B M Court (Aus)
Aberavon	J Fassbender (FRG)	Mrs B M Court (Aus)
Torquay	R J Moore (SA)	Mrs B M Court (Aus)
R Albert Hall	I Nastase (Rom)	Mrs B M Court (Aus)
1973 Aberavon	M Cox (GB)	Miss S V Wade (GB)
Edinburgh	R Taylor (GB)	Miss S V Wade (GB)
Billingham	R Taylor (GB)	Miss S V Wade (GB)
Nottingham/R Albert Hall	J S Connors (USA)	Miss S V Wade (GB)
1974 Cardiff	M Cox (GB)	Miss J M Heldman (USA)
Edinburgh	M Cox (GB)	Miss S V Wade (GB)
Billingham/R Albert Hall	T S Okker (Hol)	Miss S V Wade (GB)
1975 Edinburgh/R Albert Hall	E Dibbs (USA)	Miss S V Wade (GB)
1976 Islington/R Albert Hall	R Ramirez (Mex)	Miss S V Wade (GB)

Events no longer held

The traditions of lawn tennis belong to the events of the past and some have disappeared. There are records that merit preservation.

The historian must regret the paucity of early records. Those of the tournament that used to be staged at Prince's Club prior to the Wimbledon Championships would contribute to knowledge of the founding fathers of lawn tennis. The Prince's Club, in Knightsbridge, London, continued as a tennis and rackets club until the Second World War but lawn tennis had ceased many years before.

The records of the Olympic Games proved very elusive. They have added interest in view of the probable revival of lawn tennis as an Olympic Sport.

Some events no longer held, the British Covered Court Championships, the old All England Championships and the Dewar Cup, will be found under the section on British Domestic Events.

OLYMPIC GAMES

Lawn tennis was a part of the Olympic Games from the start of the movement and feature in the Athens meeting of 1896 when it was described in the official report as 'this most charming athletic game'. Only men's singles and men's doubles were played. The entry was 13 from 4 different nations. The winner, John Pius Boland, from Ireland, does not feature in the game's history other than for his gold medal.

Women came on to the scene for the Paris meeting of 1900. British players made a clean sweep of the gold, Laurie and Reggie Doherty and Charlotte Cooper, later Mrs Sterry, winning all four events between them from a total entry of 24.

The St Louis games of 1904 marked the nadir of Olympic lawn tennis fortunes. Only men's singles and doubles were staged and the total entry was no more then eight, all Americans.

Beals Wright acquired a cheap gold medal.

Lawn tennis fortunes in the Olympics subsequently improved, even though the tournaments in London in 1908, when an indoor event was staged at Queen's Club and an outdoor tournament put on at Wimbledon following the Championships, made it clear that lawn tennis players were regarding their own traditional annual events as of greater importance. There were numerous withdrawals.

Even so there were 49 men and 42 women for the outdoor meeting in Stockholm in 1912. In Antwerp in 1920 women's doubles were granted a place, giving the orthodox five events. The Paris games of 1924, when lawn tennis was put on at the newly built Stade Colombes, were the peak of Olympic lawn tennis fortunes. There were 82 men and 31 women—all top class—from 27 different nations.

But the weather was bad and the tournament not well run. The International Lawn Tennis Federation, newly strengthened by the USA at last becoming a member, disputed with the Olympic Committee about the control. Furthermore there were differences about the definition of an amateur. The upshot was that the ILTF withdrew the game as an Olympic sport.

In recent years, with pressure strong from the nations of Eastern Europe, there have been moves to have lawn tennis included again as one of the Olympic sports. With the Mexican games of 1968 lawn tennis was included as a 'demonstration' sport. The results and those of the 1906 games in Athens, which were officially sanctioned but not numbered as an Olympiad, are included in the data below.

The **greatest number** of Olympic medals was won by Max Decugis of France, with **6** (4 gold, 1 silver, 1 bronze) 1920–1924. His **4 gold** is a record also.

The **greatest number** of medals won by a woman was **5** by Kitty McKane of Great Britain 1920 and 1924 (1 gold, 2 silver and 2 bronze).

RESULTS

OLYMPIC MEDALISTS

		Gold Medalists	Silver Medalists	Bronze Medalists
1896	Men's Singles	J P Boland (Ire)	D Kasdaglis (Gre)	
Athens	Men's Doubles	Boland & F Traun (Ger)	Kasdaglis & D Petrokokkinos (Gre)	
1900	Men's Singles	H L Doherty (GB)	H S Mahony (Ire)	R F Doherty (GB)/A J B Norris (GB)
Paris	Men's Doubles	H L & R F Doherty	M Decugis (Fra) & S de Garmendia (USA)	A Prevost (Fra) & G de la Chapelle (Fra)/Mahony & Norris
	Women's Singles	Miss C Cooper (GB)	Mlle H Prevost (Fra)	Miss M Jones (USA)/ Miss H Rosenbaumova (Cze)
	Mixed Doubles	R F Doherty & Miss Cooper	Mahony & Mlle Prevost	A A Warden (GB) & Miss Rosenbaumova/ H L Doherty & Miss Jones
1904	Men's Singles	B C Wright (USA)	R LeRoy (USA)	
St Louis	Men's Doubles	E W Leonard (USA) & Wright	A L Bell (USA) & LeRoy	
1906	Men's Singles	M Decugis (Fra)	M Germot (Fra)	Z Zemla (Cze)
Athens	Men's Doubles	Decugis & Germot	X Kasdaglis & I Ballis (Gre)	Z & L Zemla (Cze)
	Women's Singles	Miss E Simiriotu (Gre)	Miss S Marinou (Gre)	Miss E Paspati (Gre)
	Mixed Doubles	Decugis & Mme M Decugis (Fra)	G Simiriotis & Miss Marinou (Gre)	Kasdaglis & Miss A Matsa (Gre)
1908	Men's Singles	A W Gore (GB)	G A Caridia (GB)	M J G Ritchie (GB)
Indoors	Men's Doubles	Gore & H Roper Barrett (GB)	Caridia & G M Simond (GB)	W Bostrom & G Setterwall (Swe)
Queen's Club	Women's Singles	Miss G Eastlake Smith (GB)	Miss A N G Greene (GB)	Mrs M Adlerstrahle (Swe)
Wimbledon	Men's Singles	M J G Ritchie (GB)	O Froitzheim (Ger)	W V Eaves (GB)
	Men's Doubles	R F Doherty & G W Hillyard (GB)	Ritchie & J C Parke (GB)	C H L Cazalet & C P Dixon (GB)
	Women's Singles	Mrs R Lambert Chambers (GB)	Miss D Boothby (GB)	Mrs R J Winch (GB)
1912	Men's Singles	A H Gobert (Fra)	C P Dixon (GB)	A F Wilding (NZ)
Indoors	Men's Doubles	M Germot & Gobert (Fra)	C Kempe & G Setterwall (Swe)	A E Beamish & Dixon (GB)
Stockholm	Women's Singles	Mrs F J Hannam (GB)	Miss S Castenschiold (Den)	Mrs E G Parton (GB)
	Mixed Doubles	Dixon & Mrs Hannam	H Roper Barrett & Miss F H Aitchison (GB)	Setterwall & Mrs H Frick (Swe)
1912	Men's Singles	C L Winslow (SA)	H A Kitson (SA)	O Kreuzer (Ger)
Stockholm	Men's Doubles	Kitson & Winslow	F Pipes & A Zborzil (Aus)	A Canet & M Meny (Fra)
	Women's Singles	Mlle M Broquedis (Fra)	Frl D Koring (Ger)	Miss M Bjorstedt (Nor)
	Mixed Doubles	H Schomburgk & Frl Koring (Ger)	G Setterwall & Mrs H Frick (Swe)	Canet & Mlle Broquedis
1920	Men's Singles	L Raymond (SA)	I Kumagae (Jap)	C L Winslow (SA)
Antwerp	Men's Doubles	O G N Turnbull & M Woosnam (GB)	S Kashio & Kumagae (Jap)	P Albarran & M Decugis (Fra)
	Women's Singles	Mlle S Lenglen (Fra)	Miss E D Holman (GB)	Miss K McKane (GB)
	Women's Doubles	Mrs R J McNair & Miss McKane (GB)	Mrs A E Beamish & Miss Holman (GB)	Mlle Lenglen & Mlle E d'Ayen (Fra)
	Mixed Doubles	Decugis & Mlle Lenglen	Woosnam & Miss McKane	M Zemla & Miss M Skrobkova (Cze)
1924	Men's Singles	V Richards (USA)	H Cochet (Fra)	H de Morpurgo (Ita)
Paris	Men's Doubles	F T Hunter & Richards (USA)	J Brugnon & Cochet (Fra)	J Borotra & R Lacoste (Fra)
	Women's Singles	Miss H N Wills (USA)	Mlle J P Vlasto (Fra)	Miss K McKane (GB)
	Women's Doubles	Mrs H Wightman & Miss Wills (USA)	Mrs E Covell & Miss McKane (GB)	Mrs D Shepherd-Barron & Miss E L Colyer (GB)
	Mixed Doubles	R N Williams & Mrs Wightman (USA)	Richards & Mrs M Jessup (USA)	H Timmer & Miss C Bouman (Hol)
1968	Men's Singles	M Santana (Spa)	M Orantes (Spa)	H Fitzgibbon (USA)
Mexico City	Men's Doubles	R H Osuna & V Zarazua (Mex)	J Gisbert & Santana (Spa)	P Darmon (Fra) & J Loyo-Mayo (Mex)
	Women's Singles	Frl H Niessen (FRG)	Miss J Bartkowicz (USA)	Miss J M Heldman (USA)
	Women's Doubles	Frl E Buding & Frl Niessen (FRG)	Mme P Darmon (Fra) & Miss Heldman	Miss Bartkowicz & Miss V Ziegunfuss (USA)
	Mixed Doubles	Fitzgibbon & Miss Heldman	J Fassbender & Frl Niessen (FRG)	J I Osborne & Miss J Bartkowicz (USA)

MEN'S SINGLES FINALS

1896 J P Boland (Ire)	beat D Kasdaglis (Gre)	7–5 6–4 6–1
1900 H L Doherty (GB)	beat H S Mahony (Ire)	6–4 6–2 6–3
1904 B C Wright (USA)	beat R LeRoy (USA)	6–4 6–4

1906 M Decugis (Fra)	beat M Germot (Fra)	7–5 6–2 6–4
1908 A W Gore (GB) (indoors)	beat G A Caridia (GB)	4–6 6–3 5–7 6–1 6–4
1908 M J G Ritchie (GB)	beat O Froitzheim (Ger)	2–6 6–1 6–4 6–1
1912 A H Gobert (Fra) (indoors)	beat C P Dixon (GB)	8–6 6–4 6–4
1912 C L Winslow (SA)	beat H A Kitson (SA)	7–5 4–6 10–8 8–6
1920 L Raymond (SA)	beat I Kumagae (Jap)	5–7 6–4 7–5 6–4
1924 V Richards (USA)	beat H Cochet (Fra)	6–4 6–4 5–7 4–6 6–2
1968 M Santana (Spa)	beat M Orantes (Spa)	2–6 6–3 3–6 6–3 6–4

WOMEN'S SINGLES FINALS

1900 Miss C Cooper (GB)	beat Mlle H Prevost (Fra)	6–1 6–4
1906 Miss E Simirotou (Gre)	beat Miss S Marinou (Gre)	6–1 6–4
1908 Miss G Eastlake-Smith (GB) (indoors)	beat Miss A N Greene (GB)	6–2 4–6 6–0
1908 Mrs R Lambert Chambers (GB)	beat Miss D B Boothby (GB)	6–1 7–5
1912 Mrs E M Hannam (GB) (indoors)	beat Miss T G S Castenschiold (Den)	6–4 6–3
1912 Mlle M Broquedis (Fra)	beat Frl D Koring (Ger)	4–6 6–3 6–4
1920 Mlle S Lenglen (Fra)	beat Miss E D Holman (GB)	6–3 6–0
1924 Miss H N Wills (USA)	beat Mlle J P Vlasto (Fra)	6–2 6–2
1968 Frl H Niessen (FRG)	beat Miss J Bartkowicz (USA)	6–4 6–3

MEN'S DOUBLES FINALS

1896 J P Boland (Ire) & F Traun (Ger)	beat D Kasdaglis & D Petrokokkinos (Gre)	6–2 6–4
1900 H L & R F Doherty (GB)	beat M Decugis (Fra) & S de Garmendia (USA)	6–3 6–3 7–5
1904 E W Leonard & B C Wright (USA)	beat A L Bell & R LeRoy (USA)	6–4 6–4 6–2
1906 M Decugis & M Germot (Fra)	beat I Ballis (Gre) & X Kasdaglis (Gre)	6–4 6–2 6–1
1908 H Roper Barrett & A W Gore (GB) (indoors)	beat G M Simond & G A Caridia (GB)	6–2 2–6 6–3 6–3
1908 R F Doherty & G W Hillyard (GB)	beat J C Parke & M J G Ritchie (GB)	9–7 7–5 9–7
1912 M Germot & A H Gobert (Fra) (indoors)	beat C Kempe & G Setterwall (Swe)	6–4 12–14 6–2 6–4
1912 H A Kitson & C L Winslow (SA)	beat F Pipes & A Zborzil (Aut)	4–6 6–1 6–2 6–2
1920 O G N Turnbull & M Woosnam (GB)	beat S Kashio & I Kumagae (Jap)	6–2 5–7 7–5 7–5
1924 F T Hunter & V Richards (USA)	beat J Brugnon & H Cochet (Fra)	4–6 6–2 6–3 2–6 6–3
1968 R H Osuna & V Zarazua (Mex)	beat J Gisbert & M Santana (Spa)	6–4 6–3 6–4

WOMEN'S DOUBLES FINALS

1920 Miss K McKane & Mrs R J McNair (GB)	beat Mrs G Beamish & Miss E D Holman (GB)	8–6 6–4
1924 Mrs H Wightman & Miss H Wills (USA)	beat Mrs E Covell & Miss K McKane (GB)	7–5 8–6
1968 Frl E Buding & Frl H Niessen (Ger)	beat Miss J M Heldman (USA) & Mme P Darmon (Fra)	6–3 6–4

MIXED DOUBLES FINALS

1900 R F Doherty & Miss C Cooper (GB)	beat H S Mahony (Ire) & Mlle H Prevost (Fra)	6–2 6–4
1906 M Decugis & Mme M Decugis (Fra)	beat G Simiriotis & Miss S Marinou (Gre)	6–1 6–2
1912 C P Dixon & Mrs E M Hannam (GB) (indoors)	beat H Roper Barrett & Miss H Aitchison (GB)	4–6 6–3 6–2
1912 H Schomburgk & Frl D Koring (Ger)	beat G Setterwall & Mrs S Fick (Swe)	6–4 6–0
1920 M Decugis & Mlle S Lenglen (Fra)	beat M Woosnam & Miss K McKane (GB)	6–4 6–2
1924 R N Williams & Mrs H Wightman (USA)	beat V Richards & Mrs M Jessup (USA)	6–2 6–3
1968 H Fitzgibbon & Miss J M Heldman (USA)	beat J Fassbender & Frl H Niessen (FRG)	6–1 6–3

WORLD CHAMPIONSHIPS

The World Championships, staged on grass, hard courts and wood, began in 1912 with the institution of the hard court event at St. Cloud, Paris. The first task of the International Lawn Tennis Federation, formed the following year, was to sanction the world titles. The world title on grass was granted to Wimbledon in per-petuity. The United States made a condition of their joining the Federation that the titles be dropped and all three world championships came to an end after 1923.

The only difference the world titles made to Wimbledon was to inspire the promotion of women's and mixed doubles as full championship events in 1913. The dropping of the hard court championship had little effect in 1924 since the French were concerned with staging lawn tennis as part of the Olympic Games at the Colombes Stadium in Paris. In 1925 the old French Championships, which had become restricted to native players, were made open to all nationalities and effectively replaced the former World title meeting.

The grandiose reverberations of the World Championships on Covered Courts died away. These were the world titles that had prospered least.

In the records noted below it needs be remembered that they are shared by Wimbledon for the years 1913 to 1923.

The **greatest number of World Championship titles** was won by **Suzanne Lenglen**, 9 singles, 8 women's doubles and 5 mixed doubles, a total of **22 in all.**

Elizabeth Ryan won **13 world titles** in all, 8 doubles and 5 mixed.

Henri Cochet won **most men's titles,** 3 singles, 3 doubles and 2 mixed, a total of **8 in all.**

The longest men's singles final was that on hard courts in Paris in 1923 when William Johnston (USA) beat J Washer (Bel) 4–6 6–2 6–2 4–6 6–3, a total of **45 games.**

The longest women's singles final was that at Wimbledon in 1919 when Suzanne Lenglen (Fra) beat Dorothea Lambert Chambers (GB) 10–8 4–6 9–7, a total of **44 games.**

The longest men's doubles final was in 1920 on covered courts at Queen's Club, London, when P M Davson and T M Mavrogordato (both GB) beat F M B Fisher (NZ) and A E Beamish (GB) 4–6 10–8 13–11 3–6 6–3, a total of **70 games.**

The longest women's doubles final was at Wimbledon in 1919 when Suzanne Lenglen (Fra) and Elizabeth Ryan (US) beat Mrs D R Larcombe and Dorothea Lambert Chambers (both GB) 4–6 7–5 6–3, a total of **31 games.**

The longest mixed final was indoors at Stockholm in 1913 when M Decugis and Mme Fenwick (both Fra) beat G Setterwall and Mrs Fick (both Swe) 7–5 12–10, a total of **34 games.**

WORLD HARD COURT CHAMPIONSHIPS

Date	Venue	Men's Singles	Women's Singles	Men's Doubles	Women's Doubles	Mixed Doubles
1912	Paris	O Froitzheim (Ger)	Mlle M Brocquedis	O Froitzheim (Ger) & O Kreuzer (Ger)		M Decugis & Mme de Borman
1913	Paris	A F Wilding (NZ)	Frl M Rieck (Ger)	R Kleinschroth (Ger) & Baron von Bissing (Ger)		M Decugis & Miss E Ryan (USA)
1914	Paris	A F Wilding (NZ)	Mlle S Lenglen	M Decugis & M Germot	Mlle S Lenglen & Miss E Ryan (USA)	M Decugis & Miss E Ryan (USA)
1915–1919 not held						
1920	Paris	W H Laurentz	Miss E D Holman (GB)	A H Gobert & W H Laurentz	Miss E D Holman (GB) & Miss P Satterthwaite (GB)	W H Laurentz & Mme J Golding
1921	Paris	W T Tilden (USA)	Mlle S Lenglen	A H Gobert & W H Laurentz	Mlle S Lenglen & Mme J Golding	M Decugis & Mlle S Lenglen
1922	Brussels	H Cochet (Fra)	Mlle S Lenglen (Fra)	J Borotra (Fra) & H Cochet (Fra)	Mlle S Lenglen (Fra) & Miss E Ryan (USA)	H Cochet (Fra) & Mlle S Lenglen (Fra)
1923	Paris	W M Johnston (USA)	Mlle S Lenglen	J Brugnon & M Dupont	Mrs A E Beamish (GB) & Miss K McKane (GB)	H Cochet & Mlle S Lenglen

SINGLES FINALS

	MEN				WOMEN		
Date	Winner	Finalist	Score		Winner	Finalist	Score
1912	O Froitzheim	O Kreuzer	6–2 7–5 4–6 7–5		Mlle M Brocquedis	Frl M Rieck	6–3 0–6 6–4
1913	A F Wilding	A H Gobert	6–3 6–3 1–6 6–4		Frl M Rieck	Mlle M Brocquedis	6–4–3–6 6–4
1914	A F Wilding	Count Salm	6–0 6–2 6–4		Mlle S Lenglen	Mme J Golding	6–2 6–1
1915–1919 not held							
1920	W H Laurentz	A H Gobert	9–7 6–2 3–6 6–2		Miss E D Holman	Sen P Subirana	6–0 7–5
1921	W T Tilden	J Washer	6–3 6–3 6–3		Mlle S Lenglen	Miss F Mallory	6–2 6–3
1922	H Cochet	Count de Gomar	6–0 2–6 4–6 6–1 6–2		Mlle S Lenglen	Miss E Ryan	6–3 6–2
1923	W M Johnston	J Washer	4–6 6–2 6–2 4–6 6–3		Mlle S Lenglen	Miss K McKane	6–3 6–3

WORLD COVERED COURT CHAMPIONSHIPS

Date	Venue	Men's Singles	Women's Singles	Men's Doubles	Women's Doubles	Mixed Doubles
1913	Stockholm	A F Wilding (NZ)	Miss H Aichison (GB)	M Decugis (Fra) & M Germot (Fra)		M Decugis (Fra) & Mme Fenwick (Fra)
1914–1918 not held						
1919	Paris	A H Gobert	Miss E D Holman (GB)	A H Gobert & W H Laurentz	Mrs A E Beamish (GB) & Miss K McKane (GB)	M Decugis & Mrs A E Beamish (GB)
1920	London Queen's Club	F G Lowe	Mrs A E Beamish	P M Davson & T M Mavrogordato	Mrs A E Beamish & Miss K McKane	F M B Fisher (NZ) & Mrs G Peacock (Ind)
1921	Copenhagen	W H Laurentz (Fra)	Frk Brehm	M Germot (Fra) & W H Laurentz (Fra)	Frk Brehm & Frk E Meyer	E Tegner & Frk Brehm
1922	St Moritz	H Cochet (Fra)	Mme J Golding (Fra)	J Borotra (Fra) & H Cochet (Fra)	Mme J Golding (Fra) & Mme Vaussard (Fra)	J Borotra (Fra) & Mme J Golding (Fra)
1923	Barcelona	H Cochet (Fra)	Miss K McKane (GB)	H Cochet (Fra) & J Couiteas (Fra)	Mrs A E Beamish (GB) & Miss K McKane (GB)	W C Crawley (GB) & Miss K McKane (GB)

SINGLES FINALS

	MEN				WOMEN		
Year	Winner	Finalist	Score		Winner	Finalist	Score
1913	A F Wilding	M Germot	5–7 6–2 6–3 6–1		Miss H Aichison	Mme Fenwick	6–4 6–2
1914–1928 not held							
1919	A H Gobert	M Decugis	6–3 6–3 6–4		Miss E D Holman	Mme J Golding	6–3 6–4
1920	F G Lowe	W C Crawley	6–1 6–3 6–1		Mrs A E Beamish	Miss K McKane	6–2 5–7 9–7
1921	W H Laurentz	A E Beamish	6–2 6–4 6–2		Frk Brehm	Frk E Meyer	6–2 6–4
1922	H Cochet	J Borotra	4–6 2–6 6–3 6–3 6–0		Mme J Golding	Mme Vaussard	6–2 7–5
1923	H Cochet	J B Gilbert	6–4 7–5 6–4		Miss K McKane	Mrs A E Beamish	6–3 4–6 6–2

(Note: The records for the World Grass Court Championships 1913–1923 are those for the Wimbledon Championships.)

WORLD TEAM TENNIS

For five summer seasons 1974–78 World Team Tennis staged, on indoor courts, a commercially inspired inter-city league championship in the USA. Each match consisted of a men's singles, women's singles, men's doubles, women's doubles and a mixed doubles, each a short set of six games comprising seven points at most, deuce and advantage not being played. Spectators were encouraged to be noisily partisan at all times. Many of the world's leading players, especially women, took part and were generously paid. The venture failed.

TEAMS PARTICIPATING

1974	1975	1976	1977	1978
Baltimore				
Boston	Boston	Boston	Boston	Boston
Chicago				
Cleveland	Cleveland	Cleveland	Cleveland	
Denver				
Detroit				
Miami				
Golden Gaters	Golden Gaters	Golden Gaters	Golden Gaters	Golden Gaters
Hawaii	Hawaii	Hawaii		

1974	1975	1976	1977	1978
Houston				
Los Angeles	Los Angeles	Los Angeles	Los Angeles	Los Angeles
Minnesota				
New York	New York	New York	New York	New York
Philadelphia				
Pittsburgh	Pittsburgh	Pittsburgh		
Toronto/Buffalo				
	Indiana	Indiana	Indiana	Indiana
	Phoenix	Phoenix	Phoenix	Phoenix
	San Diego		San Diego	San Diego
		San Francisco		
			Sea-Port	
			Soviets*	
				Anaheim
				New Orleans
				Seattle
Winners				
Denver	Pittsburgh	New York	New York	Los Angeles

* A non-territorial side consisting of USSR players.

Note: Under the title Team Tennis the venture made a modest revival in 1981 with four teams, all Californian—Anaheim, Los Angeles, Oakland and San Diego.

It enlarged to eight teams in 1982, involving the same four locations plus Chicago, Dallas, Houston and Phoenix.

BP CUP

International team championship on indoor courts for players under 21.
Format: 2 singles, 1 doubles, except for final when reverse singles were played.
Played in Torquay 1973–78, Hamburg 1979, 1980.

FINALS RESULTS

Men				Women		
1973	Great Britain	beat USA	4–1	Czechoslovakia	beat Great Britain	3–2
1974	Great Britain	beat USA	5–0	Great Britain	beat USA	3–2
1975	USA	beat France	4–2	Great Britain	beat USA	4–1
1976	USA	beat Great Britain	3–2	Great Britain	beat USA	5–0
1977	USA	beat Italy	4–1	Great Britain	beat USA	5–0
1978	Great Britain	beat Italy	4–1	USA	beat Great Britain	3–1
1979	USA	beat Sweden	4–1	Sweden	beat USA	3–2
1980	Sweden	beat Great Britain	3–2	Great Britain	beat USA	4–1

The **most successful player** in the BP Cup was **Sue Barker** of Great Britain. She played for four years, 1974 to 1977, and was always on the winning side. She competed in 20 ties. She played 35 rubbers, winning 34, divided between 20 singles, in which she was one hundred per cent successful, and 15 doubles, where she was beaten once.

GREAT BRITAIN IN THE BP CUP

Men

1973	beat	Czechoslovakia	2–1	
	beat	Spain	2–1	
	beat	Italy	3–0	
	beat	France	2–1	
	beat	USA	4–1	Won
1974	beat	Italy	3–0	
	beat	West Germany	3–0	
	beat	Spain	2–1	
	beat	France	3–0	
	beat	USA	5–0	Won
1975	beat	Italy	3–0	
	beat	West Germany	3–0	
	beat	Spain	3–0	
	lost to	France	1–2	
1976	beat	Czechoslovakia	2–1	
	beat	Spain	2–1	
	beat	France	2–1	
	beat	Sweden	2–1	
	lost to	USA	2–3	
1977	beat	Canada	2–1	
	lost to	Italy	1–2	
	lost to	USA	1–2	
1978	beat	Netherlands	3–0	
	beat	Czechoslovakia	3–0	
	beat	Spain	2–1	
	beat	USA	2–1	
	beat	Italy	4–1	Won
1979	beat	Czechoslovakia	2–1	
	beat	West Germany	3–0	
	beat	Spain	3–0	
	lost to	Sweden	0–3	
1980	beat	Spain	2–1	
	beat	West Germany	2–1	
	lost to	Sweden	1–2	
	beat	Austria	3–0	
	lost to	Sweden	2–3	

Women

1973	beat	Netherlands	2–1	
	beat	France	3–0	
	beat	Czechoslovakia	2–1	
	lost to	Czechoslovakia	2–3	
1974	beat	Czechoslovakia	3–0	
	beat	Netherlands	3–0	
	beat	USA	2–1	
	beat	USA	3–2	Won
1975	beat	Czechoslovakia	3–0	
	beat	Netherlands	3–0	
	beat	USA	2–1	
	beat	USA	4–1	Won
1976	beat	France	2–1	
	beat	Netherlands	3–0	
	beat	Czechoslovakia	3–0	
	beat	USA	5–0	Won
1977	beat	Ireland	3–0	
	beat	France	3–0	
	beat	Canada	3–0	
	beat	USA	5–0	Won
1978	beat	France	2–1	
	beat	West Germany	2–1	
	beat	Czechoslovakia	2–1	
	lost to	USA	1–3	
1979	beat	Italy	3–0	
	beat	Netherlands	3–0	
	lost to	Sweden	1–2	
	lost to	USA	0–3	
1980	beat	Czechoslovakia	3–0	
	beat	Sweden	3–0	
	beat	Italy	3–0	
	beat	France	3–0	
	beat	USA	4–1	Won

BRITISH PLAYERS

MEN	**Years Played**
J W Feaver	1973
J M Lloyd	1973, 1974
S A Warboys	1973
M J Farrell	1974
P Siviter	1974
R A Lewis	1975
C M Robinson	1975, 1976
J R Smith	1975, 1976
W Davies	1976
R H Beven	1977, 1978
J M Dier	1977, 1979, 1980
A H Lloyd	1977
C Bradnam	1978
A M Jarrett	1978
N Rayner	1979

A Simcox	1979
K Gilbert	1980
K Harris	1980

WOMEN	
Miss V Burton	1973
Miss L J Charles	1973
Miss G L Coles	1973
Miss S Barker	1974, 1975, 1976, 1977
Miss L Blachford	1974
Miss L J Mottram	1974, 1975, 1976
Miss A Coe	1975
Miss M Tyler	1976, 1977
Miss J M Durie	1977, 1978, 1979, 1980
Miss A E Hobbs	1978, 1979
Miss D A Jevans	1978, 1980
Miss A Cooper	1979
Miss D Taylor	1980

Miss Barker as a junior in the exalted company of Rod Laver (left) and Ken Rosewall.

Sue Barker, a British heroine of the BP Cup.

CHAMPIONSHIPS OF EUROPE

The spacious days of the early 1900's are echoed in the Championships of Europe, first staged in 1899. The men's singles was entirely peripatetic until its demise in 1913. The only other event, the men's doubles, was held throughout in Bad Homburg, Germany, and had a brief revival in the 1930's. The following acquired the title:

Year	Venue	Men's Singles	Men's Doubles
			Doubles played in Bad Homburg throughout.
1899	Bad Homburg	H S Mahony (Ire)	
1900	Ostend	M J G Ritchie (GB)	
1901	Paris	M Decugis (Fra)	
1902	Queen's Club (Indoors)	H L Doherty (GB)	G C Ball-Greene (GB) & G W Hillyard (GB)
1903	Scheveningen	R Le Roy (USA)	W C Grant (USA) & R Le Roy (USA)
1904	Stockholm	M J G Ritchie (GB)	W C Grant (USA) & I C Wright (USA)
1905	Bad Homburg	A F Wilding (NZ)	G C Ball-Greene (GB) & G W Hillyard (GB)
1906	Leicester	F L Riseley (GB)	G M Simond (GB) & A F Wilding (NZ)
1907	Dublin	J C Parke (Ire)	O Froitzheim (Ger) & K von Lersner (Ger)
1908	Queen's Club (Grass)	M J G Ritchie (GB)	C von Wessely (Ger) & A F Wilding (NZ)
1909	Newcastle	M J G Ritchie (GB)	H A Parker (NZ) & L O S Poidevin (Aus)
1910	Liverpool	B C Wright (USA) & J C Parke (Ire) div'd	O Froitzheim (Ger) & O Kreuzer (Ger)
1911	Singles not held		H Kleinschroth (Ger) & F W Rahe (Ger)
1912	Hythe	A R F Kingscote (GB)	O Kreuzer (Ger) & F G Lowe (GB)
1913	Scarborough	J C Parke (Ire)	O Froitzheim (Ger) & O Kreuzer (Ger)
1914–1929	not held		
1930			H C Hopman (Aus) & J Willard (Aus)
1931	not held		
1932			H C Hopman (Aus) & C Sproule (Aus)
no more held			

THE GRAND SLAM

The term 'Grand Slam' came into being after the win of the British Fred Perry in the French Championships of 1935. He was currently the holder of both the US and Wimbledon titles. He had won the Australian in 1934 and was thus the first player in the history of the game to have taken the men's singles in all four acknowledged major championships.

He was not, however, the current holder of the Australian title. The term 'Grand Slam' was tacitly reserved for one who might become hol-

der of those four titles at one and the same time.

That record was achieved in 1938 when the Californian Don Budge won the French Championship and was thus able, had he so wished, to display the trophies of Wimbledon, America, Australia and France together on his mantelpiece. He maintained that unique status for some time when he successfully defended his singles titles at Wimbledon and at Forest Hills. Only at the turn of the year when, having become a professional, he failed to defend his

GRAND SLAM WINNERS

	Qualifying Championships	Tenure of Grand Slam
Men's singles		
Don Budge (USA)	Wimbledon, US 1937, Australia, France, Wimbledon, US 1938	6 months
Rod Laver (Aus)	Australia, France, Wimbledon, US 1962	3 months
Rod Laver (Aus)	Australia, France, Wimbledon, US 1969	3 months
Woman's singles		
Maureen Connolly (USA)	Wimbledon, US 1952, Australia, France, Wimbledon, US 1953	6 months
Margaret Court (Aus)	US 1969, Australia, France, Wimbledon, US 1970, Australia 1971	10 months
Men's doubles		
Frank Sedgman (Aus)	With J E Bromwich US 1950, with Ken McGregor Australia, France, Wimbledon, US 1951, Australia, France, Wimbledon 1952	15 months
Ken McGregor (Aus)	With Frank Sedgman Australia, France, Wimbledon, US 1951, Australia, France, Wimbledon 1952	12 months
Women's doubles		
Maria Bueno (Bra)	With Christine Truman Australia 1960, with Darlene Hard France, Wimbledon, US 1960	3 months
Mixed doubles		
Margaret Smith (Aus)	With Fred Stolle US 1962, with Ken Fletcher Australia, France, Wimbledon, US 1963, Australia, France 1964	12 months
Ken Fletcher (Aus)	With Margaret Court Australia, France, Wimbledon, US 1963, Australia, France 1964	9 months
Owen Davidson (Aus)	With Donna Fales US 1966, with Lesley Turner Australia 1967, with Billie Jean King France, Wimbledon, US 1967	5 months
Billie Jean King (US)	With Owen Davidson France, Wimbledon, US 1967, with Dick Crealy Australia 1968	5 months

Australian title did he cease to be the current holder of the four championships that mattered most.

It may be noted that Rod Laver, who emulated Budge in 1962, did even better. As a makeweight he also won the championships of Italy and Germany, the two next in line after the big four. Then in winning the Grand Slam for the second time in 1969 he set a standard of performance unlikely to be equalled.

Similarly Margaret Court added gloss to her own performance when, emulating Maureen Connolly as women's Grand Slam winner, she also took the prestigious South African title in the same period. Mrs Court had already ruled as the invincible mixed doubles performer some years before.

J D BUDGE

Don Budge became the current holder of the four major singles championships on winning the French title in June 1938. He maintained his invincible status through the Wimbledon and US meetings of that year, only ceasing to be the Grand Slam winner when he failed to defend the Australian title in January 1939.

His detailed performance was:

Wimbledon 1937

beat N G Farquharson (SA)	6–3 6–2 6–1	
G P Hughes (GB)	6–2 6–2 6–2	
C Boussus (Fra)	6–1 6–4 6–2	
L Hecht (Cze)	6–4 6–2 6–2	
V B McGrath (Aus)	6–3 6–1 6–4	
F A Parker (USA)	2–6 6–4 6–4 6–1	
G Von Cramm (Ger)	6–3 6–4 6–2	Final

US Championships 1937

beat W V Winslow (USA)	6–3 6–3 6–3	
J L Abrams (USA)	6–0 6–1 6–1	
Y Petra (Fra)	6–0 6–3 6–1	
J R Hunt (USA)	6–1 6–2 6–4	
F A Parker (USA)	6–2 6–1 6–3	
G Von Cramm (Ger)	6–1 7–9 6–1 3–6 6–1	Final

Australian Championships 1938

beat L Hancock (Aus)	6–2 6–3 6–4	
H Whillans (Aus)	6–1 6–0 6–1	
L A Schwarts (Aus)	6–4 6–3 10–8	
A K Quist (Aus)	5–7 6–4 6–1 6–2	
J E Bromwich (Aus)	6–4 6–2 6–1	Final

French Championships 1938

beat A Gentien (Fra)	6–1 6–2 6–4	
G Mohammed (Ind)	6–1 6–1 5–7 6–0	
F Kukuljevic (Yug)	6–2 8–6 2–6 1–6 6–1	
B Destremeau (Fra)	6–4 6–3 6–4	
J Pallada (Yug)	6–2 6–3 6–3	
R Menzel (Cze)	6–3 6–2 6–4	Final

Wimbledon Championships 1938

beat K Gandar-Dower (GB)	6–2 6–3 6–3	
H Billington (GB)	7–5 6–1 6–1	

G L Rogers (Ire)	6–0 7–5 6–1	
R A Shayes (GB)	6–3 6–4 6–1	
F Cejnar (Cze)	6–3 6–0 7–5	
H Henkel (Ger)	6–2 6–4 6–0	
H W Austin (GB)	6–1 6–0 6–3	Final

US Championships 1938

beat W Van Horn (USA)	6–0 6–0 6–1	
R Kamrath (USA)	6–3 7–5 9–7	
C E Hare (GB)	6–3 6–4 6–0	
H C Hopman (Aus)	6–3 6–1 6–3	
S B Wood (USA)	6–3 6–3 6–3	
G Mako (USA)	6–3 6–8 6–2 6–1	Final

R G LAVER

Rod Laver achieved the first of his two Grand Slams in 1962 when, putting himself in a class of his own, he also won the lesser championships of Italy and Germany. The details of his Grand Slam effort were:

Australian Championships 1962

beat F Sherriff (Aus)	8–6 6–2 6–4	
G Pares (Aus)	10–8 18–16 7–9 7–5	
O K Davidson (Aus)	6–4 9–7 6–4	
R A J Hewitt (Aus)	6–1 4–6 6–4 7–5	
R S Emerson (Aus)	8–6 0–6 6–4 6–4	Final

French Championships 1962

beat M Pirro (Fra)	6–4 6–0 6–2	
J A Pickard (GB)	6–2 9–7 4–6 6–1	
S Jacobini (Ita)	4–6 6–3 7–5 6–1	
M F Mulligan (Aus)	6–4 3–6 2–6 10–8 6–2*	
N A Fraser (Aus)	3–6 6–3 6–2 3–6 7–5	
R S Emerson (Aus)	3–6 2–6 6–3 9–7 6–2	Final

* Mulligan had a match point in the fourth set

Wimbledon 1962

beat N Kumar (Ind)	7–5 6–1 6–2	
J A Pickard (GB)	6–1 6–2 6–2	
W Reed (USA)	6–4 6–1 6–4	
P Darmon (Fra)	6–3 6–2 13–11	
M Santana (Spa)	14–16 9–7 6–2 6–2	
N A Fraser (Aus)	10–8 6–1 7–5	
M F Mulligan (Aus)	6–2 6–2 6–1	Final

US Championships 1962

beat E Davidman (Isr)	6–3 6–2 6–3	
E Zuleta (Ecu)	6–3 6–3 6–1	
B Nitsche (USA)	9–7 6–1 6–1	
A Palafox (Mex)	6–1 6–2 6–2	
F A Froehling (USA)	6–3 13–11 4–6 6–3	
R H Osuna (Mex)	6–1 6–3 6–4	
R S Emerson (Aus)	6–2 6–4 5–7 6–4	Final

Laver's professional status barred him from the traditional events 1963 to 1967. After open lawn tennis came about in 1968 he reasserted his invincibility:

Australian Championships 1969

beat M di Domenico (Ita)	6–2 6–3 6–3	
R S Emerson (Aus)	6–2 6–3 3–6 9–7	
F S Stolle (Aus)	6–4 18–16 6–2	
A D Roche (Aus)	7–5 22–20 9–11 1–6 6–3	
A Gimeno (Spa)	6–3 6–4 7–5	Final

French Championships 1969

beat K Watanabe (Jap)	6–1 6–1 6–1	
R D Crealy (Aus)	3–6 7–9 6–2 6–2 6–4	
P Marzano (Ita)	6–1 6–0 8–6	
S R Smith (USA)	6–4 6–2 6–4	
A Gimeno (Spa)	3–6 6–3 6–4 6–3	
T S Okker (Hol)	4–6 6–0 6–2 6–4	
K R Rosewall (Aus)	6–4 6–3 6–4	Final

Wimbledon Championships 1969

beat N Pietrangeli (Ita)	6–1 6–2 6–2	
P Lall (Ind)	3–6 4–6 6–3 6–0 6–0	
J Leschly (Den)	6–3 6–3 6–3	
S R Smith (USA)	6–4 6–2 7–9 3–6 6–3	
E C Drysdale (SA)	6–4 6–2 6–3	
A R Ashe (USA)	2–6 6–2 9–7 6–0	
J D Newcombe (Aus)	6–4 5–7 6–4 6–4	Final

US Championships (Open) 1969

beat L Garcia (Mex)	6–2 6–4 6–2	
J Pinto-Bravo (Chi)	6–4 7–5 6–2	
J Fillol (Chi)	8–6 6–1 6–2	
R D Ralston (USA)	6–4 4–6 4–6 6–2 6–3	
R S Emerson (Aus)	4–6 8–6 13–11 6–4	
A R Ashe (USA)	8–6 6–3 14–12	
A D Roche (Aus)	7–9 6–1 6–2 6–2	Final

MISS M C CONNOLLY

Maureen Connolly emulated her compatriot Don Budge in gaining her Grand Slam crown by taking the French Championships. Similarly her surrender came when she failed to defend her Australian title in 1954.

Wimbledon 1952

beat Mrs C G Moeller (GB)	6–2 6–0	
Miss A Mortimer (GB)	6–4 6–3	
Miss J S C Partridge (GB)	6–3 5–7 7–5	
Mrs T D Long (Aus)	5–7 6–2 6–0	
Miss S J Fry (USA)	6–4 6–3	
Miss A L Brough (USA)	7–5 6–3	Final

US Championships 1952

beat Mrs G Heldman (USA)	6–0 6–1	
Mrs E Carroll (USA)	6–1 6–0	
Mrs R Kiner (USA)	6–2 6–4	
Miss S J Fry (USA)	4–6 6–4 6–1	
Miss D J Hart (USA)	6–3 7–5	Final

Australian Championships 1953

beat Miss C Boreilli (Aus)	6–0 6–1	
Mrs R W Baker (Aus)	6–1 6–0	
Miss P Southcombe (Aus)	6–0 6–1	
Mrs K Hawton (Aus)	6–2 6–1	
Miss J Sampson (USA)	6–3 6–2	Final

French Championships 1953

beat Miss C Mercelis (Bel)	6–1 6–3	
Mrs R Verber Jones (Fra)	6–3 6–1	
Miss J S V Partridge (GB)	3–6 6–2 6–2	
Mrs D Knode (USA)	6–3 6–3	
Miss D J Hart (USA)	6–2 6–4	Final

Wimbledon Championships 1953

beat Miss D Killian (SA)	6–0 6–0	
Miss J M Petchell (GB)	6–1 6–1	
Miss J A Shilcock (GB)	6–0 6–1	
Mrs E Vollmer (Ger)	6–3 6–0	
Miss S J Fry (USA)	6–1 6–1	
Miss D J Hart (USA)	8–6 7–5	Final

US Championships 1953

beat Miss J Fallot (USA)	6–1 6–0	
Miss P Stewart (USA)	6–3 6–1	
Miss J Arth (USA)	6–1 6–3	
Miss A Gibson (USA)	6–2 6–3	
Miss S J Fry (USA)	6–1 6–1	
Miss D J Hart (USA)	6–2 6–4	Final

MRS B M COURT

Margaret Court had the longest tenure as holder of all four major singles titles. It might be a moot point as to which of the two American Championships staged in both 1968 and 1969 (the old style National Championships were continued for those years at Boston with the new US Open meeting starting at Forest Hills) should count for Grand Slam purposes. As it happens Mrs Court, who made her starting point at that time, resolved all difficulties by winning both in 1969 and each is recorded below:

US National Championships (Boston) 1969

beat Miss B Kirk (SA)	6–1 6–3	
Miss V Ziegenfuss (USA)	6–2 6–2	
Mrs G M Williams (GB)	6–1 6–1	
Miss K Melville (Aus)	6–2 6–2	
Miss S V Wade (GB)	4–6 6–3 6–0	Final

US Open Championships (Forest Hills) 1969

beat Miss S Peterson (Bra)	6–1 6–0	
Miss B A Grubb (USA)	6–1 6–0	
Miss E Burrer (USA)	6–0 6–2	
Miss K M Krantzcke (Aus)	6–0 9–7	
Miss S V Wade (GB)	7–5 6–0	
Miss N Richey (USA)	6–2 6–2	Final

Australian Championships 1970

beat Miss R Langsford (Aus)	6–0 6–0	
Miss K Wilkinson (Aus)	6–0 6–1	
Miss E F Goolagong (Aus)	6–3 6–1	
Miss K M Krantzcke (Aus)	6–1 6–2	
Miss K Melville (Aus)	6–3 6–1	Final

French Championships 1970

beat Mrs M Jansen-Schaar (Hol)	6–1 6–1	
Miss O Morozova (USSR)	3–6 8–6 6–1	
Miss L Hunt (Aus)	6–2 6–1	
Miss R Casals (USA)	7–5 6–2	
Miss J M Heldman (USA)	6–0 6–2	
Miss H Niessen (Ger)	6–2 6–4	Final

Wimbledon 1970

beat Miss S Alexander (Aus)	6–0 6–1	
Miss M E Guzman (Ecu)	6–0 6–1	
Mrs V Vopickova (Cze)	6–3 6–3	
Miss H Niessen (FRG)	6–8 6–0 6–0	
Miss R Casals (USA)	6–4 6–1	
Mrs L W King (USA)	14–12 11–9	Final

US Open Championships 1970

beat Miss P Austin (USA)	6–1 6–0	
Miss P S A Hogan (USA)	6–1 6–1	
Mrs P Faulkner (Aus)	6–0 6–2	
Miss H Gourlay (Aus)	6–2 6–2	
Miss N Richey (USA)	6–1 6–3	
Miss R Casals (USA)	6–2 2–6 6–1	Final

left Roy Emerson, the Australian who won many championships just prior to the open era.

below Guillermo Vilas of the Argentine in Paris in 1982.

Ilie Nastase of Romania, one of the greatest of all touch players and with a sometimes controversial sense of humour.

John Lloyd with his wife Chris Lloyd.

Evonne Cawley, Wimbledon champion, with her British husband Roger.

Mixed doubles champions at Wimbledon, Betty Stove and Frew McMillan.

Australian Championships 1971

beat	Miss P Coleman (Aus)	6–1 6–1
	Miss H Gourlay (Aus)	6–0 6–4
	Miss L Hunt (Aus)	6–0 6–3
	Miss E F Goolagong (Aus)	2–6 7–6 7–5 Final

In the French Championships Mrs Court's Grand Slam was ended with defeat.

French Championships 1971

beat	Mrs E Wennerstroem (Swe)	6–0 6–1
	Miss K Melville (Aus)	6–2 6–1
lost to	Mrs J B Chanfreau (Fra)	3–6 4–6 Third Round

TRIPLE CHAMPIONS IN DUPLICATE

At one time the hall mark of supreme success was to win all three events, singles, the men's or women's doubles and the mixed doubles. With the onset of the open game and the increasing separation of men's and women's events the achievement has become scarcer.

Since the open game only two players have made themselves triple champions and both were women. Margaret Court was triple champion at the US Open meeting in 1970, Billie Jean King at Wimbledon in 1973. In recent years it has been rare for a man with a reasonable prospect of winning the singles to take part in the mixed doubles.

The value of a triple championship can vary. Until the open game in 1968 the five events making up the US National Championships were not staged at the same place at the same time. Don Budge must have found it less exhausting to become triple champion of the US in 1938, since he took the men's doubles and mixed at Boston and the singles later in New York, than in bringing off the same feat at Wimbledon with all events taking place in the same period.

Three women and one man have achieved the feat of becoming triple champion at two of the major championships within the same year, a titanic task. They are:

Suzanne Lenglen (Fra)—triple champion France and Wimbledon 1925
Don Budge (USA)—triple champion Wimbledon and USA 1938
Alice Marble (USA)—triple champion Wimbledon and USA 1939
Billie Jean King (USA)—triple champion Wimbledon and USA 1967

TWO-FOLD CHAMPIONS IN DUPLICATE

The lesser feat of winning both singles and doubles in more than one major championship in the one year has not been commonplace:

Laurie Doherty (GB)—singles, doubles champion Wimbledon and USA 1903
Rene Lacoste (Fra)—singles, doubles champion France and Wimbledon 1925
Helen Wills Moody (USA)—singles, doubles champion France and Wimbledon 1930
Jack Kramer (USA)—singles, doubles champion Wimbledon and USA 1947
Billie Jean King (USA)—singles, doubles champion France and Wimbledon 1972
John McEnroe (USA)—singles, doubles champion Wimbledon and USA 1981

THE COMPLETE CHAMPIONS

Players Winning the Singles in the Four Major Championships

	TIMES SINGLES CHAMPION					
	Australia	France	Wimbledon	USA*	Total	
Margaret Court** (Aus)	11	5	3	5	24	Grand Slam winner
Billie Jean King (USA)	1	1	6	4	12	
Roy Emerson (Aus)	6	2	2	2	12	
Rod Laver (Aus)	3	2	4	2	11	Grand Slam winner twice
Maureen Connolly (USA)	1	2	3	3	9	Grand Slam winner
Fred Perry (GB)	1	1	3	3	8	
Don Budge (USA)	1	1	2	2	6	Grand Slam winner
Doris Hart** (USA)	1	2	1	2	6	
Shirley Fry (USA)	1	1	1	1	4	

* US National Championships 1881–1969; US Open Championships 1968 et seq.
** Mrs Court and Miss Hart also won women's and mixed doubles in all four championships.

THE INVINCIBLES

Players winning over 30 sequential singles in the major championships (Statistics refer exclusively to the period of the winning sequence)

Player	Event	Wins in Sequence	Years	End of Sequence	No. Titles Won	Sets Won	Lost	% Sets Won
Helen Wills Moody	Wimbledon	50	1927–1938	Retirement	8	100	4	96·15
Helen Wills Moody	US Champs	47	1923–1933	Retired in 1933 final	7	94	6	94
William Tilden	US Champs	45	1920–1926	Defeat in Q/F 1926	6	126	21	85·71
Bjorn Borg	Wimbledon	41	1976–1981	Defeat in final 1981	5	123	21	84·24
Suzanne Lenglen	Wimbledon	32	1919–1926	Retirement in 3rd rd. 1926	6	64	1	98·46
Rod Laver	Wimbledon	31	1961–1970	Defeat in 4th rd. 1970	4	93	17	84·54
Chris Lloyd	US Champs	31	1975–1979	Defeat in final 1979	4	62	2	96·87

LENDL'S WINNING RUN

Ivan Lendl of Czechoslovakia, the Grand Prix winner of 1981 and subsequent victor in the Grand Prix Masters' Tournament at Madison Square Garden, New York, in January 1982, was invincible in six Grand Prix tournaments and won 33 singles matches in sequence September 1981 to January 1982.

After losing to Vitas Gerulaitis of the USA in the fourth round of the US Open at Flushing Meadow, New York, on 9 September 1981 Lendl began his winning sequence in the Madrid tournament starting 28 September. In successive weeks he won the tournaments in Madrid, Barcelona, Basle, Vienna and Cologne. He took his sixth Grand Prix tournament in Buenos Aires on 22 November.

In early January he won his first two singles in an invitation tournament at Rosemont, Illinois, before losing to Jimmy Connors on 9 January.

Lendl's invincible sequence comprised:

	Won	Lost
Singles	33	0
Sets	70	4
Games	432	190

Lendl later won the Masters' event after surviving a match point in the final against Gerulaitis. It brought the tally of his sequential success in the Grand Prix to 35 matches.

PRECOCIOUS SKILLS

The youngest winners of a major open championship were Jimmy Arias and Andrea Jaeger, both Americans, when they won the mixed doubles in the French Championships in Paris on 7 June 1981. Arias was 16 years 296 days and Miss Jaeger was 15 years 339 days and their combined age of 32 years 270 days was the lowest.

The youngest competitor in a major open championship was Kathy Horvath of the US. She qualified for the US Championships at Flushing Meadow, New York, 1979. At the start of the tournament she was 14 years 3 days old. She lost her opening match in the women's singles to the sixth seeded Dianne Fromholtz (Australia) by 6–7 2–6.

The youngest winner in a major open championship was Kathy Rinaldi of the US. She was 14 years 63 days old at the start of the French Championships in Paris 1981. She won three rounds before losing in the quarter-final to Hana Mandlikova (Cze), the winner of the event.

Miss Rinaldi was also the youngest player to win a match in the Wimbledon Championships when in 1981 she beat Sue Rollinson of South Africa in the opening round of the women's singles. She was then 14 years 92 days old. On 3 August 1981 Miss Rinaldi became a professional at the age of 14 years 132 days, the youngest player to do so.

The winner of the first women's championship, the Irish women's singles title in Dublin in 1879, was May Langrishe of Ireland. At the time of her victory, which makes her the doyenne of all women champions, she was 14 years 6 months old.

LONGEST SPAN

The longest span as a major champion was by Ken Rosewall; he was Australian singles champion 1953 and again in 1972, 19 years.

The longest span as a finalist in a major championship was also by Rosewall; he was first a finalist in winning the Australian singles 1953 and he was the finalist in the US Open singles 1974, **21 years.**

The longest span as **covered court champion** was by Jean Borotra; he was French Champion 1922, British Champion in 1949, **27 years.**

Among women the longest span as a **major champion** was by Nell Hopman; as Miss Hall she was Australian mixed doubles champion with Harry Hopman 1930, and with Maureen Connolly she was French women's doubles champion 1954, **24 years.**

The longest span as a **competitor** in a major championship was by Arthur Gore; he first played at Wimbledon in 1888 and, never missing one year, last in 1927, **39 years.**

The longest span by a **woman competitor** in a major championship was by Blanche Hillyard; she first competed at Wimbledon 1884 and last in 1913, **29 years.**

The longest span as a **national number one** was by Jadwiga Jedrzejowska, ranked top in Poland 1929 and in 1959, **30 years.**

The longest span as a **Davis Cup player** was by Felicissimo Ampon; he played first for the Philippines in 1939 and again in 1968, **29 years.**

The longest span as a **national champion** was by C Alphonse Smith; he was US Boys' 15 singles champion in 1924, US men's 70 doubles champion 1979, **55 years.**

The longest span as a **British tournament winner** was by H Roper Barrett; he was singles winner at Saxmundham 1898, men's doubles winner in 1927 (and doubles finalist after 33 years in 1931), **29 years.**

The longest span as a **British county player** was by Henry Billington; he first played for Wiltshire in 1926, last in 1961, **35 years.**

The longest span as an **American tournament winner** was by May Sutton, Pacific Coast singles champion 1901, Pacific South West singles champion as Mrs Bundy in 1928, **27 years.**

The longest span as a **Wightman Cup player** was by Ann Jones, who played first in 1957 and also in 1975, **27 years.**

The longest span as an **American Wightman player** was by Billie Jean King; she first played 1961 and also in 1978, **17 years.**

The **longest continuous tenure as national singles champion** was by Miss K M Nunneley. She won the women's singles championship of New Zealand every year 1895 to 1907, that is **13** consecutive years.

A **title winner for the highest number of times** was Roper Barrett of Great Britain. He won the men's singles first in the Suffolk Championships at Saxmundham in 1898 when he was 24. He won for the **17th time** at the age of 47 in 1921. He won in 1898, 1899, 1902 and then every subsequent tournament 1904 to 1914, 1919 to 1921. In 1912 he retained the title but the final was not played because of rain. He was thus unbeaten in 14 consecutive tournaments.

The Australian women's singles championship was won by Margaret Smith, later **Mrs Court,** 1960 to 1966, 1969 to 1971 and in 1973, **11 times.**

Eric Sturgess won the men's singles in the South African Championships 1939, 1940, 1946, 1948 to 1954 and 1957, **11 times.**

The **longest tenure as a challenger in a major championship** was by Arthur Gore. He first played in the Wimbledon Championships in 1884 and, never missing a year, competed for the **40th time** in 1927. He died, aged 60, in 1928.

BEST ALL-ROUNDERS

The **best all-rounder** in lawn tennis was arguably **J C Parke** (born Clones, Monaghan, Ireland, 26 July 1881, died 27 February 1946.)

At lawn tennis he was ranked world number six in 1914, number four in 1920. He was semi-finalist in the men's singles at Wimbledon 1910 and 1913, a finalist in the men's doubles 1911, 1912, 1913 and 1920. He won the Irish men's singles championship 8 times, 1904, 1905, 1908, 1909, 1910, 1911, 1912, 1913, the men's doubles 5 times, 1903, 1909, 1910, 1911, 1912 and the mixed twice, 1909, 1912. He played for the British Isles in 1908, 1909, 1912, 1913, 1914, 1920 in the Davis Cup.

He was a good chess player. At the age of five he played for his native town, Clones.

He was a noted sprinter.

At golf he was scratch and played for Ireland.

He was a first class cricketer.

At rugby he was capped 20 times for Ireland 1903 to 1909 and was three times Irish captain.

The **best woman all-rounder** was probably **Lottie Dod.** She was born in Cheshire 24 September 1871, died 27 June 1960.

She was the youngest player to win the women's singles at Wimbledon, becoming champion at the age of 15 in 1887 and she won it four other years, 1888, 1891, 1892 and 1893, never being beaten at Wimbledon.

She played hockey for England in 1899 and 1900.

She won the British women's golf championship at Troon in 1904.

She won a silver medal at archery in the Olympic Games 1908.

244 INDIVIDUAL PERFORMANCE

RENEE RICHARDS

Dr Renee Richards, born New York, 19 September 1934, is unique in having been beaten in **both the men's and women's singles** in the US Championships and, moreover, in **losing to the American and Wimbledon champion** in both events.

In 1960, under the identity of Richard Raskind, he was beaten, 6–0 6–1 6–1, by Neale Fraser (Aus), then the Wimbledon champion and defending US title holder, in the men's singles first round of the US Nationals at Forest Hills.

In 1977, following a sex change operation and under her new identity as Renee Richards, she was beaten, 6–1 6–4, in the first round by Virginia Wade (GB), the current Wimbledon champion. In 1979 she was beaten, 6–2 6–1, in the third round by Chris Lloyd (USA), the defending holder.

Miss Richards partnered Bettyann Stuart (USA) to reach the final of the women's doubles. They lost, 6–1 7–6, to Martina Navratilova (Cze) and Betty Stove (Hol).

JAROSLAV DROBNY

Jaroslav Drobny, born 12 October 1921, is unique in having competed in the Wimbledon Championships under **four different national descriptions.**

He first played in 1938 as from 'Czechoslovakia'. In 1939, following political events, he was listed as from 'Bohemia-Moravia'. From 1946 to 1949 he was again 'Czechoslovakia'.

In the years 1950 to 1956 he was, as from 'Egypt', that nation having given him a passport on his becoming a refugee. Under that description he became the men's singles champion in 1954.

Subsequently he was naturalised as an English resident. From 1960 on he became 'Great Britain'.

As a competitor in the championship events Drobny played five times as a Czech, once as a Bohemian-Moravian, ten times as an Egyptian and once as British. In veteran events he appeared 12 times as British.

MISCELLANEOUS ACHIEVEMENTS

The most consistent record of success since 1946 over 12 years was achieved by Chris Lloyd. In twelve challenges in the US Open Championships 1971–1980 she never failed to

The success of Louise Brough includes winning eight championships in 3 years 1948–50 and 22 singles in sequence 1948–51.

reach at least the semi-final of the women's singles. Nor did she ever fail to reach the semi-final of the singles in her twelve challenges in the Wimbledon Championships 1972–1982. In the same period she played in the French Championships seven times and was in the singles semi-finals seven times. She also challenged seven times in the Italian Championships with seven semi-final appearances. In the same period Mrs Lloyd went on to win the Wimbledon Championship three times, the US Championship six times, the French Championship four times and the Italian Championship five times.

A comparable record over a decade was by Louise Brough 1946–55. She was nine times singles semi-finalist at Wimbledon (which she won four times) and six times semi-finalist in the US National singles, which she won once.

The longest sequential success in singles since the game became open in 1968 was by Chris Lloyd who as Chris Evert in 1974 won **56**

matches. On 31 March she was beaten 6–3 3–6 6–2 by Billie Jean King in the final of the US National Indoor Championships at Madison Square Garden, New York. Her next loss was 160 days later in the semi-final of the US Nationals at Forest Hills when Evonne Goolagong beat her 6–0 6–7 6–3. During her invincible spell she won three singles in the Federation Cup in Naples, the Italian Championship in Rome, the French Championship in Paris, the Wimbledon Championship, the US Clay Court Championship in Indianapolis, the Canadian Championship in Toronto as well as other tournaments. Her winning sequence began at Sarasota on 9 April and was halted on 8 September.

The longest sequential winning sequence in men's singles since 1968 was by Guillermo Vilas in 1977. He lost in the third round at Wimbledon on 23 June to Billy Martin. On 12 July he won his first match in the Austrian Championships at Kitzbuhel and went on winning at Washington, Louisville, Orange, Colombus, the US Open singles at Forest Hills, the Coupe Poree in Paris, before retiring to Ilie Nastase, then using the 'spaghetti' racket that was subsequently outlawed, in the final at Aix-en-Provence. His run of success totalled **50 matches.**

The following performances are other than those achieved in the four major championships and international team events:

HIGHEST TOTAL OF NATIONAL TITLES

Miss K M Nunneley won **32** New Zealand championships 1895 and 1909. She took the women's singles 13 successive years 1895 to 1907, never being beaten and losing only one set. She won the women's doubles ten times and the mixed doubles nine.

Miss Nunneley, born in Market Harborough circa 1876, learned her lawn tennis in England. She beat Mrs G W Hillyard at Nottingham in 1893. She was New South Wales champion in 1896.

HIGHEST TOTAL BY A MAN

Eric Sturgess (born 1920) won the South African men's singles championship first in 1939 and the men's doubles in 1958 when he pushed his total up to **25.** He won the singles eleven times, the men's doubles nine and the mixed five.

LONGEST SPELL AS NATIONAL NUMBER ONE

Jadwiga Jedrzejowska (born 1912) was ranked top in Poland 1929 to 1959, a spell of **31 years.**

GREATEST TOURNAMENT DOMINATION

H Roper Barrett (born 1873), member of the first British Davis Cup team in 1900, achieved unique dominance in the Suffolk Championships, played originally at Saxmundham, later at Framlingham, when he had an unbroken tenure of **18 years** as men's singles champion. Having first won the title in 1898 he had continuous success 1904 to 1921. He kept his title in 1912 when the final was unplayed because of rain and there was no tournament 1915 to 1918. He was singles champion 17 times.

Between 1906 and 1914 he won the mixed doubles with **Miss A M Moreton** who also won the women's singles and women's doubles in those years. At that time there was no men's doubles event. Accordingly Roper Barrett and Miss Moreton had 9 consecutive years when they won all the open events between them.

HIGHEST NUMBER OF MATCHES IN ONE EVENT

The highest number of matches won in one event of an open tournament was **13 by Marianne Van Der Torre** of the Netherlands (born 1961). In February 1981 in the Avon Futures Tournament at Hershey, Pennsylvania, she won the women's singles by winning five matches in the pre-qualifying rounds, three in the qualifying competition and five in the main event. In her 13 matches she won 26 sets to 3, 173 games to 94.

LONGEST GAP BETWEEN NATIONAL TITLES

C Alphonse Smith (born 1909) won his first US title when in August 1924 he became National Boys' Singles Champion, the Under 15 title. In August 1979, **55 years** later, he won the US 70 Hard Court Men's Doubles title.

HIGHEST NUMBER OF AMERICAN TITLES

Dorothy Bundy-Cheney (born 1917) won her first US National title, the Indoor Women's Doubles Championship, in 1941. In 1982 she acquired her **116th.**

Mrs Cheney's best success was in the US Clay Court Championships in 1944 when she won the singles. The vast majority of her triumphs were in the age group titles. Notably she was the US Hard Courts Women's 40 Champion 13 times 1957 to 1969 and she played in the US Wightman Cup side 1937 to 1939.

Ranking

Ranking lists are almost as old as the game itself. The first known one was issued for British players by Lt Col R D Osborn for 1881. He placed seven men in an order of merit. Like all compilers of such lists he had difficulties and compromised by bracketing two in the second place.

The Americans have been the most enthusiastic rankers by far. The USLTA issued its first ranking list, for men only, as early as 1885. Their women's grading did not follow until 1913.

It was not until 1929 that the British LTA began to issue ranking lists.

The definition of a ranking list varies with the views of the compiler. My own view of a world ranking list is that it should represent a guide to the future historian of how the players stood in relation to each other and in the measure of their achievement for a particular period.

That may be very different from such national ranking lists compiled on the outcome at specified events. And certainly very different from a seeding list as it used to be compiled for particular tournaments.

Both the main players' associations, the Association of Tennis Professionals of the leading men and the Women's Tennis Association of the leading women, have of recent years maintained computer based lists which are updated every two weeks or so. Their main purpose is to have a merit order of admittance to the leading and most profitable tournaments. In that, though there might be argument about the minutiae of the programming, they serve their purpose admirably. Opinions differ as to the credibility of such computer listings for other purposes.

The USA continues as the outstanding proponent of ranking. The men's ranking ranges from the normal singles list (which can extend to 75 players or more) to a men's doubles rating for players over the age of 80. The women's lists run to the age of over 65. For 1980 a girl could claim to be the 99th best player under the age of 12 and a boy the 109th in the same age group.

WORLD CHAMPIONS

Awards as 'World Champions' were instituted by the International Tennis Federation for the year 1978, the choice being made by two panels of judges comprising former great players. The selections were:

Man	Woman
1978 B Borg (Swe)	Miss C M Evert (USA)
1979 B Borg (Swe)	Miss M Navratilova (Cze)
1980 B Borg (Swe)	Mrs J M Lloyd (USA)
1981 J P McEnroe (USA)	Mrs J M Lloyd (USA)

In addition junior world champions were named, the choice being governed by a points system based on junior tournaments round the world.

Boy	Girl
1978 I Lendl (Cze)	Miss H Mandlikova (Cze)
1979 R Viver (Ecu)	Miss M L Piatek (USA)
1980 T Tulasne (Fra)	Miss S Mascarin (USA)
1981 P Cash (Aus)	Miss Z Garrison (USA)

WORLD RANKING

(World ranking was initiated in 1913 by A Wallis Myers, lawn tennis correspondent of the *Daily Telegraph* and the *Field*. It was at first confined to the men. Women's ranking started in 1925. Sir F Gordon Lowe compiled the 1939 lists. Those for 1946 and 1951 were by Pierre Gillou. For 1947 to 1950 they were by John Olliff of the *Daily Telegraph* and from 1952 by Lance Tingay of the same newspaper.)

Most ranked as World number one was Helen Wills Moody of the US, graded top for 1927, 1928, 1929, 1930, 1931, 1932, 1933, 1935 and 1938—for 7 successive years and for **9 years** in all.

Margaret Court of Australia was ranked number one for 1962, 1963, 1964, 1965, 1969, 1970 and 1973, **7 years.**

The man most ranked as World number one was William Tatem Tilden of the US, rated best for 1920, 1921, 1922, 1923, 1924 and 1925, **6 successive years.**

The youngest number one was Maureen Connolly of the US. She was top in 1952 and was, on 17 September 1952, **aged 18.**

The youngest man to be **number one** was Ellsworth Vines of the US. He was graded best in 1932 and was, on 29 September 1932, **aged 21.**

The oldest number one was Jaroslav Drobny, formerly of Czechoslovakia, in 1954. On 12 October 1954 he was **33 years old.**

The oldest woman to be **number one** was Althea Gibson of the US in 1958. On 25 August 1958 she was **aged 31.**

Billie Jean King of the US was ranked in the world's top ten the greatest number of times. Between 1963 and 1980 she was selected **17 times.**

Ann Jones of Great Britain (1957-70), Margaret Court of Australia (1961-75) and Virginia Wade of Great Britain (1967-79) were all selected **13 times.**

Louise Brough of the US was ranked (1946-57) in all of **12 years.**

The men to be **ranked the greatest number of times** were Tilden (1919-30), Ken Rosewall of Australia (1952-74) and Rod Laver of Australia (1959-75), who were selected **12 times.**

The longest span of years between first and last ranking was by Rosewall. He was ranked at number 10 in 1952 and at number 2 in 1974—a span of **22 years.**

The longest span of years **by a woman** was by Billie Jean King. She was ranked first in 1963 at number 4 and in 1980 at number 6, a span of **17 years.**

The youngest player to be ranked among the world's best ten was Andrea Jaeger of the US. She was rated number 7 for 1980 and she was **15** years old on 4 June 1980.

The second youngest player to have world ranking was Betty Nuthall, of Great Britain, who was rated number 6 in 1927. On 23 June 1927 she was **aged 16.**

The youngest man to achieve world ranking was Lew Hoad of Australia, number 10 in 1952. On 23 November 1952 he was **aged 18.** Bjorn Borg of Sweden was rated number 4 in 1974 and was aged 18 on 6 June 1974. Vincent

Ellsworth Vines (USA) was in 1932 the youngest man at 21 to be rated the world's number one.

Richards of the US was ranked 3 in 1921 and was 18 on 20 March 1921.

The oldest player to rank in the world's top ten was Ricardo Gonzales of the US, number 8 in 1969. On 9 May 1969 he was **aged 41.**

The oldest woman to have world ranking was Elizabeth Ryan of the US who was number 5 in 1930. On 5 February 1930 she was **aged 38.**

BRITISH RANKING

The first British ranking list and, as far as is known, the first anywhere, was issued by Lt Col R D Osborn for the year 1881. It was:

> 1 W Renshaw
> 2 { H F Lawford
>   { R T Richardson
> 4 O E Woodhouse
> 5 E Renshaw
> 6 E Lubbock
> 7 J T Hartley

The Renshaw twins were 20 years old on 3 January 1881. William won the Wimbledon singles when he beat the Rev John Hartley 6–0 6–1 6–1 in the Challenge Round. In the second place match Richardson, who was beaten 6–4 6–2 6–3 by William Renshaw in the All-comers' final, defeated Lawford 6–3 4–6 6–1 3–6 7–5. Woodhouse was beaten by William Renshaw in the quarter-finals. Lawford also lost to William Renshaw in the semi-finals.

Lubbock won the South of England championship in 1881.

The **most ranked as Britain's number one** was Virginia Wade. She headed the list 1968, 1971, 1972, 1973, 1974, 1975, 1976, 1977, 1978, 1979, 1980—including 10 consecutive years and **11 times** in all.

Most ranked as Britain's number one men were Mark Cox and Buster Mottram. Cox was top in 1968, 1969, 1971, 1974, 1975 (jointly with Mottram), 1976. Mottram was top in 1975 (with Cox), 1977, 1978, 1979, 1980, 1981, **6 times**.

The **youngest number one** was Christine Truman. She was top in 1958 and, on 16 January 1958, was **aged 17**.

The **youngest man** to be **number one** was Buster Mottram in 1975. He was, on 26 April 1975, **aged 20**.

The **oldest number one** was Virginia Wade. She was, on 10 July 1980, **aged 35**.

The **oldest man** to be **number one** was Mark Cox. He was, on 5 July 1976, **aged 33**.

Virginia Wade was ranked **in the top ten the greatest number of times**. Between 1963 and 1981 she was ranked every year, a total of **19 times**.

Among men Bobby Wilson and Mark Cox were ranked the greatest number of times. Wilson was rated in the top ten 1952–69, Cox 1962 to 1980 missing 1964, **each 18 times**.

The **youngest** player to achieve **top ten ranking** was Christine Truman. Rated number 4 in 1956 she was, on 16 January 1956, **age 15**.

The **youngest man** to achieve **top ten ranking** was Bobby Wilson. He was rated number 9 in 1952 and was, on 22 November 1952, **age 17**.

The **oldest** player to be ranked in the **top ten** was Mark Cox. Ranked number two in 1980 he was, on 5 July 1980, **age 37**.

The **oldest woman** to be ranked in the top ten was Shirley Brasher. Ranked number ten in 1972 she was, on 13 June 1972, **age 36**.

US RANKING

The United States initiated a ranking list for men as early as 1885 and for women in 1913. Currently the USTA issues a multiplicity of lists, ranging from boys and girls under 12, singles and doubles, to men over 80, singles and doubles.

The **most ranked** American was William Larned. Between 1892 and 1911 he was ranked in the top ten **19 times**.

The **most ranked woman** was Billie Jean King. Between 1960 and 1980 she was ranked **17 times**.

The **most ranked number one** was William Tatem Tilden. He rated best for 1920, 1921, 1922, 1923, 1924, 1925, 1926, 1927, 1928, 1929— **10 times**.

The **women** to be **ranked number one** most often were Billie Jean King (for 1965, when joint with Nancy Richey, 1966, 1967, 1970, 1971, 1972, 1973) and Helen Wills Moody (for 1923, 1924, 1925, 1927, 1928, 1929, 1931) **each 7 times**.

The **youngest top ranking player** was Maureen Connolly for 1951. On 17 September 1951 she was **aged 17**.

The **youngest top ranking man** was Oliver Campbell for 1890. On 25 February 1890, **aged 19**.

The **oldest player** to **rank number one** was Gardner Mulloy in 1952. On 22 November 1952 he was **aged 39**.

The **oldest woman** at **number one** was Molla Mallory. In 1926 she was **aged 34**.

The **greatest span** achieved in top ten ranking was by Vic Seixas. He rated number nine in 1942 and was also rated nine in 1966, bridging **24 years**.

Margaret du Pont was ranked seven in 1938 and five in 1958, a span of **20 years**. Billie Jean King rated number four in 1960 and number five in 1980, a span also of **20 years**.

MARRIED WOMEN

The following appear in the records under differing identities:

Later Description	Original Description	Later Description	Original Description
Mrs R Allister	Miss A de Schmidt (SA)	Frau I Kuehn	Frl I Riedel (Ger)
Mrs R Anderson	Miss R Jarvis (GB)	Mrs G Lamplough	Miss G Eastlake-Smith (GB)
Mrs E B Arnold	Miss E Burkhardt (USA)	Mme N Landry	Mlle N Adamson (Fra)
Frau L Barting	Frl L Berton (Ger)	Mrs D R Larcombe	Miss E W Thompson (GB)
Mme M Billout	Mlle M Brocquedies (Fra)	Mrs J L Leisk	Miss H Aitchison (GB)
Mrs N W Blair	Miss W M Lincoln (GB)	Frau A Lent	Frl A Heimann (Ger)
Mrs N Bolton	Miss N Wynne (Aus)	Mrs J M Lloyd	Miss C M Evert (USA)
Mrs E W A Bostock	Miss J Nicoll (GB)	Mrs T D Long	Miss T Coyne (Aus)
Mrs W W Bowrey	Miss L R Turner (Aus)	Mme G Lovera	Mme J B Chanfreau (Aus)
Mrs C W Brasher	Miss S J Bloomer (GB)	Mrs J F Luard	Miss C M Wilson (GB)
Mrs T C Bundy	Miss M G Sutton (USA)	Mrs R Lycett	Miss J Austin (GB)
Mrs R A Cawley	Miss E F Goolagong (Aus)	Mrs R D McKelvie	Miss A E L McOstrich (GB)
Mrs R L Cawley	Miss H Gourlay (Aus)	Mrs F I Mallory	Miss M Bjurdstedt (Nor)
Mrs L Cawthorn	Miss L Cornell (GB)	Frau H Masthoff	Frl H Niessen (Ger)
Mme J B Chanfreau	Miss G Sherriff (Aus)	Mrs M Menzies	Miss K E Stammers (GB)
Mme P Chatrier	Miss J S V Partridge (GB)	Mrs J Meulemeester	Mlle J Sigart (Bel)
Mrs R Lambert Chambers	Miss D K Douglass (GB)	Mrs L R C Michell	Miss P Saunders (GB)
Mrs D M Cheney	Miss D M Bundy (USA)	Mrs E H Miller	Miss E L Heine (SA)
Mrs A L Clapp	Miss A L Brough (USA)	Mrs F S Moody	Miss H N Wills (USA)
Mrs B Collier	Miss B Penrose (Aus)	Mrs J Moore	Miss F Toyne (Aus)
Mrs E T Cooke	Mrs M Fabyan (USA)	Mrs O Morozova	Miss O Morozova (USSR)
Mrs B M Court	Miss M Smith (Aus)	Mrs A J Mottram	Miss J Gannon (GB)
Mrs B C Covell	Miss P L Howkins (GB)	Mme H Nicolopoulo	Mlle H Contosavlos (Fra)
Mrs R Cozens	Miss D Akhurst (Aus)	Mrs L G Owen	Miss M V Chamberlain (GB)
Mrs J H Crawford	Miss M Cox (Aus)	Mrs E C Parton	Miss M B Squire (GB)
Mrs Crundell-Punnett	Mrs Nutcombe-Quick (GB)	Mrs O Plessis	Miss O Craze (SA)
Mrs D E Dalton	Miss J A M Tegart (Aus)	Mrs J B Pittman	Miss E A Goldsack (GB)
Mme P Darmon	Sen R M Reyes (Mex)	Mrs E C S Pratt	Miss B Rosenquest (USA)
Mrs G Davidson	Miss B Scotfield (USA)	Mrs Q L Pretorius	Miss P M Walkden (SA)
Mrs J Du Ploy	Miss A M Van Zyl (SA)	Mrs L E G Price	Miss S Reynolds (SA)
Mrs W D du Pont	Miss M E Osborne (USA)	Mrs E Raymond	Miss L Hammond (USA)
Frau E Eilemann	Frl U Rosenow (Ger)	Mrs G E Reid	Miss K Melville (Aus)
Mrs R T Ellis	Sen A Lizana (Chi)	Mrs S Reitano	Miss M Carter (Aus)
Mrs J Emerson	Miss J Blackman (Aus)	Mrs I Rinkel-Quertier	Miss J Quertier (GB)
Mrs M Fabyan	Miss S Palfrey (USA)	Mrs H W Roarke	Mrs F S Moody (USA)
Mrs J G Fleitz	Miss B Baker (USA)	Mrs A Robertson	Miss E Boyd (Aus)
Mrs K Ford	Miss K Baker (USA)	Mrs C Robinson	Miss F E Truman (GB)
Frau M Galvau	Frl M Rieck (Ger)	Frau von Satzgar	Frau N Neresheimer (Ger)
Mrs A C Geen	Miss D P Boothby (GB)	Mrs M Schaar	Miss M J Jansen (Hol)
Mrs P F Glover	Miss N M Lyle (GB)	Frau A Schneider	Frau A Pietz (Ger)
Mrs L A Godfree	Miss K McKane (GB)	Mrs A Segal	Mrs H Brewer (Ber)
Mrs G Greville	Miss L Austin (GB)	Mrs B I Shenton	Miss E M Watson (GB)
Mrs K S Gunter	Miss N Richey (USA)	Mrs D C Shepherd-Barron	Miss D Shepherd (GB)
Mrs R Hales	Miss P E Ward (GB)	Fru S Sperling	Frl H Krahwinkel (Ger)
Mrs W C J Halford	Miss M Whitmarsh (GB)	Mrs A Sterry	Miss C Cooper (GB)
Mrs M Hare	Miss R M Hardwick (GB)	Mrs A D Stocks	Miss M McKane (GB)
Mrs R Harper	Miss S Lance (Aus)	Frau P Stuck	Frl P von Reznicek (Ger)
Mrs C Harrison	Mrs B E Hilton (Aus)	Mrs V Sukova	Miss V Puzejova (Cze)
Mrs P Haygarth	Miss R R Schuurman (SA)	Mrs J R Susman	Miss K Hantze (USA)
Mrs E L Heine-Miller	Miss E L Heine (SA)	Countess de la Valdene	Sen E. de Alvarez (Spa)
Mrs G W Hillyard	Miss B Bingley (GB)	Mrs V Vukovich	Miss B Carr (SA)
Frau H Hoesl	Frl H Schultze (Ger)	Mrs B Walter	Mrs B Carris (GB)
Mrs H C Hopman	Miss N Hall (Aus)	Mrs E F Whittingstall	Miss E Bennett (GB)
Mrs P D Howard	Mlle D Metaxa (Fra)	Mrs G W Wightman	Miss H V Hotchkiss (USA)
Mrs G T Janes	Miss C C Truman (GB)	Mrs K Wooldridge	Miss W M Shaw (GB)
Frau M L Jencquel	Frl M L Horn (Ger)		
Mrs J B Jessup	Miss M Zinderstein (USA)		
Mrs P F Jones	Miss A S Haydon (GB)		
Mrs C W Kelleher	Miss G Wheeler (USA)		
Mrs R Kiner	Miss N Chaffee (USA)		
Mrs L W King	Miss B J Moffitt (USA)		
Mrs M R King	Miss P E Mudford (GB)		
Mrs D P Knode	Miss D Head (USA)		
Mrs F Kovacs	Miss V Wolfendon (USA)		

SUBJECT AND PICTURE INDEX

(picture references in *italics*)

Acknowledgement is made to the following for the reproduction of illustrations on the following pages:

Australian Information Service, London 123 (lower); Betteman Archive 11 (centre), 92 (right); British Petroleum Ltd 235; Cincinnati Enquirer 47 (upper right); Cornell University 90 (centre); John Dewar & Son Ltd 226 (right); Tommy Hindley 1, 14 (lower), 33, 42, 43, 47 (left and lower right), 48, 69, 70, 89 (right), 92 (centre), 102 (left), 103, 104, 113, 114, 115, 116, 124, 135 (centre), **137**, **138**, **171**, **172**, 178, 186, 188, 193, 198, 205, 206, 220, 239, 240; Le Roye Productions Ltd 51 (left), 141, 244; Marquis de Marman 112; Press Association 54, 128; The Scotsman Publications Ltd 226 (left); Sport and General 92 (centre); Sporting Pictures (UK) Ltd 87 (centre); Stanford University 18; A Tonelli **36** (upper); University of California, Berkeley 50 (left); University of California and Los Angeles, Los Angeles 102 (right); West Hants Lawn Tennis Club **36** (lower); Wimbledon Lawn Tennis Museum **2**, 10, 11 (centre and lower), 12, **35**, 37, 39, 41, 45 (right), 50 (right), 51 (right), 76, 87 (left), 92 (right), 112, 125, 131, 135 (lower left), 247

Figures in bold type refer to colour illustrations